EARLY CHRISTIAN THEOLOGY

Early Christian Theology

- A History -

J. Warren Smith

William B. Eerdmans Publishing Company
Grand Rapids, Michigan

Wm. B. Eerdmans Publishing Co.
2006 44th Street SE, Grand Rapids, MI 49508
www.eerdmans.com

Published 2026
Printed in the United States of America

32 31 30 29 28 27 26 1 2 3 4 5 6 7

ISBN 978-0-8028-7477-1

Library of Congress Cataloging-in-Publication Data

A catalog record for this book is available from the Library of Congress.

To the Duke PhD and ThD students
who have served as preceptors for Early and Medieval Christianity.

You have been my colleagues and co-teachers, giving clarity to my lectures and devoting hours teaching first year students how to interpret, write, and argue as historians and theologians. I could not have done it without you. And the students' education would have been poorer for your absence.

Deum de Deo, lumen de lumine,
gestant puellae viscera
Deum verum, genitum non factum:
Venite adoremus,
Venite adoremus,
Venite adoremus Dominum

—John Francis Wade (1743)

Veil'd in Flesh, the Godhead see,
Hail th' Incarnate Deity!
Pleas'd as Man with Men t' appear
JESUS, our Immanuel here!

—Charles Wesley (1739)

Contents

Abbreviations

1 Apol.	Justin Martyr, *First Apology* (*Apologia i*)
2 Apol.	Justin Martyr, *Second Apology* (*Apologia ii*)
1 Clem.	1 Clement
2 Clem.	2 Clement
2 Ep. Cyr.	Nestorius, *Second Letter to Cyril* (*Ad Cyrillum Alexandrinum II*)
3 Ep. Nest.	Cyril of Alexandria, *Third Epistle to Nestorius* (*Ad Nestorium III*)
Abl.	Gregory of Nyssa, *To Ablabius: On Not Three Gods* (*Ad Ablabium*)
Adol.	Basil of Caesarea, *To Young Men* (*Ad Adolescentes*)
Aen.	Vergil, *Aeneid*
Agr.	Philo, *On Agriculture* (*De agricultura*)
Amb.	Maximus the Confessor, *Difficulties* (*Ambigua*)
An. res.	Gregory of Nyssa, *On the Soul and Resurrection* (*De anima et resurrectione*)
Anakeph.	Apollinaris, *Recapitulation* (*Anakephalaiōsis*); Lietzmann, Hans. *Apollinaris von Laodicea und seine Schule*. Tübingen: Mohr, 1904
ANF	*The Ante-Nicene Fathers: Translations of the Writings of the Fathers Down to A.D. 325*. Edited by Alexander Roberts and James Donaldson. 10 vols. 1885–1887. Repr., Peabody, MA: Hendrickson, 1994
Ann.	Tacitus, *Annals* (*Annales*)
Antirrh.	Gregory of Nyssa, *Refutation of the Views of Apollinaris* (*Antirrheticus adversus Apollinarium*)
Ap. John	Apocryphon of John
Apoc. Pet.	Apocalypse of Peter
Apod.	Apollinaris, *Demonstration* (*Apodeixis*). Hans Lietzmann, *Apollinaris von Laodicea und seine Schule*. Tübingen: Mohr, 1904
Apol.	Eunomius of Cyzicus, *Apology* (*Apologia*); Tertullian, *Apology* (*Apologia*)

Apos. Con.	Apostolic Constitutions
Arbitr.	Methodius of Olympus, *On Free Choice* (*De libero arbitrio*)
Arium	Marius Victorinus, *Against Arius* (*Adversus Arium*)
Ascen. Isa.	Ascension of Isaiah
Ast. fr.	Asterius, fragment in *Asterius von Kappadokien: Die Theologischen Fragmente*. Edited by Markus Vinzent. Leiden: Brill, 1993
Autol.	Theophilus, *To Autolycus* (*Ad Autolycum*)
Avit.	Jerome, *Letter to Avitus* (*Epistula ad Avitum*)
B.J.	Josephus, *Jewish War* (*Bellum judaicum*)
Bapt.	Tertullian, *On Baptism* (*De baptismo*)
Barn.	Epistle of Barnabas
Beat.	Augustine, *On the Happy Life* (*De vita beata*); Gregory of Nyssa, *Homilies on the Beatitudes* (*De beatitudinibus*)
Bell. civ.	Appian, *Civil Wars* (*Bella civilia*)
BLC	Bardaisan of Edessa, *Book of the Laws of Countries*
Bon. conj.	Augustine, *The Good of Marriage* (*De bona conjugali*)
Brev. Chald.	*Breviarium iuxta Ritum Syrorum Orientalium id est Chaldaeorum*
C. Ar.	Athanasius, *Orations Against the Arians* (*Orationes contra Arianos*); Phoebadius, *Against the Arians* (*Contra Arianos*)
C. Jul.	Augustine, *Against Julian* (*Contra Julianum*)
Cand.	Candidus, *Epistle of Candidus* (*Candidi Epistola*); Marius Victorinus, *Letter to Candidus* (*Ad Candidum*)
Carn. Chr.	Tertullian, *On the Flesh of Christ* (*De carne Christi*)
Cat. hom.	Theodore of Mopsuestia, *Catechetical Homilies* (*Homiliae catecheticae*)
Cat. myst.	Cyril of Alexandria, *Mystagogical Catechesis* (*Catecheses mystagogicae*)
CB	Church's Bible
Cels.	Origen, *Against Celsus* (*Contra Celsum*)
Chr. un.	Cyril of Alexandria, *On the Unity of Christ* (*Quod unus sit Christus*)
Civ.	Augustine, *City of God* (*De civitate Dei*)
Coll.	John Cassian, *Conferences* (*Collationes*)
Comm. Cant.	Origen, *Commentary on the Song of Songs* (*Commentarius in Canticum*)
Comm. Diat.	Ephrem the Syrian, *Commentary on Tatian's Diatessaron* (*In Tatiani Diatesseron*)
Comm. Gal.	Marius Victorinus, *Commentarius in epistulam Pauli ad Galatas*
Comm. Jo.	Origen, *Commentary on John* (*Commentarii in evangelium Joannis*)
Comm. KG.	Babai the Great, *Commentary on the* Kephalaia gnōstika *of Evagrius* (*Commentarius ad Evagrii* Kephalaia gnōstika)

Comm. Matt.	Origen, *Commentary on Matthew* (*Commentarium in evangelium Matthaei*)
Comm. Num.	Origen, *Fragments of the Commentary on Numbers* (*Selecta in Numeros*)
Comm. Ps.	Diodore of Tarsus, *Commentary on the Psalms* (*Commentarii in Psalmos*)
Comm. Rom.	Origen, *Commentary on Romans* (*Commentarii in Romanos*); Pelagius, *Commentary on St. Paul's Epistle to the Romans* (*Expositio in epistulam Pauli ad Romanos*)
Conf.	Augustine, *Confessions* (*Confessiones*)
Corrept.	Augustine, *On Correction and Grace* (*De correptione et gratia*)
CSCO	Corpus Scriptorum Christianorum Orientalium. Edited by Jean Baptiste Chabot et al. Paris, 1903
Decr.	Athanasius, *On the Nicene Council* (*De decretis*)
Dem.	Aphrahat, *Demonstrations* (*Demonstrationes*)
Dial.	John of Damascus, *Dialectic* (*Dialectica*); Justin Martyr, *Dialogue with Trypho* (*Dialogus cum Tryphone*)
Did.	Didache
Didasc.	Didascalia
Div. nom.	Pseudo-Dionysius, *Divine Names* (*De divinis nominibus*)
Doctr. chr.	Augustine, *Christian Instruction* (*De doctrina christiana*)
Dogm. fr.	Theodore of Mopsuestia, *Dogmatic Fragments* (*Fragmenta dogmatica*)
Dogm. inc.	Proclus of Cyzicus, *Sermon on the Dogma of the Incarnation* (*Sermo de Dogmate Incarnationis*)
Dom.	Ephrem the Syrian, *Sermon on Our Lord* (*Sermo de Domino nostro*)
Eccl. theol.	Eusebius of Caesarea, *Ecclesiastical Theology* (*De ecclesiastica theologia*)
Enarrat. Ps.	Augustine, *Enarrations on the Psalms* (*Enarrationes in Psalmos*)
Engastr.	Origen, *On the Belly-Myther* (*De engastrimytho*)
Engastr. c. Orig.	Eustathius of Antioch, *On the Belly-Myther, Against Origen* (*De engastrimytho contra Origenem*)
Enn.	Plotinus, *Enneads* (*Enneades*)
Ep.	Ambrose, *Epistulae*; Basil, *Epistulae*; Cyril of Alexandria, *Epistulae*; Gregory of Nazianzus, *Epistulae*
Ep. 28	Leo the Great, *Tome of Leo* (*Tomus*)
Ep. Adelph.	Athanasius, *Letter to Adelphius* (*Epistula ad Adelphium*)
Ep. coll.	Ambrose, *Letters Outside the Collection* (*Epistulae extra collectionem*)
Ep. comm.	Marcus Aurelius, *Letter to the Common Assembly of Asia* (*Epistula ad commune Asiae*)

Ep. Dion.	Apollinaris, *Letter to Dionysius* (*Epistula ad Dionysium*)
Ep. fid.	Evagrius Ponticus, *Letter on Faith* (*Epistula fidei*)
Ep. Marcell.	Athanasius, *Letter to Marcellinus* (*Epistula ad Marcellinum*)
Ep. Mel.	Evagrius Ponticus, *Letter to Melania* (*Epistula ad Melaniam*)
Ep. Serap.	Athanasius, *Letters to Serapion Concerning the Holy Spirit* (*Epistulae ad Serapionem*)
Epil.	Leontius of Byzantium, *Solutions to the Arguments Proposed by Severus* (*Epilyseis*)
Epiph.	Ephrem the Syrian, *Hymns on Epiphany* (*De Epiphania*)
Eun.	Basil of Caesarea, *Against Eunomius* (*Contra Eunomium*); Gregory of Nyssa, *Against Eunomius* (*Contra Eunomium*)
Eun. fr.	Theodore of Mopsuestia, *Against Eunomius* (Syriac fragment from *Contra Eunomium*)
Exc.	Clement of Alexandria, *Excerpts from Theodotus* (*Excerpta ex Theodoto*)
Exp. fid.	Eunomius of Cyzicus, *Confession of Faith* (*Expositio fidei*); John of Damascus, *Exposition of the Orthodox Faith* (*Expositio fidei*)
Exp. prop. Rom.	Augustine, *Exposition on Propositions from Romans* (*Expositio quarundam propositionum ex epistula ad Romanos*)
Faust.	Augustine, *Against Faustus the Manichaean* (*Contra Faustum Manichaeum*)
Fid.	Ambrose, *On the Faith* (*De fide*)
Flor.	Ptolemy, *Letter to Flora* (*Epistula ad Floram*)
Frag. E	Valentinus, Fragment E
Gal.	Julian the Apostate, *Against the Galileans* (*Contra Galilaeos*)
Gen. litt.	Augustine, *On Genesis Literally Interpreted* (*De Genesi ad litteram*)
GNO	*Gregorii Nysseni Opera*
Gos. Thom.	Gospel of Thomas
Gos. Truth	Valentinus, Gospel of Truth
Gramm.	Severus of Antioch, *Against the Impious Grammarian* (*Liber contra impium grammaticum*)
Grat.	Augustine, *On Grace and Free Will* (*De gratia et libero arbitrio*); Faustus of Riez, *On Grace* (*De gratia*)
Grat. Chr.	Augustine, *On the Grace of Christ and Original Sin* (*De gratia Christi, et de peccato originali*)
Haer.	Irenaeus, *Against Heresies* (*Adversus haereses*)
Her.	Philo, *Who Is the Heir?* (*Quis rerum divinarum heres*)
Heracl.	Nestorius, *The Bazaar of Heracleides* (*Liber Heraclidis*)
Herm. Mand.	Shepherd of Hermas, Mandates
Herm. Sim.	Shepherd of Hermas, Similitudes
Hist. eccl.	Eusebius of Caesarea, *Ecclesiastical History* (*Historia ecclesiastica*);

	Philostorgius, *Ecclesiastical History* (*Historia ecclesiastica*); Socrates Scholasticus, *Ecclesiastical History* (*Historia ecclesiastica*); Theodoret, *Ecclesiastical History* (*Historia ecclesiastica*)
Hom. 125	Severus of Antioch, *Homily on the Trisagion* (*De Trisagio*)
Hom. 170	Jacob of Serugh, homily 170 in *Jacob of Sarug's Homilies on Women Whom Jesus Met*. Edited by Sebastian P. Brock, Reyhan Durmaz, Rebecca Stephens Falcasantos, Susan Ashbrook Harvey, Michael Payne, and Daniel Picus. Piscataway, NJ: Gorgias, 2016
Hom. bapt.	Narsai, homily 22, "On Baptism," in *The Liturgical Homilies of Narsai*. Edited by Richard Hugh Connolly and Edmund Bishop. Cambridge: University Press, 1909
Hom. Cant.	Gregory of Nyssa, *Homilies on the Song of Songs* (*Commentarius in Canticum Canticorum*); Origen, *Homilies on the Song of Songs* (*Homiliae in Canticum*)
Hom. Const.	Jacob of Serugh, *Homily on the Baptism of Constantine*
Hom. Eccl.	Gregory of Nyssa, *Homilies on Ecclesiastes* (*In Ecclesiasten homiliae*)
Hom. epiph.	Jacob of Serugh, *Homilies on the Feast of the Epiphany* in *The Epiphany Feast*. Translated by Mary F. A., Monica Mitri, and Michael Stefanos. Edited by Tadros Malaty. Alexandria: Saint George Church, 2021
Hom. mart. Sahd.	Jacob of Serugh, *Homily on Three Baptisms*
Hom. Num.	Origen, *Homilies on Numbers* (*Homiliae in Numeros*)
Hom. opif.	Gregory of Nyssa, *On the Making of Humanity* (*De hominis opificio*)
Hymn. epiph.	Anonymous, *Hymn on Epiphany* (*Hymni de Epiphania*); Brock, Sebastian. *Treasure-House of Mysteries: Explorations of the Sacred Text Through Poetry in the Syriac Tradition*. Yonkers, NY: St. Vladimir's Seminary Press, 2012
Hymn. fid.	Ephrem the Syrian, *Hymns on Faith* (*Hymni de fide*)
Hymn. haer.	Ephrem the Syrian, *Hymns Against Heresies* (*Hymni contra haereses*)
Hymn. virginit.	Ephrem the Syrian, *Hymns on Virginity* (*Hymni de virginitate*)
Idol.	Tertullian, *On Idolatry* (*De idololatria*)
Ign. *Eph.*	Ignatius of Antioch, *To the Ephesians*
Ign. *Magn.*	Ignatius of Antioch, *To the Magnesians*
Ign. *Phld.*	Ignatius of Antioch, *To the Philadelphians*
Ign. *Rom.*	Ignatius of Antioch, *To the Romans*
Ign. *Smyrn.*	Ignatius of Antioch, *To the Smyrnaeans*
Ign. *Trall.*	Ignatius of Antioch, *To the Trallians*
In Isa.	Cyril of Alexandria, *On Isaiah* (*Commentarius in Isaiam prophetam*)
In Jo.	Cyril of Alexandria, *On John* (*Commentarius in Johannem*)
Inc.	Athanasius, *On the Incarnation* (*De incarnatione*)

Inscr. Ps.	Gregory of Nyssa, *On the Inscriptions of the Psalms* (*In inscriptiones Psalmorum*)
Jos.	Ambrose, *On the Patriarch Joseph* (*De Joseph patriarcha*)
Jul.	Cyril of Alexandria, *Against Julian* (*Contra Julianum*)
KG	Evagrius Ponticus, *Chapters on Knowledge* (*Kephalaia gnōstika*)
Laud.	Victricius of Rouen, *Praising the Saints* (*De laude sanctorum*)
Laud. Paul.	John Chrysostom, *In Praise of Saint Paul* (*De laudibus sancti Pauli*)
Leg.	Athenagoras, *Plea for the Christians* (*Legatio pro Christianis*); Philo, *Allegorical Interpretation* (*Legum allegoriae*)
Lib.	Augustine, *On Free Choice of the Will* (*De libero arbitrio*)
Lib. arb.	Pelagius, *On the Defense of Free Will* (*Pro libero arbitrio*)
Lib. un.	Babai the Great, *On the Union* (*Liber de unione*)
LXX	Septuagint
Macr.	Gregory of Nyssa, *Life of Macrina* (*De vita Macrinae*)
Mag.	Augustine, *On the Teacher* (*De magistro*)
Mar. fr.	Marcellus of Ancyra, fragment in *Markell von Ankyra: Die Fragmente und der Brief an Julius von Rom*. Edited by Markus Vinzent. Leiden: Brill, 2015
Mar. imp. Pall.	Marcian, *Letter to Palladius* (*Marcianus Imperator in sacra ad Palladium*)
Marc.	Tertullian, *Against Marcion* (*Adversus Marcionem*)
Marcell.	Eusebius of Caesarea, *Against Marcellus* (*Contra Marcellum*)
Mart.	Origen, *Exhortation to Martyrdom* (*Exhortatio ad martyrium*)
Med.	Marcus Aurelius, *Meditations* (*Meditationes*)
Mem. fid. Spir.	Philoxenos of Mabbug, *Memra on the Faith by Questions and Answers*. Part 1. *On the Indwelling of the Holy Spirit*
Migr.	Philo, *On the Migration of Abraham* (*De migratione Abrahami*)
Mor. eccl.	Augustine, *On the Morals of the Catholic Church* (*De moribus ecclesiae catholicae*)
Mort.	Gregory of Nyssa, *On Those Who Have Fallen Asleep* (*De mortuis oratio*)
Mort.	Lactantius, *The Death of the Persecutors* (*De mortibus persecutorum*)
Mos.	Gregory of Nyssa, *Life of Moses* (*De vita Mosis*); Philo, *Life of Moses* (*De vita Mosis*)
Myst.	Ambrose, *On the Mysteries* (*De mysteriis*)
Myst. theol.	Pseudo-Dionysius, *Mystical Theology* (*De mystica theologia*)
Nat. grat.	Augustine of Hippo, *On Nature and Grace* (*De natura et gratia*)
Nest.	Cyril of Alexandria, *Five Tomes Against Nestorius* (*Libri quinque contra Nestorium*)

Nest. Eut.	Leontius of Byzantium, *Against Nestorius and Eutyches* (*Contra Nestorianos et Eutychianos*)
Noet.	Hippolytus of Rome, *Against Noetus* (*Contra Noetum*)
NPNF	*A Select Library of Nicene and Post-Nicene Fathers of the Christian Church*. Edited by Philip Schaff and Henry Wace. 28 vols. in 2 series. 1886–1889. Repr., Peabody, MA: Hendrickson, 1994
Od.	Homer, *Odyssey* (*Odyssea*)
Odes Sol.	Odes of Solomon
Off.	Ambrose, *On the Duties of the Clergy* (*De officiis ministrorum*)
Opif.	Philo, *On the Creation of the World* (*De opificio mundi*)
Opusc.	Maximus the Confessor, *Little Theological and Polemical Works* (*Opuscula theologica et polemica*)
Or.	Evagrius Ponticus, *Chapters on Prayer* (*De oratione*); Gregory of Nazianzus, *Orations* (*Orationes*); Origen, *On Prayer* (*De oratione*)
Or. Bas.	Gregory of Nazianzus, *Panegyric on Basil* (*Oratio in laudem Basilii*)
Or. cat.	Gregory of Nyssa, *Catechetical Oration* (*Oratio catechetica*)
Or. dom.	Gregory of Nyssa, *On the Lord's Prayer* (*De oratione dominica*)
Orat. paneg.	Gregory Thaumaturgus, *Address on Origen* (*Oratio panegyrica in Origenem*)
Pan.	Epiphanius, *Refutation of All Heresies* (*Panarion*; containing Basil of Ancyra's *Synodal Letter of the Council of Ancyra*)
Pasch.	Melito of Sardis, *On the Pascha* (*Peri pascha*)
Pecc. merit.	Augustine, *Guilt and Remission of Sins* (*De peccatorum meritis et remissione*)
Perf.	Gregory of Nyssa, *On Perfection* (*De perfectione*)
Persev.	Augustine, *On the Gift of Perseverance* (*De dono perseverantiae*)
PG	Patrologia Graeca. Edited by J.-P. Migne. 162 vols. Paris, 1857–1886
Phaed.	Plato, *Phaedo*
Phaedr.	Plato, *Phaedrus*
Philoc.	Origen, *Philocalia*
Praed.	Augustine, *On the Predestination of the Saints* (*De praedestinatione sanctorum*)
Praescr.	Tertullian, *On the Prescription against Heretics* (*De praescriptione haereticorum*)
Prax.	Tertullian, *Against Praxeas* (*Adversus Praxean*)
Princ.	Origen, *On First Principles* (*De principiis*)
Protr.	Clement of Alexandria, *Exhortation to the Greeks* (*Protrepticus*)
Pulch.	Cyril of Alexandria, *To the Empresses Pulcheria and Eudoxia* (*Ad Pulcheriam et Eudociam*)

Quaest. dub.	Maximus the Confessor, *Questions and Doubts* (*Quaestiones et dubia*)
Quaest. Thal.	Maximus the Confessor, *Questions to Thalassius* (*Quaestiones ad Thalassium*)
Reg.	Tyconius, *Book of Rules* (*Liber regularum*)
Rep.	Cicero, *On the Republic* (*De republica*)
Res.	Methodius of Olympus, *On the Resurrection of the Dead* (*De resurrectione mortuorum*)
Resp.	Plato, *Republic* (*Respublica*)
Retract.	Augustine, *Retractions* (*Retractationum libri ii*)
Sacr.	Ambrose, *On the Sacraments* (*De sacramentis*)
Sanct. Pasch.	Gregory of Nyssa, *On the Holy Pascha* (*In sanctum Pascha*)
Sanct. quadr.	Basil of Caesarea, *On the Holy Forty Martyrs* (*In sanctos quadraginta Martyres*)
SC	Sources chrétiennes
Serm.	Augustine, *Sermons* (*Sermones*)
Simpl.	Augustine, *Letter to Simplicianus* (*De diversis quaestionibus ad Simplicianum libri duo*)
Skemm.	Evagrius Ponticus, *Reflections* (*Skemmata*)
Solil.	Augustine, *Soliloquies* (*Soliloquiorum libri ii*)
Spir.	Basil of Caesarea, *On the Holy Spirit* (*De Spiritu Sancto*); Didymus the Blind, *On the Holy Spirit* (*De Spiritu Sancto*); Gregory of Nazianzus, *On the Holy Spirit* (*De Spiritu Sancto*; poem 1.1.3)
Spir. et litt.	Augustine, *On the Spirit and the Letter* (*De spiritu et littera*)
Spir. Syr.	Basil of Caesarea, *The Syriac Versions of* De Spiritu Sancto *by Basil of Caesarea*. Translated by David G. K. Taylor. CSCO 576. Leuven: Peeters, 1999
Stat.	John Chrysostom, *Homilies on the Statues* (*Homiliae xxi de statuis ad populum Antiochenum*)
Strom.	Clement of Alexandria, *Miscellanies* (*Stromateis*)
Symp.	Methodius of Olympus, *Banquet of the Ten Virgins* (*Symposion seu convivium virginum*)
Syn.	Athanasius, *On the Councils of Ariminum and Selucia* (*De synodis*); Hilary of Poitiers, *On the Councils* (*De synodis*)
Synt.	Aetius, *Syntagmation*, quoted in Thomas A. Kopecek, *A History of Neo-Arianism*. Vol. 1. Cambridge: Philadelphia Patristic Foundation, 1979
Thal. fr.	Arius, fragments of *Thalia* in *De synodis* 15
Theaet.	Plato, *Theaetetus*

Theol. oec.	Maximus the Confessor, *Chapters on Theology and the Economy* (*Capita theologica et oeconomica*)
Theoph.	Gregory of Nyssa, *To Theophilus: Against the Apollinarians* (*Ad Theophilum*)
Tom.	Athanasius, *Tome to the Antiochenes* (*Tomus ad Antiochenos*)
Tract. ep. Jo.	Augustine, *Tractates on the First Epistle of John* (*In epistulam Johannis ad Parthos tractatus*)
Tract. Ev. Jo.	Augustine, *In Evangelium Johannis tractatus* (*Tractates on the Gospel of John*)
Tract. Vat.	Babai the Great, *Tractate* (*Tractatus Vaticanus*)
Treat. Res.	Treatise on the Resurrection
Trin.	Augustine, *On the Trinity* (*De Trinitate*); Hilary of Poitiers, *On the Trinity* (*De Trinitate*)
Un. corp.	Apollinaris, *On the Union of Body and Divinity in Christ* (*De unione corporis et divinitatis in Christo*)
Unit. eccl.	Cyprian, *On the Unity of the Catholic Church* (*De catholicae ecclesiae unitate*)
Urk.	Opitz, Hans-Georg. *Urkunden zur Geschichte des arianischen Streites 318–328*. Berlin: de Gruyter, 1934
Urk. 1	Arius, *Letter to Eusebius of Nicomedia*
Urk. 4b	Alexander of Alexandria, *Circular Letter*, preserved by Athanasius
Urk. 6	Arius, *Letter to Alexander of Alexandria*
Urk. 14	Alexander of Alexandria, *Letter to Alexander of Byzantium*
Urk. 18	*Letter of the Council of Antioch 325*
Urk. 22	Eusebius of Caesarea, *Letter to His Churches*
Urk. 30	Arius, *Confession of Arius and Euzoius*, in Socrates Scholasticus, *Ecclesiastical History* 1.26.8
Ver. rel.	Augustine, *On True Religion* (*De vera religione*)
Virg.	Ambrose, *On Virgins* (*De virginibus*)
Virginit.	Gregory of Nyssa, *On Virginity* (*De virginitate*)
Vit.	Gregory of Nazianzus, *On His Own Life* (*De vita sua*)
Vit. Ant.	Athanasius, *Life of Antony* (*Vita Antonii*)
Vit. Georg.	Babai the Great, *Life of George* (*Vita Georgii*)

Introduction

A book's subtitle is often a good and necessary qualifier that reveals the actual content of the volume. So it is in this case. Although I think of myself as a historical theologian, this volume is not properly speaking a work in historical theology but in history. For I understand historical theology to be a mode of doing theology, that is, thinking through questions about the nature of God and salvation history, by thinking alongside and through the writings of theologians of the past with the goal of arriving at some tentative answers—"broken lights," as Tennyson put it—and possibly constructive suggestions that might contribute to the millennia-old conversation among Christians. Such is not the project of this volume. There is no epilogue that presumes to sum up the greater significance of these many pages.

Instead, it is, as advertised on the cover, "A History," meaning that it offers an account of what various authors from classical antiquity to the eighth century AD wrote and how I understand what they meant. Its goal is to introduce modern readers, some just beginning, to their thought, the meaning of which is often less than transparent. As such, this is not a history with a capital "H." For I am not offering a theology of history. In these pages there is no grand narrative of Marxist or Hegelian character that explains the significance of the Church's developing understanding of the meaning and implications of its faith. Rather, I try to keep my account of causal relationships between various thinkers across time to a narrow time frame. Consequently, in a very un-Hegelian mode, I offer no speculations about the actual agency of God's Spirit in inspiring or shaping the development of Christian thought. My job as the historian is to represent as accurately as I know how what I deem to be the features of an author's thought that proved most significant for the conversations and debates about various theological loci both in their historical moment and for later generations. I do not presume this is a "just the facts" narrative. The facts presented here are not wholly objective. They reflect historical judgments about which voices I deem to have been most important in a given historical setting or whose thoughts had and have enduring significance for later generations of Christian theologians.

While I have tried to include voices that were left out of histories written by earlier generations of scholars in whose debt I stand, there are others that are omitted, not because they lack merit but because of their relative lesser influence on the conversation. Some of the authors or positions I discuss were either at the time or subsequently deemed heretical. That was often as much a judgment about the author's moral failure—for example, a refusal to submit to correction—as it was because of the theological error itself. And, as we shall see, from the early heresiologies that traced deviation from the apostles' teachings to the magician Simon Magus to later polemical writings, the motives behind authors' heterodox teachings were called into question and often imputed to them the basest of motives. Unless there is historical evidence of perfidy or nefarious intentions, I bracket such judgments. Instead, I concentrate on representing the religious commitments and theo-logic guiding the author's thinking—even if that logic came to be called into question. I always took it as a compliment when my students would say that they found my presentation of an author's thought so persuasive that it was not until later in the lecture that they were surprised to learn that the position was ultimately condemned. That is intentional on my part. For the history of early Christian theology is the story of many false starts that, even as Augustine admits, had the value of forcing the Church to clarify its position and come to a deeper understanding of the logic guiding its interpretations of Scripture. It is crucial for a right understanding of the Church's history, therefore, that no thinker be treated as a theological straw man whose positions could be facilely dismissed with the slightest gust of polemical breeze.

It is unavoidably a story of winners and losers. Gregory of Nazianzus's Christology carried the day; Apollinaris's did not. Augustine's account of grace and original sin was judged normative in the West; Pelagius's was rejected. Therefore, to whatever degree my narrative shifts from mere description of a thinker's ideas to causal explanation, the story of early Christian theology as I tell it does attempt to explain why certain theological positions, in spite of imperfections inherent in all attempts to speak about God, prevailed in becoming normative and why others, in spite of their kernels of truth, did not. Nevertheless, what I am offering should not be represented as confessional history in contrast with a theologically neutral religious studies approach. That is a false dichotomy. For no method of inquiry in this or any other field is without its first principles that are unspoken givens rarely if ever expressly acknowledged. Yet all good scholarship assumes that scholars are self-aware and honest enough to admit how their perspective influences their analysis. As my colleague and friend the late Elizabeth A. Clark wrote in the introduction to her masterful monograph *The Origenist Controversy:*

The Cultural Construction of an Early Christian Debate, "My approach, as even the inattentive reader will soon note, is admittedly partisan. . . . It is . . . an attempt to raise up for consideration a defeated theology that for a few years stirred the Christian world to new intellectual creativity."[1] So, following her example, I will confess my own partisanship. One of my presuppositions is that theology is not a mere epiphenomenon in the Marxist sense. That is, theology cannot be explained entirely by the social or economic world its authors inhabited. Even when political and ecclesial rivalries between episcopal sees enter the picture—as they will—the doctrinal content is not reducible to those rivalries. Were the opposite the case, then ideas discussed in this book would be neither intelligible nor meaningful to people outside the author's historical context. Yet, for all the differences between the world of late antiquity and the age of artificial intelligence in which we live, many of these ideas have enduring meaning for Christians seeking to understand the message of their Scriptures. Because Christians of late antiquity and their modern heirs share, by and large, the same Scriptures, they are similarly troubled by many of the same lacunae and so pose similar questions of the text. For this basic reason, many students of late antique Christianity find in these authors, for all their differences, resources for thinking through the enduring enigmas of Scripture.

One of my concerns as an interpreter of ancient theological texts is to explain why an author chose to express his thought in a particular way. Nevertheless, I assume that for these theologians, as for all people, their words have a surplus of meaning that say more—or possibly imply more—than the author intended. This is what invited either criticism for problematic implications or appreciative interpretations by successive generations of theologians that expanded the author's meaning. This is what allows these texts, even today, to be a resource for enduring theological conversation. Yet patristic theology cannot be a resource if modern theologians fall into the error of presentism, which assumes an idea or term from late antiquity held the same valence as it does today. For as these ideas have passed down the generations from late antiquity to the present, they have acquired a history of interpretation and with it layers of theological accretions. Their meanings have acquired further nuances. So if any particular author of late antiquity is to serve as a resource for present theological reflection, the modern theologian must make sure that her use of a given figure, say Gregory of Nyssa, is consistent with the Gregory of the late fourth century and not the Gregory as may have been passed on in our selective contemporary memory. Only then can modern constructive theologians be confident they are fairly representing

1. Elizabeth A. Clark, *The Origenist Controversy: The Cultural Construction of an Early Christian Debate* (Princeton: Princeton University Press, 1992), 10.

Gregory as a conversation partner. This book, therefore, seeks to give readers a knowledge of the historical Gregory so as to give them a reliable foundation for further engagement and reflection.

Because I assume that this book is something of an introduction to patristic thought, I have, for the sake of simplicity, confined my references to the primary sources. In the bibliography at the end of each chapter, I list a few of the classic or contemporary works of scholarship that have informed my presentation and should be consulted for further study. Furthermore, because this book is written for Anglophone readers who may not know the Greek, Latin, or Syriac, I have given references for primary sources in recent English translations rather than the critical editions.

A word about my language. No theologian of the early Church who was judged orthodox taught that God was a man. Since God is incorporeal while gender is a feature of the body, the divine nature was viewed as sexless. Nevertheless, since Jesus taught his disciples to address God as "Father" and spoke of the one who sent him as "the Father," patristic authors used the masculine pronoun when referring to God. To be authentic, I do as well. In the case of human beings, I alternate the use of gender on the theological assumption that the common human nature shared by women and men is fully expressed in individuals of either sex. Therefore, I will say "the Christian . . . she" or "the philosopher . . . he," using the gendered term in its generic, inclusive sense. I also alternate between speaking of "Church" and "church." The latter refers to a particular historic community, as with "the church in Ephesus." The former denotes the universal community of Christian believers whom Paul refers to as "the body of Christ" and that the Nicene-Constantinopolitan Creed refers to as "one, holy, catholic, and apostolic." Furthermore, I use "Catholic," as did Irenaeus, to refer to the Christian community—that Celsus spoke of as "the Great Church"—in contrast with sects, such as Gnostics and Marcionites, that identified as Christian but were outside the Catholic community.

1

The Foundation

Church, Doxology, Scripture, and Pagan Wisdom

Historians should not be afraid to begin their narratives by stating the obvious. Precisely because the obvious is obvious, it can be, and often is, taken for granted and overlooked. Yet the obvious may contain the kernels of truth necessary for deeper understanding.

The obvious fact on which our narrative rests is this: all the authors whose writings and ideas are the material of this narrative—from Ignatius of Antioch to John of Damascus—before they were theologians and shapers of Christian doctrine, were simply members of a community, a community of worshipers. Before they applied ink to parchment or papyrus or dictated lines to a scribe, they were people engaged in practices of doxology. Before any of them composed a single sermon or pastoral letter, prepared a biblical commentary or philosophical dialogue, wrote an apology for outsiders, composed a catechesis for neophytes, or crafted a single prayer or poem or hymn, they gathered with fellow believers, would-be believers, and the simply curious to worship their God. Their communities were distinct from other religious assemblies of the late antique Mediterranean—Jews, Manichees, devotees of Isis or Mithras, or the Magna Mater in Rome—because they offered their praise and invocations to the God of Israel revealed in Jesus of Nazareth whom they identified as *Christos*, the Messiah and Son of God (Matt 16:16).

The kernel of truth contained in this obvious fact is that early Christian theology grew out of doxology. Not the praise of a lone individual, it was the collective worship of Jesus's followers first called "the Way" (Acts 9:2; 19:9) and eventually the Church (*ecclesia*). As communities that began as sects within Judaism, their worship centered upon ritual readings from the Torah, the Psalms, and the Writings. To these were added the first-century texts collected from authors who could claim direct familiarity either with Jesus or with his most intimate associates, the apostles. These texts were collected and anthologized from an early date and preserved in written form the oral tradition about Jesus's life and ministry. They also offered a witness to the significance of Jesus, which they commonly spoke of as "the gospel" (Gal 1:6–7) or "the faith" (Jude 3). These texts, which came to comprise the New Testament, not only provided the content of the Church's liturgical practices and doctrines; they also established models of exegesis imitated by later generations of interpreters. The result was a distinctive interpretation of Israel's Scriptures in light of the Christian community's confession of Jesus's identity as Israel's Messiah and the only-begotten Son of God (John 1:18).

As we historians assess the purpose of the theological enterprise undertaken by these early Christian authors, we have to recognize that the worshiping life of the Church as informed by both oral tradition and written documents of the Old and New Testaments was foundational for the production and transmission of the theological texts from the beginning of the second century to the eighth century where our narrative ends. A central contention of this history is that the doxological life of the Church is prior in the order of explanation to the theological texts on which this history focuses. That does not mean, however, as some nineteenth-century theologians contended, that theology was merely a second order reflection on religious experience. While certain worship practices may be episodic and punctiliar, the life and thought of the authors discussed here were not easily compartmentalized into worship and intellectual reflection. The familiar words of the Psalms or of the Great Thanksgiving chanted during the liturgy did not recede from consciousness at the end of the worship service. Like the words of Scripture, the language of the liturgy lingered in their minds, shaped their thoughts, and sparked haunting questions that acquired expression in a variety of theological genres. Thus, the *lex orandi lex credendi*—the norms of praying and the norms of believing or understanding—existed in a mutually informing dialectic. Even in periods when the shared articulation of the Church's confession experienced disruption, the debates and polemical exchanges moved the Church from an initial intuitive comprehension of the meaning of the liturgies and Scriptures to a more refined and nuanced understanding of the same liturgies and Scriptures.

At the same time our authors were formed by language and practices of the *ecclesia*, many, though not all, were also formed by their education in the philosophical and rhetorical literature of classical and Hellenistic culture. There was, however, a consciousness of the differences between Athens and Jerusalem that meant that the wisdom of Academy or Lyceum or Stoa could not be perfectly harmonized with the wisdom of God revealed in Jesus Christ. When young Augustine was enraptured by the description of philosophy in Cicero's *Hortensius* while studying rhetoric in Carthage, his first impulse when seeking out the wisdom of which Cicero wrote was to turn to the Christian Scriptures (*Conf.* 3.4.7). Though the rhetorical crudeness of the Bible's prose left the immature Augustine unimpressed, nevertheless his instinct to turn to Scripture was the product of a sensibility instilled in him by his mother Monica and the Catholic community of Thagaste. Regardless of their awareness of certain profound differences between the pagan and Christian wisdom, these authors, even the most ardent critics of philosophy such as Tertullian, drew from their intellectual training in the pagan classics to find tools for their theological undertakings.[1]

From examining this kernel found in the obvious, this chapter provides an overview of the four foundations of patristic theology: Church, worship, Scripture, and classical learning.

Church

The Community of the New Israel

By the turn of the second century, the divide between Christianity and Judaism had become sharper than it had been in the minds of the first or second generation of Christians. Paul's lament in his Letter to the Romans for unbelieving Israel (9:2–4) and his eschatological hope that Israel, which was cut off by its unbelief, would be regrafted into the covenant (11:22–24) indicate an early consciousness of growing divisions between Jews and Christians. After the Jewish Revolt and the destruction of the temple in AD 70 by the legions of Titus, and then certainly after Hadrian's expulsion of the Jews from Jerusalem in response to the Bar Kokhba rebellion of 132–135, Christians no longer thought of themselves or were viewed by the larger gentile world as a sect within Judaism. Christianity was a separate and distinct religion.

In this context, one of the central questions facing Christians was how to understand their identity as members of the new covenant that Jesus inaugurated at the Last Supper: "This is my blood of the new covenant poured out for you and for many for the forgiveness of sins" (Matt 26:28). What is the relationship between this new covenant recognized by Christians and God's previous covenants with Israel? This question was already in the minds of the New Testament authors. Is faith in Christ sufficient to make gentile believers children of Abraham and thus heirs of God's promises made to Abraham and his descendants, or must they be also circumcised and observe the Mosaic law (Gal 3:23–29)? Or is Christ the "true High Priest" whose sacrifice of himself and entry into the heavenly holy of

1. "Pagan" (Latin, *paganus*) was derived from *pagus*, which means "one who dwelt in a rural village"; but, reflecting the prejudice of urbanites, it carried the derisive connotation of "hick," someone unsophisticated who was a follower of superstitions. By the fourth century, Christians, following Marius Victorinus's precedent, commonly used the term as a synonym for the Greek *Hellēn*, which in the New Testament referred to a gentile (Latin, *gentilis*) but eventually was used to speak of a non-Christian.

holies established a new covenant in his blood that rendered the Mosaic covenant obsolete, as when an old will is superseded by a new will (Heb 8:13)? Christian answers to these questions ranged widely in the second century from affirmations of continuity between the two covenants to outright repudiation of any connection between them.

Justin Martyr (AD 100–165): Continuity Between the Covenants

Among those who affirmed a continuity between the covenants, the Church was spoken of as Israel. The foundation of this claim was Paul's argument in Galatians (3:6–9) that even as Abraham was reckoned righteous before God because of his faith, so too gentile believers in Christ were justified by their faith without obedience to the Mosaic law, especially circumcision. Justin Martyr (100–165), in his dialogue with a Jew named Trypho who was a member of the Jewish diaspora after the Bar Kokhba rebellion, explains to his interlocutor that the Church is the "true Israel." Christians, he assures Trypho, do not worship a God different from the God of Israel but that Jesus himself, as the Christ, is the "final law" and the "new covenant" that has abrogated the Mosaic law and rendered it obsolete (*Dial.* 11.1–2). Therefore, like the patriarchs who lived by faith before the law, the Christians are "the true spiritual Israel, and the descendants of Judah, Jacob, Isaac, and Abraham, who, though uncircumcised, was approved and blessed by God because of his faith and was called the father of many nations" (*Dial.* 11.5).

Central to the ensuing argument was the issue of circumcision. Trypho criticized the Christians for failing to follow the example of proselytes who obeyed the law and were circumcised and thereby distinguished themselves from pagan gentiles (*Dial.* 10.2–3). Justin countered that God, foreknowing the Jews' murdering the prophets and "the Just One" (Christ), and their cursing and persecuting Jesus's disciples, commanded circumcision as a sign of their sins, so that they might be distinguished from the gentiles and expelled by Hadrian from God's holy city (*Dial.* 16.2–4). Although Abraham was eventually circumcised (Gen 17:10–11), Justin argues that it was only *after* his faith had been deemed righteous by God (Gen 15:6; Rom 4:3; *Dial.* 23.4). Indeed, Abel, Noah, Enoch, and Melchizedek were not circumcised, but they were nevertheless judged righteous because of their faith (*Dial.* 19.2–4). Their righteousness through faith prior to circumcision was paradigmatic of Christian righteousness. Moreover, for Justin, the gentile Christians' faith in Christ and the repudiation of pagan idolatry were evidence that they possessed the true spiritual circumcision, a circumcision not of the flesh but of the heart (Rom 2:28–29; *Dial.* 43.1).

Justin's view of the Jews, for historians on this side of the Holocaust, is complicated. It must be remembered that Justin's view is ultimately exegetical, not a theory of racial superiority. He wrote from his position as a teacher and leader of a persecuted minority—a smaller minority in the Roman world than the Jews—and lived only a few generations removed from the death of Jesus and the persecution of Christians by Saul of Tarsus. Justin follows Paul's declaration that "not all who are descendants from Israel belong to Israel, and not all are Abraham's children because they are his descendants" (Rom 9:6–7), and his distinction between those Jews who are children of the flesh and those true Jews who are children of the promise (Rom 9:8). Thus, he tells Trypho that, even as there are nominal Christians who do not adhere to right teachings, so too there are Jews (e.g., the Sadducees) who are Jews in name only because they deny the resurrection of the dead (*Dial.* 80.4) and by extension Jesus's resurrection. Such nominal Jews are cut off from the hope of salvation and have forfeited their inheritance as Abraham's descendants unless they repent and "come to know Christ [and are] baptized" (*Dial.* 26.1; 44.4). Paradoxically, he says that all people endowed with free will have the capacity to repent and convert (*Dial.* 141.1)—indeed "every day" Jews are converting and becoming disciples of Christ (*Dial.* 39.2)—yet he also says that a special grace is necessary to recognize the signs in Scripture that confirm Jesus's identity as the Messiah (*Dial.* 119.1). Although Justin demurs on the question of the salvation of the Jews—"I shall not be bold enough to state whether or not any one of your race, by the grace of the Lord Sabaoth, may be saved"—he nevertheless is confident that "those Jews who attain salvation are saved through [Christ] and are his partisans" (*Dial.* 64.2–3). It is such grace that Justin seemingly has in mind when he repeatedly tells Trypho that he prays for the conversion of the Jews (*Dial.* 142.3).

Since God's covenant with Abraham was based on his faith in Christ who would in time come as a "light for revelation to the Gentiles" (Isa 49:6; Luke 2:32), the "new covenant" is simply the Abrahamic covenant now grounded in Christ's death for the forgiveness of sins and extended to the gentiles (*Dial.* 11.4). As such, the gift of the new covenant, for Justin, marked a return to the older—and therefore more venerable—covenant of righteousness based on faith rather than the covenant of righteousness based on adherence to the Mosaic law.

Epistle of Barnabas (ca. AD 130): Different Covenants for Jews and Christians

A more radical view of the relationship of the Mosaic covenant to the new covenant was expressed in a letter composed around 130 and attributed to Barnabas. The epistle contends that the Mosaic covenant and the new covenant given by Christ are two completely different covenants. Its argument rests upon an analysis of the narrative in Exodus 31–34 of the giving of the law. The first covenant was inscribed on the two tablets by the finger of God (Exod 31:18). This was the covenant God intended to give to Israel now liberated from slavery in Egypt. However, upon seeing the golden calf whom the Israelites were worshiping, Moses broke the tablets. This, according to the Epistle of Barnabas, signified that Israel was not ready to receive that covenant. They needed discipline to be prepared to receive this covenant. Therefore, Moses returned to Sinai where Moses, not God, wrote the Decalogue (Exod 34:27–28). The covenant that the Church received from Christ—"the covenant of the beloved Jesus"—was the first covenant inscribed by God on the tablets that Moses broke. Israel was unready and unworthy (Barn. 14.4) and so needed the law as a teacher and disciplinarian, whereas Christians received the first covenant from Jesus sealed upon their hearts because of their faith in him (Barn. 4.8).

This distinction between the two covenants, one for Jews and one for Christians, did not mean that torah was of no value for Christians. Rather, the Epistle of Barnabas drew heavily on the prophets of Israel and their critique of the Jews' focus on the *literal* observance of the sacrifices, fasts, and Sabbaths. What the Jews missed, therefore, was the spiritual meaning the law was intended to teach. The epistle, therefore, gives extensive allegorical interpretations of the torah's dietary prescriptions. For instance, Moses's instruction to eat "anything that has a divided hoof" teaches that the righteous must have a divided gaze that looks both to their lives in this world but also to "the holy age to come" (Barn. 10.11). Because the commandments in the law are types or *typoi* of spiritual truths, by understanding the spiritual meaning of the types, the Christian is able to fulfill the moral demands of the law and attain a spiritual life of holiness. Moreover, the books of Moses were useful because they contained prophetic *typoi* that pointed to the coming of Christ.

Marcion (AD 85–160): Two Covenants, Two Gods

Although the Epistle of Barnabas separated the Mosaic covenant and the new covenant, nevertheless, it contended that both were revelations of one and the same God. A teacher in Rome in the middle of the second century—a contemporary of Justin—named Marcion took a decidedly different approach. A Pontic fisherman who converted to Christianity and settled in Rome, Marcion broke from the church in Rome to establish his own community around 150. His teaching revolved around an idiosyncratic reading of Paul's letters, especially Galatians and Romans. Based on Paul's claim that salvation was given to the gentiles through faith in Christ rather than adherence to the law of Moses, Marcion envisioned a radical opposition between the Christian gospel and the Jewish torah from which Christ had liberated the gentiles. He found confirmation for this opposition in points of contradictions between the Jewish Scriptures and the Christian Scriptures, which he compiled in a text known as the *Antitheses*. Among the points of contradiction that he discovered were these:

> No. 3: Joshua conquered the land with violence and cruelty, but Christ forbade all violence and preached mercy and peace.
>
> No. 7: The prophet (i.e., Moses) of the Creator God, when the people were locked in battle, climbed to the top of the mountain and stretched forth his hands to God, that he might kill as many as possible in battle; our Lord, the Good, stretched forth his hands (sc., on the cross) not to kill men but to save them.
>
> No. 20: *Maledictio* characterizes the law; *benedictio* characterizes faith.
>
> No. 25: The Creator of the world ordained the Sabbath, but Christ takes it away.
>
> No. 26: The world-Creator rejects the publicans as non-Jewish and profane; Christ accepts the publicans.
>
> No. 27: The law forbids the touching of a woman who has an issue of blood; Christ not only touches them but heals them as well.

Marcion explains these contradictions as the result of two separate revelations of two separate Gods. The God of the Jews is the Creator god or demiurge who also gave the law. This God Marcion calls the God of righteousness—a righteousness measured by torah. He is a God of wrath who punishes the unrighteous and who made the Jews his chosen people. By contrast, the God revealed by Jesus is not the Creator of the world or the God of Israel but the true God, an alien God because he had never revealed himself before the coming of Jesus. In contrast with Israel's God of righteous judgment, the alien God is a God of mercy, forgiveness, and love who seeks the redemption of all people.

Although Marcion's life and teachings—especially, as we shall see, his creation of a New Testament canon—is more complex than the narratives offered by Tertullian, Irenaeus, Epiphanius, and other sources, what is important for the development of early Catholic doctrine is the radical separation of the old and new covenants that his thought represented. Marcion's dichotomous treatment of creation and redemption, law and grace, and Israel and the Church became a negative standard by which heresy would be separated from orthodoxy. To put it another way, Marcion's thought as interpreted by Tertullian and Irenaeus forced them to articulate an account of the apostolic faith that illustrated the essential unity of the two covenants and the God whom they disclose.

Gnostic Sects: Radical Division Between Jew and Christian

Various gnostic sects, such as those who accepted the Apocryphon of John, made a similar divide between the God of Israel who was the demiurge and the God of the Christ. For their narrative, the Creator god was ignorant Ialdabaōth, who was the abortion of one of the aeons, Sophia (Ap. John 10.1). She conceived Ialdabaōth when she attempted to see the true God who transcends all knowing. Although the Apocryphon of John does not identify the God of Israel with Ialdabaōth, its climactic poem has no reference to Israel or any connection between Israel's God and the Savior who descended to deliver humanity from ignorance and the prison of the body (Ap. John 30.11–31.27).

Similarly, Basilides, a gnostic teacher in second-century Alexandria, taught that the world was created by the lowest rank of angels who established themselves as gods over the material world. The God of Israel, therefore, was not the true God but one of the angels who created the world (*Haer.* 1.24.4). The cosmologies of Marcion and the Gnostics created a more radical division between Jews and Christians than that implied in the Epistle of Barnabas. The Epistle of Barnabas viewed the Mosaic covenant and the new covenant of Jesus as altogether distinct in a way that separated the Jews from both the Old Testament patriarchs who lived before the law and the Christians who lived under the new covenant; the Epistle of Barnabas still viewed both covenants as coming from the same God and both as authoritative for Christian knowledge of God and of righteousness.

Irenaeus (AD 130–202): Unity of the Covenants and the Divine Economy

In his treatise *Against Heresies*, the Asian-born Gallic bishop Irenaeus of Lyons countered Marcion by arguing that the apparent discrepancies between the covenants in torah and the new covenant were the necessary consequence of God's gradual revelation of himself in history. Because human beings were created from nothing and therefore were born in a state of immaturity (*Haer.* 3.22.4), it was necessary that humanity undergo a process of education. They had to learn how to see God.

This learning process occurred over time through the unfolding of the divine economy (*oikonomia*). Irenaeus took the term "economy" from Ephesians 1:9–10, which speaks of God's cosmic plan (*oikonomia*) of salvation by which all things would be united in Christ. The economy, for Irenaeus, is God's progressive self-revelation in history through a series of dispensations (*in universis dispositionibus*

Dei) that climax in Jesus and the giving of the Holy Spirit (*Haer.* 4.33.1).[2] In contrast with the intra-Trinitarian relations of the Father, Son, and Spirit that are veiled in eternity, in the economy the Trinity is revealed in the persons' activities in history, specifically through the covenants God made with his people. Each covenant or dispensation built on the previous ones to reveal some new dimension of God's nature. The covenants were imperfect, but indispensable, revealing in a fragmentary way a partial image of the divine. The Mosaic covenant, for instance, with its prescriptions and prohibitions and the corresponding punishments for failure to abide by the law, made manifest God's justice and holiness so that Israel might indeed be a "kingdom of priests and a holy nation." Since forgiveness and mercy are meaningless where there is no condemnation to be forgiven or punishment from which to be freed, God's justice and wrath revealed in torah, far from being contrary to the new covenant, were necessary prerequisites for appreciating Christ's deliverance from condemnation.

Commenting on Jesus's words that the scribes of the kingdom of heaven are like a householder "bringing forth out of his treasure things new and old" (Matt 13:52), Irenaeus argues that the old and the new did not come from different sources but from one and the same God. God reveals himself according to the status and capacity of those to whom he makes himself known. Both the old and the new come from the treasure of God's grace: the old covenant given to slaves who needed to be disciplined by the law, and the new given to those liberated from sin and condemnation through their justification by faith in Jesus (*Haer.* 4.9.1). In Jesus's parable of the prodigal son (Luke 15:11–32), the two sons represent the Jews and the gentile Christians, but there is one father representing the one God common to both. Similarly, in the parable of the workers in the vineyard (Matt 20:1–16), Jesus offers a figure of the one householder who offers the same wages to those who came early (i.e., Jews) and those who came late (i.e., gentiles). "There is but one vineyard, since there is but one righteousness and one dispenser, for there is one Spirit of God who arranges all things; and in like manner there is one hire, for they all receive a penny for each man, having stamped upon it the royal image and superscription, the knowledge of the Son of God, which is immortality" (*Haer.* 4.36.7).

For Irenaeus, the new covenant is greater than the old, but since Christ is the content of both, the covenants are of the same substance. How, though, can one be greater than the other if they share a common content, Christ? Irenaeus answers that the new is greater because, having been liberated by Christ's grace, the

2. The terms "dispensation" and "economy" are English synonyms corresponding to the Greek *oikonomia*, which, in the Latin texts of *Against Heresies*, is translated *dispositio*, which means "order" or "arrangement." At times, Irenaeus uses the singular to refer to the overall plan of salvation or in the plural when referring to the covenants.

love of those liberated is greater than those who are slaves to the law (*Haer.* 4.9.2). Yet even the new covenant is not wholly new, since it was foretold by Isaiah who exhorted the exiles, "Sing to the Lord a new song" (Isa 42:10), and by Jeremiah who prophesied, "Behold, I will make a new covenant, not as I made with your fathers" (Jer 31:31). Thus, Israel was being prepared "that they might always make progress through believing in him, and by means of [successive] covenants, should gradually attain to perfect salvation. For there is one salvation and one God; but . . . the steps which lead man to God are not few" (*Haer.* 4.9.3).

Irenaeus, following Justin, also sees the Church as supplanting the Jews from their covenantal relationship with God. Commenting on Jesus's parable of the vineyard and the wicked tenants (Matt 21:33–46), he explains that the vineyard is a figure for creation planted by the one true God. The tower built over the vineyard is a figure for Jerusalem, and the winepress represents the receptacle for the prophetic Spirit. The first servants dispatched by the owner of the vineyard were the prophets sent by the one God to call Israel to give up to him fruits of righteousness. The owner of the vineyard, who puts out the tenants who killed his son and heir, gives the vineyard, that is, the kingdom of God, to "a nation producing the fruits of it" (Matt 21:41, 43). The parable, therefore, foretells the transfer of the kingdom from the Jews to the Church. The tower that overlooked the vineyard is, Irenaeus argues, no longer a figure of Jerusalem but is "the beautiful elect tower being raised everywhere. For the illustrious Church is now everywhere, and everywhere is the winepress dug: because those who do receive the Spirit are everywhere" (*Haer.* 4.36.2). Although most contemporary commentators interpret the wicked tenants as referring not to Jews generally speaking but specifically to the chief priests and Pharisees, who rightly recognized that the parable was "told about them" (Matt 21:45), Irenaeus understood "the other tenants" (v. 41) to be those who recognize the prophets of Israel, receive the vineyard owner's son, and bear the fruit of righteousness. In this way, the Marcionites and the Gnostics who denied the authority of Israel's prophets were every bit as cut off from the one true God as were Jews who rejected Jesus's messianic authority. For Irenaeus, acknowledging the Son meant recognizing the prophets who foretold his coming, and there was no acknowledging the prophets without recognizing the Messiah whose coming they foretold. Following Paul's argument in Galatians, Irenaeus asserts that the faith of Abraham was the faith of the Church. The patriarchs were given prophetic vision by which they were able to look into the future to behold Christ and the gentiles who would, through faith in Christ, become heirs of the promise given to Abraham (*Haer.* 4.21.1).

Tertullian (AD 160–220): The Case for Unity of the Covenants

Another strong case in the second century for the unity of the covenants came in the refutations of Marcion and the Gnostics by the North African theologian Tertullian (160–220). He also grounds the unity of the old and new covenants in the "mystery of the dispensation [*oikonomia*]" in which the one God of the covenants is Father, Son, and Holy Spirit (*Prax.* 2).

Tertullian's strongest defense of the unity of the covenants comes in his treatise *Against Marcion.* Since the ground of Marcion's argument was his reading of Paul, Tertullian exposes Marcion's misreading of those letters. On Galatians, where the apostle Paul makes the severest contrast between the law and the gospel, Tertullian makes the obvious point: the problem of the law lay not in its having come from another god but because it came from the same God revealed in Jesus. Even as gentile converts to Christianity were expected to give up pagan practices, if the Jewish law had come from another god, the Galatians would have been expected to have given it up (*Marc.* 5.2). But when Paul attacks the teachers of circumcision in Galatia, he accuses them of preaching "another gospel" (Gal 1:7), not "another god" or "the gospel of another God" (*Marc.* 5.2). Nor does he accuse his opponents of apostasy—that is, abandoning the one true God of Jesus for the Creator god of Israel (*Marc.* 5.4). Neither does he repudiate all of the torah—as one would expect if this law were from a pagan deity—but only circumcision (*Marc.* 5.3).

Indeed, commenting on Paul's allegorical reading of Sarah and Hagar (Gal 4:21–31), Tertullian agrees with Marcion that God has liberated those who were once slaves to the law. Yet since only a slave's master can grant manumission, the only God who can grant liberty from the law of Israel is the God who gave the law that made them slaves to begin with (*Marc.* 5.4).

Unity and Continuity with the Church of the Apostles

Two other closely related elements central to early Christian identity were unity of the Scriptures and their continuity with the teachings of the apostles. A prevalent origin myth describes the Church as born at Pentecost with the gift of the Holy Spirit who formed Jesus's followers into a single community united in beliefs and practices. This myth claims that any diversity and division that produced heretical teachings arose from the corruption of the original pure Christianity through the addition of teachings traced ultimately back to the arch-heretic, Simon Magus (Acts 8:9–24). Justin Martyr, in his treatise *Syntagma.* traced all heresies of the mid-second century back to Simon. Such a narrative of decline from unity to diversities is simplistic. Even the evidence from the New Testament indicates that not all followers of Jesus traced their origins to Pentecost or even shared certain basic beliefs. In Ephesus, for instance, Paul encounters Christians who knew only the baptism of John and did not know about the Holy Spirit (Acts 19:1–5). Even the educated Apollos of Alexandria was familiar only with John's baptism of repentance (Acts 18:24–25). Nevertheless, early Christians, who would in time be called by later generations members of the "Catholic and Apostolic Church" (Canons of

Nicaea) or by a pagan critic Celsus "the Great Church"—in contradistinction from smaller sects that identified as Christian themselves—insisted on the unity and uniformity of the one true Church.

Ignatius of Antioch (d. circa 113): Witness of Harmonious Love

One of the earliest advocates of the unity of the Church was Ignatius of Antioch. In his letter to the Ephesians, he exhorted Christians to be as a chorus that sings its witness to Christ in its "unanimity and harmonious love" (Ign. *Eph.* 4.2). Indeed, God the Father recognizes them as members of his Son when he hears their uniformity. In this ecclesial chorus, the bishop sets the pitch to which all must attune their voices (Ign. *Eph.* 4.1). Even as Jesus did nothing apart from his Father, neither should the members of the Church do anything apart from the bishop. United by conformity to the mind of the bishop, the Church should "run together as to one temple of God, as to one altar, to the one Jesus Christ, who came forth from one Father and remained with the One and returned to the One" (Ign. *Trall.* 7.2). The mission of the Church, therefore, mirrors the mission of Christ who, even in his being sent from the Father into the world, preserved his unity with the Father who is the one source of his being.

By the second century, the office of bishop (*episkopos*) or "overseer" had developed from its original role described in the New Testament (Phil 1:1; 1 Tim 3:2) and the earliest ecclesial order, the Didache (late first to early second century), where it was synonymous with an elder (*presbyteros*) serving as senior pastor or priest of the largest congregation in an urban center. Ignatius speaks of a single bishop over elders and deacons (*diakonoi*). All three offices should be viewed with reverence and unfailing obedience. The bishop is to be honored as Christ and the elders and deacons as the apostles. Thus, each individual congregation mirrors the community of the first disciples.

Sometimes Ignatius presses the analogy further: "Let everyone respect the deacons as Jesus Christ, just as they should respect the bishop, who is a model of the Father and the presbyters as God's council and as a band of the apostles. Without these no group can be called a church" (Ign. *Trall.* 3.1). Indeed, a failure to respect or attempt to deceive the bishop, who is seen, is tantamount to deceiving and cheating God the Father, "the One who is unseen" (Ign. *Magn.* 3.2). Such offenders will face a reckoning, not with men but with God himself. For as Christ is "the Father's mind" and so revealed the Father to his disciples, the bishop is "the mind of Christ" who reveals his will for the Church (Ign. *Eph.* 3.2). As such, the bishop protects the community from the deceit of heretics who "mix Jesus Christ with poison" (Ign. *Trall.* 6.2). Those, however, who are puffed up with pride and presume to separate themselves from "the bishop and the commandments of the apostles" have rendered themselves unclean (Ign. *Trall.* 7.1–2). Moreover, those who are not inside the sanctuary do not have access to God's bread, that is, the Eucharist, which is the "medicine of immortality" (Ign. *Eph.* 5.2; 20.2). They are, in effect, cut off from salvation.

Irenaeus: Apostolic Succession

Although Ignatius closely associates the bishop, elders, and deacons with the apostles and as having authority analogous to the apostles', he does not ground that authority on some notion of a passing of authority from the apostles to their successors. The idea of apostolic succession emerged in the late second century in Irenaeus to counter gnostic claims to a secret knowledge passed down from Christ to certain apostles and then to the gnostic teachers. The Gospel of Thomas, for instance, renarrates the episode from the Synoptics (Matt 16:13–20; Mark 8:27–32) in which Jesus asks the disciples who he was. In the Synoptic version, Peter declares, "You are the Christ, the Son of the living God"; but the Gospel of Thomas reads,

> Simon Peter said to him, "A just angel is what you resemble." Matthew said to him, "An intelligent philosopher is what you resemble." Thomas said to him, "Teacher, my mouth utterly will not let me say what you resemble." . . . And [Jesus] took him, withdrew, and said three sayings to him. Now, when Thomas came to his companions they asked him, "What did Jesus say to you?" Thomas said, to them, "If I say to you one of the sayings that he said to me, you will take stones and stone me, and fire will come out of the stones and burn you up." (Gos. Thom. 34.30–35.10)

Instead of imparting knowledge of his identity to be shared by all the apostles, Jesus shared such knowledge only with Thomas—a knowledge that the other apostles and their followers were unable to receive. This line of transmission from the favored Thomas to the spiritually mature *gnōstikoi* was the basis for their claim to hidden *gnōsis* that distinguished the intellectual Gnostics from other Christians.

For Irenaeus, there was no hidden gospel given only to one of the apostles. On the contrary, there was one gospel proclaimed openly across the world (*Haer.* 1.4.3; 3.3.1). This universally recognized gospel first proclaimed by the apostles served as the standard for doctrinal norms that united the Church. The apostolic faith—what Tertullian called in Latin the *regula fidei*—was passed on to their disciples, the presbyters; it was, Irenaeus claimed, the common belief spread over the whole world and affirmed univocally, as if by a single soul (*Haer.* 1.10.2). The advantage to such univocity, he explains, is that the transmission of the gospel was not dependent on the rhetorical skill of the preacher. A lack of eloquence does not corrupt the content of the message preached.

Irenaeus's confidence in the continuity of the gospel proclaimed by the apostles and later preached in his own time was found in the succession of bishops who could trace their instruction in the faith directly to the apostles. Irenaeus himself could draw a line from John the Beloved Disciple to Polycarp of Smyrna, from whom he heard the gospel preached (*Haer.* 3.3.4). Thus, he could claim to be only two generations removed from Jesus's inner circle. Although all bishops could show their apostolic pedigree, bishops from the oldest communities had greater authority (*Haer.* 3.4.1). Of churches that could claim to have been founded by an apostle, the church at Rome had pride of place because it was traceable to both Peter and Paul (*Haer.* 3.3.3).

Worship

Central to the identity of early Christian communities, like their Jewish counterparts, was worship. "Worship" as spoken of in the New Testament did not, as Andrew McGowan has observed, refer to liturgy or ritual specifically so much as it did to a posture of reverent submission and gratitude. This posture, in either its literal sense of prostrating (*proskynēsis*) oneself before the Lord or the more common figurative sense, was a bodily confession of the reality inaugurated with Christ's incarnation, death, resurrection, and the gift of the Holy Spirit. The liturgical or ritual forms this confession took were a symbolic or sacramental expression of that reality. When Paul warned the Christians in Corinth that their failure to "discern the body" (1 Cor 11:29) brought condemnation on them, he was rebuking them not for a failure to observe the proper ritual forms or to believe rightly about the elements but for a failure as a community to live in the reality of unity in Christ's body that the meal signified.

Earliest Sources

One of the earliest accounts of Christian worship practices dates from the first decades of the second century and comes from a pagan, Pliny the Younger, who wrote a letter to the emperor Trajan to share information he received through interrogating some residents of Pontus-Bithynia who had been exposed as Christians. Based on the testimony, extracted under torture, from two slave women who were deaconesses (*ministra*), Pliny concluded that, contrary to rumors of immoral conduct (e.g., cannibalism, incest, etc.), the Christians were a harmless if "degenerate superstition." His report to Trajan ran thus:

> The sum total of their guilt or error amounted to no more than this: they met regularly before dawn on a fixed day to chant verses alternately among themselves

> in honor of Christ as if to a god, and also to bind themselves by oath, not for any criminal purpose, but to abstain from theft, robbery and adultery, to commit no breach of trust and not for any criminal purpose and not to deny a deposit when called upon to restore it. After this ceremony it had been their custom to disperse and reassemble later to take food of an ordinary, harmless kind. (*Ep*. 96.6–7)

This pagan description of Christian worship practices proves consistent with later Christian accounts.

The earliest systematic account of Christian liturgical practices comes from the Didache or Teaching of the Twelve Apostles, which is one of the earliest church orders later incorporated in the Apostolic Constitutions and dated by scholars between the period before the destruction of the temple and the early second century. Chapters 7 through 10 establish liturgical instructions. The first of these is baptism. Following the Jewish practice, the Didachist stipulates that the neophyte is to be baptized in "living or flowing water" (*en hydati zōnti*); should there not be a source of running water, it is permitted to pour the water three times "in the name of the Father and of the Son and of the Holy Spirit" (Did. 7.1–3). As preparation for baptism, both the officiant and the neophyte are required to fast for one or two days (Did. 7.4). Fasting was associated with baptismal purification; therefore, the Didachist warns against imitating the hypocrites who fast on Mondays and Thursdays rather than on Wednesdays and Fridays (Did. 7.4–8.1). The Didache proceeds to repeat the form for the Lord's Prayer, to which is added "for yours is the power, and the glory for evermore" (Did. 8.2) and for the "Great Thanksgiving" of the Eucharist, which was reserved for the baptized (Did. 9.5). The liturgy is divided into three parts. The first, over the cup, is an offering of thanks for "the holy vine of David" revealed through Jesus. Rather than a reference to the blood of Christ, the cup signifies the covenantal line from David to Jesus and then to the Church. The second blessing focuses on the bread as a symbol of eschatological unity when "your church may be gathered together from the ends of the earth into your kingdom" (Did. 9.4). The final thanksgiving occurs after a meal. For the prayer gives thanks for "food and drink" for people's enjoyment and for "spiritual food and drink, and eternal life through your servant" (Did. 10.3). The Eucharist climaxes with a plea for Christ's return and the coming of his kingdom, "May grace come and may this world pass away. . . . Maranatha (O Lord, come)!" (Did. 10.6).

Worship Rituals

For the purposes of this chapter, the focus is on the theological understanding of these worship rituals and how those understandings developed over time. One way to imagine how important worship was for theological formation is to examine the order in which early Christians would have entered into the life of the worshiping community.

Initiation of Baptism

A person's introduction to this community would have come in only a limited exposure to rites of worship. Whether the person's introduction came when she was a child—taken to worship by her parents—or as an adult curious to learn more about this religion, she would have participated in the singing of hymns and the antiphonal recitation of psalms. Then she would have heard the Scriptures read and interpreted in homilies. After the sermon, however, she would be dismissed together with all the unbaptized. The celebration of the Eucharist that followed was reserved for those initiated into the faith through baptism. It was a holy thing not to be given to dogs (Matt 7:6), that is, nonbelievers who did not recognize and affirm the holy reality that it signified.

Those wishing to join the community underwent a period of instruction in the faith or catechesis. The culmination of this instruction was baptism, which in many communities came during the Easter vigil. For the initiates or catechumens (those undergoing instruction), the baptism for which they prepared was a secret. Initiation into the Christian community, like the initiation into various Greco-Roman religions such as the cults of Isis or Mithras, was treated as a mystery so that the catechumens might come to their initiation with fresh eyes unprejudiced by preconceptions. By the fourth century, Cyril of Jerusalem, Ambrose of Milan, and John Chrysostom preserved collections of homilies delivered to the newly baptized. These homilies—postbaptismal catechesis often delivered the week after Easter—were originally preserved to provide their episcopal confreres a model for instruction of the neophytes. For historians, they pull back the curtain to allow a glimpse of the secrets of the baptismal rite and the theological significance attached to the ritual.

Christian baptism clearly had antecedent forms in Second Temple Judaism and parallels in pagan initiations. Pools for washing were at Herod's Temple in Jerusalem and at Qumran. These, however, were likely used repeatedly to preserve ritual cleanliness. By contrast, the baptism of John in the Jordan was a onetime event signifying the entry into a new life through the repentance of sin to be prepared for the judgment at the Messiah's imminent coming. Within twenty to thirty years after John the Baptist, Paul was providing the core interpretation that set Christian baptism as a participatory union with Christ in his death and resurrection (Rom 6) and as new birth in the Spirit (Rom 8), a theme also central to the understanding in the Gospel of John (John 3).

Justin Martyr: Baptismal Rebirth as Illumination By the mid-second century, Justin interpreted baptismal rebirth (*anagennēsis*) in terms of illumination (*phōtismos*). He explicitly grounds the imperative for baptism in Jesus's words, "Except you are born again, you will not enter into the kingdom of heaven" (John 3:3), and Isaiah's words, "Wash, become clean. . . . Though your sins be as crimson, I will make them white as snow" (Isa 1:16, 18).

Appealing to the apostolic practice and teachings of Paul, whom he simply calls "the apostle," Justin provides the logic behind baptism. Human beings' first birth is from "wet seed" of their parents' intercourse from which they are born in ignorance and therefore live as children of necessity reinforced by bad habits and an evil education—perhaps a reference to participation in the pagan rituals that paid honor to demons in the guise of gods who deceived devotees. The second birth is from the water of baptism, now cleansed of sins by their repentance of sin and illumination in the name of "God the Father and Master of all . . . and of Jesus Christ, who was crucified under Pontius Pilate, and in the name of the Holy Spirit, who through the prophets foretold all things about Jesus" (*1 Apol.* 61). This last clause, with its reference to the Spirit's inspiration of the Old Testament prophets' foretelling Jesus coming, whether intended or not, would have drawn a clear dividing line between Justin's community and Marcion's.

Justin is quick to distinguish Christian washing from the removal of shoes and the washing before entering pagan temples. The latter initiated by the demons, he explains, was a perverse imitation of baptism and of Moses's removing his shoes before the burning bush and receiving "mighty power from Christ" (*1 Apol.* 62). Thus, Justin implicitly treats Moses's putting off his sandals and entry into Christ's luminous presence in the burning bush as figures of baptismal purification and illumination.

Tertullian: Baptism as Spiritual Healing Tertullian, writing a generation after Justin, shares with him the view of baptism as the source of salvation through the forgiveness of sins, but Tertullian places his emphasis on baptism as a spiritual healing or recapitulation of God's creation of humanity in the beginning. Even as the Spirit of God hovered over the waters of chaos at the creation of the world (Gen 1:2), so too the Spirit hovers over the water of the font. From the Spirit's hovering, the water borrowed its holiness—"the sacramental power of sanctification"—by which the initiate is cleansed of her sin (*Bapt.* 4).

Tertullian weaves together the Genesis creation narrative with the story of the angel's disturbing the water in the pool of Bethesda (John 5:1–8). Similarly, the baptized were purified by the angel present at the font so that they might be made ready to receive new birth in the gifts of the Holy Spirit that came from the laying on of hands by the bishop and priests (*Bapt.* 6). This conferral of the Holy Spirit was, Tertullian explained, a symbolic reenactment of the creation of the first man who was fashioned in the image of God when God breathed into him the life-giving Spirit, which was taken away from him in punishment for the first sin (*Bapt.* 5).

Ephrem the Syrian (AD 306–373): Baptism as Recapitulation of Israel's Salvation History Baptism as a recapitulation of Israel's salvation history was a prominent theme in Ephrem the Syrian. Not only did his hymns offer a richly typological connection between baptism and its prefiguration in the flood and the exodus narrative, but Ephrem imagined, as Everett Ferguson has noted, a line of succession from Moses to the Church. God laid hands on Moses and Aaron, and then the line of the priests of the Old Testament, and finally from John to Jesus and from Jesus to the apostles (*Hymn. haer.* 22.18–19).

As a recapitulation of the anointings of the Old Testament, in his baptism Jesus fulfilled the righteousness of the Old Testament and so brought an end to the law and the baptism of John (*Comm. Diat.* 4.2). Since Jesus already had the Holy Spirit, when he was baptized by John he mixed the Spirit with the water. Therefore, those receiving Christian baptism would receive new life in the Spirit. For, says Ephrem, as the neophyte feels the wetness of the water washing over her body, she knows that the Spirit is flowing inwardly over her soul (*Dom.* 55 [53]). The Christian's new birth was a participation in Christ's own new birth. For, Ephrem says, as Christ was begotten first by the Father and then as man in Mary's womb, in the Jordan he was begotten in order to cleanse the stain of humanity's sin (*Dom.* 2.5). Thus, the neophyte receives forgiveness of her sins by partaking in Jesus's baptism and is born anew by receiving the Spirit from Christ.

This theme of participation was expressed in the third-century Syrian text, the Didascalia. The neophytes understand the Father's words at Jesus's baptism, "You are my beloved Son, this day I have begotten you" (Ps 2:7; Mark 1:9–11), as spoken to them as well, declaring their adoption as children of God (Didasc. 2.32–41). Now being in Christ, they receive for themselves the Father's expression of filial love he has for Christ.

Cyril of Jerusalem (AD 313–386): Baptism as Imitation of Christ's Death Paul's interpretation of baptism (Rom 6:4–11) as a participation in Christ's passion and resurrection did not acquire prominence until the fourth century. Whereas Origen, the third-century Alexandrian catechist, saw baptism primarily as a sign that the believer had *already* died to sin, as Robin Jensen has explained, Cyril of Jerusalem equated the act of being baptized as an imitation of Christ's death. As Christ was stripped naked, so the initiate removed his tunic, symbolizing that he is "putting off the old man with his deeds" (Col 3:9). In his nakedness before all, Cyril explains, the initiate is not ashamed. He has acquired the purity and innocence of the first parents in Eden who were not conscious of their nakedness (*Cat. myst.* 2.1). The oil with which the naked body was rubbed signified being grafted into the good olive tree (Rom 11:17–24), that is, Jesus (*Cat. myst.* 2.3). As Jesus was taken from the cross and laid in the tomb where he remained for three days, so the initiate was led to the font and there immersed three times in the name of the Father, Son, and Holy Spirit. "And at the selfsame moment," Cyril tells the newly baptized, "you were both dying and being born; and that water of salvation was at once your grave and your mother" (*Cat. myst.* 2.4). Then, quoting Paul, "For if we have been planted with the likeness of his death, we shall also be with the likeness of his resurrection" (Rom 6:5), Cyril concludes, "in your case, there was only a likeness of death and suffering; [however,] in the case of your salvation, there was not a mere likeness, but the reality" (*Cat. myst.* 2.7).

Ambrose (AD 339–397): Baptism as Cleansing of Sin In Milan in the late fourth century, Ambrose noted that being raised from the font was not the end of the ritual. After rising from the pool, the neophyte was anointed with *myron* or chrism, which Ambrose explained signified her reception of divine wisdom through her initiation in the holy mystery (*Myst.* 6.29–30; *Sacr.* 3.1.1). Ambrose, imitating Christ's humility, then knelt before the neophyte and washed her feet. He interpreted the water of the font as the cleansing of personal sin, while the washing of the feet—specifically the heel bruised by the serpent's deception—signified cleansing of original sin (*Myst.* 6.33; *Sacr.* 3.1.5–6). Even as Jesus told Peter, "Unless I wash your feet you have no part in me" (John 13:8), so Ambrose tells the newly baptized that they are sanctified and made part of Christ.

For Ambrose, the white robe given to the newly baptized has a number of levels of significance. It denotes that the neophyte has put off the old life and "put on Christ" (Rom 13:14). Its color signified both the purity of having been sanctified and sharing in Christ's glorified and perfected humanity of the resurrection. Furthermore, with an eye to the bride's confession in the Song of Songs, "I am black and beautiful," Ambrose explains that the neophytes, like the bride, are black inasmuch as they have a fallen condition but are beautiful through grace received in the sacrament of faith (*Myst.* 7.34). Then the initiate received the "spiritual seal" through being marked with the sign of the cross (*Myst.* 8.42) before being led into the cathedral to witness for the first time the mystery of Eucharist.

Baptism as a symbolic participation in Christ's was represented differently in the architectural style of the baptistry and font. Some, like the font in the Vitalis basilica in Sufetula, may have been designed in the form of the birth canal to present baptism as the time of being born anew. Other fonts, like those at Bulla Regia and Meninx, were cruciform. In other cases, as in Milan, the font was octagonal either to form the shape of a tomb or to signify resurrection.

Common Meal: Eucharist

While the initiation ritual of baptism occurred occasionally, the regular gathering of the Christian community was for the "breaking of bread" or Eucharist (*eucharistia*) in a common meal. These meals were shared originally in small, private apartments (*insulae*) and later in free-standing family homes (*domi*). The "breaking of bread" was not merely one phase of a set liturgy; it was the occasion for Christian worship. Given how much of Jesus's ministry and proclamation of the kingdom of God occurred during table fellowship—indeed, his eating and drinking with tax collectors and sinners was the fulfillment of his ministry to call the lost sheep of Israel (Matt 15:24)—it made sense that his disciples would continue his ministry by teaching, as their teacher had, while reclining at a table. Although in Greco-Roman culture it was common for meals to be followed by a time of drinking wine and offering discourses or conversation (*symposia*), the Christians of the first and second centuries consciously distinguished their table worship from that of their pagan neighbors by following Jewish practices. Thus, as Tertullian relates, the dinner was preceded by prayer followed by the singing of hymns to God (*Apol.* 39.17–18).

Eucharist and the Reality of the Incarnation Differing views about the nature of the elements of the meal, the bread and wine, represented a dividing line within some Christian communities. The docetic Christians, who were possibly some early Gnostics in Antioch, stayed away from the meal because they denied the reality of the incarnation and thus also the reality of Christ's bodily presence in the Eucharist. For Ignatius, the power of the bread as the medicine of immortality (Ign. *Eph.* 20.2) was a corollary of his ardent insistence on the reality of the incarnation (Ign. *Trall.* 9). The bread and wine could convey the gift of immortality because Christ was really present. Ignatius offers nothing analogous to a metaphysical theory of transubstantiation that would be developed in the Middle Ages; nevertheless, he has an implicit sense of the Eucharist as a participation in the power of Christ present in his body.

The elements of bread and wine, however, were not the totality of the Eucharist. Rather, it was the community's gathering and partaking together that signified the reality inaugurated by a believer's incorporation into Christ's body at baptism. This sensibility goes back to Jesus's words in the Last Supper: As McGowan has noted, in the words "This [*touto*] is my body. This [*touto*] do in remembrance of me" (Luke 22:19), "This" (*touto*) is neuter and so cannot refer to "bread" (*artos*), which is masculine. Therefore, "this" may refer to the action of the community of disciples' eating together. Since the Eucharist is the collective act of worship in which the community embodies what it confesses, namely the body of Christ, Ignatius perceived docetism to be both an ecclesiological problem and an errant doctrine. By denying the christological foundation of the Eucharist, docetism was a threat to the identity and integrity of the *ecclesia* (Ign. *Smyrn.* 7.1).

Eucharist and the Unity and Continuity of Familial Identity The Eucharist was also understood to link the Church with Israel. In the Didache, the Eucharist carries a blessing of the cup that signifies "the holy vine of David" (Did. 9.2). The wine, as the fruit of the grape vine, is a figure of Jesus as the descendent from the line of David. By receiving the fruit of the "holy vine," the Christian, even if a gentile, is incorporated into the line of David, that is, the house of Israel.

This sense of worship as the confession and embodiment of familial bonds of the community was expressed in the "kiss of peace." While Origen (*Hom. Cant.* 1.1) interpreted it as symbolic of the kiss exchanged between the Christian (i.e., the bride) and her bridegroom, Christ, this expression of love of Christ and the believers was mediated through other believers. Since the public kiss in Greco-Roman culture was reserved for people with whom there was a sexual or family relationship, the kiss with which the community greeted the newly baptized (*1 Apol.* 65.1–2)—a greeting reserved only for the baptized and associated with the Eucharist liturgy—was a symbolic recognition of their membership in the family of believers.

The Eucharist was not only a sign that reminded the community of believers of their family identity; it was, as a participation in Christ, *enacting* the familial relationship it signified: "Now you are the body of Christ and individually members of it" (1 Cor 12:27). Augustine explained these words from Paul in a homily addressed to the newly baptized who had seen and participated in their first Eucharist:

> So if it is you that are the body of Christ and its members, *you* are the mystery that has been placed on the Lord's table; the mystery you receive signifies who you are. You affirm what you are when you reply "Amen." . . . So be a member of the body of Christ, in order to make that "Amen" true. . . . When you were baptized it is as though you were mixed into dough. When you received the fire of the Holy Spirit, it is as though you were baked. Be what you see and receive what you are. (*Serm.* 272)

The worshiper's "Amen" in response to the priest's declaration, "the body of Christ," was a recognition of the twofold significance of the bread. The loaf signified Christ's bodily presence with the community. It also signified the union of the individual members of the community—the grain from which the loaf was formed—united in Christ as his body by the gift of his Spirit. The community's receiving the bread together was a participation in the one who made them one. Thus, the corporate worship was every bit as much an enactment of the community's collective identity as the body of Christ as it was the praise of God's mighty works (Ps 145:4; Acts 2:11).

Early Christian Doxology

Early Christian doxology took on many more forms than those described here. Prayers to Mary the mother of Jesus, the God-bearer (*Theotokos*), and to the saints requested their intercession for God's mercy (cf. Socrates Scholasticus, *Hist. eccl.* 7.32). The relics of holy men and women were honored as loci of sanctification, where divine holiness came into contact with the world and was imparted to the souls of the faithful (cf. *Laud.* 5). Delight in the Lord was expressed in dance (cf. *Stat.* 19.1) and song whose value Augustine extolled: "Our minds are more deeply moved to devotion by those holy words when they are sung, and more ardently inflamed to piety, than would be the case without singing" (*Conf.* 10.33.49). The meaning of the liturgy was interpreted in mystagogical preaching. And the community was called to social holiness in sermons of moral exhortation. Out of these doxological practices emerged expressions of piety that took the form of visual art.

From the third-century paintings of Christ the good shepherd in the catacombs of Priscilla in Rome to the sculpted relief of Christ's trial on the fourth-century sarcophagus of Junius Bassus to the sixth-century mosaic depiction of Abraham's sacrifice of Isaac in the Basilica San Vitale and the icon of Christ Pantocrator in Saint Catherine's monastery at Mount Sinai, these were sensual representations and interpretations of the faith that early Christian preachers sought to express in catechetical treatises, pastoral letters, and dogmatic formulations. Early Christian theology ought not be thought of in isolation from the sensible images that formed the cultural space in which the life of theological reflection was lived out. However limited the sample of worship practices described here, they do fairly represent those public expressions of piety that were foundational for the early Christian theology discussed in the ensuing chapters. Above all other sources, however, the primary source of the language of Christian doxology and theological reflection was the Church's Scriptures.

Scripture

Around 325, when Constantine sought to provide an anthology of the Christian Scriptures for worship for the churches in Constantinople, he sought the advice of Eusebius of Caesarea. The set of texts recommended by Eusebius was not something new as much as it was confirming or canonizing the prevailing practices of the Great Church. In a sense, the canon of Christian Scriptures that was more or less settled by the fourth century had come to be through a process begun centuries before.

Formation of Christian Scripture

When 2 Timothy 3:16 speaks of "all Scripture" as being "God-breathed," "Scripture" (*graphē*)—though it can have the general meaning of "writings"—has here a technical meaning referring specifically to the texts that Christians would come to call the Old Testament. Furthermore, this term refers not to their (mostly) Hebrew originals but to the Greek translation of these documents, that is, the Septuagint (LXX) produced between the late third and first centuries BC.

For the first and second generations of Christians, teachings about Jesus's life and its significance were passed on through oral transmission and spoken of as "the tradition [*paradoseis*] which you were taught . . . either by word of mouth or by letter" (2 Thess 2:15) or simply "the faith [*pistei*] which was once for all delivered to the saints" (Jude 3). Although the letters of Paul had from an early date been collected, preserved, and circulated as an anthology, there was no fixed canon or collection of Christian writings that was deemed authoritative for the purpose of establishing the norms of Christian belief and practice.

Within the second or third generation of Jesus worshipers, Christian writings were being spoken of as "Scripture." Second Peter, which scholars date between AD 60 and 160, says of Paul's letters, "There are some things in [his epistles] hard to understand, which the ignorant and unstable twist to their own destruction, as they do other scriptures [*tas loipas graphas*]" (3:16). Here "scriptures" refers to writings, presumably the Old Testament, whose content had the status of divine revelation in the early Church. Earlier 2 Peter declared, "First of all you must understand that no prophecy of scripture [*graphēs*] is a matter of one's own interpretation, because no prophecy ever came by the impulse of people, but people moved by the Holy Spirit spoke from God" (1:21).

Whatever the exact content of *graphē*, it is clear that 2 Peter gives Paul's letters an authority on par with other texts of divine revelation. This association corresponds to Paul's own understanding of his gospel. In his first letter to the church in Thessalonica, he says, "when you received the word of God which you heard from us, you accepted it not as the word of men but as what it really is, the word of God, which is at work in you believers" (1 Thess 2:13). Given Paul's insistence on his apostleship (e.g., Galatians), it is doubtful that Paul thought of his written works as any less authoritative than the word of God he preached.

Vernacular Editions of Biblical Texts

Among the Western churches, the vernacular edition of biblical texts in Latin translation is known as the *Vetus Latina* (*VL*). The first attempt to regularize these came in 384 when Damasus of Rome asked Jerome to make revisions of the *VL* versions of the Gospels and the Psalter. Jerome made alterations by comparing the *VL* texts to Greek manuscripts. This was the beginning of the Latin Vulgate edition. Later while living in Bethlehem, he produced the Vulgate edition of the Old Testament, drawing on Hebrew editions in the library at Caesarea and Origen's Hexapla, Origen's six-columned parallel edition of the Old Testament based on Greek and Hebrew editions, including those produced by Jews as well as Christians.

The translation for the Syriac-speaking churches is the Peshitta, which means "common" or "ordinary." The earliest of these was Tatian's *Diatessaron* from which the *Vetus Syra* edition was taken. By the second century, much of the Old Testament had been translated from Hebrew into Syriac. By the seventh century, scholars had produced the *Syrohexapla*, which was a translation of the Greek taken from Origen's Hexapla.

The Problem of Authority

The proliferation of gospels (Gospel of Thomas, Gospel of Peter, Gospel of Judas), acts (Acts of Paul and Thecla), and letters (Epistles of Paul and Seneca) confronted the church with the problem of determining which were authoritative, which were viewed favorably but deemed of a lower authority, and which were to be rejected. One example is Polycarp of Smyrna's *To the Philippians*. The letter was a response to a request from the church at Philippi for copies of the letters of Ignatius of Antioch. Though the final form of the letter is a combination of an earlier and a later text, it reflects the use of New Testament texts in the first half of the second century. In it, Polycarp quotes or expresses themes found in the three Synoptic Gospels, the Acts of the Apostles, all the letters attributed to Paul except Colossians and Philemon, 1 Peter, and 1 John, but also the letter known as 1 Clement.

Other times historians are able to draw on lists of texts. The most famous is the Muratorian Canon—also known more neutrally as the Muratorian Fragment—which is a text of eighty-five lines discovered in the eighteenth century in Milan by L. A. Muratori. The text, the beginning and ending of which are missing, has traditionally been dated—based on the reference to Pius bishop of Rome—to the second half of the second century. The fragment gives a list and description of books that correspond to the modern New Testament except for James, the two letters of Peter, and Hebrews. In addition to those books later recognized as canonical in the fourth century, the list also mentions as spurious pseudepigraphic letters to the Laodiceans and Alexandrians, which Marcionites attributed to Paul. The Wisdom of Solomon and the Shepherd of Hermas are mentioned favorably, though the Shepherd should not be read publicly. The fragment ends by mentioning gnostic authors and Marcion, whose writings are not accepted. What is implicit is the criteria by which the judgments of the texts are made. First is concern for apostolicity, that is, whether the text is connected with an apostle; and the catholicity, that is, whether it is widely accepted. Even if a text, like the Shepherd, may be edifying, it is still not given the same standing as other texts because it was written later than the period of the apostles.

One instance where we see the criteria being explicitly named appears in a late second-century correspondence between the church at Rhossus and Serapion, bishop of Antioch. When he visited the congregation at Rhossus, near Antioch, Serapion was asked about the Gospel of Peter, with which he was unfamiliar. His initial reaction was to sanction its reading, since, as he wrote, "For our part, brothers, we receive both Peter and the other apostles as we do Christ, but the writings which falsely bear their names (*pseudepigrapha*) we reject . . . knowing that such were not handed down to us" (Eusebius, *Hist. eccl.* 6.12.3). Subsequently, however, Serapion was informed by others who had made a study of this gospel that "the most part of [the gospel] indeed was in accordance with the true teaching of the savior, but some things were added which we [list] below for your benefit" (*Hist. eccl.* 6.12.6). On the basis of these additions, which seemed to deny the reality of the incarnation, he concluded that it was not of genuine apostolic origin.

These fragments of Serapion's correspondence preserved by Eusebius are revealing about the status of the canon at the end of the second century. On the one hand, that the church at Rhossus had to ask about the Gospel of Peter and that Serapion was theoretically receptive to the gospel on the grounds of apostolicity indicate that the canon was not closed; they were open to the possibility that there are other legitimate gospels than the four recognized Gospels. On the other hand, that Serapion rejected the Gospel of Peter on the grounds that it did not conform to the apostolic teachings—presumably contained in the other gospels and the oral tradition—indicates that those texts together with the oral tradition served as an important standard for judging apostolicity of other texts.

Marcion's New Testament and the Adoption of a Canon

One of the events—if not *the* event—that pushed the Great Church toward the adoption of a canon or fixed sets of texts as being authoritative for determining Christian belief and practice was Marcion's creation of his New Testament. This anthology consisted of his version of the Gospel of Luke (*Euangelion*) and the Letters of Paul (*Apostolikon*). The latter included all the letters attributed to Paul in the modern New Testament minus the Pastoral Epistles (1 and 2 Timothy and Titus). Conspicuous by their absence were the books of the Old Testament as well as Matthew, Mark, John, Acts of the Apostles, and other Christian writings that held an authoritative status in the Catholic community of Rome.

Marcion's collection was intended to function for his communities as the Torah and the prophetic writings did for Jewish communities. By both Marcion's choice of the books included and his deliberate exclusion of others, the anthology served as a standard or canon that implicitly ruled out claims about the essential unity between the God of ancient Israel and the God of Catholic Christianity. The exact content of Marcion's Luke and the letters is uncertain and is as highly contested among scholars today as in the second and third centuries. Marcion expunged what he deemed to be later interpolations of direct quotations or allusions to the Old Testament that identified Jesus as Israel's Messiah foretold by her prophets. Irenaeus described Marcion's version as "mutilations" that excised textual evidence that connected Jesus with the God of Israel. Marcion, according to competing modern interpretations, was either simply preserving the version of Luke and Paul he had—the only books he knew—or, as Irenaeus claimed, redacting the Catholic versions recognized by the Church.

Regardless of which modern reconstruction of Marcion's New Testament most closely corresponds with his lost *Euangelion* and *Apostolikon*, Jason BeDuhn notes "it is precisely in closing a canon, however provisionally, that Marcion suddenly and exponentially elevated the status of particular texts, and launched them into an undeniably superior authority relative to any others, in a way no one before him had dared to do. . . . By including them within a limited canon, . . . he set boundaries on what could be used as touchstones in evaluating various positions put forward as 'Christian,' narrowing the range of permissible variety within the Christian movement."[3] From Irenaeus's perspective, certainly the Catholic Church had already recognized the "elevated status" of the texts that comprised its Scriptures in practice, but it remains the case that Marcion forced the issue in a new way.

The question of canon formation, therefore, is not whether Catholic communities had collections of texts—some in anthologized form and some not—closely resembling the modern New Testament that they held to be authoritative along with implicit lists of other texts they judged to be heterodox. The former, if not a canon in the strict sense, clearly held a privileged status; they were, one might say, a protocanon. Although Catholic communities in the mid to late second century preserved an openness vis-à-vis which texts were, in varying degrees, authorita-

3. Jason D. BeDuhn, *The First New Testament: Marcion's Scriptural Canon* (Salem, OR: Polebridge, 2013), 60.

tive, after Marcion's publication of his canon, bishops like Irenaeus felt compelled to justify the inclusion of some texts excluded by Marcion and the exclusion of others deemed authoritative by sects they deemed heretical.

A Standard for Interpretation

Adjudicating which documents were authoritative was only the first textual challenge faced by early Christians. Simply having the right texts did not mean that one was able to interpret them correctly. For the sake of right doctrine, what was needed was a standard or model to guide how the various claims of the numerous texts should be read as a coherent whole.

The Diatessaron *(c. 160–175)*

The quest for unity did not, however, require a harmonization of the writings. This was attempted in the second half of the second century by Justin Martyr's protégé, Tatian the Syrian, in his *Diatessaron*. Originally written in Syriac, the *Diatessaron* interwove sections from the Four Gospels into a single narrative. For instance, it begins with John's prologue (John 1:1–5), followed by Luke's narrative of the annunciation (Luke 1:5–80), shifting to the appearance of the angel to Joseph in Matthew (Matt 1:18–25), then returning to Luke's birth narrative (Luke 2:1–39), back again to Matthew and the visit of the magi (Matt 2:1–23), and ultimately ending with the remainder of John's prologue and the preaching of John the Baptist (John 1:7–28).

Though viewed as canonical in certain Syrian churches, its harmonization was an outlier and ultimately condemned in the fourth century by Rabbula of Edessa. Irenaeus, rather than conflating the narratives, argued that the Four Gospels should be kept discrete because each, based on the evangelists' perfect knowledge derived from the Spirit, presented Christ to different geographic centers and depicted different dimensions of Christ's life (*Haer.* 3.3.1; 3.11.8).

The Gnostics' Use of Texts and Apostolic Teaching

Of greater concern was the need to refute the ways that Gnostics used documents shared with the Catholic Church in order to defend gnostic texts. Merely having the right texts without the guidance of a reliable pattern was not sufficient for right interpretation. Like an artist who tries to craft a mosaic portrait of a king but assembles the tiles to form the image of a fox because he has not seen the king, the Gnostics, according to Irenaeus, lacked a true pattern of the economy and relied on dubious narratives of nonapostolic origin (*Haer.* 1.8.6). Indeed, their use of apostolic texts and orthodox language made them wolves in sheep's clothing who deceived the simple or uninformed (*Haer.* 3.16.8).

Precisely because of the verbal similarities between the gnostic sects and the teachings of the Great Church, the oral tradition passed down by bishops with demonstrable links to the apostles was critical to be able to adjudicate the right meaning of words. This sentiment was summed up by Papias, bishop of Hierapolis in Asia Minor, who was a contemporary of Ignatius and Polycarp. In a fragment from his *Sayings of the Lord Explained in Five Books*, he expressed suspicion of novel doctrines; when encountering preachers whom he did not know, he would interrogate them about their knowledge of Jesus's disciples: "For I imagined that what was to be got from books was not so profitable to me as what came from the living and abiding voice" (Eusebius, *Hist. eccl.* 3.39). Thus, the oral tradition, as late as the early second century, functioned both negatively to detect heterodoxy and positively to guide the interpretation of documents recognized to be apostolic. The recollection by later generations of oral transmission of the teachings of the apostles would be the source of the pattern for right interpretation of Christian Scriptures.

Irenaeus and the Rule of Faith

Irenaeus located this unifying pattern in the Apostolic Witness or Rule of Faith, as it was known in the West. Like other protocreedal statements, such as 1 Corinthians 15:1–11, the Rule of Faith was a concise statement of the essential Christian beliefs—or as Paul called them, "things of first importance." For Irenaeus and Tertullian, the core of the Rule of Faith was the affirmation of the singular identity of the Creator God of the Old Testament and that of the Trinity worshiped by Christians.

> The Church, though dispersed throughout the whole world, even to the ends of the earth, has received from the apostles and their disciples this faith: in one God, the Father almighty, maker of heaven and earth, and the sea and all things that are in them; and in one Christ Jesus, the Son of God, who became incarnate for our salvation; and in the Holy Spirit, who proclaimed through the prophets the dispensations of God, and the advent, and the birth from a virgin, and the passion, and the resurrection from the dead, and the ascension into heaven in the flesh of the beloved Christ Jesus, our Lord, and his manifestation from heaven in the glory of the Father "to gather all things in one" and to raise up anew all flesh of the whole human race, in order that to Christ Jesus, our Lord, and God, and Savior, and king, and according to the will of the invisible Father, "every knee shall bow, of things in heaven, and things in earth, and things under the Earth, and that every tongue should confess" to him, and that he should execute just judgment toward all; that he may send "spiritual wickednesses"

> and the angels who transgressed and became apostates, together with the ungodly, and unrighteous, and wicked, and profane among men, into everlasting fire; but may, in the exercise of his grace, confer immortality on the righteous, and holy, and those who have kept his commandments, and have persevered in his love, some from the beginning and others from their repentance, and may surround them with everlasting glory. (*Haer.* 1.10.1)

The Rule of Faith does not presume to be comprehensive or exhaustive. Rather, as an expression of the essential teachings of the apostles, it articulates the fundamental points of doctrine that distinguish orthodox doctrine from the heterodox teachings of various rival sects of Christianity. As such the *regula* serves as a standard both to distinguish documents of apostolic origin from those of dubious origin and to ensure right interpretation of the ambiguous passages within apostolic writings.

Hermeneutics and Interpretive Methods

If the Rule of Faith functioned to set boundaries that could separate interpretations consistent with the oral tradition of the apostles from novel interpretations that were from nonapostolic sources, the task of interpreting the documents of the Old Testament as Christian Scripture tested the claims of Irenaeus and others that the old and the new dispensations revealed one and the same God. Irenaeus and Tertullian's theories of the divine economy exposed weaknesses in Marcion's view of the gospel and provided a theoretical alternative to explain the unity of the covenants. Nevertheless, many of the passages that Marcion had pointed to as contradicting the teachings of Jesus demanded a hermeneutic that could explain how the Old Testament narratives and prescriptions could be seen as consistent with the evolving canon of Christian Scriptures. The hermeneutic adopted by the Catholic Church was derived from the apostolic gospels and, ironically, given Marcion's ostensible reliance upon Paul, from Paul's own method of interpreting the Jewish Scriptures: allegory.

In Paul's letter to the churches of Galatia, he attacks his opponents from the church in Jerusalem who came preaching "another gospel" that required the gentile converts be circumcised. The effect, Paul insisted, was to render Jesus's death null and void, thereby returning them to slavery under the law. To illustrate his claim, he pointed those who claimed that torah was still binding on Christians to the torah—to the story of Sarah, the free woman, and Hagar, the slave woman, and their respective sons Isaac, the child of promise, and Ishmael, the child born of the flesh. Isaac and Ishmael are figures of two covenants: Ishmael the slave representing the covenant of Sinai and Isaac the freeborn representing Jerusalem.

The story of Sarah and Hagar, Isaac and Ishmael, Paul says, is an allegory (*allēgoroumena*) that prophetically distinguishes those who are under the old covenant, and so are in slavery to the law's demands and condemnation, from those who are under the new covenant through faith in Christ, and so are set free from the law's judgments (Gal 4:24).

The Greek verb *allēgoreō*, which means to read or speak with another meaning, was a strategy of interpretation that gives to a text a different meaning than what appears at first reading. What the passage really means lies cloaked in details that are figures or symbols pointing to some other reality. The Stoics, for instance, employed this strategy when interpreting passages from Homer—especially the more dubious depictions of the Olympian gods—to refer to forces of nature. Thus, a troubling passage proved, in fact, to have a more salutary reading.

In Christian circles, allegory was spoken of in terms of the relationship of literal (*kata ton logon*) or clear (*to saphes*) or narratival (*to tēs historias gramma*) meaning and the hidden or spiritual meaning. The latter, Gregory of Nyssa said, was referred to variously as anagogy (*anagōgē*) or allegory (*allēgoria*) or tropology (*tropologia*), all of which he treated as virtually synonymous (*Hom. Cant.* preface 1–5).

It is common among some biblical scholars today to suspect allegory of being a form of eisegesis (imposing a meaning on a text from the outside) rather than exegesis (extracting the meaning inherent to the text). Yet this was not how early Christian allegorists saw it. They understood themselves to be uncovering a divinely implanted meaning in the text, a truth expressed using details of the texts that served as types or figures or symbols (*typoi*). One warrant for such interpretation was given in Luke's account of Jesus's explanation to the two disciples on the road to Emmaus that the Messiah had to die and be raised: "And beginning with Moses and all the prophets, he interpreted to them in *all* the scriptures the things concerning himself" (Luke 24:27). Similarly, John's Gospel presents the bronze serpent lifted up by Moses in the wilderness (Num 21:9) as a figure for Jesus's being lifted up on the cross (John 3:14–15), implying that all the Old Testament revealed the Messiah's coming. If Jesus is the subtext of all Scripture, then Christians find the enduring value of the Old Testament by discovering the ways his life, passion, and resurrection were prophetically prefigured by its authors.

Early on, this christological hermeneutic became a dividing line between Jewish and Christian interpretations of torah. In 2 Corinthians, Paul explained the difference between Jewish and Christian readings by making an analogy between Jewish interpretations and Moses's covering his face with a veil after he had been transformed by his vision of God on Sinai (Exod 34:29–35). Because "their minds were hardened" (2 Cor 3:14), when Jews read torah, there remains a veil over their minds so that they cannot see the glory of God. That is, because of their unbelief, they were not able to recognize the torah's prophetic representations of Jesus.

Christians, however, behold the glory of the Lord revealed in torah because Christ has taken away the veil (2 Cor 3:12–18). Because Christ is the content of torah, those who know Christ are rightly able to recognize the way Christ is prefigured in torah. Moreover, since Christians have received the Spirit of the Lord, the Spirit lifts the veil so that they, as Moses, can behold the glory of Christ and are transformed into a likeness of his glory. Thus, Paul's hermeneutic is both christological and pneumatological: Christians are able to recognize Christ's prefiguration in the old covenant because they have the Spirit who has revealed Jesus as the Christ. Only by looking backward through the lens of Jesus's life could one rightly understand the Jewish Scriptures.

Although other later Christians, following the examples of Paul and the authors of the Four Gospels, employed this figural reading strategy, the most systematic account of Christian allegory appeared in book 4 of Origen's *On First Principles*. There he argued that the primary misinterpretation of Scripture was the result of reading it according to the literal sense. Ironically, this was a mistake common to Jews and heretics, like Marcion (*Princ.* 4.2.1). Jews denied that Jesus was the Messiah because his advent had not ushered in a literal peace between predator and prey, with lions now preferring to eat hay than lamb's flesh (Isa 65:25); while the Marcionites' literal reading of the Old Testament led them to see only contradictions with the New Testament. The second erroneous interpretation is of the simplistic-minded (*simpliciores*) who, though they subscribed to right doctrine generally, ended up attributing to God or the fathers and mothers of the faith unbecoming deeds—such as when Lot's daughters had sexual relations with their father (Gen 19:30–36)—and so gave a distorted picture of God (*Princ.* 4.2.2). To arrive at the true meaning of Scripture, it was necessary to recognize the other levels of meaning inherent in Scripture. Discerning these other layers of meaning was possible through allegory.

Pagan critics, such as Celsus, asserted that the slave culture of the Jews was too intellectually impoverished to know what allegory was. Therefore, the authors of the Hebrew Scriptures could not have employed figural modes of expression. Yet Origen enumerated many passages where the literal sense was incoherent or unedifying apart from being read symbolically. Responding to Celsus's implicit assumption that the meaning of a text lay in the author's intention, Origen could point to Psalm 78:1–3, "Give ear, O my people, to my law, incline your ears to the words of my mouth. I will open my mouth in parables, I will utter mysterious sayings of old, which we have heard and read, and our fathers have told us," as evidence of the Jewish authors' self-awareness in their use of figural speech (*Cels.* 4.49).

Despite his concern about exclusively literal readings of Scripture, the goal of Origen's hermeneutics was not to dispense with the literal sense. Rather, the literal and the spiritual or figural meanings remained intertwined. Origen distinguished three levels of scriptural meaning based on Solomon's prescription: "And you represent these things for yourself *thrice*, in counsel and knowledge, and so you may answer the words of truth to those who have asked you" (Prov 22:20–21): first, the *bodily* meaning, which is the ordinary narratival sense and edifying for simple folks who interpreted such passages within the bounds set by the Rule of Faith; second, the *psychic* meaning, which is accessible to those who have made progress in the interpretive art of contemplation; and third, the *spiritual* meaning, which is the highest meaning accessible to those whose minds have been perfected by the Spirit and become themselves spiritual (*Princ.* 4.2.4).

This highest spiritual sense expressed in enigmas are foreshadowings of God's unfolding economy. These prefigurations of Jesus's life, the Church, and the eschatological restoration of all things were, Origen maintained, firmly grounded in the body of the text with its myriad details (historical, geographical, linguistic). That is why he insisted on the importance of a liberal education in many fields of learning precisely so that one might uncover the symbolic significance of the text's literal details. Thus, even as Origen maintained that eschatologically the material body of this life is not eliminated but transformed into a spiritual body, so too the body or letter of Scripture was not dispensed with but was, in the meditations of the mature, spiritually minded Christian, transformed like the transparent, ethereal body of the resurrection into a spiritual lens through which one could behold the divine reality to which it pointed. In the fifth century, John Cassian (360–430) expanded Origen's threefold layer of meanings to four: (1) the literal sense of the historical narrative; (2) the allegorical sense or the prefiguration of another mystery, that is, of Christ and the Church; (3) the tropological sense that teaches the moral and practical implications of the passage; and (4) the anagogical sense that points to the "more sublime and sacred heavenly secrets" of the age to come (*Coll.* 14.8.2–3).

What cannot be overlooked if one is to understand Origen's allegory is, as Peter Martens has shown, the deep connection between the quest for the spiritual meaning and the spiritual life. Allegory was neither simply a technique of interpretation nor merely the spiritual meaning and understanding gained by use of that technique. Because God is spirit, to know God revealed in Scripture, one must seek him in its spiritual meaning (*Princ.* 1.1.2). For Origen, apprehending the spiritual meaning of Scripture was the fruit of the spiritual life. That is, only the interpreter who has risen above a carnal disposition and habits of thought is able to rise above the letter to see the spiritual meaning. Following the logic of Paul's metaphor in 2 Corinthians 3:14–17, the veil is not lifted to see God in the Old Testament apart from believing in Christ (*Princ.* 4.1.6). But the lifting of the veil is possible only because of the work of the Holy Spirit who renews the interpreter's "inner man" by its indwelling that illuminates the mind and fills it with spiritual understanding (*Comm. Rom.* 7.4.8).

It is easy to find instances of early Christian allegory that seem arbitrary—as when the Epistle of Barnabas interprets the prohibition against eating hare (Lev 11:5) to be a condemnation of pederasty (Barn. 10.6). But Origen's allegorical readings were not capricious. Rather, they rested on a methodology that combined the principle of intertextuality learned from the rabbis and the christological hermeneutic from Paul. Intertextuality, for the rabbis, meant that Scripture was self-interpreting; an unclear passage could become clear when read in the light of similar but clearer passages elsewhere in Scripture. For Origen, the intertextual play was between the Old Testament and the New Testament. Such an interpretation was possible because, Origen believed, both testaments were inspired by the same Holy Spirit. Having a single ultimate author, all Scripture possessed a common underlying meaning, and terms or images used in multiple portions of Scripture had a shared meaning; thus, the meaning of a term from the New Testament could be transferred to a passage using the same word or image in the Old Testament. Consequently, Origen's interpretation of Old Testament passages as providing types of Christ was not a random association but grounded in the New Testament.

One example is found in Origen's homilies on the Song of Songs. The Canticle, Origen says, was in its literal sense a love song written for a wedding. Its spiritual significance, however, was the union of the soul, represented by the bride, with Christ, represented by the bridegroom. The association of the bridegroom with Christ was not arbitrary. Rather, Origen took the bride's description of the bridegroom, "your anointing oils are fragrant and your name is oil poured out" (Song 1:3), as a clear indication that the bridegroom is the Christ, that is, the Anointed One. This association was based on the declaration in Psalm 45:7, "You have loved justice and hated iniquity: therefore God, your God has anointed you with the oil of gladness" (*Hom. Cant.* 1.2). Origen then draws in Paul's description of followers of Christ, "We are the good odor of Christ in every place" (2 Cor 2:14), to describe the deifying effect of the believer's union with Christ. As the Father has anointed Christ with the oil of gladness, that is, holiness and righteousness, so Christ the bridegroom anoints the souls of those united to his body in a spiritual consummation, like the bride, who then take on the sweet fragrance of his holiness and righteousness. Thus, Origen's allegorical interpretation of the bridegroom as a figure for Christ lies within the bounds of the Rule of Faith and is supported by both messianic prophecy in the Old Testament and the soteriology of Paul's gospel in the New Testament. Like Irenaeus, Origen's interpretation interweaves the language of the two testaments to demonstrate in the spiritual meaning of the passage the essential unity of Scripture as the revelation of Christ.

As Henri de Lubac expressed it, for Origen "the new lies hidden in the old; and the old is manifest in the new."[4]

While Paul's christological hermeneutic was the source and warrant for Christian allegorical readings, such readings also presupposed a participatory metaphysics. As Plato divided reality between the intelligible realities (ideas or forms that are the perfect and eternal models on which the Creator fashioned the world) and the sensible realities (particular instantiations of intelligible realities), Origen similarly divided creation between the hidden, spiritual realities of heaven (*occulta*) and the sensible, material realities of earth (*manifesta*). Though Origen's "spiritual realities" are not identical with Plato's forms, nevertheless for both Plato and Origen, the ontological connection between the spiritual and the sensible things created an epistemological connection between heaven and earth. In other words, because the hidden, intelligible realities were the models or patterns (*exemplaria*) after which the sensible, earthly creatures were fashioned, the mind could ascend to the spiritual knowledge (*spiritualis intelligentia*) of heavenly things through the contemplation of the sensible creature that embodied the forms (*formata*) of the heavenly realities (*Comm. Cant.* 3.12). Origen found biblical warrants for these metaphysical claims in Paul's assertion that God's "invisible nature, namely his eternal power and deity, has been clearly perceived in the things that have been made" (Rom 1:20), or his distinction between visible things that are transitory and the invisible things that are eternal (2 Cor 4:18). Similarly, Origen concluded, Scripture used earthly things, such as the form of the tabernacle or Israel's thirsting in the wilderness, to reveal hidden, heavenly mysteries (*Comm. Cant.* 3.12). The result was what scholars Matthew Levering and Hans Boersma have termed a "sacramental exegesis." Because the words of Scripture signified the transcendent, heavenly realities, through the contemplation (*theōria*) of Scripture the believer is brought into communion with those realities. Thus, Scripture was sacramental in that it allowed the Christian to participate in the divine.

A century after Origen, Gregory of Nyssa would argue in his refutation of Eunomius of Cyzicus's correspondence theory of language that there is no direct connection between human speech about God and God's nature—God is not identical with the words used to describe him in Scripture. Nevertheless, the metaphors of Scripture are not mere metaphors, but as scholar Frances Young has written, the analogies of Scripture are "a sacramental vehicle of truth . . . the word evokes the [divine] presence."[5] Gregory describes how the contemplation of Scripture allows the soul to ascend into God's presence in his *Commentary on the*

4. Henri de Lubac, *Scripture in the Tradition* (New York: Crossroad, 2000), xxi.

5. Frances M. Young, *Biblical Exegesis and the Formation of Christian Culture* (Peabody, MA: Hendrickson, 2002), 145.

Song of Songs. If Proverbs has prepared the childish, carnally minded Christian to desire wisdom by thinking of her as a woman of great beauty, Solomon's Song uses erotic imagery that the reader might be drawn into higher, spiritual intimacy with God in "the divine bridal chamber" (*Hom. Cant.* 1, 23). There the soul of the reader suffers the wound of love when the Father, the great archer, penetrates her soul with his arrow, the Word. The reader is thus united to the Word who now dwells within. Impregnated with the divine love, her loves are transformed from fleshly desire into an insatiable, heavenly longing for God. Though this wound of love is incurable since her desire is insatiable, nevertheless, because the Word is eternally united to the Father—such that wherever the Word is, there is the Father—the soul now united to the indwelling Word is raised into heaven and abides in the presence of the Father (*Hom. Cant.* 4, 141). Gregory elsewhere makes a similar point, writing that Christ, in teaching his disciples to pray, "Our Father who art in Heaven," acts as high priest who leads humanity with him into the true holy of holies not made with hands, eternal in the heavens (*Or. dom.* 3).

Augustine of Hippo, writing 150 years after Origen, explained the participatory nature of reading Scripture through his semiotics or theory of signs and illumination. In his treatise *Christian Instruction*, he explains that all teaching involves communication using words. Words, like all creation itself, are signs that point beyond themselves to the realities (*res*) they represent. He compares words to an orator's hand gesture that directs his audience's gaze to the thing he wants them to think about (*Doctr. chr.* preface 5–6). Yet the word's ability to communicate the reality is possible, Augustine explains, only if there is prior knowledge of the word's referent. That knowledge comes from the indwelling light of the Teacher, Christ, who illumines the intellect by revealing the reality to which the words of Scripture point (*Mag.* 38). Even then, however, the poetic nature of the language of Scripture does not give immediate understanding. Rather, its metaphors are enigmas that both arouse aesthetic delight—and thus spiritual desire—that moves the will and stimulates the intellect with puzzles that draw the mind into deeper and deeper consideration of Scripture's meaning (*Doctr. chr.* 2.11–12). Thus, participation through the contemplation of Scripture is the result of the biblical signs and the Spirit's inner illumination that fulfills in the believer the goal of all Scripture: the cultivation of the love of God and neighbor. Augustine went so far as to say that even if an explication of a passage of Scripture was technically errant, if the punch line of the text was love, then the interpreter had arrived at the passage's ultimate meaning (*Doctr. chr.* 3.54). For in loving God—and by extension the neighbor and self whom God loves—human beings find the happiness for which God made them (*Doctr. chr.* 1.64–65).

Augustine's emphasis on love was in many ways consistent with the view of Scripture among earlier exegetes. Among Origen's heirs as well as critics, the ultimate aim of the study of Scripture was the transformation of the reader. Since Christ, who is the image of the Father, was the content of all Scripture, the contemplation of Scripture was a participation—like the sacramental or mystical participation through baptism and Eucharist—in Christ through whom the image of God might be renewed in the mind of the reader. In his *Hymns of Faith*, Ephrem the Syrian articulated the parallel between the Word's accommodation of humanity in the incarnation and in the words of Scripture: "We should realize that, had He not put on the names of [earthly] things, it would not have been possible for him to speak with us human beings. By means of what belongs to us did He draw close to us; He clothed Himself in our language, so that He might clothe us in His mode of life. He asked for our form and put this on, and then, as a father with his children, He spoke with our childish state" (*Hymn. fid.* 45–47). As in the incarnation, the Word assumed human nature that human beings might behold and then be clothed in baptism with Christ's sanctified humanity, so in Scripture God who is above all speech revealed himself in human language so that these words might re-form the thought and speech of his children.

Critics of Allegory

Origen and other allegorists were not without their critics—often referred to as the Antiochene school—who contended that the spiritual meanings in allegorical interpretations did not do justice to the literal sense of the text. One of these critics was the fourth-century bishop of Tarsus, Diodore. Although Diodore recognized Paul's use of *allēgoria* in Galatians, he contended that Paul's method was not strictly allegory in the Greek understanding but was better described as *theōria*. Allegory, as employed by pagans and their Christian imitators, violated the historical sense of the text by imposing symbolic significance on figures and events that were completely alien to the narrative.

In his *Commentary on the Psalms*, Diodore gives as an example the interpretation of the myth of Zeus's abduction of Europa by changing himself into a bull and carrying her away across the sea. Because it was impossible for a bull to swim, the myth was interpreted by Stoics to signify Europa's sailing in a ship with the figurehead of a bull. Such a reading completely denied the events of the story. By contrast, Paul's technique of *theōria* was an alternative to both Hellenism, which introduced something completely foreign to the biblical narrative, and Judaism, which saw no deeper into the text than the literal meaning and so missed the higher sense of Scripture. In the allegory of Sarah and Hagar, by contrast, Paul gives a higher meaning to Isaac and Ishmael without denying the historical nature of the events related in the Genesis account.

Similarly, Diodore saw his interpretation of the story of Cain and Abel as prophetic of the relationship of the Jewish synagogue and the Church (*Comm. Ps.* prologue). This form of *theōria* he called figuration (*tropologia*) that "turns words with an obvious meaning into an expanded illustration of what [the author] is saying." The expanded meaning, however, is not derived from something external to the narrative but is grounded in other details internal to the passage. For example, the "vine" removed from Egypt and transplanted (Ps 80:8) is a figure for the people of Israel. Diodore finds confirmation for this interpretation in two places. First, just a few verses later, David quotes the Lord speaking to the vine as to a people: "Why have you broken down the hedge so that all who pass by on their way pick its fruits?" (Ps 80:12). Second, he finds further confirmation in Isaiah's use of the same figure: "For the vineyard of the Lord of hosts is the house of Israel" (Isa 5:7).

Diodore was hardly oblivious to errors or problems resulting from literal interpretations of Scripture that Origen sought to solve by employing allegory. The solution to the problems, he contended, was by recovering the historical sense (*historia*) and giving a careful analysis of the plain sense of the text (*lexis*). Such problems, common in the books of Moses, were enigmas (*ainigmata*) that, Diodore said, could often be solved by the application of reason. For instance, Diodore noticed that the Psalms were not in chronological order. Although Psalm 3 pertained to Absalom's revolt, it was placed before Psalm 143, which was about David's triumph over Goliath. The nonchronological order, he hypothesized, was the result of the loss of the psalms during the Babylonian captivity. Their present order reflected when individual psalms were rediscovered after the return of the Jews to Palestine.

Another such problem Diodore mentions is the strange phenomenon of the talking serpent in Genesis 3. Reason tells the reader that the serpent is a nonrational creature and therefore incapable of speaking, much less formulating an argument to ensnare the first woman. Instead of dismissing the serpent as a figure for the devil, Diodore insists that there was a serpent, just as the plain sense of the passage states. The serpent, however, spoke because the devil used it as his mouthpiece to speak words of guile. It is reasonable to infer that the speaker was the devil, Diodore explains, because Jesus calls the devil "a liar and the father of lies" (John 8:44). Since the serpent's words were the first lie, then the devil as "the father of lies" was the true speaker (*Comm. Ps.* 118). Although Diodore intended to distinguish his exegesis from that of allegorists, his interpretation of Genesis 3 suggests that their exegetical methods were more similar than he claimed. Like Origen, Diodore here used the technique of intertextuality by which an Old Testament enigma is explained when read through the lens of the New Testament.

The difference between Origen's exegesis and that of his Antiochene critics cannot be reduced to a difference in the seriousness with which they took the historical veracity of the Old Testament narratives. Their disagreement about the witch (or belly-myther) of Endor's summoning the ghost of Samuel from hell (1 Sam 28:3–19) is an example of the complexities of their differences. In Origen's homily on this passage, he says that although not all narratives in their literal sense are edifying for Christians, the historical sense of this passage does have important theological implications for Christians (*Engastr.* 5.2.1). Specifically, it raises the serious question whether a holy man, like the prophet Samuel, would actually be consigned to hell. The exegetical point on which Origen's argument rested was whether the witch lied when she said that she saw Samuel. Origen resolves the question by attending to the literal or narratival sense, not by offering an allegorical reading of the passage. Arguing that the "narrative persona" is the author and that the author was the Holy Spirit, one should take the narrative as factual. Thus, "When the woman saw Samuel, she cried out" (v. 12); Origen says this is the voice of the narrator, the Spirit, and the Spirit's report of the witch's words should be taken to be true (*Engastr.* 5.4.2). Origen supports this interpretation with theological arguments: since demons do not have prophetic powers, the ghost summoned by the witch could not have been a demon. The deeper point, however, driving Origen's interpretation is christological. The descent of holy Samuel to hell foreshadows Jesus's own descent into hell. Samuel went to preach to the imprisoned souls in hope of liberation through Christ's descent (*Engastr.* 5.6.3–7).

Origen's interpretation would be challenged generations later by Eustathius of Antioch (c. 280–345) in his only surviving treatise, *On the Belly-Myther, Against Origen*. Eustathius, employing the tactics of forensic oratory, placed Origen on trial, arguing that he, like the belly-myther (*engastrimythos*) herself, was the creator of unreliable myths that drew dubious spiritual meanings from perceptible things. Like Origen, Eustathius's exegesis arises from both details of the passages and theological assumptions. Against Origen, Eustathius rejects the assertions that the prophet was in hell and that a necromancer possessed the power to raise the spirits of the dead. The narrative voice does not, Eustathius insists, say that the woman saw Samuel. Such was only the belly-myther's claim. The reader knows, however, that the belly-myther was unholy, and therefore the reader would know that her words were untrustworthy (*Engastr. c. Orig.* 4.8). He finds further evidence that she was lying in her description of Samuel clothed in a prophet's cloak, for spirits of the dead do not wear clothes. Samuel's clothes would have remained with his body in the grave (*Engastr. c. Orig.* 6.3–4). Eustathius concludes that the apparition was not in fact Samuel but a demon in the guise of the prophet. Ultimately, the bigger point of Eustathius's exegesis was both that the holy prophet of God was not in hell and that Origen, by saying so, was every bit as much a conjurer of mendacious myths as the witch of Endor herself.

Perhaps the true significance of these competing interpretations is that they do not represent a conflict of allegory versus historically attentive *theōria*. Both

Origen and Eustathius were concerned with the historical sense of the text, and their respective treatments of the historical narrative were governed by the theological conclusion each intended his audience to reach.

Perhaps the most systematic analysis of a christological hermeneutic in the West was provided by Tyconius, a fourth-century contemporary of Diodore and Ambrose. Although a member of the Donatist church in North Africa, Tyconius had tremendous influence well beyond North Africa because of his influence on Augustine. In his *Book of Rules*, he offered guidelines for figural interpretations of the Old Testament. These *regulae* were broken down into seven groups that (1) distinguished the Lord and his body, (2) concerned the Lord's bipartite body, (3) distinguished the promise of grace and the law, (4) separated species and genus, (5) the times, (6) recapitulation, and (7) the devil and his followers. These rules, he said, were "keys and windows" to unlock the secret treasure hidden in the law (*Reg.* prologue).

One of Tyconius's core theological tenets that informed his exegesis was Paul's description of the Church as Christ's body. Tyconius reasoned that where Christ was spoken of figurally in the Old Testament, there, too, was the Church. The exegetical challenge was determining when the text shifted from speaking about Christ to speaking about his body. For instance, when Daniel speaks of "the stone hewn from the mountain" (Dan 2:34), he is referring to the Lord, the head, who comes from the Father. But when Daniel goes on to say, "the stone *became* a mountain and filled the whole earth," the stone must be the Lord's body, since the Lord himself, possessing divine glory before the world was made (John 17:5) and "all power in heaven and on earth" (Phil 2:10-11), did not experience growth. So the stone here is Christ's body the Church, which becomes a mountain in the way that Paul described in Ephesians 4:15–16 the Church as growing up into its head, Christ (*Reg.* 1.2).

Older binary presentations of patristic exegesis that made a sharp division between Alexandrian allegorical exegesis and Antiochene typological interpretation served as a valuable heuristic device. Yet, as we have seen, both Origen and anti-Origenists valued the literal or literary character and structure of the text as the field that held the spiritual meaning. Therefore, neither took a supersessionist view of the relationship between the letter and the spirit; that is, neither held that once the spiritual meaning was discovered one could dispense with the text's literal meaning. Rather, early Christian interpreters, like Jewish rabbis who held that all possible interpretations of torah were delivered by God on Sinai, viewed Scripture as having a surplus of meaning. A single passage of Scripture did not have a single meaning, that is, the human author's intention; it had many. Nor was there a sense that the Christian could attain such a transcendent communion with the divine that she would not need the special revelation of Scripture. Augustine's surprising comment that those who are perfect can live in solitude without the Scriptures (*Doctr. chr.* 1.93) is surprising precisely because it is an anomaly in patristic theology. Therefore, these early Christian commenters returned again and again and again to the letter to discover yet further insight into the nature and character of the infinite God whom they revealed and to be perfected in the holiness expected of the community of his worshipers.

Wisdom and Rhetoric of Classical Culture

While the practices of the worshiping communities and the Christian Scriptures were the primary touchstones for early Christian theology, the intellectual traditions of the Greco-Roman culture left no insignificant imprint. The degree of influence varied widely. Some figures, like Ignatius of Antioch, reveal very little philosophical education, while others, like Clement of Alexandria whose writings are pedantically peppered with allusions to classical philosophy and literature, wore their intellectual pedigree on their sleeves. Justin Martyr narrates his movement through the philosophical schools until he found an intellectual home in Platonism before his conversion to Christianity. Tertullian and Ambrose were trained in Roman law. Origen was a student of the Alexandrian philosopher Ammonius Saccas, who may or may not have been the same Ammonius who was the teacher of Plotinus, the father of Neo-Platonism. Basil of Caesarea, Gregory of Nazianzus, Gregory of Nyssa, and Augustine of Hippo all studied rhetoric and were teachers of oratory before they were bishops. And Marius Victorinus, before his conversion, was so distinguished a Neo-Platonist philosopher and teacher of rhetoric—*rhetor urbis Romae*—that a statue was erected to his honor in the Forum of Trajan. With few exceptions, most of their writings reflect a mixture of appreciative indebtedness and critical ambivalence to classical culture.

Theological Engagement with Philosophy

Tertullian famously asked, "What indeed has Athens to do with Jerusalem? What concord is there between the Academy and the Church? What between heretics and Christians? Our instruction comes from 'the porch of Solomon,' who had himself taught that 'the Lord should be sought in simplicity of heart'" (*Praescr.* 7). Although often treated as an example of a fideistic tendency within patristic thought, read in isolation from his larger corpus it belies his familiarity with and deployment of philosophy for his own theological purposes. Tertullian's concern was not with Christians' *using* pagan learning per se but with making Christian belief *contingent* on demonstration based on philosophical arguments. The result he feared was an adulteration of the faith that compromised the essential mystery it contains.

Basil (AD 329–379): Compare Pagan and Scripture Texts to See Truth

A commonly held approach to pagan learning was summed up by Basil in his *Address to Young Men*—namely, that Christians should not "surrender to [pagan authors] once for all the rudders of your mind, as if of a ship, and follow them wheresoever they lead," but instead take from them only that which is useful (*Adol.* 1.5). The star by which the young men ought to navigate is the hope of life in the age to come; and they ought to deem as useful those teachings that prepare them for that life (*Adol.* 2.2–3). Such, said Gregory of Nazianzus in his funeral oration for Basil, was the ordering principle of their friendship when they were studying rhetoric together in Athens (*Or. Bas.* 20).

Explaining his own pedagogical method, Basil compared his use of pagan philosophy and poetry to the way a dyer of cloth uses certain treatments that enable wool or cotton to hold the color of the dye (*Adol.* 2.8). By juxtaposing the pagan authors with those of Scripture, the pagan texts highlighted the truth of holy teachings either because of their affinity or because of the drastic contrast in teachings (*Adol.* 3.1). That is, by comparing pagan and Christian texts, the students learned the critical skills that better enabled them to discriminate traditions that were faithful to the apostolic teachings from those that were not. Such a practical pedagogical approach merely built on that of the theological voices of prior generations. Of these, for Basil, none surpassed Origen.

Origen (AD 185–254): "Plundering the Egyptians"

Although Origen saw an uncritical dependence on Greco-Roman culture as the source of the errors of Gnostics, he did not see a problem with pagan authors per se. Rather, the failing of the Gnostics lay in their appropriation of ideas that were "alien" to Christianity in the sense of being antithetical to the teachings of Jesus (*Cels.* 5.61). Rather than an equally uncritical and categorical rejection of classical and Hellenistic wisdom, Origen encouraged a critical appropriation of the nobler elements of pagan learning known subsequently as "plundering the Egyptians."

In his *Letter to Gregory*—possibly his protégé, Gregory Thaumaturgus—preserved in the *Philocalia*, Origen illustrated the right use of philosophy by appealing to the Israelites' request on the eve of their exodus from Egypt for vessels of silver and gold and for clothing of their Egyptian masters (Exod 11:2; 12:35). They took the treasures of the Egyptians that they might be converted into "holy vessels" for the worship of the Lord in his holy tabernacle (*Philoc.* 13.2). So too, Gregory, though "applying [himself] with all the power of [his] innate ability to Christianity, . . . [should] accept those things from the philosophy of the Greeks that can serve as a general education or introduction to Christianity and . . . that are useful for the interpretation of the Holy Scriptures." Just as the fields of geometry, music, grammar, rhetoric, and astronomy are treated as "adjuncts to philosophy" (*hōs synerithōn philosophias*), so should philosophy be used as an aid for Christianity (*Philoc.* 13.1).

Origen justified the auxiliary role of philosophy on the premise that all knowledge comes from God (*Hom. Num.* 18.3.2). While Origen affirms the value of pagan learning, the subtext of his interpretation is that Christians, not the pagan authors, know the proper use of philosophy, namely for the worship of God (*theosebeia*). As a result, Gregory Thaumaturgus relates, Origen warned his students not to be committed to any one philosophical school (*Orat. paneg.* 14). Such dogmatic adherence to a single philosophical tradition would make philosophy an idol—like the Israelites erecting the golden calf at Bethel—rather than a servant of God (*Philoc.* 13.2). As was evident with the Gnostics, he concluded, heresy was the fruit of such idolatry.

Gregory of Nyssa (c. 335–394): Tension Between Philosophy and Theology

In his allegorical reading of the exodus story, *Life of Moses*, Gregory of Nyssa stresses the life according to reason and formative value of education. In contrast with the tyranny of the nonrational passions—represented by both Pharaoh and the rushing waters of the Nile, which would sweep the person away to his death—the life born of "sober and prudent rational thoughts" cultivated through an "education in different disciplines," represented by the boy child Moses in the ark that carries him to firm ground of the river bank, allows one to rise above the life of turmoil (*Mos.* 2.7–8).

The education he has in mind, however, is not philosophy. He proceeds to interpret Pharaoh's childless daughter who took Moses in as a figure for "profane philosophy" with its "barren wisdom," which "is always in labor but never gives birth" (*Mos.* 2.10–11). This seems ironic, given Gregory's knowledge and use of wisdom from the major philosophical traditions in his own theology. Yet here he is using a stock argument about the insufficiency of philosophical knowledge. Not only is there no consensus among the various schools, but even when they do hit upon truth it is only a partial truth often corrupted with some errors. For example, the Platonists are right for believing in the immortality of the soul but wrong for adding to this their idea about the transmigration of souls. It is precisely such errors that are apt to have a corrupting effect on Christian theology if introduced to Church teachings (*Mos.* 2.40).

Later Gregory repeats Origen's interpretation of the Hebrews' "plundering the Egyptians" as a figure for the "wealth of pagan learning" (i.e., moral and natural philosophy, geometry, astronomy, dialectic) by which the "divine sanctuary of mystery must be beautified with the riches of reason" (*Mos.* 2.115). Gregory then cites the example of his brother Basil the Great as one who took his training in rhetoric and philosophy as a "gift" for the adornment of the Church even as the Hebrews used Egyptian gold to adorn the ark of the covenant (*Mos.* 2.116). Gregory builds upon Basil's argument in his *Address to Young Men*: it is those who have been nourished by the milk of the Church's doctrine who are best able to assess which elements of philosophy are gifts edifying to the Church and which must be rejected.

Augustine (AD 354–430): Philosophy on the Journey to Faith

In few places is the tension between an appreciation for pagan literature and Christian theology more evident than in Jerome and Augustine. During his hermitical sojourn in Chalcis (near modern-day Aleppo), Jerome fell gravely ill to the point that the community was making arrangements for his funeral. While under a fever, he had a nightmare that he was taken up before the judgment seat of God. There castigating him for his love of classical literature, the Lord declared, "You are a Ciceronian, not a Christian" (*Ep.* 22.30). Jerome's dream reveals his awareness of the tension between his identity as a follower of Christ and his love of classical literature, which he recognized was not fully compatible with the Christian teachings.

In *Confessions*, Augustine recounts the tremendous value he found in the "books of the Platonists" that gave him the intellectual resources to resolve questions that had become major obstacles in his progress toward the Catholic faith. One question was explaining the existence of evil in a universe brought into existence by an all-good, all-wise, and all-powerful Creator. From the Platonic notion that evil is merely a privation or absence of the good, he was able to see that evil, contrary to the Manichees' doctrine of dark matter, is not a substance. Rather, it is like darkness that is not a thing but merely the absence of light. Similarly, evil was not a thing that God created but the diminution of the goodness of creation that resulted from the misuse of human free choice (*Conf.* 7.12.18). Indeed, evil lay in the will itself that was not directed by the love of God.

Similarly, the Platonic theory of immaterial, intelligible realities—that is, ideas or forms—enabled him to conceive of God's incorporeal nature and thus his being both transcendent and immanent in creation. Even as ideas, such as the number five, are not confined to a single place or time but are fully present in the minds of thinkers in different places at the same time, so, Augustine realized, God was able to be fully present in all places simultaneously (*Conf.* 7.10.16).

But for all these benefits, Augustine recognized the ultimate failure of Platonism to arrive at the wisdom that was the goal of dialectic. In *City of God*, he praises Porphyry as the philosopher who came closest to the truth (*Civ.* 22.3). Perhaps ironically, the Platonists' confidence in their ability to transcend the sensible realm and ascend to the knowledge of the eternal, intelligible realities through dialectic was the source of pride that erected a wall of separation between themselves and the highest truth revealed in Jesus. "They disdained to learn from him, for 'he is weak and humble of heart'" (*Conf.* 7.21.27). They denied their own need for the deathless Logos to put on mortal flesh in order to deliver mortals from their mortality. Their pride was Augustine's own pride: "I began to want to give myself airs as a wise person . . . but I shed no tears of penitence. Worse still I was puffed up with knowledge. But where was the charity which builds on the foundation of the humility which is Jesus Christ?" (*Conf.* 7.20.26).

Like Basil, Augustine reflected on his study of the books of the Platonists and saw them as part of his preparation for conversion. Unlike Basil, Augustine saw their preparatory value not as training in the analysis of dialectic but for formation in humility. Addressing God, Augustine prays,

> I believe you wanted me to encounter [the books of the Platonists] before I came to study your Scriptures. Your intention was that the manner in which I was affected by them should be imprinted in my memory, so that when later I had been made docile by *your books* and my wounds healed by your gentle fingers, I would learn to discern and distinguish the difference between presumption and confession, between those who see what the goal is but not how to get there and those who see the way which leads to the home of bliss. (*Conf.* 7.20.26)

Augustine abandoned hope of attaining perfection through philosophy. Yet his intellectual sensibilities, especially his illuminationist epistemology, remained formed by the Platonic tradition throughout his life as bishop-theologian. Augustine's relationship to pagan learning, like that of most of the figures discussed in this book, reflects an attitude that is both appreciative and critical.

Philo of Alexandria (20 BC–AD 50): A Jewish Model for Christian Theologians

Among the non-Christian philosophers whose thought Christians directly plundered, few ranked as highly as Philo of Alexandria. Philo was raised in one of the two districts reserved for Jews in Alexandria, Egypt, the most hellenized of cities outside of Greece. The Jews of Alexandria were also highly hellenized. In the third century BC under the patronage of King Ptolemy II, Greek translations of the Hebrew Scriptures, the Septuagint, reflected a union of Jewish and Hellenistic cultures. There was a certain sustained tension—even violence—between Jews and gentiles, however, in part because of gentile resentment at Jewish privileges such as control over their taxation and laws set by their own senate that dealt with internal affairs.

As the scion of one of the wealthiest families in Alexandria, Philo was educated by a Greek tutor. Although he was fully observant of the Mosaic law, there is no evidence that he knew Hebrew; rather, he studied the Torah only in its Septuagintal form. He used his knowledge of both intellectual traditions not only to act as an apologist of Alexandrian Jewry but also to create a genuine synthesis of Jewish and Hellenistic thought through his allegorical interpretations of the Torah and philosophical treatises. Having argued—as would Christian apologists for centuries after him—that the Greek sages derived much of their wisdom from Moses, Philo viewed his project not as syncretistic conformity to his Hellenistic culture but as a union of traditions that ultimately drew their wisdom from one and the same source. Such eclecticism was fully consistent with the temperament of Middle Platonism to synthesize the thought of Plato and reconcile it with Stoic ethics and Peripatetic logic.

The union of Jewish and Hellenistic thought that would prove most influential for Christians appeared in Philo's cosmological treatise *On the Creation of the World*. He begins by posing a basic question: Why does the Torah begin with the story of creation? What, in other words, does cosmology have to do with the Law? Philo's answer reflects the Stoic view that human flourishing or *eudaimonia* lies in the virtuous life, which the Stoics spoke of as a life according to nature or a life according to reason. The Law of Moses is a revelation of the virtuous life that reflects the reason underlying the cosmic order of God's creation. Even as *Timaeus*, Plato's creation myth, provides the cosmological basis for the proper ordering of the soul and the polis according to the right relationship between the intelligible and sensible world—the realm of the forms and the realm of material things—described in *Republic*, so Genesis provides the cosmological foundation for the decalogue. "The cosmos," Philo writes, "is in harmony with the law and the law with the cosmos, and the man who observes the law is at once a citizen of the cosmos, directing his actions in relation to the rational purpose of nature" (*Opif.* 3). A life not according to nature is a life dominated by the passions, that is, emotions and impulses arising from mistaken judgment about the goods proper to human flourishing. The source of this errant judgment of passion was human traditions and social customs that were at odds with reason and nature. The fear of death, for instance, came from the mistaken belief in the stories told by the poets of the torments of those souls ferried across the River Styx into Hades. Virtuous individuals who followed reason reject such fanciful myths because they are contrary to a rational understanding of nature. Therefore, they are not distressed or deeply grieved by death because they rightly understand death as part of nature and accept the inevitable end of life over which we have no control. When an individual's mind is aligned with nature, she is a citizen of the cosmos and her life is undisturbed by foolish social conventions.

Such, Philo says, was the condition of the first man: "The cosmos was his home and city. . . . He resided in the cosmos with complete safety like in his native land, wholly without fear. . . . And so he lived in the enjoyment of peace without conflict" (*Opif.* 142). When Philo speaks of the blessedness of Adam's Edenic existence as a citizen of the cosmos, he draws on language shared by Platonism and Judaism. As Plato in *Theaetetus* (176a–c) describes the virtuous life as a likeness to God who is perfect wisdom and justice, Philo employs similar language of the *imago Dei* from Genesis 1:26–27. Whereas the Stoics defined human flourishing in terms of nature (material universe) and the Platonist in terms of the transcendent divinity (heavenly, intelligible realm), Philo weds the two. Like Adam, the virtuous person is able to flourish by living in conformity to nature (the material world) as a citizen of the cosmos because she has been made in the image of God. That is, living in harmony with the cosmos is possible only by conforming to the image of the cosmos's Creator. Adam "was closely related and akin to the Director [of the cosmos], because the divine spirit had flowed into him . . . so that all his words and actions were undertaken in order to please the Father and King . . . because only those souls are permitted to approach him who consider the goal of their existence to be assimilation to the God who brought them forth" (*Opif.* 143).

Philo's God, who is humanity's *summum bonum*, is not identical with nature as in Stoic pantheism but is closer to the transcendent God of Platonism. Precisely because Philo's God is nature's Creator, human flourishing as a citizen of the cosmos living in harmony with nature is possible only by conforming to the image of the God who ordered the cosmos. In this way, Philo reconciles the Stoic and Platonic accounts of *eudaimonia* with the Genesis narrative of God's relationship with creation.

Philo's allegorical interpretation of the Jewish Scriptures set a model for early Christian allegorists. Not only his method but also the content of his interpretations influenced Christian explanations of creation, the nature of human beings, and the life of virtue for early Christian theologians, including Origen, Basil of Caesarea, Gregory of Nyssa, Jerome, and Ambrose of Milan. Philo's greatest impact on Christian dogma came in his theology of the Logos, which proved foundational for Christian interpretations of the prologue to John, "In the beginning was the Logos . . . and the Logos became flesh" (John 1:1, 14).

Christian Preachers and Pagan Rhetoric

No small portion of the pagan treasure plundered by Christians was the craft of oratory. Since the days of Socrates, philosophers coming out of the Platonic tradition lauded the superiority of dialectic over the suspect *technē* of rhetoric. Plato had argued that while the sophists taught the skill of using words to give the appearance of truth, dialectic allowed the discovery of truth itself (*Phaedr.* 266b, 274d–276e).

Those who gave theological insight into the meaning of Scripture were not academics in the modern sense. Rather, they were pastors tasked with interpreting Scripture for their congregations through homilies. Naturally, therefore, they appreciated the power of carefully crafted words to edify their congregations. Many, if not most, had been schooled in the rhetorical arts from adolescence. They were cognizant of the vanity of the cult of oratory that pervaded the Hellenistic world.

As with philosophy, so too the theologians expressed ambivalence about the craft. Macrina, sister and teacher of Basil of Caesarea and Gregory of Nyssa, shamed both her brothers for allowing their love of rhetoric and classical literature to divert them from the humble service of God (*Macr.* 8.3 in Silvas). Augustine, reflecting on the days immediately following his conversion experience in the garden of Milan, recounts that the first action he took to "make no provision for the flesh and its lusts" (Rom 13:14; cf. *Conf.* 8.12.29) was to resign the once highly coveted position as a teacher of rhetoric to the sons of the Milanese elite. Augustine decided to "quietly retire from my post as a salesman of words in the markets of rhetoric. I did not wish my pupils, who were giving their minds not to your law nor to your peace, but to frenzied lies and lawcourt squabbles, to buy from my mouth weapons for their madness" (*Conf.* 9.2.2).

It was in the prideful purpose of his students and their parents that the problem lay. Augustine did believe in the ecclesial purposes rhetoric might serve. Earlier in *Confessions*, as he reflected on his training at the hand of the vainglorious *grammatici* who were more troubled by an infelicitous turn of phrase or syntactical slip than by the immoral pictures they painted with their words, he prayed, "May I dedicate to your service my power to speak and write and read and count" (*Conf.* 1.15.24). He knew that the preacher's words grounded in prayer might inform, delight, and move his parishioners' wills toward the love of God and neighbor (*Doctr. chr.* 4.14.31). Even more fundamentally, he understood that words were given by God that human beings might find their highest good in the happiness of doxology: "Accept the sacrifice of my confession offered by 'the hand of my tongue' which you have formed and stirred up to confess your name" (*Conf.* 5.1.1).

The Apostle Paul and Rhetorical Technique

Not surprisingly, early Christian theologians drew heavily upon their training in rhetoric to serve ecclesial purposes. In this respect, they were following the example of Paul, who undoubtedly was schooled in rhetoric while a boy in the academic communities of Tarsus and employed the techniques of protrepsis and paraenesis in his letters. In his First Letter to the Thessalonians, for instance, Paul uses the paraenetic tactics of *reminding* his readers what they already know, namely what sort of man Paul was and how he labored and suffered on their behalf (1 Thess 1:5; 2:9), such that they need *no further instruction* by him (1 Thess 4:9), and praising them for what they are *already doing* and encouraging them to *continue* to *imitate* his example of the life that is pleasing to God (1 Thess 4:1).

It should not be surprising that preachers such as John Chrysostom (347–407) not only presented Paul as a model for their congregations' imitation but, as Margaret Mitchell has shown, drew on their knowledge of rhetorical theory to paint portraits of virtue on the souls of their audience (cf. *Resp.* 9.588b; *Hom. 2 Cor.* 7.7). The goal was to make the text of Scripture come alive in the minds of their congregants through the technique of ekphrasis, which recounted the scenes of his life with unforgettable vividness. In his homilies *In Praise of Saint Paul*, Chrysostom depicts Paul's soul as "a meadow of virtues and a spiritual paradise" (*Laud. Paul.* 1.1). In the grand style of epideictic or show oratory, he then paints in vivid images the various plants, each of which represents Paul's virtues. These baroque word pictures served not only the purpose of impressing the images into his listeners' memories but also the complementary nature of the virtues by showing that the beauty of Paul's soul lay not in a single virtue but in the beauty of the garden of his soul seen as a whole (*Laud. Paul.* 1.1, 16). Whereas Plutarch in his *Lives of Great Men* or Ambrose in his catechetical homilies on the lives of Israel's patriarchs presented each figure as representing a single particular virtue, for Chrysostom Paul's greatness is manifest in the presence of all the virtues united in a single life.

Tell Their Story: First-Person Narrative Technique

Another rhetorical technique was prosopopoeia, which is direct, first-person speech that the orator places in the mouth of the individual being presented to his audience. In essence, the orator takes on the persona of the individual so that the audience feels that they are not simply hearing *about* the figure but actually hearing him or her speak *directly* to them. In his instructions on the craft of oratory, *The Institutes*, Quintilian enumerates the advantages of prosopopoeia. In a court of law, an advocate's words will have a far greater emotional impact on the judge and jury if they seem to hear the victim of an injustice speak directly of her suffering (6.1.26). Although it bordered on presumption for Christian preachers to adopt the persona of Jesus himself and put words into his mouth, because the rhetorical technique was recognized by their audiences, prosopopoeia allowed the preacher to summon the Lord into the presence of the congregation.

In a series of homilies on women in the gospels, Jacob of Serugh (451–521) uses prosopopoeia in his homily on the woman with the issue of blood (Mark 5:25–34) to allow his congregation to enter the woman's thoughts and hear the frustration and desperation of one not only excluded from normal social intercourse but barred by the law of Moses from access to Christ, who is her hope of being healed. "She saw the needy who had their needs met . . . but then realized her illness was something different . . . and that the Law does not give permission to uncleanness to enter, without a cleansing, a crowd that is ritually clean. . . . The wretched woman realized that it was not possible to go in among the great crowd and tell of her illness—for Moses had excluded her from the people" (*Hom.* 170.209–214, 217–219). Then Jacob gives words to her unspoken thoughts to arouse among his listeners sympathy for the woman; out of this sympathy, compassion for the afflicted and helpless is aroused in their souls. This woman is not passive. Boldly believing in Jesus's power and pity (*Hom.* 170.204), she defies the law that separates her from Jesus and prevents her from being healed. In defiant hope, she declares,

> This illness (of mine) has gone beyond the bounds (faced) by all other women,
> So accordingly I am going to go beyond the bounds (set) for all women in a state of uncleanness.
> Let the women whose (flow of) blood is kept within the norm keep the norm,
> But not in the case of a wretched woman whose flow knows no law. . . .
> I am not afraid of the Law that threatens me.
> I shall show my illness to the Lord of Moses . . .
> And he will heal me—then let Moses become aware and see me. . . .
> For [Jesus] is entirely open to everyone who comes to Him with love. (*Hom.* 170.225–231, 254)

Here Jacob uses prosopopoeia to lift up this nameless woman as an example of the boldness of faith that wisely—he expressly calls her a "sage"—recognizes both Jesus's authority over the law and his power and compassion to heal those who come to him. Prosopopoeia served as a tool to allow the preacher or hymn writer to make a theological point, in this case about the nature of faith in Christ's mercy, by going beyond what is expressly said in Scripture but what is consistent with the character of these actors in the biblical drama. Consequently, through their empathetic connection with the characters and deeper insight into their interaction with Jesus, the congregation is able to reflect more deeply about their own need for salvation and God's saving condescension.

Oratory and the Word as Mimesis of the Creator

These orator-theologians thought of themselves as craftsmen who were imitating the divine Craftsman, the Word "through whom all things were made" and who fashioned humanity in his image and who in the incarnation sought to restore that image defaced by sin. In his *On the Making of Humanity*, Gregory of Nyssa described God's fashioning humanity in his image by using the metaphor of God as a portrait artist. As the artist conveys the distinct personality of the archetype by casting their image using different hues, so too the imageless God the master painter confers his image to the first human beings by making them partakers of his virtues (*Hom. opif.* 5.1). Later in his treatise on the Psalms, Gregory recognizes the parallel between God's craftsmanship in the beginning and the preacher's skilled depiction of virtue in the lives of the saints: "Then by means of the form of virtue, [the Word] forms Christ in us in accordance with whose image we existed in the beginning and in accordance with which we again come to exist" (*Inscr. Ps.* 2.134). Through the words of the orator extolling the virtues of the saints, the Word re-forms the mind of the listener in his image.

Gregory's brother Basil also employs the metaphor of the painter to speak of the Christian rhetor to explain how Christian oratory re-forms the listener in virtues that are the mark of the divine image. The vivid painting of a great battle is an imitation (*mimēsis*) of the deeds of noble men that inspires imitation of their heroism. The painting not only arouses an admiration for their bravery but also stirs up a feeling of courage in the soul of the viewer. "In this very way," Basil declares in his sermon *On the Holy Forty Martyrs*, "let us too remind those present of these men's virtues, and as it were, by bringing their deed to their gaze, let us move their conduct towards the imitation [*mimēsin*] of those who are noble and appropriate" (*Sanct. quadr.* 2).

Such preaching, as Morwenna Ludlow has pointed out, was not a form of allegory that used metaphors to point the listener beyond the letter of Scripture. Rather, their word pictures sought to draw the congregation more deeply into the narrative and thus consider the moral and spiritual implications of the passage. Just as earlier patristic exegesis treated Scripture as a sacramental medium for entering into the presence of God, similarly the preacher's use of ekphrasis and prosopopoeia to animate the biblical narrative allowed the congregation to have a more active, participatory relationship with the biblical text and through it with God.

Conclusion

New Testament scholar Abraham Malherbe, when discussing Paul's classical allusions or deployment of the rhetorical strategies from Hellenistic moral philosophers, used to put into Paul's mouth the words of Tennyson's Ulysses: "I am part of all that I have met." The theologians of the early Church themselves had "met" many people in person or in their writings. Some were pagan, some Jewish, and even in the waning years of the patristic period, some Muslim. It should not be surprising, therefore, that their worldview and their manner of defending the Christian faith was informed by a range of cultural sources that converged in the Hellenistic world of late antiquity. Yet out of that convergence emerged a Christian culture that would be strikingly different from the pagan culture that went before or either the medieval culture of the Latin West or the Islamic culture that spread across North Africa and Asia Minor and eventually jumped the Bosporus into Macedonia and the Balkans.

The theology produced by this culture would form a living intellectual tradition in the Catholic and Protestant churches of the West and the Orthodox and non-Chalcedonian churches of the East. At times one understandably may question the saintliness of some of these luminaries, whom the Church, both East and West, has called its teachers (*doctores ecclesiae*). Nevertheless, when one considers their ideas against the background of the worshiping communities in which they lived and taught, one sees their ultimate end: to arrive at a right understanding of Peter's famous declaration of Jesus's identity as "the Christ, the son of the living God" (Matt 16:16). For them, the right understanding of Peter's confession was not a speculative matter. It was a matter of life and death—quite literally, as the martyrs among them could attest. The life they sought was the eternal life inescapably tied to the person of Jesus of Nazareth. Truly, the impetus underlying their search for theological knowledge rested on a belief in Jesus's prayer, "This is eternal life that they may *know* you, the only true God, and Jesus Christ whom you have sent" (John 17:3). Such knowledge was both the beginning and the end of the journey; and between the beginning and the end—along the journey—was, they hoped, a distinctive way of life that conformed to the knowledge they found in Christ.

Bibliography

Primary Sources

Ambrose of Milan. *The Mysteries* and *The Sacraments*. In *Theological and Dogmatic Treatises*. Translated by Roy J. Deferrari. Washington, DC: Catholic University of America Press, 1963.

Apostolic Fathers. 2 vols. Translated by Bart D. Ehrman. Loeb Classical Library. Cambridge: Harvard University Press, 2014.

Apostolic Fathers. Translated by J. B. Lightfoot and J. R. Harmer. Edited by Michael W. Holmes. Grand Rapids: Baker, 1989.

Augustine. *Concerning the City of God Against the Pagans*. Translated by John J. O'Meara. London: Penguin Books, 1972.

———. *Confessions*. Translated by Henry Chadwick. Oxford: Oxford University Press, 1991.

———. *On Christian Teaching*. Translated by R. P. H. Green. Oxford: Oxford University Press, 1997.

Gregory of Nyssa. *Life of Macrina*. In *Macrina the Younger: Philosopher of God*. Translated by Anna M. Silvas. Turnhout: Brepols, 2008.

———. *On the Making of Man*. *NPNF* 2/5.

Irenaeus of Lyons. *Against Heresies*. *ANF* 1.

Jacob of Serugh. *Homily on the Baptism of Constantine*. Translated by Arthur Lincoln Frothingham. Pages 167–242 in *Memorie della Reale Accademia Nazionale dei Lincei*. Classe di Scienze morali, storiche e filologiche III.8. 1882.

———. *Jacob of Sarug's Homilies on Women Whom Jesus Met*. Translated by Susan Ashbrook Harvey, Sebastian P. Brock, Reyhan Durmaz, Rebecca Stephens Falcasantos, Michael Payne, and Daniel Picus. Piscataway, NJ: Gorgias, 2016.

John Cassian. *The Conferences*. Translated by Boniface Ramsey. Ancient Christian Writers. New York: Paulist, 1997.

Justin Martyr. *Dialogue with Trypho*. Translated by Thomas B. Falls. Washington, DC: Catholic University of America Press, 2003.

———. *The First and Second Apologies*. Translated by Leslie William Barnard. Ancient Christian Writers. New York: Paulist, 1997.

Origen. *Commentary on the Epistle to the Romans: Books 6–10*. Translated by Thomas P. Scheck. Washington, DC: Catholic University of America Press, 2002.

———. *On First Principles: A Reader's Edition*. Translated by John Behr. Oxford: Oxford University Press, 2019.

Secondary Sources

BeDuhn, Jason D. *The First New Testament: Marcion's Scriptural Canon*. Salem, OR: Polebridge, 2013.

Boersma, Hans. *Scripture as Real Presence: Sacramental Exegesis in Early Christianity*. Grand Rapids: Baker Academic, 2017.

Dawson, John David. *Christian Figural Reading and the Fashioning of Identity*. Berkeley: University of California Press, 2002.

Gamble, Harry Y. "The New Testament Canon: Recent Research and the Status Quaestionis." Pages 267–94 in *The Canon Debate*. Edited by L. M. McDonald and J. A. Sanders. Peabody, MA: Hendrickson, 2002.

Greer, Rowan A., and Margaret M. Mitchell. *The "Belly-Myther" of Endor: Interpretations of 1 Kingdoms 28 in the Early Church*. Atlanta: Society of Biblical Literature, 2006.

Jensen, Robin M. *Baptismal Imagery in Early Christianity: Ritual, Visual, and Theological Dimensions*. Grand Rapids: Baker Academic, 2012.

Lieu, Judith. *Marcion and the Making of a Heretic: God and Scripture in the Second Century*. Cambridge: Cambridge University Press, 2014.

Ludlow, Morwenna. *Art, Craft, and Theology in Fourth-Century Christian Authors*. Oxford: Oxford University Press, 2020.

Malherbe, Abraham J. *Moral Exhortation: A Greco-Roman Sourcebook*. Philadelphia: Westminster, 1986.

Martens, Peter W. *Origen and Scripture: The Contours of the Exegetical Life*. Oxford: Oxford University Press, 2012.

McDonald, Lee M. *The Formation of the Christian Biblical Canon*. Peabody, MA: Hendrickson, 1995.

McGowan, Andrew B. *Ancient Christian Worship: Early Church Practices in Social, Historical, and Theological Perspective*. Grand Rapids: Baker Academic, 2014.

Mitchell, Margaret M. *The Heavenly Trumpet: John Chrysostom and the Art of Pauline Interpretation*. Louisville: Westminster John Knox, 2002.

———. *Paul, the Corinthians, and the Birth of Christian Hermeneutics*. Cambridge: Cambridge University Press, 2010.

Siker, Jeffrey S. *Disinheriting the Jews: Abraham in Early Christian Controversy*. Louisville: Westminster John Knox, 1991.

Witherington, Ben, III. *The Living Word of God: Rethinking the Theology of the Bible*. Waco, TX; Baylor University Press, 2009.

Young, Frances M. *Biblical Exegesis and the Formation of Christian Culture*. Peabody, MA: Hendrickson, 2002.

2

Persecution, Apologetics, and Polemics

From Justin Martyr to Augustine

On a day around the year 150, a teacher of one of the Christian communities in Rome went to the Curia or Roman Senate House in the *Forum Romanum*, which from the days of the early Republic was the center of political life in Rome. There he stood in line outside the Curia to present a petition to the Senate and to the emperor Antoninus Pius (AD 86–161). The petition sought an end to the arrest and punishment of people who identified as Christians. The mere name "Christian" did not merit such treatment, the petition argued. For the grounds of such persecution were founded on base prejudice and misunderstanding (*1 Apol.* 4). The petition sought to demonstrate that the teachings and practices of Christianity were neither without parallel in pagan Roman culture nor threatening to the peace of the empire and as such did not warrant arrest and execution. The petitioner was Justin to whom later generations would add the sobriquet "Martyr." As this honorific title suggests, Justin's petition was not successful. Indeed, given the length of the first petition especially, it is hard to imagine that Justin thought the petition would ever get a fair hearing. Yet these petitions, now known as the *First Apology* and *Second Apology*, were preserved by the Christian community in Rome and became the prototype of the genre of Christian theological literature—indeed a veritable cottage industry in the second and third centuries—called apologetics.

Justin's *First* and *Second Apologies*, like the many apologies that followed, reflected the impulse of Christians asserting their voice as a minority community on the margins of a larger society that did not rightly understand their beliefs and practices. Apologetics, as a genre of discourse, may be defined as a defense of Christianity in response to attacks by opponents. Thus, apologetics narrowly construed is different from other genres such as polemics, which poured contempt and critique on the beliefs and practices of the larger culture, and protreptic speech, which though equally critical was a form of exhortation that sought to convert the reader. Yet, all these genres, whose style and tone were often virtually identical, shared a similar function: to define Christian identity and instill confidence in the rightness of their faith against that of the majority culture. Some apologetic works were ostensibly addressed to non-Christians, in Justin's case to the emperor and the Senate. Yet it is highly unlikely that these missives got past the scrutiny of the *scrinia* whose job was to vet which petitions were worthy of being passed up the chain of command to the emperor's notice. Therefore, the authors of apologies were really writing for their fellow believers to model for them responses to objections to their faith that they may have heard from hostile neighbors. At the same time, they may have had a secondary audience, namely those who were potentially sympathetic to Christianity but also misunderstood it because of popular rumors and mischaracterizations of the faith. By debunking such misrepresentations, apologetics sought to clear the air of prejudices to make the first step toward opening the minds of pagan bystanders to the truth Christians claimed.

Apologetics were also of further value by explaining the relationship between Christian teachings and the wisdom of the larger non-Christian world. In this respect, the author and the audience represent a peculiar type of Christian. As historian Robert Grant observed, apologists were people not entirely at home in either the Christian or the pagan worlds. Their interests were too broad to be confined to a narrow set of Christian teachings. Yet their religious commitments created certain points of intellectual tension with the larger pagan culture. Therefore, at the same time that apologists sought to defend Christianity against outsiders, they were also trying to reconcile competing cultures and worldviews. Because apologists had one foot, so to speak, in the non-Christian world, they shared an affinity for the wisdom of the philosophical schools and the literary achievements, the epic poetry and oratory, with their non-Christian neighbors. Therefore, the apologists sought common ground—shared truths—between Christianity and pagan culture, not only to persuade their friends but to give themselves an account of how Christians and pagans can arrive at the same or similar conceptions of reality. Therefore, apologetics provided, as D. H. Williams has suggested, "a cerebral and pastoral 'lift' for believers who were supposed to live within, but not partake of, the pagan culture that was all around them."[1] Second, at the same time, the apologists recognized profound points of divergence between Christian and pagan cultures. So, in defending Christianity, they sought to understand the reason for the deeply ingrained defects in non-Christian culture that set it at odds with Christianity. This raised further questions about appropriate boundaries between their cultures. Consequently, apologetics bled over into protreptics or polemics. For by exposing

1. D. H. Williams, *Defending and Defining the Faith: An Introduction to Early Christian Apologetic Literature* (Oxford: Oxford University Press, 2020), 12.

the incompatibility of certain Christian truth claims with those of rival intellectual traditions, apologetics implicitly or explicitly called their hearers to make a decisive choice between the cultures and commit themselves to what Kavin Rowe has called "one true life." At other times, however, they were called to the more moderate judgment of assessing how to assimilate elements of pagan culture that were compatible with Christianity. Moreover, as we shall see, these dilemmas led to further questions about the relationship between Christianity and the state. The Scriptures taught that Christians should honor those in authority and be obedient members of society. What are the limits of that obedience? How deep can that loyalty go? More importantly—indeed the ultimate question at the heart of all apologetics—how much can the believer's identity be defined by their associations with the larger society that does not understand Christian teachings and practices but also is at times openly hostile to Christ and his followers? As such, the question of Christian identity vis-à-vis the world outside the Church would endure long after Christianity became the accepted religion of the empire in the fourth century.

Roman Perceptions and Prejudices

The Roman reaction to Christianity was in part the by-product of prejudice shaped by gossip. Rumors of incest and cannibalism, based on misunderstandings of Christian rituals such as the kiss of peace between members who addressed each other as brother or sister and the ritual of the Eucharist or Lord's Supper, made Christians, as the Roman historian Tacitus records, "a class hated for their abominations" (*Ann.* 15.44). Thus, it was easy for the emperor Nero to make scapegoats of Christians in order to redirect public attention from himself to the Christians as the cause of the great fire in Rome (AD 64). But there was a deeper source of animus for Christians that lay in the conflict between Roman piety with its endorsement of religious pluralism and Christian monotheism.

The core of Roman religious sensibilities was summed up in the idea of *pietas*. Originally, *pietas* meant showing respect for one's parents and ancestors by abiding by the *mos maiorum*, that is, the customs and norms of one's ancestors. Generally speaking, the Romans were temperamentally conservative. What was old was good because it had been tested over time by generation upon generation and proven reliable. By contrast, what was novel was highly suspect because it was not tried and true. New customs had not yet withstood the test of time. Following the *mos maiorum* was a form of piety because it honored the wisdom of the generations that had gone before and who had built an empire that stretched from Hadrian's Wall in Britain to the pillars of Hercules at Gibraltar to the headwaters of the Tigris and Euphrates Rivers. The building of the empire, however, was not the work of the great men of Rome's illustrious history alone; it came about through the favor of the gods. Rome's myth of origins, epically recounted by Vergil in his *Aeneid*, traced Rome's founding to Venus's sending Aeneas from Troy to Italy. As time passed, the gods raised up an elite class of men, the members of the senatorial aristocracy during the Republic and the emperors during the principate, who extended Roman rule throughout the Mediterranean world. Thus, the Roman political authority was tied to the gods. Therefore, it was necessary to show piety to the gods by building temples and making sacrificial offerings to the deities on whose favor Rome depended. Moreover, to honor the gods was a way of recognizing the foundation of Roman political authority. *Pietas* for the gods was as much or more a political matter than a theological one.

The Romans, being pragmatic in their policies, treated other religions with a greater or lesser degree of tolerance. Prudently, the Romans wanted to engender trust and a spirit of cooperation among the elites of the provinces. Destroying or desecrating the temples of these local gods would militate against building the sort of cooperative relations necessary to pacify the peoples of the provinces. Moreover, as polytheists, the Romans assumed that their gods were not the only gods. Although they were confident that Jupiter, Juno, and their siblings and offspring were the greatest deities, the Romans also recognized the possibility that in other parts of the world other gods might have greater power. Therefore, wherever the Romans went they build temples to their gods, but often they built temples to honor the local deities as well. Such mutual recognition of each other's gods created an atmosphere of religious pluralism. For Christians, as for Jews, the theological claim expressed in the Shema, "Hear, O Israel, the LORD is God; the LORD is one" (Deut 6:4), precluded the possibility of their remaining faithful to the one and only God while at the same time participating in many Roman public affairs that included some expression of *pietas* to gods that, from a Christian or Jewish perspective, were not gods at all. Because of Judaism's undeniable antiquity, Jews, though looked upon as truly peculiar people with incomprehensible idiosyncrasies, were granted various privileges and exemptions that freed them from participating in the pagan religious features of Roman social practices. With the division of Judaism and Christianity that emerged after the Jewish War (AD 66–73), Christians were no longer viewed as members of a venerable, ancient faith but devotees of a newfangled superstition. Not surprisingly, therefore, they were no longer granted the religious exemptions given to Jews. Consequently, their withdrawal from civic and political life not only made them appear misanthropic but also made them guilty of impiety.

Martyrdom: Ignatius of Antioch and the Price of Impiety

In the autumn of 111, Pliny the Younger arrived in the Asian provinces of Pontus and Bithynia on the southern coast of the Black Sea to assume his imperial appointment as governor. Prudently, he began his tenure by taking a tour of the provinces to acquaint himself with the people, their culture, and their needs. During his travels, he heard two repeated complaints. First, the temples were empty, and consequently offerings were not being made to the gods. Second, butchers selling meat in the agora complained that people were not buying their meat. The explanation he received was the rise of Christianity whose adherents neither frequented the temples nor bought meat that had been part of pagan religious rituals. Obviously, these Christians were disruptive of the religious and commercial life in his provinces, but, for all of Pliny's experience in the imperial civil service, he was unsure how to proceed. He had never been present at the interrogation of Christians, nor were there legal precedents to guide him (*Ep.* 96.1–2). Therefore, he wrote the emperor Trajan seeking counsel.

This letter, epistle 96, provides a window to early Christian practices as well as the formation of official Roman policy toward them. From the information Pliny gleaned through the torture of slave women who served as Christian deaconesses (*ministrae*), he determined that the wild rumors about them were inaccurate. The Christians were not cannibals but shared a common meal where they ate "food of an ordinary, harmless kind." Moreover, they met "to bind themselves by oath, not for any criminal purpose, but to abstain from theft, robbery, adultery, to commit no breach of trust, and not to deny a deposit when called upon to restore it." All this led him to conclude, "I found nothing but a degenerate superstition carried to extravagant lengths" (*Ep.* 96.7). Nevertheless, Pliny's ad hoc policy required the accused to repudiate Christianity by repeating "a formula of invocation to the gods" and making an offering of wine and incense before a statue of the emperor and images of the gods. If they refused, they were put to death or, in the case of Christians with Roman citizenship, sent to Rome to make their appeal before the emperor himself. The reason for this harsh punishment Pliny explained, "Whatever the nature of their admission, I am convinced that their stubbornness and unshakeable obstinacy ought not go unpunished" (*Ep.* 96.4).

Pliny's rationale for treating Christianity—not merely the crimes associated with it but simply confessing the name "Christian"—as a capital offense is telling about the place of religion in Roman political life and why Christians incurred the suspicion of imperial magistrates. The invocation of the gods and the sacrifices to the emperor's statue were acts of political as well as religious *pietas*. For Pliny, these gestures of piety were not about one's theological convictions but about one's recognition of Roman imperial authority through a public display of submission to that authority. Therefore, the Christians' refusal simply to say some prescribed words and perform some token acts of obedience—a refusal that seemed baffling to Pliny—was not merely an act of impiety in the modern religious sense;

it was tantamount to political sedition. Consequently, Rome could not allow the refusal to submit to the imperial authority of the emperor's representative to go unchecked. In Pliny's mind, such insubordination was a threat to the peace and prosperity of the provinces. For however innocuous their teachings and ritual practices were, the Christians' example of defiance, if unchecked, might give hope to other malcontents or potential rebels in the region. Whatever the Christians of Pontus and Bithynia thought of Rome's political authority, their "unshakeable obstinacy" rested on a fundamental theological commitment: there is only one God, and he alone should be worshiped. Thus, the difference between the Roman political view of *pietas* and the Christian theological view of faithfulness to Christ created a social impasse. There was no room for compromise by either group.

The intractability of some, though not all, of the Christians that Pliny found so detestable was not confined to the Christians of Pontus-Bithynia. Around the same time as Pliny's governorship, the Christian bishop of Antioch, Ignatius, was arrested and taken under armed guard to Rome where he would stand trial and be put to death by being thrown to the beasts in the Flavian amphitheater. During his journey to Rome, Ignatius composed letters to churches along the way. Although he does not say explicitly why he was arrested, the tone of his letters conveys the sort of obstinate defiance that Pliny deemed worthy of death. Ignatius reflects constantly about the significance of his impending death. He envisions his death as an imitation of Christ's suffering and death (Ign. *Eph.* 10; Ign. *Rom.* 6). Therefore, instead of encouraging the churches to find a way to enable him to escape or be freed, he veritably pleads with them that they not liberate him so that he may see his witness through to its end (Ign. *Rom.* 2.1). Though he never speaks of his martyrdom as the result of refusing to submit to imperial authority, he sees a parallel between his relationship with the world and that of Christ. As Jesus and the apostles were persecuted by the world, so shall he be if he has Christ's life in him (Ign. *Magn.* 5). One hears this in his antagonism toward his captors whose abusive treatment he saw as preparing him for his martyrdom (Ign. *Rom.* 4) by breaking his attachments to the world (Ign. *Rom.* 7.2). Rather than trusting that it is by reasoned argument that people will see the truth of the gospel, Ignatius instead declares, "The work [of the Church] is not a matter of persuasive rhetoric; rather, Christianity is greatest when it is hated by the world" (Ign. *Rom.* 3.3). Therefore, he believed, it was in the arena with the beasts that he would attain Christian perfection and become a true disciple (Ign. *Rom.* 1.2). Ignatius's rhetoric reflected—and likely inspired—a zeal for martyrdom that inspired some Christians to hand themselves over to be killed, which, far from proving persuasive to the Romans, only roused contempt among those, like Marcus Aurelius, who saw Christians as throwing away their lives (cf. *Ep. comm.*).

Justin Martyr's *First* and *Second Apologies*

Some forty to fifty years later, Justin's petitions assumed a more erudite posture with appeals to Plato and the Stoics, but the thrust of his arguments is a more direct attack upon Roman religion and the political structure it supported than Ignatius's impassioned rhetoric. Although his *First Apology* begins by appealing to the emperor and his sons' philosophical commitment to the pursuit of truth rather than blindly following social custom (*mos maiorum*), the implication is that by sanctioning the deaths of Christians based on rumor and innuendo, they show themselves not to be seekers of the truth (*1 Apol.* 2) and that they are led by their passions rather than reason (*1 Apol.* 3). Thus, he challenges them to prove that they are true philosophers by listening to the truth about Christianity. Justin then lays out the case that Christians are not politically subversive but in fact are model citizens. Contrary to the misinterpretation of Jesus's proclamation of the kingdom of God, he assures the emperor that they are not looking for another human kingdom. If they were, it would be better to curse Christ in order to escape death, which is a debt that all—including the emperor—must pay (*1 Apol.* 11). Although Christians' primary focus is not on the present but the future, they are not indifferent to life's present obligations and so are the emperor's "helpers and allies in promoting peace" (*1 Apol.* 12) by complying with Roman laws. Justin proves the point by rehearsing Jesus's moral teachings on adultery, self-restraint in matters of sex, love of enemies, giving to those in need, and seeking heavenly treasure that is eternal rather than worldly, that is, corruptible and transitory (*1 Apol.* 15). Justin, by focusing on the upright morals taught by Christianity, is making the case that Christians should not be killed simply for bearing the name "Christian" since Christians are not guilty of crimes falsely attributed to them. Indeed, he says that if there are people who claim the name "Christian" but are guilty of crimes prohibited by Roman law, such people are not Christians and should be punished (*1 Apol.* 16). Cleverly, Justin cloaks Christians' refusal to observe the rituals of Roman *pietas* with the assurance that Jesus commanded (Matt 22:17–21) his followers to pay taxes (*1 Apol.* 17). The implication was that taxes, not sacrificial offerings of wine and incense, were the tribute Caesar really wanted.

On the surface, the *First Apology* appears to be making the benign argument that Christians should not be killed because they are law-abiding citizens. Yet not far below the surface is a challenge to imperial authority. First, Justin's explanation for why Christians obey the emperor's laws is that Christians are primarily acting in obedience to God whose power to see and punish crimes—even those only meditated upon in the heart—is greater than Caesar's (*1 Apol.* 12). Thus, Christians comply with the law of Rome only where it overlaps the commands of God to whom their true duty lies. Second, even Justin's explanation of Jesus's words

"Render unto Caesar the things that are Caesar's and to God the things that are God's" (Matt 22:21) establishes a limit to the emperor's authority at the same time that it recognizes it—which means the emperor has the authority to exact taxes, but he has no claim to worship: "Whence to God alone we render worship, but in other things we gladly serve you, acknowledging you are kings and rulers of men." But then Justin issues a warning. Because the emperor's power is ultimately from God, those who misuse that power—as when they put to death Christians who are innocent of any crime except refusing to render worship to anyone other than the true God—will ultimately be answerable to God. The emperor's fate, if his policies against the Christians persisted, was clear: "Every man will suffer punishment in eternal fire according to the merit of his deed, and will render an account according to the power he has received from God" (*1 Apol.* 17).

If Pliny had perceived Christian impiety as an implicit act of political sedition, Antoninus Pius certainly would have interpreted Justin's attack upon Roman religion as openly seditious. In his refutation of the charge of atheism, Justin explained that Christians do in fact believe in and worship God, the one true God rather than the false Roman gods. This, not the fallacious stories spread by malicious neighbors, was, he explained, the reason they were persecuted. For the gods of the Roman pantheon, far from being divine, were demons that were the offspring of angels who had mated with mortals (*2 Apol.* 5). These demons set themselves up as gods by corrupting the seed of reason implanted within all people (*1 Apol.* 10).[2] Consequently, because of the demonic deception, people ceased to follow reason in worshiping the one true God—the Logos or seminal reason of the cosmos—and worshiped the demons instead. Not only was Justin's theory of the demons a denial of the divinity of the Roman gods, but it pitted Antoninus Pius's philosophical commitment to Stoicism and its doctrine of the Logos against the Roman religion that the emperor, as *pontifex maximus* or high priest of the state religion, was to uphold. A philosopher's capitulation with pagan religion was antithetical to a philosophical devotion to the truth and, therefore, was base hypocrisy. This was a personal attack against the emperor and his sons. Justin's appeal to the idea of the Logos as a point of common ground shared by philosophers and Christians was also a weapon with which to discredit both Roman religion and these most prominent devotees of Stoicism.

The charge of demonic worship turned a theological and philosophical indictment of Roman *pietas* into an indictment of imperial political authority. For if honoring the gods was a recognition of the foundation of Roman political authority, then Justin's declaration that the gods were demons implied that the emperor's rule was not divinely sanctioned but was grounded in a great lie.

2. For Justin's discussion of the *spermatikos logos*, see chapter 4, pp. 123–24.

Therefore, those who exercised authority and required the worship of these gods on pain of death were deceived and were themselves propagators of deception and injustice. Moreover, since the demons exerted influence by the corruption of reason, the religious foundation of the Roman political system was itself corrupt and contrary to reason.

Chief evidence of the demonic corruption of political leaders was their persecution of those whom the demons hated because they exposed this deception (*2 Apol.* 1). That ordinary Christians were no longer deceived by the demons and were able to live virtuously rather than being enslaved to lust inspired by the demons (*1 Apol.* 14–15) was evidence that they were followers of the Logos, the one true God, who is more powerful than the pretender deities of Rome. One such example was that of the teacher Ptolemaeus who was imprisoned and likely executed by the state for being a Christian. The charge was leveled by a man infamous for his unnatural behavior because Ptolemaeus had converted his wife who repudiated the life of immorality she had led with her husband and divorced him (*2 Apol.* 2). The tragic irony was that the Roman judge Urbicus, acting under the authority of the emperor, championed the cause of an utter reprobate but imprisoned a teacher of virtue solely for the name "Christian." Even before the coming of Christ, the incarnation of the whole Logos, the demonic gods inspired the death of followers of the Logos, like Socrates, whom they, too, accused of atheism (*1 Apol.* 5). Therefore, the demonic deities, who gave legitimacy to Roman political power and rule, were the source of the injustices against the innocent perpetrated by Rome's rulers. Although Justin, following Paul (Rom 13), maintained that political authority is from God, his identification of the state religion with the worship of demon-gods challenged the Roman myth of origins that located Roman power and greatness in these so-called deities. If the legitimacy of Roman power resided in myths of divine approval, then the exposure of the gods as demons called into question that political legitimacy. Because Roman politics and religion were inseparable, Justin's exposure of the corrupt nature of Roman religion also exposed the corruption of Rome's political foundations.

The political implications of his argument against the state religion Justin never stated explicitly. He did not need to. The point would have been clear to the emperor, to the Senate, and to his Christian readers. Justin was all too conscious of the implications this critique would have for him personally: "I too, therefore, expect to be plotted against and fixed to the stake, by some of those I have named" (*2 Apol.* 3). It also reveals for us the complex character of these first Christian apologies. On the one hand, they affirmed elements of Roman high culture—for example, the Platonic and Stoic theories of the Logos—to make connections between the truth claims of philosophy and the truth claims of Christianity, connections most likely recognized by those already professing Christianity. So they allowed Christians to reconcile their own religious convictions with confidence in the teachings of revered philosophers such as Socrates and Plato. On the other hand, Justin wielded these features of the philosophical tradition against the state that persecuted Christians for their atheism and impiety. His attack on the foundation of Roman *pietas*, far from persuading the emperor and the Senate to end the persecution, would have been seen as a form of impiety that posed a threat to the political system. What Pliny inferred from his interrogation of Christian deaconesses Justin spelled out theologically: Roman *pietas* and Christian piety could not be reconciled. In Roman eyes, Justin was guilty of impiety and sedition, and for that he paid with his life. Yet, as works written primarily for and preserved by Christians, the *First* and *Second Apologies* provided a theological account of their moral innocence and the justice of their cause.

Apologetics in Alexandria: Clement and Origen

Alexander the Great's program of eastward conquest had two purposes: first, to ensure that Persia would never again threaten Greece and, second, to disseminate Greek culture to the barbarians, that is, the non–Greek-speaking world. Nowhere was his project of Hellenization more successful than in the Nile Delta and in the city that bore his name, Alexandria. There was a thriving Jewish community whose culture was infused with all things Greek. They adopted Alexander's language and produced the Greek translation of Israel's Scriptures. And in the figure of Philo, the intellectual legacy of Greece became wed to the teachings of Moses. For Christians living in the Delta, their myth of origins claimed Saint Mark as their founder. The earliest biblical reference to the presence of Christians in Alexandria is the description in Acts (18:25) of Paul's rival in Corinth, Apollos, as a learned Alexandrian. The Pseudo-Clementine homilies, however, credit Barnabas with bringing the gospel to Alexandria. While both Judaism and Christianity in Alexandria were imbued with Hellenic culture, that did not mean they were free from critique by the intelligentsia of Alexandria. Learned critics, Celsus and the Neo-Platonist philosopher Porphyry, attacked Christians, not for rumors of moral abominations, like incest and cannibalism. Rather, they challenged the claims at the heart of the gospel, namely the identity of Jesus and the authenticity of the narratives of his life. Therefore, late second- and early third-century Christian apologetics in Alexandria required an intellectually robust counterattack to meet the serious challenge posed by their Hellenistic opponents.

The first of those to lead the counteroffensive was Titus Flavius Clemens (d. ca. 220). Born to pagan Athenian parents in the middle of the second century, Clement eventually traveled to Alexandria for his education. There he came under the tutelage of the Stoic teacher Pantaenus who himself was also a convert to Christianity. Under Pantaenus's influence, Clement became a Christian and a teacher in Alexandria until he fled Egypt to escape the persecution under Septimius Severus. Between 193 and 211, Clement composed four influential works, including his analysis of Jesus's exchange with the so-called rich young ruler (Mark 10:17–31), that represent the rigorously ascetic as well as Hellenistic character of the early Alexandrian school of Christian theology.

Clement's chief apologetic work was the *Protrepticus* or *Exhortation to the Greeks*. Since critics like Celsus and later Porphyry rested their critiques of Christianity on their familiarity with Christian writings, Clement was determined to demonstrate, if rather pedantically at times, his command of pagan literature. At the very outset, Clement goes on the offensive, ridiculing the pagan legends of celebrated minstrels Amphion, Arion, and Orpheus whose music had the fantastic power to uproot trees and tame wild beasts (*Protr.* 1). Even more troubling, he says, are the tragic demon-inspired dramas whose depiction of evil deeds "gladdens your hearts." In contrast with these dubious minstrels of pagan myth, Clement declares that he will "bring down truth, with wisdom in all her brightness, from heaven above, to the holy mountain of God and the holy company of the prophets" through whom came the song of the Logos (*Protr.* 1). Speaking to the Roman prejudice that favored the ancient over the novel, Clement explains that the song of the Logos is both old and new. It appeared new because the Logos was only recently incarnate. But the content of his message is ancient—far older than the songs of the demons—because the Logos himself was before the morning star and was in the beginning with God (*Protr.* 1). And his song is the cosmic harmony that was the expression of the fatherly purpose of God manifest in the arrangement of the world in the beginning. It feels new only because the truth always seems new when it breaks in exposing the deception under which humanity has lived and now offers an alternative to chaos offered by the demons. The life the Logos offers *today*—if only today we would hear the voice of the Word (cf. Heb 3:13)—is an image of "the everlasting age"; for "the day is a symbol of light, and the light of men is the Word, through whom we gaze upon God" (*Protr.* 9). Those who are drawn to the song of the Logos and find life Clement contrasts with Odysseus who might have been drawn to his death by the sirens' song. Whereas "the old man of Ithaca" longed only "for the smoke from the hearth" (*Od.* 1.57–58), which was a figure of this world, the Christian yearns for the true fatherland (*patridos*) in heaven (*Protr.* 9). The Logos alone is able to impart to believers true piety (*theosebeia*) that seeks as far as possible to bear a likeness to God because "he alone has the power worthy to conform man to his own likeness" (*Protr.* 9). For the Logos is the master teacher and orator whose exhortations have the power to instruct them in righteousness (*pros paideian tēn en dikaiosynē*) because he is the Lord and unsurpassed lover of humanity (*philanthrōpos*).

The Logos is a minstrel whose song of truth surpasses the potency of Orpheus since the music of the Logos can tame the most savage of beasts, that is, human beings, turning those whose souls were petrified and inured to the truth by their worship of stone idols into children of Abraham (*Protr.* 4). Because the Logos, he explains, is the Creator who ordered the cosmos in the beginning, he can restore the cosmic harmony that was overturned by the violence promoted by demonic myths so central to pagan literature. Employing the Pythagorean language of the Monad (*monada*) to speak of God, Clement, mixing his metaphors, says that the Logos as the universal light of God that shines upon all people is able to transform the cacophony of many scattered peoples into a single symphony (*mia symphōnia*). The crescendo of the Logos's symphony comes when the many nations, now divided into many religions, will confess the one who is truth itself when with one voice they cry out in doxology, "Abba! Father!" (*Protr.* 9).

One recurring pagan argument of which Clement was conscious was that Christianity lacked credibility because its adherents, the common and uneducated, took the claims of the Church on faith (*pistis*), which is a form of mere opinion (*doxa*) that stood in contrast with true knowledge (*epistēmē*) attained through dialectic. Therefore, Clement sought to give faith epistemic credibility and emphasize the essentially philosophical character of Christianity. Building upon Justin's argument that, because Christians worshiped the Logos, Christianity was inherently rational, Clement depicted the Logos as the sagely orator whose exhortations that led people from paganism to the truth worked both through supernatural wonders for the hard-hearted and by reason through the teachings of "all-wise Moses and truth-loving Isaiah." Then comparing the Logos to a good physician who applies different healing methods to different patients depending on their particular conditions—a common *topos* employed by Hellenistic moral philosophers—Clement explained that the Logos revealed himself using different modes of revelation: rebuke and encouragement, a burning bush and a pillar of fire. Ultimately, emptying himself in the incarnation, the compassionate Word revealed the form of salvation God desires for humanity, divinization: "the Word himself now speaks to you plainly, putting to shame your unbelief . . . the Word speaks, having become a man in order that you might learn from man how it is even possible for man to become a god" (*Protr.* 1).

The divinizing vision of God comes through reason, that is, through the Logos who is the door through whom one must pass. But the key to the door is faith. Clement appeals to a Middle Platonic doctrine of the ineffable nature of God who is knowable only through the mediation of the Logos. Quoting Jesus, "No one knows God but the Son and him to whom the Son reveals him" (Matt 11:27), he declares that faith in the Logos "opens this door that was previously shut and unveils what is within and shows what could not have been discerned before, except we had entered through Christ, through whom alone comes the vision of God" (*Protr.* 1). Since God in his transcendence is unknowable apart from his self-disclosure in the Logos, the soul's ascent to God through reason must begin with faith in the Logos as the only way to God. By treating faith in the Logos as the precondition for the mind's coming to the true knowledge of God, Clement locates faith within the philosophical life by synthesizing Stoic and Aristotelian epistemologies. Faith corresponds to what Aristotle held to be one's strong confidence in indemonstrable first principles (*hypolēpsis sphodra*) that are the starting points for rational judgments. At the same time, faith, far from being blind, is what Epicurus described as the preconception necessary for that deliberation by which the mind gives its assent (*synkatathesis*) to carefully scrutinized perceptions. In other words, faith, for Clement, is the mind's assent to impressions left by one's encounter with God's Spirit. Faith, therefore, is rational because it is the a priori or preconception that is the necessary beginning of all cognitive judgments while also retaining the meritorious character proper to an act of the will in obedience to God (*Strom.* 2.4.16–17). Consequently, faith is the beginning of humanity's liberation from the demonic deceptions that keep the soul a prisoner of irrational passions. For faith's assent to the cognitive impressions left by God's Spirit counters the errant impressions left upon the mind by the deceptions of demons, sophists, and sensual pleasures. Thus, faith, far from being antithetical to the life of reason, actually frees the mind so that it may ascend to the truth of God.

Although Clement knew the objections to Christianity leveled by philosophically disposed pagans, he does not name these critics or quote their texts. The reader, therefore, can only infer what these anti-Christian arguments were. It is from Clement's fellow Alexandrian, Origen, that we know in considerable detail the arguments of one such learned critic, Celsus. Justin's defense of Christianity did not end persecution, but it may have changed the character of the debate between Christians and their pagan critics. Regardless of who Justin's real audience was, his *First* and *Second Apologies* made their way into the hands of some non-Christians, in particular a second-century philosopher—more likely a Platonist than an Epicurean—named Celsus who felt compelled to write a response to Justin, entitled *True Doctrine*. Written in the 170s, Celsus's arguments reflected a shift in the focus of pagan critiques. Not surprisingly, he repeated the stock accusation, first heard by Tacitus and Pliny, that Christianity was a cult or superstition and the charge that Christians were fideists, who assented to the claims of the religion without any understanding or rational basis. What was distinctive about Celsus was that, unlike Suetonius or Tacitus or Galen, he had actually read the Scriptures of the "Great Church," which was his term to distinguish the church of Justin from smaller sects, like the Gnostics. Moreover, instead of focusing on Christians themselves, Celsus directed his attack against the centerpiece of Christian faith and worship, Jesus.

This may have been because Christianity was better known at a popular level, and through Justin's description of Christian practices, the misconceptions and prejudices of an earlier generation of critics had been exposed as erroneous. However, for an intellectual like Celsus, the moral decency of Christians did not negate the absurdity of Christian doctrine. The only thing that really mattered was the veracity of Christian claims about Jesus's identity. Therefore, Celsus concentrated his refutation on Jesus's divine sonship by exposing him as unworthy of worship based on the details of his life.

Cleverly, Celsus did this by putting the criticisms of Jesus in the mouths of his fellow Jews. Unlike Marcion and some Gnostics, Celsus recognized that the identity of Christianity was tied to Judaism. Christian claims about Jesus's divinity were tied to his identity as the long-awaited Messiah of the Jews. That Jews did not recognize him as the one foretold by Israel's prophets cast doubts on whether he was the Son of the God of Israel. If Jews were unpersuaded by Christian interpretations of the Jewish Scriptures—and who should understand the Torah better than Jews—then the Christian arguments were exegetically suspect. Indeed, by breaking with the moral and ritual prescriptions of Torah, Christians could no longer claim to stand within the tradition of Israel. Although Celsus's attack had not attracted any immediate response from Christians, sometime before the middle of the third century, Origen penned a line-by-line refutation so thorough that from it one can reliably reconstruct the content of Celsus's tome. Indeed, without Origen's extensive quotations, Celsus and his text would be lost to history.

Origen, in the second book, takes up the question of Christianity's relationship with Israel. The disbelief of the Jews should hardly be taken as definitive proof against Jesus's messiahship. The history of Israel was, Origen wrote, a long narrative of their failure to believe. For instance, the Israelites, who had passed through the Red Sea, been fed with manna from heaven, and drank water from the rock, still—even after having witnessed these miracles—did not believe Moses's authority (*Cels.* 2.75). To begin with, not all Jews rejected Jesus's messianic claim (e.g., Ebionites). Nor did Christians abandon torah, as in Acts 10:9 where Peter keeps kosher (*Cels.* 2.1). The Jews' general rejection of Jesus as the Christ lay in their inability to learn from his instruction the spiritual meaning of torah and so remained in bondage to the letter of the law. Jesus recognized this when he said, "I still have many things to say to you, but you cannot bear them now" (John 16:12). The Mosaic law is but a shadow of the true law, which is understood only when read through the lens of Jesus's crucifixion and resurrection (*Cels.* 2.2). For only with the resurrection does one see Jesus as the firstborn from the dead (Col 1:18) and so gain both a confidence in eternal life and with that the hope that one's life can be reformed and reoriented to the heavenly things (*Cels.* 2.77).

Origen's argument for Jesus's transformative power dovetailed with his defense of Jesus's miracles. Celsus, rather than questioning whether Jesus's miracles actually happened, granted that Jesus had performed the wonders that he was purported to have accomplished. However, these so-called miracles were not, he argued, evidence of divine power. Instead they were the work of daimonic power that magicians manipulated for their own chicanery (*Cels.* 1.6). Since the practice of magic was prohibited by Roman law, Celsus's assertion impugned Jesus's moral character, placing him in the category of criminals and charlatans. Origen countered the charge of magic by arguing that the moral transformation that occurred in the lives of believers was evidence of the divine character of Jesus's miracles and his divine identity. The healing narratives in Scripture reveal the spiritual healing of the Logos who reorders a person's affections and gives him the new life of the inner man when the rational soul receives the Logos's illumination (*Cels.* 2.48). The divine source of these miracles is thus proven by the transformation in the lives of Jesus's followers. Since the life of virtue is a life according to the Logos, the moral conversion of those who worship Christ is evidence that through Jesus they have received the power not of an ordinary man but of the Father's wisdom (*Cels.* 2.79). The very fact, as Celsus is wont to repeat, that Christians were among the common and uneducated was proof that the power of Jesus exceeded that of philosophers whose influence extended only to a small following of educated individuals. Since there is no virtue apart from truth, one cannot be led to virtue through deception. Consequently, the conversion of Christians to the virtuous life was evidence that Jesus's miracles were no conjurer's trick (like Pharaoh's magicians in Exod 7:10) but a display of the power of the supremely good God—a power now active in the lives of believers (*Cels.* 2.50).

Ambrose and Augustine

Constantine the Great's patronage of the Church, whose members still represented only a minority of the population of the Roman Empire, remains an enigma to historians. Although he did not make Christianity the official religion of the empire as would his son Constantius II, his Edict of Milan of 313, which he issued together with his fellow Augustus Licinius, marked the formal end of an era of persecution: "Concerning the Christians and any one of these who wishes to observe the Christian religion [they] may do so freely and openly, without molestation . . . [and] those Christians [are given] free and unrestricted opportunity of religious worship." Furthermore, it established that each resident of the empire had "the right of open and free observance of their worship for the sake of the peace of our times, that each one may have the free opportunity to worship as he pleases" (*Mort.* 48). The edict was viewed by some as a year of Jubilee, an emancipation from an oppressive and hostile political order. While the edict allowed practitioners of ancient non-Christian religions to carry on—some of Constantine's inner circle of advisors remained pagan—Christians celebrated the coming to be of a government that extended its favors to the Church by restoring property seized or destroyed during the Great Persecution of Diocletian.

Others, however, were less triumphalistic. Ambrose of Milan had been born into a family at the heart of the imperial power structure. His father, as praetorian prefect of Gaul, was second in authority only to the emperor in the Western half of the empire. After his father's death—likely an assassination—young Ambrose moved with his Christian family from Trier back to Rome, where he received an education that would prepare him to climb the political ladder in civil administration. Ultimately, he was appointed governor of the northern Italian province of Liguria-Emelia, whose capital was Milan. Following the death of the Homoian bishop of Milan, Auxentius, Ambrose, who was not yet baptized, was made Milan's bishop through a combination of public acclamation and imperial endorsement. Because Milan at the time also served as the capital of the Western empire, Ambrose served as pastor to the emperor.

Although Ambrose expressed the belief that the flourishing of the empire was dependent on divine blessing that was linked to the degree of influence the Church was allowed (cf. *Fid.* 2.143), he was not naive about his new position or the complicated social relations that those close to the emperor's court had to navigate. His years in the imperial civil service had taught him how tenuous positions of privilege were. In his homilies on Joseph, he interprets the story of Pharaoh's cupbearer and baker who were imprisoned because they had fallen from the king's favor (Gen 40:1–23) as a warning to catechumens who served close to the emperor. Alluding probably to Calligonus, Valentinian II's grand chamberlain who fell from grace and was executed, Ambrose says of the cupbearer and baker, "They ought to serve as an example to other eunuchs that their standing is fragile and weak and all their hopes lie in the will of the king; for them a slight offense is a very great danger, while prosperity is a paltry condition of service" (*Jos.* 6.29).

In this early period of the state's patronage of Christianity, Ambrose saw the need to set boundaries that defined the place of the Church within an empire ruled by an emperor who himself was a member of the Church and therefore under the spiritual authority of the bishop. The first testing of boundaries came in 384 when the great Latin orator and prefect of Rome, Symmachus, petitioned the emperor Valentinian II to restore to the Senate house in Rome an altar to the goddess Nike. Symmachus's *Relatio* III was a plea that Rome should retain a spirit of religious pluralism and toleration and so give to pagans the same rights as Christians. It appealed to a Roman sense of *pietas* that was committed to honoring the *mos maiorum* as Rome's rightful teacher about the gods. "For since reason is totally in the dark, surely knowledge of the gods comes to us most directly through memory and records of the past. If long passage of time gives religious practices their authority, we must keep faith with so many centuries, and we must follow our parents as they, prosperously, followed theirs" (*Ep.* 72a.8). Ambrose counters with a letter of his own to the young emperor. Repeating the stock argument that the gods whom Symmachus honors are not divine but demonic, Ambrose declares, "There is no way that salvation can be assured other than that everyone truly worships the true God, that is the God of the Christians" (*Ep.* 72.1). Therefore, the true impiety would be to use imperial funds to support the worship of demons. Moreover, he warns Valentinian not to take seriously Symmachus's revisionist history that envisions a past where religious toleration and pluralism were the norm: "The people who are now complaining . . . are the same men who never spared our blood, who demolished the very walls of our churches from the foundations . . . [and] denied our spokesmen the right of speaking and teaching" (*Ep.* 72.4). Valentinian cannot serve two masters; to honor Nike would be an act of apostasy. Should the emperor restore the altar of Victory, Ambrose offers a thinly veiled threat of excommunication: "The Church does not want your gifts, because with your gifts you have adorned temples of the pagans. The altar of Christ rejects your offerings with contempt because you have built an altar of graven images" (*Ep.* 72.14). Such arguments were directed not only to the emperor but also to a minority of Christian senators who endorsed the appeal of their pagan colleagues. Valentinian yielded to Ambrose and an important precedent was established; a Christian emperor could not extend patronage to pagan religions.

Other important precedents about Church-state relations were established. Ambrose extended the precedent of the altar of Victory to nullify the emperor's authority to require a church to use its own funds to rebuild a Jewish house of worship. This came after a synagogue in the eastern town of Callinicum was destroyed in 388/9 by a mob of Christians roused to violence by their bishop's incendiary, anti-Jewish rhetoric. Although Ambrose acknowledged that "the bishop was somewhat too zealous in burning the synagogue" (*Ep.* 74.6), compelling the bishop to rebuild the synagogue would be giving the Jews a "triumph over the Church of God" (*Ep.* 74.20).

Earlier during Holy Week of 386, Ambrose and his congregation occupied a basilica that Valentinian II's mother, Justina, attempted to requisition so that she and her fellow Homoians would have a sanctuary for Easter services. Refusing to surrender the basilica, Ambrose and his congregants occupied the church. Surrounded by imperial troops, the congregation sang hymns, likely some composed by Ambrose, and Ambrose preached a sermon in defiance of Justina. In the homily addressed to Valentinian, Ambrose drew on his knowledge of Roman law to argue that the basilica belonged to the Church, not to the state, and therefore the emperor had no authority to seize the building. Relating the episode in a letter to his sister Marcelina, Ambrose wrote that when word was sent demanding his surrender of the building, he responded quoting Jesus's words, "'What is God's to God, what is Caesar's to Caesar. Palaces belong to the emperor, churches to the bishop. The jurisdiction entrusted to you is over public buildings, not sacred ones" (*Ep.* 76.19). In both the case of the basilica crisis and the synagogue at Callinicum, Ambrose asserted the Church's independence. The state might extend patronage *to* the Church, but that did not give the state authority *over* the Church.

While Ambrose recognized a division between the ecclesial and the civil spheres, those boundaries were not hard and fast. Around the year 390, Theodosius retaliated against the citizens of Thessalonica for a riot over taxes in which an imperial official was killed. Under his orders, the citizens were summoned to an amphitheater where, surrounded by soldiers and their paths of retreat cut off, they were cut down. Too late, Theodosius had come to his senses and dispatched new orders countermanding his previous instructions; the new orders did not arrive in time to stop the bloodshed. Ambrose responded by assuming the posture of the prophet Nathan, who confronted David with his adultery with Bathsheba and the death of her husband Uriah the Hittite. In a letter that begins with a pastoral tone so as not to rouse the emperor's passions, Ambrose required Theodosius to perform public penance for the massacre by abstaining from the Eucharist for a period of time (*Ep. coll.* 11.6). The act of censure established the precedent that the emperor's position did not give him the freedom to act without moral constraints. On the contrary, as a Christian, the emperor was accountable to the bishop for political actions that were morally egregious.

During the Easter vigil of 387, Ambrose baptized a North African teacher of rhetoric named Augustine. Having abandoned his ambition for social advancement following his conversion experience, Augustine shared Ambrose's temperate expectations about the state's relationship to the Church even under a Christian emperor. Although a Christian emperor was preferable to a pagan one who waged war on the followers of Christ (*Civ.* 5.24–26), it was foolish, Augustine thought, to place one's hope for happiness and a just society in the political structures and personalities of this age. In a telling passage in *Confessions*, Augustine relates the experience of Ponticianus, who, though a member of the emperor's inner circle, nearly gave up such to follow the path of monasticism. "What is our aim in life?" Ponticianus exclaims, "What is the motive of our service to the state? Can we hope for any higher office in the palace than to be Friends of the emperor? And in that position what is not fragile and full of dangers? How many hazards must one risk to attain a position of even greater danger? . . . Whereas, if I wish to become God's friend, in an instant I may become that now" (*Conf.* 8.6.15).

Augustine's tome *City of God* gave full voice to his doubts about the pagan foundation upon which Roman political order was built. Its subtitle, *Against the*

Pagans, which is often overlooked, reveals the apologetic and polemical character of the work. Likely influenced in its structure by the *Divine Institutes* of Lactantius (240–320), *City of God*, like the *Institutes*, progresses from a critique of Roman politics and religion, culminating in his account of the summum bonum. Although Lactantius wrote from the Great Persecution to the ascendency of Constantine the Great, and Augustine in the period of Christianity's acceptance as the official religion of the empire, both men's works sought not only to refute pagan critics but also to instruct their people in right doctrine. In August 410, the Visigothic king Alaric sacked Rome and set his troops on the "Eternal City" for three days of looting and raping. News of Rome's capture by barbarians sent waves of disorientation through the empire. Jerome, living in Jerusalem, expressed the shock of many when he wrote, "Rome had been besieged and its citizens had been forced to buy their lives with gold. . . . My voice sticks in my throat; and, as I dictate, sobs choke my utterance. The city which had taken the whole world was itself taken" (*Ep.* 127.13). In pagan quarters, Rome's fall was blamed on the Christians. Rome had been safe for centuries while the gods of the Roman Pantheon protected her and were honored. It was only after Rome's conversion to Christianity that the city fell to the barbarians. The fall of Rome was an indictment of Christian impiety and the impotence of their God. As Williams observes, the destruction of Rome in 410 might have been seen as a vindication of Symmachus's warning to Valentinian twenty-six years earlier that a refusal to restore the altar of Victory was an impiety that left Rome naked and unprotected against her enemies. Augustine counters the pagan assertion by enumerating numerous occasions in which Rome suffered calamities in the pre-Christian era. Then he asks rhetorically, where was the protection of Rome's gods then (*Civ.* 3.15–31)? By contrast, even during Alaric's savage assault, signs of God's protection are evident, most notably that the Goths, who were Christians, did not destroy Christian basilicas and shrines where Christians and pagans alike were able to seek sanctuary and so escape violence and death. More than those arguments, *City of God* offered an explanation for the fall of Rome through a theological critique not just of Roman paganism but of all earthly polities that embody the disordered love that was the seed of Rome's destruction.

Augustine explains Rome's inherent character flaw by distinguishing between two cities: the earthly city or city of man and the heavenly city or city of God. The citizens of the heavenly city are characterized by the virtue of humility (*virtus humilitatis*) that makes no claim to self-sufficiency but trusts entirely in God's grace. By contrast, the earthly city is populated by those who bear the marks of fallen humanity, who in pride and undue confidence in their own power turned from God. As exhibit A in his prosecution of Rome and its pagan defenders, Augustine points to the hubris of Roman pride (*superbia*) summed up in Vergil's description of Rome's self-appointed mission: "To spare the conquered and beat down the proud" (*Aen.* 6.853). For in her imperial ambitions to secure for herself peace through the conquest and subjugation of all the peoples of the Mediterranean, Rome arrogated to herself the dominium that belongs to God alone of whom the Epistle of James (4:6) says, "God resists the proud, but he gives grace to the humble" (*Civ.* 1, preamble). Both the earthly and the heavenly cities share the same goal, peace. Whereas the heavenly city knows that such peace is to be attained only in its eschatological rest in God, the earthly city imagines that peace is achieved when it can ensure security from all external threats. Thus, while citizens of the city of God are motivated by a trust in and love for God, citizens of the city of man are driven by its lust for dominion (*libido dominandi*).

The irony at the heart of the earthly city—an irony of which its citizens are oblivious—is that the quest for autonomy and security through domination leaves the city enslaved to its insatiable lust for dominion. Rather than peace, the earthly city continually experiences the sufferings brought on by an endless succession of wars waged against the ever-present threat lying just over the empire's frontier (cf. *Civ.* 3.15). "When," Augustine asks, "can that lust for power in arrogant hearts come to rest until . . . it arrives at sovereignty?" (*Civ.* 1.31). Rome's quest for the supposed security of sovereignty through the complete domination of her neighbors began with the destruction of Carthage in the Third Punic War. Free from any threat in the western Mediterranean, Rome became complacent. Instead of using earthly peace to pursue nobler ends, Rome's citizens replaced their prior lifestyle of austerity, self-restraint, and vigilance with self-indulgence. Presciently, Augustine notes, Scipio opposed Cato the Elder's interminable cry, "Carthage must be destroyed," because "he was afraid of security, as being a danger to weak characters; he looked on citizens as wards, and fear as a kind of guardian, giving protection they needed." Without such a guardian to unite them, "the Romans, who in a period of high moral standards stood in fear of enemies, suffered a harsher fate from their fellow-citizens when those standards collapsed . . . and lust for domination . . . crushed the rest of an exhausted country beneath the yoke of slavery" (*Civ.* 1.30)—slavery to ambition, avarice, and sensuality. Such was not merely Augustine's opinion; it was the judgment of the Roman historian Sallust who wrote, "After the destruction of Carthage, there came the highest pitch of discord, greed, ambition, and all the evils that generally spring up in times of prosperity" (*Civ.* 2.18). Rome's pursuit of security and sovereignty through conquest was, Augustine saw, an expression of pride—that is, a confidence in their own self-sufficiency to secure for themselves peace and prosperity. Yet Rome would not enjoy true peace without justice. That insight led Augustine to turn his apologia to an analysis of the nature of political relations.

Augustine appeals to Cicero to provide an explanation for Sallust's assessment. Concord in the state is analogous to harmony in music when each instrument or voice exhibits restraint performing only its part. In *On the Republic*, such concord, which is "the best and closest bond of security," cannot exist without justice (*Rep.* 2.42). Through the voice of Scipio, Cicero defines a commonwealth, regardless of whether it is a monarchy or aristocracy or democracy, as "an association united by a common sense of right and a community of interest" (*Rep.* 1.25). Whereas Sallust believed that the decline of the Roman Republic "into the depths of depravity" was due to a lack of justice—a lost sense of right and regard for common interest—Augustine instead insists that Rome never was a true commonwealth because it never was a just community. For true justice exists only in the city of God whose founder and ruler is Christ (*Civ.* 2.21). Rome's founder, however, was not Christ but followers of demons in the guise of gods. Therefore, since justice entails giving to each her due, because Roman piety was directed not to the one true God but to her pantheon of false gods, Rome was inherently unjust. For if the soul is not submissive to God, it does not give God his due and so is unjust. And if individual souls are unjust, the community of such people is also unjust. Indeed, they are not a "people" at all but a mob (*Civ.* 19.21). Rather, a true commonwealth Augustine defines as "a people [that] is the association of a multitude of rational beings united by a common agreement on the objects of their love" (*Civ.* 19.24). Justice, therefore, Augustine identifies with loving the right object rightly. The justice of a society, therefore, is determined by the object of its collective love.

Since justice—this rightly ordered love—is the true source of peace and security while injustice is its greatest threat to concord, the injustice of Roman paganism, present at its founding, was the seed of its degeneration and fall. The earthly city's quest for peace is illusory. It seeks happiness by securing the things of this life that, as inherently imperfect and temporal, cannot provide happiness. The fall of Rome was but one illustration of that truth. Augustine's political analysis of the two cities, therefore, provides an apologia to reassure Christians unsettled by the pagan charge against their religion. Not only are they not responsible for the very real suffering that resulted from Alaric's seizure of the "Eternal City" but, as citizens of the heavenly city—that commonwealth united by a common love of God—they have access to true peace and happiness that the earthly city cannot provide. That is, because ultimate peace, and with it happiness, are fully attained only eschatologically, citizens of the city of God are *peregrini*—wayfaring strangers, resident aliens whose commonwealth (*politeia*) is in heaven. Therefore, in this life the saints can experience at most a *proleptic* happiness. Nevertheless, that happiness, though imperfect, is real because the object of their hope is real and perfect. In that hope, the citizens of the heavenly city can derive a peace the earthly city cannot give. For the hopelessness of the earthly city is itself the source of suffering. As Augustine writes, "Present reality without that hope is, to be sure, a false happiness, in fact, an utter misery. For the present does not bring into play the true goods of the mind; since no wisdom is true wisdom if it does not direct its attention, in all its prudent decisions, its resolute self-control and its dealings with others, toward that ultimate state in which God will be all in all, in the assurance of eternity and the perfection of peace" (*Civ.* 19.20). It is not surprising that the climax of the tome concerns eschatology. In the penultimate chapter of book 22, Augustine paints an image for his readers of the peace of the heavenly city where in an unending Sabbath its citizens will behold the invisible deity in the resurrected bodies of one another—a true community united in the perfect love of God (*Civ.* 22.29).

Conclusion

Although apologia was a technical genre of literature in antiquity that was distinct from polemic and protrepsis or paraenesis, the goal was the same: to convert the thinking of one's opponents or neutral bystanders or to reassure and confirm the thinking of insiders. Thus, strategies typical of protrepsis and paraenesis were employed in defenses of Christianity. Similarly, for Christian theologians, the difference between apologetic and constructive theologies was at times negligible. For the objections against Christianity that took the form either of bigoted slander at the popular level or carefully crafted critique at the level of the intelligentsia forced Christian teachers to explain the faith by elaborating theological themes or making theological connections not explicit in their Scriptures. Their *arguments* advanced Christian thinking about their beliefs and practices and also established precedents for Christian engagement with various schools of philosophy that later generations would imitate and build upon. Regardless of whether Justin was familiar with the prologue to John's Gospel, his Logos theology would prove influential for later interpreters of the Fourth Gospel. Augustine, likewise, turned the scapegoating of Christians into an occasion for a metanarrative not only of Rome's history but that defined the character of the present age (*saeculum*) in contrast with the age to come. This allowed him to invite Christians to consider how they have been shaped by the former even while through baptism they are called to the latter. The result was that between the second and fifth centuries, Christian apologists, in defending the Church and its people, beliefs, and practices against critiques by hostile pagans, also defined their understanding of the Church's relationship to the larger intellectual culture as well as to the state whether administered by hostile pagans or Christian emperors.

Bibliography

Primary Sources

Ambrose of Milan. *Political Letters and Speeches*. Translated by J. H. W. G. Liebeschuetz with Carole Hill. Liverpool: Liverpool University Press, 2005.

Augustine of Hippo. *On the City of God Against the Pagans*. Translated by Henry Bettenson. London: Penguin Books, 1972.

Clement of Alexandria. *Exhortation to the Greeks*. Translated by G. W. Butterworth. Loeb Classical Library. Cambridge: Harvard University Press, 1982.

———. *Stromateis*. Translated by John Ferguson. Fathers of the Church 85. Washington, DC: The Catholic University of America Press, 1991.

Justin Martyr. *First and Second Apologies*. Translated by Leslie William Barnard. Ancient Christian Writers. New York: Paulist, 1997.

Lactantius. *Divine Institutes*. Translated by Anthony Bowen and Peter Garnsey. Liverpool: Liverpool University Press, 2003.

Origen. *Against Celsus*. Translated by Henry Chadwick. Cambridge: Cambridge University Press, 1953.

Secondary Sources

Edwards, Mark. "The Flowering of Latin Apologetic: Lactantius and Arnobius." In *Apologetics in the Roman Empire: Pagans, Jews, and Christians*. Edited by Mark Edwards, Simon Price, and Christopher Rowland. New York: Oxford University Press, 1999.

Grant, Robert M. *Greek Apologists of the Second Century*. Philadelphia: Westminster, 1988.

Rowe, C. Kavin. *One True Life: The Stoic and Early Christian as Rival Traditions*. New Haven: Yale University Press, 2016.

Wetzel, James, ed. *Augustine's City of God: A Critical Guide*. Cambridge: Cambridge University Press, 2012.

Wilken, Robert L. *The Christians as the Romans Saw Them*. New Haven: Yale University Press, 1984.

Williams, D. H. *Defending and Defining the Faith: An Introduction to Early Christian Apologetic Literature*. Oxford: Oxford University Press, 2020.

3

"By One Man Came Death"

Humanity's Creation and Fall

Jesus of Nazareth was the center of the Great Church's reflection on human nature. Although viewed, first and foremost, as the divine Word, he was also the second Adam. Few texts from the New Testament were as central to early Christian anthropology as Paul's Adam typology in Romans 5:18–19: "Then as one man's trespass led to condemnation for all men, so one man's act of righteousness led to acquittal and life, for by one man's disobedience many were made sinners, so by one man's obedience many were made righteous." What was recognized was that the first man's sin was not only a moral and existential problem, but it also created an epistemic problem. In the present life under sin, human beings cannot know themselves as God intended. Augustine expressed the point succinctly: "I have become an enigma to myself" (*Conf.* 10.33.50). Only through Christ who, as the second Adam and the image of the invisible God (Col 1:15), reveals human nature untainted by sin can human beings know themselves rightly. Therefore, the biblical story of creation and fall was read through the lens of the Christ event. For our purposes, however, before discussing early Christian views of the person of Christ and that saving work by which he brought human nature to the fulfillment God intended, it is helpful to start with the various conceptions of the fall and its effect on humanity. In other words, it helps to understand different accounts of that from which the Savior delivered his fellow creatures. Yet, as the early Christian teachings about the fall emerged in the second century, they did so within competing conceptions of the very nature of creation itself.

The Creation from the Fall in Gnostic Scriptures

In the Hellenistic world, no classical text was as commented upon as Plato's creation narrative, *Timaeus*. In this dialogue, Plato offered a cosmological explanation for his division of reality between the heavenly intelligible realm of the forms and the earthly, sensible realm of material things. Although Plato's metaphysics assumed a causal relationship between the intelligible and sensible realms, many passages in his corpus that attributed pain, ignorance, and distraction to the material body opened the door for highly dualistic readings of his cosmology. It should not be a surprise, therefore, that various gnostic authors, who intellectually were influenced by Plato, integrated ideas from *Timaeus* into their interpretations of the early chapters of Genesis. Of the six hundred quotations from the Old Testament found in the documents at Nag Hammadi, a third are from the chapters of Genesis detailing creation and the antediluvian age. Furthermore, when they read the creation narratives of Genesis alongside the binary language of "spirit" and "flesh" or "light" and "darkness" in Paul (Rom 6; 8) and John (1:5), the result was a dichotomous ontology in which material creation itself was the source of evil. This only raised the classic question of theodicy: Why would an all-wise, all-good, and all-powerful God have ever created a material world that is the cause of sin? This was one of the central questions motivating the Sethian Apocryphon of John (Ap. John). This text, which Bentley Layton has said was the principal articulation of the myth of origins adopted by many gnostic sects, has provided historians with "the distinguishing mark of gnostic literature; without [which] classic gnostic scripture could not be recognized."[1]

The myth purports to be based on a revelation that John, the son of Zebedee, received from the Savior (Ap. John 1.1). In the apophatic language typical of Middle Platonism, the myth begins by describing God as the "monad" and the "parent of the entirety . . . [who] presides over . . . incorruptibility; existing in uncontaminated light, toward which no vision can gaze . . . it is ineffable and perfect in incorruptibility: not imperfection, nor in blessedness, nor in divinity; rather as being far superior to these" (Ap. John 2.26–32; 3.22–24). From the Parent's thinking came the second principle, the Barbēlō, the source of the Entirety or Plērōma, which included various intelligible entities including the "only begotten offspring," who will be known as the Christ, and twelve aeons (ideas such as loveliness, truth, form, etc.). The twelfth of the aeons was Sophia or wisdom. Desiring to know the unknowable Parent, Sophia tried to conceive in herself the idea of God. Since, however, God is radically transcendent and beyond all thought or conception, Sophia's progeny was not a true image of God but a misshapen being called Ialdabaōth. Because Sophia's child was conceived without knowledge of the Parent ("the invisible spirit") and thus alien to the immaterial realm of light, she aborted him, casting Ialdabaōth out of the realm of light into a realm of darkness. Finding himself alone and being ignorant of his mother and the realm of light whence he came, Ialdabaōth assumed that he was God (Ap. John 11.21).

1. Bentley Layton, *The Gnostic Scriptures*, 2nd ed. (New Haven: Yale University Press, 2021), 9.

The figure of Ialdabaōth corresponds to the Creator or demiurge in *Timaeus* who is inferior to the true God. For, in his hubris and ignorance, Ialdabaōth used the power that he derived from his mother to create the material universe. However, unlike Plato's demiurge who modeled the material world on his vision of the eternal and perfect forms, Ialdabaōth lacked *gnōsis* of the intelligible realities in the realm of light. Consequently, his material creation was merely a reflection of its Creator's ignorance and madness. The life of Ialdabaōth's creatures naturally was not one of blessedness and incorruptibility, as in the realm of light, but one of suffering from the instability and corruption inherent to matter. Thus, the demiurge "brought darkness down upon all the earth" and sent a "counterfeit spirit" among humanity who gave gifts of gold, silver, and other materials that filled them with "great anxieties" (Ap. John 29.14, 23–33). Beguiled by the counterfeit spirit, humanity was ignorant of the God of truth, "and thus was the whole creation perpetually enslaved, from the foundation of the world to the present time. And [men] married women and begot children out of the darkness, after the image of their spirit. And their hearts became closed and hardened with the hardness of the counterfeit spirit down to the present time" (Ap. John 30.4–9). Creation's only limited degree of likeness to the heavenly reality was the spark of power Ialdabaōth received from his mother and passed on to his creation.

Following Genesis, the Apocryphon of John briefly renarrates the events from the making of humanity to Noah and the flood. According to this retelling, when Ialdabaōth made Adam, he breathed some of Sophia's power into Adam (Ap. John 19.27–28) and from Adam the power passed in varying degrees to his offspring. Ialdabaōth defiled Eve, and from their intercourse were begotten Cain and Abel (Ap. John 24.15). Adam and Eve's child was called Seth. To him Sophia sent down a spirit in the female form who would prepare him and his descendants to receive the gift of *gnōsis* brought by heavenly beings. In later iterations of the myth, the three sons of Adam and Eve correspond to the three classes of people Paul describes in 1 Corinthians 2:14–15. The children of Cain are the Carnal ones who have no spark of Wisdom's power. They are incapable of receiving enlightenment and are content to live in their ignorance believing that the material world is the highest degree of reality. Seth's offspring are called the Spiritual who have the lion's share of Sophia's power; they are the gnostic elect who will receive enlightenment seeing the material creation for the flawed thing it is. Between them are the descendants of Abel who are called the Psychics or Soul people. They received enough of a spark of wisdom that they may or may not be able to come to *gnōsis* given by the coming of the Christ, or Barbēlō, who was sent by the Parent in his compassion for the residents in the realm of darkness.[2]

2. For further discussion of the Barbēlō, see chapter 4, pp. 129–30.

Not all Gnostics were satisfied with this narrative. Ptolemy's *Letter to Flora*, for example, rejects the identification of the Creator with the author of evil. Rather, its demiurge, the Logos of John's prologue, was an intermediary being between the true God and the devil. Therefore, Logos's creation was not inherently evil, as was Ialdabaōth's. Yet because its maker was ontologically inferior to God—merely "the image of the better God" (*Flor.* 7.4)—it was imperfect and so vulnerable to corruption.

In the Sethian myth of origins, creation and fall are coterminous. The material world, and the misery that resulted from its creation, was not the plan of God. The gnostic answer to the question, "Why would a good, powerful and wise God create a world of suffering and evil?" was "He would not." The Creator of the material world is neither good nor wise nor all-powerful. The miseries inherent in the material universe bear testimony to his ignorance and folly. The world did not begin as paradise that then fell into corruption; it was corrupt from the beginning. Therefore, as we shall see, the gnostic narrative of salvation depicts not a redemption of the world but deliverance from it. Even Ptolemy's counternarrative depicts creation's imperfections and susceptibility to the distortion of evil as being due to the imperfections of a lesser god. The gnostic myths proved compelling narratives. Communities shaped by them stretched from Mesopotamia and the upper Nile across the Mediterranean Sea to Gaul and North Africa and endured from the second into the eighth century.

The gnostic myths of origin that emerged in the second century were not the first such narratives. The author of the Pastoral Epistles complained about false teachers whose "myths and endless genealogies which promote speculations rather than divine training" (1 Tim 1:4) purported to provide *gnōsis* (1 Tim 6:20) that seduced people with "itching ears" (2 Tim 4:3). But their alternative account of the fundamental nature of the world and its origin posed a theological challenge to the Great Church in the second and third centuries. One who took up that challenge was Irenaeus of Lyons.

Irenaeus: To Behold God's Glory

Against the gnostic and Marcionite claims that the evils inherent to creation were the result of an ignorant Creator, Irenaeus offered an account of creation within a salvation narrative in which creation and redemption were the work of one and the same God. Whereas the Apocryphon of John divided reality between the Parent who is the Creator of the heavenly Entirety and Ialdabaōth who created the material world, Irenaeus insists that there is one God who is the source of all things. "It is important, then, that I should begin with the first and most important point, that is, God, the Creator.... There is nothing either above him, or after him.... Since he is the only God, the only Lord, the only Creator, the only Father, alone containing all things, and himself commanding all things into existence" (*Haer.* 2.1.1). God himself is the Plērōma, who "contains all things in his immensity" (*Haer.* 2.1.2); for, Irenaeus notes, in Hebrew God's name *Elohim* means "that which contains all" (*Haer.* 2.35.3). The Creator is the one God; but this single Creator is triune: "There is only one God, the Creator—he is above every principality, and power, and dominion, and virtue: he is the Father . . . who made these things by himself, that is, through his Word and Wisdom [i.e., the Son and Spirit]" (*Haer.* 2.30.9).

Irenaeus's affirmation of the single Creator only raises the gnostic question whether the imperfections and blemishes patently manifest in the material world do not logically imply that its Creator is either evil, ignorant, impotent, or all of the above. Irenaeus rests his counterargument on an ontological divide between creatures and their Creator. God's perfection is manifest in his aseity. Because God never came into being but is eternal, God is entirely self-subsisting, fully possessing all his virtues and powers. By contrast, creatures, because they were made from nothing—passing from nonbeing to being—necessarily change and develop over time. The inherently developmental character of creatures means that their imperfections are not the result of some imperfection or impotence on the part of their Creator. Rather, what the Gnostics deemed evil simply reflected the immaturity in creation's process of maturation and the inherent mutability of creatures.[3] Based on this fundamental ontological difference, Irenaeus contends that a creature by definition is imperfect in the sense that it is not what it shall eventually become. Creatures are simply born into a state of immaturity—even infancy—out of which they shall grow over time (*Haer.* 4.38.1). Therefore, the Gnostics cannot claim that creaturely mutability is evidence of some deficiency in the Creator. Indeed, far from being a sign of God's weakness, it is a sign of God's wisdom that the divine economy uses creation's mutability and its concomitant imperfection to bring it to perfection. Like newborn infants whose eyes are not able to see at first because they must gradually become capable of taking in the light and focusing on distant objects, the first human beings in their imperfection or immaturity were not able to receive the full knowledge of God and the vision of God's glory. Therefore, although human beings were endowed with the rational faculties for receiving the gifts of God's self-revelation (*Haer.* 4.38.3), this capacity had to be developed. Irenaeus compares the first human beings to the gentile converts on whom Paul had laid hands. For although they had received the gift of the Spirit, Paul gave them milk rather than solid food (1 Cor 3:2) because, due to

3. Building on this view, Gregory of Nyssa will later argue that this inherent mutability that may be the source of evil is paradoxically also essential for creaturely perfection. For Gregory's theory of *epektasis*, see chapter 13, pp. 486–87.

their lack of spiritual discipline and maturity, they were not yet ready to receive more advanced teachings (*Haer.* 4.38.2). For the same reason, when Christ came, he did not reveal the Father in his immortal glory but gave himself as milk to infants by coming in an accessible form. By appearing in a familiar form, Christ trained humanity by providing a vision of God that would prepare them for the greater vision of his glory that was to come.

Perhaps even more provocatively, true knowledge comes through experience. Human beings were endowed with a rational nature proper to the image of God that allowed them to know the difference between good and evil. But a firmer knowledge comes when theoretical knowledge is confirmed by personal experience. This premise affects the way Irenaeus interprets the fall of the first human beings. Although Adam and Eve should have trusted the command of their Creator not to eat of the forbidden fruit, their immaturity mitigates against their guilt. They acted in ignorance rather than intentional rebellion against God (*Haer.* 3.23.8). Therefore, although the fall brought death, they gained the experiential knowledge that obedience preserves union with God who gives life and that disobedience, which separates the creature from God, leads to death (*Haer.* 4.39.1). Moreover, since the good is not achieved except by struggle in the face of trials (*Haer.* 4.37.7), the lessons learned through disciplines in the face of worldly hardships teach mortals to cling all the more tenaciously to God. Through the imitation of Christ's example, his followers shall attain that perfection Scripture speaks of as "the image and likeness of God" (*Haer.* 3.20.2). In the midst of struggles—for Irenaeus's community that meant persecution—they learned to await in patience for the hand of the Creator to bring to completion his plan (*Haer.* 4.39.1).

Irenaeus sees a close connection between the perfection of humanity and the beatific vision. For the vision of God is both the end and the means of humanity's perfection. In a famous passage, Irenaeus declares, "The glory of God is a living man, and the life of man consists in beholding God" (*Haer.* 4.20.7). Life in this case does not mean mere existence but corresponds to the Greek idea of *eudaimonia*, commonly translated "happiness" or "flourishing." A person's life attains its fulfillment in seeing God's glory. This vision requires the cultivation of the rational nature proper to the "image of God" in which humanity was made in the beginning. Creation itself trains the rational faculty for this purpose. For, Irenaeus goes on to say, "if the manifestation of God through the creation affords life to all living on the Earth, much more does that revelation of the Father, which comes through the Word, give life to those who see God" (*Haer.* 4.20.7). Such a passage illustrates the radical difference between the gnostic view of creation and that of Irenaeus. Not only is material creation not intrinsically evil or the source of evil; it is the way God reveals his glory, a glory that is life-giving to humanity. For, in Jesus, who is the perfected creation in microcosm, the Father's glory is revealed and imparted to creation. All, therefore, who behold the Father's glory in the Son share in his glory. Indeed, the glorification of humanity, as the fulfillment of God's plan for humanity, is God's greatest display of glory. Thus, the glory of God is manifest in his munificence toward all creation, but especially in his glorification of humanity in Jesus.

Beholding God is not only the source of human *eudaimonia*; it is the source of immortality. When the human race has been brought to maturity through Christ, Irenaeus explains, it shall be brought near to God and receive the vision of the Creator. In receiving the vision of the one who is life itself, those who shall behold God's immortal glory shall become like him and be clothed in his immortality (*Haer.* 4.38.3–4). Although the human race after the fall required training to see God through God's self-revelation in the Old Testament covenants or dispensations, the training of humanity's spiritual sight comes through the incarnation where the glory of God is revealed in the glorification of creation. The glorification of creation through the union of Creator and creature in the incarnation was not, for Irenaeus, merely an afterthought in reaction to the fall. Rather, it was God's intention for humanity prior to and independent of the fall. After quoting Jesus's parable of the feast given by a king in honor of his son's wedding (Matt 22:1–10), Irenaeus explains the parable's significance: "Now, by these words, does the Lord clearly show all that there is one King and Lord . . . and that he had *from the beginning*, prepared the marriage for his Son, and, with the utmost kindness, called, by the instrumentality of his servants, the men of the former dispensation to the wedding feast" (*Haer.* 4.36.5). The marriage God willed from the beginning was the union of his Son with humanity. It also illustrates that, while the coming of sin did not prevent God's ultimate fulfillment of his plans, it required added preparation through the teachings of the prophets to prepare humanity for the incarnation. In the context of the fall, the incarnation was all the more necessary to overcome sin. Now humanity had to be delivered not only from ignorance but also from willful error and death. Sin meant that humanity had to endure discipline under the pedagogy of the law and prophets before it was ready to receive the revelation of the incarnation. Had humanity not fallen into sin, there would have been an incarnation but no cross.

As a result of sin, there was the need for atonement. Yet, as John Behr has shown, Christ's atonement for Irenaeus is not punitive but simply the accomplishment of God's original purpose. Commenting on Paul's description of Adam as "the type of the one who was to come" (Rom 5:14), Irenaeus says that Adam was the prefiguration of the perfected humanity to come in Christ. For Adam who was "psychical," that is, an animate creature with a rational soul, needs to be saved and taught to be spiritual by the one who is spiritual (*Haer.* 3.22.3). For the perfection of human nature in the incarnation reveals the divinization of mortal flesh that will occur with Christ's gift of the Spirit; "when the weakness of the flesh is absorbed, it manifests the Spirit as powerful; and again, when the Spirit absorbs the weakness, it inherits the flesh for itself, and from both of these is made a living human being: living, indeed, because of participation of the Spirit; and human because of the substance of the flesh" (*Haer.* 5.9.2). In Christ's passion and resurrection, there are both the atonement for sin and education of humanity through the revelation of the Creator's nature:

> when the Word of God bestows on humanity the resurrection to the glory of God, the Father, who secures immortality for the mortals and bountifully bestows incorruptibility on the corruptible, because the power of God is made perfect in weakness that we may never become puffed up, as if we had life in ourselves nor exalted against God, entertaining ungrateful thoughts, but learning by experience that it is from his excellence, and not from our own nature, that we have eternal existence, that we should neither undervalue the true glory of God, nor be ignorant of our true nature. (*Haer.* 5.2.3)

Human beings are by no means passive recipients of God's gifts or mere victims of ignorance. Rather, their ability to receive God's gifts, especially the knowledge of the giver, comes through participation in God's nature. This participation was possible because being made after the image of its Creator brought with it the gift of free choice (*Haer.* 3.37.4). Against the gnostic view that the children of Cain were so deprived of any spark of Sophia's power that they are consigned to ignorance and cut off from the hope of immortality (*Haer.* 3.37.6), Irenaeus maintains that all human beings have the possibility of receiving God's redemptive revelation. If individuals were good or bad by nature, they would be worthy of neither praise nor blame (*Haer.* 3.37.2). Thus, the possibility of faith lies within God's creation of each individual with the capacity to choose (*Haer.* 3.37.5).

Reading *Against Heresies* primarily as a polemical response to the Gnostics, one is tempted to see Irenaeus's account of the creation and fall as merely a work of theodicy. Yet as his argument unfolds it becomes clearer that Irenaeus's anthropology is more than theodicy. He seeks to offer a coherent narrative of God's unfolding, single economy whose plot traces the gradual maturation and perfection of a humanity fit for intimate fellowship with God. As there was one God, the single source of all things visible and invisible, so too creation and redemption were but two dimensions of a single divinely ordained process that had a single end determined from before the foundation of the world. For Irenaeus presents the biblical narrative of creation and redemption as resting on two fundamental principles: humanity's *growth* toward perfection in Christ and its *reception* of God's gift of life in the Spirit.

Origen: The Fall of Preexistent Minds

Among the antignostic theologians of the early centuries of the Church, Origen is distinctive for positing God's creation of the material world as the result of the fall and the coming of sin. While gnostic narratives, such as the Apocryphon of John, viewed humanity's sin as merely the consequence of the inherently fallen condition of the material universe, Origen's narrative differs because the creation of the material world was the result of the sin of rational beings but also the response of an all-wise God for the ultimate redemption of those fallen beings. Thus, like Irenaeus but unlike the Gnostics and Marcion, Origen maintains an essential unity between creation and redemption.

Origen's narrative was driven by two theological concerns: first, his absolute confidence in the justice of God's nature, and second, a concern for the inequality among rational creatures. Why were rational beings divided into three general classes (i.e., angels, human beings, and demons) each with different degrees of blessedness or suffering, or both? And among human beings, why were some endowed with health and beauty while others suffered debilitating, physical and mental conditions? Such inequality would appear to be capricious and unjust and so was unworthy of a perfectly wise, benevolent, and just Creator. But God is perfectly just. Therefore, Origen sought an account of creation that would explain the inequality among rational creatures and uphold the justice of God. If God's justice would not allow him to fashion rational beings in disparate states without a reason, the reason must lie with the merit or demerit of the rational creatures themselves. From this premise, Origen developed his theory of the preexistence of rational beings.

In the beginning, so runs his narrative, God created the full number of rational creatures, the *logikoi*, in his image. Through sharing in the rational nature of the Logos who created them, they were capable of attaining the highest degree of blessedness through the contemplation of God's beauty and goodness revealed to them through the Son and Spirit (*Princ.* 4.4.9). Per his justice, God gifted the *logikoi* with an equal share in his rational nature and therefore an equal ability to behold his splendor. Because God in his justice created all the rational beings with an equal degree of rationality, he also endowed them with free will. For it would not be just to compel their attention, devotion, and worship. All had equal opportunity for the blessedness of contemplating God, but whether they exercised that native capacity was a matter of their individual choice. Therefore, in paradise, their choice to be united to God was expressed in their love for God. Since, in the physics of Origen's day, heat was understood as the force responsible for binding elements together, Origen described the *logikoi*'s union with God as the result of their fiery love for God. The hotter their love for God, the more intense their union and blessedness.

Being a teacher and lover of learning, not surprisingly, Origen described paradise as a great classroom where the *logikoi* received instruction from the Logos. This paradise was in the ethereal realm of the heavens, and so the *logikoi* were also endowed with ethereal bodies suitable for such habitation. This paradisical state did not endure. In time, the rational beings' love for God began to cool. As the fiery ardor of their love for God waned, the bond uniting them to God loosened, and, all except one, the *logikoi* turned from God and fell away. Then the rational beings became souls (*Princ.* 2.8.3). (The Greek word for soul, *psychē*, was derived from *psychesthai*, which means "to cool.") For, whereas heat rises, that which is cool hardens and falls. But why? How could a rational being ever turn away from that which is supremely beautiful and desirable? Origen's answer was twofold: free will and satiation. He insisted that the fall was an act of free choice (*Princ.* 2.9.2). Thus, the fall was not necessary but the result of sloth, which reflected a failure of the will (*Princ.* 1.6.2; 2.9.2). There was nothing in God's creation of the *logikoi* that meant a fall was inevitable. The fact that there was one of the *logikoi*, that is, the rational being that would be incarnate as the mind or *nous* of Jesus, who did not fall away was, for Origen, evidence of the voluntary nature of the fall (*Princ.* 2.6.3). Still, why would a rational creature *choose* to turn from God? His answer was that the *logikoi* became satiated with the vision of God. Although Origen believed that God was infinite, he compared the mind's satiation with God to a scholar of mathematics or medicine who after having attained perfect knowledge of the subject became complacent and neglectful. Consequently, his knowledge would over time wane (*Princ.* 1.4.1). The free will–satiation explanation allowed Origen to make the *logikoi* culpable for the fall and with it responsible for the inequality among angels, people, and demons. The angels were those whose love for God cooled only slightly, whereas the demons' love became contempt. And the souls of human beings fell into a middle position. Even among the human race, their disparity in intelligence or health or beauty plainly visible among its members was the result of the degree to which they had turned from God. Within this scheme, inequality was not the result of divine caprice but of God's just judgment of the merits or demerits of each of the *logikoi* (*Princ.* 2.9.6).

How could God rekindle the *logikoi*'s love in order to renew their union? God's solution was to create the material world. For the material world was suitable to the changed physical condition of the soul. The cooling of the *logikoi*'s love for God not only changed their moral character; it also changed the nature of their body. Instead of an ethereal body suitable for heaven, their bodies became hard and heavy, corresponding to the heavy nature of the soul. Thus, the material world that God created as the new habitat for fallen souls corresponded to conditions of the rational beings' bodies (*Princ.* 1.7.4–5). As the bodies of the angels, human beings, and demons differed from their original ethereal bodies, so the material world was the antithesis of the heavenly realm. Unlike the light and easy existence of the *logikoi*'s ethereal bodies in heaven, the coarse and heavy nature of the material body meant that the souls labored under the weight of their own heaviness. They experienced all the burdens and sufferings of a body composed of ever-fluctuating matter. It was a natural condition appropriately proportionate to the nature of the fallen being.

This causal relationship between the soul and the material world revealed the wisdom of God's providential fashioning of creation. The material body's condition not only justly corresponded to the merits or demerits of the particular soul, it was also created to be the vehicle for the individual's redemption. Origen imagines the material body not as a prison in which punitive justice was meted out but as a place where the fallen soul might convalesce and reacquire its proper health as a lover of God. During its sojourn in the material world, amid all the miseries of the flesh, the soul experiences an appreciation for the blessedness of its life in heaven in fellowship with God. Being enfleshed cultivated a certain homesickness for heaven. The soul's ardor for God is reignited in its longing to return to its heavenly home. Through its time in the flesh, therefore, the soul begins its rehabilitation and is predisposed to receive the invitation of Jesus's gospel to the kingdom of heaven.

Gregory of Nyssa: Origen Corrected

Few fourth-century theologians appreciated Origen's teachings as did the Cappadocians, Basil the Great, Gregory of Nazianzus, and Gregory of Nyssa. They went so far as to compile an anthology of Origen's writings, the *Philokalia* or *Love of Beauty*. At the same time, however, they recognized problems inherent in some of Origen's speculations. One of these was his theory of the preexistence of the rational beings. The task of correcting this error was taken up by Gregory of Nyssa. This alternative vision of humanity's origins Gregory developed in the treatise *On the Making of Humanity*, which together with *On the Soul and Resurrection* provided the earliest, extended works in theological anthropology.

The central question Gregory poses in *On the Making of Humanity* is how human beings, creatures made in the image of the perfectly blessed God, have lives of misery. His method, as he explains in the preface, is to understand the human condition in the present by contrasting it with human nature as God intended it in the beginning and as it shall be at the resurrection (*Hom. opif.* preface). Here Gregory follows the Aristotelean logic that one cannot understand the acorn without first seeing the oak tree that is both its source and its telos. The final blessed state of the eschaton, initially revealed in Christ's resurrection, is the consummation of, and therefore the key to understanding, God's creative purpose for humanity in the beginning. As will be shown in the final chapter, Gregory speaks of the eschaton as the "restoration" (*apokatastasis*) of humanity to paradise; in fact, the resurrection is less the restoration of perfect human nature and more its attainment.

Gregory's rejection of Origen's theory of the preexistence of rational beings (*Hom. opif.* 28) reflects his concern that it renders material creation a mere epiphenomenonal state for the rehabilitation of fallen creatures. By contrast, Gregory affirms the goodness of the material creation, and with it man's material body, as declared by God in Genesis 1. Human beings, he explains, are an amphibious creature possessing both the rational nature of angels and the corporeal nature of nonrational animals. The rational nature allows them to apprehend the intelligible, heavenly realities that are beyond the grasp of the senses. Thus, humanity was equipped for fellowship with God. Gregory adapts Aristotle's threefold hierarchy of the soul to explain this hybrid nature (*Hom. opif.* 8.4). The soul is passed on from the father's seed. As the source of the body's activities, it begins in the womb with only the basic functions of the vegetative faculties, that is, respiration, ingestion, digestion, elimination, and so on. Soon, however, the soul acquires the faculties of the sentient soul, that is, the ability to perceive the external world as do the nonrational animals. As sentient beings that apprehend the environment, these creatures experience elements of their environments as pleasant or unpleasant, desirable or repellant, objects to be pursued or avoided. These reactions to sense experience are the emotions or passions (*pathē*). The two sources of emotion proper to the sentient soul are the appetitive and spirited faculties, which together act as the soul's principle of movement. The appetitive faculty reacts to perceptions as either goods to be pursued or dangers to be avoided, and the spirited faculty is the fight or flight impulse by which goods are sought or threats are shunned. As the child matures, her soul develops the rational faculties proper to its highest nature. Because of its rational faculties that allow it to apprehend intelligible realities that cannot be known by the faculties of the sentient soul, the intellectual soul is able to recognize the beauty of God's creative artistry and power revealed in his material creation. Thus, through this union of the rational and nonrational, the angelic and the bestial, human beings are able to know God through material creation. "By his enjoyment [of the sensual goods of the material world]," Gregory writes, "[God intended that] man might have understanding of the giver, and by the beauty and majesty of the things he saw might trace out that power of the maker which is beyond speech [*hyper logon*]" (*Hom. opif.* 2.1). The intellect's reflection on the sensual experience will lead to the worship of the Creator and at the same time to an awareness that God transcends the intellect's capacity to describe or comprehend. Although Gregory did not develop the idea thoroughly in *On the Making of Humanity*, Gregory sees the hybrid nature as a microcosm of creation and essential for creation's perfection. Because human nature can participate in the divine nature and shares the bodily nature of the physical world, it is the ideal nature to which Christ can be joined in the incarnation to leaven all of creation with divinity (*Hom. opif.* 16.1).

Gregory had a lofty view of human nature as God intended it expressed in God's words, "Let us make man in our image, after our likeness" (Gen 1:26). Since God is incorporeal and therefore without a visible form, Gregory interprets "image" to refer to the regal beauty of God manifest in his virtues (*Hom. opif.* 5.1). Human beings possess the divine image inasmuch as they embody the virtues proper to and derived from participation in God's nature. Gregory recognized a connection between God's making humanity in his image and his dominical purpose for humanity to "rule over" the nonrational creatures. If human beings were to act as God's viceroy governing creation on his behalf (*eis basileias energeian*), then they should be self-governing (*autarkeia*) creatures whose actions are not determined by the material world they govern (*Hom. opif.* 4). Like Origen, therefore, Gregory insists that a central characteristic of the divine image is freedom of choice (*proairesis*), that is, freedom from necessity. Free choice is not, for Gregory, a faculty separate from the intellect. Rather, it is the intellect's ability to adjudicate between competing goods and assess how they promote the highest good of serving God. Thus, the intellect is the source of self-transcendence that frees people from the automatic reaction of impulses or urges (*orexis*) arising from bodily pleasure or pain. Human beings, as God intended them, possess a twofold resemblance to God: structural and moral. Likely following Irenaeus's image-likeness distinction, Gregory locates the structural image in the hardwiring of the soul with its faculties of perception, understanding, and free choice; while the moral likeness consists in purity (*katharotēs*), freedom from irrational passion (*apatheia*), and most of all love (*agapē*), the highest of all virtues without which "the whole stamp of the likeness is distorted" (*Hom. opif.* 5.2). By the pursuit of virtue (*aretē*), attained through participation in God's nature, human beings grow into the likeness of the divine archetype.

This trichotomous view of the soul Gregory maps onto similar threefold descriptions of humanity in Scripture. Paul's distinction between body, mind, and spirit (1 Thess 5:23) corresponds to the nurturing, sensing, and reasoning faculties. Jesus's description of loving God with heart, soul, and mind (Mark 12:30) Gregory interprets as paralleling Paul's description of the three dispositions of the soul (1 Cor 2:14–15): carnal, natural, and spiritual. "Heart" refers to the corporeal or carnal orientation toward sensual pleasures. "Mind" refers to the spiritual orientation that "perceives the perfections of the godly life" (*Hom. opif.* 8.5–6). "Soul" denotes an intermediate disposition between heart and mind; it is the "natural" man—the state of the virtuous pagan—whose life is not dominated by carnal vice but that lacks the highest virtues devoted to the things of the Spirit.

Gregory gives a fuller description of the emotions and their relationship to the life of virtue in *On the Soul and Resurrection* or *De anima et resurrectione*. Written about the same time as *On the Making of Humanity*, *On the Soul and Resurrection* is Gregory's deathbed dialogue with his sister, the ascetic matriarch of the family whom Gregory calls "my teacher" (*An. res.* preface 7; Silvas, 172). Modeled on Plato's *Phaedo*, where Socrates, who, as he is waiting to drink the hemlock, consoles his grieving students by turning them to a right knowledge of the immortal soul, *On the Soul and Resurrection* presents Macrina playing the role of Socrates and assuaging Gregory's sorrow over her immanent death by reordering his emotions through philosophical argument that restores Gregory's hope of the soul's immortality and the body's resurrection. Against the Epicureans, Stoics, and Peripatetics, Macrina grounds her argument about the immortality of the soul in the doctrine of the image of God. As an image of the divine nature, the soul, she explains, is not identical to God but like a small piece of glass that contains the reflection of a much larger object in miniature. God's relationship with creation is reflected in the soul's relationship with the body. As the invisible God, the archetype of human nature, is known by the displays of his creative and providential powers in the world, so the invisible soul's presence can be confirmed by its activities in the body (*An. res.* 2.41–43; Silvas, 184–85). As God is present in all things and yet distinct from them, so too is the soul present in but distinct from the body. Although Gregory says that the structure of the body with its erect posture and opposable thumbs is necessary for the soul's rational faculties that bear the divine image (*Hom. opif.* 8.1–2), through the voice of Macrina, he contends that the essence of human nature is the rational soul. For a thing's essence is that distinctive feature (*idia*) that distinguishes its species from all others (*An. res.* 3.11–12; Silvas, 190). In the case of human beings, it is the rational nature that bears the image of God other creatures lack. Since the vegetative and sentient faculties, including the appetitive and spirited faculties, are alien to the divine nature, Macrina argues, they are not part of the image of God.

However, drawing on biblical examples of holy grief for sin, zeal for righteousness, and the longing for God, Gregory nudges his sister into a more nuanced account of the relationship of virtue and the emotions. Although the emotions are not part of the divine image, they are not themselves vices. On the contrary, the emotions of desire (*epithymia*) and gumption (*thymos*) are in themselves morally neutral. On the one hand, if they are not controlled by the moderating force of reason, they are like wild horses that pull the reins from the hands of the charioteer and so drag the chariot pell-mell to destruction. On the other hand, if they are controlled by reason directing them in obedience to God, they are virtues

(*An. res.* 3.47; Silvas, 195). When oriented to God by the intellect, these nonrational faculties are transformed and serve the higher, intelligible goods of God known by the rational soul through the Spirit's illumination. Desire (*epithymia*) for sensual goods becomes holy love (*agapē*) for God, and irascibility (*thymos*) is turned into courage to resist the temptations of the devil. As the soul's principles of movement, they are necessary for the end of the virtuous life, friendship with God (*Mos.* 2.320). For without a desire for God and the courage to endure hardships and overcome the pull of pleasure or the fear of pain, the soul could not ascend to God. Therefore, Macrina concludes that the emotions lie on the "borderland" of the soul and serve the spiritual and material needs of the present life (*An. res.* 3.30; Silvas, 192).

Because *On the Making of Humanity* focuses mostly on Genesis 1 rather than its second and third chapters, Gregory offers no allegorical interpretation of the fall of Adam and Eve. Rather, his account of the fallen condition of humanity is located in his explanation of gender. Given Paul's declaration that "in Christ there is neither male nor female" (Gal 3:28), Gregory concludes that, since Christ is the archetype after whose likeness humanity was made, the division of the human race into male and female like the nonrational animals is alien to the divine image and so not part of God's original intention for human beings. Moreover, given Gregory's use of the resurrection as the lens through which to interpret Genesis, Gregory takes Jesus's eschatological prophecy that "those worthy of the resurrection will be like the angels" (Luke 20:34–36) to mean that God's original design of human beings did not include gender differences. He then proceeds to speculate that originally humanity would have engaged in a spiritual, asexual mode of procreation like that of angels. Since the division of male and female is contrary to the divine image, why did God make some male and some female? His answer is that Genesis 1:26 and 1:27 represent two "stages" of creation. First, God's words "Let us make man in our image, after our likeness" (1:26) refer to God's creative decision to endow humanity with a rational nature like the Logos, in which there is no division along gendered lines. Here, too, God establishes at the level of his foreknowledge the whole human race (*plērōma*), that is, all the human beings that will ever be (*Hom. opif.* 16.16). This "first fashioning" (*kataskeuē*) of humanity is the perfect, collective image of God that humanity will bear in the resurrection (*Hom. opif.* 16.17). The second stage described in Genesis 1:27, "And God made man in his image; male and female he made them," is the actual making of the first human beings in God's image but with the addition of gender. Gregory explains the fashioning of humanity with gender is the result of God's anticipation of the fall. Since God foreknew that humanity would turn away from him to seek transitory, sensual goods and so become subject to death, God gave humanity a bestial mode of procreation that reflected their fallen, sensual orientation.

The two "stages" theory of creation is significant at a number of levels. First, although Gregory is not always consistent, it affirms the possibility for moral equality between men and women. Because God's intention from the beginning was that human beings share in his rational nature—with gender only an afterthought—the image of God, not one's gender, is the primary locus of humanity's essence. Therefore, men and women are equally capable of being rational and by extension of being virtuous. When Gregory, in his *Life of Macrina*, says that by her ascetic life she "transcended her nature" (*Macr.* 1.3; Silvas, 110), he does not mean that she became male but that she became like the angels transcending the division of male and female. Even if the bodies of the resurrection retain the marks of gender, sexuality will pass away along with death at Christ's return. Consequently, people's primary sense of identity should be that of creatures made in the image of God who will ultimately be free of gender, social status, nationality, and other identities that divide the human race in the present age and distract from humanity's proper focus on God.

Second, gender actually contributes to the corruption of human nature. In a controversial section of *On the Making of Humanity*, Gregory says that being created for sexual procreation oriented the first human beings to the sensual pleasures that precipitated the fall in the first place. Commenting on the cause of humanity's misery in the present life, Gregory writes,

> For [Adam] truly was made like unto the beasts, who received in his nature the present mode of transient generation, on account of his inclination to material things. For I think that from this beginning all our passions issued as from a spring, and pour their flood over man's life. . . . These attributes, then, human nature took to itself from the side of the brutes; for those qualities with which brute life was armed for self-preservation, when transferred to human life, became passions. (*Hom. opif.* 17.5–18.2)

As a result, when humanity's appetites are not oriented toward God but to worldly goods, both natural, sensual pleasures and socially constructed worldly honors, then the rational faculties become enslaved to the passions. When the rational faculties are directed to the service of the passions by calculating the most effective means to achieve those worldly goals, then human beings become the most vicious of beasts, inflicting suffering on one another (*Hom. opif.* 18.3–4). Thus, the passions, which are the source of greed for wealth or dominion over others, lead to the misuse of free choice and consequently of much of human misery.

Further explanation of how the passions prejudice human nature against virtue lies in the development of the soul. Because the rational faculties develop later than the sentient faculties, the appetitive and spirited impulses of the sentient soul are naturally inclined to sensual rather than intelligible goods. Therefore, when an individual's intellectual faculties emerge, her appetites are not neutrally disposed so as to be easily moved to intelligible goods. Therefore, it is difficult for the intellect to exert control over the sensually oriented appetites. Consequently, their habitual orientation toward transient worldly goods must be broken, like a bad habit, through the disciplines of *askēsis*. The body reflects the condition of the soul; it is a "mirror of the mirror" that reflects the character of the objects toward which the soul is directed (*Hom. opif.* 12.11). If the soul's appetites are oriented toward the corruptible things of the world, then the body itself will be liable to corruption. Conversely, once the appetites are directed by the spiritually inclined intellect to the divine goods, then the body through the soul participates in God's incorruptibility. However, precisely because the soul has participated in the transitory and corruptible world, the body retains the corrupting effects of the passions until the body is broken down in death and then remade in the resurrection free of such corruption. Because death is the beginning of the healing of the body that is completed at the resurrection, it is not to be feared. Rather, Gregory, following Origen, speaks of the mortal body as the garments of skins with which God graciously clothed Adam and Eve after the fall in order that through mortality they might be ultimately delivered from the ravages of sin upon the soul and the body (*Or. cat.* 8).

Gregory's speculative intellectual temperament, like Origen's, made him comfortable exploring various possible theological trajectories. He was, as Rowan Greer has put it, a prismatic rather than a systematic thinker; his theological vision has coherence even if the pieces are not systematically arranged. He was comfortable living with paradox; Christians, this side of the resurrection, see only as in a glass darkly. His paradoxical thinking is on full display in his anthropology. At one level, Gregory has a more positive view of the body and the material world than Origen does. And he rejects Origen's view that the material creation is the result of sin. Yet in the relationship between the passions and gender, it appears that humanity was created in the very condition that caused the passions and the fall to begin with. Here is the paradox of human nature, the contradiction between what God in the beginning intended humanity to be and its divided condition in the present. Humanity is at one moment fashioned with the capacity for royal dignity and beauty surpassing all other animals. As Gregory writes in his *Homilies on the Beatitudes*, "that which is called [the image of God] . . . should also be held blessed, inasmuch as it participates in the true beatitude. . . . [For in human nature], which is the image of the transcendent, the beatitude is itself marked by the beauty of goodness when it reflects in itself the blessed features [of God]" (*Beat.* 1). At the same time, people are also guilty of brutality against one another surpassing the most vicious of all animals. The dignity of one bearing the image and likeness of the King of the cosmos was the goal into which humanity had to mature. The bestial desire and irascibility was something to be overcome not by the elimination of the emotions but by their transformation. As we shall see, God the Father made possible this deliverance from the destructive force through the transformation of base passions by sending Christ. In putting on Christ in baptism, the believer lays hold of the source of perfection by "put[ting] on the humanity 'which is created after the image of him that created him' (Col 3:9–10)" (*Hom. opif.* 30.33–34). For Christ is the second Adam whose humanity embodies God's original purpose. This perfection is ultimately attainable, Gregory says, because through Christ the believer participates in his divinity and so attains the likeness that God intended in the beginning. Thus, Christ is "our great high priest" who makes humanity worthy of entering with him into the true holy of holies (*adyton*) not made with hands to enjoy communion with "our Father who is in heaven" (*Or. dom.* 3).

Gregory's interpretation of Genesis 1 and his account of the psychosomatic unity of the person allows him to distinguish between humanity's rational soul and the material body while at the same time including both in God's original purpose. Moreover, since he uses the distinction between God's eternal being and humanity's eternal becoming to draw the ontological divide between Creator and creature, mutability is inherent to the soul as well as to the body. Paradoxically, therefore, although the mind's rational ability to participate in God allows it to share in his immortality, its inherent mutability allows it to be eternally formed and reformed in the image of its infinite Creator. This laid the foundation, as we shall see in a later chapter, for his theory of Christian perfection or *epektasis*.

Augustine and the Latin West

As the legacy of gnostic dualism dominated much of theology in the Greek-speaking East, the dualism of the Manichees would pose a rival to the Catholic theology of Latin-speaking North Africa in the fourth and fifth centuries. The classic instance of this rivalry is found in the early writings of Augustine of Hippo. In the midst of this controversy, which we will examine in detail in a later chapter, emerged Augustine's first attempt to understand human nature through his exegesis of Genesis 1–3. After a number of false starts, Augustine finally composed his extended exegesis, *On Genesis Literally Interpreted.* By "literally" Augustine simply means what the details of the creation narrative signify; the result is largely an allegorical interpretation of Genesis. When he turns to the creation of humanity on the sixth day, he faces the basic exegetical problem: What is the relationship between the two accounts of creation? Is Genesis 2 a detailed recapitulation of God's creative work described generally in Genesis 1, or is it a separate act of creation? His answer is that the two creation stories represent two stages. Genesis 1 is the hidden (*in secreto*), invisible creation (*Gen. litt.* 6.1.1) in which God fashions all things at the level of his will, while Genesis 2 narrates the beginning of the visible world as it unfolds in time (*Gen. litt.* 6.3.4). Based on Sirach 18:1, "God created all things together," Augustine conjectures that God instantaneously, without any interval, willed the existence of all things, and they existed "in their potency [*potentialiter*] and cause" (*Gen. litt.* 6.4.5). This creation is different from the light or created wisdom that contains the forms of all things that were to be made (*Gen. litt.* 5.12.28). The forms are species or universals, the natures of all the creatures. The beings created on the subsequent days are the particular instances of those natures. Thus, on the sixth day (Gen 1:26–27), God willed all individual human beings who ever would exist and who, therefore, were seminally present (*Gen. litt.* 6.5.8) in the first person from whom all the rest of human beings would come. For this reason, God could say to Jeremiah, "Before I formed you in the womb, I knew you" (Jer 1:5), and Levi was met by Melchizedek (Heb 7:9–10) while he was still in Abraham's loins (*Gen. litt.* 6.8.13).

Unlike Origen, who, as we have already seen, sees the creation of the material body as an epiphenomenon, a consequence of the fall of rational beings, Augustine affirms the goodness of the material body by making it, together with the soul, constitutive of human nature generally and of all people in their particularity. The fruit on the trees created on the third day was after all intended to sustain the body; therefore, Augustine concludes, God willed that humanity possess a material body from the beginning. Thus, although the "image of God" refers to the spiritual and intellectual nature proper to the soul, he rejects the possibility that the creation of humanity in Genesis 1 refers only to the soul apart from the body. Genesis 2, therefore, is not an account of a separate creation of the body (*Gen. litt.* 6.7.12). Augustine does ascribe to the rational soul greater dignity than the body, because the soul bears the image of God and through this image is able to know and commune with God; nevertheless, he says that the form of the body with its erect posture, different from that of other animals that walk on all fours, is honored by God with a dignity befitting creatures made in his image (*Gen. litt.* 6.12.22).

What was the nature of this body that God willed for humanity on the sixth day? Is it the "natural," as he calls it, mortal body, which human beings have in the present age or the spiritual body they will receive at the resurrection? Affirming continuity between the good of creation in the beginning and the perfection of nature in the eschaton, Augustine reasons that the body God willed for humanity and gave Adam in the beginning was essentially the same body—a spiritual body—that Paul describes in his account of the resurrection in 1 Corinthians 15:44: "it is sown a natural body and it is raised a spiritual body" (*Gen. litt.* 6.19.30). Augustine does not understand Paul's distinction between a natural and a spiritual body to be between a body composed of earthly matter and one that is immaterial or ethereal, as was the body of Origen's rational beings before the fall. Rather, "natural" refers to a mortal body, and "spiritual" refers to an immortal one. Augustine's answer to the question "natural or spiritual" is "both" in different respects. His first premise is that eschatologically human nature shall be *renewed* in the image of the heavenly man so that it will recover that nature Adam originally possessed. Therefore, since the resurrected body will be spiritual in the sense that it will not be subject to death, Adam's body must also have been spiritual because it was not prone to death before his sin. Augustine's point is that sin, not God, is responsible for humanity's mortality; "your bodies are dead because of sin" (Rom 8:10). The logic, Augustine explains, is that the body derives life from the soul, which derives its life from its participation in God, who is life itself. When Adam and Eve turned from God by their disobedience, their bodies became mortal in the sense that they no longer were united to the divine source of life. When the saints will be perfectly united with God in the eschaton—as are angelic citizens of the "heaven of heaven"—they will be restored to an Edenic immortality.

Yet the spiritual body of the resurrection will be an improved version of the prototype. Jesus alludes to the superiority of the spiritual body of the resurrection when he describes the father's calling for his servants to clothe the prodigal son with "the best robe" (*Gen. litt.* 6.20.31). In what sense is the spiritual body of the resurrection superior to the spiritual body of Eden? Before the fall, the body was not spiritual and immortal by nature; it was immortal only in a provisional sense. Whereas angels are by nature immortal, which means that they "cannot possibly die," Adam and Eve were immortal only in the sense that as long as they ate of the fruit of the tree of life they were "able not to die" (*Gen. litt.* 6.25.36). The immortality of Eden was a gift from God rather than a constituent element of their nature. Consequently, Augustine interprets Jesus's prophetic utterance that in the resurrection the saints "shall enjoy equality with the angels" (Matt 22:30) to mean that the resurrection body shall become *naturally* immortal as the angels and thus not able to suffer death. They will be made alive by their immediate participation in God's immortality and so will not need to be sustained by corruptible food (*Gen. litt.* 6.24.35). This naturally spiritual and immortal body is the "best robe" with which the heavenly Father will clothe prodigal humanity at the resurrection.

What humanity shall become in the resurrection is in fact what the first people would have become in time had they not succumbed to temptation and fallen into sin. Their bodies would have become by nature what they were by gift. By virtue of their soul's union with God, the mortal nature of their bodies would have become immortal, reflecting the spiritual nature of their souls (*Gen. litt.* 6.23.34). For Augustine, the transformation of the human soul and body into permanently spiritual being was both an organic process and a matter of justice. It is organic in the sense that through prolonged participation in God's nature, one's own nature becomes divinized. But it is also a matter of justice. Adam and Eve were not made naturally spiritual in the beginning because they needed to merit the blessings of immortality (*Gen. litt.* 6.27.38). Therefore, they were *provisionally* spiritual, capable of not sinning (*posse non peccare*). If they had grown firm in fellowship with God and proven themselves faithful to him, this justly ordered relationship would have become permanent. They would have come to that perfect liberty in which they were incapable of sin (*non posse peccare*). Through the gift of grace by which human beings are restored to a just relationship with God, the soul begins in the present age the process of becoming what Adam and Eve were intended to become. For through grace, believers are being "renewed in the knowledge of God" (Col 3:9–10) and thus being restored to the image of God that the first people partially lost due to sin (*Gen. litt.* 6.27.38). Thus, the *renewal* of the "spirit of your minds" (Eph 4:23) begun in baptism and completed at the resurrection is, for Augustine, not simply a return to Eden but the perfection of human nature as it was made to become (*Gen. litt.* 6.28.39).

"Male and Female He Made Them"

Augustine views God's division of humanity into male and female quite differently from his predecessors, Latin or Greek. The key texts are Genesis 1:27b and Genesis 2:18, God's pronouncement, "It is not good that the man should be alone. Let us make for him a helper." The specific sort of helper Adam needed was neither one to share his toil, since there was no toil in the growing of crops in Eden, nor one to be a companion to dispel his solitude. Were Adam simply in need of someone to be a friend, God would have fashioned another male. Here Augustine follows the logic from classical antiquity that in order for a friend really to be a second self, friends must be equals. Therefore, a man's friend was another man and a woman's friend was another woman (*Gen. litt.* 9.5.9). Since Adam needed neither a colaborer nor a friend, the distinctive contribution a woman would add to their life together was for procreation (*Gen. litt.* 9.3.5). Augustine is not saying that God created woman *merely* as an instrument for sexual reproduction. Against the backdrop of the Jovinian controversy that concerned the question whether the married life was inferior to the life of celibacy, Augustine sought to articulate a positive view of marriage that nonetheless did not make it equal with virginity. In *The Good of Marriage*, which had been written in 401 before he composed the later books of *On Genesis Literally Interpreted*, he speaks more positively about the salvific benefits of a cooperative relation between man and wife. "God did not create [man and woman] as strangers but made them from one and the same flesh, indicating the strength of the union between them. They were destined to be joined to one another side by side, as they walked together looking toward the goal of their journey" (*Bon. conj.* 1.1). Man and woman are not naturally strangers—as would be man and dog—but share a common nature formed after the divine image and so are able to be fellow pilgrims on their common journey to their heavenly homeland. Perhaps the clearest instance in Augustine's writings of how women and men can be travel companions on their spiritual pilgrimage is the account of his relationship with Monica after his baptism. His narration of the mystical union they shared at Ostia is a foreshadowing of the union of minds in which the saints share at the resurrection. "Alone with each other, we talked very intimately. 'Forgetting the past and reaching forward to what lies ahead,' we were searching together in the presence of the truth which is you yourself. . . . Our minds were lifted up by an ardent affection toward eternal being itself. Step by step we climbed . . . by internal reflection and dialogue and wonder at your works and entered into our own minds" (*Conf.* 9.10.23–24). Monica and Augustine experienced "the eternal life of the saints" in which barriers between people are broken down and human minds meet and are united in mutual intimacy with the one who is eternal being itself. Augustine's explanation for the creation of woman, therefore, simply identifies the feature that distinguishes her from man and by which she makes her distinctive contribution, qua woman, to their life together.

Augustine's explanation for the creation of woman ultimately leads him to an account of sexual relations between man and woman that is distinctive among patristic theologians. Whereas Gregory of Nyssa, for instance, saw procreation through sexual intercourse as God's accommodation of sin rather than a part of God's will for humanity had there been no fall, Augustine envisions sex as having a natural place in Eden. Since God issued the commandment "Be fruitful and multiply" (Gen 1:28) before the fall, Augustine concluded that, even though the first human beings did not have time for sex before they fell and were expelled from the garden, they would have had intercourse in paradise. Sex in Eden, however, would have been different from sex after the fall. Whereas in the present age procreation is motivated by carnal desire and the manner of intercourse is passionate and frenetic, in paradise sex would have entirely been governed by the higher faculties of the soul. Thus, man and woman would have come together only for the purpose of procreation, and their coming together would be "without the tumultuous ardor of passion" since the body would have been entirely submissive to the will of the intellect (*Gen. litt.* 9.3.6). Although Augustine is certain that holy virginity is superior to the married state, he is equally emphatic that even incontinence that characterizes humanity's present condition does not in itself render marriage evil. Rather, God uses the institution of marriage not only to provide an allowable outlet for sexual desires but also to turn humanity's weakness into an instrument to serve the good of procreation. Unlike wisdom, health, and friendship, which are goods in themselves, marriage and sexual intercourse, like food and sleep, are instrumental goods necessary for those higher goods, especially friendship (*Bon. conj.* 9.9). Augustine's point is not that the goods of friendship are experienced in sexual intimacy but that the propagation of the species is necessary for enjoying the "social bonds of friendship" (*societas amicalis*). Beyond these goods, marriage also teaches humanity the virtue of fidelity to each other. Even when the motive for sexual intimacy is lust rather than procreation, intercourse within the mutual pledge of faithfulness is a good (*Bon. conj.* 5.5), for in it a spouse is supporting his or her mate in times of weakness (*Bon. conj.* 6.6). Even in cases where a husband would prefer to be continent, he nevertheless "should give to his wife her conjugal rights" (1 Cor 7:3), as the wife also would her husband, so that neither falls into sin during a time of vulnerability to sexual temptation. Marriage also serves as a sacrament that models the indissoluble union of the saints in paradise. So while virginity is a foretaste of the angelic life of the resurrection, the union of man and wife in marriage is in its own way a foretaste of the eschatological bonds of fellowship (*Bon. conj.* 18.21).

Augustine's Account of the Fall

Eating the forbidden fruit was not, for Augustine, the first sin. It was merely the inevitable consequence of a prior sin, a prior act of turning away from God that made the serpent's deception of Eve possible and caused Adam to choose the companionship of his mate over obedience to God. The theological challenge posed by the narratives of Genesis 2–3 was not simply explaining how humanity, abiding in the bliss of fellowship with God, could rebel against that God. Rather, for Augustine, it was how Adam and Eve, whose intellects were illuminated by the light of created wisdom, could fall prey to the wiles of the serpent. This light of wisdom was that light created on the first day and itself provided the model for the fashioning of all other creatures. It was the light by which the inner teacher of the soul gave innate knowledge that allowed the intellect to understand the world rightly. It was through the illumination of the light of wisdom that Adam discerned what names to give the animals because it revealed the distinctive nature of each. How, therefore, could they fail to recognize the falsehood of the serpent's words that contradicted the explicit command of their Creator?

Although Augustine was careful not to conflate Platonism and Manichaeism, his account of the fall ruled out both Manichaean arguments about the inherently corrupting nature of matter and Platonist attribution of the soul's ills to the body (*Civ.* 14.12). After all, the devil, that former angel of light, did not have a material body like that of humans, and yet he fell (*Civ.* 14.3). His turning from God was not the result of disordered sensual appetites, such as sexual desire or a fondness for drink, but of the more subtle, cerebral vices of pride and envy. Sin, therefore, originates in the intellect and will, not the body. The disobedience to God's command was an act of the will contrary to God's, but it was not deliberate or premeditated. Rather, Augustine says, the evil began in secret and "slipped into open disobedience" through pride (*Civ.* 14.13). Such pride (*probia*) arises from a failure to recognize that God is the "ground of our being" and the foundational condition for all life. Then the soul exalts itself by trusting in its own ability to know and judge the good by which happiness is achieved rather than relying upon the illumination of the mind by God. Adam and Eve became self-complacent (*cum sibi nimis placet*); they were pleased with themselves and self-confident in the power of their intellect. So they made themselves their own standard of truth rather than relying on one who is the Changeless Good (*Civ.* 14.13). In that moment, self-love superseded love of the Changeless Good. No longer bound to God in proper creaturely love for the Creator, they sought goods for themselves that were other than God and contrary to God's will. When their love did not cleave to God, they ceased to abide in the light of God's wisdom. Without the illumination of their intellects by God, shadows fell over their minds, and they did not see the world clearly as they had. Now they saw what they desired to see. Confused by pride, Eve was susceptible to the serpent's pandering promise to make her like God. In pride she believed the serpent's lie that God was not telling the truth when he said they would die if they ate the fruit of the tree of the knowledge of good and evil. Likewise, Adam's pride caused him to trust Eve's words because he had ceased to love Eve *in God* and instead loved her more than God. Eve had replaced God as the source of Adam's pleasure and happiness. Therefore, he chose to disobey God rather than to abandon Eve. It is this identification of sin as disordered love manifest in the self-complacency of pride that ultimately provides Augustine with an alternative to the Manichaean identification of the source of evil with the material world.

Augustine and the Idea of Original Sin

Augustine's exegesis of Genesis offered an account of the nature of sin that explained how humanity would turn from God without blaming material creation. The next challenge was to explain the consequences of Adam and Eve's sin for their progeny. What was the "death" that Paul said came from Adam, and how did it "pass" to all (Rom 5:18)? To be sure, Augustine's answers to these questions developed over the years. Yet, contrary to enduring narratives that present Augustine's doctrine of original sin as the result of the Pelagian controversy, Augustine's anthropology and his account of the corruption of human nature developed a full decade and a half before he clashed with Pelagius and his erstwhile protégé, Caelestius, over the effect of the fall upon human nature.

In early writings, such as *On True Religion*, Augustine argued that the primary consequence of Adam's sin for his posterity was mortality. But there was no fundamental alteration of human nature. The divine image in which humanity was made was not lost or corrupted. The power of free choice (*liberum arbitrium*) remained intact. While his reading of Romans in the 390s caused him to qualify the extent of free will before and after the fall, Augustine first articulated a theory of original sin in 411 when he rebutted Caelestius's assertion that infants were not born with any sin of their own and therefore did not need to be baptized.[4] Indeed, it was then in his *Punishment and Forgiveness of Sin and the Baptism of Little Ones* that he coined the term "original sin" that has haunted Western theology ever since.

Although Pelagius himself did not go so far as his disciple in repudiating the practice of infant baptism, Caelestius's view of baptism rested upon Pelagius's view of human nature. Both maintained that Adam and Eve were mortal beings who, even if they had not sinned and been expelled from Eden, would have grown old and died. Therefore, the punishment of death that Adam received was not the death of the body but of the soul. Central to this claim was their interpretation of the warning that accompanied God's commandment not to eat of the tree of the knowledge of good and evil: "for in the day that you eat of it you shall die" (Gen 2:17). Had this death applied to the body, they reasoned, then Adam and Eve would, like Ananias and Sapphira (Acts 5:10), have dropped dead instantly upon eating the forbidden fruit. Instead, they lived to a ripe old age and then died. The only way they died on the day they ate of it was a spiritual death. Although Augustine early on followed Ambrose in distinguishing the death of the soul (i.e., the soul's separation and estrangement from God) and the death of the body (i.e., the body's separation from the soul), unlike Pelagius, he saw both forms of death as the consequence of sin. Augustine countered Caelestius by restating the view he had developed in *On Genesis Literally Interpreted*: Adam's body was mortal only in the sense that it was capable of dying but was spiritual, like the body of the resurrection, because it was sustained by the fruit of the tree of life. Had they not sinned but remained faithful, their bodies eventually would have become immortal, spiritual bodies incapable of death. To illustrate the point, he uses a pedestrian analogy: although a person *may* become ill with some disease, that does not mean that he necessarily or inevitably will die with that disease (*Pecc. merit.* 1.5.5). He responded to the Pelagian interpretation of Genesis 2:17 by saying that the punishment of death was not an instantaneous event; rather, it was the aging and decaying of the body over a period of time, sometimes short and other times spanning many years. Therefore, while Adam and Eve's souls died *spiritually* on the day of their disobedience, this spiritual death initiated the gradual *physical* death—that is, that long process of decay that climaxed when their hearts stopped beating (*Pecc. merit.* 1.3.3). The key verse from Genesis that he

4. For historical background on Caelestius, see chapter 3, p. 109; chapter 12, pp. 456–57.

uses to challenge Caelestius's view was God's pronouncement, "Dust you are and to dust you shall return" (Gen 3:19). Since the body, not the immaterial soul, was formed from the dust of the earth, the punishment of which they were warned in Genesis 2:17 was the death of the body, not the soul (*Pecc. merit.* 1.2.2).

Augustine finds strong confirmation of this reading in Paul's statement that "the body is indeed dead on account of sin" (Rom 8:10b). Here was his trump card. "I do not believe that so clear and so obvious a statement needs anyone to interpret it; it merely needs someone to read it" (*Pecc. merit.* 1.4.4). The body is not mortal, that is, capable of dying, but dead, that is, actually will die and is even now decaying, because of sin. The "obvious" meaning of this verse is confirmed by Paul's contrast between the dead body of sin and "the spirit [that] is life on account of righteousness" (Rom 8:10). Augustine finds a similar contrastive parallel of soul and body in Romans 7:22–24 where the apostle opposes the interior self that delights in the law of God with "the body of this death" that bears the punishment of unrighteousness because its members war against the law of God in the inner self (*Pecc. merit.* 1.6.6). In *City of God*, Augustine explains why the body, whose members feel the impulse of sin, resists the governing authority of the mind. It is a poetically just punishment in which the body's rebellion against the mind mirrors the mind's resistance to the authority of God, its rightful Lord (*Civ.* 13.13). The unjust and disordered relationship of the higher faculties of the soul and the lower faculties of the body is a reflection of the disorder of fallen creation in miniature. Adam and Eve's condemnation and punishment were passed to their descendants because, due to "the magnitude of that offence, the condemnation changed human nature for the worse. . . . Human nature in [Adam] was vitiated and altered so that he experienced the rebellion and disobedience of desire in his body and was bound by necessity of dying and he produced offspring in the same condition to which his fault and its punishment had reduced him" (*Civ.* 13.3). Here is a critical shift from the earlier view of *On True Religion*. Not only do Adam's progeny inherit mortality—that is not surprising since, no longer living in the garden, they would not be sustained by the fruit of the tree of life—but their nature itself is corrupted such that they experience *involuntarily* impure desires and impulses that are at variance with the judgment of their intellect.

How, though, can the sin of the first people have such catastrophic consequences for all subsequent generations? The answer hinged on Augustine's and Pelagius's vastly different interpretations of Paul's two-Adams theory in Romans 5. Even as the first Adam's disobedience to God brought sin and death into the world, the perfect obedience of the second Adam, Christ, brought life to many. On Pelagius's reading, the first Adam's sin spread to his descendants through contagion; that is, they imitated the sinful example of their parents (*Comm. Rom.* 5.12). Adam's sin, however, was his own, and he alone bore the guilt and punishment.

His nature was not made mortal by his sin. Nor was either his guilt or its punishment passed on to his children. They died because of their own sins. In following the pattern or precedent set by Adam, they were guilty of a similar disobedience to God. From this explanation, Caelestius could reasonably argue that since infants are not capable of imitating their parents' pattern of life, they do not have any sins of their own that need to be washed away through baptism (*Pecc. merit.* 1.9.9).

Augustine counters Pelagius's theory of contagion by arguing first that if the spread of sin were a matter of imitation, then the one who set the pattern of disobedience that sinful humanity followed was not Adam but the devil (*Pecc. merit.* 1.9.10). The heart of Augustine's counterargument is that sin and death were passed from Adam to his descendants even as righteousness and eternal life are passed from Christ to his spiritual children. Augustine reasons backward from salvation to the fall. One understands the manner of humanity's corruption in Adam by understanding the manner of humanity's healing by Christ. Pelagius, too, followed a similar logic, contending that as Adam corrupted his children by his example of sin, so too Christ liberated humanity by providing them an example of righteousness that they might imitate and so become righteous. Yet Pelagius's Christ is more than mere moral exemplar. In Jesus, "God demonstrates his love" (Rom 5:8), "so that we might see whether anything should be valued more highly than one so generous and holy. . . . [Consequently, God] becomes the object of love when he conveys how much he loves us" (*Comm. Rom.* 5.6–8). Not only does Christ reveal the goodness of a righteous life such that people will desire to live righteously themselves, but by revealing the unmerited love of God for his disobedient children, Christ sparks within the sinner a love for God that is the essence of all righteousness.

While Augustine agrees that Christians imitate Jesus's righteous life, the example itself, he contends, is not enough to make one righteous. Were that the case, then Christians would attain righteousness by imitating the examples set by Peter, Paul, and a myriad of other holy people (*Pecc. merit.* 1.10.11). Paul, who offered himself as an example for imitation, recognizes that imitating him is not sufficient for a life of holiness; for he tells the Corinthians, "Neither the one who plants [i.e., Paul] nor the one who waters [i.e., Apollos] is anything; it is, rather, God who gives the increase" (1 Cor 3:7). The "increase" or fruit of righteousness comes from Christ, "the one in whom all are brought to life [and who] also gives the faithful the most hidden grace of the Spirit" (*Pecc. merit.* 1.9.10). Therefore, in baptism, Augustine writes, "those who believe in him are justified in Christ on account of the *hidden communication* and inspiration of spiritual grace which makes whoever clings to the Lord one spirit" (*Pecc. merit.* 1.10.11). The spiritual grace that is communicated in baptism is the believer's participation in the divine nature through the Spirit of Christ from whom she derives life and righteousness by partaking of his body and blood in the Eucharist. In the sacraments, believers are united to Christ and become members of his body. As Jesus's earthly body was divinized through union with his divine nature in the incarnation, so too those who are united with him in baptism and Eucharist are justified (*iustificare*) by participating in his righteousness (*iustitia*). Augustine believes that salvation comes to humanity by a sacramental union of natures. The Christian's humanity is healed and sanctified because it is conjoined with the divinity of Christ through the Holy Spirit who is poured out into the heart of the believer. Therefore, since humanity is healed of its sinfulness and mortality by this sacramental participation in Christ's nature, the whole human race, which derived its nature from the first human beings, must have been corrupted by a participation in Adam's sin and the corrupting effect it had upon his nature.

Central to this argument, for Augustine, is Romans 5:12, which Augustine interprets radically differently from Pelagius. The Old Latin translation of the verse that Augustine read is as follows: "Through one man sin entered the world and through sin death and thus passed on to all human beings in whom [*in quo*] all have sinned." Whereas the Greek manuscripts and the Vulgate specify that "death passed on to all" the Old Latin does not specify the subject of "passed on" (*pertransiit*). Consequently, Augustine inferred that the subject was "sin" not "death." Thus, he read the passage as "and sin passed on to all" (*Pecc. merit.* 1.9.9).[5] Moreover, Augustine took the following clause "in whom all sinned" to mean that not only did Adam's descendants derive their nature from Adam, but they were *in Adam* when he sinned.[6] In *City of God*, Augustine famously writes, "But man was willingly perverted and justly condemned and so begot perverted and condemned offspring. For we were all *in that one man*, seeing that we all *were that one man* who fell. . . . We did not yet possess forms individually created and assigned to us for us to live in them as individuals; but there already existed the seminal nature from which we were to be begotten" (*Civ.* 13.14). Therefore, Adam's children inherit not only whatever corruption of his nature occurred by virtue of Adam's sin; they also inherit Adam's guilt. Adam's children share in his guilt and therefore also in his punishment, death, because being part of Adam, they sinned in Adam.

The death of Adam and the death of his descendants, therefore, result from two different sins. Adam died because of his own sin, while his descendants die

5. On this technical point, see Roland J. Teske, *Answer to the Pelagians*, part 1 (Hyde Park, NY: New City, 1997), 76 n. 14.

6. Both the Old Latin and the Vulgate are misleading here. They translate the Greek expression *eph' hō*, which means "because," as *in quo*, which means "in whom." Thus, Augustine's text of Rom 5:12 is decidedly different from the sense of the Greek: "and death passed to all people because all people sinned." Although Augustine's overall argument does not stand or fall entirely on his reading of this verse, the errors in the Old Latin text contributed to his argument about the transmission of original sin.

because of their parents' sin. This distinction Augustine finds in Romans 5:14: "But death reigned from Adam to Moses in those sins that were not like the transgression of Adam who was a type of the one who is to come." For Pelagius, there is no essential difference between the sin and death of Adam and those of his children. Both were mortal by nature and would experience bodily death regardless of sin. Both sinned by their disobedience and so suffered the death of their souls. The only difference between the two, Pelagius guesses, is that Adam's sin was by disobedience to an explicit commandment from God, whereas his descendants' sin was disobedience to the natural law (*Comm. Rom.* 5.14). For Augustine the difference is that Adam's death resulted from a voluntary sin, whereas his children lived under death because of sin that was theirs by inheritance, not by an act of will. "Hence, [death] reigned in those 'who did not sin in the likeness of the transgression of Adam,' that is, in those who did not sin, as he did, by their own personal will, but contracted *original sin* from him 'who is the pattern of what was to come'" (*Pecc. merit.* 1.11.13); here is Augustine's first use of the term "original sin."

Caelestius's rejection of infant baptism was a logical implication of his view of sin as individual and personal rather than corporate. Yet it begged a new question about the death of infants. If the death of the soul is the result of disobedience to God that is entirely voluntary, then infants who do not possess the capacity for making moral decisions are not in sin. Since, however, "the wages of sin is death" (Rom 6:23), why do sinless infants die? While Caelestius could have replied that this was merely the death of the body, not the death of their soul, he would still have had to explain the source of infirmity that causes the naturally mortal infant to die an unnaturally early death. For Augustine, since death is the punishment for sin, if infants are indeed sinless, then their death would be wholly unjust. The only way to make sense of the death of infants, which was an existential reality for many families in late antiquity, was their inheritance of original sin. Second, if infants are without sin and so not subject to divine punishment, do these infants have need of a savior? The logic of Caelestius's position would be "no," yet this answer exposed a profound weakness in his theory that flew in the face of orthodox teaching and practice. And Augustine knew how to exploit this vulnerability. Is Christ the Savior of all who are saved or is there another savior? He is the lone Savior of all. Is he, therefore, the Savior of infants? Who would deny it? To say otherwise would be to suggest that some people have no need of Christ's saving mercy. If, on the other hand, he is the Savior of infants who have not committed any sin on their own, then from what does he save them but "the disease of original sin" (*Pecc. merit.* 1.23.33)? Without Christ's grace that forgives original sin, infants who die before baptism, though they have the mildest of punishments (*Pecc. merit.* 1.16.21), nevertheless are not saved from God's anger. Augustine finds biblical support for the presence of sin in infants from birth in the words of David's great penitential psalm: "For I was conceived in sin and amid sins my mother fed me in the womb" (Ps 51:5). In what sense was David "conceived in sin"? One option, Augustine says, is that David was conceived in fornication. Since, however, David's mother and father were lawfully married, he was not conceived in illicit sexual relations. The only alternative is that he was born in original sin (*Pecc. merit.* 1.24.34). Children, therefore, need to receive the grace of baptism in order to expunge the guilt of original sin that they inherit from Adam.

How did corruption pass from Adam to his descendants? Although Augustine expressly rejected a traducianist theory of the soul, which held that the soul passed from parent to child through the father's seed, his notion that all of Adam's race was seminally present in Adam and so participated in his act of disobedience seems to follow the logic of a traducianist model. While a traducianist model worked to explain the transmission of original guilt, it was more problematic to explain the corruption of nature. In the thirteenth book of *City of God* written around 417, Augustine explains that Adam's nature was corrupted because of his sin. That corrupted nature was in turn passed down to his progeny: "in [Adam's] person, human nature was so changed and vitiated that it suffered from the recalcitrance of a rebellious concupiscence and is bound by the law of death. And what the first man became *by perversion and penalty*, this his descendants are *by birth*—natures subject to sin and death." According to this account, then, all human beings were born with Adam's corrupt and willful concupiscence. Ten years later, however, Augustine was forced to change his mind in response to the argument of his most challenging critic, a second generation Pelagian, Julian of Eclanum (386–455). More knowledgeable about human physiology and reproduction than Augustine, Julian was able to expose flaws in Augustine's argument at the level of biology and theology. The most damning theological argument, however, spoke to the nature of the incarnation. If the corruption of human nature in Adam had been passed down through procreation, then children simply inherit the corrupt nature of their parents. If that were the case, Julian reasoned, then Mary, too, possessed a corrupt human nature she received from her parents and that she in turn passed on to Jesus. Thus, Jesus's nature, too, was corrupt and so subject to the inner conflict between the disordered love (*concupiscentia*) in his members and the law of his mind. In one of his last works, *Against Julian*, Augustine revised his position. Instead of contending that human nature after Adam was corrupt in itself, Augustine claimed that the corruption occurred in the act of coitus. This marked a distinct revision of an earlier position. In his earlier works, Augustine rejects the Manichaean attribution of sin to sex. His commentary on Psalm 51:5 ("in sin did my mother conceive me") emphatically rejected this position: "It is not, therefore, that men are conceived in iniquity . . . because it is sin to have to do with wives; but because that which is made is surely made of flesh deserving of punishment. This chaste operation in a married person has no sin, but the original sin draws with it condign punishment" (*Enarrat. Ps.* 50.5). Sin and mortality were consequences of the flesh, not the act of sex. In his response to Julian, he reverses this position, quoting Ambrose's *On the Sacrament of Regeneration*: "Evilly did Eve give birth, thereby leaving to women the inheritance of childbirth, and the result that everyone formed *in the pleasure of concupiscence* and conceived in it in the womb and fashioned in it wrapped as in swaddling clothes, first undergoes the *contagion of sin* before he drinks the gift of life-giving air" (*C. Jul.* 2.6). Here Augustine follows a common view that the condition of the parents' souls during intercourse influenced the character of their child's soul. For instance, having marital relations while intoxicated, Plutarch believed, would produce children prone to alcoholism. Similarly, Augustine reasoned, the father's lust for his wife—the "vital fire" of concupiscence—at the time of conception meant that the father's seed was vitiated and thereby he passed on his own disordered concupiscence to his offspring through his seed (*C. Jul.* 3.13.26). Since Jesus's conception was by the Holy Spirit without sexual passion, his nature was not corrupted. In response to Julian's objection that Augustine's view of sex as the source of sin reflected a lapse back into his old Manichaean views (*C. Jul.* 3.12.24), Augustine countered that, contra the Manichees, he did not view sex itself to be evil (*C. Jul.* 3. 7.15). Chief evidence of this is that God made Adam and Eve for sexual relations, which they would have enjoyed in paradise without disordered passion. In such a case, their offspring would have experienced no corruption of their nature. Sex in the present age, however, is not as sex in Eden would have been. After the fall, no act of sex wholly escapes the disordered concupiscence that is the source of the contagion (*C. Jul.* 3.12.27). Thus, Augustine concludes that humanity is born from and with concupiscence. Although the birth itself is good, nonetheless the child is born with a corrupted nature that must be healed by grace (*C. Jul.* 3.21.46).

At the heart of Augustine's dispute with the Pelagians about original sin is a disagreement about the nature of nature. Nature for Pelagius is a substantial reality, and only substances can interact with each other so as to create a change in their respective natures. While milk is life-giving, if a poisonous substance is added to it, its nature changes, and it ceases to be the source of nourishment and becomes lethal. An act of the will, however, is not a substance. Therefore, Pelagius reasons that the will cannot alter human nature (*Nat. grat.* 19.21). Augustine counters that, though the will is not substantial, an act of the will can in fact alter nature. Someone who chooses to abstain from food will weaken his constitution such that he will become frail and vulnerable to illness or injury (*Nat. grat.* 20.22). The "absence of food" is not a substance; nevertheless, the lack of substance does materially affect a person's nature. Another more gruesome example is that a person can choose to cut his tongue out with a knife. That act of the will has irreparably altered his nature, depriving him of the natural capacity of speech (*Nat. grat.* 45.53). A more subtle example that is more analogous to the sin of the first parents is that of a man who voluntarily closes his eyes and shuts out the light. Not only does his choice deprive the eyes of the light necessary to see, but if he were to choose to keep his eye covered for an extended period of time—wearing a patch over one eye—eventually that eye's natural ability to see would be compromised. His eyesight would be weakened in that eye because of his choice to shut out the light. Therefore, Augustine reasons, an act of the will can affect capacities of one's nature. Moreover, the ability to see is not entirely a matter of either one's natural ability or will; it is dependent upon the presence of light (*Nat. grat.* 47.55). So too, when Adam closed his eyes to the light of wisdom, he became ignorant, and through him the human race dwelt in darkness and came to love the darkness rather than the light. Without the illuminating grace of baptism, which both heals the will, giving it the love of the light of wisdom, and heals the eyes of the soul by illuminating it with divine wisdom, sinful humanity will remain spiritually blind (*Pecc. merit.* 1.25.37).

The difference between will and nature is a critical point in Augustine's argument with Pelagius, because it gets to the heart of whether sinlessness is possible in this life. Both men agreed that Adam was free not to sin; thus, the fall was neither inevitable nor necessary. They also agreed that no person other than Jesus had in fact lived a sinless life. The point of departure was whether in this age sinlessness was possible. As Pelagius put it, the question is not whether any of Adam's descendants *are* in fact sinless, "what is the case," but whether anyone *might* be perfect, "what can be the case" (*Nat. grat.* 7.8). That is, is there anything about the human condition that makes sin inevitable? The only way sin would be inevitable is if there were some defect or corruption in the human nature that Adam's children inherited. Such a conclusion, for Pelagius, flew contrary to the logic of Scripture. Not only do the commandments of law assume the ability to obey those commands, but Jesus's command to his disciples, "Be perfect even as your heavenly Father is perfect" (Matt 5:48), assumes that human beings are able to fulfill this command and thereby merit the reward of eternal life. Pelagius went further to say that if people in an era before Christ had lived just lives, God would be unjust if he did not reward their justice. Such justice was possible independent of the revelation of Christ because they had the natural law (*Nat. grat.* 2.2). Appealing to Romans 10:2–4, "they, not knowing the justice of God, and seeking to establish their own, have not submitted to the justice of God. For the end of the law is Christ, so there may be justice for everyone who believes," Augustine counters that Pelagius is positing a source of justice and thus salvation apart from Christ. For the justice of God (*iustitia Dei*) is not contained in the precepts of the law—or presumably in the natural law—but is the gift of grace in Christ. Pelagius's argument that some might be righteous independent of the revelation of Christ, either prophetically in the Old Testament or the incarnation, contradicts Paul's pronouncement in Galatians 2:21: "For if justice is through the law, Christ died in vain" (*Nat. grat.* 1.1). Pelagius, Augustine argues, is positing a path to salvation not dependent on Christ, who as the great physician came to bring healing to those whose nature bears the wounds of sin.

The lives of holy men and women, whom Scripture speaks of as just, were for Pelagius obvious examples of those who at least by the end did not leave this life in a state of sin (*Nat. grat.* 35.41). In addition to biblical examples, including Enoch, Melchizedek, Abraham, Hannah, John the Beloved Disciple, Pelagius points to Mary the mother of Jesus as the definitive example of one who was perfect and who "we are obliged out of piety to confess was without sin" (*Nat. grat.* 36.42). Sharing Pelagius's pious devotion to Mary, Augustine here grants that Mary was without sin because she received such an abundance of grace that she was able to be sinless. Yet in the case of all the rest, he asks rhetorically who of them would not have prayed, "forgive us our sins," or confessed with John, "If we say we have no sin, the truth is not in us" (1 John 1:8)? Or would such confessions be mendacious expressions of insincere humility? Whether all the holy individuals Pelagius mentioned were sinless, Augustine counters, misses the point. The real question is whether these holy ones were holy simply by exercising a *natural* capacity for faithfulness and righteousness or because they were endowed with grace that *healed* their nature and enabled them to possess "the love of God to such a degree of perfection that nothing can be added" (*Nat. grat.* 42.49). Such sinlessness, Augustine concedes for the sake of argument, is at least theoretically possible but is not possible without the aid of grace. While humanity was endowed with free will at its creation in Eden, since then humanity's condition is not that of Adam before the fall but of the man in Jesus's parable, whom the good Samaritan, a figure of Christ himself, rescues from death on the roadside, binds his wounds, and carries him to an inn to convalesce (*Nat. grat.* 43.50). At present, humanity remains in the inn undergoing treatment and awaiting restoration to full health at Christ's return. Even then in a state where nature has been entirely healed and mankind is in perfect health, as Adam and Eve experienced in Eden, humanity will be sustained in sinless perfection through grace "as light gives aid to healthy eyes" (*Nat. grat.* 48.56). Yet in the present where the corruptible body is such a burden upon the soul, being sinless is even less possible apart from the aid of grace. Augustine's central point is that human nature is insufficient either to attain or retain sinless righteousness. Human nature was graced in the beginning inasmuch as it was capable of receiving the illumination of the Wisdom of God. For Adam this was through partaking of that Wisdom represented by the tree of life, so that he was given immortality and with it the ability to enjoy the natural end for which he was made, namely unceasing fellowship with God. Since the fall, his descendants' nature is so compromised that they are unable to turn to God for help, much less live a life of perfect love and obedience, apart from the healing and sustaining work of grace. Such healing and divinizing of fallen humanity would fall to the incarnate Christ and the Spirit given to Adam's descendants.

Bibliography

Primary Sources

Apocryphon of John. In *The Gnostic Scriptures*. Translated by Bentley Layton. Garden City, NY: Doubleday, 1987.

Augustine of Hippo. *Against Julian*. Translated by Matthew A. Schumacher. Fathers of the Church 35. Washington, DC: Catholic University of America Press, 1957.

———. *City of God*. Translated by Henry Bettenson. London: Penguin Books, 1972.

———. *Literal Meaning of Genesis*. Translated by John Hammond Taylor. Ancient Christian Writers. New York: Paulist, 1982.

———. *On True Religion*. Translated by Edmund Hill. In *On Christian Belief*. The Works of Saint Augustine: A Translation for the 21st Century 1/8. Hyde Park, NY: New City, 2005.

———. *Punishment and Forgiveness of Sins and the Baptism of Little Ones*. In *Answer to the Pelagians*. Part 1. Translated by Roland J. Teske. Hyde Park, NY: New City, 1997.

Gregory of Nyssa. *Catechetical Oration* [*GNO* 3/4]. Pages 268–325 in *Christology of the Later Fathers*. Edited by Edward R. Hardy. Philadelphia: Westminster, 1954.

———. *Gregory of Nyssa: On the Human Image of God*. Translated by John Behr. Oxford: Oxford University Press, 2024.

———. *On the Making of Humanity* [*GNO* 4/2; PG 44:125–256]. In *Gregory of Nyssa: Dogmatic Treatises*. *NPNF* 2/5. Translated by William Moore and Henry Austin Wilson. Grand Rapids: Eerdmans, 1988.

———. *On the Soul and Resurrection* [*GNO* 3/3]. Pages 171–248 in *Macrina the Younger, Philosopher of God*. Translated by Anna M. Silvas. Turnhout: Brepols, 2008.

Irenaeus of Lyons. *Against Heresies*. *ANF* 1.

Origen of Alexandria. *On First Principles: A Reader's Edition*. Translated by John Behr. Oxford: Oxford University Press, 2019.

Ptolemy. *Epistle to Flora*. In *The Gnostic Scriptures*. Translated by Bentley Layton. Garden City, NY: Doubleday, 1987.

Secondary Sources

Behr, John. *Asceticism and Anthropology in Irenaeus and Clement*. Oxford: Oxford University Press, 2000.

———. *Irenaeus of Lyons: Identifying Christianity*. Oxford: Oxford University Press, 2013.

Blowers, Paul M. *Drama of the Divine Economy: Creator and Creation in Early Christian Theology and Piety*. Oxford: Oxford University Press, 2011.

Boersma, Hans. *Embodiment and Virtue in Gregory of Nyssa: An Anagogical Approach*. Oxford: Oxford University Press, 2013.

Cadenhead, Raphael A. *The Body and Desire: Gregory of Nyssa's Ascetical Theology*. Oakland: University of California Press, 2018.

Couenhoven, Jessie. *Stricken by Sin, Cured by Christ: Agency, Necessity, and Culpability in Augustinian Theology*. Oxford: Oxford University Press, 2013.

Greer, Rowan A. *Broken Lights and Mended Lives: Theology and the Common Life in the Early Church*. University Park: Pennsylvania State University Press, 1986.

Meconi, David Vincent. *On Self-Harm, Narcissism, Atonement, and the Vulnerable Christ*. New York: Bloomsbury Academic, 2020.

Smith, J. Warren. *Passion and Paradise: Human and Divine Emotion in the Thought of Gregory of Nyssa*. New York: Herder & Herder, 2004.

Wessel, Susan. *On Compassion, Healing, Suffering, and the Purpose of the Emotional Life*. New York: Bloomsbury Academic, 2020.

Wetzel, James. *Augustine and the Limits of Virtue*. Cambridge: Cambridge University Press, 1992.

Zachhuber, Johannes. *Human Nature in Gregory of Nyssa: Philosophical Background and Theological Significance*. Leiden: Brill, 2000.

4

"So Through One Man Came Life"

Christology Before Nicaea

Around the year 112, the Roman governor of the Asian provinces of Pontus-Bithynia, Pliny the Younger interrogated a group of Christians whom frustrated pagans blamed for the emptiness of the pagan temples and the decline in the sale of meat used in pagan religious rituals. Lacking a knowledge of any precedent for dealing with Christians, he wrote a letter to the emperor Trajan seeking his counsel. In the letter, Pliny recounts the information about this new superstition that he extracted from the accused under torture, "the sum of their guilt or error amounted to no more than this: they had met regularly before dawn on a fixed day to chant verse alternatively among themselves in honour of Christ as if to a god" (*Ep.* 96.7). In roughly the same period, the Christian bishop of Antioch, Ignatius, wrote a series of letters to churches of Asia Minor and Rome in which he described Jesus as "the mind of God" (Ign. *Eph.* 3.2) who is "united with the Father" (Ign. *Magn.* 1.2) and "who before the ages [*pro aiōnōn*] was with the Father and appeared at the end times" (Ign. *Magn.* 6). Of this appearance, Ignatius declares to the Christians of Smyrna, "our Lord . . . is truly of the family of David in respect to human descent, Son of God with respect to will and power" (Ign. *Smyrn.* 1.1).

In both Pliny's account of the Pontic Christians' testimony and Ignatius's quasi-creedal confessions, Jesus was the object of worship and was declared to be divine. Yet neither explains exactly how Jesus's divine status is to be understood. From Pliny's perspective, did the honor Christians gave to Jesus as divine mean nothing more than that he was viewed as an apotheosized hero, like Hercules? What, for a Christian insider like Ignatius, did it mean to say that he is the Son of God according to will and power? Were his will and power understood to be a gift from the Father, or are they held to be intrinsic to his nature as Son of God? If they are his by nature, is Christ equal to the Father in divinity, or does he possess a lesser degree of divinity? Did saying that he was "before the ages" mean that his life was coextensive with the Father's or he simply came from the Father for the purpose of fashioning creation?

At its core, Christology in the second and third centuries follows two lines of reflection. The first is the Trinitarian question about the relationship of the Father and the Son—how to make sense of John 1:1: "In the beginning was the Word, and the Word was with God, and the Word was God." The second line concerns the incarnation, making sense of John 1:14: "And the Word became flesh." A strong commitment to the divinity of Christ among some Christians provoked the concern that union with flesh would compromise his divinity or that it was simply impossible. How could an all-powerful God become a helpless infant? How could a supremely blessed deity remain blessed while enduring the passion of the cross? How could the immortal God who is life itself be said to die? In sum, how could the divine Word take on the finitude of a mortal creature and still retain all the attributes of his divinity? Both lines of inquiry wrestle with the theological task of reconciling God's transcendence and immanence. Unlike the god of Aristotle, who as the first efficient cause sets all in motion but otherwise is entirely turned in upon himself contemplating his own perfection, the God revealed in the narrative of the Jewish and Christian Scriptures is the Creator who remains engaged with his creation and is involved in the lives of individuals. Christians, however, were not the first to face the challenge of holding together God's transcendence and immanence. This task had already been taken up a century before Ignatius by the Jewish philosopher Philo of Alexandria.

Philo of Alexandria: The Beginnings of a Logos Theology

The early Church historian Henry Chadwick has observed that "the history of Christian philosophy begins not with a Christian but with a Jew, Philo of Alexandria."[1] Nowhere are Philo's influence on and anticipation of later Christian theologians more clearly seen than in his Logos theology. In his allegorical interpretation of Genesis, *On the Creation of the World*, Philo draws upon elements of both Plato's cosmology developed in *Timaeus* and the Stoic idea of the *spermatikos logos* or seminal reason. From Plato, he took the idea of the Craftsman (*dēmiourgos*) who used the eternal ideals of the intelligible realm as patterns (*paradeigmata*) by which he fashioned the material universe. From the Stoics, he adapted the idea of a seminal reason that pervades the cosmos and provides order and regularity. Philo identified this seminal reason (*logos spermatikos*) with the word or Logos in Psalm 32:6 (LXX): "By the word of the Lord [*tō logō tou kyriou*], the heavens were made, and all their host by the breath of his mouth." The material world

1. Henry Chadwick, "Philo," in *The Cambridge History of Later Greek and Early Medieval Philosophy*, ed. A. H. Armstrong (Cambridge: Cambridge University Press, 1967), 137.

that God creates is for Philo, as for Plato, a reflection of an intelligible cosmos or realm of ideals or archetypes. However, unlike *Timaeus,* in which the ideals that serve as patterns for the material world are eternal and uncreated, in Philo's *On the Creation of the World,* the patterns are not eternal but are created and correspond to "the heavens and the earth" that God fashioned on the first day of creation (Gen 1:1). In his wisdom, Philo explains, God "understood in advance that a beautiful copy [i.e., the material world] would not come into existence apart from a beautiful model. . . . Therefore, when he decided to construct this visible cosmos, he first marked out [*proexetypou*] the intelligible cosmos so that he could use it as an incorporeal and most god-like paradigm . . . [to fashion] the corporeal cosmos" (*Opif.* 16).

What then was the relationship between the intelligible patterns and the Logos? Even as the Stoic Logos was the rational principle that orders nature, so too the Platonic patterns impose a rational order on chaotic, primal matter by giving it form. Yet because the God of Judaism, unlike the entirely immanent Stoic Logos, transcends his creation, Philo adapts the Stoic Logos, giving it a transcendence akin to the intelligible forms of Plato's cosmology. And yet because Philo's God alone is eternal and is the lone necessary being on which all other things depend, Philo's patterns must somehow express the beauty and goodness of God's eternal nature while at the same time being contingent creatures. Philo's solution is to locate the patterns in God's Logos, that is, in God's mind or reason, as when an architect first designs the blueprints for a building in her mind (*Opif.* 20) before beginning construction. Initially, therefore, the Logos is identical with the intelligible cosmos; for the Logos is simply God's creative reasoning (*Opif.* 24). Even as "the entire sense-perceptible cosmos . . . is a representation of the divine image," Philo reasons, "the archetypal seal, which [is] the intelligible cosmos, would itself be the model and archetypal idea of the ideas, the Logos of God" (*Opif.* 25). In calling the Logos the "idea of ideas," it is comparable to Plato's form of the Good that is the one source of all other forms and so is the principle of unity for creation. It also implies that the patterns are an image of the divine beauty proper to God's Logos. Because God is self-sufficient and needs no other being, God does not need to create; rather, he does so out of his munificence. He fashions finite creatures in order that they might share in the goodness of his divine being (*Opif.* 21). Of these creatures, humanity is supremely blessed because God fashioned no model for people but made his own Logos the pattern in whose likeness humanity was made (*Opif.* 129). Therefore, human beings share more directly and more fully in God's intelligible beauty and goodness than any other material creature.

Against the backdrop of this allegorical reading of the first day of creation lie certain key questions. Earlier in *On the Creation of the World,* Philo draws a line between the visible and the invisible realms. The visible, material creation is inherently mutable and so belongs to the realm of beginning and becoming (*en genesei kai metabolais*), whereas the invisible realm is ingenerate (*agenēton*) and eternal (*Opif.* 12). One sees in Philo's cosmology a tension between, on the one hand, his preservation of the Platonic division of the eternal, intelligible realm of being and the temporal, sensible realm of becoming and, on the other hand, his Jewish commitment to preserving the uniqueness of God's eternal being. Yet Philo's final position is ambiguous. At times he appears to be saying that the intelligible cosmos corresponds to God's Logos and thus the intelligible patterns are eternal ideas in the mind of God. In other places, he seems to say that the Logos was not eternally a part of God but itself gained being only when God planned creation.

Speaking of God as Maker and Father, Philo identifies God as the "active cause" in contrast with the passive object and then attributes to God the active cause a transcendence above all universals. He is "absolutely pure and unadulterated intellect of the universe, superior to excellence and superior to knowledge and even superior to the good and the beautiful itself" (*Opif.* 7–8). God is not one beautiful or good thing among other good and beautiful things. He is the source of goodness and beauty but in his transcendence is not himself conditioned by them. When Philo comments on the seventh day, he explains its significance by appealing to the Pythagorean account of the number seven—a number that neither generates nor is generated—to speak of God's transcendent holiness as "superior to every form of speech . . . [and] more wonderful than the words to describe it" (*Opif.* 89–90). Here he echoes Plato's famous pronouncement in *Timaeus* (28c): "Now to discover the Maker and Father of this universe were a task indeed; and having discovered him, to declare him unto all men were a thing impossible." Quoting the fourth-century philosopher Philolaus, Philo declares, "The only being who neither changes nor is changed is the very ancient Ruler and Director, of whom seven would fittingly be an image . . . [to quote Philolaus] 'There exists the Director and Ruler of all things, God who is one, always existent, abiding, unchanged, himself identical to himself and different from all others'" (*Opif.* 100). God transcends human speech because in his eternal and immutable nature he is absolutely unique.

Commenting on God's assessment of Adam's solitude, "It is not good that the man should be alone, let us make for him a helper like unto him" (Gen 2:18), Philo explains that such solitude properly belongs only to God. "It is good that the alone should be alone; God being One is alone and unique, and there is nothing like God . . . [meaning] that neither before creation was there anything with God, nor, when the universe had come into being, does anything take its place with him; for there is absolutely nothing which he needs" (*Leg.* 2.1–2). Such a description affirms the Jewish Creator-creature distinction expressed in the words of the psalmist, "Who,

O God, is like you?" (Ps 72:20 LXX), and is an apt description for the God confessed in the Shema, "Hear, O Israel, the LORD is God. The LORD is one" (Deut 6:4). Nevertheless God's uniqueness raises a problem. God's simplicity creates an epistemic gulf between God and rational creatures. If like is known by like and yet God is utterly unique, then he stands beyond human comprehension and verbal expression. How then is theology or worship possible? How can humanity have genuine knowledge of God or at minimum speak truthfully about the divine? The only categories or names that can aptly be applied to God are "the one" (*to hen*) and "the monad" (*hē monas*) (*Leg.* 2.3), which express God's uniqueness, or "the Most High" (*ho hypsistos*), which Scripture uses to express God's transcendence of all creatures (*Leg.* 3.82). Here, too, lies the essential problem that Middle Platonists faced. The solution—indeed Philo's most significant contribution to Middle Platonism—he located in the idea of God's Logos. For Philo, the Logos became not simply a faculty of the divine mind but a mediator between God and creation. This mediatorial work began with the Logos's role as God's instrument (*organon*) of creation (*Leg.* 3.96). When he speaks of the Logos in this instrumental capacity, Philo draws a distinction between God the archetype (*archetypon*) or pattern of the image (*paradeigma tēs eikonos*) and the Logos, which is the shadow of God (*skia theou*) or image of the pattern. Therefore, when he interprets Genesis 1:27, "And God made man after his image," Philo, equating the image with the Logos, concludes, "the image had been made such as representing God, but man was made after the image when it had acquired the force of a pattern" (*Leg.* 3.96; cf. 1.31). Thus, in Philo's anthropology, there is a threefold distinction between God (archetypal pattern), the Logos (image of God and pattern for human nature), and Adam (image of the image/Logos).

As mediator, the Logos is described by Philo in personal terms. In his treatise *On Agriculture*, Philo says that the good of shepherding is so great that it is attributed to God "the All-Sovereign" in Psalm 23. The flora and fauna on earth and the celestial bodies of the heavens are God's "hallowed flock," which he "leads in accordance with right and law, setting over it his true word and firstborn son (*logon kai prōtogonon huion*) who shall take upon it his government like some viceroy of a great king" (*Agr.* 50–51). Philo identifies the Logos as the Son of God in his *Life of Moses*. Having said that the high priest who intercedes for the forgiveness of sins is consecrated to the Father of the world, he says that the priest should have the "Father's son with all his excellence to plead his cause" as a "pattern enshrined in his heart and so in a sense be transformed from a man into the nature of the world" (*Mos.* 2.134–135). Thus, the priest must bear the image of the Logos who himself was the pattern for the world. Indeed, the high priest in his vestments is an image of the heavenly high priest, the Logos (*Migr.* 102). As mediator, the Logos seems to occupy a middle place in the hierarchy of being between God and creatures. It is precisely because he holds a place between the Creator and his creation that the Logos is able to mediate the knowledge of God to humanity—as he does in the theophany of the burning bush—but also forgiveness and mercy.

> His Word, His chief messenger, highest in age and honour, the Father of all has given the special prerogative, to stand on the border and separate the creature from the Creator. This same Word both pleads with the immortal as suppliant for afflicted mortality and acts as ambassador of the ruler to the subject. He glories in this prerogative and proudly describes it in these words "and I stood between the Lord and you," that is neither uncreated as God, nor created as you, but midway between the two extremes, a surety to both sides; . . . [declaring] "I am the harbinger of peace to creation from that God whose will is to bring wars to an end, who is ever the guardian of peace." (*Her.* 205–206)

As the image of the Father, the Logos is able to reveal the transcendent, uncreated one to created beings and to be active providentially in their lives. In this way, Philo was able to apply a Platonic metaphysical account of the first principle to articulate the transcendence of the God of Israel's faith while at the same time providing an explanation of God's immanent presence.

While the Logos allows Philo to reconcile God's transcendence and immanence, another set of questions arises. His description of the Logos as the shadow or image or only begotten Son of God implies a distinction between God and his Logos. As the image, the Logos is intimately connected to God and yet is not simply God's reason. Indeed, the Logos has to be something other than the transcendent God in order to fulfill its mediatorial or high priestly function. So it appears to be an entity whose existence is distinct from the Father. Yet, ontologically speaking, how can the Logos stand between the created and the uncreated? Is the Logos a semidivine being who is not God but not one of the creatures that the Logos itself made either? Moreover, if the Logos is indeed distinct from the Father, when did it gain its discrete identity and existence? Has it always coexisted with God, or did God alone beget the Logos for the purpose of creation? One option is that the Logos existed seminally in God but was begotten later to be the Father's agent of creation and his mediator. In this case, the Logos has no independent existence from eternity but acquires a hypostatic identity in relation to creation. This would certainly make sense if the Logos is identified with the intelligible cosmos, the idea of ideas that nonetheless reflects the Father's goodness and beauty.

For the purpose of Christian theological history, these questions do not need to be answered. Nevertheless, they are worth raising precisely because they are implicit in Philo's reading of key passages of shared Scripture and because they anticipate the christological questions with which Christians from the second century on would have to grapple. If Christians were familiar with Philo's theory of the Logos, as they most certainly were, and were influenced by the theory as they began to think through the logic of the prologue of John's Gospel, then these same questions consciously hung over their contemplation of the Logos who as the only begotten Son abided with God in the beginning but who in the fulness of time "became flesh and dwelt among us" and by his death, resurrection, and ascension became the Church's "Great High Priest." To be sure, because Christians of late antiquity possessed a Bible that expanded beyond the Jewish Scriptures to include Jesus's life and the mission of the apostolic Church, the gospel narratives would have confronted them with theological problems about the relationship of God the Father and his Son even if they had no previous knowledge of Philo. The task of Christian theologians, therefore, was not primarily to solve the riddles in Philo's interpretation of Torah but to explicate what John means when he identifies Jesus of Nazareth with the Logos. Indeed, the Christian narrative in which the Logos assumes a mortal human nature and is crucified and dies adds a level of complexity for thinking about the Logos far beyond what Philo encountered in narratives of Genesis and Exodus. How does one explain the ontological relationship of God the Father and the Logos who hangs upon Golgotha's tree? Nevertheless, the attraction of Philo for the early Christians lay not only in his Platonized readings of the Pentateuch but in their shared fundamental challenge: reconciling God's transcendence with his immanent participation in the life of creation.

Justin Martyr: A Christian Logos Theology

Writing well over a century after Philo's death, Justin, a teacher in the Catholic community in Rome, drew on the Stoic idea of the Logos in his defense of Christianity during a period of persecution in the capital. In two petitions addressed to the emperor Antoninus Pius, his sons, and the Senate, his main tack was to argue that people should not be arrested and executed solely because they bore the name "Christian" but rather only for actual crimes—crimes that ignorant men had falsely attributed to Christians (*1 Apol.* 4; *2 Apol.* 2). Within this apologetic project, Justin's theology of the Logos arises in response to two specific accusations leveled against Christians: first, that they were atheists, and second, that their religion was mere opinion (faith) without a rational foundation. Responding to the first accusation, Justin dismisses the charge of atheism by distinguishing the Roman deities, which were not gods at all but demons born of intercourse between angels and mortals, from the Christian God. Although he speaks of God as "Father of righteousness" (*1 Apol.* 6), "Father and Ruler" (*1 Apol.* 12), "Father and King of the heavens" (*2 Apol.* 2), and "Father of all" (*2 Apol.* 6), Justin almost always speaks of

God together with his Son and prophetic Spirit. Yet the Father is clearly distinct from the Son, whom he identified as the Logos. For the Father is transcendent, being unbegotten (*1 Apol.* 14), eternal and immutable (*1 Apol.* 13), and possessing ineffable glory (*1 Apol.* 9); whereas the Son is begotten by the Father (*1 Apol.* 14) and therefore holds second place to the Father (*1 Apol.* 13).

Justin's identification of Christ, whom the Christians worship, with the Logos served the apologetic purpose of aligning the God of Christianity with the one entity that the emperor and his sons, as adherents of Stoicism, viewed to be the true God, the *spermatikos logos* or the seminal reason that was the ordering principle of the cosmos. Years later, writing on campaign with his legions on the German frontier, Marcus Aurelius in his *Meditations* would explain Stoic pantheism. All things in the universe, he explains, are material; there is no transcendent spiritual or intelligible substance, such as Plato advocated. But there is one reason that pervades the universe and is common to all rational creatures (*Med.* 7.9). Although the Logos is not a personal entity, the *spermatikos logos* not only functions as the ordering principle of nature but also the source that imparts a share of the rational nature to human beings. As such the *spermatikos logos* is, as Marcus describes it, the beginning and end of all things and so governs the eternal cycles of nature from the big bang that is the beginning to the conflagration of all things with which each cycle ends (*Med.* 5.32). So the emperor, speaking to himself about himself, concludes, "You have subsisted as part of the whole. You shall vanish into that which begat you or rather shall be taken again into its seminal reason [*logon spermatikon*] by a process of change" (*Med.* 4.14). Because the human intellect is derived from the all-pervading reason, human beings are able to live the virtuous life of conforming to reason and nature.

By invoking the *spermatikos logos*, Justin's apology sought to stake out common ground with the philosophically minded emperor. Since Christ is the Logos, he argued, Christians worshiped the same being whom the Stoics recognize as the source of all things. Therefore, the Christian life of obedience to Christ the Logos is not a life contrary to reason but a life in conformity with the supreme reason that is the guiding principle of the virtuous life for Stoics (*1 Apol.* 14). Consequently, Christian faith, which philosophers denigrated as mere opinion rather than reasoned understanding, is not at all antithetical to reason. Rather, God endows human beings with reason that they might be persuaded rationally of the truth of Christianity and so be led by reason to faith (*1 Apol.* 10). Furthermore, the Stoic idea that in each human being was implanted a seed of reason from the *spermatikos logos* also provided an analogy for incarnation of the Logos in Jesus (*1 Apol.* 5). In sum, his argument creates a link between Christian belief in one God and the incipient monotheism in certain philosophical schools. In other words, the God whom the Christians worship is the God of whom all people have some innate knowledge and who, at a very basic level, corresponds to the God taught by Socrates. Therefore, not only are Christians not atheists, but their faith, far from being irrational, accepts rational doctrines about God that were maintained by philosophers—doctrines, Justin asserts, the philosophers first learned from Moses (*1 Apol.* 59).

More than demonstrating common ground between Christianity and philosophy, Justin's appeal to the Logos gave him ground to launch a counterattack against philosophical critics of Christianity—a tactic more apt to reassure Christians of the righteousness of their cause than to persuade their persecutors. For by invoking the Logos, Justin sought to pit the emperor's philosophical commitments against pagan Roman religion. As philosophers, the emperor and his sons should have a more sophisticated view of divinity than the common Roman who went to temples to offer sacrifices to Jupiter *Optimus Maximus*. Like philosophers, Justin was suggesting, the emperor should know that the many gods and goddesses whose conduct was ruled by base passions rather than reason were not the divine reason that governed the universe. The implication was that the emperor, if he were true to his philosophy, would not believe in the Roman gods any more than the Christians did. Therefore, if Christians are to be charged with atheism and impiety, Justin is arguing, then let us, as men of reason, be clear that we are talking about the true God. Indeed, the surest evidence that the pagan religion was incompatible with philosophy, Justin argued, was that also Socrates, whom all the major philosophical schools revered, was persecuted by defenders of the pagan religions because the demons in the guise of gods hated him, fearing that lovers of wisdom who honored the true God would expose them as mere pretenders to divinity (*2 Apol.* 8). By supporting the persecution of Christians in defense of pagan religion, the emperor and the Senate were not on the side of philosophers who seek truth but the demons who corrupt reason by their deceptions. Far from possessing wisdom, they have allowed themselves to be deceived and are acting out of ignorance rather than knowledge (*1 Apol.* 2–3). As such, the persecutors of Christianity are on the side of the Athenian jury that sentenced Socrates to death—something no true philosopher would do.

Although Justin's approach is designed to give philosophical credibility to Christianity—if not in the opinion of pagan philosophers, at least in the minds of his fellow Christians—it also allowed him to make the case for the superiority of Christianity not only to the pagan religions but to the various philosophical schools as well. On the one hand, since Socrates, Heraclitus, and Plato's souls were endowed with a greater share of the Logos, which allowed them to see through the demons' deceptions, they possessed much of the same wisdom that Christians had (*2 Apol.* 13). Thus, Christians can and should appreciate the truths of philosophy and use those insights to express or deepen their understanding of

Christian doctrine. On the other hand, however, Jesus was not simply possessed of a seed of reason from the Logos, as was Socrates, but was the Logos in its totality revealed in human form (*2 Apol.* 8). Therefore, since Jesus is the whole Logos and not merely a part of the Logos, Christian doctrine possesses greater wisdom than do the philosophers (*2 Apol.* 10). Christians have a fuller, and therefore more profound, knowledge of God. Moreover, by claiming that Christ the Logos is second in power to God the Father who begat the Logos (*1 Apol.* 32), Justin is able to assert that the God of Christianity is greater than the Stoic *spermatikos logos*.

Justin's adaptation of the Stoic *spermatikos logos* serves more than an apologetic purpose. For Justin was writing not solely to nonbelievers but to his fellow Christians. Regardless of whether one believes Justin knew the prologue of John's Gospel, Justin certainly uses the Logos, possibly adapted from Philo, as a way of addressing problems surrounding both the relationship between God the Father and Jesus and humanity's ability to know the transcendent Creator. Justin draws on Plato's description of God in *Timaeus* (28c) as beyond human speech—quoting the passage twice—to stress God's incomparable otherness and superiority to all things. He explains that God has no proper name, because such a name can be given only by one who is superior (*2 Apol.* 6), as when a parent names their child. Since, however, God is unbegotten, there is no one prior or superior to God who could give him a name. "Father" and "Creator" are not truly names but appellations given by the creatures based on God's deeds. Even "God" is not a name but merely signifies the idea or opinion that such a first, unbegotten being exists—an idea implanted in the mind by virtue of humanity's being endowed with a rational nature. Justin is not going so far as to say that God is incomprehensible. Plato after all says that finding God is only difficult, not impossible. Indeed, the Son's role as teacher was to reveal the transcendent Father and to exhort human beings to seek understanding through rational contemplation (*2 Apol.* 10).

In what sense is the idea of God "implanted" in humanity? One possibility is that "God" is an innate idea such as Socrates advocates in *Meno*. This seems unlikely since Justin nowhere argues for the human soul's preembodied existence in the heavenly realm of ideas, where the vision of the ideas becomes implanted in memory and is later recovered by dialectic. More likely, Justin maintains as Paul argues in Romans 1:20–21, that because human beings have been made rational, they are able to reason from nature to the existence of nature's Creator. Though such is plausible, the idea of God in Paul's argument is grasped through inferences drawn from nature rather than implanted. The other possibility is that by virtue of being made rational, humanity possesses a natural affinity with the divine Logos. Moreover, by being conscious of their own rationality, human beings have an innate knowledge of the divine that is the source of their rational nature.

Even with this natural knowledge of God, the Father remains transcendent and therefore is ineffable. Although Justin finds confirmation for this view in *Timaeus*, the source of this view is Jesus's declaration, "No one knows the Father except the Son; nor the Son except the Father, and those to whom the Son will reveal him" (Matt 11:27). Since the ineffable Father is known only through the revelation of the Son, Justin interprets the Old Testament theophanies, such as God's appearance to Moses in the burning bush on Mount Horeb, as the work of the Logos (*1 Apol.* 63). Because the Logos—the Word who spoke to Moses—is the Son begotten by the Father, the Logos is able to disclose the will of the Father to humanity.

One point of complication in Justin's Logos theology is his interpretation of "the angel of God" (Exod 3:6) as the Logos. Likely drawing on Jewish angelology, he describes the Logos and the Spirit in the same terms as angelic beings called "Powers" to indicate their authority and capacity to act on behalf of God. Furthermore, Justin explains that the Logos is called an angel in Exodus because he took the form of an angel just as he took the form of the pillar of fire and cloud and finally the form of man, Jesus. Yet Justin also writes that, while the Logos appeared in the likeness of an angel, Jesus is both divine and yet possesses an outward resemblance to human beings because he possesses a genuine human nature taken from his earthly mother, Mary. "The Father of the universe," Justin writes, "has a Son; who also, being the first-begotten Word of God, is even God . . . [but now has] become man by a virgin, according to the counsel of the Father, for the salvation of those who believe in him" (*1 Apol.* 63). The Christian's saving belief in the ineffable Father is given in baptism, which Justin calls the washing of illumination in which the initiate is forgiven, reborn, and given a new understanding of the Father (*1 Apol.* 61). Thus, Justin links the mediatorial role of the Logos with the redemptive ritual of baptism.

This then raises the question: If the Logos primarily serves this mediatorial role of divine angel and apostle, how did Justin understand the Logos's divinity? Was the Son begotten solely to fulfill this mediatorial role? It is essentially the same ambiguity in Philo's account of the Logos. Was the Logos begotten from eternity or was he begotten simply before God's plan of creation was set in motion? If the former, the Logos would have a relationship intrinsic to the Father's being. If the latter, the Logos as mediator would exist only in an instrumental relationship between God and creation. Justin never resolves the question. Nor does he even seem conscious of the problem. Nevertheless, he asserts the Son's divinity. Unlike theologians in the third and fourth centuries, he makes no explicit connection between his claim that the Logos is "begotten" by the Father as his "only proper son" (*1 Apol.* 23) and the Father's nature. Indeed, the language of "nature" is altogether absent. Although he compares Jesus with the sons of Jupiter, his point is merely apologetic: Romans should not think Jesus's being born of a virgin peculiar if they believe in the numerous progenies born of Jupiter's amorous liaisons with mortal women.

Rather, Justin speaks of the Logos's divinity in two ways. First, he justifies the claim that Jesus is the Logos incarnate by appealing to Old Testament prophecy. That Jesus's birth, life, and passion were foretold by prophets was, he asserted, confirmation of Jesus's identity as the Logos since only the Logos and his prophetic Spirit could be the source of the mortal prophets' foreknowledge. Second, and more importantly, Justin speaks of Christ's divinity in terms of his divine power. Writing in an almost creedal formula, Justin links divine sonship and power: "Jesus Christ is the only proper Son of God who was begotten by God, being his *Logos* and *first-begotten* and *power*; and becoming man according to his will, he taught us these things for the conversion and restoration of the human race" (*1 Apol.* 23). Jesus's persuasive ability to make the sexual profligates chaste, to turn devotees of magic from their demonic arts, and to convert enemies driven by tribal hatred into brothers who pray for their enemies was evidence that his words were not the product of sophistic artistry but the power of God (*1 Apol.* 14). Although Jesus was "a man by ordinary generation," his identity as Son of God was confirmed by his wisdom and the actions in which the Father's wisdom was revealed (*1 Apol.* 22). Although intellectual faculty marks humanity's share in the *spermatikos logos*, Jesus's ability to free men from the deception of the demons and to arouse such trust in his words that his followers would die for him rather than submit to the demons—the greatest evidence of their conversion to the life according to the Logos—could be explained only in his possessing "power of the ineffable Father, and not the mere instrument of human reason" (*2 Apol.* 10). Even though Justin refers to the Logos as "in the second place" to the Father (*1 Apol.* 13) and as "the power of God, and the first power after God" (*1 Apol.* 32), Justin envisions a hierarchical relationship between the Father and the Son based on the Son's having been begotten by the Father. From the hindsight of the fourth century, the absence of "nature" language makes it unclear whether Justin maintained an ontological hierarchy in which the Father is superior in his divinity to the Son. Justin endeavored to make sense of the occasionally contradictory evidence in Scripture itself by means of a Middle Platonic system that promised to resolve such tensions, but only at the cost of a trinitarian theology that would soon prove untenable from the perspective of pro-Nicene efforts two hundred years later to affirm the Son's consubstantiality with the Father.

Marcion and the Gnostics

As Plato's demiurge and patterns in *Timaeus* allowed him to build a bridge between the eternal realm of forms and the sensible material realm described in *Republic*, the Logos of Philo and Justin functioned similarly, linking the transcendent I AM with his creation. With Marcion and the Gnostics of the second century, that connection is either wholly absent or tenuous at best.

In Marcion's case, Christ is a mediator neither as the transcendent Father's agent of creation nor as the revealer of the Creator and his law to Israel. Rather, Marcion's catalogue in his *Antitheses* of the contradictory descriptions of God in the Jewish Scriptures and those in the letters of Paul and the gospel led him to posit two deities. One, the God of Israel, was the demiurge who in his foolishness created the material world that is the cause of error, ignorance, and the passions. He is the God of righteousness who offers salvation to those who adhere to the law that he gave to his servant Moses. The other God is the God revealed by Jesus. This God Marcion calls an alien God, because prior to the preaching of Jesus, this God was unknown to the world. He did not create the world; therefore, he could not be known indirectly through nature. Moreover, there were no prophets to whom he revealed himself and who then foretold the coming of Jesus. Marcion did not have a developed Christology. Nothing was said of Christ's relationship with the alien God before Jesus's ministry. It is likely that he did not maintain a doctrine of the incarnation. Since he believed that matter was the source of evil and corruption, Marcion's Jesus was not truly human. Although he had the outward appearance of a person, he was not truly embodied. The heart of Jesus's message, as properly understood by Paul, was that salvation lies not in obedience to the law of the Creator God but through faith in God the merciful and compassionate who commands love of neighbor and enemy alike. Marcion's Christ brought salvation by liberating humanity from the dominion of the Creator God and the burdensome demands of the law.

Far more extensive than Marcion's influence were the sects of Christians who identified themselves as Gnostics (*gnōstikoi*) or "the knowing ones." While, generally speaking, they shared Marcion's view of the material world and its creator, they possessed a highly developed Christology based on their elaborate cosmological myths. Although the teachings of the various sects of Gnostics bore a certain family resemblance to each other, there was no monolithic religion called Gnosticism. Nor is it clear how the gnostic schools were connected to each other, if they were at all. Nevertheless, there were communities of Gnostics from Gaul to the Upper Nile and from Carthage to Mesopotamia. By the mid-third century, most of these communities were absorbed into the Valentinian church. But in the fourth century, the Gnostics had split into smaller groups: the Archontics, Sethians, and Barbelites.

The Gnostics adopted this name because the salvation they received was the gift of *gnōsis*, which means "knowledge." This salvific knowledge was not propositional knowledge—what the Greeks would call *epistēmē* or Romans *scientia*—but a personal knowledge or acquaintance associated with "self-awareness" or more specifically "God-self-consciousness" derived from revelation of secret teachings of Jesus. The Gospel of Thomas, for example, purports to contain the "obscure" or "hidden" utterances of Jesus that he disclosed to Didymus Jude Thomas. The salvific power of these intentionally cryptic sayings is that by their very obscurity, they provoke the quest for understanding (cf. Gos. Thom. 33.10). However, the liberating truth to which they point is not available to all. For Jesus did not reveal it to all the disciples; only to Thomas. Thus, the Gnostics see themselves as an intellectual elite who are heirs of Thomas who possess knowledge to which other Christians do not have access.

The secret *gnōsis* that separates the Gnostics from other people, Christian or otherwise, is that the kingdom of God is inside of them and that they are "children of the living father"; herein lies their identity: "If you do not become acquainted with yourselves, then you are in poverty, and it is you who are the poverty" (Gos. Thom. 32.19–33.2). Indeed, the reason Jesus pulled Thomas aside from the other apostles is that he would become the apostle of the Gnostics because he is Didymus, the Twin, who knows that he is Jesus's twin. As Jesus says to him, "Now, since it is said that you are my double and my true companion, examine yourself and understand who you are, how you exist, and how you will be. Inasmuch as you are going to be called my sibling, it is not fitting for you to be unacquainted with yourself. . . . So for this reason, Thomas, my brother, you have personally seen what is obscure to humankind" (Gos. Thom. 138.4–20). Thus, Thomas is the paradigmatic Gnostic, and through his gospel, his followers escape the poverty of self-ignorance and acquire the self-acquaintance of God-self-consciousness—that is, the awareness of one's inner spark of divinity.

The identity of Christ who brings the salvation of self-awareness is complex. There is no single normative christological grammar governing gnostic theology. Yet the Apocryphon of John, which Bentley Layton calls the "classic gnostic myth," provides a cosmological narrative that contains many of the themes common in gnostic texts. According to the secret of John, in the beginning there was only the Realm of Light in which dwelt God the First Principle, who is called alternatively the Father-Mother or Virgin Spirit. God is the uncontaminated monad (Ap. John 2.26) who is unlimited (Ap. John 3.6) and entirely self-sufficient (Ap. John 3.1). The First Principle is unique and therefore transcends all categories of human thought or speech. Consequently, God can be spoken of only in entirely negative language: he is superior to deity (Ap. John 2.35) and neither corporeal nor incorporeal (Ap. John 3.24). As such, God exists, but not as one of the things that exist (Ap. John 3.26); nevertheless, from God flows the spring of living water that overflows, giving life to all that is (Ap. John 3.21). From the Parent emanates (Ap. John 5.10) the Second Principle or Barbēlō—also known as the Beforehand or Forethought (Ap. John 3.31)—who gazes upon the Parent alone and gains for itself acquaintance because of what shines out from the Parent (Ap. John 4.1–16) and therefore is the image (Ap. John 4.32) or spark (Ap. John 6.13) of the Parent. The Barbēlō is the active intellect of the Parent; therefore, from Barbēlō emanates the Plērōma or Entirety, which consists of intelligible entities or aeons. Among the beings in the Plērōma are the Holy Spirit or Afterthought (Ap. John 27.33ff) and the Christ who is described as either the spark of the Barbēlō anointed by the Holy Spirit (Ap. John 6.23) or the offspring of Barbēlō and the Holy Spirit (Ap. John 7.18–19).

It is the Christ of the Barbēlō who is sent to deliver the children of Adam and Eve trapped in the material Realm of Darkness fashioned by the demiurge, Ialdabaōth. Sophia, mother of the demiurge, took pity on humanity and through Afterthought, the Holy Spirit, gave Eve the gift of Life (Zoē) so that she possessed *gnōsis* of the Realm of Light. The children of Adam and Eve—Cain, Abel, and Seth—were allegorized as representing the three races of men. The descendants of Cain were materialists who were so lost in error and ignorance that they lay beyond hope of redemption. The children of Seth were spiritual by nature and so could be awakened to the truth. These were the gnostic elect. Abel's offspring were called the animates or Soul people who were a middle sort between the materialists and the spirituals. They might or might not be receptive to the gnostic gospel. So they possessed the hope of deliverance, but it was not a certain hope. Into the darkness, Christ as the spark or memory of the Barbēlō came to reveal the reality of the Spiritual Realm to those whose soul possessed the spark of life and wisdom given by Sophia and were capable of receiving the truth. He awakened them to the truth that the world in which they lived was ultimately not real. It was a fraud and an illusion. Christ declares, "O Listener, arise from heavy sleep. . . . It is I who am the thinking of the virgin spirit (i.e., the Parent) and who am leading you to the place of honor. . . . And be wakeful (now that you have come) out of heavy sleep and out of the garment in the interior of Hades" (Ap. John 31.4–20). It is unclear how literally to take the language of deliverance to a "place" where the soul is liberated from the body and the corruption of material existence. Most likely it is simply a place of right self-knowledge where one is no longer deceived by the senses and lives with a certain knowing detachment from the material world and its illusory forms of happiness.

Valentinus (100–175) was an influential teacher of a school in Rome in the middle of the second century—the same time as Marcion and Justin—and may even have aspired to become bishop of Rome. He simplified and adapted the narrative of the classic gnostic myth so that it more closely resembled the language of Catholic Christianity. In his sermon the Gospel of Truth, Valentinus presented his salvation narrative. The intellectual entities that comprised the Plērōma were the thoughts of the Father. The Son or Word was an emanation from the Plērōma (Gos. Truth 16.33) who was predestined by the Father to bring hope to humanity.

The Word came into the world for proclamation of the truth so that those people who were ignorant of the Father might be ransomed (Gos. Truth 17.1). In their ignorance, people suffered from fear and agitation and so became subject to the erroneous opinion that material beauty was real and true (Gos. Truth 17.14–17). The fog of ignorance and error led to a state of forgetfulness, forgetfulness of God their source and thus their own identity (Gos. Truth 17.33). Therefore, the Word came as a teacher to reveal the *gnōsis* that the Father is God and is to be discovered within themselves (Gos. Truth 18.27–31). The Word thus revealed "the living book of the living" that was the thought of the Father from the foundation of the world but that had been incomprehensible until it was revealed by the Word (Gos. Truth 19.34–20.3). But such truth is available only to the gnostic elect whose names have been spoken by God (Gos. Truth 21.25).

Although Valentinus wrote that Jesus "became patient and accepted the sufferings even unto taking up that book" (Gos. Truth 20.10), the Gospel of Truth gives no account of the incarnation. In a fragment preserved by Clement of Alexandria, Valentinus wrote cryptically, "Jesus digested divinity: he ate and drank in a special way, without excreting his solids. He had such a great capacity for continence that the nourishment within him was not corrupted" (frag. E). The implication was that the Word was not born in the manner of a typical human being. Irenaeus relates a gnostic doctrine that held that the Word passed through Mary's womb like water through a tube. Still others held the heavenly Savior descended upon the man Jesus and through him declared the Father before returning to the Plērōma. The actual union of the Word with a human body is less important to Valentinus than his outward appearance; for he writes that Jesus "appeared [and] wrapped himself in that document [i.e., the living book]" which he published when he was nailed to the cross (Gos. Truth 20.19–27). Jesus's crucifixion is principally an image for the elect of being awakened to the truth, which entails a death to the world, a putting off of the corrupt rags of human flesh and clothing oneself in an incorruptible knowledge that frees one from fear, error, and forgetfulness. Those who receive the teaching of Christ discover their identity as being "enrolled in the book of the living, learning about themselves, recovering themselves from the father to return to him" (Gos. Truth 21.3).

The Egyptian Gnostic Basilides—possibly a teacher of Valentinus—taught that the material world was created by some lower angels, the chief of whom established himself as the God of the Jews. The unbegotten Parent took pity on humans and sent Christ, the firstborn Intellect, to save people from the angels that created the world. He only "appeared on earth as a man and he performed deeds of power" but did not suffer on the cross. Rather, Christ gave Simon of Cyrene the form of Jesus so that he was crucified in the place of Christ, who all the while stood by laughing at his enemies (*Haer.* 1.24.3–7).

Because of their highly dualistic view of matter and spirit, Gnostics tended to speak of Christ as having only the outward, visible "appearance" of a man—like a ghost or a hologram—but without assuming corruptible and corrupting flesh. It is a Christology that later historians would call docetic—coming from the Greek *dokein* meaning to "appear" or "seem." The Gospels of Luke and John, if responding to teachers of a docetic Christology, at least felt the need to affirm the material nature of Jesus's resurrected body by including accounts of the risen Jesus's asking for a bit of fish to eat when he appeared to the disciples after the resurrection (Luke 24:39). Among earliest evidence for this docetic Christology is found in the letters of Ignatius of Antioch. Writing to the Trallians, he warns them, "Be deaf, therefore, whenever anyone speaks to you apart from Jesus Christ, who was of the family of David, who was the son of Mary, who *really* [*alēthōs*] was born, who both ate and drank, who *really* was persecuted under Pontius Pilate, who *really* was crucified and died . . . who, moreover, *really* was raised from the dead when his Father raised him up" (Ign. *Trall.* 9.1–2). Ignatius's repetition of the intensifier "really" suggests that people against whom he is warning the Trallians were teachers who taught that Christ was not in fact born of Mary and therefore lacked a mortal human body capable of suffering death on a cross. Ignatius seems to have had a similar concern when he emphatically reminded the Christians at Smyrna, "Regarding our Lord, you are absolutely convinced on the human side that he was actually sprung from the line of David . . . truly born of a virgin . . . truly nailed in the flesh. . . . And after his resurrection, he ate and drank with [the disciples] like one who is composed of flesh, although spiritually united with the Father" (Ign. *Smyrn.* 1.1–2; 3.3). But then Ignatius goes to the existential heart of the matter by linking the doctrine of the incarnation with his own martyrdom: "For if these things were done by our Lord in appearance only, then I am in chains in appearance only. Why, moreover, have I surrendered myself to death, to fire, to sword, to beasts?" (Ign. *Smyrn.* 4.2). His point: unless Christ truly possessed a mortal body, and not merely its visible form, then he did not truly die. If he did not truly die, then there was no bodily resurrection. And if Jesus's crucified body was not raised from the dead, then Ignatius, like Paul, was most pitiful of all men because he had no hope of life beyond death. Then the dismemberment of his body at the claws of the beasts in the arena was the end of his life, and all its pleasures he would have thrown away for nothing. Even if he were to have believed in the immortality of the soul—a point for which there is no evidence in the letters—Ignatius's focus is on Jesus's incarnation, death, and resurrection as the foundation of the hope that enabled him to face his fear of the horrific death that awaited him in Rome. Thus, this docetic Christology posed an existential threat to Ignatius personally and to a Church grounded in the hope of the resurrection.

Ultimately, Valentinus and the gnostic tradition offered a thoroughly intellectualized account of the gospel. It appealed to a certain type of self-styled Christian intellectual who thought of salvation as knowledge. Such knowledge set them apart from the naive and simplistic Christians whose lives were caught up in this world as if it were ultimately real. Therefore, Christ did not need to have a real body in order to reveal what was real. Their focus on salvific *gnōsis* meant that other details of Jesus's life and ministry included in the Four Gospels of the Catholic Scriptures were omitted altogether or drastically reinterpreted. The cross, for instance, was not depicted as an altar where Christ the high priest offered himself as a sacrifice for the forgiveness of sin. For Christ did not come to reconcile the Creator with his creatures who turned away in disobedience and fell into death. Rather, Christ's death and resurrection were given an entirely spiritualized meaning. Jesus is the prototype of the Gnostics who rises above the fear of death and the love of the material world. He is dead to the world, which has no hold on him because he knows it is not ultimate reality. He is risen in the sense that he is freed from the prison of the Creator's deception and lives in the liberating knowledge that he is a spark of the divine and so can transcend the bondage of the material world.

This docetic Christology ultimately rested upon a cosmology that narrated a radical divide between the heavenly intelligible realm of God and the material world of the demiurge. Therefore, the gnostic theory of salvation is neither a healing perfection of creation nor a restoration of the paradise that was in the beginning. It has a negative character—"deliverance from" more than an "actualization of." Christ is not the fulfillment of a divine plan but the rectifier of the ill-conceived act of an ignorant demiurge. Even when the Gnostics preserve, through allegorical interpretations, elements from the Jewish Scriptures, their salvation myth is disconnected from the history of Israel and the Creator who was the God of Abraham, Isaac, and Jacob. It was, therefore, a Christianity not only without a creation story but without an exodus narrative or the law of Sinai, without a Davidic kingdom or the prophetic promises of a Messiah, without the psalms or apocalyptic visions. In short, it was Christianity without a past, without a historical trajectory. As we have already seen, by the mid-second century the Great Church had gone its own way and was a religion distinct from Judaism. And the theological writings of the period sought to confirm the Church's identity—over against Judaism—as the true heirs of God's promises to Israel. Nevertheless, Gnosticism posed for Catholic Christianity a central theological question: Can a religion that worships Jesus as the Christ, the Son of the living God, have coherence apart from the narrative of the Creator's covenantal relationship with Israel and his providential design to draw all peoples to himself? Or to put it in christological terms, what is the relationship of Jesus to the God of Israel's history? The Great Church, therefore, faced two christological challenges: first, the need to demonstrate that the Creator God of Israel was the same God whom Jesus called

Father; second, the need to refute the various docetic or Adoptionist Christologies by showing the oneness of Christ as the Father's Son truly incarnate in the fully human Jesus of Nazareth. These challenges were taken up by Irenaeus of Lyons (120/140–203) in his *Against Heresies*.

Irenaeus and the Christ of Salvation History

Unlike the Gnostics' dualist ontology, the ontological foundation of Catholic theology was its teaching that there is one God and God is one. This is a theme that Irenaeus repeatedly underscores. Having summarized various doctrines of God he deems heretical in book 1, he begins laying out the Catholic position in book 2, declaring, "It is important, then, that I should begin with the first and most important head, that is God the Creator. . . . There is nothing either above him or after him . . . since he is the only God, the only Lord, the only Creator, the only Father, alone containing all things and himself commanding all things into existence" (*Haer.* 2.1.1). Whereas in the classic gnostic myth, there are two worlds, one within the Plērōma and one outside the Plērōma, each coming from a different Creator (*Haer.* 4.19.3), the only true God is himself the Plērōma because he "contains all things in his immensity" (*Haer.* 2.1.2), which is the meaning of the Hebrew names for God, *Elōeim* and *Elōeuth* (*Haer.* 2.35.3). Irenaeus, however, is not advocating a form of Stoic pantheism. For God contains all things but is himself uncontained (*Haer.* 2.30.9). This is the way Irenaeus affirms the marvelous relationship between God's transcendence of creation and his immanence with the whole of the created order. God can be the principle of unity for creation precisely because he is "the uncreated One" (*Haer.* 4.38.3). All that is exists because he willed their existence; therefore, nothing stands outside of his will. Yet he alone is "the Lord of all, [who] is without beginning and without end, being truly and forever the same, and always remaining the same unchangeable being" (*Haer.* 2.34.2). Therefore, God himself is uncircumscribed and unconditioned by anything that he created. Furthermore, God the Father of all is unknown except by his Son (*Haer.* 4.6.3). Yet because his Son eternally coexists with the Father and is the one through whom the world was made and in whom the Father is manifest to his creatures (*Haer.* 2.30.9), God has always been active in creation.

For Irenaeus, it was this ontology that lent theological coherence to the divine economy—that is, the salvation narrative of Scripture from Genesis to the Apocalypse—and it was precisely this theological coherence that the gnostic and Marcionite narratives lacked. Thus, the goal of *Against Heresies* was to offer a sweeping account of salvation history that would demonstrate the essential unity of the ministry of Jesus and the Old Testament's narrative of creation, fall, and redemption in the covenantal history of Israel. In other words, Irenaeus's goal was to show that Jesus's life and proclamation of salvation as related in the Catholic Scriptures, which were also read by the heretical groups, made no sense apart from Israel, and therefore, that the narratives of the two testaments should be read as a single integrated whole. Irenaeus articulated this with his theory of dispensations, the climax of which was Jesus in whom Christians see most fully both the face of the one God, their Creator, and the face of humanity as God intended it from the beginning.

The biblical passages that provided the organizing principle for Irenaeus's Christology and his vision of the unity of the testaments were Matthew 11 and Paul's Adam typology in Romans 5 and 1 Corinthians 15. Summing up his position, Irenaeus writes, "The Son of God did not then [i.e., in incarnation] begin to exist, being with the Father from the beginning; but when he became incarnate, and was made man, he commenced afresh the long line of human beings . . . so that what was lost in Adam—namely the image and likeness of God—we might recover in Christ Jesus" (*Haer.* 3.18.1). As Adam had been the father of the human family, now in the incarnation, Irenaeus declares, Jesus has become the progenitor of a line of Adam's family remade in the image and likeness of God. Thus, Christ is the second Adam; for Irenaeus goes on to quote the apostle: "Paul knew no other Christ besides him alone who both suffered and was buried and rose from the dead, who was also born and whom he speaks of as man. . . . [Paul] continues, rendering the reason for the incarnation, 'For since by man came death, by man [came] also the resurrection of the dead' (1 Cor 15:12)" (*Haer.* 3.18.3).

Irenaeus explains Christ's fashioning a new line of humanity as a "recapitulation" (*recapitulans*)[2] of the first Adam (*Haer.* 3.18.7) and as a new "dispensation" of liberty in the knowledge of God. Christ, as the second Adam, is a recapitulation of the first Adam in two senses. First, following Paul's typology, Irenaeus depicts Jesus's life as an inversion of Adam's. It is not simply that Adam, who was disobedient and brought death to himself and his descendants, was the antitype of Jesus, who was perfectly obedient and so restored life to Adam's family. But in Jesus and the Virgin Mary, Irenaeus imagines a reenactment of Adam and Eve's life—their lives as they should have been. He does so to illustrate Paul's insight: God in the incarnation was remaking humanity by making a new founder of the human race. So that Jesus might truly be a recapitulation of Adam, it was appropriate that Jesus have a beginning analogous to that of Adam. Therefore, as the Word had formed the first Adam taking his substance from virgin soil that had never been tilled, now the Word formed the second Adam in the womb of a virgin (*Haer.* 3.21.10). As Eve, who was still a virgin since she was not yet an adult, brought death upon herself and her offspring by her disobedience, so now Mary, who was yet a virgin, brought salvation to herself and the human race by her obedient submission to God. "For what the virgin Eve had bound fast [i.e., humanity] through unbelief, this did the

2. From the verb *recapitulo*, which is the Latin translation of the Greek *anakephalaioō*.

Virgin Mary set free through faith" (*Haer.* 3.22.4). As Adam had by his disobedience descended into the house of death, now Christ in his obedience descended to the house of death to "bind the strong man and spoil his goods," setting the first Adam and his descendants free (*Haer.* 3.23.1). Thus, as Satan had held disobedient humanity captive in death, now by an obedient man was Satan held captive. As the first parents were deceived by the serpent, now the second Adam has crushed the head of the serpent who bruised the first Adam's heel (*Haer.* 3.32.7; 5.21.1).

The second sense of Christ as the recapitulation is that, since Jesus is Son of God as well as a Son of Man, he possesses the perfect image and likeness of God and therefore *sums up* human nature as God intended it to become from the beginning. No human being had—or could—reflect the virtues of his Creator as Jesus did precisely because he himself is the image of God, the archetype, in whose likeness humanity was originally fashioned. Yet whereas the divine image in the first Adam was immature—and ultimately corrupted by sin—the second Adam is mature humanity. The potential for perfection with which the first Adam had been endowed at his creation was fully actualized in the second Adam. And through Christ, those who are his descendants through being united with him in baptism receive the potential to share in his perfection as far as humanly possible through the restoration of the image and likeness of God in themselves (*Haer.* 4.38). For as Adam was a type of Christ, so Christ's life is a type or model for the life of the new line of humanity of which he is the father. At his baptism in the Jordan, the Spirit anointed Jesus not because he received from the Spirit anything that he did not already possess as Son of God. Rather, the Spirit's anointing of him in his humanity, as a son of Abraham, set a model for the anointing of the descendants of the second Adam at their baptism (*Haer.* 3.9.3; 3.17.1). For in receiving Christ's Spirit in baptism, the believer is united to Christ and is renewed in his image and likeness. Indeed, in the Christian's baptism, there is a recapitulation of the birth of the first Adam. For as God breathed into Adam his living Spirit, which was later lost due to sin, now in baptism God breathes his Spirit on the believer (*Haer.* 5.1.3). Only through the gift of the Spirit is one made perfect—in the sense of being the complete human being God wills one to be—by becoming spiritual (*Haer.* 5.6.1). Through the Spirit's indwelling, the soul is turned from a carnal orientation to the spiritual goods of the Father. Playing with Paul's analogy of the wild olive branch that is engrafted into the cultivated olive tree, Irenaeus says that by the Spirit the baptized are engrafted onto Christ and begin to bear the spiritual fruit that is the sign of "the pristine nature of man—that which was created after the image and likeness of God" (*Haer.* 5.10.1).[3] Thus, little by little as the believer comes to partake of fellowship with her adoptive heavenly Father, she is being made perfect

3. For a fuller account of Irenaeus's pneumatology, see chapter 7, pp. 280–83.

as she more and more conforms to the image of Christ (*Haer.* 5.8.1). This image of the Spirit engrafting the baptized into Christ gives another sense to the word recapitulation. Etymologically, the root of both the Latin *recapitulo* and the Greek *anakephalaioō*, which are translated "recapitulation," is the word for "head" (*caput* and *kephalē*). Therefore, recapitulation is literally "receiving a new head." Such may be in Irenaeus's mind when he explicates Paul's image of Christ as the head of the body. As firstborn from the dead (Col 1:18), the risen Christ is the head of the body—that is, those who are united to him by baptism. As the head of the body, Christ who by his obedience overcame sin and death now gives the hope of resurrection to those who were under condemnation because of disobedience but now are members of his body through the Spirit's engrafting (*Haer.* 3.19.3). The head of the serpent has been crushed. The human family has a new head, no longer the first Adam but Christ Jesus in whose resurrection Irenaeus sees an image of the perfected humanity that awaits at the general resurrection.

The theory of recapitulation, as an elaboration of Paul's Adam typology, drew a clear line between gnostic narrative with its docetic Christ and the Catholic confession of the incarnation. The salvific work of Christ, for Irenaeus, was not reducible to the disclosure of hidden knowledge. It was nothing short of the re-creation of humanity in himself. Assuming the mere outward form of a man was not enough. In order to become the second Adam, the Son of God had to be a full member of Adam's family through an actual incarnation. Irenaeus, therefore, rejected the gnostic two-substance Christology in favor of a unitive Christology. When characterizing the gnostic view as "dividing the Lord . . . saying that he was formed of two different substances [*altera substantia* or *allēs hypostaseōs*]" (*Haer.* 3.16.5), he does not mean by "different substances" different natures, since he describes the incarnation as the union of divine and human natures. Rather, "substance" here means "discrete entities" or "persons." Thus, Irenaeus characterizes the Gnostics as subscribing to a "two-subjects" Christology.[4] Whereas the Gnostics maintained two Christs, one the heavenly Savior and the other the man Jesus on whom the heavenly Savior descended for a time before ascending to heaven rather than sharing in the man Jesus's passion on the cross (*Haer.* 3.11.3), Irenaeus affirmed the union of the Word and a human nature in a single person. Against those who maintained "that Jesus was he who was born of Mary but Christ was he who descended from above," Irenaeus pressed back, asking where the gospels make such a distinction. Matthew (1:18), for instance, does not say, "Now the birth of Jesus was thus," but, "Now the birth of Christ was thus" (*Haer.* 3.16.2). Therefore, Matthew makes no distinction; the Christ who descended was the same Christ who was born a helpless infant. The Logos who had always been present with the human race now in Mary's

4. For the later development, see chapter 8, pp. 328–36.

womb became "united to and mixed with his own creation," to form a human being who was divine and human (*Haer.* 3.16.6). The logic was that if the Christ were to be the recapitulation of the human race, he must participate in the full spectrum of the human experience from birth to death (*Haer.* 3.18.7). This is why Irenaeus emphasized so strongly the role of Mary. Not only must Christ have the same nature as Adam's family; he must derive it from one of Adam's children (*Haer.* 3.23.1). Otherwise, he would not be a member of the family but a mere copy (*Haer.* 3.21.10). Nor was it satisfactory, as one sect of Gnostics taught, that the heavenly Christ was incarnate but passed through Mary's womb like water through a tube. "Superfluous," Irenaeus retorted, "is his descension into Mary; for why did he come down into her if he were to take nothing of her?" (*Haer.* 3.22.2). Only by being born of woman could he possess a nature that was susceptible to all the weaknesses of Adam's children—hungering in the wilderness or being weary after his journeys or weeping over the loss of a friend or "exceedingly sorrowing in his soul"—that Scripture records he experienced.

Indeed, perhaps in no place does Irenaeus better confront the difference between heretical views of the incarnation and orthodox views than in the question of Christ's impassibility. Earlier in the second century, Ignatius argued vehemently against those who held such a lofty view of Christ's divinity that they denied the reality of Christ's birth as a human being, his death on the cross, and his bodily resurrection. Irenaeus builds upon this point, insisting that Christ is one and therefore Christ truly suffered and died even as he was truly raised. Pointing to Jesus's reply to Peter's confession, "You are the Christ, the Son of the living God" (Matt 16:16), Irenaeus argues that Jesus not only affirms Peter's words but then explains what it means for him to be the Christ, namely that he must go to Jerusalem where he would be crucified. Matthew gives Irenaeus further ammunition against those who denied Christ's passion when he tells that Jesus explicitly rebuked Peter for refusing to believe that the Christ would suffer and die (*Haer.* 3.18.4). Moreover, appealing to Jesus's rebuke of the disciples on the way to Emmaus, "O thoughtless ones and slow of heart to believe" (Luke 24:25), Irenaeus argues that Jesus's passion should not have been a surprise since it was the fulfillment of the teachings of Moses, the prophets, and the Psalms (*Haer.* 3.16.5). While such an argument would not be persuasive to heretical groups that denied the authority of the Old Testament, nevertheless it illustrates that—unless, like Marcion, one imagines all the Old Testament references in Luke to be later interpolations—the gospels take as a given that the Old Testament foretells the Christ's advent and passion. Therefore, Irenaeus contends it is not appropriate to divide Christ into Jesus who suffered and died and the heavenly figure who was "incomprehensible, invisible, and impassible" and therefore did not share in Jesus's passion. Rather, he sums up the orthodox alternative:

> There . . . is one God the Father, and one Christ Jesus, who came by means of the whole dispensational arrangements, and gathered together all things in himself. But in every respect too, he is man, the formation of God; and thus he took up man into himself, the invisible becoming visible, the incomprehensible become comprehensible, the impassible become capable of suffering, and the Word being made man, thus summing up all things in himself; so that as in super-celestial spiritual, and invisible things, the Word of God is supreme, so also in things visible and corporeal he might possess the supremacy, and, taking to himself the preeminence, as well as constituting himself the head of the Church he might draw all things to himself at the proper time. (*Haer.* 3.16.6)

Irenaeus here envisions the incarnation not simply as God's condescension to human nature but also the elevation of humanity into union with God. As he put it elsewhere, "the Son of the Most High . . . would become the Son of Man for the purpose that man also might become the son of God" (*Haer.* 3.10.2). Yet drawing humanity into fellowship with God as children of God was possible only by the condescension of the Son. If, therefore, the incarnation is a true union of the divine and the human into a single Christ, then that union meant that in Christ one sees properties and powers belonging to both his humanity and his divinity. In other words, Irenaeus assumes that the Word in his divinity is invisible, incomprehensible, and impassible. But in his accommodation of humanity, he takes on the human qualities of being visible, comprehensible, and capable of suffering. Yet rather than seeing these creaturely qualities as diminishing or compromising Christ's divinity, Irenaeus envisions the Word's union of the divine and human natures giving Christ preeminence as the second Adam by allowing humanity to participate in the supremacy of his divinity.

What, for Irenaeus, was the salvific benefit of the impassible Word's entry into creaturely suffering? How does Christ's passion contribute to the recapitulation of Adam in Jesus? The incarnation as a true union of the divine Word and with human nature in one man was necessary for the redemption of humanity. Irenaeus's logic follows the Pauline typology. If Jesus is to be the father of a new humanity, then he must be fully like the first Adam in order to correct his error. Since it was by the disobedience of a man that humanity became subject to death and the devil, it was necessary that a human being be the one to perform the act of obedience. God, he explains, "caused man to cleave to and to become one with God. For unless man had overcome the enemy of man, the enemy would not have been legitimately vanquished" (*Haer.* 3.18.7). Even though humanity was God's creature, humanity voluntarily handed itself over to sin and death and so had made the devil its master. Therefore, God could not simply seize humanity from Satan; humanity had to break Satan's claim by a genuinely voluntary act of perfect obedience. Yet Irenaeus recognizes that weakened human nature was not capable of securing the victory all by itself: "And again: unless it had been God who had freely given salvation, we could never have possessed it securely" (*Haer.* 3.18.7). The law exposed that Satan had no ultimate claim on Adam and his heirs. Though the law exposed sin, it could not free humanity from sin and death. Therefore, the one who would reconcile God and humanity must be the God-man in whose single person Creator and creature exist in true fellowship of unity. Christ the God-man is the archetype for the communion between God and human beings characteristic of the new humanity from the line of the second Adam. For by his humanity, Jesus was a man who rightly owed the perfect obedience that the first Adam failed to give. But in order for Jesus to be a true recapitulation of the first Adam, Jesus, too, had to be tempted. In other words, his act of obedience had to be the deliberate choice of submission to God over the false promises of Satan. Therefore, the Word, instead of overpowering Jesus's humanity and rendering him impassible and therefore incapable of suffering temptation, held back his divine power so that the second Adam might endure temptation, suffering, and death (*Haer.* 3.19.3).

Although Irenaeus does say that Jesus became, to use Paul's language (Gal 3:13), a curse for us (*Haer.* 3.18.3), his emphasis is primarily on Jesus's obedience as the means of reconciling God and humanity. Nevertheless, because Jesus is the God-man, his humanity was empowered by his divinity such that he was enabled to conquer Satan both by resisting his tempting promises and by breaking the bonds of death. For by virtue of the union of divinity and humanity in the second Adam, mortal Jesus was able to descend to Hades—again passing through all the first Adam endured—where in his immortal divinity he might bind the Strongman and plunder his house, liberating humanity from death's clutches.

The resurrection and ascension mark the climax of Christ's recapitulation. For as Jesus's humanity allowed him to be tempted and die, his divinity allowed him to be glorified and partake of the Father's immortality. Indeed, the very weakness and vulnerability of the flesh allow the power and glory of God to be revealed. Jesus's triumph over Satan's temptations and his resurrection from the dead are evidence that the flesh and spirit are not antithetical as in the gnostic cosmology. Countering the gnostic appeal to Paul's words "flesh and blood cannot inherit the kingdom of God" (1 Cor 15:50), Irenaeus points to the incarnation as evidence of the adaptable nature of matter. The flesh, by itself, is weak and subject to decay. But the union of the Spirit with flesh gives to the flesh a potency that overcomes its weaknesses. Indeed, the frailty of the flesh is absorbed into the life-giving force of the Spirit (*Haer.* 5.9.2). The "flesh and blood" that will not inherit the kingdom of God does not refer to the material substance of the person; rather, it refers to those who lack the Spirit and so are spiritually dead. Since "without the Spirit of God we cannot be saved," Irenaeus explains, "the apostle exhorts us through faith and chaste conversation to preserve the Spirit of God, lest, having become nonparticipators of the divine Spirit, we lose the kingdom of heaven" (*Haer.* 5.9.3). Rather, the flesh can be ruled and given a spiritual character by the Spirit. As Irenaeus puts it, the flesh may not inherit the kingdom, but it can be inherited—that is, claimed and raised up—by the Spirit (*Haer.* 5.9.3). Then the body becomes, as God intended it, a temple in which his Spirit dwells (*Haer.* 5.7.2). The believer knows this, says Irenaeus, when the Spirit bears witness to her adoption in the cry "Abba Father" (Rom 8:15). Through this adoption by Christ's Spirit as children of God, the baptized become members of the new line of Adam's family. Through the Spirit of adoption, believers participate in Christ's recapitulation of the first Adam by being remade in the image of the second Adam. Yet, although the Christian is restored to the image and likeness of God, she also surpasses the first Adam because her likeness is that of Christ who is the perfect image and likeness of the Father.

Irenaeus's theory of Christ's recapitulation of the first Adam and of the believer's participation in that reality through the Spirit's adoption articulates the fundamental difference and incompatibility of the gnostic and Catholic narratives of salvation. Using Paul's Adam typology, he affirms not only that the Father through his Son was the Creator of embodied humanity in the beginning but that salvation is rightly understood as the redemption of that material creation. The gnostic narrative of God's liberation of humanity from the material mess created by an ignorant demiurge is replaced with the perfecting of the good but fallen world through the hallowing of the material creation. Whereas the gnostic divide of spirit and matter remains an irreconcilable conflict, the incarnation and bodily resurrection prove the greater power of God in the harmonious integration of spirit and matter. For the descendants of the second Adam become immortal not by being liberated from the body as from a prison but when the flesh is made spiritual by the gift of Christ's Spirit (*Haer.* 5.8.1). This divinization of weak and mortal flesh was, for Irenaeus, proof of God's words to Paul, "My power is made perfect in weakness" (2 Cor 12:9); for then "that flesh shall [at the resurrection] be found fit for and capable of receiving the power of God, which at the beginning received the skillful touch of God" (*Haer.* 5.3.2). The Marcionite and gnostic theodicy shielded God from any responsibility for evil of the material world. Such responsibility falls entirely upon the demiurge. The heavenly Savior makes a path through the darkness for humanity to escape the evil world in which they were made and of which they were victims. By contrast, Irenaeus's God descends into the moral chaos by becoming a passible creature so that creation might be healed of evil. By the union of God and humanity in Jesus the one Christ empowered humanity to take responsibility for the evil created by their disobedient use of free will. By his perfect and voluntary obedience—even unto death—the second Adam overcomes the adversary so that death itself might be overcome. This reconciliation of God and Adam's family in Christ perfected the fellowship that God desired for humanity from the beginning.

The incarnation, for Irenaeus, was not simply the recapitulation of Adam's story but of God's self-revelation. Because Christ is the Son of the one and only God, the incarnation provided humanity with its fullest picture of their Creator who alone is the source of all things. Yet the early generations of Adam's family were not ready for such a revelation. Because the first people were created from nothing, as Irenaeus explains, they were not perfect creatures. That is, Adam and Eve, far from being adults, were born in a state of immaturity. They were, at most, adolescents. Although they were made in the image of God, such that their souls had the capacity to come to the knowledge of God, their cognitive functions had to be trained in order to see God. Not surprisingly, when God commanded Adam and Eve not to eat of the fruit of the tree of the knowledge of good and evil, they did not comprehend why. Consequently, their ignorance and immaturity naturally made them particularly susceptible to the serpent's deceptions. Irenaeus is clear that their ignorance did not excuse their disobedience; they should have trusted that their Creator had good reason for his command even if that reason was obscure to them. Nevertheless, their disobedience introduced sin and death into the world, which only further diminished humanity's ability to know God. Therefore, the human race had to undergo a process of remedial education that trained their cognitive faculties to think about God rightly. This training occurred through what Irenaeus called dispensations.

By dispensations, Irenaeus meant the gradual process of God's self-disclosure through a series of covenants: the first with Adam, then Noah, then Abraham, and finally Moses. Each covenant revealed different aspects of God's nature. Each covenant represented a new stage in humanity's understanding of God, and each built upon the knowledge of the prior stage. The incarnation was the capstone of humanity's education. As the Father's Word incarnate, Christ is the highest revelation of God. Irenaeus is emphatic: "For in no other way could we have learned the things of God unless our master, existing as the Word, had become man. For no other being had the power of revealing to us the things of the Father, except his own proper Word" (*Haer.* 5.1.1). Because the one Christ is God and man, the incarnation is God's direct revelation of himself rather than the indirect revelation through prophets. In Jesus, humanity sees and hears not one of God's representatives but God himself. Therefore, God's new covenant in Christ represents the final dispensation that itself is a recapitulation of the previous dispensations. This final covenant of the gospel "sums up [*recapitulata*] all things in itself by means of the gospel, raising and bearing men upon its wings into the heavenly kingdom" (*Haer.* 3.11.8). That is, the revelation of God in the incarnate Word unites all the characteristics of the divine that had been revealed in part in each of the previous dispensations. The prior covenants, though each incomplete, nevertheless provided glimpses of God's nature that were suitable to humanity's stage of religious development. As Christ recapitulated the first Adam revealing the true nature of humanity as God intended, so Christ, in providing the perfect disclosure of God, was the consummation of God's providential plan for training humanity to see the divine. Therefore, in Jesus humanity beholds both perfected humanity and the perfect image of the Father. This is the double sense of recapitulation.

Irenaeus's theory of the gospel as the recapitulation of the prior dispensations is critical for his rebuttal of those heretical groups, most particularly the Marcionites, that separated the Old Testament covenants from the New. In his *Antitheses*, Marcion's enumeration of contradictions between the Old and the New allowed him to posit two different deities, whose different characters were reflected in the different covenants. Whereas the Creator God's covenant with Moses revealed him to be a God of righteousness, who executed justice in his wrath, the (new) covenant that the alien God made through Christ revealed him to be not a God of justice and judgment but a God of love and mercy. For Marcion, justice and judgment were diametrically opposite of love and mercy. Therefore, the covenant of the gospel was completely antithetical to the covenant of the Creator God. This posed the serious challenge for those who affirmed the unity of the Jewish Scriptures and the gospel to explain these contradictions. Irenaeus's theory of dispensations provided an answer. Yes, the early covenants were imperfect in the sense that they were incomplete. They revealed only partial knowledge of God. Nevertheless, each taught humanity to think about God's nature in ways appropriate to their level of development at that time. Christ, who recapitulates the previous dispensations, far from abandoning the prior covenants, reveals their unity in their revelation of the one God. Contra Marcion, Christ does not repudiate justice and judgment in favor of love and mercy. Rather, for Irenaeus, he shows that justice and mercy are but two sides of the same coin. There is no idea of mercy without a prior sense of justice and condemnation. For mercy is deliverance from just judgment. Therefore, before Christ could bring forgiveness of sins, there first had to be the law that revealed humanity's sin and their need for forgiveness. Ultimately, for Irenaeus, Christ is the recapitulation of the law because he reveals in God's love for humanity that love fulfills all the righteousness of the law. As such, the dispensation of the law and the dispensation of the gospel are not only not contradictory but, from the vantage point of humanity's education, mutually dependent.

Early Syriac Christology

Among the Syriac Christian communities of the second and third centuries, two poetic texts, strikingly different in genre from those previously discussed in this chapter, offered their own Christologies that were seemingly unaffected by doctrinal conflict: Odes of Solomon and the Ascension of Isaiah. The Odes, what James Charlesworth has dubbed "the earliest Christian hymnbook," were not composed by a single author but developed over time, originally—given the parallels with documents from Qumran—out of a community of Jewish Christians in the second century writing in Aramaic or Syriac. The Odes repeat many themes and elements of Paul's letters. The seventh ode focuses on Christ's condescension to humanity, using the language of the "great exchange." As in the Christ hymn of Philippians 2, here Christ humbles himself (cf. 41.12) "without envy," giving up some portion of his heavenly majesty (Odes Sol. 7.3) that, by his taking on human form, human beings might receive and clothe themselves with him (7.4). For in this shared likeness, he might be comprehended so that the mind of mortals might not turn from him (7.6). Perhaps drawing on imagery from the Song of Songs, Odes of Solomon 42 describes Christ as the bridegroom who yokes himself in love to his bride. For those who believe in him, the bridegroom's love refashions their heart in a bridal chamber (42.7–9).

The Odes sing of Christ as the giver of life. Odes of Solomon 19 describes the Virgin's womb as "trapping" the Son and being made so strong by his indwelling that she gave birth without labor pains, for "he gave life to her like a man" (19.6). Although Odes of Solomon 42 speaks of Christ's stretching forth his hands on the wood of the cross (42.1–2), the emphasis is not upon his death but upon Christ as the power of life. The forty-first ode opens with an offering of praise: "We are alive in the Lord through grace; we receive life through his Messiah" (41.3). He declares, "I was not rejected even if I seemed to have been . . . and I did not perish even if they thought so of me" (42.10); for when he descended to Sheol, the power of death was weakened and, unable to contain him, vomited him up (42.11). With him, Christ delivered from Sheol "the congregation of the living among the dead" whom he made while in death's house (42.14). These souls called out to him as their Savior (42.18), and hearing their faith, Christ set their names on his head and made them a free people (42.19–20). Because he is risen from the dead, Jesus is alive and with those who proclaim him (42.5–6).

Only in Odes of Solomon 19 is there an express reference to the Trinity. It describes the Father as the source of sweet milk that is the kindness of the Lord, which believers drink from the cup that is the Son. The Spirit is the one who milked the Father's breasts to fill the Son (19.1–2). Although the Spirit is mentioned third in order, the Spirit seems to be a middle figure between the Father and Son. That, however, may simply refer to the role of the Spirit in the incarnation—the cup being Jesus's humanity that is filled with the divine milk coming from the Father through the Spirit's overshadowing Mary. All the Odes that have a christological element make a definite distinction between the Father and the Son—even if they are made obscure by ambiguous pronoun references. The seventh ode declares, "He let him appear to those who are his, so that they might recognize the one who made them" (7.12). Here the Son is sent by the Father, the Most High (7.16), that he might reveal the Father as their Creator. Thus, the Son is the one through whom the Father is known by his creatures. Through this knowledge, the Son becomes a path for the Father's creatures. This the Son can do because his knowledge of the Father and creation is "a path extending from the beginning to the end" (7.15). The Son, who is the Word and Messiah, has appeared in the fullness of the Father (41.13) and therefore is the giver of life because he was in the Father "from the beginning" (41.14) and has been known "since the foundation of the world" (41.15). This "beginning" is not the beginning of creation but is the birth of the Son from the Father as "the thought of [the Father's] heart" (41.9–10). The poetry of the Odes articulates a relationship between the Father and Son that is, if not explicitly eternal, at least prior to and independent of creation—a relationship that allows the Son to reveal the Father to human beings and makes them recipients of his life-giving power.

Although there is no consensus on its date or provenance, the Ascension of Isaiah has a strong textual connection with Syria going back as early as the second century. The anonymous author recounts the prophet Isaiah's mystical rapture into the heavens. During an audience with King Hezekiah, Isaiah's mind is seized by the Holy Spirit who speaks through him. But after falling silent, the prophet undergoes an ecstatic experience in which he can no longer see those around him but finds himself led by an angel through the spheres of heaven until he reaches the seventh where he receives the beatific vision. Throughout his ascent, his angelic guide refers to God variously as "the Lord of Righteousness, the exalted one who is in the exalted world" (Ascen. Isa. 1.8–10) and "the most exalted one" (5.7). As the ascent begins, the angel tells the prophet that one greater than he will speak to him and that he will see "the Father of the greater one" (2.7–8). Whenever God is spoken of, he is almost always spoken of together with "the greater one." God is his Father, and the "greater one" is Christ who is spoken of as the Father's "beloved" (2.22), "his chosen one whose name is not known" (3.7). The inhabitants of the seventh heaven worship "the Primal Father, the beloved Christ, and the Holy Spirit" (3.17–18). Although the three are spoken of here together, there is a clear hierarchy. The Father exists in total transcendent glory that Isaiah and his guide cannot behold; only the Son and Spirit can see the Father (5.2–4). Consequently, the Father transcends verbal description and is called "the one who is not named" (3.7). The Son, even though he is identified as "your Lord God, the beloved, Christ, who will be called in the world Jesus" (4.5), nevertheless is depicted as bowing with the Spirit before the Father (4.30). Although all three are the object of worship and the Son is called God, the author treats them as discrete entities and ascribes to the Father priority. This hierarchy extends to the relation of the Son and Spirit—the Son being treated as superior to the Spirit, who is repeatedly spoken of as "the angel of the Spirit" (4.39).

After the prophet receives this vision in the throne room of the seventh heaven, he is made witness to the Father's commissioning of the Son. At the end of days (4.13), the Father will send the Son through the heavens, but none of the angels will honor him, because he has the appearance of one of them (5.8). He was from Mary, who was of David's seed, and after a miraculous two-month gestation period appeared to Mary and Joseph—rather than being birthed in the normal manner (6.7–9). The author does not seem to have subscribed to a docetic Christology, for he says that Jesus will be thought a human in the flesh (4.13) and as an infant suckled at Mary's breast (6.17). Isaiah's vision includes the scene of his crucifixion, his descent to the angel of Sheol, and his resurrection on the third day (6.20–21). Then in the glory that of right was his by nature, the Lord ascends from Sheol through the six heavens until he returns to the seventh where he is seated at the right hand of the Father, whom Isaiah describes as "that great glory, whose glory I have told you I was not able to see" (6.32).

The Rise of Monarchianism

Jesus's divine status as Son of God was, as we have seen, generally accepted by the Great Church and smaller sects alike in the second century. But by the end of the century, there emerged groups of Christians who were concerned that this description of Jesus compromised a core theological principle expressed in the words of the Shema from Deuteronomy 6:4: "Hear, O Israel, the Lord is God. The Lord is one." This doctrine is repeated in the first mandate of the Shepherd of Hermas: "First of all, believe that God is one, who created all things . . . and who contains all things but is himself uncontained" (Herm. Mand. 1.26.1). Indeed, the confession that the God of Israel and the Church is the one and only God was the central point of doctrine that set Christians in conflict with the spirit of religious pluralism that was the norm in the Roman Empire and led to their persecution. Yet was the confession of Jesus's divinity compatible with the confession of the Shema? Didn't the claim that he was the Son of God in effect posit two divine beings: "the God and Father of our Lord Jesus Christ" (2 Cor 1:3) and Jesus the Father's "only begotten Son" (John 1:18)? Although the worship of the Holy Spirit, as we shall see, further complicated the Christian confession of one God, it was chiefly the confession of Jesus's divine sonship that was the bone of contention from the late second through the fourth century.

Adoptionism

For two groups of Christians in the late second and third centuries the theological challenge was reconciling Jesus's sonship with the oneness of God. These Christians became called Monarchians because they both strongly affirmed above all else that there is only one God. Yet each had decidedly different approaches to affirming Jesus's identity as Son of God within their doctrine of God's absolute singularity. The first group solved the problem by emphasizing the difference—an ontological difference—and separateness between the Father and Jesus. These were the Adoptionists. Their name comes from their view that when Scripture calls Jesus the Son of God, it means that he is God's *adopted* son. The first of the Adoptionists, Theodotus the Cobbler (late second century), noticed that at Jesus's baptism in Luke, the words spoken by the voice from heaven, "You are my beloved son; with you I am well pleased" (Luke 3:22), were from Psalm 2, which was sung at the coronation of Israel's kings. In verse 7, God, speaking to the new king, declares, "You are my son; today, I have begotten you." The psalm was a celebration of God's adoption of the king as his son, with whom he invests the authority to rule God's people. But the king, ontologically speaking, remains what he always was, a man. He contended that when Scripture speaks of the Father, it is referring to the one and only God. Jesus, therefore, was a mere man whom God anointed as his son. As the anointed son, Jesus proclaimed the "word of God," which denoted the commandments that God inspired Jesus to preach. Similarly, "the Spirit" was not a divine person but refers to the grace of God that dwelt in the apostles. Thus, the appellation "son of God" did not, for the Adoptionists, denote Jesus's divinity. Rather, like the Old Testament prophets, he was simply a man inspired to proclaim God's message.

One figure who is often associated with Adoptionism is Paul of Samasota, bishop of Antioch (260–268). Yet it would be inaccurate to equate Paul's Christology with that of Theodotus. Paul does not go as far as Theodotus's claim that Jesus was simply an inspired man delivering God's word. For Paul held to a doctrine of the incarnation and virgin birth. However, it was his description of the incarnation that sounded Adoptionistic and became the source of controversy just a few years after his consecration. Most of our knowledge of his Christology is based on fragments from a stenographer's report of a debate between Paul and an Antiochene priest, Malchion, around 268 and the letter of the Synod of Antioch that same year that condemned and deposed Paul. At the heart of his position was a sharp distinction between the Word—alternatively called Wisdom—and the man Jesus (frag. 1). Because the Word was divine and did not need to be anointed with power, only Jesus the man was made wise through the anointing of Wisdom. Thus, Paul confessed, "We know one unbegotten God and one begotten Christ [who] became his Son. The Word [is] the Son, the Word [is] God-begotten" (frag. 8). From this, Malchion concluded that Paul believed in two sons: the Word begotten by the Father, and Jesus who is the son of Mary. Although Paul maintained that Mary did not give birth to the Word (frag. 2), he did contend that the Word was united to Jesus by dwelling with him such that Jesus became the temple in which the Word dwelt.

Was such an indwelling different from the relationship of Wisdom and the prophets or Moses? Paul's answer is both yes and no. No, it was not essentially different in that the Word similarly had indwelt Abraham, Moses, David, and the lesser prophets (frag. 6). Nevertheless, the Word's indwelling of Jesus was greater than in any prophet before (frags. 3 and 4); "filling [Jesus] in every way," the Word "dwelt in him as it never did anyone else" (frag. 5). Thus, Paul held that Jesus was unique. Yet Jesus was different from the holy men of Israel not by the *manner* of his union with the Word but simply by *degree* or *extent* of the Word's indwelling (frag. 22). This indwelling Paul understood not as the result of a *substantial* joining of the divine and human natures but as the *participation* of Jesus's intellect in Wisdom (frags. 12 and 25). Had it been a substantial union, he argued, the divinity would be deminished—as if a part of the Word were separated and joined to Jesus—and so lose something of his divine honor (frag. 14). The result of this thoroughgoing participation in the Word meant that Jesus possessed not the substance of the divine but his divine qualities (frag. 20).

Paul's critics found his strong distinction between the Word and Jesus contrary to the more unitive character of the incarnation they believed was implied by Scripture. Jesus, Malchion contended, was the one Son and Christ, the Son of God who suffered and died. "It is not fitting," he wrote, to distinguish him who is from before the ages from this one who was begotten at the end of days. Indeed, I am terrified to speak of two sons; I am terrified to speak of two Christs" (frag. 9). Although Paul resisted speaking of two sons, the bishops in their synodal letter argued that if Christ were treated as one thing and the Word another and each was called a son, then there were two, not one (frag. 24). Indeed, because God is the Father of the Word, he is therefore the Father of Jesus who was "constituted from the Word and from Mary's body" (frag. 27). In other words, because Jesus is the Word in human form, he could claim the same unique relationship with God.

While the bishops would claim that Jesus was a compound being, Word and flesh, they placed the emphasis on his divinity. For instance, the magi, they wrote, came offering gifts primarily to God and only secondarily to the "human body that carries the God" (frag. 28). Jesus could receive the magi's worship because he was God's Word infleshed. Malchion called Christ a single hypostasis existing as a substantial unity (frag. 11) of the Word and a human body taken from the seed of David. Therefore, Paul's analogy of the temple could not be descriptive of a true union. A person may live in a house (frag. 12) and put on clothes (frag. 23), but no one would think that she is united to her house or clothes. The person and her house are not one thing. Nor are the clothes she wears genuinely part of her. Therefore, a Word, who simply inhabits a human body, would not truly share in all the essential dimensions of human life. That would be possible only if the Word shares in the human substance. Malchion then proceeded to differentiate substance and participation. In the substantial union, the divine and human substances are parts that combined to make the one Lord. By contrast, that in which one participates is "not like a part of that in which it exists" (frag. 15), but it remains external as in the case of our participation in God (frag. 22). Far from being external, however, the incarnate Word was what Paul (2 Cor 4:16) called the "inner man" (frag. 21). With their commitment to the substantial unity of Jesus, the bishops went so far as to affirm that "in a secondary sense," God was in Mary's womb (frag. 26) and suffered on the cross by sharing in human weakness (frag. 30).

While affirming the unity of the Word and body, Malchion and the bishops inserted language that drew some distinction between the suffering of Jesus in his divinity and in his humanity. Whereas the magi gave gifts *primarily* to Jesus as the Word and *secondarily* through his body, the Word suffered *primarily* in his body and only *secondarily* by virtue of his union with the body (frag. 30). Similarly, Malchion said that as a result of the substantial union that occurred in the incarnation, it appeared "as if" what happened to Jesus's body also happened to the Word (frag. 11).

Paul of Samosata clearly did not subscribe to Theodotus's narrative of Jesus's adoption at his baptism in the Jordan. Nevertheless, his rejection of the language of substantial union in favor of a model of cognitive participation failed, in the eyes of his critics, to demonstrate Jesus's uniqueness among men. If the indwelling of the Word in Jesus differed only in degrees from that of Moses and David, whom the Father had adopted through just such an indwelling, then it raised the question: How was Jesus not simply the greatest in a long line of prophets adopted by the Father's anointing? The Synod of Antioch in 268, with its emphasis on the incarnation as a substantial union, made suspect any Christology that divided the Word and the man. In Jesus, the Word had not simply become dressed in human form. Nor was the Word merely the source of inspiration. Jesus was a single person: the Word made flesh. Indeed, it was around this very point 160 years later that the Christology of another Antiochene, Nestorius bishop of Constantinople, would become a bone of contention that would divide the Church.

Modalists

While the Adoptionists preserved the Father's unique identity as God by denying Jesus's divinity, the second group of Monarchians, subsequently called Modalists, sought to preserve the true oneness of God without reducing Jesus's sonship to a mere title. Whereas the Adoptionists defended the singularity of God by affirming an ontological divide between the Father and his Son, these other Monarchians upheld Jesus's divinity by erasing the ontological divide between the Father and the Son. They did this by collapsing all distinctions between the Father and Son into a single person. Writing in the late second or early third century, Noetus of Smyrna reasoned that since Scripture teaches that there is one God (Gen 46:3; Exod 20:3; Isa 44:6) and that both Christ and the Father are God, then Christ must be the Father. Hippolytus's *Against Noetus* summarizes Noetus's position: "Christ himself was the Father, and the Father had been born, suffered, and died" (*Noet.* 1.2). Whereas Justin had distinguished the transcendent Father from the Logos who spoke for the Father in the Old Testament theophanies, Noetus and his disciples maintained that it was the Father himself who appeared in the burning bush. Sabellius systematizes the logic of Noetus's syllogism. God, Sabellius claimed, is a monad, a perfectly singular entity but a being with three distinct operations spoken of in Scripture in the personal language of "Father," "Son," and "Holy Spirit." These, however, are not three discrete persons but merely three modes of God's self-expression. In other words, within God's economy of salvation, God revealed himself in three forms at times spoken of by the authors of Scripture as "Father," at other times as "Son," and at others as the "Holy Spirit." Before the incarnation, God reveals himself as the Father of Israel who reveals himself through the prophets, promising to deliver them. In the incarnation, God then appears as the Son whose coming God promised. Then after Jesus's ascension, the Holy Spirit becomes the mode by which God abides with the disciples.

Similarly, Praxeas reasoning from Isaiah's words, "[God] alone stretched out the heavens" (44:24), and God's declaration, "There is no God beside me," concluded that only the Father may rightly be called God (*Prax.* 19–20). Taking this as his hermeneutical key, Praxeas interpreted Jesus's words "I and the Father are one" (John 10:30) to mean that they are one entity, a single person. Therefore, he reasoned that Jesus could tell the disciples, "If you have seen me, you have seen the Father" (John 14:9), only because the Son was simply the Father's incarnate form (*Prax.* 1). Although Praxeas ultimately repented of this view, his name is forever associated with Modalism because Tertullian used his name as a catchall to speak of the heresy.

This Modalist or, as it would also be called, Sabellian Christology was, to speak anachronistically from the perspective of the orthodoxy established nearly two centuries later at the Council of Constantinople, a rejection of the Trinity. If the Father, Son, and Holy Spirit were not separate persons, the implication was that "Father," "Son," and "Holy Spirit" are merely nominal distinctions used by Scripture to speak of God's actions in history. God *in se* is not triune. The Trinity is merely a verbal construct designed to accommodate human finitude. It is simply a way of thinking about God based on God's activities in creation. Such a view glossed over passages where the Scripture treats the three as discrete and distinct. When, for instance, Jesus says in his Farewell Discourse, "But when the Counselor comes, whom I shall send to you from the Father, even the Spirit of truth, who proceeds from the Father, he will bear witness to me . . . if I do not go away, the Counselor will not come to you" (John 15:26; 16:7), the Sabellians would say that Scripture is speaking merely figuratively (*Prax.* 9). There is no actual sending of the Son by the Father; rather, the "Father" is simply God taking the human form of the "Son." Nor now is the Son seated at the Father's right hand making intercession as the great high priest. Rather, because God is one, the Father has no mediator between himself and humanity but himself is united to his creatures.

The most problematic implication of Modalism was the crucufixion. How from a Modalist perspective does one make sense of Jesus's praying from the cross, "Father, forgive them; they know not what they do" (Luke 23:34), or the cry of dereliction, "My God, my God, why have you forsaken me?" (Mark 15:34). Indeed, if God is a monad, then it is the Father who died on the cross (*Prax.* 2). Thus, Noetus and the Modalists were open to the charge of heresy called patripassionism or theopassionism, the view that the Father suffered and died.[5] Not all Monarchians followed Noetus's claim that the Father suffered. Callistus of Rome, who may have been the real target of Tertullian's *Against Praxeas*, held that the Son and Father are not distinct since the Father is the animating spirit of all things. The spirit of the Son was the Father now made visible in the Son, Jesus. Thus, the Son is the Father's incarnate form. But Callistus's distinction between the man Jesus and the Father's indwelling spirit allowed him to attribute Jesus's passion to the man rather than to the Father's spirit.

Tertullian and the Trinity

Tertullian's Christology, like that of Irenaeus, largely emerged in his polemical responses to various heretical groups. It is in the context of Tertullian's polemic against Praxeas's Monarchianism that one finds his doctrine of the Trinity. In fact, here is the first instance of the term Trinity (*trinitas*) being used in the his-

5. Patripassionism and theopassionism will be discussed in chapter 8, pp. 342–44.

tory of Christian literature. He begins his disputation by appealing to the Rule of Faith (*regula fidei*), which "came down to us from the beginning of the gospel" and declares that there is only one God who in the order of the divine plan or dispensation (*dispensatio* or *oikonomia*) is revealed to be Father, Son, and Holy Spirit (*Prax.* 2). Like Irenaeus, Tertullian argues that God is rightly known only in the context of the economy; that is, within the unfolding revelation of God in the narrative of salvation history. The Son was sent by the Father into a virgin so that he was both Son of God and Son of man. The Spirit whom the Son sends from the Father sanctifies the faith of believers. Praxeas falls into error, Tertullian suggests, because he so focuses on the single principle of God's oneness that he ignores the distinctions between the persons implied by the biblical narrative. Tertullian recognizes that Praxeas's error is common among the simpleminded, who comprise the majority of believers. They rightly take the Christian belief in one God to be what sets them apart from the pagan polytheism of their earlier life. Not wanting to fall back into their previous error, they fear that the Trinity compromises the unity and oneness of God (*Prax.* 3). Yet this was to ignore the biblical descriptions of the members of the godhead. Divine unity, Tertullian says, is distributed in "a Trinity [*unitatem in trinitatem*], placing in their order the three [i.e.,] Father, Son, and Spirit" (*Prax.* 2). Yet the unity of the three presupposed that they are distinct from each other. Since the Word is "of the Father" and the Spirit is "of God," then the Word and Spirit must be other than the one to whom they belong. Therefore, the Son and Spirit are not the same person as the Father (*Prax.* 26). The theological challenge that faced Tertullian was devising language with which to speak about both the oneness of Father, Son, and Holy Spirit—affirming the *monarchia* of God—and the difference between them so that, contra Praxeas, the three cannot be collapsed into each other. Thus, Tertullian went beyond Irenaeus who lacked the language, such as *persona*, with which to give as clear a distinction between Father, Son, and Spirit. In other words, he sought to reconcile the monarchy of God, which set Christianity and Judaism apart from polytheism, and the biblical presentation of God as three in the divine economy.

The Son and Spirit are, Tertullian contends, one with the Father in that they share the same substance (*substantia*) as the Father and so share the Father's divinity. Since the Son was not created from nothing, Tertullian reasons, he has to take his substance or being from the Father who begat him. Similarly, since the Spirit of God comes from the one whose spirit he is, the Spirit derives his substance from the Father from whom he and the Son proceed (*Prax.* 4, 26). And since they share the same substance or nature, they hold the same status ontologically speaking. Thus, the Spirit is rightly called God for the same reason as is the Son. Yet by itself, the focus on the shared *substantia* would not necessarily mean that the Trinity maintained the monarchy of God in contrast with polytheism.

For were *substantia* understood simply to mean "nature," then the same might be said of the Greco-Roman deities as well. Ontologically, Jupiter, Juno, and Apollo were of the same nature that distinguished them from mortals. Yet Tertullian sees in the substantial unity of Father, Son, and Spirit something more than simply a shared nature as in the case of the pagan gods. For him, to say that the Son and Spirit share the same substance as the Father means that they possess not only the same power (*potestas*) as the Father (*Prax.* 3) but also the same will (*voluntas*). The Son not only has the power to carry out the Father's will, but he does so because he wills what the Father wills. For, Tertullian claims, in the case of God, his power and will are one; what he is able to do he wills, and what he wills he accomplishes (*Prax.* 10). The implication is that God's power and will that are manifest in the economy are expressions of God's substance and so are identical with his substance. Herein lies the critical difference between the Trinity and the gods of the pagan pantheon. Because the Son and Spirit come from the Father's substance, they are bound to the Father by a mutual love. There is a familial relationship within the Trinity between the Father and Son by which the Son loves the Father with the same love out of which the Father begat the Son. As the Father declared in the words of the psalmist, "My heart has emitted my most excellent Word" (Ps 45:1). That is, the Word was begotten from the Father's love for him who returns that love. "The Father took pleasure evermore," Tertullian writes, "in him, who equally rejoiced with a reciprocal gladness in the Father's presence" (*Prax.* 7). Commenting on John 10:15–18, Tertullian explains that the Son "was so wholly loved by the Father, that he [i.e., the Son] was laying down his life, because he had received this commandment from the Father" (*Prax.* 22). Thus, the economy of salvation itself is a revelation of the Son's and Spirit's love of the Father and his love for them. In a monistic view of God, such as Praxeas espoused, there is no mutual affection within the Godhead; for there is no other whom God can love. Within Tertullian's Trinitarian framework, however, such reciprocal love is possible because God is not one person (*unus*) but one thing (*unum*) existing "in a unity, an essential likeness, the intimacy of friendship [*conjunctionem*], the love [*ad dilectionem*] of the Father who loves the Son and the submission of the Son who submits to the Father's will" (*Prax.* 22).

Yet how was Tertullian to deal with favorite Modalist prooftexts from Scripture, such as Isaiah 44:24, "He alone stretched out the heavens," and John 14:9–10, "I and the Father are one"? His exegetical move was to read Jesus's words to Philip within the context of the opening line of John's prologue that provided the identity of Jesus and his relationship with the Father, which provided the interpretive framework for the rest of the gospel. Therefore, John's opening declaration "and the Word was with God and was God" (John 1:1) treats Christ as the Word of God and therefore as being distinct from God the Father whose Word he was. Since he is other than God the Father, the Son is not identical with the Father. But nor is he separate from the Father by division, because the Word exists in an eternal union of will and substance; only in this sense are the Father and Son one (*Prax.* 21). John's prologue also provided Tertullian the key for interpreting Isaiah 44. God creates through his Son, who employs the Father's power to accomplish the Father's creative will. But because the Son abides in an eternal substantial union with the Father, God "stretched out the heavens" through nothing external to himself. Since the Son created the world according to the wisdom of the Father's will and with his power, which are intrinsic to the Father's will, the cosmos was created by none other than God. Confirmation of this Tertullian locates in the psalmist's almost exact parallel of Isaiah 44: "By the Word of the Lord were the heavens made and all the hosts of them by his Spirit" (Ps 33:6). Therefore, God alone was the author of creation (*Prax.* 19).

Having demonstrated that the plurality of the persons did not threaten the divine *monarchia*, Tertullian sought language to describe the distinctness of Father, Son, and Holy Spirit. If the members of the Trinity are collectively one thing (*unum*), then what are they individually? Tertullian's answer was to say that within the economy, the three are different from each other by degree (*gradus*), aspect (*specie*), and form (*forma*). These are terms of particularity and individuality that stand in contrast with the general or essential (i.e., *substantia, status, potestas*) qualities shared among the three (*Prax.* 2). By virtue of being "begotten of God, in a way peculiar to himself, from the womb of [the Father's] own heart," the Son shares the Father's divine substance and so is equal to the Father (*Prax.* 7). Yet although the Son is equal in his ontological status as God—in contrast with "all things" that he created from nothing—Tertullian was troubled by Jesus's deferential words, "My Father is greater than I" (John 14:28). Initially, Tertullian explains that the Father is first among equals, so to speak, because he is the source of the Son's being. That is, since the entire divine substance of the Son was derived from the Father, then the Son's *substantia* is a portion of that substance. Since the begetter is greater than the only begotten, the Son is a second degree within the hierarchy of the Trinity, and the Spirit is a third degree (*Prax.* 9).[6] Although his description of the Son as a "portion of the whole"—in contrast with the Father who is the whole—comes close to asserting an ontological hierarchy, nevertheless, Tertullian's distinction of the three degrees must be seen within the dispensation of the economy. He shifts from the distinction between begetter and the begotten to the difference between the Father who is the sender and the Son who is the one sent. The Son is the one who will deliver up the kingdom, and the Father is the one to whom the kingdom will be delivered. Tertullian's point is that within Scrip-

6. For the relation of the Son and the Spirit, see chapter 7, pp. 276–83.

ture's salvation narrative, the Father and Son are distinct agents in the economy (*Prax.* 4). Does the economic hierarchy imply an ontological hierarchy as well? Tertullian is inconsistent. Although Tertullian's distinction of the three degrees refers to a distinction within the economy, his description of the Son as a "portion of the whole"—in contrast with the Father who is the whole—comes close to asserting an ontological hierarchy (cf. *Prax.* 5).

Tertullian shifted away from speaking of the relationship for Father and Son *within the Trinity* to speaking of the hierarchy of Father and Son in the context of their *external* relationship with creation (*Prax.* 9). Tertullian's logic is that the Son is inferior to the Father because in both his creative activity and the dispensation of the incarnation, the Son reveals only a portion, not the totality, of the Father's divinity. In his transcendence, the Father retains the fullness of his divine glory and power, while the incarnate Son's immanent presence in the world is but a partial revelation of that glory. To put it another way, in Christ humanity sees only the image of the Father. The image, economically speaking, is a lower degree of divinity than the Father, who is the archetype. Even though the Son derived *all* the divine power from the Father by virtue of having been begotten from his substance, nevertheless the Son exercises only that degree of power necessary to accomplish the Father's will for the creation and redemption of the world (*Prax.* 4).

This economic account of the Trinity, however, raises the question whether Tertullian has reduced the Trinity to God's creative and salvific activities. As we saw with Philo, the critical question regarding Tertullian's Christology is whether the Son exists in an eternal relationship with the Father or whether he was begotten by the Father simply to be his agent of creation and redemption. Although he devotes little time to speculating about the intra-Trinitarian relations of Father, Son, and Spirit—that is, what the persons were doing before the world was created—Tertullian does separate the Son's existence with the Father from his activity as Creator of the world. For instance, he rejects the claim that the Genesis creation narrative begins with the making of the Son through whom other things were made. Rather, following the prologue of John, he asserts that the Son was with the Father prior to and perhaps independent of his work of creation. Taking advantage of the double meaning of *logos* as both "word" and "reason," Tertullian distinguishes between the Son who was in the beginning with the Father and the Son "through whom all things were made." Before creation, the Father possessed his Logos or reason (*ratio*). When God created by speaking the cosmos into existence, the Father's *ratio* became the Father's spoken Word (*sermo*). The Son's intra-Trinitarian relation with the Father was as the *ratio* by which God "silently planned and arranged within himself everything which he was about to utter through his Word [*sermonem*]" (*Prax.* 5). Thus, the Son's discrete identity vis-à-vis the economy was manifest when the Father "sent out" the Son as his spoken Word. Because the Son as the Father's eternal reason was identical with the Son as spoken Word, the Son could reveal the Father in the economy.

Yet this raises the question: Did the Son have a discrete existence as something other than the Father before he acted as the Father's spoken Word? The evidence is conflicting. On the one hand, Tertullian treats the move from inner thought to spoken word as the Word's advent in creation. Speaking of God's command, "Let there be light," Tertullian says, "This is the perfect nativity [*nativitas*] of the Word when he proceeds forth from God—formed by him first to devise and think out all things under the name of Wisdom . . . then afterwards begotten [*generatus*] to carry all into effect" (*Prax.* 7). Thus, the Son is the Wisdom of the Father by whom the plan of creation was set in order, but the Wisdom was begotten as Word (*sermo*) at the Father's spoken command. So here it appears that the Son becomes a person discrete from the Father when he deploys him as *sermo* for the creation of the world. On this reading, the Son has an embryonic existence in the Father only to become his own person, so to speak, in the act of creating. In other words, to counter the Monarchianism of Praxeas, Tertullian adopted a two-stage theory of the Logos. Though incipiently with the Father in the beginning (stage 1), the Logos goes out from the Father (stage 2), becoming a discrete entity to accomplish God's economic purposes. On the other hand, from his familiarity with Irenaeus, Tertullian was aware of Valentinus and certain troubling similarities that his two-stage theory of the Logos had with Valentinus's separation of the Father from the Son, who was one of the aeons. Tertullian sought a way of thinking of the Son as being both united to and at the same time discrete from the Father *before creation* (*Prax.* 5, 8). He explains this by way of analogy with human cognition. There is, he says, a discursive quality to reason even before one's thought is expressed outwardly in written or audible form. When in private meditation we are thinking through a matter, our thoughts are already verbal; we are conversing within ourselves. One's reason, he says, is like a second self with whom one engages in deliberation. So too, the Son as the Father's *ratio* already had the character of *sermo* when the Father planned the creation. In other words, the Father conversed with his Wisdom as an interlocutor. Furthermore, even as we are not identical with our thoughts, neither is the Son identical with the Father. As the thoughts of the thinker stand apart from the one thinking the thoughts, similarly the Logos exists discretely apart from the Father whose thinking generates his Logos. The result was not a nicely coherent doctrine. Rather than fully reconciling these positions, Tertullian simply affirms both. The Son *exists separate* from the Father when the Father spoke his inherent *ratio* into existence as the economic *sermo* (contra Praxeas). Equally true, the Son is *eternally united* to the Father as both *ratio* and intradiscursive *sermo* in the Father's mind (contra Valentinus).

Tertullian on the Unity of Creation and Redemption

While Tertullian's reliance on the economy proclaimed in the Rule of Faith allowed him to counter the Monarchians, it also set him at odds with Marcion and his separation of the Creator and the redeemer. Like Irenaeus, Tertullian focused his argument against Marcion on the incoherence of a Christian theory of salvation separated from the Old Testament. Christ's identity lay entirely in his relationship to the one and only God, the Creator, who sent Christ into his creation (*Marc.* 3.1). Marcion's theory of salvation lacked a narrative that offered a theory of Christ's origin. Rather, Marcion's Christology began with what Tertullian took to be a patent absurdity: that Christ came announcing a God who was previously entirely unknown. If Marcion's god were truly a god of goodness and love who cared enough about humanity to become involved in human affairs, why would he have hidden himself from humanity for so long? The only way Christ's message as the Son of the Father could have any credibility would be if the God in whose name he came already had some authority among the people to whom he preached. In other words, the people would believe his message only if they first recognized the authority of the one who sent him. The authority and credibility of the messenger, who is sent, depend on the authority of the one who sends (*Marc.* 3.2). The Son could be believed because the Father who sent him was already known. More than a question of credibility, however, Christ's coming reflected, for Tertullian, the orderly nature of God's ways. Far from acting suddenly or impulsively, God acts according to a plan ordered according to his wisdom. Moreover, God prepares humanity for the unfolding of his plan by announcing his plan ahead of time. By contrast, Marcion's Christ simply appears on the scene. If the people to whom he was sent did not know the God who sent him, then his preaching would carry no authority for them (*Marc.* 3.4). There would, in other words, have been no prior criterion to which he could appeal to prove his identity. Anticipating a Marcionite's appeal to Christ's miracles, which would reveal his authority as coming from one who had power far surpassing the Creator's, Tertullian counters that miracles by themselves were no proof of divine authority. For Christ himself warned his disciples against "many" who would come after him claiming to be Christ by performing signs and wonders. Unlike Marcion's unannounced Christ, the identity of Tertullian's Christ could be confirmed by his conformity to the announcement of his coming by his Father's prophets (*Marc.* 3.3).

More than simply a question of credibility, the Son's authority rested upon the Father's just claim over both his creation and the people of Israel grounded in a relationship that stretched back to the very beginning. By contrast, the unheralded appearance of the Christ of the unknown god would have been an unjust usurpation of the creator's authority. For the material world was not his domain but belonged to the Creator who made it. Therefore, Marcion's god would be unjust because he trespassed where he had no rightful claim. If, on the other hand, the unknown God had a proper claim to dominion over the material creation but had for millennia not exercised his claim, then he would have been guilty of an unjust neglect of his domain and of those who were depending on his beneficence (*Marc.* 3.4). The other possibility, Tertullian hypothesized, was that the failure of Marcion's god to intervene was not a dereliction of duty but evidence of his weakness and impotence to impose his will on the Creator. Tertullian's Christ, like the son in Jesus's parable of the vineyard and the wicked tenants (Matt 21:33–41), came to reclaim what was lawfully his Father's from tenants who had repeatedly rejected and killed the Father's servants (*Prax.* 26). Indeed, the Son had already been active in the creation and had himself prepared Israel for his later coming by having spoken, as the Spirit of the Creator, through the prophets (*Marc.* 3.6). In contrast with Marcion's hidden god, whom Tertullian accuses of being idle, the one God who is Lord of his creation was the Creator of time itself and of the ages, which he ordered so that, as Paul declared (Gal 4:4), Christ would come in the fullness of time—that is, when the plans that had made suitable preparation for Christ's advent had been fulfilled (*Marc.* 5.4).

Tertullian on the Incarnation

When it came to the incarnation, Tertullian did not lay out his Christology straightforwardly, much less systematically. Rather, his view of the Word's assumption of human nature emerges over the course of his refutations of the docetic Christologies espoused by various heretics. The docetic views that he confronted lay along a continuum. On one end of the spectrum, there was Marcion's view, what one might call hard docetism: Christ did not have a body of any type but merely the appearance of a body. On the other end was what one might call soft docetism, of which Valentinus was a representative: Christ has a fleshly body, but he was not actually born. In between these poles were the views of figures like Appelles that Christ's body was of an angelic substance or that his flesh was his soul.

The hard docetism of Marcion was, in Tertullian's thinking, the most vulnerable position. To begin with, it went against Marcion's own insistence that there was only one meaning of Scripture and it lay in the literal sense. The literal sense of the Gospels' identification of Jesus as "the Son of Man" was that Jesus was a human being and therefore actually possessed the human qualities, including the properties of a human body. However, Marcion's claim that Jesus was a mere phantom violated his own exegetical principle. If Jesus did not have a true human body, not only would it call into question the veracity of Scripture, but it would make God a liar. By taking only the outward form of a man and not the body, then God deceived people into believing that Christ was something he was not (*Carn. Chr.* 3). If Christ was but a phantom, his birth was imaginary. If he had no body, then the miracles were not real displays of power. Without a body, Jesus did not really walk on the water. Without a body of mortal flesh, the crucifixion was but an illusion (*Carn. Chr.* 5). Infinitely more antithetical and more degrading to God's nature than taking on corruptible human flesh would be for God, who is Truth, to pretend to be something he was not or to do anything that was untrue. Tertullian went so far as to say that, if God found man's carnal nature so loathsome that he would not condescend to join himself to it, then it was hard to imagine how God could love such vile creatures in the first place (*Carn. Chr.* 4).

Against the more moderate form of docetism that held that Christ's body was not of earthly matter but was soul consisting of an ethereal substance, Tertullian put forward an argument that anticipates Gregory of Nazianzus's dictum: "that which Christ did not assume he did not redeem." If the soul could be saved only by being united to Christ—"by him having it [i.e., the soul] within himself"—then, since human beings are composed of body as well as soul, the only way human beings could be saved was if Christ united himself to the body as well. For human beings are composed of body as well as soul (*Carn. Chr.* 10). Tertullian's logic follows that of Irenaeus's application of Paul's Adam typology: Christ can save humanity only by becoming one of those he came to save. This reasoning led him to conclude that a Christ whose soul is his flesh not only lacks a human body but is bereft of a human soul, and so is powerless to save either.

On the opposite end of the spectrum from Marcion was a certain Alexander who maintained that Christ did have a material body proper to human beings but that the purpose of this union was that Christ might deliver humanity by abolishing the body. Drawing on Paul's description of Jesus as having "the likeness of sinful flesh" (Rom 8:3), Alexander concluded that earthly flesh was inherently sinful. Therefore, if flesh were the source of evil, Christ triumphed over evil only by means of its destruction. Tertullian countered that Christ did not destroy the body but raised it up and honored it by carrying it to the right hand of the Father. Moreover, when he returns, Christ will appear in the same flesh in which he arose and ascended. Indeed, the incarnation exposed Alexander's erroneous interpretation of Romans 8:3, namely that flesh is intrinsically evil. Christ clothed himself with a body of the same substance as that of any human being. Therefore, Paul could say it had the "likeness" of sinful flesh. Yet by calling it the "likeness" of sinful flesh, Paul means that Christ's body had the material and anatomical characteristics of human flesh but that Christ's flesh was not corrupted by sin as is the flesh of the rest of Adam's family. Moreover, Tertullian corrects Alexander's interpretation of Paul's phrase "sinful flesh" (*carnis peccati*) by noting that Paul goes on in the same verse to say that Christ "abolished sin in the flesh" (*peccatum carnis*). Thus, Paul is distinguishing the body itself from the sin that infects it. As evidenced by his resurrection, what Christ abolished was not the substance of the body but the corruption that inheres in bodies as a result of human sin. Tertullian concludes, "For in putting on our flesh, he made it his own; in making it his own, he made it sinless" (*Carn. Chr.* 16). Since Christ's body was without sin, the flesh cannot be inherently sinful. Furthermore, Jesus's ability to keep his body pure and free from sin and corruption was a sign generally of Christ's power over evil and particularly of his power to free bodies from sin and corruption.

Valentinus posed a different challenge. Unlike either other gnostic sects or Marcion, the Valentinians held that Christ did have an earthly body but that it was not born of Mary. It was not enough, for Tertullian, that Christ have a human nature; he must take that nature from the line of Adam and not be a new sort of human being made like Adam but not one of his descendants. Although he does not use Irenaeus's language of recapitulation, he appeals to Paul's Adam typology and calls Christ "Adam" through whom God restored the divine image in which the first Adam was created. Moreover, like Irenaeus, Tertullian invokes the comparison between Eve and Mary. As by Eve's belief in the devil's mendacious and ensnaring words did humanity turn from God, so by Mary's belief in the angel's declaration of the Word of God would humanity be set free from the devil and restored to its true Master. As the womb of Eve produced Cain, that "fratricidal devil," Mary's womb would bring into the world "one who was one day to secure salvation to Israel, his own brother after the flesh, and the murderer of himself. God, therefore, sent down into Mary's womb his Word, as the good brother, who should blot out the memory of the evil brother" (*Carn. Chr.* 17). Cain's murder of Abel was the first death that their parents' disobedience introduced to the world. This, Tertullian held, was undone by the faithfulness of Mary and her progeny. Jesus's death was the recapitulation of the first death; for by the death of Mary's Son at the hands of his brothers (the Jews), God freed Jesus's brothers (all humanity, Jew and gentile) from death. Contra Valentinus, unless Jesus's humanity is truly taken from Mary, then he is not as Elizabeth declared of her cousin's child "the fruit of your womb" (Luke 1:42). If Jesus were not from Mary, but a mere stranger inhabiting her womb as a holding place until his appearance, then he would not truly be of the line of David (Isa 11:1), and it would be wrong in calling him the stem of Jesse's rod (*Carn. Chr.* 21).

At the same time that Jesus's receiving his human nature from Mary provides continuity between the line of the first Adam and the second Adam—something lacking in Valentinus's account of the incarnation—Tertullian explains the significance of Jesus's being born from a virgin as the reformation of the human race. "He who was going to consecrate a new order of birth [*novae nativitatis dedicator*], must himself be born after a novel fashion [*nove nasci*]. . . . Accordingly, a virgin did conceive and bear 'Emmanuel, God with us'" (*Carn. Chr.* 17). From Mary, Jesus takes the "flesh of an ancient race" and so is true brother to Adam's descendants. But Jesus is conceived with a new seed so that the humanity re-formed in Mary's womb might be purified of its "ancient filth" (*antiquitatis sordibus*). The novel union of God and humanity—"a man born in God" and "in this man God was born"—means not only that Jesus's particular humanity was pure of sin's corruption but all those who are united to Christ in baptism share in the new birth and the new humanity inaugurated by Jesus's birth.

Tertullian's Christ is both Son of God and Son of Man. As Son of Man, he was born in flesh with a human soul (*Carn. Chr.* 11) and so was vulnerable to human weaknesses and death. As Son of God, his origin was not through birth from a mortal mother—unlike the sons of Jupiter—but was from the Father. Therefore, his was a spiritual substance that was exceedingly powerful and incapable of death (*Carn. Chr.* 5). But Tertullian, playing on Paul's contrast between the wisdom of the world and the foolishness of God (1 Cor 1:25), writes that the foolishness of God lies in the fact that this eternal and immortal Son of God was born and crucified, which prompts his famous declaration, "it is by all means to be believed, because it is absurd" (*Carn. Chr.* 5). The union of divinity and humanity in Jesus was possible because the Son was born of the Father's seed, that is, the Spirit, that took to itself human flesh from Mary (*Carn. Chr.* 18). Did this birth entail a change in God? Tertullian was familiar with an objection by certain heretical groups that, since a thing ceases to be one thing when it is changed into something else, the Son's change from a spiritual state into a material state would necessarily entail a loss of divinity. Tertullian replied that this is generally true because such creatures lack permanence. God, by contrast, is eternal and so possesses permanence to his nature. Therefore, God can change into any state he chooses without ceasing to be what he is. If, for instance, one can believe that angels took on the form of human beings and yet remain angelic in their core nature, how, Tertullian presses, could you think that God, who is superior in nature to angels, does not also retain his divine nature while assuming a human form (*Carn. Chr.* 3)? Tertullian is content affirming that the incarnation did constitute a change for God but not one that alters his essential nature. Having affirmed God's immutability, Tertullian appears unconcerned with the question of divine impassibility. On the contrary, he is more concerned to affirm Christ's suffering both as evidence of the earthly nature of his body and as the means of his redemption of humanity (*Carn. Chr.* 9). Against Marcion, who wanted to affirm the goodness of his god but feared the corruption of his god by a true incarnation, Tertullian points to God's condescension in the incarnation as evidence of God's true goodness. For Jesus is "the Witness and Servant of the Father, uniting in himself man and God,

God in mighty deeds, man in weak deeds in order that he may give to man as much as he takes from God. . . . [In Jesus] God held converse with man that man might learn to act as God. . . . God was found little that man might become very great" (*Marc.* 2.27). Here, as in Irenaeus, Tertullian's theology of salvation through the "great exchange" of divine greatness and human weakness expresses in an embryonic form the logic of the divinization soteriology that would be further articulated in the Alexandrian theologians of the third and fourth centuries.

Origen and the Father's Eternally Begotten Wisdom

More than any other author of the third century, the figure whose brilliance as an interpreter of Scripture and speculative theologian casts his shadow over the centuries to come is Origen of Alexandria. Yet he stands as the great enigma of the patristic era. First, he is an enigma because some of his writings that may have served as a foundation for doctrine in the early fourth century have been lost in part or whole or are preserved only in Greek fragments or a Latin translation by Tyrannius Rufinus (345–410). The classic instance is the treatise *On First Principles*, the authenticity of which has recently been called into question.[7] Second, because Origen's speculative method within the bounds of the Rule of Faith allowed him to offer a wide range of possible trajectories of interpretation of Scripture, one is not always sure which positions he held firmly, and which were contingent hypotheses. Therefore, any synthesis of Origen's Christology from his major works must be acknowledged to be highly provisional from the beginning.

In *On First Principles*, Origen's Christology begins with an account of the relation between God and creation. Whereas creation is material and embodied and therefore restricted to place and time, the divine is, as Christ told the woman at the well (John 4:24), spirit, immaterial and incorporeal (*Princ.* 1.1.4). Therefore, God is not fixed in place or time, confined either to Mount Zion where the Jews worshiped or Mount Gerizim where the Samaritans worshiped. As spirit, God is a simple intellectual substance, which means that he is noncomposite, without magnitude, and utterly one. In other words, God is irreducible; he cannot be broken down into constitutive parts. Because Origen's account of God and creation was derived from Jesus's words to the Samaritan woman, he immediately moved from metaphysics to its spiritual implication: the Christian's understanding and worship of God must put off material or bodily conceptions of the divine so that God is worshiped as he is, in spirit and truth.

Origen's was a dualist ontology of spiritual Creator and material creature in

7. Mark Edwards, *Origen Against Plato* (Burlington, VT: Ashgate, 2002).

contrast with the monism of Stoic pantheism that made no distinction between the divine and nature. Yet Origen's dualism was unlike that of the Gnostics that expressed the radical divide between the divine and the material as a moral distinction between light and darkness, good and evil. Rather, Origen described the immanent relation of the Creator to his creation using the metaphor of the sun and its rays: "the works of divine providence and the plan of this universe are as it were rays of God's nature in contrast to his real substance and being . . . [for] unable to behold God as he is, [the rational creature] understands the parent of the universe from the beauty of his works and the comeliness of his creatures" (*Princ.* 1.1.6).

To these attributes of God's simplicity, Origen adds one more: God is "without delay or hesitation" (*Princ.* 1.1.6). That is, God's will is eternal and immediate; there is no interval between God's will and its accomplishment. For a delay or interval would imply either that some external force caused the delay or that God acquired a new potency or that the divine will changed. In such a case, God would not be the first principle of all things but would himself be conditioned by something outside of himself. Since there is in him no delay or hesitation that separated God's will from his actions, Origen concluded that God's creative will and powers never "ceased from performing works worthy of themselves and have been inactive" (*Princ.* 1.4.3). This reasoning led Origen to conclude that creation itself has always existed, without beginning. That said, Origen was fully conscious of how problematic such a deduction was. He worried about the conclusions about the divine made by "feeble and limited" human intelligence, and he peppered his account with qualifiers such as "if we may say so" that expressed the contingency of all such theological judgments (*Princ.* 1.4.4). Origen's conclusion did not emerge entirely from his doctrine of divine simplicity. Rather, God's goodness is inherently generative. Drawing on Ecclesiastes 1:9–10, he concluded that God's creative will was an expression of his self-diffusive goodness. Since God's goodness is by nature self-giving, there never was a time when God did not impart a share of his goodness to others (*Princ.* 1.4.5). Since God did not *become* a Creator, all creation existed in an embryonic state of potentiality—"form and outline"—in God's Wisdom (*Princ.* 1.4.4.). In other words, in his goodness God willed the existence of other beings, and in his wisdom God determined those forms of life that would mirror and share in his goodness. This leads to the question: Who is the Father's Wisdom that fashioned creation?

Origen's Christology here and in his *Commentary on John* is an explication of the biblical names for Christ. Of all such names and titles, Wisdom is, for Origen, the name that establishes his relationship with God and with the world. He begins by identifying the figure of Wisdom with the Son based on Paul's description of Christ in 1 Corinthians 1:24 as "the power of God and the wisdom of God." Moreover, Wisdom is rightly called the Son because as Wisdom declares, "The Lord created me at the beginning of his ways for his works. Before he made anything, before the ages he established me" (Prov 8:22). This is what Paul meant when he speaks of Christ as "firstborn of all creation" (Col 1:15). In the next century, the difference between being "created" (*genēton*) and "begotten" (*gennēton*) would become critical to the theological grammar by which the Creator would be distinguished from creatures. And although Jerome (*Avit.* 2) reported that Origen held that the Son was created, more than the words themselves the key to understanding Origen's Christology is found in the implications he drew from the title Wisdom. Since God in his nature is pure intellect, then his Wisdom is necessarily of the same rational nature (*Princ.* 1.2.1). Moreover, since God in his simplicity is eternal and unchanging, his Wisdom could not be an acquired or accidental property. On the contrary, since God is eternally wise, it is unthinkable that the Father did not always have his Wisdom. Therefore, Origen concluded that it was blasphemous to hold that the Son had a beginning. For if the Son came into being some time "after" the Father, then the Father was once without his Wisdom and so is not eternally wise (*Princ.* 1.2.3).

The Son as Wisdom is, therefore, intrinsic to and derived from the Father. Commenting on John 1:1, "In the beginning was the Word," Origen argues that the "beginning" or *archē* does not denote a point of time. Rather, the beginning is the Father from whom the Word came and in whom the Word eternally abides (*Comm. Jo.* 1.101–102). The Word "through whom all things were made" is the Wisdom that contains the forms of creatures. Therefore, he is the *archē* of creation. But the Father, as the source of his Wisdom, is the absolute *archē*. Indeed, speaking of God as "the beginning" is a synonym for "Father." Yet for Origen, "Father" is primarily descriptive of God's relation with his Word and not creation. Whereas Plato in *Timaeus* 28c spoke of God the artificer as "the Father of all" by virtue of his creation of the world, Origen understood "Father" primarily to denote his relationship with the Son whom he begat. For whatever else "Father" implies, offspring is a necessary corollary. Moreover, the language of "Father" implies a shared nature; the Son, as the Father's only begotten offspring, possesses the Father's spiritual nature. Because the rational creatures were not begotten by the Father and so do not possess the Father's nature, they are not naturally children of God. They may enter into a familial relationship with God by their baptismal union with the Son who gives them, as partakers of the Father's spiritual nature, the power to become spiritual and thus children of God. To put it another way, before their union with the Son, Christians who were slaves to carnality and death, like Moses and the prophets, knew God only as Lord and Master (*Comm. Jo.* 19.5). But when they were united to the Son who confers the gift of the Spirit, believers renounced their carnal mode of life and instead became spiritual as God is spiritual. Then the God, who is spirit, becomes the one they call "Our Father who art in heaven"; as Origen says, "those who are begotten by the word of faith in him are called sons" (*Or.* 22.2–3). In contrast with creatures who must be raised by Christ from a Lord-servant relationship to a Father-child relationship, the Son never knew God as Lord but only as Father. Thus, the biblical language of "Father" and "Son" drew for Origen a line between the unique intra-Trinitarian relationship and that between God and creatures.

Like Tertullian, Origen saw a difference between God and his Wisdom, between the begetter and the begotten. Therefore, Origen concludes, by virtue of being begotten by the Father, the primal Wisdom has a hypostatic existence (*Princ.* 1.2.2). That is, Wisdom is an entity discrete from the Father. The Son is rightly called Wisdom economically because he is the one who imparts wisdom to rational creatures. He is able to make individuals wise in respect to God because the Son is the image of the invisible God (Col 1:15) and is the source of all knowledge of the transcendent Father (*Princ.* 1.1.8). But he also confers wisdom about the world because as the firstborn of all creation who was created at the beginning of the Father's ways, all creation had their formal existence in Wisdom. Therefore, in coming to humanity in the form of a man, the Son revealed the logic that ordered the cosmos. Precisely because the Father's Wisdom is self-disclosing, revealing the mysteries contained within him before all creation, Wisdom is called the Word (*Princ.* 1.2.3).

The unity of the Father and the Son as well as their discrete subsistence Origen explained by focusing on the Son's having been begotten by the Father. The language of "begetting" should not, Origen states up front, be misinterpreted as resembling the carnal form of procreation proper to animals and human beings. Because God, unlike animals, is spirit and pure rationality, the manner of the Father's begetting is unique. It is not like the asexual reproduction of creatures for whom procreation entails a splitting or dividing of the parent into parts (*Princ.* 1.2.6). Since God is simple, he is indivisible and cannot, therefore, be divided. Indeed, were the Son begotten by division, the Father would undergo change by being lessened, forfeiting some powers and properties to the Son. Rather, since the Father is eternally wise and has never been without his Wisdom, the Father's generation of the Son must be by "an eternal and everlasting begetting" analogous to the brightness that is continually emitted by a light (*Princ.* 1.2.4). In saying that the Son is eternally begotten, Origen means that the Son's generation was outside of time. That is, it was not a moment in the life of God but simply the way God eternally is. The Son, as Wisdom, unceasingly flows from the Father as thoughts flow from the intellect of a rational being. Moreover, even as thoughts, which are intelligible rather than material, are fully present in the mind of the thinker at the same time that she imparts them to others through speech, the Logos remains fully united with the Father at the same time that he goes out from the Father to fulfill the Father's will (*Princ.* 1.2.6). Thus, the Son is both eternally united to the Father and eternally subsisting as a discrete hypostasis.

The metaphor of light and its brightness Origen took from the description of the Son in Hebrews 1:3 as "the brightness of God's glory and the express image of his substance." Because the Son is begotten from the Father, the Son is not like human beings who become united to the Father through adoption (*Princ.* 1.2.4). Thus, the Son is divine by nature because he possesses the nature of the one from whom he is eternally generated even as the light generated by the flame is of the same nature as the flame whence it emanates (*Princ.* 1.2.5). As the brightness is of the same nature and therefore the image of the light itself, so too the Son as the brightness of the Father's glory is also "the invisible image of the invisible God" (*Princ.* 1.2.6.) For the Son, in doing all that the Father does and wills, presents the image of the Father. Thus, at the same time that Paul calls the Son "the wisdom of God," he also calls him "the power of God," which Solomon expresses when speaking of "the glory of the Almighty" (Wis 7:25). For to be the glory of the Almighty Father is to share the Father's power and might. Even as God is not wise without his Wisdom, neither is the Father Almighty without his power (*Princ.* 1.2.10). Therefore, the Son is "power proceeding from the power" (*Princ.* 1.2.9). Indeed, as the brightness that is the illuminating power of the light reveals the nature of the light, so the Word in exercising the Father's power is the image that discloses the Father's divinity to rational beings. It is precisely this dual aspect of the Son as wisdom and power that makes the Son the living image of the Father. In other words, the Son as the Father's wisdom is not the mere blueprint of the Father's plans for creation. When the Wisdom of Solomon (7:25) describes "the glory of the Almighty" as "an unspotted mirror of the energy or working of God," it adds a nuance to the Pauline description of the Son as the image of God. For, Origen explains, unlike a statue or mosaic portrait that is static, a person's reflection in a mirror is active and fluid, exactly matching the movements of the person (*Princ.* 1.2.12). This is what Jesus meant when he said, "The Son can do nothing of himself, but what he has seen the Father doing" (John 5:19). These words cannot be taken to imply some weakness or limitation on the part of the Son. Rather, they are simply Jesus's affirmation of his perfect union with the Father. What the Father does at the level of his will in heaven is mirrored in the Son's actions on earth. Thus, Origen concludes that "there is absolutely no dissimilarity between the Son and the Father" (*Princ.* 1.2.12). In this way, Hebrews's metaphor of brightness and image expresses both the immanent relation of the Father and Son and also the economic activity of the Son as mediator between God and creation (*Princ.* 1.2.7).

Although Origen affirmed both the unity of the Father and Son as well as the discrete hypostatic existence of each, it was his description of the latter that was the source of perhaps his most controversial christological legacy. In his reading of the prologue of the Fourth Gospel, Origen addresses the curious phrase, "and the Word was with God [*pros ton theon*] and the Word was God [*theos*]" (John 1:1). What sense does it make to say that the Word both was *with* God and *was* God? In the first instance, "and the Word was with God," the word "God" (*theos*) is preceded by the definite article (*ton*) and so should be interpreted, "and the Word was with *the* God" (*Comm. Jo.* 2.13). Here, therefore, John is distinguishing the Son from the God, who is the Father. In the second instance, "and the word was God," the word for God is without the definite article. In this instance, *theos* describes the Word as divine and names him "God," but God as distinct from "the God." By designating the Father as *the* God, Origen maintains, John recognizes the Father's primacy as "the uncreated cause of the universe" in distinction from *the* Word who is "that reason which is in each rational being" (*Comm. Jo.* 2.14–15). Jesus himself uses the definite article "the" to make the same distinction when, addressing the Father in his high priestly prayer, he says, "This is eternal life that they may know you the [*ton*] only true God [*theon*]" (John 17:3).

Origen recognized that the opening line of John's Gospel could be confusing for the simpleminded who confuse the statement to mean that the Word is a second God. In his identification of the Father with the one true God—"the God of gods" (Ps 50:1)—Origen thinks he has put that confusion to rest. However, if the Father is "the true God," is the Son not truly God? "To be sure," Origen answered, "[the Word is] 'the firstborn of every creature,' inasmuch as he was the first to be with God and has drawn divinity into himself [and so] is more honored than the other gods beside him . . . that they might be deified" (*Comm. Jo.* 2.17). Not only is the Son treated as divine only in a derivative sense, but he appears to be the first of a series of divine creatures who become gods because the Son made them partakers of the Father's divinity. The chief difference between the Word and other creatures lies in the Word's having been "with the God" from the beginning and so was divine from his begetting, whereas the other beings were not divine from their beginning but came to divinity by adoption and participation in the Word (*Comm. Jo.* 2.19). The Father, as true God, is the archetype. The Word is the natural image of the archetype. And rational creatures, who are made "according to the image" (i.e., the Word), are images of the image (*Comm. Jo.* 2.20).

The historical upshot of Origen's distinction between *the* God and *the* Word is that Origen has been interpreted to advocate a subordination of the Son to the Father. In other words, if the Word is not the true God and yet still divine, he must be a lesser order of deity. Consequently, when Origen's later interpreters read his explication of John 1:1 in light of a fourth-century theological grammar, committed as it was to an absolute divide between God and creature, they concluded that Origen was guilty of either subordinationism that denied the ontological equality of the persons of the Trinity or of a proto-Arianism that placed the Son on the creatures' side of the Creator-creature divide. While one can see both trajectories leading out of certain passages in his *Commentary on John*, Origen's Christology taken as a whole cannot be reduced to either of these alternatives. Although he does subordinate the Son to the Father—following, it must be said, other passages within the New Testament besides John 1:1, such as Matthew 24:36, John 14:28, 1 Corinthians 15:28, and so on—Origen did not conceive of the Son as being *ontologically* inferior to the Father. Origen expresses the Son's ontological unity with the Father by saying that he is the "natural" and "living" image of the Father, who, in begetting the Son, imparted to him the totality of his wisdom and power. In other words, Origen envisions the Son as having the same nature or being of the one from whom he is eternally begotten and of whom he is an eternal expression. Moreover, his distinction between being divine by virtue of being begotten by the Father and becoming divinized by participation in the Logos the mediator is critical to understanding his Christology. It reflects an incipient grammar for speaking about the ontological divide between God and creatures that places the Son on the side of the Godhead. Nonetheless, Origen's ascription of *theos* to the Father who eternally begets his Logos, to the Son who was divine by virtue of being with the God, and to rational creatures who become gods illustrates how elastic the term *theos* was in the third and early fourth centuries. Thus, it was possible for various groups within the Great Church, and even the gnostic sects, to confess that Jesus was the Son of God and was God while meaning quite different things by those words.

When Origen's Christology turns from speaking of the nature of the Logos to the union of the Logos with humanity in Jesus, his narrative of the incarnation begins in the beginning with the Logos's relation to the rational beings or *logikoi*. As we have already seen,[8] Origen, drawing on Plato's notion of the preexistence of souls, imagined that God created all the *logikoi* in a state of equality. All possessed ethereal bodies suitable to their existence in the heavenly ether. And all possessed the freedom to contemplate the beauty of the Father through contemplative union with the Logos who mediated the vision of the transcendent Father. Therefore, each of the rational beings had the potential for the blessedness of unceasing fellowship with God through the Son. But not all were equally blessed. For their degree of blessedness from the Logos's illumination was contingent on "the degree of participation proportionate to the loving affection with which each had clung to him" (*Princ.* 2.6.3). Those who received the revelation of the Logos were filled with a desire to see more. For these, their love was rewarded with further and fuller revelations of God's glory.

Eventually, however, all the *logikoi* cooled in their desire for contemplation of God and so fell, in various degrees, into bodies appropriate to the degree of

8. See chapter 4, pp. 89–90.

intellectual and spiritual apathy. However, one mind, of all the rational beings, did not fall but remained united with the Logos in rapt contemplation of the glories of the Father. This was the mind or *nous* of Jesus. The result of this union was that the prolonged contemplation of the Logos formed the thoughts and, therefore, the nature of the *nous* of Jesus. For through its contemplative participation in the Logos that took in the intellectual vision of God, Jesus's mind was divinized through a process known as *communicatio idiomatum*—that is, the communication or transmission of the divine properties (*idiomata*) to the mind of the thinker. Origen subscribed to the principle that you are what you think about. As Jesus's mind progressed in the knowledge of God and became more and more like God, this likeness increased his love of God. For Origen took as axiomatic that like is known by like, and like is attracted to like. The result was that the *nous* of Jesus eventually became permanently united to the Logos and perfectly conformed to the Logos in knowledge and love. Therefore, Origen says, Jesus's "inseparable unity with God" was no accident but the reward for the virtuous use of his free will. Because he chose in love fellowship with God above all, God, as the psalmist put it, "has anointed thee with the oil of gladness above thy fellows" (Ps 45:7) and made him the Christ (*Princ.* 2.6.4). Thus, it was the *nous* of Jesus that was sent to draw his fellow rational beings back to the Father and their proper home in heaven.

Although Jesus's mind never cooled, as did the other *logikoi*, his ethereal body was transformed into a material human body. The union of the Logos and the *nous* became the soul that mediated the union of the divine with mortal flesh. There was a reciprocal indwelling—the *nous* in the Logos and the Logos in the *nous*. The Word and *nous* of Jesus coexisted in perfect unity by a mutual indwelling, as Paul writes, "he who is joined to the Lord is one spirit" (1 Cor 6:17). Consequently, the very process of *communicatio idiomatum* by which the *nous* was divinized conferred divinity to Jesus's body in a great exchange: "throughout the whole of Scripture, while the divine nature is spoken of in human terms the human nature is in its turn adorned with the marks that belong to the divine prerogative" (*Princ.* 2.6.3).

Although Jesus possessed a rational soul, like all other human beings, his soul was not truly a soul like other souls because his mind never cooled in its devotion to God. The result was that, whereas the souls of other human beings were capable of choosing good and evil and so felt the tension and temptation that come with freedom of the will, the soul of Jesus had transcended that tension. Because his soul, before its descent, had exercised free will to cleave to God in love for God's righteousness, his will became permanently fixed on the good of God's will. Thus, Origen concluded, "by firmness of purpose, immensity of affection, and an inextinguishable warmth of love, all susceptibility to change or alteration was destroyed and what formerly depended upon the will was by the influence of long custom changed into nature" (*Princ.* 2.6.5). Jesus's soul was so thoroughly divinized by virtue of its affectionate union with the Logos that it was not susceptible to sin. Origen illustrates the point with the analogy of iron placed in a blacksmith's furnace. Though the iron by nature could be either hot or cold, the fire of the furnace so thoroughly penetrates the iron that the iron is "completely changed into fire" and remains so as long as it is in the furnace. So too, the soul of Jesus that permanently abides in fellowship with the Father's wisdom is rendered divine in all its thoughts and feelings (*Princ.* 2.6.6). Thus, like someone touching a glowing hot piece of iron, the woman with the issue of blood (Matt 9:20–22) was healed by touching the hem of Jesus's garment because in touching him she felt the power of divinity that completely suffused his humanity. This thoroughgoing union did not, for Origen, negate Jesus's free will and therefore compromise his full humanity. On the contrary, it was the perfection of a rational nature that was made to be forever united to God in love. Therefore, before his descent in the incarnation, Jesus's *nous* over time had come to such a clear vision of God's goodness that he did not will anything other than to be united to the Good.

The union of divinity and humanity in Jesus resembles the union of the Father and the Son. As Origen described the Son using the image in a mirror that perfectly reflects the movements of the person looking in the mirror, he employs a variation of that metaphor when speaking of the incarnation. Jesus's soul is, Origen says, like a shadow that is inseparable from the body and matches the movements of the body; for his soul matched every impulse and volitional movement of the Logos to whom it was united (*Princ.* 2.6.7). So too, the souls of Jesus's followers, as is written in Lamentations 4:20, "shall live under his shadow among the nations," participating in the Logos by being united to Christ. The parallel between Origen's analogies of a body's shadow and of the image of a face in a mirror is significant christologically in two ways. First, even as the image in a mirror has a greater resemblance to the face than the shadow does to the movements of the body, the divinized humanity of Jesus, and that of his followers, is not identical to the Logos in the way the Son is identical in his nature with the Father. Although Origen here is quoting Lamentations, neither the shadows of Plato's cave nor the earthly tabernacle as a shadow of heavenly things from Hebrews (8:5) was far out of his thoughts. In this way, Origen can speak of a unity between the human and the divine while nonetheless preserving the distinction between the creature and the Creator. Second, the exact parallel between the movements of the body and its shadow illustrates Origen's unitive Christology. Although the divine power is manifest in a creaturely form, the divine Logos is the ruling principle in union. Jesus's humanity voluntarily moves in accordance with the will of the Logos. This synchronicity of Logos and humanity allows those with spiritual eyes to behold in Jesus the Son the image of the Father.

Here Origen's view of contemplative participation is central to the ontology that governs his Christology. It is a participatory ontology that is thoroughly relational. The union of the Logos and the *nous* of Jesus becomes the paradigm for understanding the deification of the souls of the saints who abide in Logos and once again become spiritual beings. Yet now they are permanently united to the Logos and so transformed by their participation in God. They are made unchangeably holy by virtue of their union with the eternal and unchanging God.

At the beginning and the end, for all its audacious speculations, Origen's Christology retains the humility of awe. "When we consider these great and marvelous truths about the nature of the Son of God, we are lost in the deepest amazement. . . . When, therefore we see in him some things so human that they appear in no way to differ from the common frailty of mortals, and some things so divine that they are appropriate to nothing else but the primal and ineffable nature of deity, the human understanding with its narrow limits is baffled" (*Princ.* 2.6.1–2).

Bibliography

Primary Sources

The Gnostic Scriptures. Translated by Bentley Layton. Garden City, NY: Doubleday, 1987.

Irenaeus of Lyons. *Against Heresies*. *ANF* 1.

Justin Martyr. *First and Second Apologies*. *ANF* 1.

Melito of Sardis. *On Pascha*. Translated by Alistair C. Stewart. Yonkers, NY: St. Vladimir's Seminary Press, 2016.

Origen. *Commentary on the Gospel According to John: Books 1–10*. Translated by Ronald E. Heine. Fathers of the Church 80. Washington, DC: Catholic University of America Press, 1989.

———. *On First Principles: A Reader's Edition*. Translated by John Behr. Oxford: Oxford University Press, 2019.

Philo of Alexandria. *On Creation*. Translated by F. H. Colson and G. H. Whitaker. Loeb Classical Library 226. Cambridge: Harvard University Press, 1991.

Secondary Sources

Behr, John. *Irenaeus of Lyons: Identifying Christianity*. Oxford: Oxford University Press, 2013.

———. *The Way to Nicaea*. Crestwood, NY: St. Vladimir's Seminary Press, 2001.

Briggman, Anthony. *God and Christ in Irenaeus*. Oxford: Oxford University Press, 2019.

Heine, Ronald. "The Christology of Callistus." *Journal of Theological Studies* 49 (1998): 56–91.

———. *Origen: An Introduction to His Life and Thought*. Eugene, OR: Cascade Books, 2019.

Lashier, Jackson. "Tertullian's Inconsistent Anti-Monarchianism: Against Praxeas 8 and the Influence of Irenaeus." Pages 293–310 in *New Narratives for Old: The Historical Method of Reading Early Christian Theology; Essays in Honor of Michel René Barnes*. Edited by Anthony Briggman and Ellen Scully. Washington, DC: Catholic University of America Press, 2022.

Osborn, Eric. *Irenaeus of Lyons*. Cambridge: Cambridge University Press, 2001.

Waers, Stephen E. "Monarchianism and Two Powers: Jewish and Christian Monotheism at the Beginning of the Third Century." *Vigiliae Christianae* 70 (2016): 401–29.

5

"I and the Father Are One"

Nicaea, Its Critics, and Its Champions

During Diocletian's Great Persecution (303–305), when Egyptian bishops were imprisoned or, as in the case of Peter bishop of Alexandria, fled or were in hiding, the churches in the region of the Nile Delta suffered a weakened episcopal presence. Without conferring with the imprisoned bishops, Melitius, bishop of neighboring Lycopolis, took advantage of the situation to extend his episcopal jurisdiction into the region of the Delta by ordaining presbyters who became loyal to him. The result was a schism in Alexandria between the supporters of Peter and those of Melitius that lasted from 305/6 to 311. In this same period, there emerged in the Delta another source of contention in the form of a radical ascetic, Hieracas, who seems to have preached heterodox opinions about the resurrection of the body, celibacy, infant baptism, and the Holy Spirit. Such was the theologically confused and disordered state of the Church in Lower Egypt, when in 313 Alexander was elected to the archepiscopal see of Alexandria. In an effort to consolidate his authority and promote unity of doctrine, Alexander entered into conflict with one of his priests, a man named Arius.

If, as the historian Sozomen relates, Arius was one of the other candidates in the episcopal election of 313, Alexander surely would have been acquainted with him prior to his demand for samples of Arius's exegesis. Whenever Alexander became familiar with Arius's theology—the chronology and precise dating of events are hazy at best—Alexander summoned a gathering of Alexandrian clergy in 321, which condemned Arius's teachings contained in a creedal statement that he issued the previous year. Although he remained in Alexandria, gaining supporters among fellow priests, eventually Arius and his followers either were exiled or voluntarily fled to Palestine where they were welcomed as refugees by Paulinus of Tyre, Patrophilus of Scythopolis, and Eusebius of Caesarea. While in exile, Arius began courting allies among bishops of Asia Minor and Syria as well as Palestine. He laid out his case in his letter to Eusebius of Nicomedia and his *Thalia*. Alexander launched a letter-writing campaign of his own, seeking support from Alexander of Byzantium, Philogonius of Antioch, Eustathius of Beroea, and even Sylvester of Rome. In 323, a synod of Egyptian and Syrian bishops called together by Alexander issued a statement of condemnation. Later that year, Eusebius of Nicomedia, who extended his episcopal patronage to Arius, summoned a synod to Bithynia to condemn Alexander.

In 324, the emperor Constantine dispatched Ossius of Corduba as his envoy to Egypt to reconcile Alexander and Arius. Unsuccessful, Ossius departed Egypt for Antioch, when in December Philogonius died and was succeeded by Eustathius. This gave Alexander an ally in one of the most prestigious and influential episcopal sees. Eustathius summoned a council of some fifty bishops to Antioch to address doctrinal and ecclesial divisions in Syria but also to weigh in on the Egyptian controversy. The council produced a creedal statement that aligned with Alexander's theology and included an anathema, implicitly directed against Arius and his followers, condemning those who held that the Son was a creature made by God (*poiēton*) and therefore was not eternal. Three bishops, including Eusebius of Caesarea, refused to approve the condemnations and so were themselves provisionally condemned if they did not accept the Antiochene creed by the time of an impending council at Ancyra. At this point, Constantine, likely under the influence of Arius's chief ecclesial patron Eusebius of Nicomedia, intervened, changing the venue of the council to the town of Nicaea, near his capital, and setting the date for June of 325. In Nicaea, the emperor would be able to preside over the deliberations to ensure a final solution to the conflict that, to him, seemed a tempest in a teapot. Yet, as we shall see, the Council of Nicaea, far from calming the stormy ecclesial seas, would only stir up a greater theological tempest that would dominate the empire into the early fifth century.

Although Alexander's dispute with Arius precipitated a theological debate that stretched across the empire, theologians and historians (ancient and modern) have distorted our picture of the fourth century by attaching Arius's name to a controversy that extended far beyond Arius's particular theological positions. Indeed, the events of the second decade of the fourth century elevated to prominence an otherwise obscure priest whose emphasis on the absolute uniqueness of the Father and its corollary, the radical ontological subordination of the Son, brought into conflict bishops whose theologies represented two divergent views of the Father's relationship with the Son.

Although both views, which I will call the subordinationist and the antisubordinationist positions, reflect concerns that found expression in various trajectories of Origen's theology, more basically they represent what Arthur Wainwright calls "the problem of the Trinity" inherent in the New Testament. This problem centers around key questions based on claims about Jesus and his relationship with the God whom he called Father and the Spirit whose coming he promised. These questions were neither raised explicitly nor resolved by the authors of the texts of the New Testament. Indeed, bishops in both groups affirmed in their churches' liturgies and their own writings the distinction between God and creation, the Father's begetting the Son, the Son's role as the Father's agent of creation and of redemption, the Son's divinity, the Spirit's sanctifying work, and initiation with the baptismal formula "in the name of the Father and of the Son and of the Holy Spirit." In other words, Alexander, Arius, and Arius's allies shared the core beliefs, confessional language, and liturgical practices associated with the Great Church in the early fourth century.

Yet as their respective understandings of these shared points of confession emerged, it became clear that they were not using the words to mean the same thing. In particular, Arius and Alexander were both influenced by Origen and his varied approaches to thinking through the New Testament's "problem of the Trinity." Each, however, followed different answers Origen gave to the problems. Whereas Arius, with his strong antimaterialist and anti-Sabellian sensibility, emphasized the difference and separateness of the Father and the Son, and by extension the Son's subordination, Alexander placed the accent on the unity and thus coeternality of the Father and Son. Each saw that the other's emphasis threatened essential elements of their own confession. Arius's extreme subordinationism, and Alexander's condemnation of Arius and his explanation for the condemnation, exposed what they perceived to be mutually exclusive differences in their understanding of the shared confessional and liturgical language. Arius's own views differed, in some ways subtle and in some ways drastic, from those of his allies and subsequent generations of subordinationists. By contrast, the antisubordinationists saw a family resemblance in the christological and soteriological implications of all subordinationist views—no matter how diverse. So much so, in fact, that the antisubordinationists accepted Athanasius's branding all subordinationist positions, for both polemical and theologically substantial reasons, "Arian."

Even though this controversy that stretched from the second to the early decades of the fifth century was by no means confined to the particulars of Arius's thought, it is helpful to begin with Arius. For here we see how his idiosyncratic form of subordinationism exposed theological fault lines within the Great Church and forced the Church to fashion a truly catholic theological grammar that would govern its teaching about and proclamation of the one God, Father, Son, and Holy Spirit.

Arius's Theology

The starting point of Arius's theology was the absolute singularity of God. As he explained in his *Letter to Alexander*, the Father is unique. There is none other like him; for he alone is ingenerate (*Thal. fr.* 5) and without beginning (*anarchos monōtatos*)—a view he claims to have learned from Alexander himself (*Urk.* 6). He affirms the Father's radical transcendence and otherness: "We acknowledge one God who *alone* is ingenerate, *alone* eternal, *alone* without beginning, *alone* true, *alone* possessing immortality, *alone* wise, *alone* good" (*Urk.* 6.2). Arius expanded on this point in his *Thalia*, a presentation of his theology in the form of a banquet song written likely during his exile. Arius follows the logic of God's uniqueness as unbegotten to its epistemological conclusion: God is ineffable (*Thal. fr.* 4). Because God's nature is unlike that of any creature, he is beyond comparison with any phenomenon in humanity's experience. Consequently, Arius, following the logic of the generally accepted Greek maxim that "like is known by like," concludes that God lies beyond all analogical reasoning. One is able to say neither what God is nor even what God is like. One can say only what he is not, using words with negative prefixes, for example, unbegotten, or that are implicitly negative, such as "simple," which is a positive way of saying he is noncomposite. None is his equal in glory; therefore, none can truly tell of his glory. Precisely for this reason, Arius, adopting the logic of Middle Platonic Logos theology, contends that God's transcendence requires a mediator between himself and the very creatures whose existence he wills. The Father, therefore, begets a Son to be the beginning of other begotten things (*Thal. fr.* 6).

Being begotten from the Father's will, the Son is not without beginning. Therefore, the Son is not eternal or coeternal with the Father. Were the Son eternal, that would mean that there were two first principles or two unbegottens (*Urk.* 1.4). Even more basically, Arius reasons that, since a cause is necessarily prior to its effects, the Father who begets the Son must also be prior. Therefore, since the eternal and unbegotten Father is begetter or cause of the Son, "there was once when [the Son] was not" (*Urk.* 4b.7). Nevertheless, the Son is timeless (*achronos*) because he was begotten before all things of which he himself is their Creator (*Urk.* 6). Arius's claim that the Son has a beginning and yet is timeless comes from the ancient identification of time with the movements of the heavens (Plato) or the coincidental or relative movement of objects (Aristotle).[1] Thus, when Arius asserts, "there was once when the Son was not," he can contend that there is a necessary interval between the existence of the Father and the coming to be of the Son and yet affirm that, unlike all other creatures, the Son is a being created outside of time. In a letter written around 327 when Arius petitioned for his restoration to communion, he confessed that the Father is prior to the Son but not in a temporal manner (*Urk.* 30). This, however, rather than being an affirmation that

1. For example, the time of a runner's sprint between two points is simply an interval relative to the movement of the hands of a stopwatch. Cf. Aristotle, *Physica* 4.

the Son is eternal, may simply be another way of saying that the Son's beginning was outside of time.

Although the Son does not share the Father's singularity as being unbegotten, he is unique in his own way; he is a unique creature. Following Proverbs 8:22, "The Lord created [*ektisen*] me at the beginning of his works, the first of his acts of old," Arius contended that the Son is the Father's perfect creature who is unlike any other creature. For the Son was "begotten [*gennētheis*] timelessly by the Father, and created and established before the aeons" (*Urk.* 6.2–5). Arius saw no distinction between "begotten" (*gennētos*) and "created" (*ktimenos*). Because he is created according to the Father's will, he derives his being, life, and glory from the Father. This generation, however, is not from the Father's being, as if God were composed of some matter out of which the Son was fashioned. Therefore, as he explains in his letter to Eusebius of Nicomedia, the Son was made "out of nothing" (*Urk* 1.5). Because he is begotten by the unbegotten Father, the Son is a distinct hypostasis from the Father (*Thal. fr.* 7). Arius draws a further line between the Father and Son with his comment that when there was no Son, God was still God (*Thal. fr.* 14/15). The implication is that the Father is a necessary and self-sufficient being, but the Son is a contingent being who is entirely dependent on his begetter. Therefore, although the Son is Wisdom, spoken of in Proverbs 8, the Father is eternally and essentially wise independent of the Son. Indeed, the wise Father is the teacher of Wisdom (*Thal. fr.* 8). Wisdom, therefore, came into existence by the will of the wise Father (*Thal. fr.* 16). Although the Son is not coeternal with the Father, Arius does say that the Son is as old as the Father's will (*Thal. fr.* 20) and has subsistence from the moment of the Father's will. Like Philo, Arius is asserting that, when the Son as Wisdom was begotten from the Father's will, the Father was giving his eternal wisdom a discrete or hypostatic existence for the purpose of fashioning creation according to the Father's wise will. This has two important implications. First, the Son is the perfect image of the Father's will and wisdom. And second, the Son is able to mediate the Father's will to creation.

There is another important implication of the Son's having been created by the Father. The Son is immutable in his likeness to the Father and so was *not subject* to change as are other creatures. Nevertheless, the Son is *capable* of experiencing change in his passion. Therefore, unlike the immortal and impassible Father, the Son can become a human being, suffer, and die for the redemption of humanity.

The letter Arius wrote to Alexander explaining his theology reveals that Arius sees his position as standing firmly on the side of right teachings over against those of the heretics who dominated the second and third centuries. Saying that the Son is begotten from the Father's will cannot be confused with the quasi-materialist description of the Son's generation found in Valentinus's theory of emanation, or Mani's view that the Son was taken from the substance of the Father, or Hieracas's comparison of the Son's generation to the division of a single torch divided in two. Nor could it be confused with Sabellian Modalism in which God is a monad nominally divided into Father, Son, and Spirit. And he certainly was not an Adoptionist, like Paul of Samosata, who imagined that Jesus became Son at some later time. What was the alternative to these except that the Son was a hypostasis "begotten timelessly by the Father, and created and established before the aeons" (*Urk.* 6.2–5). Out of what was the Son begotten? Whence did he derive his being? Unless one subscribed to Valentinus's view that the Son was an emanation of the Father's being, the only alternative Arius could see was that the Son was created out of nothing. Anything else would compromise the Father's independence and autonomy. If the Son were consubstantial (*homoousios*) with the Father or were an emanation of the Father, then the Father would appear to be composite, that is, composed of some divisible substance rather than being immaterial and incorporeal (*Urk.* 6.5). If the Son were begotten by taking his being from the Father's being, he would be either a part of the Father or sharing the same substratum (*Urk* 1.5). And if the Son were taken from the Father (something analogous to the asexual reproduction of a single cell organism), then the Father would have undergone some change. God would be diminished by the transfer of some portion of his substance to the Son. Such was unthinkable to Arius. And since the incorporeal Father is indivisible, the Son could not have been begotten from the Father's being. Therefore, the Son could not have derived his being from the Father and so is not consubstantial with the Father.

The most radical dimension of Arius's subordinationism—a point of disagreement even with Arius's episcopal sympathizers—is the gap between the Father and the Son's knowledge of the Father. In the *Thalia*, Arius writes that God is invisible to all, including the Son, adding only that the Son sees the Father through the Son's own self-perception (*Thal. fr.* 9/10). In another fragment, Arius says that God is ineffable to the Son and even to himself (*Thal. fr.* 22). Although the Son comes from the will of the Father, this does not mean that he knows either his own being or the being of the one who begat him. For how can one who comes into being comprehend the one who is without beginning? These fragments have been the source of confusion and frustration for interpreters ever since. No one is fully confident of a final solution. What is important is the conflict between God's transcendence and the mediatorial role of the Son. If the Father is ineffable even to the Son, how can the Son reveal the Father to rational creatures? One of the most plausible solutions is that, although the Son knows neither the Father's essence nor his own, he is the image of the Father's will. Therefore, in his imperfect knowledge of himself, his power and will, the Son is imperfectly able to reveal the Father.

Arius's view of the Son's being begotten from the unique Father ontologically subordinated the Son to the Father. The Son is the perfect image of the unbegotten Father, but he is not the same being as the Father. He does not share the same nature as the Father. He certainly is not equal to the Father. As with Plato's division between the eternal/intelligible and transient/sensible realms and then Philo's Jewish adaptation of the Platonic tradition, Arius makes, at least implicitly, a radical division between the transcendent and unknowable Father and the visible and knowable creation. By virtue of his radically transcendent otherness, however, God cannot directly enter into creation. He must do so indirectly through the Son who bears his wisdom to his creatures. The theological problem then is what ontological status to give the Son. On which side of the God-creature divide does the Son fall? As the Father's *begotten* Word, does the Son fall on the side with other creatures? Or does the Son, who is clearly ontologically distinct from the Father and yet also unlike any other creature, nevertheless occupy a unique, liminal, quasi-divine state between the eternal, transcendent Father and the temporal, material creation? Is the Son, as the Father's subsisting Wisdom, a divine creature? Can Arius in any sense call the Son "divine" or "God"? His notion of God's uniqueness would seem to restrict the category "divine" in its fullest and most proper sense to the Father alone. Yet, as we shall see, at this time the language of "divine" was not confined to the God side of the God-creature divide.

Alexander and the Eusebians

Although both the theological sensibility that emphasized the unity of the Father and the Son and the contrary position that stressed their separateness as distinct hypostases predated Arius's eruption on the Alexandrian scene, Alexander's condemnation of Arius's subordinationism drew a line in the sand that Arius's fellow subordinationists could not leave unchallenged. Alexander's condemnation was perceived to be an attack on the anti-Sabellian sensibility at the heart of their Christology. Both groups were forced to clarify their respective positions in response to the issues raised by Arius.

Alexander followed a trajectory in Origen's theology that emphasized the Son's essential, and therefore eternal, union with the Father. If the Father is eternally Father, it is because he eternally begets the Son. The Father's perfection lies in his eternally begetting the Son. For the Son is the Father's Logos and Wisdom that are intrinsic to the Father's being. If the Father had ever been without his Logos, he would not have been eternally wise. Similarly, if the Son is the image of the eternal Father, then the image also must be eternal. Thus, the Son is an eternal corollary of the Father's eternally wise being. Therefore, the Son, as the Father's Wisdom, is eternally constitutive of the Father's being the Father. Since the Son is intrinsic to the Father's being, Alexander argued, Arius was wrong to claim that the Son is a creature and that "there was once when he was not." For the word "creature" necessarily implies time. Since a creature is made and so comes into being, there necessarily was some period before the creature existed. Since, however, the Son is intrinsic to the Father, there could not have been an interval when the Father was without his Son. Since the Son is intrinsic to the Father's being, Alexander concludes, the Son must share the Father's nature. Writing to Alexander of Byzantium, Alexander declares, "The essential sonship of the paternal birth, which results not from attention [via foreknowledge] to [Jesus's] conduct nor a discipline of progress, but by a distinct property of nature [*physeōs idiōmati*]," which makes the Son proper to the very thing that makes the Father God (*Urk.* 14.34). Therefore, the Son is divine, not a creature. Arius's designation of Christ as a creature—albeit a perfect creature—stemmed, according to Alexander, from his focusing on passages from the gospels that emphasize his role in the economy, especially his humiliation in his incarnation and passion, which led Arius to ignore other passages that affirmed Christ's "indescribable glory with the Father" (*Urk.* 14.4). Alexander goes so far as to impute to Arius an Adoptionist Christology. On the contrary, Alexander insists, while believers are children of God by adoption through the Spirit in baptism, Christ alone is Son of God by nature (*Urk.* 14.31).

While Alexander followed Origen in emphasizing the Son's identity as Word and Wisdom as being a necessary and eternal corollary of the Father's being eternally wise—with its contrast between the eternal and the created—such a view was normative even for some of Origen's critics. Methodius of Olympus, for instance, used the distinction of the eternal and the temporal to establish an absolute ontological dividing line between the divine and the creature. For this reason, Methodius, in his lost work *On Created Things* (*De creatis*), attacked Origen's view of the eternity of creation, arguing that God is unchangeable and self-sufficient and therefore alone is Father and Creator. By contrast, all things that were created had beginnings and therefore were not eternal and so were not God. Following this logic of the Creator-creature divide, he argues in his *Symposium* for the superiority of the Son to all creatures because the Son, being from the eternal Father, had no temporal beginning. Commenting on the Father's declaration at Jesus's baptism, "You are my Son, today I have begotten you" (Ps 2:7; Mark 1:11), Methodius stresses that the present tense, "You *are* my Son"—in contrast with saying, "You have become"—indicates that Jesus is the Son of God "unconditionally and without regard to time . . . [having] neither recently attained to the relation of a son . . . but having been begotten before [time]; that he was to be, and to be the same . . . [for he] already existed in the heavens before the ages" (*Symp.* 8.9). The baptism, therefore, is not a moment of adoption but of the Father's revelation of the Son to humanity as his eternal and unchanging Son. Yet even here there is an ambiguity. For, as John Behr notes, Methodius's description of the world as being "more recent" than the Son may imply that the Son has a "quasi-temporal" beginning after the Father but before all things. If that is the case, his view would be close to Arius's view of time. Yet Methodius's assertion that the Son is timeless and therefore "the same" conforms with his earlier correlation of immutability with the Father's eternity. In this respect, his logic is closer to Alexander's.

Although saying that the Son is intrinsic to the Father's being implies an essential unity between them, Alexander did not, as Sabellius, conflate the Son with the Father. As with Origen's interpretation of John 1:1, "the Word was with *the* God and the Word was God," that distinguished the divine Word from the Father who is *the* God, Alexander interpreted the title "Son of God" as describing the unique status of the Logos as being both one with the Father and yet distinct from the Father. For a son may be the image of his father but is not the same person. In this way, Alexander built on Origen's notion of the Son's being "eternally begotten" to move Logos theology well beyond Philo. Whereas Philo imagined the Logos as abiding in God before acquiring a hypostatic existence for the purpose of creation, Alexander contended that the Logos as eternally begotten from the Father was nonetheless eternally a subsistent hypostasis discrete from the Father. For Philo,[2] the Logos's subsistence is associated with the beginning of creation; for Alexander, by contrast, the Logos's subsistence is tied to God's being and so entirely prior to and independent of creation. Whereas Arius made the Son a separate hypostasis by subordinating the Son ontologically—a perfect creature in contrast with the Father's unique divinity—Alexander made the Father and Son distinct entities by insisting that the biblical language of "image" and "Son" implied a distinction between Father and Son while at the same time implying that the Son is intrinsic to and therefore coeternal with the Father. For Arius, as for virtually all his second- and third-century predecessors, the Logos has no eternal subsistence but only an economic relation with the Father as an expression of the Father's creative and redemptive will. For Alexander, by contrast, the relationship of Father and Son is timeless and therefore prior to and independent of the economy. Moreover, Alexander could hold that the Son is a discrete entity without making him ontologically subordinate or inferior to the Father.

It would be simplistic to reduce the dispute between Alexander and Arius to a dispute about the divinity of the Son. For, as Lewis Ayres has argued, the term "divine" had an elasticity in its semantic range rather than the dogmatically restricted meaning it acquired in the late fourth century. Following various examples in Scripture, angels and human beings could be called "divine" or "gods." Neverthe-

2. For Philo, see chapter 4, pp. 117–22.

less, what Alexander recognized—perhaps we might say intuited—was that there was no ontological middle ground between the divine and the creature. A being was one or the other; there was no such thing as a quasi-divine being. This is why in his letter to Alexander of Byzantium, the bishop of Alexandria says expressly that Arius was guilty of "denying the divinity of our Savior" (*Urk.* 14.4). Such a charge must have sounded like polemical hyperbole to those subordinationists who saw themselves as enemies of both the Adoptionist Paul of Samosata and the Modalist Sabellius. Not surprisingly, therefore, it would take the next sixty years for Alexander's theological grammar to be definitively canonized.

Alexander's theological and ecclesial opponents, who were Arius's episcopal patrons, are often called the Eusebians because the two most prominent members of this faction were Eusebius of Caesarea and Eusebius of Nicomedia. Although these two bishops were hardly theologically identical, they supported Arius because they agreed that the Son as distinct from the Father was also ontologically subordinate to the Father. Therefore, they united in opposition to Alexander's claim that the Son was ontologically equal to the Father.

Eusebius of Nicomedia, whom Arius addresses as a "fellow Lucianist," may have been a student of the Lucian, a presbyter from Antioch, who was Paul of Samosata's successor and was martyred in January 312 (Eusebius, *Hist. eccl.* 8.13.12). Lucian taught that the Son was the "image of the Father" and thus an entity discrete from the Father. Likely to distinguish himself from Paul, Lucian seems to have taught that in the incarnation, the Logos assumed a mortal body of which the Logos was its soul. Such a robust view of Jesus as the Word made flesh would clearly distinguish Lucian's Christology from Paul's Adoptionism. Following his teacher, Eusebius leaned toward the language of "image" to speak of the Son's relationship with the Father. With Arius, Eusebius held strongly to the uniqueness of the Father, who was the lone unoriginated. Wanting to avoid a materialist concept of the generation of the Son implied in Alexander's claim that the Son was "proper" to the Father's nature, Eusebius insisted that the Son was from the Father's will and bore the *likeness* of the Father's goodness and power—rather than being the Father's power and goodness per se.

Another ally of Arius and possible disciple of Lucian was the Cappadocian priest Asterius. He distinguished two types of essential divine qualities. On the one hand, there were the *unique* essential properties that distinguished God from all other beings. Of these properties, Asterius identified two: being "ingenerate" and, by extension, being "eternal." On the other hand, there were *nonunique* essential properties that God shared with other beings. These attributes in which others could participate include such things as divinity, progenitor, light, Logos, wisdom, savior. Thus, Asterius could explain how the Son, as the wisdom and power of God, was the first begotten of many powers that were created by the Father and participated in the essential features of his divinity. Asterius could also say of the Father and the Son, "One [begat] one, the God [begat] God, the indistinguishable [*aparallaktos*] image of his being and will and glory and power" (*Ast. fr.* 10). This was important for the divine economy since God's transcendence prevented him from having immediate contact with creation such that he required an intermediary to be his agent of creation. In this mediatorial role, the Son could not be counted the Father's equal. Rather, he necessarily was different ontologically; for if he were equal in divinity with the Father's nature, he could not fulfill his mediatorial role in the economy of creation and salvation. Asterius was thus content to speak of the Son as the image of the Father's will and therefore was a discrete hypostasis. Nevertheless, as the Father's image, Asterius thought, the Son should be thought of as divine in the sense of his possessing the nonunique essential properties. Therefore, he was content to refer to the Son as a second God.

Asterius's support for Arius is an example that the maxim "Politics makes strange bedfellows" was an apt description of fourth-century ecclesial politics. Arius agreed with Asterius's view of unique essential properties except that he added two more: ineffability and oneness. Yet whereas Asterius held that all the essential divine characteristics, except ingenerate and eternal, were possessed by the Son, Arius held that the Son was essentially unlike God, who is one. And whereas Asterius claimed that God was always Father—even before the Son gained hypostatic existence—because God possessed within himself the salvific power of the Word that would be manifest in Christ, Arius held that God was not always Father but became Father only when he begat the Son. Asterius, therefore, seems to have supported Arius, not because their doctrine was identical, but because of a shared opposition to, what they perceived to be, Alexander's failure to distinguish the Son from the Father.

Eusebius of Caesarea, about whom more will be said below, shared Arius's hierarchical view of the relation of the Father and Son. Yet, paradoxically, he spoke of the relationship using the language of participation similar to that of Alexander and the antisubordinationists. The Father, who is the ingenerate source (*archē*) of divinity (*Eccl. theol.* 1.2), begat the Son "before all ages" (*Marcell.* 1.4.23) in a manner analogous to the sun's emitting a ray of light. This begetting, however, was entirely immaterial and without passion as with human procreation. The Son was from the Father's will and not of the same nature as the Father. Nevertheless, the Son was also life because, as an overflow of the Father's goodness, power, and being, he participated in the Father's nature so that he could communicate life to creatures. Eusebius's description of the Son as the "overflow" did not, however, mean that his generation was from the Father's being. Such would carry the materialist connotation that the Son was composed of some divine substance taken from the substance of the Father. Rather, the Son was endowed with the gift of the Father's life and power in order that he might be the gift of the Father to the world. As the Father's gift, the Son brought eternal life to the world through his revelation of the Father. As with Eusebius of Nicomedia and Asterius, Eusebius of Caesarea was content to speak of the Son using the language of "image" and "likeness" that differed from Arius's account of the Son's essential unlikeness and ignorance of the Father. Nevertheless, he, too, shared greater concerns about Alexander's doctrine of the Son than whatever differences he had with Arius.

The Council of Nicaea: The End of the Beginning

When the three-hundred-some-odd bishops responded to the imperial summons to Nicaea, they gathered to deal with more issues than resolving the conflict between Alexander and Arius's supporters. Among the other issues were settling the Melitian schism in the Nile Delta. Out of this episcopal competition likely grew Nicaea's prohibition against bishops moving from one episcopal see to another. They also addressed the problem of how to treat the lapsed who apostatized during the persecutions. Yet it was the clash between the subordinationists and the antisubordinationists that hung most heavily over the deliberations.

The tendency of such councils is not to generate new positions so much as confirm existing practices and beliefs. This is both true and not true of Nicaea. The creedal statement that was produced expressed theological sensibilities and reflected language that predated June 325. One of the antecedent documents was the creedal statement composed earlier that year at the Council of Antioch. It affirmed that the Son was not created *ex nihilo* but was begotten from the Father and as such was immutable. Thus, it drew some line between creatures that were created from nothing and the Son. It did not specify what is meant by saying that the Son is from the Father except to say that he was not simply begotten from the Father's will. That was a clear rejection of Arius's position. It did, however, say that the Son was the true image of the Father's *hypostasis* (*Urk.* 18). Here the ambiguity of the word *hypostasis* confused rather than clarified. Did *hypostasis* mean a "nature" derived from the Father? Or did it mean that the Son was a reflection of the Father's identity as a "discrete entity"? Rather than breaking new ground or giving clarity to prior language, it simply echoed the language of Hebrews 1:3, which, contrasting the Son with the prophets and angels, says, "He reflects the glory of God and bears the very stamp of his *hypostasis* upholding the universe by his word of power" (RSV). While the language of "true image" carried a semantic range that made it attractive to subordinationists and antisubordinationists alike, the bishops at Antioch did not define its meaning except as implied by the anathemas. The Son who is the Father's true image could not be spoken of as a creature. Nor could his immutability be attributed simply to his will. They also condemned Arius's assertion that "there was once when he was not" (*Urk.* 18).

At Nicaea, Eusebius of Caesarea, as he wrote in a letter to his churches explaining his involvement at the council, said that he put forward his own creed. In it, he offered a string of attributes: "Word of God, God of God, Light of Light, Life of Life, only begotten Son, firstborn of all creation, begotten from the Father before all ages" (*Urk.* 22). Thus, he affirmed the Son's identities as being "of" the Father from whom he was begotten, but without any reference to the Father's nature or substance. Eusebius also echoed Arius's description of the Son's generation as being prior to all things and, quoting Colossians 1:15, "firstborn of all creation," which distinguished the Son from other creatures made in time. Yet without repeating Arius's description of the Father, Son, and Spirit as *hypostaseis*, Eusebius affirmed that the three exist discretely as "truly Father, truly Son, and truly Spirit" (*Urk.* 22)—"truly" implying a *real* rather than a merely *nominal* identity as was the case with Sabellius's interpretation of the divine monad.

The influence of these formulae or prior local creeds is evident in the language of Nicaea's creedal statement:

> We believe in one God, the Father, the Almighty, Maker of all things, seen and unseen.
>
> And in one Lord, Jesus Christ, the Son of God, begotten from the Father, only begotten, from the being of the Father, God from God, Light from Light, true God from true God, begotten not made, consubstantial with the Father, through him all things came to be, things in heaven and things on earth, for the sake of us human beings and our salvation he came down and was incarnate and became a human being. He suffered and arose on the third day. He ascended into the heavens, he is coming to rule the living and the dead.
>
> And in the Holy Spirit.
>
> And those saying, "There was once when he was not" and "before being begotten he did not exist" and that "he came into existence from nothing" or who affirm the Son of God is of another *hypostasis* or *ousia* or mutable and changeable, these the Catholic and Apostolic Church condemns.

The words of the creed, even apart from the anathemas clearly directed against Arius, ruled out Arius's identification of the Son as a creature. Whereas Arius interpreted the begetting of the Son to be an act of the Father's creative will, Nicaea, changing Eusebius's language from "of" to "from" (*ek*), affirmed that the Son was begotten "from the being [*ousia*] of the Father." Whereas Arius, making no distinction between the terms "begotten" and "made" or "created" in Proverbs 8:22, called the Son a "perfect creature," Nicaea made a distinction between being "made" (*poiēthenta*) and being "begotten" (*gennēthenta*). The logic of the distinction is that whereas something that is made, such as a wooden chair, is fashioned of some material different from the carpenter's own flesh and blood, a child is begotten by her parents and is composed of the same flesh and blood as her parents because she derives her nature from her parents. So too with the Son of God. To be begotten is to take one's *ousia* (being or nature) from one's progenitor; therefore, the Son is begotten from the Father's being (*ousia*) and so possesses the same being or nature (*ousia*) as the Father. The creed expressed this point with the insertion of the declaration that the Son is "consubstantial [*homoousios*] with the Father."

From these positive judgments about the Son, the creedal statement moved on to their negative corollaries in the anathemas or condemnations directed at Arius's assertion that the Son was a creature. Since the Son was begotten from the being of the Father and was consubstantial with the Father, he could not be said to be created from nothing (*ex ouk ontōn egeneto*). Nor could he be said to be made from some other substance or nature (*hypostasis* or *ousia*) than the Father's. Since he was begotten from the being of the eternal and immutable Father, the Son, too, is unchangeable and immutable. Therefore, he cannot be described as being changeable (*treptos*) or mutable (*alloiōtos*) as are creatures that come into being and so are inherently changeable. Although the creed avoided Origen's language of "eternally begotten," it seems to have followed the logic that if the Son is begotten by an eternal and unchangeable Father from that Father's nature and so possesses the Father's eternal divinity, then the Son himself must be eternal as well. Thus, there can be no interval between the Father's existence and that of the Son's. Therefore, Arius's assertion of such an interval with his expressions "there was once when he was not" (*ēn pote hote ouk ēn*) and "before he was begotten he was not" (*prin gennēthēnai ouk ēn*) were anathematized.

In the end, all but two bishops from Libya signed the creedal statement. Even the Eusebian supporters of Arius put their name to the document. Eusebius of Nicomedia did not assent to the condemnation of Arius. Nevertheless, Arius's subordinationism that assigned the Son to the status of a creature was condemned, and Arius was sent into exile. Even though the council did not embrace Origen's and Alexander's preferred language of "eternally begotten," it did confirm Alexander's affirmation of the Son's divinity as a result of his being begotten from the Father's nature. Moreover, with its anathemas against the Son's separation from God by some interval, the creedal statement implicitly affirmed Alexander's view that the Son was eternally with the Father and therefore was intrinsic to the Father's being. Thus, Nicaea set the grammar for speaking of Christ the Word as the "Son of God": the Son is divine and not a creature because he shares the Father's nature (consubstantial) and is coeternal with the Father. Where the council was creative in its language was its insertion of the term *homoousios*, which has been translated either as "the same being" or "same-in-substance" or "same nature" or "consubstantial." Although the term was likely seen as the logical extension of the earlier phrase "from the *ousia* of the Father," the term had, as we shall see, a tainted past because of its association with Paul of Samosata and condemnations in 264 and 268 at the synod in Antioch. Ironically, it may have been one of the Eusebians who introduced the term to the council's deliberation. If Ambrose of Milan writing six decades later in his *On the Faith* is to be believed, Eusebius of Nicomedia put forward a subordinationist statement that included the claim, "if, indeed, we say that the Son of God is uncreated, then we are beginning to declare that he is consubstantial [*homoousios*] with the Father" (*Fid.* 3.15). By this comment, Eusebius was not personally affirming the Son's consubstantiality with the Father. Rather, he likely meant that if the council denied an interval between the Son and the Father, then the Son must be coeternal and therefore coextensive with the Father. Since there is one God, if the Son is coextensive with the Father, then they are the same being (*homoousios*) and no real distinction between them exists. Therefore, for Eusebius, to claim that the Son and the Father are coeternal and *homoousios* would be to fall back into Sabellianism, which Eusebius assumed the council agreed was anathema. Regardless of who introduced the term *homoousios*, whether it was Eusebius as Ambrose claimed or even Constantine himself, once the council affirmed that the Son is indeed not a creature, as Arius claimed, but is coeternal with the Father, the bishops followed the logic laid out by Eusebius that the Son must be consubstantial with the Father.

The council's condemnation of Arius's radical subordinationism was not the end of the controversy. It did not provide a definitive solution to the disagreement between the subordinationists with their anti-Sabellian concern for the distinctness of the Father and Son and the antisubordinationists with concern for the unity of the Father and Son. For while the creedal statement provided language to speak of the Father and Son's unity, it did not provide clear language for speaking of them as discrete entities. How was one to affirm their essential unity without collapsing the Son into the Father in a Modalist fashion? Furthermore, it did not provide a unifying creed universally incorporated into the Church's liturgy. Many churches continued using their own local creeds. Indeed, all of its grammar was not universally accepted. Even defenders of Nicaea, like Alexander's protégé Athanasius, did not immediately embrace the language of *homoousios*. As such, it was not the beginning of the end but merely the end of the beginning of a disagreement that would carry on into the fifth century—long after Alexander and his Eusebian opponents had died. With Arius's condemnation and Alexander's death on 17 April 326, less than a year after the council, the first phase of the controversy was at an end, and a new phase with some new players who were ready to take center stage would soon commence. Although Nicaea's imprecision about the nature of the unity and division of the Father and Son would prove the source of discontent some decades down the road, the new phase of the controversy centered around conflicting theological personalities more than Nicaea itself.

The Anti-Marcellan Phase: The Eusebians, Marcellus, and Athanasius

The next phase of the controversy shifted focus away from Arius. In time, Arius was eventually returned from exile but was not readmitted to communion by the Alexandrian church because of his lack of contrition. Yet even his sympathizers who believed he was treated unjustly never took for themselves the appellation "Arians" or championed his doctrine of the Son. Rather, the clash was between Arius's former supporters and the supporters of Alexander and reflected the Eusebians' dissatisfaction with the council's conclusion, especially its use of *homoousios*. The term was suspect, as we have seen, because it had been deployed by the Adoptionist Paul of Samosata and condemned in the mid-third century. Yet the meaning that Paul had attached to the term was considerably different from the meaning suggested by the council's formula. "If Christ did not derive from man," Paul had written, "he is therefore *homoousios* with the Father and therefore there must be three beings [*ousiai*], one chief and two deriving from it" (*Syn.* 43.45). His point was that if one claims that Christ is anything other than a human being adopted by God, then he is a member of the species "God," of which there are three members. In other words, asserting that Christ is consubstantial with the Father is tantamount to polytheism. The condemnation of *homoousios* was a repudiation of any suggestion that the Son was a second God. Although Nicaea used the term to convey the very opposite, namely that the Father and Son were one God and not two, the term remained tainted, and with it was the creed that used it.

It is one of the great ironies of fourth-century theology that the real theological objection to *homoousios* by the Eusebian critics of Nicaea was not that they feared the term implied polytheism but that it smacked of Sabellianism. Their concern was that by speaking of the Son and the Father as *homoousios*, Nicaea was collapsing the Son into the Father. For while *ousia* could mean "nature"—as in the difference between a divine nature and human nature—it could also mean "being" or "entity," as when Paul of Samosata said that *homoousios* implied "three beings" (*ousiai*). Therefore, *homoousios* could be interpreted to mean "same being" or "same entity" rather than "same in nature," as was intended by the additional description of the Son as "God from God, Light from Light, true God from true God." However, since the council used *homoousios* to speak of the unity of Father and Son without providing comparable language that distinguished the Father from the Son, the creed's critics claimed that the council reduced the Father, Son, and Holy Spirit to one being. This interpretation gained credence when one of Nicaea's champions, Marcellus of Ancyra, quite openly espoused a Modalist theology.

The autumn of 327 saw mutual recriminations by Eusebius of Caesarea and Eustathius of Antioch. The Antiochene bishop had imposed a tentative condemnation of Eusebius at the Council of Antioch in January 325 for refusing to condemn Arius. Now in 327, Eustathius was deposed, at the likely instigation of Eusebius, from his see by a council of bishops. This drew Marcellus, as a supporter of Eustathius, into conflict with Eusebius. Although the enmity between the Eusebians and Marcellus predated the Council of Nicaea, the controversy between them escalated in the 330s when Marcellus attacked the subordinationist theology of Asterius, who had been traveling through Syria defending the Eusebians. As in so many cases, Asterius's theology was tainted by his moral failings. In Asterius's case, he had apostatized during Diocletian's Great Persecution and so was denied holy orders. Nevertheless, he remained theologically vocal; in 327, he penned an apologia for Paulinus of Tyre in which Asterius maintained that the Father, Son, and Holy Spirit were three distinct hypostases united not by a common nature but by a harmony of will. The Son, therefore, was a subordinate hypostasis who proceeded from the Father's will. Consequently, the Son was only an image of the Father's *ousia* and therefore was not equal to the Father. Moreover, Asterius's claim that Christ was but the first of a number of powers to be created by God appointed to Christ the status of a creature, albeit the first among creatures.

Marcellus had been at Nicaea in 325 and was a fierce antisubordinationist who accepted the language of *homoousios*. Ironically, Marcellus shared a doctrine of God similar to that of Arius. Both men believed in the absolute oneness of God. Marcellus's God was an indivisible monad, a single being (*prosōpon*), one power (*dynamis*), and one hypostasis. Where he parted company with Arius was with respect to the status of the Son. Whereas Arius viewed the Son as a separate hypostasis ontologically unlike the Father, Marcellus viewed the Word as identical with the Father and in no way separate or discrete from God. However, the focus of Marcellus's attack was not Arius himself but Asterius. Indeed, in all his writings from the post-Nicaea period, Marcellus never names Arius.

Yet the very objections he had to Arius's separation of the Father and Son applied to Asterius as well. Marcellus's emphasis on the singularity of God led him to conclude that the biblical names, Father, Son, and Spirit, reflected a purely economic difference. That is, they did not refer to real, eternal distinctions within God but merely describe God's creative and salvific action in the world in history. The Logos, therefore, was not distinct from God but was simply the Word of God abiding in God. A person's words or thoughts, he reasoned, are not a discrete entity separate from the speaker. Rather, one's words and thoughts are identical with the speaker. "It is not possible to separate the word from a man in power, and is separated in no other way than by the activity alone of the deed" (*Mar. fr.* 87). Thus, the Logos was simply the Father's thoughts. To illustrate the point, he borrowed from Philo the example of a sculptor. The sculptor has in his mind the technical knowledge and even pattern necessary to fashion a bronze statue. The sculptor's inner planning and deliberation about the statue are not between himself and some other being. It is simply the sculptor thinking out loud to himself. So it was, Marcellus says, when in Genesis 1:26 God says, "Let us make man in our image" (*Mar. fr.* 98). God was not addressing the Logos as a person but simply planning within himself the creation of humanity. Therefore, the Word always existed as an inner capacity of will and power that was the basis for his creative and saving activities. Thus, whereas Asterius imagined the three hypostases of Father, Son, and Spirit united by a shared will, for Marcellus there was no union of separate *hypostaseis* in God; there was only the eternal oneness of God. Therefore, in the economy, when God acted to create or redeem, God's activities were expressions of God's essential being. Thus, in the salvation history, the Logos in action acted in perfect unity with God; for the Logos was nothing other than God actualizing his thought in history.

Eusebius complained that Marcellus avoided the biblical language of "Father" and "Son" in favor of "God" and "Word" (Logos); nevertheless, Marcellus was willing to say that the Word became a Son when he was begotten by the Father. This, however, occurred only in the incarnation. "Therefore, before the descent and birth through the Virgin," Marcellus wrote, "he was only Logos. For before the assumption of the human flesh . . . it was nothing other than Logos" (*Marcell.* 2.2.1). The "Son" was simply the power or *dynamis* of God's Word in action economically. In the incarnation, the Word was a Son because he, with the assumption of a human nature, was distinct from the transcendent, incorporeal God who willed the incarnation. Therefore, against Asterius's claim that the Son was the image of God separate from the Father *before* the incarnation, Marcellus argued that the identification of Jesus in Colossians 1:15 as "the image of the invisible God" applied only to the incarnation (*Mar. fr.* 36). For were the Word an image of God—in the sense of sharing a true likeness—he would also be invisible. Marcellus was also uncomfortable with the language of "image" because "image" implied "otherness"—a separation between the archetype and its image, between God and the Word. Therefore, the Word was not eternally the image of God but only became a visible image for the sake of God's self-revelation. Indeed, such revelation could be salvific only because the Word was not other than the Father but identical to him.

The clash between Asterius and Marcellus quickly expanded, drawing in Eusebius of Caesarea. As Asterius had defended the Eusebians, now Eusebius of

Caesarea returned the favor. He responded to Marcellus's *Against Asterius* with two polemical works of his own, *Against Marcellus* and *The Ecclesiastical Theology*, that sought to expose the Sabellian tendencies of Marcellus's thought. In addition to his general indictment of Marcellus for his failure to read Scripture correctly according to the wise example of the fathers of the Church—including Origen—Eusebius criticized him for an overemphasis on the language of "Logos" that, in effect, replaces the language of "Son" and "Father" with which Jesus spoke of himself and the God who sent him. Whereas "Father" and "Son" are designations for two separate persons, Marcellus's depiction of God as a monad composed of God and the Word within God made no real distinction between God and his Word. Attacking Marcellus's use of the sculptor analogy, Eusebius countered that if the Son were simply the Word abiding in the Father, then the Son would not be a person but a mere faculty of the Father (*Eccl. theol.* 2.14). Marcellus's Son, therefore, is not really "the only begotten Son full of grace and truth" who "existed and preexisted" but a "mere word" (*Marcell.* 1.1.15; *Eccl. theol.* 1.18), insubstantial (*anypostatos*) and ephemeral (*Marcell.* 1.1.32). Moreover, if the Word is simply God's communication of his will and commands through Jesus—just as he spoke through Moses and the prophets—then Marcellus's Jesus, like Sabellius's Jesus, was not substantially different from Moses and the other prophets. He was simply the visible mouthpiece for God's Word (*Marcell.* 2.4.27). If there is no real distinction, they are "one and the same thing" just as Sabellius taught; therefore, Christ is "a Son-Father" (*Eccl. theol.* 2.5). If there were no distinction between the Father and the Son, then the one who was born of Mary and suffered and died was the Father himself (*Marcell.* 2.2.5), the one God who is over all (*Eccl. theol.* 2.4). Thus, Marcellus was guilty of patripassionism just like Sabellius.

Eusebius's own theology was something of a middle ground alternative to Marcellus's conflation of the Son and Father but also to Arius's and Asterius's hyperseparation of the Son from the Father that compromised the Son's divinity. Yet neither was he willing to make the Son equal to the Father as Alexander had. Eusebius drew on Asterius's analogy of the relation of a father and his progeny to press the logic of Jesus's language of "Father" and "Son." Just as a child is distinct from the parents who begat her, so the Son begotten by the Father is hypostatically distinct. Such was necessary to make sense of Jesus's claim of being "sent" by the Father; for were Jesus simply the Father incarnate, it would not make sense to speak of his condescension to humanity as "being sent" (*Eccl. theol.* 1.20). Conscious that speaking of the Son as a second divine hypostasis could imply two gods, Eusebius drew on Origen's distinction between the Father who is the "only true God" and the Son who is divine. Countering Marcellus's and his allies' critique that Asterius's separation of Father and Son resulted in a form of polytheism, Eusebius writes, "If the notion of proclaiming two gods makes them afraid, let them know that even when the Son is confessed by us to be God, the [Father] would still be the one and only God, the only one without source and unbegotten, the one who possessed the divinity as his own, and has become the cause of being and being in such a way for the Son himself" (*Eccl. theol.* 1.11). Thus, the Father is God as source of the Son's divinity. Drawing together Jesus's claim that the Father is his head (John 20:17) and Paul's claim that Jesus is the head of the Church (1 Cor 11:3), Eusebius reasons that the Father's relationship to the Son is analogous to the Son's relationship to the Church. Thus, he concludes that, since the Father is "the one source and head . . . who possesses the divinity of monarchial authority as his own without source and unbegotten," no one can say there are two gods (*Eccl. theol.* 1.11.3). Nevertheless, he immediately proceeds to say that the Father, as the head, "has given a share of his own divinity and life to the Son" such that "when [the Son] glorified his Father in [the incarnation], the Father glorifying him in return, revealed him as Lord and Savior and God of the universe and co-regent of his kingdom" (*Eccl. theol.* 1.11.5).

Although Eusebius affirmed the divinity of the Son on the grounds that he was begotten by the Father and so drew his life and his divinity from him, the description of the Father as "only true God" suggested that the Son was not the Father's equal. Finding his scriptural warrant in Jesus's confession "the Father is greater than I" (John 14:28), Eusebius explains the Father's superior glory (*Eccl. theol.* 2.7): the Son is dependent upon the Father for his existence; he was sent by the Father and can do nothing apart from the Father (John 5:30); he was obedient to the Father's will "even unto death" (Phil 2:8). The only begotten Son received all things from the Father, "who entrusted to him alone the direction of the constitution and government of the universe" that through the Son the Father might exert his dominion over all things (*Eccl. theol.* 1.13). Thus was Paul able to say that "God was in Christ reconciling the world to himself" (2 Cor 5:19). Therefore, commenting on the Christ hymn from Philippians 2:6–8, Eusebius concludes, the Son was "honored with the divinity of the paternal glory" (*Eccl. theol.* 1.13).

Although Eusebius clearly places the Son in a subordinate position to the Father, his subordinationism is not as extreme as that of either Arius or Asterius. They treated the Son as divine only in a nominal sense—as when Scripture speaks of Moses as god—and placed him as the first and greatest of God's creatures. For Eusebius, however, the language of "image" from Colossians and Hebrews denoted the Son's actual divinity. Explaining John's curious description that the Word both "was with God" and "was God," Eusebius says, "the Word himself is God, as an image of the God . . . as in a living son, who also has been made like, in the closest way possible, to the archetypal divinity of the Father" (*Eccl. theol.* 2.17). The question, however, that would hang over the next decades was whether Eusebius's moderate form of subordinationism that warded off the errors of Sabellius could also genuinely claim that the Son was "true God of true God."

In 335 at a synod in Tyre, the Melitians and Eusebians joined forces, issuing a condemnation of Athanasius and declaring Arius to be orthodox. The next year, a council at Constantinople condemned Marcellus and his disciple, Photinus, as Sabellians. Five years later at the Council of Antioch under the influence of Eusebius of Nicomedia, now patriarch of Constantinople, and Acacius of Caesarea, the council produced an anti-Modalist document known as the Dedication Creed, so-called because the council coincided with the dedication of a newly erected church where the council met. The Eusebians wanted to repudiate the accusation leveled against them that they had been "followers" of Arius (*Syn.* 22). Indeed, the creed they produced at Antioch, despite Athanasius's charge to the contrary, was far from the Logos theology espoused by Arius. The chief object of the creed was to offer language that differentiated the Father, Son, and Holy Spirit. For instance, consistent with Nicaea's condemnation of Arius's claim that "there once was when the Son was not," the Eusebians emphasized the eternal and independent existence of the Son. Furthermore, to counter Marcellus's denial that Father and Son were distinct individuals but mere economic personas, the creed declares that the Father is "truly Father," the Son is "truly Son," and the Spirit "truly Holy Spirit" (*Syn.* 23).

A second striking feature of the Dedication Creed is its affirmation that the Son is "only begotten Son, God . . . begotten from the Father before all the ages, God from God, whole from whole, sole from sole," to which it added key biblical names "true light, way, truth, resurrection, shepherd, door." The Son, therefore, is not a mere part of God or a being endowed with some of the Father's attributes; rather, the whole of the Son is the whole of the Father's divinity. In this way, the Dedication Creed expressed the Son's independence using traditional "image" language; the Son is "the indistinguishable image of the divinity, the *ousia*, will, power, and glory of the Father." This phrase is significant because it shows an acceptance of *ousia* language employed by Nicaea without going so far as to say that the Son and Father are the same *ousia*. Moreover, the creed ends with an anathema against those who say the Son is "a creature like one of the creatures." This prohibition sought to eliminate any carnal connotation connected with *ousia* and makes clear that the Son's begetting was not in the carnal fashion of other creatures. Describing the Son as the exact or indistinguishable image of the Father was a compromise. It had the advantage over *homoousios* of being closer to the biblical sense of Colossians 1:17 while at the same time affirming a strong affinity between Father and Son. For the Eusebians, it also had the advantage of making the Son "other than" the Father. Deploying language used by Origen (*Cels.* 8.12), the council replaced language of consubstantiality with the more vague language of symphonic unity. "The names are not given [in Scripture] lightly or idly, but signify exactly the particular *hypostasis* and order and glory of each of those who are named, so that they are three in *hypostasis* but one in agreement [*symphōnia*]."

Yet, in the coming decades, the language of the Dedication Creed was troubling to some defenders of Nicaea. First, to say that the Son is a mere image of the Father's divinity implies that the Son is not divine or at least not equal in divinity with the Father. Second, the creed's third stipulation that the names "Father," "Son," and "Holy Spirit" and their appearance in the baptismal formula determine the "order and glory" suggested an ontological hierarchy treating the Son as inferior to the Father. If the Son is "God," he is a lesser God. Thus, although the language of the Dedication Creed differentiates Father and Son, the language it chooses would be viewed as subordinationist. Nevertheless, the Eusebian's Dedication Creed was a damning defeat for Marcellus. The final blow would come ten years later in 351 at the First Council of Sirmium with its condemnation of Marcellus's disciple, Photinus.

While the Eusebians were attacking Marcellus and Photinus, they were also targeting another figure who, though repeatedly condemned and sent into exile, would be an enduring voice of the antisubordinationist cause through his narrative of the saving work of the Son's incarnation. Equally enduring and damning was his construction of the category "Arian" with which to malign the Eusebians and their heirs. This figure was Athanasius of Alexandria.

Athanasius had attended the Council of Nicaea as Alexander's secretary. He, therefore, made no direct contribution to the proceedings but was only an observer. This prepared him as Alexander's protégé to succeed the bishop of Alexandria upon his death in 328. Nevertheless, the episcopal election in Alexandria was a hotly contested affair. Athanasius was opposed by clergy who were loyal to Melitius. Although Athanasius ultimately won, his election was tainted with accusations by the Melitians that Athanasius had used violence and bribery to secure his victory. Athanasius's refusal to readmit Arius to communion after a period of exile did not foster reconciliation with the Eusebians. The Eusebians, therefore, were more than happy to use the Melitian accusations against Alexander and Athanasius to undermine Alexander's legacy by attacking his heir. At a synod of bishops convened at Tyre in 335, they leveled charges of graft against Athanasius. He was judged guilty and sent into exile. The hatchet between the Alexandrians and the Eusebians clearly had not been buried. During his exile in Rome, Athanasius encountered another expatriate, Marcellus. Although Athanasius would ultimately distance himself from Marcellus's Modalism, the two found common cause in their opposition to the Eusebians.

In the period between his election to the see of Alexandria and his first exile, Athanasius penned a defense of the antisubordinationist theology of Alexander. This was the second of a two-volume work, *Against the Greeks–On the Incarnation*. The absence of a polemical tone and any reference to Arius and his allies led some scholars to date the treatise before Nicaea. More recently, scholars like Khaled

Anatolios have put its composition after his election and explained his silence on the Arians as a strategic move not to earn the ire of Constantine, who had had his fill of disruption and division in his empire created by theological controversy. Indeed, the nonpolemical tone of *On the Incarnation* may have allowed the work to have lasting influence as an expression of the antisubordinationist position of Alexander and Athanasius.

The central question of *On the Incarnation* is, "Why did the Word have to become incarnate in order to save humanity?" Athanasius's answer was that only the Word who originally made humanity in the image of God could himself restore to humanity the very image necessary to free humanity from the decline into death (*Inc.* 1). His argument required him to go back to the very beginning. There God made the world through the agency of his Son, the Word who is the image of God. Drawing on Plato's explanation for God's creation in *Timaeus*, Athanasius explained that creation was an expression of God's generosity or *philanthrōpia*. God's goodness was self-defusing. Rather than hoarding his goodness, he willed the existence of creatures with whom to share his goodness. In the case of human beings, he did not endow them with mere existence, as he did the flora and fauna. Instead, the Word fashioned them in his own likeness by endowing them with reason (*Inc.* 3). As rational creatures, Adam and Eve's experience of the world was not confined to the world accessible through the senses. Rather, reason allowed them to apprehend the intelligible reality that lay behind the sensible world, namely God himself (*Inc.* 4). Following the logic of the maxim that like is known by like and like is attracted to like, Athanasius saw the gift of the divine likeness as necessary for humanity to know the goodness of the Creator and be drawn to him. Through such knowledge of and attraction to God, human beings were able to participate in the divine nature. The logic was that, when the mind thinks about a thing, the *object* of its thought becomes the *content* of its thoughts. The mind becomes conformed to the object of its meditation. Therefore, as the mind contemplates the divine, it takes on a greater likeness to God because the mind itself is being conformed to the divine object of its contemplation. That is, the mind reflects the attributes of the God it contemplates. Not only does one, as we would say today, internalize the virtues one "sees" in God, but the mind participates in the very life of God. Thus, unstable and mortal humanity was given incorruptibility that it might not experience decay and pass away into death (*Inc.* 4–5). Consequently, the divine image allowed human beings to receive the gift of immortality through participation in God. This transformative participation in the divine is what Athanasius calls *theopoiēsis*, which means "being made divine."

With Adam and Eve's disobedience, the human race turned away from God in sin. Instead of focusing their minds on God, human beings set their thoughts on the good but corruptible material world. With their minds centered on creatures rather than their Creator, the content of their thoughts no longer conformed to God. Consequently, over time their knowledge of God waned and their likeness to God faded. As the divine image was compromised, so too was their rational nature so that they were not able to participate in the divine nature as they had in paradise (*Inc.* 12). Thus, although the image of God was not lost altogether, their rational nature diminished to the point that humanity ceased to know God rightly (*Inc.* 6). Without this likeness to God, human beings were not able to participate in God and so could no longer enjoy the gifts of incorruptibility and immortality. Rather, unstable humanity experienced death as the natural consequence of turning their minds from the God who is the source of life. Athanasius's logic was that, since human beings could be immortal only by participating in God, apart from such divinizing participation, they would return to what he called their original and natural state, namely the nothingness out of which the Word fashioned them in the beginning (*Inc.* 11). Thus, sin threatened God's gift of creation by threatening humanity with annihilation. Although God did not owe humanity anything and so was under no compulsion to redeem disobedient humanity, allowing sin to ruin creation would be a sign of weakness. Therefore, so that his will would ultimately prove sovereign, God chose to save humanity from the consequence of their disobedience. In order to stop humanity's slide toward oblivion, God had to restore to humanity the ability to participate in the divine nature. This required returning to humanity the gift of the image of God (*Inc.* 13).

Wounded by sin, humanity had not entirely lost the knowledge of God. It retained the idea that there was a God, but because their minds were set upon the material world of creatures, they thought of God in creaturely terms. Therefore, they began to fashion images of God after the form of creatures. These were the idols of pagan religion (*Inc.* 14). How, therefore, could God restore the image of God to people whose minds were filled with misconceptions of God because they thought of the divine as a falcon or jackal, or worse the passionate deities of the Greek pantheon? God's solution—the greatest expression of his love for humanity, his *philanthrōpia*—was for his Son the Word, who made humanity after his image and likeness in the beginning, to become a creature himself and take on the likeness of sinful flesh. Humanity's gaze was fixed upon the material world, and in response, the Word chose to meet humanity's gaze in the material world. In the incarnation, the Word joined himself to humanity by refashioning a new humanity in Mary's womb (*Inc.* 8). This new humanity, this new Adam, was not only made *after* the image of God; Jesus *was* the image of God, the Word made flesh. Because the Word was the Son of God and equal in divinity with the Father, the union of the Word's divinity with mortal human nature made human nature once more a participant in the divine nature and with it immortality. Like a small measure of leaven added to a lump of dough, the immortal Word joined to the lump of humanity and imparted to all humanity the resurrection principle that prevented humanity from receding into nothingness (*Inc.* 9). Now human nature would be capable of being resurrected.

The incarnation of the Word was salvific in a second way. Salvation was possible only through the knowledge of God gained through a knowledge of Jesus. As Jesus revealed in his high priestly prayer, "This is eternal life that they might know you the one true God and Jesus Christ whom you have sent" (John 17:3). Such knowledge was salvific because, for Athanasius, it was not mere propositional knowledge, as with mathematical theorems, but knowledge that allowed participation in the one who is life itself. Because the Word became flesh and dwelt among humanity in a visible form, human beings were once again able to see God—now in the flesh (*Inc.* 15). As the image of the invisible God, Jesus gave to humanity a right knowledge of God. Humanity, whose mind was fixed upon the flesh, could now know God in the flesh. No longer would they rely on images of a god of their own making; now they could rely on a true image of God's making. In the vision of the incarnate Word, humanity received a vision of God. Here again Athanasius drew on Jesus's Farewell Discourse in John, when, responding to Philip's entreaty, "Show us the Father," Jesus declared, "Anyone who has seen me has seen the Father" (John 14:9); for as he had earlier told them, "I and the Father are one" (John 10:30). Consequently, when human beings contemplated the person of Jesus the Word made flesh, the Son of God became the object of their thought. When the incarnate Word became the content of their contemplation, their minds became conformed to the Word, and they were renewed in the image and likeness of the one who is the Father's image. Thus, the Word, who made humanity in the beginning, now in the incarnation not only refashioned human nature in himself but created the condition for humanity's divinization. As Athanasius famously wrote, "He [the Word] became man that man might be made god" (*Inc.* 54). By this, Athanasius did not mean that human beings took on the metaphysical characteristics unique to God, that is, omnipotence, omniscience, and so on. Rather, he meant that humanity might share not only God's moral character, his *philanthrōpia*, but also his incorruptibility and immortality.

Athanasius illustrated the divinizing effects of the incarnation by pointing to the life of Saint Antony. As an ascetic, Antony was guided by reason (Logos) because his soul participated in the divine purity of the Word and so maintained emotional stability. Athanasius believed in the psychosomatic unity of the person according to which the soul was the ruling principle or *hēgemonikon* that governed the body. The condition of the soul affected the condition of the body. Therefore, because his soul was in an advanced stage of being divinized, it had attained a godlike stability through fellowship with the unchanging Logos. This equanimity the soul passed on to his body so that it possessed a stasis akin to that final freedom from corruption that will come at the resurrection. Although Antony had not attained to perfect incorruption and immortality—for he did die—his relative lack of decay and degeneration illustrated the deifying effects of monastic participation in the divine Word.

Such divinization provided the deep logic for the antisubordinationism of *On the Incarnation*. Although Eusebius subscribed to divinization through the knowledge of God, this saving knowledge revealed by Jesus was God's will. Thus, deification came through obedience to the Father's will. For Athanasius, divinization was the result of an ontological participation in the divine nature through the knowledge of the Father Jesus revealed in himself. If humanity is to be delivered from death by participating in the divine nature through Jesus the incarnate Word, then the Word cannot be a creature, even a semidivine or quasi-divine being. Rather, the Word can communicate the Father's life-giving divinity to human beings only if he is fully divine—that is, only if "the Son is the proper Word and wisdom and power from the Father" (*Inc.* 32). Therefore, the Son cannot be ontologically subordinate to the Father but must, ontologically speaking, be equal in divinity with the Father.

During his second exile in Rome (339–343), Athanasius launched a methodical attack on the Eusebians, whom he referred to in the title of the orations as "Arians." His goal in these discourses was both to counter the Eusebians' subordinationist interpretations of Scripture and, equally important, to create a connection in the minds of his readers between the theology of the Eusebians and their erstwhile ally, the condemned heretic Arius.

After offering a summary of Arius's *Thalia*, Athanasius challenges Arius's slogan that "there was once when the Son was not" because it renders the Son a mere creature. Although Athanasius had previously employed the language of "likeness" (*homoios*) to describe the Son's relationship with the Father, here he distinguished between being "very God" and being "like God." The former indicates that the Son is "proper to [the Father's] essence" (*idios tēs tou patros ousias*) and "existing in one essence [*homoousios*] with the Father," while the latter is applied to creatures who gain a resemblance to God by participation in the Word through the Spirit (*C. Ar.* 1.3.9). Thus, he used the language of "participation" to draw a line between creature and deity. Unlike the Son who possesses the divine attributes by virtue of his shared essence with the Father who begot him, human beings do not naturally possess these divine qualities but acquire them by "participation" so as to become "like" God. For that which possesses an attribute by "participation" can lose the attribute if separated from the one in whom it participates. But a natural attribute is intrinsic to one's being and cannot be lost. Since the Son is God by nature, the divine qualities cannot be taken away; therefore, he is unalterably divine (*C. Ar.* 1.11.37).

Athanasius proceeds to illustrate the ways Scripture distinguishes the creature from Creator. Christ is identical with the "eternal power and Godhead" to which Paul referred: "Ever since the creation of the world his invisible nature, namely his eternal power and deity, has been perceived in the things that have been made" (Rom 1:20). Yet Jesus did not answer Philip's request, "Show us the Father," by saying, "Just look at creation." Athanasius's point is that, if Jesus merely possessed a creaturely likeness to God, then the incarnation would have been superfluous; for the vision of God in Jesus would be no clearer than one would receive by looking at nature (*C. Ar.* 1.4.12).

Moreover, time is a property of creatures. Arius and his allies avoided the language of time when speaking of the Son's generation, saying, "There was once when he was not," rather than "There was a time when he was not." Athanasius countered that this is a distinction without a difference. To speak of "before" the Son's generation is to mean that the Son is not eternal but a creature who comes into being. Such becoming, with its intervals before and after coming into being, is time. Yet Jesus, in saying, "I am truth," rather than "I became truth," claims truth to be an eternal property of his being (*C. Ar.* 1.4.13). To counter the Arian argument that the term "son" necessarily implies a begetting and with it a moment before his being begotten, Athanasius explains that the scriptural terms "Father" and "Son" are not intended to convey a temporal relationship but an ontological one: a son shares the same nature as the father who begot him (*C. Ar.* 1.8.29). He goes on to argue that the eternal and immaterial Father's mode of generation is unlike that of earthly fathers. God's offspring is eternally begotten from God's perfect nature and therefore is a natural expression of God's being, even as the radiance of the light is a natural expression of the nature of the flame (*C. Ar.* 1.5.14). For the expression of a thing is inseparable from and intrinsic to the substance of which it is an expression (*C. Ar.* 1.6.20).

Although the line between creature and divinity was at times blurry for Arius and the Eusebians, Arius's concern for the Father's absolute singularity led him to use the category of "unoriginate" (*agennētos* or *agenētos*) to divide God from creatures. The Eusebians, as we have seen, adopted this position, arguing that if Father and Son were coeternal, then there would be two unoriginates or two first principles, which would make no sense. When Athanasius turns to this argument, he reasons that the term "unoriginate" properly applies to the Father but can in another sense also apply to the Son. Inasmuch as the Father is the eternal source of the Son's begetting, strictly speaking the Father alone is uncaused or ingenerate. Since the Son is begotten by the Father, he is not properly speaking "ingenerate." Yet, Athanasius argues, Asterius's definition of *agenētos* as "what is not a work but was always" also applies to the Son. For the Son, as the eternally begotten Word, Wisdom, and Power of the Father, is, in contrast with all the creatures made by the

Son, not a "work" but is eternal (*C. Ar.* 1.9.30–34). Thus, Athanasius distinguishes two meanings of *agennētos*/*agenētos*: one applying to the Son qua God and the other applying to God the Father qua Father. To put it another way, the Son *as Son* is not unoriginate or without cause, but the Son *in his divinity* is unoriginate and uncaused.

Another key question concerned the mutability of the Son. For Arius, God was unbegotten and eternal—therefore not subject to change—whereas Scripture seemingly speaks of Christ as alterable. For example, Philippians 2:9–10, "Wherefore God has highly exalted him and given him a name at which every knee shall bow," implies that the Son is given an exalted status that he earns as a reward for his faithfulness. Similarly, the psalmist speaks prophetically of Christ, "You love righteousness and hate iniquity. Therefore, God, your God, has anointed you" (Ps 45:7; cf. Heb 1:9). The Arians, according to Athanasius, took this to mean that the Word was not "very God" from the beginning but was made God at his anointing. In both cases, Athanasius sees the exaltation and anointing as being conferred not on the Word but on Christ's humanity and with it his followers. Philippians cannot, he argues, be speaking about Christ since the Son was the "King of glory" from the beginning. Rather, "exaltation" refers to Jesus's resurrection and those who will share in his resurrection (*C. Ar.* 1.11.44–45). Similarly, "anointing," he explains, cannot refer to the deification of Christ since he was God before creation. Rather, the anointing of Jesus at his baptism in the Jordan is a sign giving proof that human beings are sanctified and deified by the intimate indwelling of the Spirit (*C. Ar.* 1.12.51). In his explanation of both passages, Athanasius sees Jesus as a second Adam whose exaltation and anointing extend to those who participate in his redeemed and glorified humanity. What happens to Jesus does not mark a change in the Word but the change wrought in those who are in Christ.

Against the background of this creature-Creator grammar, Athanasius turns to the subordinationists' use of Proverbs 8:22 to claim that the Son is "a creature but not as one of the creatures." Here, too, they are guilty of a distinction without a difference. Either the Word is the Creator and so confessed to be Son by nature, or he is a creature "assigned to the same condition as the rest [of creatures] one with another. . . . For though the Son excels the rest on a comparison, he is still a creature as they are" (*C. Ar.* 2.16.20). No creature, made from nothing, can itself be a Creator (*C. Ar.* 2.16.21). Moreover, Athanasius asks rhetorically, how else would God create except through his Word and Wisdom, which are expressions of God's very essence (*C. Ar.* 2.16.22)? Athanasius cites a view he attributes to Arius, Eusebius, and Asterius, namely that God willed creation but knew "it could not endure the untempered hand of the Father" and so had to create an intermediary first who would be the agent of his will (*C. Ar.* 2.17.24). Such a position, Athanasius charges, denies that God is the Creator of all things and belies Isaiah's declaration,

"The everlasting God, the Lord, the Creator of the ends of the earth, is not faint or weary" (Isa 40:28; *C. Ar.* 2.17.25).

When he turns to the specific wording of Proverbs 8:22, Athanasius explains that proverbial speech, as Jesus himself says (John 16:25), is figurative, and its true meaning is hidden. Therefore, when Wisdom says, "The Lord created me a beginning of his ways for his works," "created" may be a synonym for "beget" if it is referring to the Word through whom all things were created (*C. Ar.* 2.19.44). On the other hand, "create" also may refer not to the Word in his preexistence but to his incarnation. In this case, "created" refers not to the generation of the Word's substantial existence. Rather, it carries the economic sense as when Ephesians (2:15) says that God has abolished the law and created in Christ one new man out of two, or when Jeremiah (31:22) declares, "The Lord created a new salvation" (*C. Ar.* 2.19.46). Therefore, Proverbs 8:22, anticipating John 1:14, "And the Word became flesh," rightly means, "My Father has prepared for me a body and has created me for men on behalf of their salvation" (*C. Ar.* 2.19.47).

Beyond its theological and exegetical arguments, Athanasius's *Orations Against the Arians* scored a rhetorical victory against the Eusebians by branding their theology as "Arian." As we have seen, although Arius and his Eusebian allies shared subordinationist sensibilities, their theology was hardly of a single piece. Nevertheless, following Athanasius's return from exile in 338, he began developing the narrative of a conspiracy against himself by a group he called "Arian madmen." The phrase "Arian madmen" may first have been used by Eustathius as a label for Arius's sympathizers, who accepted the judgment of Nicaea with clinched teeth and crossed fingers (Theodoret, *Eccl. hist.* 1.7). Athanasius deployed this language in his festal letter of 338 and then in an encyclical to denounce those who had deposed him at the Synod of Tyre. As Lewis Ayres has argued, Athanasius turned the alliance of his ecclesial opponents into a heresy, a univocal heterodox school of thought, by comparing them with the Manichees who identified themselves not by taking the name Christ but the name of the founder of their school (*C. Ar.* 1.1.3–4). The genealogy that Athanasius constructs in his *Orations* traces the Eusebians' thought to the *Thalia* before turning its focus on the exegetical arguments of Asterius.

The Homoian Ascendency

With the dawning of the mid-fourth century, a second generation of subordinationists emerged called Homoians because they employed the term *homoios*, which means "like" or "similar," to describe the Son's relationship to the Father. Their success reflected the relative weakness of the antisubordinationists, especially in the Western portion of the empire, and the imperial patronage extended them by Constantius II.

On Pentecost of 337, Constantine the Great died, which left the empire divided between his three sons, Constans, Constantine II, and Constantius II. Before a year had passed, Constantine's desire for shared dynastic rule was shattered. In the autumn of that year, Constantine II led an army from the Balkans into Italy against the forces of his teenage brother Constans. When Constans's legions surprised his brother's forces in an ambush near Aquileia, Constantine II was killed on the field of battle, which left Constans the sole *augustus* in the West. Meanwhile Constantius II, with the aid of Eusebius of Nicomedia, was securing his authority in the East. This was achieved in part by the massacre of the descendants of Constantine I's stepmother, Theodora, who had been given positions of authority in the East—positions that Constantius believed might be bases of power from which to challenge him. After Constans was deposed and assassinated in 351 in a coup d'état orchestrated by his main field general, Flavius Magnus Magnentius, Constantius turned west to consolidate his hegemonic control of the empire. At a bloody engagement on the plains outside the city of Mursa, Constantius's forces, though sustaining 50 percent casualties, defeated Magnentius, who lost two-thirds of his legionnaires. The contest for the West dragged on two more years until Magnentius, thoroughly defeated, committed suicide in August 353, which left Constantius the sole ruler of an empire that stretched from northernmost Britannia to the headwaters of the Tigris and Euphrates Rivers.

Although Constantine the Great had extended his patronage of Christianity by restoring Church land and property seized during Diocletian's persecution, published the anthology of Christian Scriptures we know as the Bible, built churches, and sought to heal the Church divisions created by the clash between the Eusebians and Alexander of Alexandria, his empire was administered by Christians and pagans alike. Constantius II, however, committed himself completely to the Christian side, specifically the opponents of Athanasius. As early as 341, he had thrown his imperial weight behind Eusebius of Nicomedia in convening the Council of Antioch that produced the Dedication Creed. But he also summoned the Council of Sirmium in 351 to hear the charges against Photinus. With Constantius's position largely secure against political rivals by the mid-350s, the leading subordinationist bishops sought to use imperial patronage to overturn Nicaea completely. Having thoroughly triumphed over Marcellus, they turned their attention to Marcellus's old ally, Athanasius. It helped their cause in no small degree that there existed deep antipathy between Athanasius and Constantius. Moreover, rumor had it that during the civil war, Athanasius had received a deputation from Magnentius making him a political as well as ecclesial enemy of the emperor. Taking advantage of Constantius's presence in the West, the Homoians led by Valens of Mursa and Ursacius of Singidunum prevailed upon the emperor to summon a council to condemn Athanasius who had already been deposed from his see in Alexandria by a synod at Antioch the previous year. Since Magnentius had sought the support of a number of other Gallic bishops, Constantius wanted to use the council at Arles as an occasion for these Western bishops to prove their loyalty to him by signing a condemnation of Athanasius. The pro-Nicene bishops, Eusebius of Vercelli and Liberius of Rome, recognized the theological subtext of Valens and Ursacius's agenda. After the council, Eusebius and Liberius sought from Constantius a reaffirmation of Nicaea as the standard for right doctrine. Not surprisingly, this plea fell on deaf ears. Moreover, being pro-Nicene was, in Constantius's eyes, tantamount to being pro-Athanasius. Recriminations against the pro-Nicenes, therefore, were soon to follow. Two years later at a council in Milan, Valens and Ursacius with Constantius's support deposed the pro-Nicene bishops occupying major sees (e.g., Liberius, Eusebius, Dionysius of Milan, and Lucifer of Cagliari) for failing to support the condemnation of Athanasius and replaced them with anti-Nicene bishops. The next year, 356, the Homoian bishops at the Council of Bezier deposed Hilary from his Gallic see of Poitiers and exiled him to Asia Minor.

With the ranks of Nicene bishops weakened, the Homoians were positioned to formulate a new creedal formula. This began in earnest at a second council in Sirmium where Constantius had his court in 357. Alongside Valens and Ursacius were their fellow Homoians, Germinius of Sirmium, and Eunomius of Cyzicus. Eudoxius of Constantinople, though not present, later endorsed the council's conclusion. The council produced a position paper that marked a deviation not only from Nicaea but also from both the Eusebian formula crafted at Antioch in 341 and the articles from the first Council of Sirmium in 351. The bishops at Second Sirmium prohibited terms that used any form of *ousia* (e.g., *homoousios*) on the grounds that such language was unscriptural. Second, they prohibited discussion of the Son's generation. "It is beyond human understanding," the bishops wrote, "nor is anyone able to explain the nativity of the Son, of whom it is written, 'Who will explain his generation?' (Isa 53:8). The Father alone knows how he begot his Son, and the Son how he was begotten by the Father." By taking the generation of the Son off the table, the pro-Nicenes were effectively prevented from speaking about the relationship of the Father and Son and thus unable to argue that those names implied a shared nature between the "only begotten" Son and the Father who begot him. Third, the bishops at Second Sirmium concluded that the biblical language of "Father" and "Son" assumes a hierarchical relationship. Therefore, the Father must be deemed superior to the Son in "honor, virtue, power, dignity, glory, and majesty." This was a more explicit subordinationist posture than that espoused in the Eusebeans' Dedication Creed.

Second Sirmium was a significant moment not just because of its extreme subordinationist position but also because of the reaction among antisubordinationists. Among these was the Gallic bishop Phoebadius of Agen. His *Against the Arians* published the same year of the council was the first response to the Homoians in the form of a defense of the creed of Nicaea. Eusebius of Vercelli and Liberius of Rome's insistence at the Council of Arles that Athanasius's condemnation be accompanied with an affirmation of Nicaea indicates that the language of 325, if imperfect, was viewed by some antisubordinationists as authoritative. Phoebadius, however, was the first to put that explicit defense in writing. For the moment, however, momentum lay with the Homoians.

In February of 358, Eudoxius invited a gathering of bishops at his see of Antioch to affirm the Second Council of Sirmium's rejection of the Eusebian Dedication Creed. He also welcomed a self-styled philosopher and ardent subordinationist Aetius.[3] Eudoxius's synod at Antioch precipitated a rupture among the anti-Nicenes. The leader of the opposition was Basil of Ancyra. Basil shared the Eusebians' concern that Nicaea's use of *homoousios* sounded Sabellian. But unlike the other anti-Nicenes, Basil's deployment of the traditional language of "likeness" did not carry the same degree of subordination. At his own assembly of bishops at Ancyra in the weeks leading up to Easter 358, Basil and his allies articulated an antisubordinationist theology that reaffirmed the Dedication Creed (*Pan.* 73.2.10) by declaring the Son to be "like the Father according to essence [*homoiousios*]" (*Pan.* 73.4.2). Hereafter, Basil's faction has been known as the Homoiousians for this claim that the Son possessed an *essential likeness* to the Father. Indeed, it was the natural connection of Father and Son that was central to Basil's argument against the Homoians and Aetius. Whereas Aetius had spoken of God as the unbegotten, Basil insisted upon using the scriptural names of Father, Son, and Holy Spirit given in Jesus's Great Commission (Matt 28:19) and used in the baptismal liturgy rather than Aetius's abstract appellations "unincarnate" and "incarnate one" or "unbegotten" and "begotten" (*Pan.* 73.3.2). Unlike these lifeless, abstract designations, Basil explained, the Church used "Father," "Son," and "Holy Spirit" "in order that, when we hear the names, based on the natural concepts, we may understand the Father to be the cause of a substance like himself . . . [and the Son] to be like the Father, whose Son he is" (*Pan.* 73.3.3). By saying that the names "Father" and "Son" were based on "natural concepts," Basil meant that they conveyed a substantial relationship analogous to that between earthly fathers and sons yet without carnal connotations. That is, "the generation of a living being that is like in substance [*homoiousios*], since every father is understood as a father of a substance like his" (*Pan.* 73.4.2). Here he used *ousia*, not simply meaning nature but a progeny distinct from its father and yet possessing its father's nature. This allowed Basil to affirm that God's relationship to his Word and Wisdom is that

3. For Aetius's heterousian theology, see chapter 6, pp. 220–22.

of Father, not Creator (*Pan.* 73.4.4), and therefore that the Son was indeed a son and not a creature (*Pan.* 73.3.4). For a son is begotten by his parents, not made. God as Father *begot* his Son; God as Creator *made* his creatures (*Pan.* 73.4.5–6). For God the Father exercises "a peculiar and unique and generative activity" by which he is Father of the only begotten (*Pan.* 73.5.3) because begetting conveys to the Son a substantial likeness that creatures do not possess (*Pan.* 73.5.4). If the Son did not possess a "likeness according to essence" that fathers and sons share, he would be a creature, not a son (*Pan.* 73.9.6). Thus, Basil integrated the grammar of the Creator-creature distinction with the Father-Son distinction in a way that prevented either the subordinationist or Sabellian errors.

Thus, in contrast with Arius, who placed the Logos in an exalted but liminal state as perfect creature between God and the temporal creation, Basil affirmed a clear line between deity and creature. The Son fell on the side of divinity and not in a merely nominal sense. Basil clearly distinguished Scripture's application of familial terms to the members of the Godhead from its application to creatures economically. In his relationship to his Word, God was the "Proper Father," and the Word was the "Proper Son" in contrast with the children of Israel of whom Isaiah (1:2), speaking the word of the Lord, says, "I have begotten sons and raised them, but they have rejected me," or John's declaration in the prologue (1:12–13), "To as many as received him he gave the power to become children of God" (*Pan.* 73.5.1). With the designation of Christ as the "Proper Son," Basil essentially distinguished the one who is Son of God by nature from those who are children of God by grace or adoption. Mortals may be made "sons of God," but only the Word is properly speaking God's Son.

As with the Eusebians' use of the traditional language of "likeness," Basil saw the term "likeness" to convey similarity of the Son to the Father without collapsing the Son into the Father, as Sabellius and Marcellus did. On the one hand, "likeness according to essence" meant that everything that could be said of the Father's divinity could also be said of the Son. After comparing the interchangeable language of Proverb 8's description of the Wisdom, and the prologue of John's description of the Word, Basil declares, "God's Word, Wisdom, and image is like [the Father] in all respects" (*Pan.* 73.8.2–5). Therefore, the Son is "perfect from perfect" (*Pan.* 73.6.6). The conferral of all the Father's perfections was entirely plausible for Basil because of God's incorporeal nature. The designation of the Son as image of the Father simply meant that the Son is Wisdom and therefore the image of the perfectly wise Father. The wisdom proper to the Father's nature is proper to the nature of the Son since, in begetting the Son, the Father conveyed to him the entirety of his wisdom. Thus, he interprets Colossians 1:15 to mean that the Son as Wisdom is "the image of the invisible God" (*Pan.* 73.7.6). Similarly, Jesus can say (John 5:26) that the Father *has* life in himself and gives it to the Son who *has* life because the

Father's generation of the Son conferred a "likeness according to essence" such that the Son possessed all that is proper to the Father's nature (*Pan.* 73.8.7). On the other hand, the letter from the Council of Ancyra made clear that the Son's essential "likeness" did not mean that the Son was the "same" as the Father. As the second anathema declares, the Son who is Wisdom is not the same as the wise Father (*Pan.* 73.10.2). For, as conveyed by John's assertion that the Word was "with God," the Son is "truly Son"—and not a mere faculty of God—because, as all sons, he is a person different from his Father (*Pan.* 73.10.4).

The language of "likeness according to essence" allowed Basil to affirm the full divinity of the Son without conflating Father and Son; "the Son who was before all ages is indeed God inasmuch as he is Son of God . . . but he is not the same as *the* God and Father who begot him" (*Pan.* 73.9.2, 5). Here Basil's distinction between the Son as God and the Father as "the" God follows Origen's hierarchical delineation of the two persons without an ontological subordination. In his interpretation of the words of the Christ hymn in Philippians 2:7, Basil explains that the Son is "equal" to God because he "has the characteristics of divinity, since he is incorporeal according to the substance and like the Father according to divinity, incorporeality, and activities" (*Pan.* 73.9.3). However, he goes on to say, the Son is not "equal to *the* God but to God, nor [does he possess divinity] absolutely as the Father does" (*Pan.* 73.9.5). Basil's point is that the Son is equal to the Father with respect to the Father's divine nature but that the Father is nevertheless superior to the Son because the Father possesses divinity in himself, whereas the Son possesses divinity derivatively from the Father's act of begetting. Therefore, the Son can be perfectly like the Father's divine perfection, and yet the Father as the source of that divinity is superior to the Son.

Basil's homoiousian theology charted a middle way between Nicaea and Second Sirmium. By replacing *homo* ("same") with *homoi* ("like" or "similar"), Basil preserved the Eusebeian language of likeness as an alternative to the Sabellian connotations of *homoousios* from Nicaea, which appeared to deny a real distinction between the Father and the Son. At the same time, it declared the Son's essential unity with the Father that differed from the subordinationism of the Homoians at Sirmium in 357 and of Aetius's heterousian theology. But by linking the language of "likeness" to "essence," Basil offered a more robust basis for the Son's ontological equality with the Father than had previously been articulated by Eusebians in the Dedication Creed. As such, Basil articulated a compromise position that erected the pylons for a bridge between critics of Nicaea's apparent Modalism and champions of Nicaea's antisubordinationism. For *homoiousios* could not be construed to mean that the Father and Son were the "same being" while at the same time affirming an essential affinity between the Father and Son that confirmed the Son's divinity. It would, however, be up to Athanasius and then later the Cappadocians, led by Basil of Ancyra's protégé Basil of Caesarea, to complete the bridge that would unite the Homoiousians and the pro-Nicenes against the subordinationism of Aetius's protégé, Eunomius of Cyzicus. Yet although the alliance against the Homoians and Eunomians would ultimately abandon the language of *homoiousios* in favor of the Nicene *homoousios*, Basil's compromise language marked a stage that advanced the evolution of the Church's understanding of the grammar of Nicene Trinitarianism.

In the year following Basil's synod in Ancyra, however, the Homoians persuaded Constantius to summon two more councils, one Eastern and one Western, to formulate a creedal statement based on the position paper that emerged from Second Sirmium. The Eastern council was convened at Seleucia, and the Western gathering took place at Ariminum. Here Constantius saw his chance to reconcile the divisions and promote ecclesial unity within the empire. For, like his father, Constantius believed that the peace and prosperity of the empire depended on the blessings of God. And those blessings would come only if the Roman people worshiped him with one voice. Unity of doxology, however, depended on a unity of doctrine.

The opening session of Ariminum, however, did not proceed as smoothly as the emperor might have hoped. The discussion centered around a document commonly known as the Dated Creed that was drafted by Valens as a compromise between the Homoians and the Homoiousians. In it, the Son was said to be "like [*homoios*] the Father in all things." The majority of the Western bishops present rejected the Dated Creed as an innovation. They also issued condemnations of Valens and Ursacius for their refusal to include anathemas against Arius and his teachings. Valens and Ursacius immediately adjourned the council and withdrew to the nearby Thracian town of Nikē to regroup. Constantius was infuriated and demanded that the bishops reconvene to arrive at some compromise statement that would reconcile the various parties. The second session of the Council of Ariminum lifted the excommunications against Valens and Ursacius. It approved the creedal provisions drafted during the interim at Nikē. This creed, called the Nikē Formula, reaffirmed Second Sirmium's prohibition of *ousia* language. It also modified the language of the Dated Creed to say the "Son is like the Father" while omitting the phrase "in all things." This omission marked a significant departure from Nicaea's language of "true God from true God" and the Eusebian language of "indistinguishable image" from the Council of Antioch. For to say that two things are "like" each other is not the same as saying that they are identical. Indeed, it implies that if they are alike in certain ways, they are also dissimilar in other ways. Its more nebulous description of the Son's resemblance to the Father gave bishops far greater latitude in describing the relationship of the Father and Son. The creed of Ariminum completely lacked a robust affirmation of the Son's identity as the wisdom and power of God. In so doing, it was able to acknowledge the Son's affinity to the Father that allowed him to reveal the Father and serve as the mediator between God and creation while at the same time preserving the Father's uniqueness.

The most controversial language in the Ariminum statement appeared in an anathema at the end of the document. The anathema condemned those who denied that "the Son was not a creature like other creatures." By insisting that the Son was not a creature, the creed could be read to affirm that the Son was divine. Yet by adding the qualifier "like other creatures," the Homoian authors of the creed were able to affirm that the Son is a unique and perfect creature—as Arius himself had taught—but a creature nonetheless and not God.

Meanwhile, the gathering of Eastern bishops at Seleucia was divided between the Homoians led by Eudoxius and Acacius and the Homoiousians under Basil who arrived late to the debate. The creed put to the synod by Acacius was largely a version of the Dated Creed with a similar rejection of *ousia* language. The homoiousian majority's victory in voting down this creed brought the council to the breaking point. Eventually, however, they capitulated, and the council approved a variation of Acacius's formula. Thus, Ariminum and Seleucia set the stage for a union of the imperial Church, West and East, around a thoroughly subordinationist creed.

The next year, in 360, at the Second Council of Constantinople, Homoian bishops from East and West convened to establish a new creed. The result was the Nikē Formula with the additions from the second session of Ariminum. It also stipulated that all previous creeds were null and void. The Homoian creed had officially replaced Nicaea as the creed of the empire.

The Nicene Counterattack

One consequence of the councils of 359 and 360 was to galvanize the pro-Nicene bishops. In the 320s, few if any, even among Nicaea's defenders, had been especially enthusiastic about *homoousios*; the general preference was for the traditional language of "image" and "likeness." Yet by the fifth decade of the fourth century, the tepid language of the Nikē Formula illustrated—at least in the minds of certain leading antisubordinationist bishops—that the language of "likeness," especially without a connection to *ousia*, was not enough to preserve the essential unity of the Father and Son.

Although Athanasius began his *Orations Against the Arians* (*C. Ar.* 1.3.9) by defending *homoousios*, this was not the terminological hill on which he was willing to die. By the middle of the fifth decade, however, he offered his first full-throated defense of Nicaea and *homoousios* in his *On the Nicene Council*. Since one of the objections to *homoousios* was that it did not appear in Scripture, Athanasius argued that the "fathers" at Nicaea did employ the biblical language "from God" to distinguish the Son from creatures that were made "from nothing." This, however, was not sufficient since all things are ultimately "from God." When Paul says that "all things are from God," Athanasius notes, he excludes the Son from "all" by adding "and one Lord Jesus Christ, through whom are all things" (1 Cor 8:6). Therefore, to give clarity to the sense that the Word, as the Son, is "from God" Nicaea added the qualifier "from the essence of God" (*Decr.* 5.19). For a child is begotten, not made, and therefore comes from the essence of her parents and shares the same nature as her parents. Yet the bishops at Nicaea knew that was still insufficient. For, Athanasius explains, they presciently anticipated the distortions of Scripture by Arians, such as Asterius, who would say that scriptural words "likeness," "image," "power," and "glory" were applied to human beings as well as the Son. Therefore, in order to affirm the Son's unique relationship with the Father as his Word and Wisdom possessing power and glory in his nature, the bishops had "to resay and rewrite what they had said before, more distinctly still" by adding that the Son is "one in essence [*homoousios*] with the Father" (*Decr.* 5.20). *Homoousios* also added another key qualifier that distinguished the Son's relation with the Father from that of human offspring and their parents. The human child, though begotten "from" her parents, is at birth no longer united to her parents but a completely separate being. By contrast, because the Son is eternally begotten by the Father, he, though distinct from the Father, nevertheless remains eternally united to the Father. The fathers of Nicaea used *homoousios* to distinguish a creaturely generation from the divine generation of the Son who is "inseparable from the essence of the Father, [since] he and the Father are one, as he himself said, and the Word is ever in the Father and the Father in the Word" (*Decr.* 5.20). Thus, Athanasius makes the case that *homoousios*, though not itself in Scripture, was merely the logical implication of the biblical language of "Son" and "Father" expressed in Nicaea's declaration that the Son is "from the essence of the Father." But it also functions to safeguard the Son's uniqueness by strengthening the boundary between creatures and the Creator. Though Athanasius's analysis of *homoousios* affirmed the unity of the Father and his Word in a way that places the Word squarely on the divine side of the ontological division of divinity and creation, it did not provide clear language to counter the Sabellian interpretation of Nicaea.

Nevertheless, Athanasius's defense of *homoousios* prepared the ground for a reconciliation between antisubordinationist defenders of Nicaea and its antisubordinationist critics, namely Basil of Ancyra's Homoiousians. Five to six years after *On the Nicene Council*, Athanasius penned *On the Councils of Ariminum and Seleucia*. There he crafted a narrative to show the common cause of those who affirmed that the Son was "from the Father's *ousia*" (*Syn.* 3.41). By affirming that the Son was a begotten son rather than a made creature, Basil held that the Father and Son were *essentially* related: the Son was "like the Father according to essence [*homoiousios*]" (*Pan.* 73.4.2). For if Christ is truly the only begotten Son of the Father, then he is begotten from the Father's nature or essence. This essential relationship, Athanasius explained, was the point the bishops at Nicaea intended when they employed the term *homoousios*. Thus, in recognizing the essential relation of Father and Son, both the Homoiousians and the pro-Nicenes rejected any Homoian claim that the Son was a creature, albeit a perfect one. Therefore, since Basil's "like in essence" and Nicaea's "same in essence" both affirmed that the Son is "of the Father's essence," the two expressions were synonyms and should not divide the two groups.

In 362, Athanasius offered another olive branch. In a letter from an Alexandrian synod of bishops to the Church in Antioch, he grants that the description of Father, Son, and Spirit as three hypostases need not imply an ontological division and therefore was not a subordination of the Son like that of the "Arian madmen." To speak of each as a hypostasis meant that each was "truly existing and subsisting" really distinct from the other. Though distinct, the Son and Spirit were not "external to but proper to and inseparable from the essence of the Father" (*Tom.* 5). The *Tome* recognized their agreement that affirming a real distinction between Father and Son did not imply that the Son was ontologically subordinate to the Father. With this point of agreement, Athanasius was accepting language used by Antiochene supporters of Basil that had been lacking in his earlier *On the Nicene Council* and *On the Councils of Ariminum and Seleucia*. Now Athanasius was affirming language that ruled out possible Sabellian interpretations of *homoousios*. This was a significant step toward making the once objectionable language of Nicaea acceptable to the Homoiousians.

The most prominent voice among the Western antisubordinationists in the middle decades of the fourth century was Hilary of Poitiers. In 356, after Valens and Ursacius deposed the pro-Nicene bishops at Arles in 353, their ally Saturninus brought charges against Hilary at a synod at Bézier. Hilary does not tell us what the charges were, and given his claim of innocence, it is doubtful that they were theological in nature—though they may have been a pretext for gaining another see for a Homoian bishop. The four years of exile in Asia Minor were transformative for Hilary. Although his doctrine of Christ in later works is largely consistent with the theology that emerged in his early commentary on Matthew, his sojourn in Asia Minor exposed him both to Basil of Ancyra and to the Homoian theology articulated at the Council of Sirmium in 357. These four years gave him a clearer understanding of the Homoian theology and their agenda. When he returned from exile in 360, he became an ardent antihomoian and even sought, though unsuccessfully, to depose the Homoian Auxentius from the see of Milan.

During his exile, he began composing his response to Sirmium in his *On the Councils* and *On the Trinity*, which expanded his earlier work *On the Faith* by building upon Basil's homoiousian arguments. Hilary, who coined the appellation "the Blasphemy of Sirmium," argues in *On the Councils* that many of the bishops who signed on were duped by the Homoians because of their lack of theological acuity and by the deceptive wording of the anathema condemning any who "denied that the Son was not a creature like other creatures." Instead of affirming that the Son was not a creature, they thoughtlessly accepted the Homoian view that the Son was a perfect creature. After an opening that declares that the discussion of the Trinity rests upon the Christian's experience of worship in which the luminous gift of the Spirit reveals the Father through the Son (*Trin.* 2.3), Hilary's *On the Trinity* turns to Homoian objections to the consubstantiality of the Father and the Son. Examining Jesus's words in John 14:11, "I am in the Father and the Father is in me," Hilary confronts the obvious question, How can the Father and Son be said to be "in" each other? The answer lies in the Father's transcendent and immaterial nature. Because the Father is immaterial, he is not located in place and time; therefore, he is able to be within all things and holding all things within himself (*Trin.* 3.2). While that may apply to one infinite being's relationship with finite beings, it does not answer how two infinite beings could be mutually penetrating. Hilary answers that because the Father is immaterial, the Son is begotten from the Father's self, not in part but in whole (*Trin.* 3.3). The whole of the Father's divinity is in the Son. However, that answer only raised the question of how such mutual indwelling is not tantamount to collapsing the Father and Son into each other. If the Son is begotten from the essence or substance of the Father, either the Son is a part of the Father, in which case the Father undergoes change and loss, or the Father and Son exist in each other without a real distinction (*Trin.* 3.8). Hilary answers the question of mutual indwelling by appealing to John 17:1–6 where Jesus speaks of the Son and Father as glorifying each other. If the Father gives glory to the Son without losing his eternal glory, and the Son gives glory to the Father without losing the immaterial glory that was his from eternity, then by analogy the Father was able to confer his whole nature to the Son in the act of begetting without compromising his own perfection (*Trin.* 3.11–12). The relationship between the divine nature and divine glory, for Hilary, is more than a mere analogy. Rather, the exchange of glory is a reflection of the power proper to the nature that is shared consubstantially by Father and Son. For the Father glorifies the Son by giving the Son the power to give eternal life to believers. And the Son gives glory to the Father by fulfilling the Father's charge to give eternal life (*Trin.* 3.13).

Perhaps Hilary's most significant contribution to Nicene Trinitarian thought was to shift the focus from Basil's emphasis on the significance of the names "Word," "Wisdom," and "Power" to the Son's nativity as that which explains all the other names. Christians call Christ the "Son of God" because of his "name [given in Scripture], birth, nature, power, and confession" (*Trin.* 7.3). Yet his birth (*nativitas*) is the source of his name, nature, power, and confession. Unlike Moses's being called "god of Pharaoh," Jesus's name "Son of God" is his by virtue of his birth from the Father in which he was given the divine nature (*Trin.* 7.9). "The name 'Word' belongs to the Son of God," Hilary writes, "from the mystery of the birth just as do the names wisdom and power" (*Trin.* 7.11). Unlike the Logos theologies of the second century that identified Christ with a divine faculty, Hilary's account of the Son being born and yet possessing the whole of the divine nature as "true substantial existence" avoids describing the Son's divine nature as an inner faculty of God. Instead, the names "Word," "Wisdom," and "Power" denote the Son's divine nature from birth. Thus, when John 1:1 says "the Word was God," "God" is not an accidental property, as with Moses, but "an eternal reality proper to his essential existence" (*Trin.* 7.11). Here lies the explanation for Paul's claim in Philippians 2 that the Son is equal to the Father: "Now it is manifest the equality consists in the absence of difference between those who are equal . . . birth can bring into existence a nature equal to its origin" (*Trin.* 7.15). Moreover, Philippians' confession of equality of Father and Son rules out two theological mistakes. On the one hand is the mistake of thinking that God is alone, because a thing is "equal" not to itself but to another. On the other hand is the mistake of thinking that there is diversity in the Trinity; for unless the persons share the same attributes, their natures are not identical (*Trin.* 7.16). Hilary finds scriptural support for the connection between "birth" and "nature" in the ironic reaction of the Jews to Jesus's claim, "The Son can do nothing of himself except what he sees the Father do." Instead of concluding, as the Homoians did, that Jesus was confessing his inferiority to the Father, the Jews rightly perceived that Jesus's claim meant "God was his own Father, making himself equal with God" (John 5:18; *Trin.* 7.16). This passage was significant for Hilary because it linked "work," "power," and "nature." The Son is able to perform the works he saw in the Father only because, by his birth, he possessed the power intrinsic to the Father's divine nature (*Trin.* 7.18–19).

Hilary's emphasis on the Son's nativity opened the door for the classic subordinationist objection: if the Son was born, which means to have a beginning, then there was once when the Son did not exist (*Trin.* 12.22). Because of the ontological difference between Creator and creatures, the analogical character of language means that "begetting" does not mean for the eternal Father what it means for creatures who are time-bound. Thus, Hilary contends, the Father's begetting of the Son is not temporal. Hilary addresses the difference between begetting and creating with an analysis of Proverbs 8:22. "The Lord created me," he explains, does not refer to the Father's generation of the Son but the creation of Jesus's humanity in Mary's womb. Such a reading, however, is made more difficult by the additional phrase, "before the beginning of his ways." Hilary's solution focuses on the word "ways." He interprets it economically through the lens of Jesus's description of himself as the "way to the Father" (John 14:6). Jesus, Wisdom incarnate, is the Way. Hilary goes on to interpret the parallel clause, "before all the hills, he begat me," to refer to the Father's preparation of creation that was from eternity: "the whole preparation of these things is coeternal with God . . . the creation of the heaven and earth and other elements is not separated by the slightest interval in God's working, since their preparation had been completed in like infinity of eternity in the counsel of God" (*Trin.* 12.40). Thus, the Son, who would be "created" in human form at the incarnation, is coeternal with the Father; for the Son is the Father's coeternal Wisdom with whom the Father took counsel in planning creation and creation's redemption through Jesus the Way.

Another Latin champion of Nicaea in the 350s and 360s was the Neo-Platonist convert to Christianity, Marius Victorinus. Born in Africa around the end of the third century, he eventually made his way to Rome where he taught rhetoric. He acquired such renown as a rhetor that a statue was erected in his honor in the Forum of Trajan. His primary contribution to Neo-Platonism was his Latin translation of Plotinus's *Enneads* and Porphyry's *Isagoge*. Following his conversion in 356, Victorinus continued to teach until 362 upon the emperor Julian's prohibition against Christian teachers. In addition to hymns and commentaries on Paul's epistles (Romans, 1 and 2 Corinthians, Galatians, Ephesians, and Philippians), he composed antihomoian and heterousian works, *Candidus Correspondence* and *Against Arius*. In these latter two works he adapted, with significant alterations, Plotinus's, Porphyry's, and other later Neo-Platonists' accounts of the triad of One, Mind, and Soul to articulate a Nicene grammar for the Trinity. Using the Plotinian model, he sought to explain how the Son was consubstantial with the Father and how the creative and salvific activity of the Trinity was a manifestation of the eternal relations of Father, Son, and Holy Spirit.

The foundational premise of Victorinus's doctrine of the Trinity was that the divine being or existence is intrinsically active; to be (*esse*) is to act (*facere*) (*Arium* 1a.3). Therefore, God's eternal being is eternally active. Victorinus explains this eternal activity in terms of the relationship of the Father, Son, and Spirit, which he often does using verbs in place of names. As the great I AM, the Father's essence or substance (*substantia*) is his existence (*existentia*). In the case of God, essence and existence are identical. Therefore, Victorinus refers to the Father as *esse* or "to be." Since doing is intrinsic to being, the Father is the first principle and source of all divine activity. Yet in order to signify that the Father is the *transcendent* source, Victorinus describes him as hidden within himself in potency. He is divinity in transcendent repose or "unacting act" (*inoperans operatio*). The Father is "unacting" in that he does not himself directly create, but he acts in begetting the Son and sending the Spirit, who are divine being in action (*operans operatio*) (*Arium* 1a.12). In other words, the Son is the activity born out of the potency or potential of the Father. Thus, whereas the Father is "unacting act," the Son is "acting act" and so is called *facere* or "to do." That is, the Son *does* what the Father in his transcendent repose *wills*. Victorinus illustrates this using the analogy of sight. The eye is the source of seeing because it has the potential to see, even when its eyelid is shut. The act of seeing is the actualization of the potentiality proper to the eye (*Arium* 3.5). The difference between the eye and God is that the Father is always exercising his potency through the Son's eternal doing. Thus, the Son's doings are an expression of being or existence of the Father. As external being in action, the Son is the image of the eternal *esse* who remains hidden within himself (*Cand.* 1.15). Because the Son is the Father's divine being (*esse*) in action, Victorinus calls the Son *vivere* or "to live," signifying the Son's outward active existence or life. In this way, Victorinus proves the intrinsic relationship of the Father and the Son. Because *to be* is inherently *to be in act*, the Father (*esse*) is never without his active Son (*facere*). For the Son is the eternal, outward, active expression of the Father's inner being. The doings of the Son are the Father's eternal activity; in this way, Victorinus's scheme is analogous to Origen's notion of the Father's eternal begetting of the Son. It also explains how the Son acts as the Father's agent of creation (John 1:4). As the Father's being in action, the Son is life and therefore is able to give being or life to creation by giving each thing its distinctive form or essence. Genesis 1:1, "In the beginning, God made," is rendered in Latin either "In principio" or "In capitulo," which literally means "In the head"; Victorinus interprets this Head as the Son (*Cand.* 1.27). Christ is the Head or Principle of creation because he, as the Father's creative action, is the source of all things that were made. After all, how, Victorinus asks, could the Son be the Father's Principle of creation fulfilling the Father's creative purpose unless the Father's life-giving power was intrinsic to the Son's essence (*Arium* 1a.3)?

As the Father is *esse* and the Son *facere/vivere*, the Holy Spirit Victorinus calls *intellegere* (to know or understand). Plotinus had made Mind (*nous*) the second principle emanating from the One to emphasize the priority of knowing the Good as the condition for making the good things in the image of the Good. Instead, Victorinus, though not disagreeing with Plotinus's logic, equates the Son primarily with doing and living, rather than intellect. He does this both because of his act ontology that equates *esse* and *facere* and because he is following the biblical depiction of the Logos as the Creator. This also may reflect the influence of Porphyry, who modified Plotinus's triad by associating the first outgoing movement from the "Father" with will rather than intellect. Victorinus identifies the Spirit with *intellegere* largely because Jesus in John's Gospel both equates eternal life with knowing God and the Son (John 17:3) and promises that the disciples will receive the Spirit of truth who gives understanding of what the Father has revealed in the Son (John 16:12–15). Even as the Son's doing is in the Father's being, similarly the Spirit's understanding is implicit in the Son's doing. For the Son is the Father's life-giving act because he knows the Father and his will. Likewise, the Spirit is the stream of life-giving water that flows from the Son to give those who receive him eternal life and the ability to become children of God (*Cand.* 1.31). The Spirit gives life by imparting to believers understanding of the Father revealed in the Son (*Arium* 3.8; *Comm. Gal.* 4.6). This the Spirit can do only because he is the external expression of the Son's understanding. Victorinus draws this dyadic relationship between the Son and Spirt from his understanding of Paul's reference to "the Spirit of the Son" in Galatians 4:6.

Victorinus's distinction between the Father as *esse* and the Son as *facere/vivere* was foundational for drawing the line between creatures and deity and therefore offering a Nicene account of the Son's divinity. At one level, simply because God is spirit (John 4:24) and Christ is spirit (2 Cor 3:17), Victorinus declares the Spirit is *homoousios* with the Father and Son (*Arium* 3.6). Victorinus's fuller account of the consubstantiality of the persons rests upon his creature-Creator distinction grounded in the difference between that which is nonexistent and that which is existent. Creatures he calls "not truly nonexistents" because, though they really exist (unlike darkness, which is the mere absence of light, or square triangles), they are also "not truly existents" because they are contingent beings whose existence is not intrinsic to who they are but given by their Creator (*Cand.* 1.4 and 1.11). By contrast, the Trinity is necessary being and therefore alone truly exists. Yet when he distinguishes the Father from the Son, Victorinus calls the Son the Existent (*ho ōn*) and the Father the Nonexistent or *pro-ōn* (*Cand.* 1.2 and 1.28). Like Plotinus, Victorinus equates "being" with "form"; for form, whether of a chair or a giraffe, gives to matter the qualities and limits that are distinctive of that type of being and distinguishes it from other beings. Thus, the nature of a thing's being is conditioned by its form. To say that God was a being would imply that God was conditioned or limited by a form external to God (*Cand.* 1.13). Consequently, Plato and Plotinus placed God the First Principle "beyond being" since God, who is the unconditioned condition of all beings, cannot himself be one being among other beings. Similarly, Victorinus insists that the Father, who like Plotinus's One is simple, is the unconditioned source of being. To call the Father "the Nonexistent" is simply Victorinus's way of affirming that the Father is beyond or before being (*pro-ōn*). The Son he calls the Existent (*ho ōn*), which corresponds to the name revealed to Moses from the burning bush, because he is the actualization of the potentiality hidden in the Father, the Nonexistent (*Cand.* 15). For, as the prologue of John declares, the Word was "in the beginning," which Victorinus takes to mean not in time but in the Eternal Father who is before being (*Cand.* 1.16). Thus, Victorinus explains the Son's consubstantiality by arguing that, given God's simplicity, to be and to act are essentially one; therefore, the Father (*esse*) is in the Son's action (*facere*), and the Son's doing is in the potentiality of the Father's existence (*Cand.* 1.19). This allows Victorinus to explain how the Son is eternally united to the Father in essence (consubstantial) and at the same time avoid the Sabellian error of failing to make a real distinction between the Father and the Son. As being in action, the Logos is "in the bosom of the Father" (John 1:18) inasmuch as, being born from the Father's potency, the Son shares the Father's substance or being. At the same time, Victorinus interprets John's declaration that the Logos is "with God" (John 1:1) to mean that the Son is distinct from the Father because he manifests externally the Father's hidden potentiality (*Arium* 1a.4–5). Because the Son is the Father's active being—Life—he is the source of form and being of all that is. Victorinus describes intelligible realities called "truly existents," intellectual souls called "mere existents," creatures with embodied souls called "not truly nonexistents," and formless matter called "nonexistent," because it is not any thing in particular but merely pure potentiality (*Cand.* 1.7–8). Thus, the Son shares the Father's necessary existence that distinguishes the Son from contingent creatures while affirming that the Son's creative activity is an outward expression of God's gracious sharing existence with creatures (*Arium* 4.22).

Victorinus is significant both as a mid-century defender of Nicaea and for the groundwork his account of the Trinity laid for later Western Trinitarian thought, particularly that of Augustine. In his *Correspondence with Candidus*, he creates a fictional interlocutor whom he uses as a mouthpiece for Homoian and Heterousian arguments against the Father's generation of the Son from his essence. Candidus argues that begetting from the essence is a form of movement. Since a movement is a form of change, if the Son were begotten from the essence of the God, then God would not be eternal and immutable (*Cand.* 1.3). Victorinus combines the doctrine of divine simplicity and his act ontology to demonstrate how the Father's begetting of the Son, far from entailing some diminution or alteration of the Father's essence, is simply the natural extension of the unique activity inherent in the Father's essence. At the same time that he responded to the Homoian triumph at Sirmium in 357, he also attacked Basil of Ancyra's substitution of *homoiousios* for *homoousios*. If the Son were *like in substance* (*homoiousios*) to the Father, he would not have the same essence as the Father and therefore would not be equal in divinity with the Father. Rather, he would have a nature, though similar, different from the Father's. The Son would be another, lesser god (*Arium* 1a.29–30).[4] It is because the Son is begotten from the Father's

4. To use a modern analogy, if the Son were not of the same nature (*homoousios*) but merely a similar nature (*homoiousios*) to the Father's, then the Son's relationship to the Father would

essence—and therefore *homoousios* with the Father—that they are equal in their shared divinity.

Conclusion

The Second Council of Constantinople in 360 was the high-water mark of Homoian theology. With the adoption of the Nikē Formula, Nicaea had been overturned. Alexander's emphasis on the essential unity of the Father and Son expressed in the language of *homoousios* was replaced with a strongly subordinationist understanding of the Son's mere "likeness" with the Father. Yet the Homoian triumphs at Sirmium in 357 and Constantinople in 360 would prove Pyrrhic victories. For some anti-Nicenes, like Basil of Ancyra who had originally worried about a creeping Sabellianism in Nicaea, Sirmium and Constantinople had gone too far. Divisions within the ranks of the anti-Nicenes grew. For others, like Athanasius who had already been sympathetic with Nicaea, there emerged a new realization that, regardless of its checkered past, *homoousios* could, if understood rightly, provide the language necessary to confess the essential unity of the Godhead and so avoid a subordinationism that placed the Son on the ontological side of creatures rather than the Father. The result was a movement toward rapprochement between various antisubordinationists, the Homoiousians and the pro-Nicenes. This was facilitated by Athanasius's rhetorical victory of branding the Eusebians and the Homoians as "Arians" through his narratives of the Homoian ascendency. However different the theology of various groups of anti-Nicenes was from Arius, Athanasius was pointing to an essential similarity that produced a common demotion of the Son to the mere nominal status of god. At the same time, the narratives carried overtures intended to unite antisubordinationist critics of Nicaea in common cause with Nicaea's defenders. This common cause would be felt more strongly in the decades after 360 with the rise of the extreme subordinationism articulated with seeming philosophical cogency by a disciple of the Heterousian Aetius named Eunomius of Cyzicus, who would make his way to the episcopal see of Constantinople. The task of cementing the alliance of antisubordinationists and of countering Eunomius's persuasive syllogisms fell to Basil of Ancyra's protégé, Basil of Caesarea. Together with his brother Gregory of Nyssa and his school companion, Gregory of Nazianzus, Basil would begin crafting a mature form of Nicene theology that would advance the antisubordinationist cause to another milestone at the Council of Constantinople in 381.

---

be like that of a chimpanzee to a human being—which are altogether different species even though their DNA is 98.8 percent the same.

Bibliography

Primary Sources

Arius. *Letters to Eusebius of Nicomedia and Alexander of Alexandria.* Translated by Mark DelCogliano. Cambridge Editions of Early Christian Writings 1. Edited by Andrew Radde-Gallwitz. Cambridge: Cambridge University Press, 2017.

———. *Thalia.* In Athanasius, *On the Synods at Ariminum and Seleucia.* Translated by Andrew Radde-Gallwitz. Cambridge Editions of Early Christian Writings 1. Edited by Andrew Radde-Gallwitz. Cambridge: Cambridge University Press, 2017.

Athanasius of Alexandria. *Against the Arians, Defense of the Council of Nicaea, On the Councils of Arimimum and Selucia, Tome to the Antiochenes. NPNF* 2/4.

———. *The Life of Antony and The Letter of Marcellinus.* Translated by Robert C. Gregg. New York: Paulist, 1980.

———. *On the Incarnation.* Translated by John Behr. Yonkers, NY: St. Vladimir's Seminary Press, 2011.

Basil of Ancyra. *The Synodal Letter of the Council of Ancyra.* Translated by Jeffrey Steenson. Cambridge Editions of Early Christian Writings 1. Edited by Andrew Radde-Gallwitz. Cambridge: Cambridge University Press, 2017.

Eusebius of Caesarea. *Against Marcellus* and *On Ecclesiastical Theology.* Translated by Kelley McCarthy Spoerl and Markus Vinzent. Fathers of the Church 135. Washington, DC: Catholic University of America Press, 2017.

Hilary of Poitiers. *On the Councils* and *On the Trinity. NPNF* 2/9.

Marius Victorinus. *Theological Treatises on the Trinity.* Translated by Mary T. Clark. Fathers of the Church 69. Washington DC: Catholic University of America Press, 1978.

Secondary Sources

Anatolios, Khaled. *Athanasius: The Coherence of His Thought.* London: Routledge, 1998.

———. *Retrieving Nicaea: The Development and Meaning of Trinitarian Doctrine.* Grand Rapids: Baker Academic, 2011.

Ayres, Lewis. *Nicaea and Its Legacy: An Approach to Fourth-Century Trinitarian Theology.* Oxford: Oxford University Press, 2004.

Barnes, Michel R., and Daniel H. Williams. *Arianism After Arius: Essays on the Development of the Fourth Century Trinitarian Conflicts.* Edinburgh: T&T Clark, 1993.

Beckwith, Carl L. *Hilary of Poitiers on the Trinity: From* De fide *to* De Trinitate. Oxford: Oxford University Press, 2008.

Behr, John. *The Nicene Faith.* Part 1 in *Formation of Christian Theology* 2. Crestwood, NY: St. Vladimir's Seminary Press, 2004.

Clark, Mary T. "A Neoplatonic Commentary on the Christian Trinity: Marius Victorinus." *Neo-Platonism and Christian Thought*. Edited by Dominic J. O'Meara. Albany: SUNY Press, 1982.

Cooper, Stephen A. "The Platonist Christianity of Marius Victorinus." *Religions* 7 (2016): DOI: 10.3390/rel7100122.

Edwards, Mark. "Marius Victorinus and the *Homoousion*." *Studia Patristica* 46 (2010): 105–18.

Hanson, R. P. C. *The Search for the Christian Doctrine of God: The Arian Controversy 318–381*. Edinburgh: T&T Clark, 1993.

Kannengiesser, Charles. *Arius and Athanasius: Two Theologians*. Hampshire: Variorum, 1991.

Löhr, Winriche. "Arius Reconsidered (Part 1)." *Zeitschrift für Antikes Christentum* 9 (2006): 524–60.

———. "Arius Reconsidered (Part 2)." *Zeitschrift für Antikes Christentum* 10 (2007): 121–57.

Weedman, Mark. *The Trinitarian Theology of Hilary of Poitiers*. Leiden: Brill, 2007.

Wiles, Maurice. *Archetypal Heresy: Arianism Through the Centuries*. Oxford: Clarendon, 1996.

Williams, Rowan. *Arius: Heresy and Tradition*. Grand Rapids: Eerdmans, 1987.

6

"One God in Three Persons"

Trinitarian Triumph, East and West

In 358, Eudoxius, bishop of Antioch, summoned a gathering of bishops to approve the judgment of the Council of Sirmium from the previous year. Among the guests Eudoxius invited was a supporter of the Homoians but who was not among the ranks of bishops. He was a deacon who had risen from relative social obscurity to be the champion of an extreme form of subordinationist theology that would come to be known as anomoian or heterousian because of his insistence that the Son was unlike (*anomoios*) the Father because he was of an altogether different essence (*heterousia*). This man was Aetius.

Born in Antioch around 313, Aetius was the son of an artisan who occupied the lower rungs of the social hierarchy. Although Aetius learned his father's craft to provide for his family, he was not content with the trade. Showing promise as a student of logic (*pros logikas theōrias*), he began to study theology under the anti-Nicene bishop Paulinus of Antioch (Philostorgius, *Hist. eccl.* 3.15). Soon he distinguished himself as a skillful debater who bettered others of higher social standing in theological disputation—something that did not endear him to the upper-class Antiochenes. After Paulinus's death, he continued his studies with other subordinationists who had been in the circle of Lucian of Antioch. Something of a social pariah, he eventually left Antioch to become an itinerant debater traveling from Asia Minor to Alexandria disputing all comers in matters of theology. While Aetius was in Alexandria, a Cappadocian named Eunomius made his way to Antioch and then Egypt sometime between 348 and 350 seeking to study with the master of theological debate. Eunomius not only became Aetius's lifelong friend and defender but would come to surpass his mentor as leader of the anti-Nicenes.

Aetius's heterousian theology was summed up in his brief work the *Syntagmation* written in 359 in response to both defenders of *homoousios* like Athanasius and his opponents among the anti-Nicenes, especially Basil of Ancyra. In the

Syntagmation, Aetius lays out thirty-seven syllogisms that exposed the fallacy of claiming any essential likeness of the Father and Son or, as he tends to refer to them, the ungenerated God and the generated one (*Synt.* introduction; Kopecek, p. 227). The major premise, explicit or implicit, of his syllogisms is that God, who is the first principle or cause of all things, must himself be ingenerate. This was not a novel claim but one that Alexander himself espoused. But Aetius went further in claiming that "ingenerate" is God's essence. Two conclusions, Aetius reasoned, necessarily follow from this. First, if God's essence is "ingenerate" or "unbegotten" and the Son is "generated" or "begotten," then by definition the begotten Son cannot be of the same essence as the unbegotten Father. Therefore, he cannot be *homoousios* with God. Moreover, since that which is not dependent on another for its existence is superior to that which is dependent, the Ingenerate God is ontologically superior to the Generated One (*Synt.* 2; p. 229).

Second, the chief error, according to Aetius, of both the defenders of *homoousios* and the proponents of its alternative *homoiousios* is that they somehow imagined that a God who is simple and noncomposite could generate another being from his essence. Aetius's logic was that, since God is essentially ingenerate, he is uncaused and unconditioned by anything. That is, there is no substratum out of which he is composed. Therefore, the Ingenerate God is necessarily simple or noncomposite. A simple and ingenerate God, however, could not generate or beget a son since the act of generation entails transferring something of the parent's substance to its offspring. In the case of God, however, that is impossible. For since God is simple, he is indivisible and so has no portion of his being that could be, as it were, broken off and used to form his progeny (*Synt.* 5; p. 230). The only alternative, Aetius argued, was that the Son was not, properly speaking, begotten from the essence of the Father but made according to the Father's will out of nothing.

Aetius's and Eunomius's theology shared subordinationist tendencies of Arius and the Homoians. Like Arius, the core of their theology was God's absolute uniqueness as the one and only Ingenerate. Arius followed the logic of their view that the Son, as begotten from the will of God from nothing, was of a different, inferior essence from the Father. Yet whereas Arius had affirmed God's unknowability—even to the point of saying that the Son does not know the Father—Aetius and Eunomius by contrast boldly claimed not only that rational creatures were capable of attaining true knowledge of God but that they could know God's very essence.[1] Although Aetius and Eunomius shared common cause with Homoians, like Eudoxius, who rejected Nicaea's language of *homoousios*, their emphasis on

1. Given Aetius and Eunomius's difference with Arius on this central point, recent scholarship no longer refers to them using the older appellation "Neo-Arians."

the difference in essence between the Father and Son diluted the Son's likeness to the Father. Therefore, while the pejorative label "anomoians" attached to them by their enemies was not an entirely fair representation of their theology, it did name a perception that grew within the ranks of the Homoians. Eventually, for many anti-Nicenes, including Eudoxius and Acacius, Aetius had gone too far. This judgment led George of Laodicea and Basil of Ancyra to the Council of Ancyra in 358 and their eventual break with the Homoians. They came to share the view of anti-Homoians that Aetius and Eunomius's heterousian theology was simply the logical extension of the Homoian rejection at Second Sirmium of the Son's essential unity with or likeness to the Father.

At the Council of Constantinople of 360, Acacius, seeking to solidify the Homoian victories at Sirmium, Ariminum, and Seleucia, deposed homoiousian bishops from their sees. But he also banished Aetius. Eunomius was obviously tainted by his close association with Aetius. Therefore, Acacius compelled him to offer a defense of his position and demonstrate its agreement with the Homoian theology. His speech met with the Homoian bishops' approval, which they expressed by appointing him to the episcopal see of Cyzicus recently vacated by the deposed homoiousian bishop Eleusius. Within that year or next, Eunomius published a polished form of this account in his *Apology*. One of the attendees at the council who likely heard Eunomius's oration was Basil of Caesarea. In 363, following the edict of toleration and Julian's death, Basil penned his own response to the *Apology* entitled *Against Eunomius*. With that began the clash between the heterousians and the pro-Nicenes led by the so-called Cappadocian fathers: Basil, Gregory of Nazianzus, and Gregory of Nyssa. Together Aetius and Eunomius leveled potentially the most damning analyses of Nicaea and its homoousion theology. Yet out of their clash with Eunomius, the Cappadocians would not only articulate a grammar governing what might and might not be said about the identity of the Son and his relationship with the Father but more generally describe the nature and limits of Nicene theology that included the proper way to read Scripture, the relationship between theology and salvation history, and the largely overlooked person of the Holy Spirit.

The Cappadocians

Christian communities had existed in Cappadocia since the late first century (1 Pet 1:1). Yet the figure who has been credited with shaping the character of Cappadocian Christianity was the third-century bishop Gregory Thaumaturgus. Gregory, together with his brother Athenodorus, were students in Caesarea of Palestine during Origen's exile from Alexandria. From Origen, Gregory learned a love of pagan wisdom and even more the divine knowledge of Scripture. Eventually, Gregory and Athenodorus were sent as bishops to Pontus, which at that time was part of Cappadocia. One of the people converted under Gregory's teaching was Macrina the Elder, the paternal grandmother of Basil and Gregory. Consequently, the Christianity they imbibed was spoken with an Origenist inflection. This appreciation of Origen was reflected in Basil's composition of the *Philocalia*, an anthology of selections from Origen's corpus.

Basil and Gregory were from the class of local elites called *decuriones* who served as counselors overseeing the governance of the province. Their father, Basil the Elder, was a teacher of rhetoric in Neocaesarea of Pontus. Together with his wife Amelia, he had five daughters and four sons. Upon Basil the Elder's death, the eldest daughter, Macrina the Younger, persuaded her mother to convert their rural estate at Annisa, northwest of Neocaesarea on the river Iris, into a monastic community. Macrina, whom Gregory would call "my teacher," was the spiritual conscience and guide of the family. Gregory would honor her in a hagiographical account of her life and a dialogue modeled on Plato's *Phaedo*.

Holy orders were not Basil's original vocation. Rather, the expectation was that he would follow in his father's profession. So Basil began his study of rhetoric first under his father's tutelage, then in Constantinople and Athens, where he connected with the son of the bishop of Nazianzus, Gregory. In school together they would be united by their devotion to the ideal of the philosophical life. In his funeral oration for Basil, Gregory, looking back on their school days in Athens, described their friendship as a relationship governed by "the law of superhuman love":

> we acknowledged our mutual affection, and that philosophy was our aim, we were all in all to one another, housemates, messmates, intimates . . . love which is godly and under restraint, since its object is stable, not only is more lasting, but the fuller its vision of beauty grows the more closely does it bind to itself and to one another the hearts of those whose love has one and the same object. (*Or.* 43.19)

In his mid-twenties, Basil left Gregory in Athens to return to Pontus to teach rhetoric. Among his students there in the capital of Neocaesarea was his younger brother, Gregory. After a couple of years, Basil came under the influence of the ascetic, homoiousian Eustathius of Sebaste. In 360, he accompanied his bishop, Dianius, to the Council of Constantinople where he saw Eustathius, among other Homoiousians, condemned by the Homoians. Although Basil and Eustathius would eventually part ways over the divinity of the Holy Spirit, in 360 Basil, seeing his mentor condemned and Eunomius, the pupil of Eustathius's nemesis Aetius, elevated to the see of Cyzicus, decided to pen a reply to Eunomius's *Apology*. Although Basil, like Basil of Ancyra and Eustathius, originally rejected the Nicene language of *homoousios*, after his ordination and his publication of *Against Eunomius*, he accepted it and worked to form an alliance between the Homoiousians and the pro-Nicenes.

Gregory of Nazianzus, like Basil, was from the landed gentry. His mother, Nonna, was from an old and wealthy Christian family. His father, Gregory the Elder, was also raised in a Christian family but did not receive baptism until shortly before his marriage to Nonna. Around his fiftieth year, Gregory the Elder was chosen as bishop of the Christian community at Nazianzus in Cappadocia. Gregory sent his two sons, Gregory and Caesarius, off to receive an education befitting young men of their class in Caesarea of Palestine, followed by periods of schooling in Alexandria and Athens. Upon returning to Cappadocia around the age of thirty, Gregory the Younger finally fulfilled his terror-stricken promise to God made in the middle of a storm on the Mediterranean, "I shall live for you," and was baptized. Gregory the Elder, who was by this point advanced in years and in need of someone to share the pastoral responsibilities, pressured Gregory into being ordained a priest and serving alongside him in Nazianzus. Ten years later, as the clash between pro-Nicenes and the heterousians intensified, Basil, now bishop of Caesarea, pressured both his younger brother Gregory and his friend Gregory of Nazianzus to be ordained to the episcopacy in order to strengthen the ranks of pro-Nicene bishops. His brother Gregory he ordained to the see of Nyssa, and his friend Gregory he ordained to an equally obscure, cultural backwater crossroad town of Sasima. Both Gregories felt used, and their relationship with Basil was strained, especially as they found themselves bearing the burden of defending Basil against his numerous critics. Yet their fraught relationship with Basil positioned them to become leaders of the pro-Nicene faction. Moreover, they would develop the seed of Basil's Nicene grammar into a fully developed Trinitarian theology.

Opening Salvo: Basil's *Against Eunomius*

Basil's response to Eunomius's *Apology* focuses considerably on the questions of what constitutes a valid creed and what is the nature of theology. Having taken the "pious tradition" that the fathers had passed down from the beginning as "a kind of rule and norm" (*Apol.* 4.6–9), Eunomius sums up that tradition: "We believe in one God, the almighty Father, from whom are all things and in one only begotten Son of God. God, the Word, our Lord Jesus Christ, through whom are all things, and in one Holy Spirit, the Paraclete" (*Apol.* 5.1–5). The virtue of this succinct statement, he says, is its very succinctness—that it is "simpler and common to all . . . so that one can say the more important points in a summary" (*Apol.* 6.1–3). Basil's objection is that this statement of faith cannot be a rule if it itself needs a rule to supplement or explain it. The real creedal commitment that serves as a rule for Eunomius's theology was not contained in the language passed on from the fathers but in the creedal statements of Aetius: "We believe that unbegottenness is the substance of the God of the universe," and "We believe that the only begotten is unlike the Father in substance" (Basil, *Eun.* 1.4–5).

Basil's chief complaint against Eunomius is that he had replaced the biblical language of the baptismal formula "Father" with "unbegotten" when speaking about God. The terms, however, are not interchangeable. For while the Father is certainly unbegotten, "Father" carries meanings not included in "unbegotten." "Father" is inherently a relational term that necessarily implies the existence of offspring (*Eun.* 1.5). Whereas one who is "unbegotten" might have been alone in the beginning, when Scripture calls the eternal God "Father," it implies an eternal relationship to the Son who is eternally begotten by the Father. Eunomius counters that father-son relationships necessarily entail an interval (of time). If God begat a son, he did so either when the son existed—which is nonsensical—or when the son did not exist (*Apol.* 13.1–7). Obviously, a son does not exist before he is begotten. Therefore, the Son cannot be coeternal with the Father and so is not of the same eternal nature as the Father. Basil responds that, since the Father is infinite, he is without beginning or end and therefore is eternal. Since the Father is eternal, God's fatherhood is coextensive with his eternal existence. And since a father is not a father without his progeny, the Only Begotten must be coeternal with the Father (*Eun.* 2.12). This, Basil argues, is confirmed by John's prologue: "In the beginning was the Word." Here "beginning" refers to the absolute beginning before anything was. It is, he argues, impossible to imagine anything before the beginning. So when John writes that the Word was in the beginning, he is revealing the supreme and eternal divine nature. For "beginning" does not refer to the beginning of creation, as in Genesis 1, but denotes God's eternity that was before all things. When John says, "and the Word was with God," he means that the Son was with the Father in his eternal nature (*Eun.* 2.15). Basil, moreover, interprets John 1:1 through Revelation 1:8, in which Jesus declares, "I am the one who is and who was, the Almighty." As the one who is and who was, the Son is eternal: "For something prior to the beginning is inconceivable, and the being of God the Word is inseparable from the beginning . . . [thus] you are unable to transcend 'was' and use reasoning to go beyond it" (*Eun.* 2.14).

The fundamental error of Eunomius, according to the Cappadocians, was his tendency to think of God in temporal terms. More accurate still, Eunomius treated the temporal language used to speak about God literally. Although Eunomius wanted to eliminate anthropomorphic ways of thinking about God, ironically, he interpreted the Father's "begetting" the Son in an anthropomorphic manner. Consequently, he asserted that the Father-Son language of Scripture necessarily meant that the Father was "before" the Son (*Eun.* 2.16). The solution was not to eliminate the language of "Father." Rather, Christ himself provided a model for speaking about God when he instructed his disciples: "Call no man father on earth, for you have one Father, who is in heaven" (Matt 23:9). Thus, Jesus "transfers terms [e.g., Father] from human beings to God as fitting for his impassibility" (*Eun.* 2.23). The solution, therefore, is not abandoning material, temporal terms, which some people misinterpret, but distinguishing between the relational properties appropriately transferred from human relations to God and the strictly creaturely properties that cannot be applied to God. By eliminating carnal elements from the idea of "begetting," Basil argues, one not only removes from one's conception of God human notions of passionate procreation but also temporal notions as well. Since God is eternal and incorporeal in nature, the Father's begetting of the Son happens neither in time nor in the fashion of material creatures. Whereas for corporeal beings that have extension in time and space there is an interval between the progenitor and the progeny, for God, who is eternal, the generation of the Son is an eternal generation and therefore without an interval between the existence of the Father and the existence of the Son.

At the heart of this conflict is a dispute about the nature of theology and the limits of language to express the nature and identity of God. For Eunomius, as for Basil, the goal of the theology was doxology. Its purpose was to honor God or, as Eunomius puts it, "[to] repay the most necessary debt," namely "confessing that [God] is what he is" (*Apol.* 8.1–5). Christians honor God when they declare the true identity of God by naming his essence (*ousia*). "What he is" is the absolute uniqueness that distinguishes God from all creatures. Eunomius distinguishes the essence of a thing from mere conceptualization (*epinoia*). Whereas *ousia* is the defining feature of a thing, *epinoia* refers to verbal expressions of qualities associated with a thing but that are not its distinguishing feature. The *ousia* is the reality. *Epinoiai*, however, are not real; they are mere words that "have an existence in name alone and when they are being pronounced . . . are dissolved together with the sounds used to say them" (*Apol.* 8.1–5). They are as ephemeral as the breath used to utter them. Eunomius is committed to this distinction because he holds a high view of theology as science—that is, a discipline that provides true knowledge. If, however, theology does not tell what God is *in se*, it does not provide real knowledge. Unless theology identifies the divine essence, its content is the product of human imagination. Moreover, since God is simple, there is only the divine essence with no distinguishable attributes of God. "Unbegotten" is no mere conceptualization but reality. All the qualities referred to with *epinoiai* are really just the essence imperfectly expressed. To speak anachronistically, Eunomius was a nominalist with regard to religious language generally but paradoxically an extreme realist when it came to speaking of God's essence.

Basil held a drastically different view of both the divine *ousia* and religious *epinoiai*. Most fundamentally, whereas Aetius and Eunomius were confident that the divine essence was knowable, Basil contended that it is unknowable. This disagreement begins with a different understanding of the definition of "essence." Eunomius thought of essence in a reductive sense; it is that single quality that distinguishes one thing from all other things. God's essence is "unbegotten" because, unlike all other things that derive their being from God, God himself does not come from some prior source; therefore, his essence is unbegotten. Basil, by contrast, thought of God's essence in a maximal sense. God's essence is God's being, the totality of his being. It includes all that is proper to God's nature, all that might ever be said about God. Moreover, since God is not a finite creature but eternal and infinite, God's being is infinite. Therefore, it is beyond the comprehension of a creature's finite intellect. We cannot, so to speak, get our minds around God. Who God is cannot be summed up in words. "There is not one name," Basil writes, "which encompasses the entire nature of God and suffices to express it adequately" (*Eun.* 1.10). Eunomius's claim to being able to name the divine essence, Basil asserts, surpasses a simply epistemological error. It reveals a moral failing, hubris. For Eunomius presumes to know what the divinely inspired authors of Scripture expressly said was beyond them. Isaiah denies that anyone can speak of the Son's origin (Isa 53:8). David declares, "I regard the knowledge of you as a marvel, as too strong—I cannot attain it" (Ps 139:6). Most of all, Paul, even after being taken up into the third heaven and receiving a vision of God's glory, says that this vision was beyond description, "[I] heard ineffable words which are impossible for a person to utter" (2 Cor 12:4). Thus, the apostle concludes, "How inscrutable are [God's] judgments, and how unsearchable are his ways" (Rom 11:33). If these truly great men confess that naming divine essence lies beyond their or any man's ability, why then, Basil asks, should anyone believe that Eunomius can sum up God's being in a single word? (*Eun.* 1.12).

Although Christians must in all humility refrain from arrogant claims to knowledge of the divine essence, the Cappadocians maintained a theory of language that is quite different from that of the Eunomians and established the contemplation of Scripture as the central task of the theologian. Unlike Eunomius, *epinoiai* for Basil are not mere puffs of breath that vanish after they are spoken. Rather, a conceptualization is an idea formed in the mind after reflection (*ennoia*) upon the concept or first impression (*prolēpsis*) implanted in one's thoughts by sense experience. Sometimes the initial concept appears simple but upon reflection gains greater detail and nuance. Basil's example is a grain of wheat. Initially, the grain appears a simple thing without many notable qualities; upon reflection, however, the intellect generates conceptualizations that give a fuller account of "grain" as a mechanism for the plant's reproduction called "seed" or as the life-giving food provided for people called "nourishment." Far from being mere words, these conceptualizations refer to realities proper to the nature of grain (*Apol.* 1.6). Thus, words allow us to make true claims about things, even things that are unitary. The body, for instance, is one thing, one whole; but *epinoiai* allow one to analyze the workings of the body by enumerating its parts and functions.

Therefore, although God's essence is unknowable and cannot be captured in human thought or speech, human beings are not rendered utterly speechless about God. "Rather," Basil writes, "there are many diverse names, and each one contributes, in accordance with its own meaning, to a notion that is altogether dim and trifling as regards the whole but is at least sufficient for us" (*Eun.* 1.10). For *epinoiai,* in the case of God, are of a higher order than the product of the mind's reflection on sense perceptions. They are the names and qualities of the divine revealed in Scripture. Jesus, for instance, spoke of God's love and redemptive grace manifest in the divine economy by using "distinguishing marks" (*idiōmasi tisi*)—for example, "door," "light," "bread"—that denote his salvific work in the world (*Apol.* 1.7). Although Christ, in his divinity, is a simple being with a single substance, nevertheless, these marks are *epinoiai* that refer to actual qualities (*propria*) of God revealed economically in his activities (*energeiai*). Creative power, providential oversight, and foreknowledge are undeniable capacities that belong to the divine substance. Yet neither individually nor collectively can they be equated with the substance. For no single *epinoia* captures the totality of God's powers. Unlike "Simon," "Cephas," and "Peter," which are polyonyms—completely interchangeable terms—"door," "vine," and "light" denote certain of Jesus's particular salvific activities but not others (*Apol.* 1.8). The same is true of "love," "wisdom," and "power"; each expresses a divine quality not included in the others. Precisely because no single *epinoia* nor even all the *epinoiai* combined sum up the totality of God's being, they fall far short of defining God's essence in the maximal sense of essence Basil has in mind.

From Basil's perspective, not only is Eunomius's theory of language defective and his confidence in the human intellect exaggerated, but his specific identification of God's essence as "unbegotten" reveals flawed reasoning. Basil objects that unbegotten cannot be the divine essence because the essence of a thing is *what it is*. "Unbegotten," however, does not say what God *is*, only what he *is not*. "Unbegotten" belongs to the vocabulary of Middle Platonic negative or apophatic theology ("ineffable," "immaterial," "incorporeal") that spoke about a God who, because of his radical otherness, can be described only by naming all the ways he is unlike creatures. Such theology does not presume to make positive claims about God's nature except to affirm the true difference between God and creatures. It does not provide knowledge about the content of God's nature; it merely purifies one's thinking about God by ruling out temporal and material analogies used to speak about God as if he were a temporal being like ourselves. As we shall see in a later chapter, apophatic theology played an important role in the Cappadocians' own theological project. Nevertheless, for Basil, Eunomius makes a categorical error in using negative language to make a positive claim about the content of God's being.

From Eunomius's perspective, however, "unbegotten" was no mere negative or privative description. Because, in his understanding, the essence of a thing is that which is distinctive about that thing and is set apart from other members of a genus, "unbegotten" gave positive knowledge about God because it named not merely what was distinctive but the absolute uniqueness of God. It affirms that God was first of all things and that there was nothing prior to him that was the source of God's existence. He writes, "that God neither existed before himself nor did anything else exist before him, but that he is before all things, then what follows from this is the unbegotten, or rather, that he is unbegotten essence" (*Apol.* 7). Consequently, there can be no entity that is coeternal with the unbegotten (*Apol.* 10). "Unbegotten" is a corollary of the Plotinian idea that the One is simple (*haplous*), which means that he is the unconditioned condition of all things. Therefore, since "unbegotten" expresses God's absolute primacy and priority before all things, it explains how he is essentially unlike all things that come after him and that are dependent on him for their existence. Since God is not dependent on anything for his existence, he is autonomous and sovereign Lord of all that depend on him for their existence. Decades later when called upon by the emperor Theodosius I in 383 to explain his theology, Eunomius avoided invoking "unbegotten" altogether but instead used language that expressed the absolute aseity of unbegotten deity: "As regards the essence in respect of which he is one . . . (for he is absolutely and altogether 'one,' remaining uniformly and invariably 'only') . . . none to divide his glory, none to inherit his authority with him . . . for the Almighty [*pantokratōr*] is the 'one and only God'" (*Exp. fid.* 2).

"Unbegotten" was indeed, for Basil, an attribute of God's substance; but, he says, it is not itself the divine substance (*Eun.* 1.11). Its value, therefore, is to distinguish the uncreated Creator from his creatures. Moreover, because God is unbegotten, God's nature is beyond human comprehension. After all, Basil reasons, when we want to understand something, we describe its first cause, its source. But since God is unbegotten and is without a first cause, then he is beyond our understanding. Thus, Basil writes, "when we ascend in our thoughts to that which is beyond the ages and peer upon the boundlessness of the life of God as if upon some vast ocean, we are unable to apprehend its origin from which he has come" (*Eun.* 1.16). The only way that one could come to know such a God would be through a mediator, the Son, who was consubstantial and coeternal and in the beginning with God. Yet, Basil points out, Eunomius by declaring that the Father and Son are unlike in nature precludes this possibility. Eunomius himself concludes that since God "could never undergo a begetting which would result in his giving a share of his proper nature to the one who is begotten . . . he would escape all comparison (*synkrisin*) or fellowship (*koinōnian*) with the one who is begotten" (*Apol.* 9.1–3). This marks a significant departure from the Eusebian and Homoian use of "image" and "likeness" language to speak of the Son. To "escape all comparison" does not mean, however, that Eunomius abandons the biblical language of image when speaking of Christ. What he means is that, since the Father's essence is unique, it is beyond comparison with the essence of the Son. Nevertheless, the Son can be spoken of as the image of the Father's will. The Son can be the image of the Father's will but not of his essence, because Eunomius makes a categorical distinction between God's essence and his will. It rests on his separation of God's essence (*ousia*) from his activity (*energeia*). God's essence is who God is in himself from eternity; God's will, however, is God's activity in time. His reason for this absolute distinction is that if God's creative and redemptive activities are expressions of his eternal being, then it would mean that creation itself is eternal. God's being alone is necessary because it is the uncaused cause of all else. If, however, God's creative activity were an expression of his eternal essence, then creation also has a necessary existence. It would also mean that the activity of creation would entail a division or motion in the essence; this, however, is impossible since God is immutable (*Apol.* 22.8–9). The activities come not from God's essence but from his will. While God's essence is necessary and eternal, creation is a contingent reality. Whereas God is without beginning or end, God's activities are neither without beginning nor without end; for if they were, they would be identical in essence to God (*Apol.* 23.7–10). Creation, however, need not have existed but exists only because God willed that it exist. God's will is an act of his free choice. The Unbegotten brought the Only Begotten into being by a simple act of his will. The Son, therefore, is an image, not of the Father's essence but of his will. As "the firstborn of creation," the Son is the perfect expression of the Father's will. Eunomius explains Colossians 1:15–16: "The word 'image,' then, would refer the similarity back, not to God's essence, but to the action unbegottenly stored up in his foreknowledge prior to the existence of the firstborn and of the things created 'in him'" (*Apol.* 24.10–13). The Son as the image of the Father's will reveals not God's essence by which human beings might know God and become conformed to God. There is no divinization soteriology operative here. Rather, the Son, as the image of the Father's will, reveals the Father's creative intention. That is, Christ reveals what the Father desires his creation to be.

Basil rejects Eunomius's separation of essence and will. For that would imply an interval within God between what God is and what he willed. Since, however, God is eternal and no such temporal gap exists within God, the will cannot be treated as something separate; rather, it is an expression of his essence. The Son cannot truly be an image of the Father revealing the Father to humanity unless the Son exists in a fellowship with the Father that allows him to know the Father's essence. The only way such fellowship could exist is if they were of the same nature. Jesus says, "The one who sees me sees the one who sent me" (John 12:45), and Paul speaks of him as the "image of God." Therefore, Scripture can call the Son an image of the divine archetype because he shares the Father's nature (*Eun.* 1.17). While falling back on the biblical language of "image" to counter Eunomius's anomoian theology, Basil must at the same time avoid the subordinationist implications of "image." His solution is to interpret Colossians 1:15 to mean that the Son is a "living image" in contrast with a wooden or marble statue or a mosaic portrait that is lifeless. This move allows Basil to interpret the traditional image Christology through the Nicene begotten-made distinction. In other words, the statue or portrait of a king has a certain resemblance to the king; yet because it is made of other material, it is not of the same nature as the king and so is another class of thing altogether. By contrast, because the Son is begotten by the Father and has the Father's life in him, he shares the Father's nature and so is a living image of the Father. The Son is, Basil writes, "self-existent life which always preserves the indistinguishability, not by likeness of shape, but in his very substance" (*Eun.* 1.18). Moreover, Basil's language of "living image" harkens back to Origen's language of "eternally begotten." Because the Son is *eternally* begotten by the Father rather than made once and for all *in time*, the Son's being eternally flows from the Father to the Son in their eternal union—like radiance of light that continually flows outward from the flame. Therefore, the Son is a living, active image of the Father's nature derived from an organic relationship between the Father and the Son (*Eun.* 2.17). Moreover, unlike the lifeless portrait that possesses only a formal resemblance to the king but lacks any of the king's actual power, the Son, as a living image, possesses all the Father's power and wisdom (1 Cor 1:24) and so is equal in divinity with the Father (*Eun.* 1.23). The Father and Son are equal in power and wisdom because, since God is simple, the whole of the Father's nature—everything that the Father is in essence—abides in the Son even as the whole image from a signet ring is impressed into a wax seal. Using an analogy more apt for speaking about wisdom and power, Basil compares the Father's conferral of his wisdom and power on the Son to a teacher's imparting knowledge of an art to her students: "the teacher loses nothing, and the disciples attain the fullness of the art" (*Eun.* 2.16). Yet whereas the teacher imparts the knowledge and skill of her art to her students over time—therefore, the knowledge is conveyed incrementally—the Father does not impart his wisdom and power incrementally over time but instantaneously, so to speak, in his act of eternal generation (*Eun.* 2.17).

One of the enduring issues faced by the pro-Nicenes was the subordinationist insistence on the preeminence of the Father based on Jesus's confession, "The Father is greater than I" (John 14:28). Eunomius located the Father's preeminence in his being, not in temporal priority. Preeminence, he argued, can be based on either temporal priority or a quality proper to the nature or an ontological superiority. The relation of Father and the Son, however, stands outside of time since time came into being only with the creation of the stars by which time is measured. Since, therefore, the Father's preeminence is not the result of his being before the Son *in time*, the Father's superiority must be located in his essence (*Apol.* 10.1–9). Basil counters that the Father's preeminence is neither due to some difference in their natures nor because the Father preceded the Son in time. Rather, the Father is superior, not ontologically, but in authority because he is the source of the Son's being. To illustrate the point, Basil invokes the analogy of light coming from a flame. The light that fills the room comes from the light of the flame. The light that radiates forth from the flame, though distinct from the flame itself, is of the same nature as the flame whence it comes. Nor is the flame temporally prior to the light. For there is never an instant that the flame exists that there is not also light. The flame and the light necessarily coexist; the light does not exist without the flame, and the flame does not exist without the light. Nevertheless, the flame is *logically prior* to the light inasmuch as it is the source or cause of the light. Basil then turns Eunomius's contempt for *epinoiai* against him, declaring, "We do not separate these things [i.e., the fire and the light] from one another by an interval, but through reasoning we conceptualize the cause as prior to the effect" (*Eun.* 1.19–20). So too, the Father is logically or naturally prior to the Son without either being temporally prior or being of a different nature. Thus, the Father is preeminent not because his nature is superior to the Son's but because he is causally prior to the Son.

Basil then uses Eunomius's argument about the priority of the Father over the Son to turn the focus of the debate back to the common nature presupposed by the terms "Father" and "Son." The scriptural evidence for this Basil finds in the story of Jesus's healing the lame man at the pool of Bethzatha (John 5:1–8). When Jesus justified his healing on the Sabbath by saying that he was working on the authority of "my Father," the Jews sought to kill him "not only [because he] broke the Sabbath but also called God his own Father, making himself equal with God" (John 5:18). Basil uses this story not simply as an ad hominem identification of the Eunomians with unbelieving Jews but to make the point that the Jews in fact grasped the obvious implication of Jesus's calling God "Father"—namely that Jesus is claiming equality with God—a point of exegetical significance lost on the subordinationists (*Eun.* 1.24). Eunomius and the Jews of John 5:1–8 may be equally impious for denying the divinity of Christ, but at least the Jews recognized that sonship implies ontological equality with the Father. Even Jesus's own words, "The Father is greater than I," presuppose that he and his Father are of the same nature. Eunomius declared that because the Father and Son are unlike each other in nature, "the one God of all things is unbegotten and incomparable" (*Apol.* 11.15–17). Yet Jesus, in saying that the Father is "greater than," is making a comparison. Two things can be compared, Basil insists, only if they are the same sort of thing (*Eun.* 1.25). If Father and Son were of different natures, they would be incomparable, like the proverbial apples and oranges. Not only here but in Jesus's earlier claim, "I and the Father are one" (John 10:30), Jesus "is making himself one (so to speak) with the Father and by these words expressing their indistinguishable nature" (*Eun.* 1.27).

If Father and Son are indistinguishable because of their common nature, what difference do the names "Father" and "Son" signify? This was an important question for the Cappadocians not just because they needed to provide language to distinguish the Father, Son, and Holy Spirit—a deficiency in the Nicene Creed—but because Eunomius argued that different names or terms imply different natures (*Apol.* 12.3–4). The Eunomians rejected Basil's doxology—"Glory be to the Father with the Son together with the Holy Spirit"—because it treated the Son and Spirit as objects of worship and therefore equal in divinity with the Father. They championed the older doxology—"Glory be to the Father through [*dia*] the Son in [*en*] the Holy Spirit"—because, they contended, the prepositional phrases designated different natures (*Spir.* 2.4). Moreover, instead of treating the Son and Spirit themselves as objects of worship, the prepositions indicate their inferior, mediatorial functions. They are simply the ones through whom worship is directed to the Father. Aetius and Eunomius found support for their correlation of essence and prepositions in texts like 1 Corinthians 8:6: "But for us there is one God the Father *from whom* are all things and *in whom* we exist and one Lord, Jesus Christ, *through whom* all things are and *through whom* we are." This verse was an obvious favorite for subordinationists because it expressly distinguished the "one God" from "the Lord Jesus Christ." Moreover, following the maxim that "things naturally unlike are expressed in unlike terms," the Eunomians claimed that the prepositions "from" and "in" when applied to the Father in contrast with Paul's repetition of "through" when speaking of the Son indicates that the Father and Son are unlike in nature. The Father is the divine source of all things, while the Son is merely the instrumental cause through whom the Father's will is accomplished.

Basil responds to Aetius and Eunomius's application of the maxim about "unlike terms" to the doxology and to 1 Corinthians 8:6 by appealing to Paul's description of the "unsearchable" and "inscrutable" God in Romans 11:36: "For *from* him, and *through* him, and *to* him are all things." Here, Paul uses a string of different prepositions to speak of the Father; thus, the prepositions do not correspond to different natures. Moreover, in Romans 11:36, Paul uses the preposition "through" when speaking of the Father even as he used it in 1 Corinthians 8:6 when speaking of the Son. Basil's more immediate point is that, given the diversity of terms used to speak of the persons of the Trinity, Scripture does not use the terms to denote different natures (*Spir.* 5.7). Thus, the two doxologies are not contradictory. Rather, when the Church recognizes the Son's glory, he is seen as worthy of praise *with* the Father. When the Church recognizes the Son's creative and redemptive work in the economy, "we acknowledge that [the Father's] grace works for us *through* him and *in* him." Basil concludes, "Therefore, the best phrase when giving him glory is *with whom* and the most appropriate for giving thanks is *through whom*" (*Spir.* 7.16). When Basil turns to the Eunomian theory of names, he notes that *what a thing is* is prior to the particular name given to it. The human nature held in common by Peter and Paul predated the names "Peter" and "Paul." The names, therefore, do not indicate a difference of nature; both are names of human beings. Rather, the names are associated with distinguishing marks (*idiōmata*) of individual members of a species. When we hear the name "Peter," Basil says, we think of the fisherman who was Andrew's brother, not his substance (*Eun.* 2.4).

Although Basil makes his own constructive suggestions about the language used to affirm the unity of and difference between the Father and Son, his arguments in *Against Eunomius* primarily expose the flaws in Eunomius's presuppositions. Basil does provide an alternative theory of language—a theory largely derived from his understanding of how the language of Scripture worked—and of theology that would be foundational for the constructive positions advanced by his successors, Gregory of Nyssa and Gregory of Nazianzus.

378: A Year of Transition

The brief period between August of 378 and January of 379 saw two deaths that would have significant consequences for the pro-Nicenes. First, on a sweltering August day, Valens, emperor of the Eastern empire and longtime antagonist of Basil and the pro-Nicenes, attacked a large army of Goths near the Thracian town of Adrianople. Believing scouting reports that mistakenly estimated the Goths' numbers to be only ten thousand, Valens, rather than waiting to be joined by his Western colleague Gratian, elected to engage the Goths on his own. What the Roman scouts missed in their reconnaissance was a large body of Gothic cavalry that swept around the Roman left flank enveloping Valens's legions. The emperor and his bodyguard fled the field only to be trapped in a nearby farmhouse where he died when the Goths surrounded and torched the building. Valens's death opened the door for Gratian to appoint as Augustus in the East Theodosius I, who, in addition to being an experienced and effective military commander, was from an old pro-Nicene family from Spain. Shortly after his elevation in January 379, Theodosius made his religious commitments clear when in August of that year he and Gratian overturned Valens's edict exiling certain key pro-Nicenes—not the least of whom were Meletius of Antioch, Eusebius of Samosata, and Gregory of

Nyssa. In the same month, they issued a new policy on religious liberty denying freedom of worship to certain heretical groups, including the Eunomians. A scant six months later, Theodosius issued another edict, this one requiring that the Christian faith preached in Constantinople conform to Nicene doctrine as taught by Peter of Alexandria and Damasus of Rome. If Valentinian I had been reluctant to follow Constantius II's heavy-handed involvement in ecclesial affairs, Theodosius's policies marked a return to the example of Constantius; this time, however, imperial support had definitively shifted to the Nicene cause.

The second death came on New Year's Day 379. Basil of Caesarea, who had forged the alliance between the pro-Nicenes and the Homoiousians against the Homoians and Eunomians, was dead. This left a leadership vacuum in the pro-Nicene camp as well as some unfinished theological business. While Basil was successful in drawing in some of the homoiousian followers of Basil of Ancyra, other Homoiousians were unmoved. This included the followers of Macedonius I, bishop of Constantinople (339–360), who accepted the Son's equality with the Father but denied the divinity of the Spirit—hence his followers received the name Pneumatomachians or "Spirit fighters." As we will see in the next chapter, Basil's willingness to compromise on the language used to speak of the Spirit in order to draw the Macedonians into the Nicene coalition was a matter of strong contention among his devoted allies, not the least of whom was Gregory of Nazianzus. Moreover, Basil's response to Eunomius's *Apology* had not proved to be the definitive refutation of heterousian theology. During his time of exile on the island of Naoxia, after he was expelled from Constantinople by Demophilus around 370, Eunomius penned his rejoinder to Basil's *Against Eunomius* entitled *Apology for the Apology*. He followed Basil's own method of quoting sections of his opponent's text before giving his rebuttal. After the death of Valens, Eunomius returned to Constantinople and distributed at least the first two books to the inner circle of his allies, perhaps hoping to rally those sympathetic to the anti-Nicene cause. With the leader of the Nicene party dead and Eunomius publishing his refutation, Gregory of Nyssa and Gregory of Nazianzus, neither of whom was temperamentally disposed to ecclesiastical politics, rose to fill the void in the pro-Nicene leadership and to meet the new theological challenge posed by Eunomius.

Gregory of Nyssa and Eunomius

Shortly after Basil's death, Gregory of Nyssa acquired a copy of Eunomius's *Apology for the Apology* and immediately began composing a defense of Basil also with the creative title *Against Eunomius*. Since Basil's death provided Eunomius with a strategic opening to galvanize his co-religionists in Constantinople, Gregory recognized the need to respond with dispatch to the first book of Eunomius's rebuttal. His replies to the second and third books were published piecemeal between 380 and 383.

While Gregory's *Against Eunomius* directly addresses arguments about the Son's relationship with the Father, in many ways it challenged Eunomius's theological project on a meta level: questioning the basic presuppositions on which Eunomius's critique of Nicaea rested. While, as has already been seen, Eunomius's claim to know God's essence rested upon his theory of language, to an even greater extent it rested on the heterousian understanding of essence as the unique or distinguishing feature of a thing. Out of his theory of God's absolute self-sufficiency and simplicity, God's uniqueness could be summed up as "unbegotten." Gregory countered by focusing on the divine attribute of "infinity" to challenge Eunomius's identification of "unbegotten" with God's essence. Gregory was not claiming that "infinity" was a substitute for "unbegotten"; rather, in affirming that God is infinite, Gregory established the epistemological and linguistic limits on the possibility of theological truth claims and thus Eunomius's ability to claim knowledge of God's essence. Gregory drew the connection between verbal and epistemological limitations from the way that the inspired authors of Scripture limited what they presumed to say about God. Appealing to the psalmist's doxological declaration that "of the magnificence of the glory of [God's] holiness . . . there is no end" (Ps 144:3, 5 LXX), Gregory reasoned that, since God's glory manifest in his innumerable works is infinite, the divine nature that is the source of the glory is also infinite. Since, therefore, it is without limits, it is impossible for the intellect to grasp it in its totality. Since God's being is infinite and therefore incomprehensible, it cannot be captured or summed up by any single word or collection of verbal expressions. "If the things about him [i.e., attributes like glory] are endless, much more he himself in his being, whatever that actually is, is in no part grasped by any definition" (Gregory, *Eun.* 3.1.3–4). Scripture does not offer definitions of the divine that would reduce the inexhaustible wonder of God's boundless being to a single feature. For that would make God finite and so deprive him of his due honor by belittling his glory.

Here one sees the conflicting intersection between Eunomius's and Gregory's respective understandings of the relationship between piety and *theologia*. For Eunomius, the task of theology was doxological because it was fulfilling the Christian's debt to God of offering him honor and praise by confessing his true nature and thus his uniqueness that exalted him above all created beings that were not unbegotten. For Gregory, too, theology sought a true knowledge of God and thus had doxology as its ultimate aim. Yet his account of the nature of what constituted the true knowledge of God led Gregory to a radically different view of human praise of the divine. Far from discovering the divine essence, true theology lay in the discovery that God's essence could not be known and that the soul could be united with God only through faith. Gregory located the paradigm for the Christian's quest for God in Abraham, who "walked by faith, not by sight" (2 Cor 5:7) and "rose up so far in the breadth of knowledge as to be reckoned the measure of perfection, knowing God as far as possible for this little, mortal power to reach out and achieve" (*Eun.* 2.86–87). Yet this perfect knowledge was characterized by a pursuit of God whose name he did not know and who was leading him he knew not where. This was not to imply that Gregory saw in Abraham an example of fideism. On the contrary, Abraham, Gregory says, applied his intellect to go beyond the limits of the materialist, pagan philosophy of the Chaldeans to grasp divine attributes, that is, power, goodness, existence without beginning or ending. Abraham, unlike Eunomius, did not treat any of these attributes as being definitive of God's being. Rather, each was like steps on a staircase that led him further upward to seek the greater glory of God that ever lay beyond his reach. In discovering that his intellect brought him to no definitive understanding of God, his mind was purified of impious efforts to reduce God to verbal expressions or concepts. In the self-knowledge of his inability to capture the divine, Abraham came to the epiphany that the only way to know God rightly was through faith. "Having cleansed his mind of such notions, [Abraham] resorted to faith, pure and unadulterated by any ratiocination," and having arrived at the true knowledge, "he believed God to be greater and higher than any epistemological indicator" (*Eun.* 2.88–89). Since God transcends the finite expressions taken from our material, creaturely existence, the intellect, which depends upon verbal concepts, cannot by itself enter into union with God. Rather, the true knowledge of God entails the recognition of the limits of the intellect—"speechless and impotent" before God. Far from being hopeless, however, Abraham comes to the glorious understanding that he may enter into God's splendor through faith, which "interposes [between the intellect and God] and itself joins the enquiring mind to the incomprehensible nature" (*Eun.* 2.90–91).

The example of Abraham and of the authors of Scripture who recognized the intellect's limits and the capacity of faith to grasp what the intellect cannot was evidence of their wisdom. Moreover, it illustrated the difference between their true piety and the hubris of the Eunomians. For the true knowledge of God's ungraspable infinity opens the way to true worship that recognizes the gap between the Creator and the creatures: "We know the height of glory of what we worship, deducing the unimaginable greatness from our inability to grasp it in our thoughts" (*Eun.* 3.1.109). By contrast, the Eunomians, in failing to recognize that the divine nature transcends terrestrial reasoning of the intellect, failed to see that "it is safer and at the same time *more reverent* to believe that the divine majesty is more than can be thought of, than to restrict his glory to certain ideas and think there is nothing beyond that" (*Eun.* 2.96). Gregory contrasts the faith of the truly pious with the impiety of the Eunomians. The pious are like children captivated by the wonder of a beam of sunlight coming through the window. They try to grasp it with their hands. When they open their hands and behold their empty palms, they laugh and clap their hands with delight. Like the children, the truly pious see the light in faith and upon reflection discover that God escapes their comprehension. But both the children and pious still take pleasure in the marvel without having to master the light for themselves. The Eunomians, by contrast, "rather than marveling at the divine generosity and the one who is thereby known, overstep the mind's limitations and clutch with logical tricks" what they cannot clutch and so are left "with nothing at all" (*Eun.* 2.80–81). The worshipful delight of the truly pious—imitators of Abraham—is discovered only in fellowship with God, enjoyed in the journey of faith to an unknown land with a God who is beyond all naming.

As in Basil before him, the reverent silence of Gregory's apophaticism did not lead to agnosticism. On the contrary, although a comprehensive knowledge of God's essence (*ousia*) was impossible, true knowledge of the divine nature was possible through his activities (*energeiai*) in salvation history by which God revealed his nature. Therefore, the Christian's knowledge of God is derived primarily from the words of Scripture that testify to God's works of benevolence toward his creation, especially humanity (*philanthrōpia*). Thus, the heart of the theological enterprise, for Gregory as for Basil, was not syllogistic reasoning but *theōria*—the contemplation of God's power expressed in Scripture. Yet even in Scripture's positive or cataphatic judgments about God, Gregory sees an implicit apophaticism in the myriad images used in Scripture to express the superabundance of God's goodness and power—that is, an implicit recognition that even the very plethora of words in Scripture is a witness to their insufficiency in conveying the infinite breadth of God's goodness. Years later in his *Commentary on the Song of Songs*, Gregory says of the bride—that figure of the soul seeking God—"[she] contrives all sorts of word meanings but every expressive power falls short and is exposed as being less than the truth. The great David himself often does the same sort of thing: calling the divinity by a thousand names and then confessing that he has fallen short of the truth" (*Hom. Cant.* 12, 377–379). If neither David nor Paul found a single word sufficient to sum up God's infinite being, Eunomius's claim to have done just that is, in Gregory's judgment, the height of hubris and evidence of his true ignorance of God's nature. Gregory pressed his attack by turning Eunomius's logic against him. If, as Eunomius maintained, a thing's name reveals its essence, then Scripture's use of the same names to speak of the divinity of *both* the Father and the Son necessarily means that they are consubstantial (*symphyēs*) (*Eun.* 1; *GNO* 1:161).

Eunomius certainly knew that Scripture provided many of the same names for the Father and the Son—for example, "Light," "Truth," "Wisdom," as well as "God." That did not mean that the terms were used equivocally. After all Scripture also speaks of human beings similarly as "the light of the world" and "gods" without implying that human beings are "god" or "light" in the same sense—ontologically speaking—as the Father. Gregory countered by establishing a rule central to Nicene grammar for distinguishing uncreated being from created beings: uncreated Divinity *is* eternally divine *by nature*; created beings *become* divinized *by participation*. Eunomius accepted the point only to say that the Son is "divine" by participation. Gregory countered by pointing out the profoundly unorthodox implications of this assertion. Since a piece of iron, which is not hot by nature, is hot only by its close proximity in time or space to fire, which is hot by nature, then the iron may become cold when separated from the fire by a certain distance for a certain length of time. So too, Gregory reasons, if the Son and Holy Spirit are not consubstantial with the Father and therefore are good and holy not by nature, but only by creaturely participation as Eunomius claimed, then there would exist the possibility that the Son and Spirit might become evil and unholy (*Eun.* 1; *GNO* 1:110). It was unthinkable that the Son could fall, as did creatures; the Son's holiness could not be compromised by an innate fragility as with creatures who are holy only by participation in some external source of holiness. If the Son could not become anything other than what he was, then the Son could not be said to be divine by mere participation. If he was not divine by participation, the only alternative was that he was divine by nature.

Gregory's reasoning out the implications of God's infinity exposed the logical flaw in Eunomius's syllogistic reasoning. He thereby disqualified the major premise upon which Eunomius's rejection of the Son's consubstantial relationship with the Father rested. If God's essence is unknowable, then one cannot claim that the only begotten Son is necessarily of a different essence from the unbegotten Father. This victory, however, would have been a Pyrrhic one if Gregory had not been able to give a positive argument for the Son's consubstantiality with the Father. That account came in his argument for the necessary correlation of power (*dynamis*) or natural property (*symphyēs* or *physikē idiotēta*) and nature (*physis*).

The relationship of a being's distinctive powers and its nature provided an important development of the earlier distinction between activities and essence. Although the divine essence in its totality was unknowable, it could be known indirectly and partially through God's activities in the economy that manifest God's power. Such revelations of God's power in Christ's creative and redemptive activities revealed his divine nature that he derived from and shared with the Father who begat him. Thus, Gregory came to articulate a central premise of the pro-Nicene grammar, as Michel Barnes has succinctly summarized it: a common power implies a common nature. Gregory built upon the connection between activities and essence to challenge Eunomius's subordinationist claim that, since a cause is greater than its effect, a causal sequence of things implies an ontological hierarchy. That which is prior is ontologically different and superior to that of which it is the cause. Gregory countered that, at a commonsense level, the causal order of things does not imply a difference of nature. For example, the progenitor is not of a superior nature to its progeny. Rather, different natures are distinguished from each other based on their different powers. The power to heat is proper to the nature of fire and the power to illuminate is intrinsic to the nature of a sunbeam. Although the essence of a thing, generally speaking but absolutely in the case of God, is not reducible to its capacities, sameness and difference between essences lay in the presence or absence of different capacities. So too, there are some properties that are distinctive or unique to God that creatures do not possess. Only God, who essentially is, has the power to create from nothing, that is, giving existence to something that had no existence. Gregory reasoned that, since capacities are expressions of natures, when Scripture attributes to the Son certain distinctively divine powers, such as creating, which belonged to the Father's nature, then the Son must share the same nature as the Father. Support for Paul's declaration in 1 Corinthians 1:24 that Christ is "the power of God and the wisdom of God" Gregory found in Jesus's own words: "the Son can do nothing of his own accord, but only what he sees the Father doing; for whatever he does the Son does likewise" (John 5:19). The chief evidence of this is the Son's role as the Father's agent of creation (*Eun.* 1; *GNO* 1:126).

Drawing on the principle that a common power implies a common nature, Gregory used 1 Corinthians 1:24 to make an ontological claim: the Son, who is consubstantial with the Father, is thereby equal in divinity. This divine nature, however, did not, for Gregory, exist apart from the persons of the Trinity. It was not a fourth thing of which the Father, Son, and Spirit were hypostases. Rather, the nature is proper to the person of the Father with whom the Son and Spirit are essentially united and so shares the powers of the nature. This ontological unity of the persons meant, as implied in Jesus's words in John 5:19, that the Father, Son, and Spirit work together in a unity of operations. Any action in Scripture that is attributed to the Father is simultaneously and cooperatively an action of the Son and Spirit. For the actions of the Son and Spirit are works from the activities of the Father's power: "all these [creative] works [*erga*] [are] of the Father in that they are works of his power. . . . Since the Son is the power [*dynamis*] of the Father, all these works of the Son are the works of the Father" (*Eun.* 3.4; *GNO* 2:147).

There is another crucial rule of the pro-Nicene grammar that distinguished uncreated Divinity from temporal creatures and explained the unity of operations by persons of the Trinity: in God, there is no gap or interval between God's will and God's power. The activities of animate creatures entail series of causal steps or intervals between willing and acting spread out over time. The cheetah *first* chooses to pursue the impala and *then* at the right moment springs into motion. A human being may will something but either may not have the power to fulfill her will or must wait to exercise her power in accomplishing her will. God, however, is simple, not composite; God is one. Since his nature is a single whole, his will and power are not truly separate. Therefore, there is no interval between God's willing a thing and his act of accomplishing what he wills. Gregory illustrates the point with the imaginative image of fire endowed with a will. The flame would will to shine forth radiating heat and would in that same instant of willing exercise its power to shine forth and radiate heat (*Eun.* 20; *GNO* 2:192; *NPNF* 2/5:202). The flame's nature, will, and power would be one. So it is with the Trinity. When the Father wills a thing, the Son who is the "power of God" and Spirit who is the activity of God effect the Father's will. Thus, speaking of God's triune creative activity, Gregory writes, "For at one and the same time did [the Father] will that that which ought to be should be, and his power, that produced all things that are, kept pace with his will turning his will into action. . . . His will done suffices to effect the subsistence of existing things; for his will is his power" (*Refutation of the Creed* [*NPNF* 2/5:111]).

By focusing on the unity of nature and power, Gregory could employ 1 Corinthians 1:24 to counter Eunomius's claim that "[the Son] was not before his generation"—his rephrasing of Arius's condemned slogan, "There was when the Son was not." Instead, however, of repeating the older objection that if the Son, who is the Wisdom and Power of God, is not coeternal with the Father, then there was a time when the Father was neither wise nor powerful, Gregory offers the bolder conclusion that the Father, whose nature includes wisdom and power, did not exist. That is, to affirm that power is intrinsic to the nature of the Father necessarily affirms that the Son is consubstantial with the Father.

Paul's identification of Son, who is the Father's Word, as "the power of God" was critical to Gregory's salvific view of divinization. In his work *On Perfection*, Gregory explains that the life of virtue comes from knowing the meaning of the name "Christ." In knowing that the Christ is "the power of God and the wisdom of God," the Christian realizes that, when she prays, she is drawing into herself Christ and with him the divine power and wisdom that he in turn imparts to her soul as she gazes upon him in contemplative worship. Thus, through the indwelling *dynamis* of the Son, the believer is empowered to resist sin and wisely choose the good that she may become holy as God is holy (*Perf.*; *GNO* 8/1:183; Greer, 29).

In the years following Eunomius's *Apology for the Apology*, when Gregory offered an account of the Trinity, he employed the language of *ousia* to refer to the one nature common to each person and *hypostasis* to refer to the individual, subsistent entities, Father, Son, and Holy Spirit. Indeed, the formula of one essence (*ousia*) in three persons (*hypostaseis*) that Gregory summed up as "a distinction of persons in unity" (*Or. cat.* 1) countered interpretations of Nicaea as a Sabellian creed by clearly affirming the real distinction of the persons while also affirming their essential oneness. Yet Gregory's subsequent teachings on the Trinity were intended to go beyond polemics to provide pedagogical guidance for *theōria*—the sanctifying reading and contemplation of Scripture. The Trinity understood as one essence in three hypostases could serve as a rule for the right interpretation of the biblical narrative because the distinct identities of Father, Son, and Holy Spirit were derived from Scripture itself. That is, Gregory maintained that the immanent or eternal relations of the persons corresponded to their revelation in the economy as narrated in Scripture.

At the most basic level, Gregory distinguished the persons by saying that the Father is the unbegotten, the Son is the only begotten, and the Spirit is neither begotten nor unbegotten (*Eun.* 1; *GNO* 1:278–80). In his later epistle 38, he repeats these same distinguishing markers but in language that expresses the organic relationship of the persons as depicted in Scripture: the Father is "a certain power subsisting without begetting or beginning . . . alone from no other cause"; the Son "alone shines forth from the unbegotten light as the only begotten . . . [and] makes known the Holy Spirit," without whom we can have no conception of the Son; and the Holy Spirit "is made known after the Son and with the Son, and subsists from the Father" (*Ep.* 38.4). In his *Catechetical Oration*, where he argues for the superiority of Christian Trinitarianism over either pagan polytheism or Jewish monotheism, Gregory appeals to the category of God's perfection as manifest in God's triunity. Even as Plato in *Timaeus* had explained God's perfect goodness in his sharing his goodness through his act of creation, so too the perfection of the God of the Christian Scriptures lies in his self-expression. Unlike creaturely perfection that is ceaselessly being formed through participation in God's goodness, God's perfection lies in his boundless goodness, power, and wisdom proper to the common nature of the persons. The perfection of God's goodness is the *philanthrōpia* manifest in God's self-giving through his Word and Spirit. Transitory human beings give self-expression through uttering words that go forth into an existence distinct from the speaker; yet because the speaker is transitory, so are her words that pass away almost as soon as they are spoken. By contrast, God is eternal; therefore, his Word, in contrast with human speech, is not a fleeting subsistence but an eternal one. And the divine Breath that accompanies the Word is also an eternal subsistence (*Or. cat.* 1). Precisely because the Word and Spirit are consubstantial with the Father, they are able to make humanity truly participants in the divine goodness through communion with the Father.

Gregory illustrates the soteriological significance of the cooperative union and mutual indwelling of the persons in his *Homilies on the Song of Songs*. There

Gregory describes the divinization of the soul or the bride as the joint work of the Father and Son. The Father is the archer who lets fly his arrow, the Son, which penetrates the bride's heart and inflicts it with the wound of love. Since, as Jesus declared, "I and my Father will come and make our dwelling with him" (John 14:23), when the Son enters the bride's heart, the Father also enters therein (*Hom. Cant.* 4; *GNO* 6:127). Then the human heart, filled with the love of God, is transformed into the heavenly holy of holies. For through the Word's union with the Father, the Son's descent has made the bride's soul the Father's dwelling place and thus an image of the heavenly tabernacle (*Or. dom.* 3; SC 596.390–92). Seen from another angle, "heaven" as God's "dwelling place" is a figurative expression of the Father's transcendence. Therefore, when the Son, who eternally abides with the Father, enters the Christian's soul, he raises her up to heaven, that is, into the presence of his Father.

Perhaps Gregory's most famous and confusing work on the Trinity is his *To Ablabius: On Not Three Gods*. There Gregory sought to rebut the charge of tritheism: Peter, James, and John share a common nature (*ousia*), and yet each as an individual (*hypostasis*) is distinct from the others so that we call them "three men" rather than "one man." So, by analogy, why are the Father, Son, and Holy Spirit, who have a common nature (*ousia*) and who each is an individual (*hypostasis*) distinct from the others, not also called "three gods"? Gregory's argument becomes all the more opaque when he dismisses the analogy by saying that in fact Peter, James, and John are not really "three men" and to call them such is a thoughtless error in our common speech. His point is that, although Peter, James, and John have markers of their individual identities such that they are three *hypostaseis*, the common human nature in them is one, not three. However, the critical point where the analogy at the heart of the objection breaks down is that the relationship between Peter, James, and John is different from that of Father, Son, and Holy Spirit. For the cooperation of three mortals is unlike the unity of operations of the three members of the Trinity. Peter, James, and John may work together, but there is no necessary and immediate agreement of their wills. In the case of the Trinity, however, the eternal unity of the Son and Spirit in their common nature with the Father means that there is no gap (*diastēma*) between their wills. Rather, unlike mortals or the gods of Olympus, there is an immediate procession of a common, perfect will from the Father to the Son and Holy Spirit that corresponds to the Father's immediate generation of the Son and the spiration of the Spirit. "For the action of each [person] in any matter is not separate and individualized," Gregory explains. "But whatever occurs . . . in reference to God's providence for us . . . occurs through the three persons, and is not three separate things" (*Abl.*; Hardy, 262). Having explained that the term "Godhead" (*theotēs* from *theaomai*, "to behold"), which is associated with the single, common nature, denotes God's providential watch over creation, Gregory writes, "the principle of the overseeing and beholding power is a unity in Father, Son, and Holy Spirit. It issues from the Father, as from a spring. It is actualized by the Son; and its grace is perfected by the power of the Holy Spirit" (*Abl.*; Hardy, 263).

In sum, Gregory's Trinitarian grammar with its unity of *ousia* with distinctions among the *hypostaseis* clearly distinguishes Nicaea from the Modalism of Sabellius and Marcellus. Gregory's *hypostaseis* understood as modes of God's being is different from a Modalist distinction between three modes of God's self-revelation. Whereas Father, Son, and Holy Spirit for Modalists are simply three different forms the one God assumes when he acts economically, for Gregory, when orthodox Christians speak of the Father as unbegotten, the Son as only begotten, and the Spirit as the one who proceeds from the Father through the mediation of the Son, they are naming eternal modes of God's subsistence—the eternal immanent relations between the persons—as described in Scripture. Moreover, for Sabellius and his followers, the three modes of the one God's self-revelation are discrete actions separate from God's works when acting in another mode or form. By contrast for Gregory, all of God's works (*erga*) are the product of a single activity performed by all three persons in perfect unity. Therefore, within Gregory's Trinitarian logic, the triad of titles Creator, redeemer, and sustainer does not correspond to the divine names Father, Son, and Holy Spirit. For the Father alone is not the Creator, nor the Son alone the redeemer, nor the Spirit alone the sustainer. Rather, all three together are the Creator, all three together are redeemer, and all three providentially sustain creation.

Gregory of Nazianzus Against the Eunomians

Gregory of Nazianzus's ascendency as a leader of the pro-Nicenes was to a greater or lesser degree thanks to the patronage of Melitius of Antioch. Given the opportunity created by Valens's death and the need for a unifying leader created by Basil's passing, Meletius, once back in Antioch, saw the need to heal the divisions among the pro-Nicenes to forge a strong united front against the lingering subordinationist presence. Acting swiftly, Meletius summoned one hundred and fifty Eastern bishops to a synod in Antioch in the fall of 379. The first of the council's goals was to heal the schism among the pro-Nicene Antiochenes. The rift originated when Athanasius refused to recognize Meletius as bishop of Antioch because he had been ordained by anti-Nicenes. Even though Meletius immediately committed to the pro-Nicene party, doubts lingered in many minds, including that of Athanasius's successor, Peter, and Damasus of Rome who supported Paulinus, Meletius's rival in Antioch. The synod also recognized the need to organize countermeasures against the Eunomians who, though officially outlawed, remained a visible presence and influence in major metropolitan areas, not the least of which was Constantinople. One of the council's actions, likely pushed forward by Meletius and Eusebius, was to secure for Gregory of Nazianzus an invitation—likely from pro-Nicene aristocrats in the capital, including Gregory's cousin, Theodosia—to preach in Constantinople in order to strengthen the Nicene minority residing in the Eastern capital. Tensions in Constantinople ran high. The Homoian and Eunomian clergy looked on Gregory with his simple attire and decidedly aristocratic manner of life as a lowbrow provincial unworthy of being bishop of the imperial capital. The animus climaxed during the Easter Vigil of 380 when supporters of the anti-Nicene bishop, Demophilos, stormed Gregory's chapel and smashed the altar, throwing the eucharistic chalices and plate and hurling stones at Gregory and the congregation (*Vit.* 655–657). That summer in the small chapel of Anastasia, Gregory preached a series of sermons commonly called his theological orations (*Or.* 27–31) that laid out his Trinitarian grammar and would provide the textual lens through which the ultimate judgment of the Council of Constantinople would be interpreted.[2]

The opening sermon, rather than turning directly to the subject of God, provided prolegomena (*prodialexis*) setting the scope of the subjects Gregory would discuss. Invoking the Pauline censure of heterodox teachers and those with "itching ears" who eagerly listen to them (2 Tim 4:3), Gregory laments the irreverently casual manner in which the uneducated and unworthy openly speculate about the nature of God in the most common social gatherings (*Or.* 27.1–2). The Church's faith is turned from a holy mystery reserved for those initiated in baptism into a public spectacle—a verbal wrestling match—for mere entertainment rather than for the edification of those "who have ears to hear" (Sir 25:9). When Gregory declares, "Discussion of theology is not for everyone, I tell you, not for everyone," he is using "theology" (*theologia*) not in the broad modern sense that includes Christology, soteriology, ecclesiology, and other loci that the Eastern church referred to as "salvation history" (*oikonomia*) but in its ancient narrow sense as concerning the nature of God. Inquiry into such lofty matters he compares to Moses's ascent of Mount Sinai to stand upon holy ground. Most Christians, like most of the Israelites in the wilderness who out of pious fear did not presume to make the ascent, should not attempt to discuss such topics as the Father's generation of the Son or other mysteries proper to theology (*Or.* 28.2). Here Gregory is not treating the Church's faith as a secret *gnōsis* reserved for religious intelligentsia. On the contrary, he invites his listeners to inquire about the cosmos, the nature of the soul, the general resurrection, the last judgment, and the like. Speculations in

2. To make an anachronistic comparison, Nazianzen's Theological Orations are to the Nicene-Constantinopolitan Creed what the *Federalist Papers* are to the US Constitution.

these questions may be profitable if one's conclusions prove correct, while missing the mark in such speculations does not result in serious spiritual consequences (*Or.* 27.10). Whereas to be in error about something as fundamental as the nature of God may imperil one's soul by leading one to worship something other than the one true God. Gregory is motivated by pastoral and apologetic concerns. Pagan neighbors, who have not undergone catechesis, overhearing discussions about the only begotten Son of God who is then conceived by the Spirit and born of a human mother, may see no difference between Jesus and any number of demigods conceived during Zeus's numerous sexual liaisons with mortal women. To discuss theology with audiences hostile or uninformed, or both, gives them material they can use to defend their own religion or to give a distorted picture of Nicene Christianity (*Or.* 27.6). If one's actions and thoughts have not been purified through the teachings and sacraments of the Church, an impure carnal life is apt to lead to carnal misinterpretations of Scripture and the creed.

In this opening salvo, Gregory is establishing for the Nicene community and anti-Nicene interlopers a vision of theology that is fundamentally different from the pseudointellectual approach of the Eunomians. Grasping the nature of the triune God, he argues, is no mere wordplay (*technydrion*), a verbal *technē* or skill acquired through mastery of syllogistic reasoning (*Or.* 27.2). Rather, it is a form of contemplation (*theōria*) profitable only for those who, like a Moses or an Aaron, have attained a certain degree of purity of life and understanding in order to perceive the divine reality signified by the words of Scripture. *Theologia* penetrates the dark cloud that is mysterious divinity. It seeks, like Moses, to behold God's glory. A glory revealed not in a direct vision of the divine essence shining out from the face of God but in God's averted figure or backside seen only from the vantage point of the Rock, the Father's incarnate Logos (*Or.* 28.3). The averted figure refers to the creative and redemptive activity (*energeia*) that follows from the divine nature and is manifest in Scripture's narrative of the divine economy. In other words, the Christian beholds the Father's glory where Jesus's divine power is manifest in his human flesh. Thus, the incarnation becomes the hermeneutical lens through which the believer interprets creation as reflections of God's power (*dynamis*) and thus apprehends not the divine essence itself but particular attributes of God's nature that constitute true knowledge of God.

Gregory, like Basil, recognizes that the reason for Eunomius's theological errors lies in his errant view of language and as a consequence of his misinterpretation of Scripture. Curiously, he draws the dividing line between himself and Eunomius by invoking Plato's famous pronouncement from *Timaeus* (28c): "It is difficult to conceive God, but to define him in words is an impossibility." By this, Plato means knowing *that* there is a cause of the world lies within the intellect's grasp. But speaking about the nature of that God is impossible. This judgment became the premise of the negative or apophatic theology of Middle Platonism; the only way to speak with certainty about God is to say what God is not. Gregory is appreciative of Plato, who proves himself superior to Eunomius because he recognizes not only that apprehending God is hard but that expressing the essence of God is impossible. In recognizing this impossibility, Plato, unlike Eunomius, shows that he is not ignorant of the God he has apprehended. But for Gregory, Plato did not go far enough; therefore, Gregory declares, "to tell of God is not possible, but to know him is even less possible" (*Or.* 28.4). Human words may express convictions about the existence of the Creator whom the mind apprehends, but such convictions are not knowledge in a maximal sense since the finite intellect cannot compass the reality of God's infinite being (*Or.* 28.5). Even Jacob, who wrestled with God, "could not boast that he had taken in the nature, the total vision of God" (*Or.* 28.18). Thus, contra Eunomius, Gregory insists that any claim to know God *in se*, in the totality of his being that is his essence, is absolutely impossible.

Moreover, since language belongs to the realm of creatures and is shaped by their material and temporal context, no speech can span the ontological divide between the eternal God and temporal creation. To put it another way, because language developed to describe, among other things, the temporal relations between creatures—that is, the temporal sequence of events in the world—language is inherently temporal. Yet since God is eternal, there are no temporal distinctions within God; there is no "before" or "after" in God. To speak of God in such temporal terms would treat God as a body having extension in time and space. However, the mind is dependent upon language to think and describe God. Even as the eye is dependent on the medium of light and atmosphere to see, so too as material creatures human beings are dependent on the medium of language to reason. Therefore, we reason about the world in material and temporal terms. That is true of how we think about God as well: "Some corporeal factor of ours will always intrude itself, even if the mind be most fully detached from the visible world" (*Or.* 28.12). In other words, as material creatures, human beings naturally think with analogy, comparing material characteristics of one thing to those of another. This is what taxonomies are. So we describe God with material analogies, "Spirit" or "fire" or "light" (*Or.* 28.13). Therefore, when human beings speak about God, their language inevitably imposes temporal aspects on God. We speak as if there is a "first this" that is "before that" that is "after this" (*Or.* 29.3). Therefore, on the one hand, we should not be surprised when Scripture speaks of the relationship of the Father and the Son in temporal language: "In the beginning *was* the Word, and the Word *was* with God." On the other hand, however, we should recognize that for God there is no "was" or "will be"; the use of tenses is a limitation of our language, which God nevertheless uses to reveal himself to time-bound creatures. It is as if Gregory would have us mentally insert a qualifier, "In the beginning, so to speak, was the Word." The force of this argument was to undercut both the Eunomian direct correspondence theory of language and by extension their assertion that the temporal language used in Scripture to distinguish the Father and the Son denotes a temporal gap between the persons that would refute the Nicene claim that the Son is coeternal with the Father.

When in oration 29, the third of the theological orations preached in Constantinople, Gregory turns from the nature of theology generally to the specific relation of the Son and the Father, he begins by distinguishing the Nicene doctrine of the triune God from polytheism. Gregory took this as his starting point not because his main rival was pagan polytheism but to respond to the Eunomian charge that pro-Nicenes' belief in the Trinity was tantamount to the belief in multiple gods, like devotees of the Olympian deities. The difference is clear when one compares polytheism and monotheism with atheism espoused by the Epicureans. Polytheism is, he argues, not fundamentally different from atheism because neither view has a principle of unity that is the source of the many things that populate the universe and that holds them together in a coherent whole. Rather, a world with many gods is every bit as anarchic as one without a first cause. Each of the many gods of the Greco-Roman pantheon possesses his or her own independent will; they are no more united to one another than mortals. They have power but no unity and so cannot give unity and coherence to the world. They are simply one species among the many other species of beings. The world of the monotheist, by contrast, is not essentially chaotic because its existence is derived from a single first cause, God, whose single wise and good will establishes an orderly relationship between the many creatures that derive their being from him. This is the world of Nicene Christianity. For the persons of the Trinity are not like the pagan deities with their separate and often conflicting wills. Rather, Nicene Christianity affirms the monarchy of God: "the single rule produced by equality of nature, harmony of will, identity of action, and the convergence toward the source of what springs from unity" (*Or.* 29.2). In other words, since the Father, Son, and Spirit, though distinct from each other, are consubstantial and exist in a unity of being, they have a single will. Thus, the Son does nothing apart from the Father, and all he does is a fulfillment of the Father's will.

At the same time that Gregory affirms the superiority of monotheism over polytheism and atheism, he is equally firm that Nicene monotheism is superior to Eunomian monotheism. The God of Nicene Christianity is not a monad as in the Eunomian heresy. For, he asserts, a monad might experience an inner conflict or "self-discordant unity" (*to hen stasiazon*) that leads to an endless string of emanations (*Or.* 29.2). The consubstantiality of the Father, Son, and Spirit—and therefore the unity of wills—is important for a harmonic peace within the Godhead and within the Church. Some sixteen years before preaching the theological orations,

Gregory invoked the harmonic unity of the Trinity as a model for the Christian life in a series of orations (*Or.* 6, 22, and 23) that sought to heal a breach between his father Gregory, bishop of Nazianzus, and his monks: "we of the One have become one; we of the Trinity [are] like in nature and same in heart and in honor; we of the Logos above unreason, we of the Spirit aglow with, not against, one another" (*Or.* 6.4). Even as the ontological unity of Father, Son, and Holy Spirit confers equality of honor among the divine persons, so Christians, who are of the same nature as partakers of the divine reason and spiritual illumination, should abide together in godly unity in doctrine, faith, and hope (*Or.* 6.11). The Church's confession of God as Trinity is the surest sign of God's indwelling the community of believers: "'God is really among us' who unites those who unite him and exalts those who exalt him" (*Or.* 23.4). He finds in the host of heaven an example of creaturely unity through participation in God. The angelic host abides in harmony with each other because their collective existence is a reflection of the luminous unity of the God whom they worship (*Or.* 6.12). Consequently, "the prime mark" of their heavenly life is "peacefulness and freedom from faction, [for they] draw their unity, as indeed their radiance, from the honored and holy Trinity. For this too both is, and is believed in faith to be, one God, as much for its inner harmony as for its identity of substance" (*Or.* 6.13). Such unity is preserved in the Church through recognizing the right relationship of the Father, Son, and Spirit "not regarding the three as a single individual [*ta tria hōs hena*] (for they are not without individual reality [*kata mias hypostaseōs*], nor do they comprise a single reality) . . . but rather believing the three to be a single entity [*ta tria hen*]. For they are a single entity not in individual reality but in divinity a unity worshipped in Trinity and a Trinity summed up into unity [*monas en Triadi*]" (*Or.* 6.22). Error comes, he argues, from either collapsing the three into a single individual as if there were only one person and not three distinct hypostases or separating them as if they did not exist in the unity of a single deity. In the latter case, the Father, Son, and Spirit are "alienated and disjoined from one another" and consequently exist in a state of conflict rather than unity because of their inequality. Such inequality among the persons is demeaning to God because it implies that the Father is either envious and petty in refusing to share his divinity with an equal, or weak in being fearful that Son and Spirit would as equals be hostile and threatening to his preeminence (*Or.* 23.6). Furthermore, the Son and Spirit are dishonored and reduced to a status below that of mortal creatures. For they are looked upon merely as instrumental causes. Even as the sculptor's hammer and chisel are inferior to the marble statue, so the Son and Spirit, if they were not equal in divinity with the Father, would be mere tools that exist not as goods in themselves but simply as means for fulfilling the Father's will (*Or.* 23.7). As such, they would be the Father's slaves and unworthy of our worship. Here Gregory is pressing the logic of basic Christian piety against the Eunomians. If the Son and

Spirit are not equal in divinity with the Father, then they are unworthy of worship and adoration. "If I worshipped a creature, I would not be a Christian. Why is Christianity precious? Is it not because Christ is God?" (*Or.* 37.17).

Confessing God as Trinity honors both the Father, who is the source, and the Son and Spirit, who issue from the Father. The Father is honored because he is shown to be magnanimous, willing to share his dignity and honor of his divinity with the Son and Spirit. But neither is the Father depicted, as in pagan polytheism, as prodigal in the disorderly, boundless diffusion of his divinity. The Son and Spirit are rightly honored in worship because of the divinity they derive from their source, the Father (*Or.* 23.8). The Nicene doctrine of God as Trinity has the virtue of preserving the *monarchia* of God without conflating the persons, as with Modalists, and preserving the distinctiveness of the persons without separating them ontologically, as with the Eunomians and other subordinationists. He defines the Trinity as "a comprehensive relationship between equals who are held in equal honor; the term unites in one word members that are one by nature and does not allow things that are indivisible to suffer fragmentation when their members are divided" (*Or.* 23.10). Without diminishing the uniqueness of God and therefore the task of theology, Gregory does not see this reasoning about the Trinity as a whole, with the persons as its members, as radically different from other modes of intellectual investigation. For instance, the intellect is able to separate, at a conceptual level, things that are in reality inseparable and think of each part as reflecting the whole—as when people distinguish mind, word, and spirit when thinking about the unity that is the person. Thus, Christians are able to speak of each person as distinct from the other and yet, because of their shared nature, speak of each individually as God (*Or.* 23.11). Thus, even as each can be called light since all three illuminate with the same luminous divinity proper to their shared nature, so too each can be called God (*Or.* 31.3). To put it another way, since God is light, the Father, Son, and Spirit are the divine light existing in three discrete *hypostaseis* (*Or.* 40.5). Yet Gregory locates the uniqueness of the Trinity in its perfect, eternal movement from monad to dyad to triad. The Father is the perfectly simple *monad* who, out of his superabundance, generates his perfect image, the Son, to form the *dyad*, which transcends the binary relation of form and matter of created things, and ultimately expresses its perfection in the emission of the Spirit to form a *triad*, which is the perfect expression of the Father's generosity without an endless and chaotic diffusion of divinity (*Or.* 23.8). Thus, Gregory has portrayed Nicene monotheism as the mean between Jewish monotheism, in which the Godhead is constricted and ungenerous, and Plotinian monotheism, in which all creation is an emanation from the One.

Theological orations 29 and 30 summarize, for Gregory, the logic of the Trinity in terms of the Father's generation of the Son—a logic that is carried through in his discussion of the Spirit in oration 31. The Father is the principle of unity who is the begetter (*ho gennētōr*) of the begotten one (*to gennēma*), the Son, and the emitter (*ho proboleus*) of the emission (*to problēma*), the Spirit (*Or.* 29.2). The Father, as the first principle and principle of unity, is the monad, the single unbegotten fount of divinity. Yet because God is by his will and power inherently generative, he is always the Father who eternally generates the Son and emits the Spirit. But because the Father is the incorporeal Source, his generation of the Son and his emission of the Spirit in their subsistence do not entail diminution or loss of the Father's divine substance. Nor do they result in the Son and Spirit's separation from the Father. Rather, because the Son and Spirit derive their being from the Father, he is the principle of unity that draws them back into a convergence (*synneusis*) in him, their source (*Or.* 42.15).

To clarify the nature of the Son as the only begotten, Gregory returns to the contrast between the Christian Trinity and the Neo-Platonic triad of the One, Mind, and Soul. Plotinus's theology was largely an attempt to systematize Plato's divergent accounts of God either as the Good and the Beautiful in dialogues like *Republic* and *Symposium* or as the source of creation in *Timaeus*. As with Gregory's later account of the *monarchia* of God, Plotinus, too, depicts God as the One who is the source of all things and therefore the principle of unity. The One is simple, which means not only that it is immaterial and so noncomposite but more generally that the One is the unconditioned condition for all other things. The One, therefore, is entirely self-sufficient. This, however, raised a real conundrum: since the One is entirely self-sufficient—"at rest in itself"—why would it need to generate a second and a third principle, Mind and Soul? Following *Timaeus*, Plotinus explains the coming of all things from the One in terms of a series of emanations or the overflowing of God's goodness. This, however, only raises another quandary: since the One abides in itself and knows itself but not as an object of self-reflection—that is, the One has no transcendental ego—is the emanation of Mind from the One an act of volition or merely an automatic movement arising from the nature of the One? Since an act of will for a rational being entails a choice based on some deliberation—a form of cognition alien to the One—the answer for Plotinus is paradoxical: the emanation is neither automatic or unconscious nor willed or planned. It is a free and spontaneous expression of the One's nature analogous to the radiation of light from the sun (*Enn.* 5.1.6).

For Gregory, the Father's begetting of the Son is fundamentally different. He rejects Plato's metaphor of the divine as a bowl that cannot contain its own goodness but overflows and shares that goodness in creation (*Tim.* 41d). Such imagery is unfitting for the God of Christianity precisely because it treats God as an automaton for whom the generation of the Son is an involuntary and irrepressible excretion (*perittōma ti physikon kai dyskathekton*) proceeding from God's nature rather than from the Father's will (*Or.* 29.2). Gregory is not here denying that the Son is begotten from the Father's nature; that was the view of Arius and other subordinationists who claimed the Son was begotten from the will of the Father. Indeed, Gregory recognizes that for such people, a voluntary begetting implies an interval between the Father's act of willing and the begetting. On the contrary, since for God there is no divide between God's nature, God's will, and God's action, the Father's willing the Son is identical with his begetting the Son from his nature. Moreover, since God is by nature eternal, his willing and begetting the Son are from eternity. Consequently, there is no interval between the Father's willing and his begetting the Son (*Or.* 29.6). Ultimately, because the language of Platonic monotheism conveys a view of the relation of the first and second principles fundamentally different from that of the Father and the Son, Gregory rejects the Platonic imagery and terminology and instead relies exclusively on the language both from the prologue of John's Gospel (John 1:18)—the Word made flesh is the "only begotten God" (*monogenēs theos*)—and from Jesus's Farewell Discourse (John 15:26) where he speaks of the Spirit as the one proceeding from the Father (*ho para tou patros ekporeuetai*).

One of the major challenges facing Gregory was answering Eunomius's argument about the implication of the names "Father" and "Son." Namely, a father as the begetter of a son must be before the son; therefore, the Son cannot be coeternal with the Father. As we have already seen, Gregory objects that this line of reasoning, though perfectly sensible in the temporal context in which human fathers beget their offspring, does not makes sense when speaking about a God who is eternal and therefore exists outside of time. Therefore, the Father, as the one who begets the Son, is logically prior as the sun is to the light that radiates from it (*Or.* 29.3). Thus, whereas Levi existed in a latent state in Abraham's loins (Heb 7:9–10) until he was born, the Son did not exist *in potentiality* in the Father before being begotten. Rather, since the Son was in the beginning with the Father, the Son's being begotten "from the beginning" is the Son's eternal mode of existence (*Or.* 29.9). Moreover, if Eunomius wants to make a strict comparison between human fathers and sons and the Father and Son, then, Gregory argues, he will have to concede that begetting entails the generation not of a different sort of creature but of a being of the same nature as the parents. Therefore, because the Son is begotten by God the Father, the Son is necessarily of the same nature (*Or.* 29.10).

Eunomius had posed another more serious question: When the name "Father" is applied to God, is "Father" speaking about God's nature (*ousia*) or about a divine activity (*energeia*)? Here is the fork of the dilemma. If being "Father," the unbegotten begetter, is an essential attribute of God, then the begotten Son, who himself is not a father, is of an essence different from that of the Father. On the other hand, "works" are external economic activities of God. They refer to God's relationship with creation rather than movements internal to God's being. Therefore, if being "Father" refers to God's workings, like creating the world, then the Son is a creature—the first of God's works. Gregory counters that this is a false dilemma. Divine predicates are not simply either essential (e.g., simple, immutable, eternal) or economic (Creator, Redeemer, Sanctifier). A select few (e.g., Father and Son) refer to relations internal to the Godhead. "Father" denotes his relationship (*schesis*) to an offspring. "Father" and "son" are relational, not essential, predicates because becoming a father does not alter a man's nature; it merely establishes a unique relationship between the man and his child. Moreover, it denotes the relationship of two beings that share the same nature. In the case of the Trinity, "Father" and "Son" are not merely predicates but the names of persons. These names refer to the eternal relationship of the begetter, who is the fount of the divine nature, and the only begotten, who receives the fullness of the Father's divinity (*Or.* 29.16). Although this language is taken from human relations and as such is God's accommodation of our limited creaturely understanding, the names "Father" and "Son" are not economic terms that describe God's relationship with creation; rather, they name two modes of God's being (*to pōs echei*) (*Or.* 29.16). They name who God is eternally as Father, Son, and Holy Spirit. Thus, he sums up the unity and diversity of the Godhead: "One single nature [*mian physin*] in three distinctive characters [*en trisin idiotēsi*], intelligences, perfections, and individual subsistences [*hypostaseis*]. They are distinguishable by enumeration, not divided in deity" (*Or.* 33.16).

Nazianzen's Partitive Exegesis: A Trinitarian Approach to Interpreting Scripture

The arguments about the relation of the Father and the Son were, for Gregory, not primarily the result of the misuse of syllogistic reasoning or a defective theory of language. It was the result of a misreading of Scripture. Therefore, Gregory articulated a method of interpretation known as partitive exegesis. It emerged in his theological orations as the discussion of "Father" and "Son" leading to the larger subject of names and attributes that Scripture gives to Jesus. Here Gregory locates the chief flaw in the subordinationist interpretation of Scripture that leads them to conclude that Christ is a creature. Namely, they attribute to the Word's nature qualities and actions that properly refer to the creaturely nature that the Word assumed in the incarnation and not his divine nature from eternity. They read, for instance, that Christ slept, hungered, thirst, wept, and suffered. Therefore, they conclude that since these are not proper to immutable deity that Christ must not be God equal in divinity with the Father. This hierarchical relation between the Father and the Son seems confirmed by scriptural statements that the Son is a "slave" (Phil 2:7) or was "created" (Prov 8:22) or "grew in wisdom and favor with God and man" (Luke 2:52). In addition, they find Jesus's own declarations that the Father is "greater" than he (John 14:28) or that he is "ignorant" about when the consummation of the kingdom will come (Matt 24:36). All these Gregory acknowledges to be attributes of Christ. Where the subordinationists go wrong, however, is that they fail to distinguish between attributes proper to Christ by virtue of his assumed humanity and those proper to his eternal divinity. This distinction between the incarnate Word's divine and human natures leads Gregory to articulate the principle of partitive exegesis: the lofty or sublime descriptions (Word, wisdom, power, almighty) of Scripture refer to Christ in his divinity, and the lowly descriptions (grew, hungered, suffered, was ignorant) refer to Christ in his humanity (*Or.* 29.18). The former are proper to Christ's divine nature, which from eternity was not subject to the needs and limitations of a body. The latter are Christ's by virtue of his composite condition in the incarnation when he assumed our bodily nature with its creaturely finitude. This allows one in the interpretation of Scripture to distinguish the Word's nature from his works in the incarnation. Obviously, through the Word's works during his earthly sojourn in the flesh, the Christian is able to make inferences about the nature of God manifest in his displays of power and compassion. Nevertheless, it is a mistake if certain of Christ's experiences in the flesh, such as his suffering and death, are viewed as properties of the divine nature itself.

Applying the method of partitive exegesis to Hebrews 5:7–8 in which Christ is said to have "learned obedience by the things which he suffered," Gregory countered the Eunomian use of the passage as a prooftext of the Son's subordination to the Father. These verses, Gregory argues, refer not to the Word, who in his divinity is equal to the Father, but to the Word who in the incarnation condescended to the level of fallen humanity by taking on the "form of a slave" (Phil 2:7). When the divine Word assumed human nature, Gregory explains, he took upon himself "the whole of me, along with all that is mine, in himself so that he may consume within himself the meaner elements, as fire consumes wax" (*Or.* 30.6). In taking to himself humanity's sin, his fiery holiness purges humanity of the sin of worldly passions so that we might be partakers of his divine holiness and blessedness. Christ's suffering, which is possible for the Word clothed in a frail and mortal nature, was a demonstration of perfect obedience of God's servant and proved the honor that belongs to such faithfulness to God, the Master. Gesturing to the larger argument of Hebrews, Gregory suggests that Christ is able to be a sympathetic high priest because, by his suffering, he has experienced the frailty of those for whom he makes intercession before the Father. Thus, the Word in his eternal status as the only begotten Son did not need to learn obedience—as if he were a disobedient slave. The Eunomians dishonor the Son because they mistakenly apply the verse to the Son as he was before the incarnation rather than to the Son in his economic assumption of our human nature.

When analyzing Proverbs 8:22–23, "The Lord created me at the beginning of his ways for his works, before the ages he made me the foundation in the beginning,"[3] Gregory begins reasoning: since Godhead is uncaused, verse 22 cannot be referring to the divinity of Wisdom. The only option, therefore, is that it is referring to the humanity with which Wisdom is clothed in the incarnation. Here is a new articulation of the principle of partitive exegesis: Biblical descriptions of Christ that have "a causal implication we will attribute to the humanity; what is absolutely free of cause we will reckon to the Godhead" (*Or.* 30.2). This logic works only if one already accepts the very conclusion that is contested by the Eunomians, namely that the Son is fully divine and not god in a purely nominal sense. On what basis, then, can Gregory counter the Eunomian interpretation that Wisdom was "created" as the first of God's creatures through whom all else was made? First, he interprets "for his works" as the cause of Christ's becoming human for the salvation of the human race. This is the "work" for which Jesus was conceived and anointed with divinity. Thus, Gregory interprets verse 22 to mean either that God, foreknowing humanity's fall into sin and need for redemption, willed the incarnation or that the fashioning of Christ's humanity in Mary's womb was the beginning of the redemptive work of the incarnation. Second, to support this reading, he contrasts Wisdom's being "created" for his works with Wisdom's being "begotten [*genna*] before the hills were established" in verse 25. Whereas "created" implies a cause, "begotten," he asserts rather speciously, does not imply a cause. Although earlier he argued that causal priority need not be temporally prior, here his main point is that Christ's divine nature is not caused in the way that creatures are. Thus, Proverbs 8 allows one to speak of Wisdom as a creature in his incarnate form and as an offspring begotten by the Father.

Basil of Caesarea had similarly employed partitive exegesis to respond to Eunomian interpretations. One such concerned Peter's Pentecost sermon in Acts 2:36: "Let all the house of Israel know that God has *made* him Lord and Christ, this Jesus whom you have crucified." Eunomius used this and other such verses as evidence that the Church originally treated "begotten" and "made" as synonyms contrary to Nicaea's strict distinction between them. First, Basil says, there are some things that are said of the Father that are not said of the Son, and vice versa, not because

3. "*Kyrios ektisen me archēn hodōn autou eis erga autou pro tou aiōnos ethemeliōsen me en archē*" (LXX). "Dominus possedit me in initio viarum suarum antequam quidquam facere a principio. Ad aeterno ordinata sum et ex antiquis antequam terra fieret" (Vulgate).

of an essential difference but because of the Son's activity in the economy of salvation. Second, he says that it is illogical to say of the Son "through whom *all* things were made" (John 1:3) and then to claim that he himself was "something made" (*Eun.* 2.2). Moreover, third, Eunomius's interpretation rests upon a categorical error; he fails to recognize that here Peter "does not teach us in the mode of theology, but hints at the reason for the economy" (*Eun.* 2.3). For when Peter spoke of Jesus as being "made" Lord and Christ, he was not referring to "the very subsistence of the only begotten before the ages" but of the incarnate Son who took on the form of a slave only to be exalted as Lord. "*This* Jesus" is not the Word in his preincarnation status but the Word made flesh. Hence, Peter is not making an ontological claim about the Word but about the authority and power given to the crucified and risen Jesus.

Although partitive analysis is a standard tool in Gregory's theological kit, it is equally important to notice when Gregory does not appeal to partitive exegesis to refute a subordinationist interpretation. For example, one of the cornerstone Eunomian prooftexts was "the Father is greater than I" (John 14:28). Indeed, this seemed to be the smoking gun; Jesus is explicitly declaring his inferiority to the Father. Instead, Gregory counters the Eunomian use of John 14:28 by playing the classic Nicene trump card, Philippians 2:6: "he did not count equality with God a thing to be held onto." Since both statements are in Scripture, Gregory concludes, one must accept as true both that the Son is equal to the Father and at the same time that the Father is greater than the Son. Faced with this paradox, it might appear that the easiest response for Gregory would have been to say that in John 14 Jesus is not speaking of the Father's superiority to the Son vis-à-vis the Son's eternal divinity but of the Son who emptied himself, taking the form of a slave. For in his mortal human form, the Son took upon himself a finitude and humiliation that is far beneath the Father's transcendent glory. But this is not Gregory's first line of argument. That the Father enthroned in majesty is greater than the Son who took on the likeness of sinful flesh is so obviously true as to be trivial (*ou mega*) and not worth commenting on. Instead, he argues that the Father is superior to the Son, not ontologically but relationally. That is, the Father is not of a superior nature to the Son; for, as Philippians 2 established, they are equally God. Rather, the Father is greater because he is the source or cause of the Son's divinity (*Or.* 30.7). Even though a human parent and her offspring are equally human, the parent is, nonetheless, superior to her child in authority and is to be so honored because she is the one who brought the child into the world. Thus, two things can be equal in one respect but unequal in another. So it is with the Father and Son.

For Gregory, distinguishing of Christ's humanity and divinity is more than an exegetical principle necessary to avoid falling into theological error through misinterpretations of Scripture. It is the foundation of Christian contemplation (*theōria*) by which the mind sees through the veil of Jesus's creaturely form to behold the glory of the Father reflected in the Son's divinity. As Christ was exalted in his resurrection and ascension and given again the glory he shared with the Father from before the foundations of the world, our vision of his divine glory enables human understanding to "have done away with earthbound carnality" in its opinions of Christ and rise to meditate on eternal spiritual realities (*Or.* 29.18). As will be seen in the next two chapters, though Gregory in orations 27 and 28 restricts the activity of *theologia* proper to only a few, nevertheless he envisions the heart of Christian piety as theological and therefore Trinitarian in its structure: through the Holy Spirit's illumination of God's works in salvation history, the Christian grows in the knowledge of the Father's divinity manifest in his consubstantial and coeternal Son.

The Council of Constantinople 381

By 381, the theological tide had turned against the anti-Nicenes in Constantinople, and Gregory for all intents and purposes was its bishop. Yet, although the emperor Theodosius had already exiled Demophilus, the Homoian bishop in Constantinople, who refused to submit to the Nicene faith prescribed by the imperial edict of January 381, there were some loose ends that needed tying up: the confirmation of Gregory as bishop of Constantinople and the reconciliation of those antisubordinationists, the Homoiousians and Pneumatomachians, who were nevertheless dissatisfied with Nicaea. Therefore, later that year, Theodosius summoned a council at Constantinople consisting of 150 bishops, most of whom had attended the synod two years before to settle the divide between the Nicenes in Antioch. The council seems to have had the narrow objective of setting the theological affairs of the Eastern capital in order.

Since the Council of Constantinople was presided over by Meletius of Antioch who had endorsed the idea of sending Gregory on his missionary assignment to the capital, his appointment as bishop, though not without some controversy, was confirmed. In the midst of the council, however, Meletius died. Gregory of Nyssa was called upon to deliver the funeral oration, and Gregory of Nazianzus, as bishop of the city in which the council met, succeeded him as president of the council. Meletius's death had the unforeseen consequence of diverting focus from Constantinople to Antioch as a rift opened up between the supporters of the bishops jockeying to be Meletius's successor. Gregory stood adamantly behind Paulinus, who according to the settlement of 379, would become bishop upon Meletius's death. But Diodore of Tarsus, who saw himself as the leader of the Antiochene community, backed the presbyter Flavian. As if the question surrounding

Meletius's successor were not contentious enough to put the council on edge, Theodosius invited representatives from the Western church with the arrival of Acholius of Thessalonica who represented Damasus of Rome, and a contingent of Egyptian bishops led by Timothy of Alexandria. Upon their arrival in mid-June, they immediately called into question the legitimacy of Gregory's position as bishop of Constantinople on the grounds that it contradicted the canon of Nicaea that prohibited a bishop's being moved from one see to another. Ultimately, the council rejected Gregory's insistence that Paulinus be recognized as bishop of Antioch. Never inclined to ecclesial politics with its compromises, Gregory grew more frustrated with the council, which ultimately led to his resignation.

The theological straw that broke Gregory's back was the question concerning the divinity of the Holy Spirit and a rapprochement between the Nicenes and the Pneumatomachians, who, though affirming the divinity of the Son against the Homoians and Eunomians, rejected the Spirit's consubstantiality with the Father. Gregory felt that the council was being pressured unduly by those in "authority," namely Theodosius himself, to make compromises on the Holy Spirit that were intolerable. Upon Gregory's resignation as president of the council and as bishop of Constantinople, the bishops elected an unbaptized layman, who was an ally of Diodore, as Gregory's successor. Although Theodosius would try for several years afterward to broker a reconciliation, the Pneumatomachian bishops led by Eleusius of Cyzicus could not be moved to a compromise and walked out.[4]

Ultimately, the bishops passed four canons, most of which dealt with details of the episcopal office. The first canon, however, was theological; it affirmed the creed adopted by the Council of Nicaea. They also adopted the creedalesque statement known today as the Nicene-Constantinopolitan Creed. Here is R. P. C. Hanson's translation with the omissions from Nicaea in brackets and additions in italics:

> We believe in one God the Father Almighty, *maker of heaven and earth* and of all things visible and invisible;
>
> And in one Lord Jesus Christ the Son of God, *the Only-Begotten*, begotten by his Father before all ages, Light from Light, true God of True God, begotten not made, consubstantial with the Father, [that is, from the substance of the Father] through whom all things came into existence [the things in heaven and the things on earth], who for us men and for our salvation came down from the heavens and became incarnate *by the Holy Spirit and the Virgin Mary* and became a man, *and was crucified for us under Pontius Pilate* and suffered *and*

4. For a discussion of the clash between the Pneumatomachians and the Cappadocians, see chapter 7, pp. 294–300.

was buried and rose again on the third day *in accordance with the Scriptures* and ascended into the heavens *and is seated at the right hand of the Father* and will come again *in glory* to judge the living and the dead, *and there will be no end to his kingdom*;

And in the Holy Spirit, *the Lord and Life-Giver, who proceeds from the Father, who is worshipped and glorified together with the Father and the Son, who spoke by the prophets*;

And in one, holy, catholic, and apostolic Church;

We confess one baptism for the forgiveness of sins;

We wait for the resurrection of the dead and the life of the coming age. Amen.

Two things are curious about this statement. First, it is odd that, just having affirmed in the first canon of the council that Nicaea was the official creed of the Church—thus overturning the Homoians' Nikē Formula adopted at the Councils of Ariminum (359) and Constantinople (360)—the bishops composed their own creedal formula. Second, even more curious is that there was no verbatim account of this creed until it was recorded seventy years later in the proceedings from the Council of Chalcedon (451). This suggests that the bishops in 381 were not intending to produce a creed to supersede Nicaea but rather were elaborating on the wording of the Nicene Creed by using material from other baptismal creeds and most importantly amplifying the third article concerning the Holy Spirit, which will be discussed in the next chapter. For all of Gregory of Nazianzus's dissatisfaction with the language around the Holy Spirit, ultimately the Council of Constantinople produced a robustly Trinitarian doctrine of God. After the proceedings of the council were concluded, the canons and creed were sent to Theodosius, who in turn on 30 July 381 issued *Episcopis tradi*. This imperial edict required all bishops to "confess that Father, Son, and Holy Spirit are a single majesty, of the same glory, of one splendor" and to make "no difference [between the persons] by profane division but [preserve] the order of the Trinity by recognizing the persons and uniting the divinity."

The next year another gathering of Eastern bishops was convened at Constantinople to respond to objections from Pope Damasus and other Western bishops to the canons of the previous year's council. The letter to Damasus summed up the Constantinople 381's theological statement: "it is the ancient faith; it is the faith of our baptism; it is the faith that teaches us to believe in the name of the Father, of the Son, and of the Holy Spirit . . . there is one Godhead, Power and Substance of the Father and of the Son and of the Holy Spirit; the dignity being equal, and the majesty being equal in three perfect essences and three perfect persons" (Theodoret, *Hist. eccl.* 5.9). Without invoking the controversial terminology of *homoousios*, both the edict and the letter of 382, in offering a summary of the creed of the 381 council, affirmed the *monarchia* of the Godhead and thus the equality of Father, Son, and Spirit as objects of worship while making clear the distinction between the persons so as to avoid any misinterpretation of the creed as Sabellian or Marcellan.

Ambrose's Rearguard Action in the West

The triumph of the pro-Nicenes in 381 did not mean that the Homoians disappeared from the ecclesial landscape. Perhaps ironically, one place where they made their presence felt was at the imperial court of Valentinian II in Milan. As a result of the Gothic invasion across the Danube (376–382), many Homoians who lived in the Balkans fled to Milan, which was the imperial capital of the Western empire. There they found a patroness in the figure of Valentinian II's mother, the empress Justina, who was herself a Homoian. In Lent of 386, Justina, acting in the name of her son, who was then a mere boy, demanded that one of the basilicas in Milan be given over to the Homoians in order that they might celebrate Easter there. Ambrose, the bishop of Milan and by extension pastor to the emperor, absolutely refused. If he would not surrender it peacefully, it was to be taken forcibly. The result was that Ambrose and his congregants occupied the basilica in question and sang hymns in defiance of the imperial troops that surrounded the church. Ultimately, it was Justina who blinked; the troops withdrew without bloodshed, and the church remained in Ambrose's hands. The battle of the basilicas was only the most dramatic clash between Nicenes and Homoians in Milan in the 370s and 380s.

At the Council of Milan in 355, the Homoians, supported by Constantius II, deposed the pro-Nicene bishop of Milan, Dionysius. The see was then claimed by the Homoian bishop Auxentius. Although Constantius's successors in the West, Jovian and Valentinian I, were sympathetic with the pro-Nicenes, they, unlike Constantius, did not throw their imperial weight behind any ecclesial faction. Therefore, when Hilary of Poitiers sought to depose Auxentius—after a gathering of ninety bishops in Rome found him guilty of heresy in 370—there was no imperial backing to enforce the condemnation. Auxentius had enough popular support that, without direct imperial intervention to depose him, he remained secure in his see. Whether this reflected a strong Homoian presence theologically and demographically in Milan or simply that Auxentius was a popular pastor is not clear. What is sure is that there was not a strong pro-Nicene sympathy among the Milanese sufficient to rise up against Auxentius as Hilary had hoped.

When Auxentius died in 374, however, the divisions between the Nicenes and Homoians manifested in the contest for Auxentius's successor. According to Paulinus's *Life of Ambrose*, violence broke out potentially serious enough to bring the provincial governor, Ambrose, to restore order. Upon his arrival, the cry went up "Ambrose for bishop." Was Ambrose's selection the result of his popularity or the influence of Valentinian I, who wanted one of his own in the bishop's seat—one who would keep the peace? The question remains debated. Equally debated is Ambrose's theological affiliation in 374. Although he was from an old Christian family whose daughter, Marcellina, was a consecrated virgin and who moved in social circles with the pro-Nicene bishop of Rome, Liberius, Ambrose was not yet baptized. Moreover, his was an education that prepared him for office in the imperial civil service, not the clergy—a fact of which he was self-conscious (*Off.* 1.1.4). Nevertheless, once consecrated, Ambrose read the leading Eastern bishops and luminaries, including Athanasius, Basil of Caesarea, and Gregory of Nazianzus and other theologians such as Philo, Origen, and Didymus the Blind. He imitated their episcopal examples and incorporated their thought into his homilies and treatises. Ambrose did not begin his episcopacy by waging ecclesial war against the Homoians of Milan. His first order of business after all was to solidify his position and master the day-to-day duties of a bishop. Nevertheless, his choice of Simplicianus, a friend of Marius Victorinus and a known pro-Nicene, as his catechist was a signal of his theological and ecclesial sympathies. By 378, however, with pressure from various Homoian leaders in and outside of Milan, Ambrose rose to the task of putting forward his defense of Nicene Christianity, employing theological strategies developed by the Eastern pro-Nicenes in the 360s and 370s.

In 378, an Illyrian Homoian bishop, Palladius, charged Ambrose with heresy. In response, the emperor Gratian—son of the late Valentinian I—asked Ambrose for a statement of his doctrine of God. The result was Ambrose's most developed early Trinitarian writing, *On the Faith*. Here Ambrose employs certain strategies that were developed by defenders of Nicaea in the 370s. Two such strategies that Ambrose combined were partitive exegesis and the argument from power. He affirmed that Christ brought salvation to humanity through his assumption of the body and its weaknesses—because humanity was unable to free itself from the weakness of sinful flesh (*Fid.* 3.1.6). For Ambrose, this soteriological logic challenged "Arian" appeals to Jesus's hunger, thirst, and weeping as evidence of his mutability and therefore his inferiority to the immutable Father. Put another way, for Ambrose, Jesus's assumption of the body and its weaknesses does not attest to his mutability or inferiority to the Father but instead reveals the divine logic of salvation. These are not properties of the Son's eternal divinity and power but belong to the weakness of humanity that the Son assumed in the incarnation when he "was made man" (*Fid.* 3.2.7). Indeed, Christ was able to be a mediator between God and humanity, redeeming humanity from its weakness because of the union of divine power and human weakness in the incarnate Christ: "our redemption was made by his blood, our pardon comes through his power, our life is secured through his grace. He gives as the Most High, he prays as man. The one is the office of the Creator, the other of a redeemer. Be the gifts as distinct as they may, yet the giver is one, for it is fitting that our maker should be our redeemer" (*Fid.* 3.2.8). Not surprisingly, therefore, when Ambrose turns to Proverbs 8:22, "The Lord created me at the beginning of his ways for his works," he explains that Wisdom's "creation" does not refer to the Father's begetting the Son but the fashioning of Jesus's humanity in Mary's womb (*Fid.* 3.7.46). For, since Christ declared himself to be "the Way, the Truth, and the Life," Ambrose concludes that the "ways" in Proverbs 8:22 refers to "the way [who] is the unsurpassed power of God, for Christ is our way," who in giving us the powers (*virtutes*) of faith, love, abstinence, and so on, has given us the ways to the Father (*Fid.* 3.7.51–52). It is only because the Son himself possesses the very power (*virtus*) of the Father that he is able to impart to humanity the powers or virtues necessary to overcome weakness and ascend to the Father.

This distinction between Christ's creaturely weakness that was capable of suffering and death, on the one hand, and his divine power, on the other hand, that could overcome sin and death appeared in Ambrose's earliest treatise *On Virgins*, addressed to his ascetic sister Marcellina. Reminding his sister of the words of Pope Liberius spoken on the day of her consecration, Ambrose writes, "He was born after the manner of men, of a virgin, but was begotten of his Father before all things, resembling his mother in body and his Father in power . . . power, undivided and inseparable from the Father . . . [he is] the power of the Father, because the fullness of the Godhead dwelt in him bodily" (*Virg.* 3.1.2). Such is possible because the Word is the Father's Son begotten from the power of the Father and therefore is equal in power with the Father from whom he is begotten and with whom he is eternally united: "So he is the perfect Son of a perfect Father. For he who comes from the power comes from him whose power it is. [Thus] the perfection of the Godhead does not admit inequality" (*Virg.* 3.1.4). Unity in power implies unity and equality of nature.

The unity of nature, however, cannot be taken in a Sabellian sense. Building on Liberius's earlier emphasis on the Father and Son's unity of power, Ambrose at the beginning of *On the Faith* reasons that if both Father and Son are confessed with one name "God," then "there is one power of the Trinity." For there is one name in which Christ commanded his disciples to baptize (Matt 28:19), the common name shared by Father, Son, and Holy Spirit, God (*Fid.* 1.1.8). But then, commenting on Jesus's words, "I and the Father are one" (John 10:30), Ambrose states that the oneness of Father and Son entails an inseparable unity of power and nature yet a unity "not by confusion of persons" (*Fid.* 1.1.9). Even as the Cappadocians argued that the Father, Son, and Spirit are distinguished by their respective modes of being or generation—the Father being unbegotten, the Son begotten, and the

Spirit spirated—Ambrose, too, saw the distinction as resulting from generation: Christ is called "Word, because he is without blemish; the Power, because he is perfect; the Son because he is begotten of the Father. . . . Not that the Father is one person with the Son; between Father and Son is the plain distinction that comes from generation; so that Christ is God of God, everlasting of everlasting, fullness of fullness" (*Fid.* 1.2.16). The persons abide in unity without confusion (*confusio*) so that they are distinct entities; yet in the distinction (*distinctio*), there is no separation (*separatio*) or plurality (*pluralitas*) (*Fid.* 4.8.91). As Ayres has observed, Ambrose stands in the apophatic tradition of the Cappadocians, affirming that the unconfused unity of the Trinity is ultimately a mystery and that the divine nature or *substantia* is incomprehensible (*Fid.* 4.8.91).

Perhaps Ambrose's most lingering influence in shaping Western Nicene theology lies in his hymns that gave choral expression to the Trinitarian faith of Nicaea. As his mystagogical homilies sought to ground his catechumens in Nicene orthodoxy, his hymns set the classical language of Scripture and Nicaea to a metrical form that impressed Nicene theology in their memory, thus effecting through the senses a spiritual conversion of mind and life. Doctrinal instruction and worship were woven together. Ambrose's theological formation through hymns, however, was not flat-footed. The allusions were often subtle yet their meaning clearly Nicene to more advanced worshipers. For instance, "Eternal Maker of All Things" addresses Christ as Creator of all things, including time itself. Not only does it echo the language of John 1:3 and the creed—"through whom all things were made"—but it places Christ the Creator of the world prior to time; the Creator is no demiurge separated from the Father by some interval but is his coeternal Wisdom and Power. Similarly, the opening lines of another hymn, "Splendor of the Father's glory / ushering light from light / light of light and source of luster, shining bright, as day of days," invokes the creedal "light from light" language. Furthermore, it also links it to the language of Psalm 36:9, "In thy light shall we see light," with all its Trinitarian overtones lifted up by pro-Nicenes.

The final clash between Palladius and Ambrose came in September of 381 at a council of some thirty-four bishops from northern Italy and Gaul at Aquileia. Ambrose took a move from Athanasius's playbook by casting Palladius in the image of Arius. After reading Arius's *Letter to Alexander*, Ambrose asked Palladius whether he would condemn Arius's teachings that the Father alone was eternal. Palladius was willing to confess that Christ was the "true Son of God," which could be open to a subordinationist reading, but was not willing to go so far as to confess him to be "true God." This was, for Ambrose, a denial of the Son's divinity. For, as Ambrose had already argued in *On the Faith*, to confess the Son to be "true God" was, from Eusebius of Nicomedia's own lips, tantamount to confessing him to be *homoousios* with the Father (*Fid.* 3.14.124–125), thus eliminating ambiguity on whether the Son was equal in divinity with the Father. Ambrose, not wanting deceptive language to pull the wool over the eyes of the bishops at Aquileia as at Sirmium and Ariminum, was pressuring Palladius to be clear about any title of divinity ascribed to Christ; as Ambrose had written earlier, "You [Arians] occasionally [*interdum*] say Christ is 'God.' So then, say [he is] 'God' designating him as 'true God,' as 'the fullness of the Father's divinity.' For there are after all, those [others] who are called 'gods' in the heavens and on earth" (*Fid.* 3.16.133). Palladius held to Homoian subordinationism, ascribing the title "true God" only to the Father who sent the Son and so was, as he believed, necessarily superior to the Son whom he sent. The bishops at Aquileia were not persuaded by Palladius's answers and condemned him. This was a repudiation of the Homoian theology made normative at Ariminum and Constantinople twenty years earlier. Although the Homoian presence lingered in the West for decades, Aquileia brought about, as Daniel Williams has argued, the de facto restoration of Nicaea as the faith of the empire.

Augustine's *On the Trinity*

Nearly two decades after the Council of Constantinople and ten years after Ambrose's triumph over the Latin Homoians in northern Italy, Augustine inherited a mature formulation of Nicene Christology. Although in 393 Augustine had already offered his first commentary on Nicaea in his *On the Faith and the Creed*, his most original and enduring treatment of the Trinity was composed over a twenty-year period between 400 and 420. Far more than a commentary on the creed of Nicaea, *On the Trinity* applied the logic of Nicene grammar to explore how that grammar might be seen in the constitution of the human soul fashioned in the image of the triune God.

The early books of *On the Trinity* face the question of how to render the Greek terminology of Nicaea into a form intelligible to Latin Christians. How, for instance, was one to express the meaning of *ousia* in Latin? Is it better rendered as "substance" (*substantia*) or "essence" or "being" (*essentia*)? Since there are some substances that are capable of changing and being changed, Augustine is inclined to speak of the immutable nature of the great I AM as *essentia*. For only that being that is eternal and unchanging is true being; therefore, he reasons, the divine nature should be understood as "true being" (*verissime esse*) (*Trin.* 5.3). So long as *substantia* is understood not as "being mutable" like created substances, then Augustine is fine using *substantia* as a synonym of *essentia* to refer to "nature" or "essence." While some attributes are enduring properties of a thing's nature (*secundum substantiam*), other attributes are accidents (*secundum accidens*) that are subject to change, such as friendship, proximity, likeness, or position (*Trin.* 5.6).

Since God is unchanging according to his nature, there are no accidents in God. Therefore, based on Jesus's declaration "I and the Father are one" (John 10:30), Augustine concludes that the Son is the same in nature (*secundum substantiam*) as the Father (*Trin.* 5.4) and therefore is also immutable. Within this understanding of *substantia* when applied to God, it is permissible to translate *ousia* as *substantia* (*Trin.* 5.9). At the same time, *substantia* may be used to refer not just to the divine nature itself but to the Father, Son, and Spirit individually. Thus, the Greek formula one *ousia* in three *hypostaseis* can be translated as one *essentia* in three *substantiae* or *personae* (*Trin.* 5.10).

The problem was that the Homoians had claimed that since "unbegotten" was an attribute of the Father according to nature and the Son was "begotten" according to his nature, they were not of the same nature. Therefore, Augustine had to explain the relationship of the Father and Son other than describing the Son as merely an essential feature (*secundum substantiam*) of the Father like love or wisdom, which would make the Son a mere property and not a distinct entity, or an accidental feature (*secundum accidens*), which would make the Son a creature of the Father's activities and alien to the Father's divinity. Although the Father does not possess any accidental properties, Augustine retorted, that does not mean that everything said of the Father is said of him in his nature. Augustine's solution was to say that "Son," "begotten," "Father," "unbegotten" are neither essential nor accidental but relational terms (*secundum relatiuum*). In other words, they describe the eternal relationship between two members of the Trinity. Yet because these are divine relations, they are different from creaturely relations. Whereas mutable creatures' relationships are accidents—a person *may* be a parent to a child, but being a parent is not necessary or essential to the person's human nature—the Father and the Son abide in an eternal and immutable relationship (*Trin.* 5.6). This solution, however, was not entirely satisfactory. While "begotten" and "son" necessarily imply a relationship to a father who begat the son, "father," as the Homoians were quick to point out, is not intrinsic to "unbegotten." An unbegotten God need not be the begetter of a son. To this, Augustine gives the rather weak reply that "unbegotten" is a relational term. For one who is "unbegotten" is by definition not a "son"; therefore, the term "unbegotten" is relational inasmuch as it distinguishes the Father from the begotten Son (*Trin.* 5.7). Similarly, terms like "Word" and "image" apply only to the Son and not to the divine nature that the Father shares with the Son. They are distinct attributes of the Son because they specify the relation of the Son to the Father who begat him. Because the Father gives all that is his to the Son, the Son is the perfect image of the Father (Col 1:15). But the Father cannot be called the "image" since an image is distinct from the archetype of which it is an image. Therefore, it would make no sense to call the Father an image of himself (*Trin.* 6.11). Later he will explain that the term "gift" when applied to the Holy Spirit is also a relational term because implicit in "gift" are "giver" and "recipient" (*Trin.* 5.17). Following the tradition of the Eastern Nicenes a generation before, Augustine was not offering proofs that would entirely rebut the objections of anti-Nicenes but giving an understanding of Nicene terminology to those already committed to the Nicene faith—that is, to those who already accepted that the Father, Son, and Spirit are united in nature but exist as distinct persons.

One difference between Augustine and his Greek predecessors is that whereas in the East "God," especially as the addressee of prayer, refers to the Father as well as to the divine nature, for Augustine it refers to the Trinity. When speaking of the Son's nature (*secundum substantiam*), it is right to apply "God" to him. But when speaking of the individual persons (*secundum relatiuum*), it is not appropriate to call any one of them God. "The Father," he writes, "is not God without the Son, nor is the Son God without the Father, but they are both God together" (*Trin.* 6.3). Thus, when Augustine interprets Jesus's reply to the rich young man, "Why do you call me good? No one is good except God alone" (Luke 18:19), "God" refers not to the Father alone but to Father, Son, and Holy Spirit (*Trin.* 5.9). Likewise, when interpreting the words of Jesus's high priestly prayer, "This is eternal life that they know you the only true God" (John 17:3), Augustine says that "God" here denotes not simply the Father but the Trinity as a whole (*Trin.* 6.10). Exceptions to this, however, are common. In the prologue to John, "and the Word was with God," "God" is referring not to the Son's nature—that is signified in the next clause "and the Word was God"—but speaking relationally (*secundum relatiuum*) denotes the Father.

"God" may, however, be applied to the Son—or to any single person of the Trinity—to convey that he is full, equal, and identical in divinity with the Father and the Spirit. God is not a composite entity whose being can be divided up and measured out in quantitatively distinct units. Rather, God is simple like the number five, which, as an idea, is not confined to space and time but is fully present at the same time in the minds of all people thinking about five. Therefore, the persons cannot be thought of as parts of God; rather, each possesses the totality of the simple divine nature. Consequently, the Father and Son together are not greater than the Spirit by itself; nor are the Son and Spirit together greater than the Father (*Trin.* 6.9). No one person of the Trinity (or even two persons) possesses more divinity—more wisdom, more power, more goodness—than any other single person. Augustine interprets "The Father is greater than I" (John 14:28) to refer not to the Son in his eternal nature or even in his eternal relationship with the Father but to the Son in his incarnate form (*Trin.* 6.10). In other words, the Son is ontologically equal to the Father inasmuch as he possesses the "form of God." Yet when he in time "empties himself taking the form of a servant" (Phil 2:7) with its finite, mortal human nature, the Son takes on a lowliness or inferiority to the glory of the Father.

Augustine's insistence that each person of the Trinity is equal because each possesses the fullness of divinity—positions clearly affirmed by Greek Nicenes—leads him to question a traditional interpretation of a text foundational for Nicene argument, 1 Corinthians 1:24: "[Christ] is the wisdom of God and the power of God." Since the Son is the wisdom and power of God, so the argument runs, if there was once when the Son was not, then there was a time when God was without either power or wisdom. Therefore, the Son must be coeternal with the Father. The problem Augustine sees with the argument is that this interpretation does not affirm the Son's equality with the Father but reduces him to two attributes of the divine nature (*Trin.* 6.1). Moreover, on this interpretation, 1 Corinthians 1:24 might be used by anti-Nicenes to argue that the Son is inferior to the Father since, although he is the wisdom and power of God, he lacks other divine attributes. Furthermore, the traditional argument suggests that the Father is not wise in himself but wise only because he begat the Son who is his wisdom. This, however, defies the logic expressed in the Nicene description of the Son as "God from God, light from light." Unless the Father is wise in himself—a wisdom he passes on when he begets the Son—then one cannot say, as the Nicene formula implies, that the Son is wisdom from wisdom. Even more ridiculous, if one were to treat each of the divine attributes as a hypostasis or person, then the many names or attributes would be many sons (*Trin.* 6.2). Augustine, however, solves the problem by appealing to the doctrines of divine simplicity and equality of the persons. Since God is simple and therefore has no real division between his attributes—as if they were parts that together made up God—all the attributes are identical (*Trin.* 6.8). God's wisdom is his power. His power is his love, and so on. Therefore, 1 Corinthians 1:24 does not restrict Christ to only two attributes; rather, all the other divine attributes are implicit in "wisdom and power." Furthermore, since the Son is equal to the Father in divinity, the Son possesses all the qualities that the Father possesses that the Father conferred on him at his begetting. Naturally then, the Son is not reducible to two divine attributes. Instead, 1 Corinthians 1:24 is simply naming two of the major attributes of God that Paul wants to contrast with the foolishness and impotence of the worldly wisdom of which the Corinthian intelligentsia were so proud.

Ultimately, Augustine, still unsatisfied with the language of "person" or "being" or "substance" to speak about Father, Son, and Holy Spirit individually, concludes that the word "person" is a placeholder. It is simply a way of answering the question, "Three what?" without falling into heretical error. "What are they? We answer three 'persons' because human languages are inadequate; they cannot give us a better word. We say they are three persons to be clear that they are not three gods, which Scripture forbids" (*Trin.* 7.8). Furthermore, "persons" is preferable to "beings" (*essentiae*) lest that be misinterpreted to mean three natures (*Trin.* 7.11).

Thus, "persons" gives Christianity language that distinguishes itself from paganism with its diversity of deities and from Judaism with its view of a single God abiding forever totally alone in his singleness (*Trin.* 7.9).

The truly innovative move Augustine makes in *On the Trinity* is to seek a model of the triune God in the structure of the human soul. Since, as Genesis teaches, man was made after the image of God and since that God in whose image humanity was made is triune, then the divine image must presumably be triune as well. That is, the human soul is the image of the Trinity. At first glance, this seems like a potentially promising method for learning about the Trinity. Human beings, after all, know themselves better than they know God. It is easier, therefore, to think about the Trinity in a human being than the Trinity in its transcendence (*Trin.* 9.2).

Augustine, therefore, begins a careful analysis of the threefold structure of the human person. The first triad he considers is mind, love, and knowledge. Even as Father, Son, and Spirit are not three gods but one in substance, so too love and knowledge are of the same substance as the mind that loves and knows (*Trin.* 9.7). This is different from a mixture of wine, water, and honey, which together form a new substance altogether. And even as the members of the Trinity are distinguishable and therefore three, mind, love, and knowledge, which are distinguishable from one another, are three distinct things. This again is different from the mixture of honey, water, and wine in which each substance loses its distinctiveness in their blending. Furthermore, as the Spirit is the product of the Father and Son's mutual love, knowledge is the product of the mind's love of itself. That is, when the mind loves itself, it seeks to know itself; thus, self-knowledge is the result of the mind's self-love (*Trin.* 9.3). Moreover, even as the names of the members of the Trinity express the relation of each to the other, so too mind, love, and knowledge are relational. The knowing describes the relation of mind to itself when it is loving itself. Similarly, loving describes the mind's relation to knowledge when it knows itself. Thus, he concludes, "In a wonderful way therefore, these three are inseparable from each other, and yet each one of them is substance, and all together they are one substance or being" (*Trin.* 9.8).

The mind's generation of knowledge is akin to the Father's begetting the Son who is equal in divinity with the Father who begat him. When the mind knows something, it produces in itself a word or idea of the thing that it knows. If the thing it knows is a bodily thing, such as a horse, the word "horse" is not identical to the actual horse the mind knows. But when what the mind knows is itself, the word "mind" that captures the mind's self-knowledge is identical with the mind itself. Therefore, there is equality between the mind and the word or knowledge that the mind has of itself even as the Word of the Father is equal to the Father (*Trin.* 9.16). Yet Augustine is aware of a crack in the analogy. The mind's self-knowledge expressed in the word "mind" is identical and therefore equal to the mind that generated the word "mind" if and only if everything that is true of mind is contained in the word "mind." That is possible if the mind knows itself in its entirety. If, however, the mind's self-knowledge is only partial, then the word "mind" and mind are not identical because a person's mind is greater than her understanding of what is signified by the word "mind." That being the case, one's mind's generation of knowledge of itself is not truly comparable to the Father's generation of the Word that is the Father's perfect image.

The second triadic analogue Augustine examines is memory, understanding, and will. They are not three lives or minds or substances, but all are faculties of one mind; therefore, they share a common substance. They are interdependent yet distinct. The keener and more extensive one's memory, the more data one's mind has in order to arrive at a more profound understanding. And the will makes use of memory to come to an understanding of the goods one desires (*Trin.* 10.17). Though they are distinct faculties of the mind, they contain each other. One remembers that she has a memory, understanding, and will. She, therefore, understands that she has understanding, memory, and will. And she wills to will, to remember, and to understand (*Trin.* 10.18). Augustine later refines this, observing that the will turns one's conscious attention to the memory such that her thoughts are given form by the images in memory (*Trin.* 11.6). Again, however, Augustine sees how the triad of memory, understanding, and will falls short of being an image of the Trinity. Since the soul does not preexist its life in the body, all memories, even fabricated ones, are derived not from the mind itself but from the vision of external objects (*Trin.* 11.8). Given memory's dependence on images from external creation, the triad of human cognition is not perfectly analogous to Trinity in its self-sufficiency. Moreover, although human faculties of recollection are distinctive from nonrational creatures in allowing one to judge between the true and the untrue, memory is not unique to human beings and so cannot be included in the image of the Trinity (*Trin.* 12.1). Because practical judgment, though the product of memory, understanding, and will, is dependent on the senses and memory, it lacks the independence proper to the Trinity. The image of the triune God, therefore, can be found only in the cognitive functions that deal with eternal things (*Trin.* 12.4). What Augustine is beginning to recognize is that the image of God found in the mind is not simply about a *structural* likeness to the Trinity; it must be the *content* of the mind as well. The image of the Trinity is the result of an active participation in the Trinity through contemplation of God (*Trin.* 12.10). For fallen humanity, however, the mind has been corrupted by sin. Because of the *curvatus* of concupiscence, the mind is turned downward and focused on the finite and transitory goods of the world rather than God. Therefore, the mind, corrupted by sin, must be healed and the image in which man was originally formed must be renewed in order for us to see how the human mind is an image of the Trinity.

How, then, does the mind become conformed to the triune God through contemplation? Augustine initially locates the answer in wisdom (*sapientia*) when the mind becomes a living reflection of the God who is the immediate object of its thoughts. True wisdom, he explains, is that piety (*pietas*) properly expressed in Greek as *theosebeia* or "the worship of God" (*Trin.* 14.1). Such piety is consistent with his earlier claim in *On Christian Teaching* that the proper love of God recognizes that God is the summum bonum in whom alone human enjoyment (*fructus*) can be found (*Doctr. chr.* 1.4.4). The wise Christian is not without sin but, because she is a lover of Wisdom, loves the God who rebukes her sin (*Trin.* 14.2). Wisdom, he goes on to explain, is different from knowledge (*scientia*), even the knowledge of faith (*fides*). Although wisdom is a form of knowledge inasmuch as it is the knowledge of God, *scientia* generally speaking concerns temporal, human matters. Faith stands in the middle between wisdom and knowledge. For although the object of faith is God who is eternal, faith itself is not eternal. It is the imperfect, temporal vision of eternal things that Paul compares to seeing blurred images in an ancient mirror (1 Cor 13:12). Faith is not eternal since in the eschaton the blurred vision will give way to a direct and clear vision of God, which is true wisdom. Therefore, since Christians in the present age walk by the imperfect vision of faith rather than the sight of wisdom, the human mind reformed by faith is not a true image of the eternal God (*Trin.* 14.3). Indeed, even the mind conformed to virtue does not give an image of the triune God. The cardinal virtues, that is, prudence, moderation, justice, and courage, are not eternal but will pass away when, in paradise, the soul will not need to be in a daily contest against sin and temptation (*Trin.* 14.12). The only virtue that endures and is perfected in paradise is love. Although in the present the mind is distracted by worldly loves (*Trin.* 14.18), it retains a love of itself, which is possible only by some degree of self-knowledge. This is the source of some knowledge of God since knowing the self is knowing something of the image of God that remains (*Trin.* 14.20). Yet this knowledge is not true knowledge of God, for it is not unchangeable. Without true knowledge of God, the mind cannot be so conformed to the divine in order to be a true image of the Trinity.

Repeatedly confronted by the differences between the mind of fallen humanity and the holy Trinity, Augustine is driven to conclude that we will never be able to know the Trinity through contemplating the mind until, as Ephesians 4:23 puts it, sinful humanity is "renewed in the spirit of [its] mind" (*Trin.* 14.22). Only then will the image be renewed. Such renewal, however, does not occur at baptism; that only throws off the fever of sin but does not restore strength to humanity's weakened condition (*Trin.* 14.23). Ultimately, the renewal of the mind necessary for us to behold in itself the reflection of the Trinity is entirely an eschatological hope. The text that leads him to this conclusion is 1 John 3:2: "Beloved, we are now sons of

God, but that which we shall be has not yet appeared. We know that when [Christ] appears we shall be like him, because we shall see him as he is." While its triad of faculties, that is, memory, understanding, and will, allows the mind to cleave to God in contemplative participation, it cannot reflect the image of the Trinity until it properly beholds the Trinity in Christ. In other words, perfect renewal comes only from the pure vision of God that awaits the blessed in the resurrection. Then the mind will become like the triune one it beholds (*Trin.* 14.24). As he goes on to explain in his interpretation of the transformation of which Paul speaks in 2 Corinthians 3:18, "But with faces unveiled we, beholding the glory of the Lord in a mirror, are being transformed into the same image from glory to glory as by the Spirit of the Lord," the mind is changed into an image of the glory of God because we have beheld the vision of the Lord. He explains the connection between "seeing" and "being changed" as he explains the glory from which we are changed and the glory into which we are being transformed. It may be, he writes, "from the glory of faith to the glory of sight; from the glory by which we are sons of God to the glory by which we shall be like him, because we shall see him as he is" (*Trin.* 15.14).

Ultimately, Augustine's quest for an image of the Trinity in the human mind ends with an apophatic conclusion. For even with the eschatological rehabilitation of the mind, the radical difference between the simple Creator and the compound, complex creature means that even in the resurrection, perfected humanity fails to be an analogue for thinking about the Trinity. In other words, because God is simple, the Father, Son, and Spirit are each love, wisdom, and power. Therefore, although the Father who is unbegotten is distinct from the only begotten Son and from the Spirit who proceeds from the Father, the Son and Spirit are identical in essence with the Father. All that can be said of the Father in his divine nature can be said of the Son and the Spirit. This is without parallel in the human mind. None of the faculties of the mind are relationally distinct and yet essentially identical. The intellect may require knowledge stored in memory in order to make rational judgments, but the actions of recollection and of intellectual analysis are different cognitive functions. Likewise, will depends on knowledge and memory, but it, too, is a distinct faculty. All these are parts of one mind and share the same nature, but none possesses all these faculties together.

While the second half of *On the Trinity* may not have achieved the knowledge of God that Augustine initially hoped, it is successful in two ways. First, it reinforces the logic behind his understanding of theology as "faith seeking understanding" (*fides quaerens intellectum*) and allows him to deepen his reflection on human psychology and the *imago Dei* through the lens of the triune Archetype. Second, it tempers these claims about the Trinity and human nature with an apophatic recognition of the differences both between Creator and creature and consequently between human speech and its divine object. In this way, the conclusion of *On the Trinity* expresses an apophatic sensibility, as Lewis Ayres has argued, that is central to the grammar of Nicene theology developed by the Cappadocians.

Conclusion

The fourth-century theological debate that reached its climax at the Council of Constantinople in 381 with anticlimactic aftershocks in the West at the Council of Aquileia and the basilica crisis in 386 can be viewed as the conclusion of a conflict between two trajectories of Origen's doctrine of Christ the Logos. On the one hand are those, like Arius and the followers of Lucian, who subscribed to Origen's interpretation of John 1:1 that distinguished between the Word who was divine and the Father who is *the* God. Such a conclusion, they reasoned, meant that the Son was ontologically subordinate to or different from the Father. On the other hand, those like Alexander and the bishops at Nicaea drew from Origen's theory that Christ the Father's Word and Wisdom was eternally begotten. Thus, they concluded that the Son was intrinsic to the Father's being and thus was indeed true God from true God. Although all the ecclesial factions baptized in the name of the Father, Son, and Holy Spirit and gave honor and praise to the Son addressing him as "God," there loomed the question, In what sense is the Son divine? If he was "created" or "made" as subordinationists concluded from Proverbs 8:22, how then was one to speak of his divinity? As "the firstborn of creation" and the "image of the invisible God," was he a unique, semidivine creature? For those who affirmed the ontological unity of Father and Son based on the Christ hymn of Philippians 2 or John 10:30, how could they also speak of the real distinction and hierarchy within the Godhead? From 360 on with the emergence of the radical subordinationists Aetius and Eunomius, the pro-Nicenes in the East chiefly led by the Cappadocians worked out the grammar of the Nicene faith that drew an absolute dividing line between the divine and created beings. Along with that grammar emerged theories of biblical exegesis and theology itself that fostered a constructive tension in orthodoxy between certainty in claims about the God manifest in Jesus and the limits of such claims. More important than a Nicene grammar, the pro-Nicenes of the fourth century, in their hymns and homilies, and catechesis and commentaries, performed in verse and poetic prose the logic of the Nicene faith. It was a logic that animated the theological imagination of Christians East and West to probe the mystery of the divine economy held within the biblical narrative.

Bibliography

Primary Sources

Aetius. *Syntagmation*. In Thomas A. Kopecek, *A History of Neo-Arianism*. Vol. 1. Cambridge: Philadelphia Patristic Foundation, 1979.

Ambrose of Milan. *On the Faith*. *NPNF* 2/10.

Augustine of Hippo. *The Trinity*. Translated by Edmund Hill. The Works of Saint Augustine: A Translation for the 21st Century I/5. Hyde Park, NY: New City, 1991.

Basil of Caesarea. *Against Eunomius*. Translated by Mark DelCogliano and Andrew Radde-Gallwitz. Fathers of the Church 122. Washington, DC: Catholic University of America Press, 2011.

Eunomius of Cyzicus. *The Extant Works*. Translated by Richard Paul Vaggione. Oxford: Clarendon, 1987.

Gregory of Nazianzus. *Orations* 2, 22, and 23. In *Select Orations*. Translated by Martha Vinson. Fathers of the Church 107. Washington, DC: Catholic University of America Press, 2003.

———. *Orations* 27–31. In *On God and Christ*. Translated by Lionel Wickham. Crestwood, NY: St. Vladimir's Seminary Press 2002.

———. *Orations* 39 and 40. In *Festal Orations*. Translated by Nonna Verna Harrison. Crestwood, NY: St. Vladimir's Seminary Press, 2008.

Gregory of Nyssa. *Against Eunomius* 1. *NPNF* 2/5.

———. *Against Eunomius* 2. In *Gregory of Nyssa: Contra Eunomium II; An English Version with Supporting Studies; Proceedings of the 10th International Colloquium on Gregory of Nyssa*. Translated by Stuart George Hall. Edited by Lenka Karfíková, Scot Douglass, and Johannes Zachhuber. Leiden: Brill, 2007.

———. *Against Eunomius* 3. In *Gregory of Nyssa: Contra Eunomium III; An English Translation with Supporting Studies; Proceedings of the 12th International Colloquium on Gregory of Nyssa*. Translated by Stuart George Hall. Edited by Johan Leemans and Matthieu Cassin. Leiden: Brill, 2014.

———. *Catechetical Oration* and *To Ablabius: On Not Three Gods*. In *Christology of the Later Fathers*. Translated by Edward R. Hardy. Philadelphia: Westminster, 1954.

———. *On Perfection*. In *One Path for All: Gregory of Nyssa on the Christian Life and Destiny*. Translated by Rowan A. Greer. Eugene, OR: Cascade, 2015.

Secondary Sources

(Readers should also consult the secondary sources listed in the previous chapters.)

Ayres, Lewis. *Augustine and the Trinity*. Cambridge: Cambridge University Press, 2010.

Barnes, Michel René. *The Power of God:* Dynamis *in Gregory of Nyssa's Trinitarian Theology*. Washington, DC: Catholic University of America Press, 2001.

Beeley, Christopher A. *Gregory of Nazianzus on the Trinity and the Knowledge of God: In Your Light We Shall See Light*. Oxford: Oxford University Press, 2008.

Behr, John. *Formation of Christian Theology*. Vol. 2. *The Nicene Faith*. Part 2. Crestwood, NY: St. Vladimir's Seminary Press, 2004.

DelCogliano, Mark. *Basil of Caesarea's Anti-Eunomian Theory of Names: Christian Theology and Late-Ancient Philosophy in the Fourth Century Trinitarian Controversy*. Leiden: Brill, 2010.

Dunkle, Brian P. *Enchantment and Creed in the Hymns of Ambrose of Milan*. Oxford: Oxford University Press, 2016.

Hildebrand, Stephen M. *Basil of Caesarea*. Grand Rapids: Baker Academic, 2014.

Ludlow, Morwenna. *Gregory of Nyssa: Ancient and [Post]Modern*. Oxford: Oxford University Press, 2007.

Maspero, Giulio. *Trinity and Man: Gregory of Nyssa's* Ad Ablabium. Leiden: Brill, 2007.

McGuckin, John. *Saint Gregory of Nazianzus: An Intellectual Biography*. Crestwood, NY: St. Vladimir's Seminary Press, 2001.

Radde-Gallwitz, Andrew. *Basil of Caesarea, Gregory of Nyssa, and the Transformation of Divine Simplicity*. Oxford: Oxford University Press, 2009.

———. *Gregory of Nyssa's Doctrinal Works*. Oxford: Oxford University Press, 2018.

Smith, J. Warren. *Christian Grace and Pagan Virtue: The Theological Foundation of Ambrose's Ethics*. Oxford: Oxford University Press, 2011.

Turcescu, Lucian. *Gregory of Nyssa and the Concepts of the Divine Persons*. Oxford: Oxford University Press, 2005.

Vaggione, Richard Paul. *Eunomius of Cyzicus and the Nicene Revolution*. Oxford: Oxford University Press, 2000.

Williams, D. H. *Ambrose of Milan and the End of the Arian-Nicene Conflicts*. Oxford: Clarendon, 1995.

7

"Another Paraclete"

Early Christian Pneumatology

In his famous letter 58 composed around 372 or 373, Gregory of Nazianzus writes Basil, warning of accusations that people within the pro-Nicene alliance are leveling against him. After assuring Basil of his "good will," writing as one who still "defer[s] to your piety" and is "completely on your side," Gregory relates the story of being at a dinner party hosted by some of their ecclesial compatriots where he was relating memories of his and Basil's early friendship during their school days in Athens. As he waxed eloquently about their shared commitment to the philosophical life, one of the party, a monk whom Gregory describes as a "so-called philosopher," interrupted him and called Gregory and Basil "liars and flatterers" and protested that "Basil is wrongly praised for orthodoxy—and Gregory wrongly as well." This monk, Gregory explains, is one of "our friends" who accuse Basil and Gregory of holding "sacrilegious opinions" about the Holy Spirit or of being "cowards" for failing to be forthright about their views. Although "the great Basil speak[s] excellent and perfect things about the divinity of the Father and the Son, as no one else could easily do," he, protests the monk, passed over the matter of the Spirit's divinity like water running over rocks in a river by employing language "more political than pious, concealing the ambiguity in the power of his words."

Gregory then recounted his defense of Basil. Unlike the monk, Basil had the burden of being leader of the anti-Eunomian coalition, which included the Macedonians who affirmed the Son's divinity but denied the Spirit's consubstantiality (*homoousios*) with the Father. Consequently, Basil, having to choose his language carefully, lest his commitment to controversial terms undo the coalition, refused to apply the term *homoousios* to the Spirit. The problem, Gregory explains, is that Basil's "prudent management" of the truth about the Spirit, though intended to hold the coalition of pro-Nicenes and Homoiousians together, might actually lead to a split in the alliance with those who insisted, as Gregory himself did, that the

Holy Spirit is consubstantial with the Father and Son. What good does it do, Gregory asks, to appease those with whom he and Basil disagreed about the Spirit, only to lose the trust and support of those who shared their own position by failing to proclaim the truth forthrightly?

If the writings of the New Testament in their unsystematic way could be viewed as unclear about the relationship of the Father and the Son, they were even more ambiguous about the person of the Holy Spirit. Although Jesus in his Great Commission at the end of Matthew's Gospel commands the apostles to baptize in the name of the Father, Son, and Holy Spirit (Matt 28:19), other times he omits reference to the Spirit. In John's Gospel, for instance, Jesus, praying to the Father, declares, "This is eternal life that they may know you the one true God and Jesus Christ whom you have sent" (John 17:3), with no mention of the Holy Spirit. Similarly, in his letters, Paul greets his addressees, "Grace and peace to you from God our Father and the Lord Jesus Christ" (Rom 1:7; 1 Cor 1:3). What might be the significance of such an omission? Does it imply a subordination of the Spirit to the Father and Son? Might it suggest that the Holy Spirit is not ontologically the same as the Father and the Son but merely a ministering spirit whom God uses for his purposes? Such questions hung over the Great Church and were implicit in the earliest depictions of the Spirit from the age of the apostles into the third quarter of the fourth century.

Early Presentations in the Apostolic and Apologetic Writings

As with Jesus, the Church in the second century was clearer about the salvific work of the Spirit than the nature of his person. The Spirit's two primary works were those of prophetic inspiration and the conferral of spiritual gifts. It was the Spirit who, according to the Epistle of Barnabas, conferred on Israel's patriarchs, Abraham and Jacob, foreknowledge of the coming of Jesus (Barn. 9.7; 13.5). Athenagoras employed the image of a flute to describe the Old Testament prophets into whom God breathed his Spirit so as to reveal himself to Israel (*Leg.* 7, 9). Although Justin Martyr, too, held that the prophets were inspired by the Spirit, he asserts in his *Dialogue with Trypho* that such prophetic gifts ceased with Christ. Trypho, appealing to Isaiah 11:1–3, asks how Christ can be said to have existed before the incarnation, since Christ, as Isaiah says, is the "shoot of Jesse" empowered to do his great works by the gifts of the Holy Spirit. Justin's logic here is that Jesus would not need such gifts from the Spirit since the Logos existed before his birth as a human being. Pointing to Isaiah's words, "a Spirit of God shall rest upon him," Justin counters that Isaiah meant by "rested" that the Spirit-endowed gifts ceased with the coming of Jesus (*Dial.* 87.2–3). Though Jesus needed no such gifts (*Dial.* 88.4), he was anointed by the Spirit to signal the end of prophecy among the Jews and to free humanity from the serpent's deceit. If without the Spirit there was no longer prophecy among Jews, the Holy Spirit transferred such gifts to the Church. In his epistle to the church in Corinth, known as 1 Clement, Clement of Rome attributes the veracity and power of the apostles' preaching to their assurance of the word of God and Jesus's declaration of the coming kingdom, which they derived from their knowledge of his resurrection and the assurance (*plērophoria*) provided by the Holy Spirit (1 Clem. 42.3).

The Spirit's conferral of gifts is primarily described in terms of the sanctification of believers and ensuring the unity of the Christian community. In the first decade of the second century, the Christian communities in Syria and Asia Minor experienced various divisions, including over the doctrine of the incarnation. Ignatius of Antioch speaks of the Spirit's conferring gifts on laity and clergy alike, but his primary concern is the authority of the bishop derived from the inspiration of the Spirit. Writing to the church at Smyrna, he rejoices that they have received all spiritual gifts, which makes its members worthy of God and bearers of holy things (*theoprepestatē kai hagiophorō*) (Ign. *Smyrn.* greeting). Through Christ's cross and the Holy Spirit, which functions as a rope, their faith and love will allow them to be drawn up into heaven where they will be stones of the Father's temple (Ign. *Eph.* 9.1). However, the indwelling of the Spirit who raises believers to God does not dwell in a community divided by conflicting teachings and anger between its members. Therefore, he exhorts the churches of Asia Minor to repent and "return to the unity in God and the council of the bishop" (Ign. *Phld.* 8.1). That is, unity in God is achieved when the church submits to the teachings of the bishop, whom they should regard as the Lord himself, because the Spirit speaks through him. Such was true, he claims, of his own preaching: "I called out when I was with you, I was speaking with a loud voice, God's voice; 'Pay attention to the bishop and the elders and deacons.' . . . The Spirit itself was preaching, saying these words: 'Do nothing without the bishop'" (Ign. *Phld.* 7.1–2).

But who is the Spirit who brings unity to the Church? Although Ignatius does not address this question directly, he distinguishes Christ and the Spirit who together allow the Christian's ascent to God. Moreover, because it is the Spirit speaking through the bishop's voice that gives the divine authority to his preaching and teaching, the Spirit has divine authority to reveal truths hidden in God (Ign. *Phld.* 7.1). Yet not all writings of the first century distinguished between Christ and the Spirit. In the anonymous sermon known today as 2 Clement, the author, drawing on the image of the Church as the body or flesh of Christ, exhorts his readers to preserve the purity of the flesh in order to receive the Spirit (2 Clem. 14.3). But, the author goes on to say, the one who does not guard the sanctity of the flesh "will not receive the Spirit which is Christ" (2 Clem. 14.4). The Shepherd of Hermas offers an even more confused account of the relationship of the Son and Spirit. Explaining why the Father placed the Son and his angels over the people of his vineyard—possibly a metaphor for the Church—the author seems to speak of the Spirit as having become incarnate: "The preexistent Holy Spirit, which created the whole creation, God caused to live in the flesh that he wished. This flesh, therefore, in which the Holy Spirit lived, served the Spirit well in holiness and purity" (Herm. Sim. 5.6). Although the incarnate Holy Spirit is not expressly identified with Jesus, later an angel of repentance reveals to Hermas the identity of the Holy Spirit to be the Son of God (Herm. Sim. 9.1).

Perhaps the greatest confusion about the identity of the Spirit came with Christian appropriations of Philo's Logos theology. The primary instance of this is found in Justin Martyr. The essential problem lay in his failure to reconcile the Trinitarian doxological language of Father, Son, and Holy Spirit with the binary or binitarian relationship of God and his Logos taken from Philo. In explaining the ritual of baptism, he describes it as a "washing in water in the name of God, the Father and Ruler of the Universe, and of the savior, Jesus Christ, and of the Holy Spirit" (*1 Apol.* 61.3), whom he elsewhere describes as existing in a hierarchical relationship (*1 Apol.* 13.1–3). Such a hierarchical view of the Godhead implies a distinction between the Son, who occupies a second rank, and the Spirit, who bears witness to the Son as the King of Glory (*Dial.* 36.6). In interpreting Isaiah's Spirit-inspired prophecy that "a virgin shall conceive and bear a son" (7:14 LXX) and the angel Gabriel's words to Mary that the child within her would be of the Holy Spirit (Luke 1:35), Justin Martyr writes, "It is wrong, therefore, to understand the Spirit and the power of God as anything other than the Logos, who is also the firstborn of God" (*1 Apol.* 33). He goes on to say that the Logos is both the one who inspired the prophets and the one through whose power Mary became pregnant. The implication is that the Logos, spoken of by the gospel writers as the Spirit, overshadowed Mary to fashion for himself a body in her womb. Moreover, Justin, in identifying the Spirit with the Logos, seems to have negated any true distinction between the Spirit and the Son. Justin compounds the confusion by attributing similar works to the two. In his account of his conversion, Justin relates the words of an old man whom he met walking along the shore. The old man tells him that the human mind is unable to see God unless it is "adorned [*kekosmēmenos*] by the Holy Spirit" (*Dial.* 4.1), who he later says is the same Spirit who revealed to the Old Testament prophets a knowledge of God the philosophers lacked precisely because they lacked the Spirit (*Dial.* 7.1). A little later, however, Justin ascribes to "God and his Christ" the illumination necessary to know hidden truths "neither visible nor comprehensible" to the mind unaided by God (*Dial.* 7.3).

A distinction between the Son and Spirit began to emerge in the writings of the apologist Theophilus of Antioch (d. ca. 185). In his *To Autolycus*, he drew a clear line between the divine and creatures: God who is uncreated is not needy, whereas creatures are inherently needy. Therefore, God needed nothing external to himself to create the world. But Theophilus proceeds to explain that God created the world through his Logos who is the governing principle (*archē*) of all things. The Logos, however, is not an external helper, he explains, but is "internal within [God's] own bowels [whom he] begat emitting [the Logos] along with his own wisdom before all things" (*Autol.* 2.10). He then calls the Logos the "spirit of God" who not only governed creation but also spoke to the prophets. Unlike the "wisdom of God which was in [God] and his holy Word which was always present with him," the prophets could know God only through special revelation (*Autol.* 2.9). This revelation was provided by Wisdom, who revealed himself to Solomon, who said, "When he [God] prepared the heavens I was there and when he appointed the foundation of the earth I was by him" (Prov 8:27). Although Theophilus seems to make a distinction between the Logos and Wisdom—two things generated from within God—it is not always clear whether he is speaking of wisdom as a person, that is, the Holy Spirit, or merely as a quality of the Logos. The distinction becomes clearer in Theophilus's account of the creation of humanity. Commenting on Genesis's use of the plural pronouns "us" and "our" when God says, "Let us create man in our image" (1:26), Theophilus introduces the metaphor of the Word and Wisdom as his Hands. He explains, "For God made all things by the Word, and having reckoned them all mere [second-order] works, he reckons the creation of man to be the only work worthy of his own Hands [pl.]. Moreover, God is found, as if needing help, to say, 'Let us make man in our image. . . .' But to no one else than to his own Word and to his own Wisdom did he say, 'Let *us* make'" (*Autol.* 2.18). Two points emerge. First, the Logos and Wisdom are not beings, like the angels, that are outside of God. Rather, they are intrinsically and eternally part of God. Second, Theophilus makes a stronger distinction between the Logos and Wisdom. For although God made all creatures through the agency of his Logos *alone*, he created man using *both* his Word and Wisdom. Thus, Wisdom is something other than the Logos. Yet even here, Theophilus does not explicitly identify Wisdom with the Holy Spirit. Moreover, he neither says how Wisdom is appreciatively different from the Logos nor explains Wisdom's distinctive contribution to the creation of humanity.

Whence comes this conflation of the Son and Spirit? The answer lies both in the Middle Platonic tradition from which the Logos language is derived and in the exegetical problem of identifying the figure of Wisdom in Proverbs 8:22. First, within Philo's thought, the Logos serves the mediatorial role of giving knowledge about the ineffable and unknowable God. Yet within the second-century interpretations of Scripture, both the Son and the Spirit mediate knowledge of the Father to Israel and the Church. Given Justin's commitment to the binary logic of the relationship of God and his Logos who makes the Father known, Justin has little choice but to see the Son and Spirit as performing the work of the Logos. Indeed, in Justin's interpretation of Scripture, the Logos assumes the dual personae of the "prophetic Spirit" and Christ himself (*1 Apol.* 36). Second, since Philo's Logos is the Father's reason, which provided the model for creation as well as being his agent of creation, as in John's prologue, then the Logos reasonably was identified by Justin with the Father's Wisdom who was at the beginning of his works (Prov 8:22–23). That raises the question, Is Wisdom the Son or the Spirit? Or are they both Wisdom? If so, does this mean that there really is only, as in Philo, God and his Logos/Wisdom? If not, how are they distinct from each other? How were Christians to make sense of the Trinitarian confession of the baptismal formula?

Toward a More Systematic Account of the Spirit

The first apologist to offer a more systematic account of the Trinitarian confession was Athenagoras (133–190). Countering the charge of atheism, he declares that Christians worship one God "uncreated, eternal, invisible, impassible, incomprehensible . . . encompassed by light and beauty and spirit and power ineffable." Then he affirms that this one God is Father, Son, and Holy Spirit whom Christians confess to be united in power but distinct in order (*Leg.* 10). In the same passage, he offers a standard account of the Son as the Father's eternal Logos existing in "oneness and power of spirit" and acting as the Father's agent of creation as declared by Proverbs 8:22. When he turns to the Holy Spirit, whom he calls the "prophetic Spirit," Athenagoras compares the Spirit to a beam of light from the sun; the Spirit flows out from the Father and then returns. By speaking of the Spirit as an "outflow" or "emanation" (*aporroia*), Athenagoras is likely equating the Spirit with Wisdom spoken of in Wisdom of Solomon 7:25 as "the breath [or spirit] of the power of God, and a pure *emanation* of the glory of the Almighty." In speaking of the Spirit as an emanation that flows out and returns, he also may be integrating the Middle Platonic description of the World Soul to speak of the Spirit as providentially holding the reins of the inherently unstable creation to preserve its goodness and order. Therefore, the Spirit, though united in essence with the Father and Son (*Leg.* 24), is third in order after the Son economically as the one who oversees that which the Logos fashioned. Athenagoras articulates a distinction between the Son and Spirit in a way that Justin does not. Nevertheless, the difference is hazy. For even as Justin identified the Son and Spirit with the Logos, Athenagoras equates both the Son/Logos and the Spirit with Wisdom.

The task of clarifying the difference between the Son and Spirit was taken up by Irenaeus of Lyons. Writing at the end of the second century, Irenaeus sought to counter the dualistic cosmologies of various sects of gnostic Christianity that conceived of the material world as the creation not of God but by an ignorant demiurge together with his angelic agents of creation. Irenaeus counters this view with an argument that implicitly affirms the divinity of the Spirit. Unlike the gnostic demiurge that created angels to carry out his plan of creation, God, Irenaeus declares, needs nothing outside of himself to fashion creation: "But in fact by his Word and Spirit he makes all things, disposing and governing and giving [creatures] existence" (*Haer.* 1.22.1). Thus, the creative activity of the Word and the Spirit demonstrates that they are not themselves creatures external to God but beings intrinsic to his being and therefore are divine.

In the second book of *Against Heresies*, Irenaeus makes a first step toward distinguishing the Spirit from the Son. His distinction becomes clearer, as Anthony Briggman has shown, when Irenaeus, drawing on the influence of both the Jewish Wisdom tradition and Theophilus of Antioch, employs the image of God's two Hands. Whereas Theophilus called the Word and Wisdom God's Hands, Irenaeus identifies the Hands as the Son and Spirit (*Haer.* 4, preface 4). Then building on Theophilus's argument about God's self-sufficiency, Irenaeus expands on the metaphor of God's hands to refute the gnostic identification of creation with the work of an ignorant demiurge and his angelic assistants. "For God did not need [angels or other creatures] to do what he himself had beforehand determined to do as if he himself did not have his Hands, the Word and Wisdom, the Son and Spirit, by whom and in whom he made all things freely and of his own will, to whom he speaks, when he says, 'Let us make man in our image and likeness'" (*Haer.* 4.20.1). This serves Irenaeus's goal of uniting the divine works of creation and redemption. The Hands, that is, Word and Wisdom, who in the Old Testament narrative created man in God's image in the beginning, are the very same Son and Spirit who in the New Testament narrative refashioned and perfected in humanity the divine image once compromised by sin. As in Theophilus, the Word and Wisdom possess the creative power that belongs to God alone. Therefore, they are not ontologically other than or subordinate to the Father but are coeternal with him. Moreover, Irenaeus here goes beyond Theophilus in separating the Word and Wisdom by mapping them onto the Trinitarian baptismal formula. The Word is the Son, and Wisdom is the Spirit. Irenaeus, in identifying the Spirit with Wisdom named in Proverbs 3:19–20, 8:22–25, and 8:27–31, ascribes to the Spirit the creative power of divinity that distinguishes it from creatures. For, alongside the Word, "Wisdom also, which is the Spirit, was present with [God], *prior to all* creation" (*Haer.* 4.20.3).

Irenaeus surpasses Theophilus by distinguishing the work of the Spirit from that of the Son. While "founding and making all things . . . by the Word," God, Irenaeus explains, "arranged all things by his Wisdom" (*Haer.* 2.30.9). This arrangement he describes using the image of the lyre. Although the lyre is composed of many strings of different lengths and yet produces "one harmonious melody [though] consist[ing] of many and opposite sounds," Wisdom orchestrates many and opposing individual creatures to produce a cosmic harmony (*Haer.* 2.25.2). In this way, the Spirit completes the Word's work of forming creation. As Wisdom providentially governs (*gubernare*) the Word's creation, the same Spirit perfects (*perficere*) or completes (*Haer.* 2.25.1–2; 2.30.3) the Son's salvific work begun in the incarnation.

The saving work of the Holy Spirit can only be understood within the context of Irenaeus's salvation history. As we saw in chapter 3, this history was the progressive education of humanity through the dispensations, that is, the covenants. The incarnation was the climax of this process of maturation and education; for Jesus, as the Son of God and a son of Adam, was the recapitulation of both the divine dispensations and human nature. In Jesus's humanity, not only could people see the image of the invisible God; they saw the true nature and destiny of the human race. They saw themselves, their nature, and their destiny rightly. But it was by the anointing of the Holy Spirit that the rest of humanity, Jesus's brothers and sisters in Adam's family, could participate in the perfected humanity of the second Adam.

When Jesus was baptized in the Jordan, the Spirit's descent on him was the first of two anointings. As the dove descended, the Spirit did not anoint Jesus's humanity with any divine qualities—those were already fully conferred by the Word in his union with Jesus's embryonic flesh in Mary's womb (*Haer.* 3.19.1). Rather, in fulfillment of Isaiah's words that Jesus would quote at the beginning of his public ministry, "The Spirit of God is upon me, because he has anointed me: he has sent me to preach the gospel to the lowly" (Isa 61:1–2; Luke 4:18), the Spirit conferred on Jesus the power to fulfill his Messianic mission "in order that we, receiving from the abundance of his anointing, might be saved" (*Haer.* 3.9.3). The "abundance of his anointing" refers to the revelation of God's salvation made available in Jesus. Later in book 3 of *Against Heresies*, Irenaeus explains the joint work of the Word and Spirit in Jesus. The Word is the "Savior" whose flesh is salvation. But the Savior's life and work are "salutary" (*salutare*) because of the Spirit who is the face of Christ (Lam 4:20); for through the Spirit's anointing, the prophecy of Psalm 98:2, "God has made his salvation known in the sight of gentiles," has been fulfilled (*Haer.* 3.10.3). In other words, the anointing of the Spirit allowed the gospel proclaimed in Jesus's preaching and actions to be understood by his hearers and later by the gentiles through the preaching of the apostles so that he might be seen as the bringer of God's salvation. But not only was Jesus's humanity affected by the anointing; so was the Spirit. For Irenaeus says that because, unlike the anointing of the prophets in whom the Spirit spoke periodically, the anointing of Jesus was perpetual. Consequently, the Spirit became *accustomed* to dwelling permanently with humanity, "renewing them from oldness into the newness of Christ" (*Haer.* 3.17.1). Thus, the Spirit's indwelling of Jesus allowed the Spirit to become the fountain of living water welling up within the believer to eternal life. (Irenaeus seems unconcerned that this account of the Spirit's becoming accustomed to dwelling with humanity threw into question the Spirit's immutability.) If the Spirit's first anointing of Jesus allowed for the preaching and hearing of the gospel, the Spirit's second anointing created the possibility that the perfection of the second Adam might be actualized in the rest of Adam's race. This second anointing was the glorification or spiritualization of Jesus by which the incorruptibility, conferred by the Word, was now accessible to the rest of humanity (*Haer.* 5.7.2). Through the Spirit, the immortality and freedom from corruption given to Jesus passed to his sisters and brothers who shared in his glorified human nature. With the gift of the Spirit's indwelling at baptism, the community of believers was made into his mystical body and was thereby enabled to participate in the immortality and incorruption proper to Jesus's divinized flesh.

The Spirit in Alexandria

Written less than a century later, Origen's account of the Spirit was not shaped as much by polemical dispute with the Gnostics as was Irenaeus's but by battles against Modalists who collapsed the Son and Spirit into the single person of the Father. Nevertheless, Origen was concerned to situate the Spirit within an account of creation, fall, and restoration that recognized, contra the Gnostics, humanity's natural capacity for free choice. Since the goal of the economy of salvation was *apokatastasis*, the return of the fallen rational beings to the spiritual state whence they fell by their errant use of free will, the sanctifying work of the Spirit was critical in enabling their spiritual restoration.

Although Origen maintained the same hierarchical view of the relationship of the Father and the Spirit as he did with the Father and the Son, he nevertheless ascribed to the Spirit an eternal communion with the Father and the Son. Nothing in Scripture, he observes in *On First Principles*, suggests that the Spirit was a creature. On the contrary, the Spirit is presented as being in the beginning hovering over the primal waters of chaos (*Princ.* 1.3.3). At the same time, the Spirit was clearly distinct from the Son, for Scripture does not apply the Son's titles (e.g., Life and Word) to the Spirit. Nevertheless, Scripture repeatedly affirms the exalted status of the Spirit by its depiction of the Spirit as the one through whose overshadowing power Mary conceived Jesus and who inspired the prophets, apostles, and evangelists to compose the Scriptures. Indeed, no one can rightly know the Son except through Scripture, whose authors were inspired by the Spirit (*Princ.* 1.3.1). Such enlightenment extends to the postapostolic Church whose members cannot confess Jesus to be Lord without the Spirit's illumination (1 Cor 12:3). Such illumination is possible because the Spirit did not *acquire* knowledge of the Father and the Son but has always known them (*Princ.* 1.3.4). Thus, Origen implies, the Spirit's knowledge of the Father and Son comes from his eternal union with them in the Godhead. Lest the divine majesty of the Spirit still be doubted, Origen appeals to Jesus's warning (Matt 12:32) that, while sins against the Father and the Son may be forgiven, blasphemy against the Spirit is alone unforgivable (*Princ.* 1.3.2).

Why are sins against the Spirit unforgivable? What does this signify about the status and work of the Spirit? Origen answers these questions by explaining the hierarchical ordering of the Father, Son, and Spirit in terms of their respective roles in the divine economy. The Father, as the great I AM, is the source of existence for all things. He is the foundation and source of the cohesion of creation in its totality. The Son, by contrast, is, as the Logos, the source of the intellectual powers proper to rational beings. But the Spirit imparts holiness—without which no one may see God—only to the saints (*Princ.* 1.3.5). Because the Spirit works in a smaller subset of creation than the Father and the Son, Origen contends, his power is inferior to theirs. Yet it is the Spirit who brings the Son's work in rational creatures to its perfection. By making rational beings partakers of his rational nature, the Logos planted within them a seed of wisdom and righteousness. That is, rational beings are endowed with an innate knowledge of the Son (*Princ.* 1.3.6). This is the kingdom of God that Jesus says lies "within you" (Luke 17:20–21). This embryonic knowledge grows to perfection through the gift of the Spirit, which allows rational beings to acquire the higher wisdom and knowledge of God that makes them spiritual. However, as represented in Scripture by Adam's fall, rational beings' diminished love for God rendered them unworthy of communion with God (Gen 6:3). Consequently, the Spirit was taken away, and they fell into humanity's present corporeal condition (*Princ.* 1.3.7).

As on other subjects, Origen's view of the Spirit is difficult to interpret because of the textual issues surrounding Rufinus's translation and emending of Origen's text to make his theology conform closer to acceptable standards of the late fourth century. This is especially true of his discussion of the Spirit in *On First Principles*. Comparing *On First Principles* with other texts in his corpus only complicates the picture. For example, in his *Commentary on John*, Origen distinguishes the Spirit from the Father and the Son by numbering the Spirit among the "all things" (John 1:3) that were made through the Logos (*Comm. Jo.* 2.73) and yet says that "the Holy Spirit is more honored than all things and is first rank of all things" (*Comm. Jo.* 2.75–76). Origen can thereby counter the Modalist conflation of the Spirit and Son into the Father; each is a discrete hypostasis. At the same time, he sets the Spirit, together with the Son, apart from creatures because of the Spirit's transcendence (*Comm. Jo.* 32.187–189). Evidence of this transcendence is their unique knowledge of the Father—knowing the beginning and end of all things—that allows them to reveal him to lower beings (*Princ.* 4.3.14).

Where Origen's treatment of the Spirit becomes a bit muddled is on whether the Spirit's attributes, for example, holiness, wisdom, and justice, are essential (i.e., natural, eternal and immutable) or accidental (i.e., derivative, contingent, and capable of being lost). On the one hand, in his *Commentary on John*, Origen reasons that the Spirit's attributes, and by extension the gifts he bestows on believers, are his by participation in the Son from whom he derives his existence (*Comm. Jo.* 2.76). Therefore, since the Spirit derives his existence and his attributes from the Son, through whom he participates, the Spirit's attributes, like those of all other creatures, are not essential but accidental. Consequently, the Spirit ranks below the Father and Son. On the other hand, Origen elsewhere distinguishes the Spirit together with the Son and Father from saints, whom the Spirit sanctifies, precisely because the Spirit's holiness is not an accidental property that can be lost (*Princ.* 1.5.5; 1.8.3). Holiness is not extrinsic (*non extrinsecus*) to the Spirit's nature but proper to who he is (*Hom. Num.* 11.8.1). While the contradiction may be explained as the result of subsequent emendations of Origen to accord with later Nicene theology, another explanation is to read Origen as subscribing to a relational ontology. That is, the Spirit's nature and attributes are the product of his eternal, and therefore essential, relationship with the Father through the Son (*Comm. Jo.* 10.270; *Comm. Matt.* 12.20). For Origen also says that the Spirit is eternally with the Son and Father even as the Son is eternally with the Father. Thus, as the Son abides in an eternal participation in the Father (*Comm. Jo.* 2.18), from whom he derives his attributes, similarly the Spirit abides in an eternal participation in the Son. If the Spirit's participatory relation with the Son is eternal, then his nature and attributes are distinct from those of creatures. Unlike creatures whose attributes may be perfected or may be lost altogether depending on the degree of their participation, the Spirit's attributes, because they are derived from an eternal participation in the Son, are themselves eternal and therefore can never be lost.

Origen's use of the participation language both for creatures and for the Son's and Spirit's relationship with the Father did not bequeath to his heirs a clear dividing line between the divine and the creature. The result is a confusing picture. The Son and Spirit, like creatures, possess their attributes only derivatively and relationally through participation, unlike the Father whose predicates are wholly intrinsic and not derivative. Yet because the Son and Spirit's relationship with the Father is not accidental but eternal, the Son and Spirit's participatory mode of being, and thus their attributes as well, occupies a middle ontological status. They seem to stand between creatures whose being and attributes are noneternal and contingent and the Father whose being and attributes are eternal and necessary. This liminal status that Origen gives to the Spirit contributes in part to the fourth-century debates about the person of the Spirit.

Less ambiguous, however, is Origen's account of the work of the Spirit in the economy of salvation. Through his incarnation and resurrection, Jesus as the "new man" (Eph 2:15) and "firstborn from the dead" (Col 1:18) revealed to his apostles the spiritual humanity that they possessed in the beginning and that would be their destiny if they chose wisely. As a reward for the apostles' faith in the resurrected Christ, Jesus breathes on them and, in doing so, anoints them with his Spirit (John 20:22). Those who receive the apostle's proclamation of Christ and in whom the seed of wisdom germinates and takes the form of virtue receive the gift of the Holy Spirit. Thus, they drink of the new wine that fills them with newness of life as spiritual beings. Yet, per Jesus's parable (Matt 9:14–17), rational beings are not able to hold the new wine of the Spirit unless they first put off the old wineskins of their fallen, carnal nature. However, should they not fully repent but turn back to the fleshly mode of thinking and acting that they put off in baptism, then they have sinned against the Holy Spirit.

Here lies a tension in Origen between the agency of the Spirit and that of rational beings. On the one hand, the Spirit is presented as the *reward* for the saint's complete repentance. On the other hand, Origen also speaks of the Spirit as the *cause* of holiness. With the gift of higher wisdom from the Spirit, all stains of sin and ignorance are removed so that the saint is "unceasingly and inseparably present with him who really exists," with the result that "the loving desire for [God's fellowship] deepens and increases within us" (*Princ.* 1.3.8). Here is Origen's concern for human free agency and for the divine agency of grace. He both affirms fallen humanity's capacity for virtue and repentance necessary for the sanctifying grace of the Spirit and at the same time recognizes that the Spirit's gift is necessary for the perfection of virtuous souls that are transformed and raised to the spiritual life.

Origen explains the Spirit's perfection of the saints in his *Commentary on Romans*. Explicating the meaning of "the love of God shed abroad into our hearts through the Holy Spirit" (Rom 5:5), Origen asks, "To whom is this love of God given?" His answer is the "perfect," that is, people such as Paul, who, having received the Spirit of adoption in baptism, will not fall back into the "spirit of slavery" (Rom 8:15) to sin and with it the fear of condemnation (*Comm. Rom.* 4.10.11). They possess "perfect love [that] casts out fear" (1 John 4:18) because they have received from the Holy Spirit the highest gift, the knowledge of God's love for humanity that inspires in Christians a reciprocal love. Thus, the "higher wisdom" given by the Spirit is nothing other than the love of God. Since God is love (1 John 4:8), when the saint perseveres in this higher wisdom so as to preserve the bonds of adoption in the Spirit, then "from the fullness of the Spirit, the fullness of love is infused into the hearts of the saints so as to make them participants in the divine nature (2 Pet 1:4)" (*Comm. Rom.* 4.10.12). Through holding fast to the gift of the Spirit, who is "the Spirit of love" (2 Tim 1:7) that flows from "the one fountain of paternal love," the saints live together in the unity of love that mirrors the unity of the Trinity (John 17:21). For through the Holy Spirit, who is "the Spirit of Christ" (Rom 8:9), Christ abides in the saints and through him they are united to the Father (*Comm. Rom.* 6.13.3). By contrast, the one who does not have the Spirit is, says Origen, "not of character and stature such as to deserve to have the Spirit of Christ [and] would immediately be repudiated as belonging to Christ" (*Comm. Rom.* 6.13.4).

The Spirit's gift of love that endures in the lives of the saints is proof that their baptism was not merely "a visible anointing" of the flesh but a true, inner baptism, that is, being dead to sin and rising to newness of life (*Comm. Rom.* 5.8.2–3). The ones in whom the Spirit of Christ dwells are his true disciples who have so thoroughly put to death the "old man," and with it worldly love and ambition, that they are prepared to take up their cross and literally die as did Christ himself. This is the death to sin that must precede baptism. For only by being dead to sin can one be said to be buried with Christ and then raised in the Spirit (*Comm. Rom.* 5.7.10). This newness of life in the Spirit is the restoration of the spiritual nature that rational beings had before their fall. As the Spirit was given to Adam in the beginning, now the Spirit returns to the truly baptized in proportion to her merit (*Comm. Rom.* 6.13.7). The Spirit effects the union of the truly baptized with Christ through kindling in her the love of God's Word. Even as the rational beings prior to the fall were united to the Word with a fiery love of the divine, the saints filled with the Spirit burn inwardly with a longing for union with God. For like the two disciples whose hearts burned within them as the risen Jesus opened the Scriptures on the road to Emmaus, "the fire of the Holy Spirit may inflame the hearts" of the saints who hear or speak the word of God and "at once begin to glow and burn to carry out every teaching" (*Comm. Rom.* 6.13.8). Thus, through the indwelling of the Spirit, love and wisdom are united in the saints. For their minds now fully set upon the things of Christ have become spiritual so that their souls possess the fiery desire for the Word necessary to ascend once more to the heavenly classroom and there be united to the God they love (*Comm. Rom.* 6.13.9).

While Origen, like Tertullian, faced a polemical contest against Modalist views of the Spirit, his account of the Spirit's workings fell largely within the freedom of speculative theology. A century later, Athanasius was not so fortunate. Rather, his pneumatology was formed in the context of his battles with various groups of subordinationists. It emerged in three letters written in reply to a query about the Spirit from his loyal episcopal colleague, Serapion of Thmuis. The subordinationists with whom Serapion was contending were not the Homoians but a group that affirmed that the Son was divine and not a creature but claimed that the Spirit was an angelic creature and thus was ontologically subordinate to the Son. Athanasius christens them with the appellation *tropikoi* or "misinterpreters" because of their flawed "mode of exegesis" (*Ep. Serap.* 1.1.2). In passing, he also charges them with "fighting against the Spirit" (*pneumatomachountes*) from which the pejorative title "Pneumatomachians" will be applied to a latter group of Homoiousians who also denied the Spirit's divinity (*Ep. Serap.* 1.32.2).

Athanasius's polemical counsel to Serapion is divided between his critique of the *tropikoi*'s exegetical method and then a more constructive argument against their view of the Spirit as a creature that appeals to the shared logic by which they defend the Son's divinity.

The *tropikoi*'s argument that the Spirit is an angelic creature was grounded textually in Amos 4:12–13 and 1 Timothy 5:21. Amos, as the Lord's mouthpiece, declares, "I am the one who gives strength to thunder and who *creates spirit* and who proclaims his Christ to humanity." On this text, the *tropikoi* contended that, since the Spirit is created, it is a creature. Athanasius finds fault with their exegetical error of not distinguishing between the times Scripture uses the word "spirit" (*pneuma*) with the definite article or other modifiers and when the article is omitted. In the latter case, Scripture uses *pneuma* to refer to "wind" as when Jonah 1:4 says, "And the Lord stirred up a spirit upon the sea and a great wave arose on the sea" (*Ep. Serap.* 1.7.5). At other times, Athanasius observes, *pneuma* without any article or other qualifier may refer to the spirit or soul of a human being (Dan 3:86) or the true meaning of Scripture (2 Cor 3:6) in contrast with the letter (*Ep. Serap.* 1.7.3 and 1.8.1). By contrast, the presence of an article or possessive adjective, he argues, denotes the Holy Spirit. The example to which Athanasius refers repeatedly is Psalm 103:29–30 (LXX), which expressly contrasts the human spirit with God's Spirit: "You take away their spirit, and they die, and return to the dust from which they came. You send forth your Spirit, and they are created and you renew the face of the earth" (*Ep. Serap.* 1.9.5–6). Here, *pneuma* that gives life is something other than the air that fills the lungs. Similarly, in the gospel narratives (Luke 3:21–22), the article accompanies *pneuma* when speaking of the Spirit's descent upon Jesus at his baptism (*Ep. Serap.* 1.4.2). Likewise, Scripture uses the definite article or a possessive pronoun when speaking specifically about the Holy Spirit's coming, foretold either in Joel 2:28, "I will pour out my Spirit on all flesh" (*Ep. Serap.* 1.5.8), or by Jesus (John 14:26), "The Paraclete, the Holy Spirit, whom the Father will send in my name, will teach you all things" (*Ep. Serap.* 1.6.2). Thus, Athanasius concludes that one who rightly observes this exegetical principle will understand that "spirit" in Amos 4:12–13 refers to the wind that tossed Jonah's boat about on the waves and not to the Holy Spirit. It, therefore, is not evidence that the Spirit is a creature.

The *tropikoi*'s claim that the Spirit is an angel also rests upon 1 Timothy 5:21 where "God, and Jesus Christ, and the elect angels" are lumped together (*Ep. Serap.* 1.10.4). Athanasius counters that such a view is a reversion to the "impiety of Valentinus" (*Ep. Serap.* 1.10.5). Not only is such a view impious, but it is also, he contends, completely without scriptural foundation since nowhere does Scripture expressly identify the Spirit as an angel. On the contrary, in places where it might have done so, Scripture distinguishes between angels and the Spirit. For instance, at Gabriel's annunciation to Mary, the archangel, rather than himself being the one who overshadows Mary or foretelling the coming of another more powerful angel, declares that the Holy Spirit will come upon her (*Ep. Serap.* 1.11.1). And even though it was angels that ministered to him in the wilderness (Matt 4:11), at his baptism in the Jordan it was the Spirit, not an angel, who anointed Jesus (Luke 3:22). Were the Spirit simply an angel, the authors would have named him as one of the angels mentioned in the same or proximate passages.

After providing a catalogue of biblical examples that raise questions about the *tropikoi*'s exegetical assumptions, Athanasius offers theological counterarguments. The Trinity is, he contends, one, a unity because the Father, Son, and Spirit share a common nature. This unity is not the combination of different parts. Rather, the Father begets the Son such that the Son possesses the whole of the Father's divinity—a point on which the *tropikoi* surely would agree. Likewise, the Spirit is the whole of the Son as the Son's image and radiance (*Ep. Serap.* 1.16.5). This is possible because of the mutual indwelling of the persons. If, however, the Spirit is a mere creature, not possessing the holiness, immutability, life, and light proper to the divine nature, then the Trinity is not one but a compound of a divine nature and a creaturely nature (*Ep. Serap.* 1.2.3–4). The *tropikoi*, therefore, have lost the triune God and instead worship a dyad. Although Athanasius does not go so far as to apply the term *homoousios* to the Spirit's relationship with the Son, he defends the Spirit's divinity by explaining the exact parallel between the relationship of the Father and the Son and that of the Father to the Spirit. As the Son is said to be proper to the Father's substance (*idios tēs ousias*), because he is both *in* the Father and *from* the Father, so too the Spirit who is in God and from God must also be "proper to the Son in substance [*kat' ousian tou huiou*]" (*Ep. Serap.* 1.25.2) inasmuch as they are both from the Father. Therefore, the Spirit is able to make the Son known because he shares with the Son the same nature they both derived from the Father. He illustrates the parallel by aligning Paul's words in 1 Corinthians 1:24 and 2:8 that the Son is the "Power of God" and the "Lord of glory" with the description of the Spirit in 1 Peter 4:14 as "the Spirit of Power" and "the Spirit of glory" (*Ep. Serap.* 1.25.3). That both the Son and Spirit are described as having the power and glory of God implies a shared essence (*idios tēs ousias*) that they possess by virtue of their both being from the Father.

Athanasius's defense of the Spirit's divinity is not reducible to an argument from the Spirit's saving works. Nevertheless, the heart of his case is that, if the Spirit were a mere creature, the Spirit could not enable believers to participate in Christ's divine nature. Thus, Athanasius uses the category of participation (*metechousia*) as the key dividing line between the Creator and the creature. Creatures, who do not possess life and holiness in themselves, acquire these by participating in an outside source that possesses them by nature. Nor are creatures able to communicate these qualities to others. Therefore, Athanasius interprets Jesus's identification of the Spirit as living water that "wells up within to eternal life" (John 4:14) to imply that the Spirit is not a creature. Rather, the Spirit is a divine person in whom believers may participate in order to receive the eternal life proper to his nature (*Ep. Serap.* 1.23.3). In other words, for the Spirit to share the Son's life with believers, the Spirit must be "proper to the Word" who gives him to them (*Ep. Serap.* 1.27.1–2). The two most common images Athanasius uses to express believers' participation in the Word through the Spirit are light and water. The Father is light, and the Son is his radiance (Heb 1:3). The Spirit is the one in whom Christ's radiance enlightens "the eyes of [the Christian's] heart" (Eph 1:17–18). Similarly, Athanasius depicts the Father as the fountain (Jer 2:13) and Christ as the river (Ps 65:9) and the rock in the wilderness (1 Cor 10:4) from whom the life-giving water flows. Christ's water given to believers is the Spirit. He thus concludes, "When we are enlightened it is Christ who enlightens us in him [i.e., the Spirit]. . . . When we drink of the Spirit, we drink of Christ" (*Ep. Serap.* 1.19.1–4).

The image, however, that Athanasius uses to explain the relationship of the work of Christ and the work of the Spirit is that of the seal imprint from a signet ring. The Spirit is the Son's gift to the Church that perfects his work in it (*Ep. Serap.* 1.20.5). That is, the Spirit glorifies the Son by revealing to the Church what the Son received from the Father that the Son passed on to the Spirit (*Ep. Serap.* 1.20.6). The Son, in receiving from the Father his divinity, bears the image of the Father. Likewise, the Spirit, in bearing the Son's life, power, glory, holiness, and so on, is an image of the Son (*Ep. Serap.* 1.20.4). Therefore, when the Christian receives in baptism the gift of the Spirit (*Ep. Serap.* 1.23.4–7), she is receiving the imprint of the Son's image and is thereby conformed to the image of Christ (*Ep. Serap.* 2.12.2–3)—in whose image humanity was originally fashioned. Thus, the gift of the Spirit renews and regenerates by restoring and perfecting the Word's creation of humanity in the beginning. As the Spirit is the living image of the Son, the Son's image, which the Holy Spirit imprinted on the believer's spirit, is also a living image. For through the luminous indwelling of the Spirit, the Christian is continually participating in God and ever receiving knowledge of God manifest in the Son whose glory and divinity the Spirit makes clear and clearer (*Ep. Serap.* 1.24.1). When the Spirit of Christ dwells within the Christian, the Lord lives in her (Gal 4:19) so that her life bears the sweet odor (2 Cor 2:15) of Christ's divinity (*Ep. Serap.* 1.23.7). This aroma is like the fragrance of oil used for anointing but also of incense wafting through a temple as a sign of the deity's presence. Indeed, through the indwelling, the Christian is made the living temple (1 Cor 3:16–17) of Christ. For as the Son is in the Father and the Father in the Son, and as the Spirit is in the Son and the Son in the Spirit, the Christian now abides in the Father and Son because the Spirit abides in her (*Ep. Serap.* 2.12.5).

In the early 360s, at roughly the same time or slightly before Athanasius composed his letter to Serapion, Didymus the Blind was composing his treatise *On the Holy Spirit*. As we have seen, Didymus was teaching with the approval of Athanasius in the catechetical school in Alexandria. Having received a request from some "brothers," likely former students, Didymus offered a refutation of the dubious teachings about the Spirit that were circulating, teachings derived from neither Scripture nor the "old ecclesial authors" (*Spir.* 2). Although Didymus's original Greek text has been lost, fortunately we have Jerome's Latin translation, which nevertheless preserves some of Didymus's technical Greek vocabulary.

Although Didymus, unlike Athanasius, does not give a name to the propagators of the spurious teachings, there is a certain overlap between this group of teachers and Athanasius's *tropikoi*. Not surprisingly, therefore, Didymus employs arguments similar to those of Athanasius. For example, he appeals to the presence of the definite article to designate *the* Holy Spirit in contrast with places where "spirit" is unaccompanied by the definite article and so simply means "wind" rather than referring to the Holy Spirit (*Spir.* 8, 72). He also comments on Amos 4:12–13, which both his and Athanasius's opponents cite in support of their claim that the Spirit is a creature and not divine. More distinctive, however, is Didymus's analysis of biblical accounts of the Christian's communion with the Spirit to argue that his substance is not that of a creature but of God.

Didymus begins by saying that God's gifts, which are the goods of his divinity conferred on humanity, are nothing other than the Holy Spirit himself (*Spir.* 12). The goods of the divine nature are all forms of God's holiness; therefore, Didymus calls the Holy Spirit the "bestower and creator of sanctification" (*Spir.* 13). The process of sanctification begins with the Spirit's cleansing work in baptism; as Paul tells the Corinthians (1 Cor 6:11), "But now you have been washed, you have been sanctified, you have been justified in the name of our Lord Jesus Christ and in the Spirit of our God" (*Spir.* 15). Didymus thinks of sanctification in relational terms as the product of the Holy Spirit's communion with the believer (*Spir.* 14). God, who is the principle of all good things, confers them on others by giving of himself through the Spirit (*Spir.* 17). In language echoing Origen, Didymus says that the Christian becomes spiritual and holy by partaking of the divine nature through communion with the Spirit (*Spir.* 20). Thus, Didymus uses the language of communion to express the Christian's participation in God. In an interpretive excursus that Jerome inserts into Didymus's text, he explains that the Spirit's "capacity to be participated in" (*capabilis*) means that the Spirit "bestows a share of itself." From the perspective of the Christian, her participation (*capax*) in the divine nature occurs when the substance of her being is "filled through communion with another [i.e., the Spirit's] substance" (*Spir.* 54–55). Jerome's elaboration explains Didymus's distinction between the creature, which can participate in another, and the Spirit, which can be participated in while he himself does not participate in another (*Spir.* 13, 17). That is, the Spirit is not filled with any substance external to his own. Didymus speaks of this participatory communion in the Spirit by using the biblical language of "being filled with," "indwelling," and "pouring forth," each of which is applied only to the Spirit and not to creatures. Whereas Scripture speaks of John the Baptist being "filled with the Holy Spirit even from his mother's womb" (Luke 1:15) and the apostles likewise being filled with the Spirit at Pentecost (Acts 2:4), it does not speak of a creature being filled with another creature (*Spir.* 30). For when the Spirit fills a creature's soul, it conveys the gifts of the Spirit's divinity, that is, wisdom, knowledge, faith, and the other virtues, proper to the Spirit's substance (*Spir.* 34). Indeed, these gifts are the very substance of the Spirit (*Spir.* 43). Similarly, God is said to lavish his gifts on humanity by "pouring forth" the Spirit (*Spir.* 50). By contrast, Scripture speaks of God as "sending" rather than "pouring forth" angels (*Spir.* 28). Whereas angels have an entirely external encounter either by vision or dream, they are not said to "indwell" the person to whom they are sent. Such inner communion is unique to the Spirit. Christ is said to dwell in the "inner person" (Eph 3:16–17) through the Spirit such that those indwelt by the Spirit become the temple of God (1 Cor 3:16; *Spir.* 107–108). This inner communion by which the Spirit's substance communicates his virtues to those who receive him in faith (*Spir.* 38) is possible because, unlike angels, which are finite and circumscribed, the Spirit's divine nature is uncircumscribed. Therefore, the Spirit is not confined to one point in space and time but permeates the whole of the cosmos and inhabits many souls at once (*Spir.* 23).

Didymus employs the language of substance to speak of the Spirit's unity with the Father and Son that sets him ontologically apart from angels and other creatures. The very name "Holy Spirit" indicates the underlying essence of the Father and the Son (*Spir.* 10), which means that the Father and Son are ontologically spiritual beings whose very property is holiness and wisdom (*Spir.* 11). Thus, he also speaks of the Spirit as "the substance of the goods of God" (*Spir.* 35). By this, Didymus does not mean that the Spirit is the substrata of which the Father and Son are composed. Rather, he means simply that human beings receive the goods proper to the Father and Son's nature when they are united to the indwelling Spirit. For the Father, Son, and Spirit have a single activity that reflects their common substance, *homoousia* (*Spir.* 81). He does not say expressly that the Spirit is *homoousios* with the Father and the Son, instead using the noun *homoousia*, "same substance," to speak of the divine nature the three share. He comes closest to applying *homoousios* to the Spirit when he says that, if angels were naturally holy, they would be *homoousios* with the Trinity (*Spir.* 27). This implies that since the Spirit, unlike the angels, is naturally holy, he is *homoousios* with the Father and Son.

The shared divinity, Didymus explains, is an indivisible substance. Therefore, the Father, Son, and Holy Spirit are inseparable. Where one is present and active, there then other members are as well. Thus, the human soul can be said to be the "temple of God" because when the Spirit indwells a person's mind, the Father and Son, to whom the Spirit is inseparably bound, are there as well (*Spir.* 108). Consequently, Didymus argues, when Ananias was accused by Peter of lying to the Holy Spirit, he was also guilty of lying to God because of the partnership (*consortium*) that exists between them. Indeed, this is a natural partnership; for Didymus goes on to say, "in whatever way holiness subsists in God, in the same way deity subsists in the Holy Spirit" (*Spir.* 83). When Paul, therefore, speaks of the "only wise God" (Rom 16:27), he is not, Didymus contends, separating the Spirit from God by implying that wisdom is the unique property of the Father. On the contrary, Scripture, describing the Son as "the Wisdom of God" (1 Cor 1:24) and the Holy Spirit as "the Spirit of Wisdom" (Deut 34:9), implies that the Son and Spirit are identified with Wisdom precisely because they share the Father's wise nature (*Spir.* 92). "We will see," writes Didymus, "that the Holy Spirit, because he is the Spirit of Wisdom and Truth, possesses the same circle of unity and substance as the Son . . . [who] is not divided from the substance of the Father" (*Spir.* 94).

Didymus illustrates the single activity of the persons using the image of the hand and the fingers. He identifies the Holy Spirit as the "Finger of God" to whom Jesus refers: "If by the Finger of God I cast out demons, then the reign of God has come upon you" (Luke 11:19–20), by pointing to a parallel text in Matthew (12:28) where Jesus says that he casts out demons "by the Spirit of God" (*Spir.* 88). Though the hand and finger are distinct, they are not separate but united in nature and in a single motion of activity. Thus, the Spirit is the Son's instrument to purify and sanctify those who are unclean by imparting to them the holiness of the Father and Son as he did when Jesus exorcised demons. Such is possible because, Didymus writes, "the Holy Spirit [is] named the Finger of God because he is conjoined in nature to the Father and the Son" (*Spir.* 87). At the same time that Didymus demonstrated the ontological unity of the Spirit with the Father and Son by appealing to the unity of their actions, he wanted to avoid any reduction of the Spirit to a mere activity of God. He demonstrates the subsistent agency of the Spirit by pointing to the letter from the Council of Jerusalem (Acts 15:28) explaining the sending of Paul and Barnabas to Antioch, where it reads, "It *seemed good* to the Holy Spirit and to us to lay no greater burden on you." Here the Spirit is depicted as possessing judgment and will, which implies that the Spirit is a subsisting entity (*Spir.* 97).

The regard with which Didymus's treatise on the Spirit was held is evident not only in Jerome's production of a translation into Latin but its subsequent use by Latin authors, such as Ambrose, and Greek authors in the later stages of the clash between the pro-Nicenes and the subordinationists. Of these Greek writers influenced by Didymus, the most important was Basil the Great.

The Cappadocians and the Spirit's Divinity

Basil's defense of the Spirit's divinity was put forward in his *Against Eunomius* where he invoked Didymus's interpretation of Amos 4:12–13 to counter Eunomius's use of it as a prooftext of the Holy Spirit's creaturely nature. Distinguishing the Spirit from the Son who, as the only begotten, is unique, Basil writes, "So then, what should we call him? Holy Spirit, Spirit of God, Spirit of truth sent from God, bestowed by the Son" (*Eun.* 3.6). Then, deploying Didymus's argument (*Spir.* 72), he rebuts Eunomius's interpretation by arguing that Amos speaks of "the one who *creates* spirit." Were the Spirit a creature, Amos would have used the past tense, "the one who created" instead of the present "creates." Therefore, "spirit" refers not to the Holy Spirit who is uncreated but to the wind that God creates for his purpose at different points in the biblical narrative.

Basil's more developed account of the Spirit, however, emerged around 375 with the publication of his *On the Holy Spirit*. There he began by challenging Aetius's theory of language to argue for the unity and ontological equality of the Son with the Holy Spirit and the Father. Basil grounds his argument on the Church's baptismal liturgy, specifically Jesus's instructions to the apostles to baptize in the name of the Father, Son, and Holy Spirit. The divinity of the Spirit is implied in baptism, Basil contends, if one rightly understands the soteriological significance of baptism and the role of the Spirit in it.

In the baptismal rite, the neophytes were asked the questions "Do you believe in God the Father?" and "Do you believe in Jesus Christ?" Neither can be answered in the affirmative, Basil insists, without the illumination of the Holy Spirit. No one knows the Father except "the only begotten God who is in the bosom of the Father" (John 1:18) who reveals the Father. Yet no one can confess Jesus to be Lord except "in the Holy Spirit" (1 Cor 12:3). Therefore, one's confession of the Father and Son is utterly dependent on the Spirit whose revelation of Jesus's identity makes faith possible (*Spir.* 11.27). The reason for baptizing in the name of the three persons rather than just the Father's, Basil explains, is the twofold role of the Son and Spirit. The water into which the body is lowered is a figure of the believer's participation in Christ's death by which she is *redeemed* from condemnation and death. This same water is also an image of the life-giving power that *renews* the soul once dead in sin (*Spir.* 15.35). As Adam lost the Spirit by his disobedience, in baptism the believer experiences regeneration—the beginning of a second life—through the return of the Spirit (*Spir.* 16.39). Although the water signifies both Christ's death and the Spirit's return, it is the Spirit who makes the whole ritual efficacious. For the Spirit, who reveals the Son and Father, is the cause of the believer's *faith* confessed in baptism that is the beginning of salvation. The Spirit then perfects the baptismal faith by leading believers into the *sanctifying fellowship* with God (*Spir.* 12.28). When the soul is purified in baptism through its renunciation of "friendship with the flesh" and so returns to the beauty of its original form, then it is ready to be a suitable dwelling place for the Holy Spirit. Then the Spirit, like a beam of light from the sun that penetrates a translucent piece of glass, thereby making the glass itself luminous, imparts its luminous brilliance and makes the soul spiritual. In this way, the believer sanctified by the Spirit becomes a medium through which others may see and receive the Spirit. Basil expresses the Spirit's work of sanctification in terms of divinization: "From [the Spirit] comes . . . heavenly citizenship, a place in the choir of angels, endless joy in the presence of God, becoming like God, and, the highest of all desires, becoming God" (*Spir.* 9.23). The Spirit's work of illumination and sanctification are not separate operations. Rather, the baptized are sanctified by new life "in the Spirit" because the Spirit's luminous indwelling confirms the believer's faith through fellowship with the Father through the Son. Through such fellowship, the Spirit renews the believer in the image of God.

For Basil, the sanctifying and regenerating work of the Spirit begun in baptism is possible only because of the Spirit's place in the Godhead. He begins laying out his doctrine of the Holy Spirit—almost as if to turn Aetius's theory about names revealing essences against him—by analyzing the name "Spirit." When Jesus told the Samaritan woman at the well that "God is spirit" (John 4:24), he was making the point that, unlike corporeal creatures that are circumscribed in place and time, God as spirit is uncircumscribed and so can be worshiped not just in Jerusalem or on Mount Gerizim but anywhere. The Holy *Spirit*, therefore, as spirit is not circumscribed as are finite creatures but instead is "an intelligent being, boundless in power, of unlimited greatness, generous in goodness, whom time cannot measure" (*Spir.* 9.22). Thus, the very name "spirit" draws a dividing line between creatures and Divinity. Then, appealing to a doctrine of divine simplicity, Basil argues that "since the divine nature is not composed of parts, union of the persons is accomplished by partaking of the whole" (*Spir.* 18.45). That is, each person possesses not a limited set of divine qualities, as do divinized creatures, but the totality of the divine nature. Thus, he concludes that the Spirit is said to be *of God* not as are creatures made by God but because he "proceeds from the mouth of the Father." Yet he is spirit not as is human breath that disperses in the air once it leaves the mouth. Rather, the Spirit is the Father's "breath" in the sense that breath is life itself: "the Spirit is the essence of life and divine sanctification" (*Spir.* 18.46). Those who in baptism receive the gift of the Spirit, as when Jesus breathed on the apostles at the resurrection, belong to Christ because his life dwells in them.

Moreover, only the Spirit is able to glorify the Father and the Son and to make Christ's followers partakers of that glory because, through the Spirit's unique intimacy with the Father and the Son, he is able to impart wisdom to the believers. Basil takes the metaphor of the Spirit as life-giving breath and adds to it another biblical metaphor, light. The Spirit confers life to believers because, as light, the Spirit allows the baptized to see and to know the Son and the Father. "If we are illumined by divine power [i.e., the Spirit]," Basil writes, "and fix our eyes on the beauty of the image [i.e., the Son] of the invisible God, and through the image are led up to the indescribable beauty of its source [i.e., the Father], it is because we have been inseparably joined to the Spirit of knowledge" (*Spir.* 18.47). This knowledge—a knowledge born of the communion of the Spirit and believers—is itself life-giving.

In fact, the downward order of procession from the Father to the Son to the Spirit forms the ladder by which believers ascend to the Father. The Spirit "reveals the glory of the only begotten in himself and he gives true worshippers the knowledge of God in himself. The way to the divine knowledge ascends from the one Spirit through the one Son to the one Father" (*Spir.* 18. 47). This is the logic of the traditional doxology: "Glory be to the Father, through the Son, in the Spirit." In the light of the Spirit, believers offer worship to the Father, who is the source of all gifts of divine goodness, through the Son in whom the Father's glory is manifest. Thus, the traditional doxology, he says, is appropriate for giving *thanks* to God since it best describes the believer's economic relationship with God. Basil's own doxology, "Glory to the Father with the Son together with the Spirit," does not contradict the traditional doxology; rather, it affirms the codignity of the persons: "Whenever we reflect on the majesty of the nature of the only begotten, and the excellence of his dignity, we ascribe glory to him *with* the Father" (*Spir.* 7.16). Since the Son is worshiped together with the Father because he shares the same glory and majesty proper to the divine nature, then, since the Spirit, too, is worshiped with the Son and Father, the Spirit likewise must share the Father's and Son's nature.

Here was the bone of contention. The logic of Basil's argument is clear: since the Spirit is the object of worship with the Father and Son, then the Spirit must be equal in divinity with the Father and Son. Yet he refused to carry his own argument to its logical conclusion. Basil would not come out and declare that the

Spirit was *homoousios* with the Father and Son or call the Spirit "God." As noted in the introduction to this chapter, Basil's reticence may in part reflect his political and pastoral attempt to hold the door open for an alliance with the Pneumatomachians against the Eunomians. In addition to being politically prudent, leaving the obvious punch line of his argument hanging in the air for his reader to supply for himself reflects Basil's apologetic aim—namely, his desire to persuade his mentor and friend, Eustathius, one of those Homoiousians who denied the divinity of the Spirit. Eustathius was an ascetic who had little interest in crafting dogmatic statements, preferring instead to focus on matters of prayer and sanctification. Given Eustathius's unsystematic temperament, Basil's rhetorical tact had to be more subtle and indirect. This subtlety is evident in the first eight chapters of *On the Holy Spirit* where Basil links the logic of the homoiousian confession of the Son's divinity to the joint worship of the Son and Spirit. However, drawing the explicit line between these two points would fall to Gregory of Nazianzus.

When Gregory in the fifth of his theological orations turns to the subject of the Spirit, the target of his polemic expands from the Eunomians, his chief adversaries in Constantinople, to the Macedonians also known as the Pneumatomachians or "Spirit fighters." This sect originated either with Macedonius, bishop of Constantinople (358), who was a member of Basil of Ancyra's homoiousion party, or with Marathonius, who was consecrated bishop of Nicomedia by Macedonius. Although Gregory laments the wide range of views he found in Constantinople, he does not offer a careful delineation of the Eunomian objections from those of the Pneumatomachians (*Or.* 31.5).

Their central objection against a confession of the Spirit's divinity was that such a claim is never stated in Scripture. The Spirit is often absent from pairings of the Father and the Son as when 1 Timothy 5:21 says, "I charge you in the presence of God and of Christ Jesus and of the elect angels." Where the Spirit or "breath of God" is mentioned, the Spirit is spoken of as a creature; as Amos declares, "Behold, I formed the mountains and *made* the wind [*pneuma*]" (4:13). Gregory answers the objection that his view is unscriptural by offering a theory of God's progressive revelation in Scripture. Since the old covenant sought to make a clear distinction between the one true God of Abraham and the many gods of the Chaldeans, Egyptians, and Canaanites, Israel first had to know God as one before it was ready to grasp the one in three persons. As one with weak eyes cannot behold a bright light, so, Gregory writes in his poem on the Spirit, it is better to come to the knowledge of God "bit by bit" (*Spir.* 20–23). Therefore, the Old Testament revealed God the Father, giving only glimpses of the Son. The new covenant contained in the Gospels revealed the Son, providing only promises of another Paraclete. Indeed, Jesus's followers could not receive the Spirit as God until they had first recognized the Son as divine (*Or.* 31.26). At Pentecost, the Spirit's descent upon the apostles and the birth of the Church not only allowed Jesus's followers to know him rightly as the Father's Son but also the Spirit as Christ's abiding presence with the Church. Although the Spirit had been active in Israel before Pentecost, for example, inspiring the prophets, including John the Baptist, and overshadowing Mary, at Pentecost the Church received "the indwelling of [the Spirit's] being [*ousiōdōs*]" (*Or.* 41.11).

Gregory's account of God's progressive self-revelation in the history of Israel and the Church not only provided an explanation for Scripture's silence on the Spirit's divinity, but it also explained the work of the Spirit within the economy of salvation. Gregory, like Basil, refers to the Father, Son, and Spirit, according to their respective roles within their unity of operations, as the cause, the Creator, and the perfecter respectively (*Or.* 34.8). That is, the Spirit brings to completion the Son's accomplishment of the Father's creative will. The Son's creative activity was not simply the fashioning of the world in the beginning. It included the redemptive re-creation of humanity in his image through the incarnation. The Spirit's indwelling presence in believers accomplishes on the microcosmic level the macrocosmic plan of salvation. That is, the divinizing union of God and humanity, of which the incarnation is the archetype, is actualized in the Spirit's union with the Church, Christ's mystical body.[1] Therefore, the Spirit must be God. Either the Spirit is God, or he is a creature. There is no middle ontological status between Divinity and creature any more than there is between Lord and servant (*Or.* 41.7). One either rules or is ruled. Only God, who alone is uncreated, autonomous, and unchanging, rules. All beings that are created are dependent on God, are subject to change, and are his servants. To deny the Spirit's divinity would be to make him a slave rather than "the Lord, the giver of life." If the Spirit does not possess in his own nature the holiness necessary to sanctify the Church, then the most that could be said is that he is an incomplete deity. That, however, is nonsense. For Gregory asks, "What use is incomplete deity? Or rather what is deity if it is incomplete?" (*Or.* 31.4). Ultimately, unless the Spirit, who is active in the Church in baptism and in the total life of the Christian community, is divine, then God is not with his people. Furthermore, if the indwelling Spirit who abides in the Church is not divine, then the Church is united not to God but to a mere creature. Indeed, the Spirit can be adored and worshiped only if he is divine. If, however, he is not divine, the Church's worship is blasphemy, and believers are not partakers of the divine nature. Unless the Spirit is divine, the Church is not divinized, and baptism is ineffectual. But because the Church experiences new birth in Christ's new creation through the divinizing work of the Spirit, it can rightly confess the

1. See Christopher A. Beeley, *Gregory of Nazianzus on the Trinity and the Knowledge of God: In Your Light We Shall See Light* (Oxford: Oxford University Press, 2008).

Spirit to be God (*Or.* 31.28). Driving the point home, Gregory asks bluntly, "If [the Spirit] has the same rank as I have, how can he make me God, how can he link me with deity?" (*Or.* 31.4).

Here Gregory plays a trump card, the common liturgy of the pro-Nicenes, Eunomians, and Pneumatomachians. Inasmuch as bishops of all three groups baptize in the name of the Father, Son, and Holy Spirit, and view the Spirit as the one who sanctifies believers, Gregory was pushing them to see the implication of their liturgical practices. He was also putting pressure on those in his own party who, following Basil, resisted applying the language of *homoousios* to the Spirit as they did to the Son. They certainly agreed with him that the Father, Son, and Spirit are spoken of in Scripture as "light." When John's prologue says, "He was the true light that enlightens every man coming into the world," the "true light," they would agree, may refer to the Father and Spirit as well as the Son, for as Psalm 36 declares, "in your light we shall see light." They are, therefore, three subjects—the Father, the Son, and the Comforter—but one reality, light. "The light is one; [therefore], God is one. . . . [For] we receive the Son's light from the Father's light in the light of the Spirit" (*Or.* 31.3). Although Gregory's argument follows the same logic as Basil's—even the same biblical language of light—Gregory insists on the need for a bolder declaration. Playing with the image of the Spirit as the light who illumines the Church that it might proclaim Christ to the world, he asks, "How long should we hide the lamp under the bushel and withhold the complete divinity from others, when we ought to put it on a lampstand now to give light to all churches . . . no longer by means of images or intellectual sketches, but by a distinct declaration?" (*Or.* 12.6). So Gregory, laying aside the traditional metaphors, declares that the Trinity is the Father, the Son, and "the Holy Spirit, who is God" (*Or.* 33.16). Traditionally, following the language of Scripture (e.g., 1 Cor 8:6), the name "God" applied to the Father, with "Lord" or "Son of God" being designations for the Son. But here Gregory applies "God" to the Spirit to make explicit that the Spirit, according to nature, is equally God as are the Father and the Son.

While at times Gregory excoriated his ecclesial confreres for their cowardice in not confessing that the Spirit possessed the same consubstantial relationship with the Father and Son that they had with each other, other times he could be more diplomatic. "Yet you are distressed by the syllables and trip over the word [*homoousios*], and this becomes for you a stone of stumbling. . . . Let us agree with each other about the Spirit. . . . Grant the power of divinity and we will grant you a concession regarding the word; confess the nature through other words that you respect more, and we will heal you as sick persons" (*Or.* 41.7). If his episcopal colleagues are squeamish so as to quibble over the word *homoousios*, Gregory says that he magnanimously will concede to them so long as they recognize the Spirit's divine power. If they agree with him that the Spirit is life and gives life, is light and illumines, deifies without being deified (*Or.* 41.9), and shares all essential attributes as the Father and the Son, then they have all but invoked the term *homoousios*. If they are comfortable saying all these of the Spirit, all of which are implied in the term "consubstantial," then in time they will accept the word itself. Unfortunately, for Gregory they did not. At the Council of Constantinople in 381, the bishops, largely under pressure from the emperor Theodosius who was determined to force a compromise, rejected Gregory's entreaties to apply *homoousios* to the Spirit. Although they were willing to agree with Gregory that the Spirit should be worshiped together with the Father and Son—a tacit acknowledgment of the Spirit's divinity—this was not sufficient for Gregory, and he left the council in disgust. Nevertheless, Gregory's arguments for the Spirit's divinity, especially in his fifth theological oration (*Or.* 31) and his homily on Pentecost (*Or.* 41), became for the Eastern churches the interpretive lens through which they read the council's description of the Spirit.

Fire and Spirit: Baptism and Eucharist in Syriac Churches

The dispute between Eunomian and Pneumatomachian subordinationists and the pro-Nicene antisubordinationists over the status of the Spirit was not confined to the Greek-speaking churches. Syriac communities also took a keen interest in these debates. In particular, they were attracted to Basil's teaching on pneumatology. Within twenty-five years of the publication of *On the Holy Spirit*, likely even before the Council of Constantinople, the treatise had been translated into Syriac.[2] Indeed, Basil's writings were translated into Syriac more than those of any other Greek theologian.

What is interesting about the first Syriac translation of *On the Holy Spirit* is the liberties the translator ventured to take. For this Syriac version was not a strict translation. Rather, the translator largely offered a paraphrase of Basil's text. To this the translator freely added emendations that put into Basil's mouth the bold confession of the Spirit's divinity that Gregory had wanted him to make. Whereas Basil avoided making the Spirit consubstantial with the Father and Son, the translator makes the shared nature explicit. To the gloss of Basil's statement, "Therefore,

2. On the manuscript tradition, see David G. K. Taylor, trans., *The Syriac Versions of* De Spiritu Sancto *by Basil of Caesarea*, CSCO 576 (Leuven: Peeters, 1999), and Benjamin D. Wayman, "The Transmission of Basil of Caesarea's *On the Holy Spirit*," in *The Use of Textual Criticism for the Interpretation of Patristic Texts: Seventeen Case Studies*, ed. Kenneth Steinhauser and Scott Demer (Lewiston, NY: Mellen, 2012).

true religion teaches us to think of the Son with the Father" (*Spir.* 6.14), the translator adds, "as a result of these things that we have heard, such as they are, that the Father and the Son and the Holy Spirit are one in nature, and they are united in three persons" (*Spir. Syr.* 22, p. 18). Whereas Basil scrupulously avoided the controversial term *homoousios*, the Syriac translator inserted into his gloss, "The Spirit shares the nature [*bar keyono'*] of the divinity." Here the phrase *bar keyono'* literally translates "son of nature," which David Taylor takes to be a Syriac rendering of *homoousios* (*Spir.* 12.28; *Spir. Syr.* 58, p. 45). Not surprisingly, the translator presses the logic of this claim to the same conclusion as did other pro-Nicene defenders of the Spirit. In his discussion of the gifts of the Spirit (1 Cor 14:24–40) where Paul speaks of "God [being] among them," Basil poses the rhetorical question, "If God is recognized to be present among prophets because their prophesying is a gift of the Spirit, let our opponents determine what place they will give to the Holy Spirit. Will they rank him with God or will they push him down to a creature's place?" (*Spir.* 16.37). In his gloss of this passage, the Syriac translator substitutes Basil's seemly open-ended question with the declarative statement that, since Paul says, "God is in [the prophets]," "the Spirit of God, then, is called 'God in them' because she is the giver of prophecy" (*Spir. Syr.* 79, p. 58). Lacking Basil's political or personal ties with the Homoiousians or the Pneumatomachians, the translator clearly felt no ecclesial compunction in confessing the Spirit's Godhead.

The translator's high pneumatology was not an anomaly. Rather, over the next five hundred years, it found expression in poetry and liturgy of the four Syriac churches (the Syrian Orthodox Church, the Maronite Church, the Melkite Church, and the Church of the East), especially in their rituals of baptism and the Eucharist. Indeed, it was the Spirit who bridged the present, profane time in which the worshipers lived their ordinary lives and the sacred time. Through the Spirit, worshipers entered the sacred moments of salvation history: Jesus's baptism in the Jordan, the Last Supper, and his crucifixion and resurrection.[3] For by the Spirit, the salvific work of Christ ordained by the Father was actualized in the lives of the believers.

In his *Hymns on Faith*, Ephrem (d. 373) uses the sun as a metaphor for the Trinity: The Father is the sun from which the Son, like the rays of light, is generated, and the Spirit is the heat from the sun's rays with which the whole world is suffused and given life (*Hymn. fid.* 73.1). The life-giving operation of the Spirit is simply the single activity together with the Father and the Son; for the Spirit "is not cut off from the Radiance / being mixed with it, nor from the Sun, / being mingled with it"

3. Sebastian Brock, *The Holy Spirit and the Syrian Baptismal Tradition* (Piscataway, NJ: Gorgias, 2008), 8–10.

(*Hymn. fid.* 74.3–4). Because in the sacred time of worship, the neophyte's baptism is concurrent with Jesus's baptism, Jesus's baptism, at which all three persons of the Trinity are active, provides the model for understanding the neophyte's baptism. For Theodore of Mopsuestia (350–428), the neophyte hears the words of the Father, "This is my beloved Son," and understands that in the Son's baptism the Father is extending to him personally the gift of sonship that the Spirit confirms in baptism (*Cat. hom.* 14.25). The Spirit's unity of action with the Father and Son is grounded in their ontological unity, which was commonly expressed in the invocation of the Spirit (*epiklēsis*) at the Eucharist when the Spirit is identified as being "consubstantial with you [the Father] and your only begotten Son" (*Anaphora of Jacob of Serugh* 1) or "unchangeable and unchanging, consubstantial with you, who proceeds from you, not alien to your Godhead or to that of your only begotten Son" (*Anaphora of Timothy of Alexandria*).

The sign of the Spirit's conferral of sonship was the oil or *myron* poured into the water. Through the oil, which Ephrem calls "the dear friend of the Holy Spirit" (*Hymn. virginit.* 7.6.1–2), the Spirit's power was conveyed to the neophyte so that in receiving the Spirit of adoption, she becomes a sibling of Christ (Jacob of Serugh, *Hom. mart. Sahd.*). As a result, she also simultaneously receives the authority to address God as "our Father" in the Lord's Prayer (Philoxenus, *Mem. fid. Spir.*; Tanghe, 44). Adoption by the Spirit is interwoven with themes of divinization, signified by putting on the "robe of the Spirit" (Ephrem), also known as the "robe of glory" (Jacob), which Adam and Eve lost in the fall. In putting on the Spirit, the baptized are clothed with Christ and so put on the divinity to which Adam and Eve aspired. Thus, the Holy Spirit both returns the baptized to paradise and, by making them children of God, allows them to surpass the glory of Edenic humanity (*Anaphora of Jacob of Serugh* 2). In the sacred time of the Eucharist, the Spirit transforms the sanctuary itself into Eden. For as Ephrem writes, "We have eaten Christ's body in place of the fruit of the tree of paradise, and his altar has taken the place of the garden of Eden for us, the curse has been washed away by his innocent blood, and in the hope of the resurrection we already walk in this new life, in that we already have the pledge of it [i.e., the Holy Spirit]" (*Comm. Diat.* 21.25). Moreover, the believer herself becomes the "royal sanctuary" that Christ, "the Carpenter of salvation," has constructed for himself and in which his Spirit dwells (Ephrem, *Hymn. virginit.* 1.2).

If oil and the white baptismal robe were the outward signs of the Spirit's divinizing anointment, the metaphor for the Spirit's sanctifying power was an extension of the Trinitarian image of heat coming from the sun's ray of light—heat in its most intense form, fire. Sometimes the Spirit is spoken of as fire, and other times the Spirit is paired with fire. Indeed, the incarnation, which itself is the product of the Spirit, divinizes believers by conferring on humanity Spirit and fire. As Ephrem writes, "When the Lord came down to earth to mortal men / he created them again in a new creation, like angels, / mingling Fire and Spirit with them, / so that in a hidden manner they might be of Fire and Spirit" (*Hymn. fid.* 10.8–13). In baptism, the same Fire and Spirit that sanctified Mary's womb, uniting their divinity and humanity, joins itself to the baptized, sanctifying the Church. A common image for the incarnation was the pearl that was believed to be formed when lightning struck the ocean. When the contrary natures of fire from the lightning and the soft flesh of the oyster met in the water, the result was the creation of a brilliant pearl. So too, the analogy goes, in Mary's womb the contrary natures of divinity and humanity were united by the Fire of the Spirit to form the pearl of great price, the God-man (*Brev. Chald.* 2, p. 543). The consecrating power of the font is signified by the mixing of spiritual fire and baptismal water (*Hymn. fid.* 40.10). In the Epiphany homilies attributed to Ephrem, the sanctifying power of the Spirit in baptism is fire: "Blessed are you, my brothers, / for the fire of mercy has come down, / utterly devouring your sins, / purifying your bodies" (*Hymn. epiph.* 3.10). In fact, Jacob of Serugh in his homily on Constantine's baptism describes fire coming over the water (Jacob of Serugh, *Hom. Const.*; Frothingham, 235–36). As in baptism, the transformative power of the Spirit in the Eucharist is fire: "the Spirit is in your bread, the Fire in your Wine, / a manifest wonder, which our lips have received / . . . The new miracle / is that our mighty Lord has given to bodily man / Fire and Spirit to eat and drink / . . . the Fire of mercy descended and dwelt in the bread. / Instead of that fire which consumed mankind / you have consumed Fire in the Bread and you have come to life" (*Hymn. fid.* 10.8–13). Isaac of Nineveh (d. 700) alludes to the Spirit as the source of life and love conveyed to the believer in the Eucharist. "When we have found love," Isaac writes, "we eat the heavenly bread and are sustained. . . . He who lives in love in this world breathes in life from God; he breathes here the air of resurrection, in which the righteous delight at the resurrection. . . . Love is sufficient to feed man instead of food and drink. . . . Blessed is he who has drunk from this wine. This is the wine from which the lascivious have drunk and became chaste, the sinners drunk and they forgot the ways of offence."

The image of the Spirit as fire in the baptismal font led to another image: the font as a furnace. The liturgy for Pentecost preserved in the *Fenqitho* describes the apostles as being "poured out like gold in the furnace of the Spirit" (*Fenqitho* 6, p. 211a) for the proclamation of the gospel. Imagining the baptismal font as the goldsmith's furnace where humanity is reforged by the Spirit, Narsai (399–502), in his homily *On Baptism*, writes, "the power of the Creator has renewed our image and blotted out our iniquity. As in a furnace He re-cast our image in Baptism; and instead of our clay He has made us spiritual gold" (*Hom. bapt.* 22, p. 33). Jacob of Serugh, in his homily on Christ's baptism, imagines the font as the forge where the baptized receive the armor of Christ that equips them for spiritual warfare. Jesus, explaining his baptism to the Church, says, "I descended to the fountain not to take up a shield for myself but to forge mighty armor for warriors. I am anxious to cleanse humanity in the contest of battle so that everyone who comes to fight should fight like me. I am instituting baptism as an armory; unless man has entered and clothed himself from it, he will not fight" (*Hom. epiph.*; Malaty, 18). The heat for the forge with which Christ baptizes his Church is the Spirit and fire.

As the place of the Christian's second birth, the font invited Syriac preachers to describe it in feminine terms and with it the Spirit also. Perhaps following Jesus's reference to the Spirit as "my mother" in the Gospel according to the Hebrews, Aphrahat (270–345), in an ascetic reimagining of Genesis 2:24, identifies the Holy Spirit as Adam and Eve's mother. When a man takes a wife, he explains, the father and mother whom he leaves are "God his Father and the Holy Spirit his Mother," who are his true parents (*Dem.* 18). As Sebastian Brock has observed, in later liturgies the Spirit is not referred to as "mother," likely to disassociate Christian initiation from triads of father, mother, and son among pagan religions of Mesopotamia. Nevertheless, the Spirit is often described maternally as "hovering" over the waters of the font. "The Spirit descended from the heights / And sanctified the water as She hovered, / When John baptized Jesus / She left all others and settled on one, / But now She has come down and settled / Upon all who are reborn in the water of baptism" (*Epiph.*; Brock, 249). "To hover" (*rahhef*) carried the connotation of motherly compassion and mercy over her children. The interweaving of maternal images of the font as a womb with those of the font as a forge represents the Spirit as the full expression of God's forgiving mercy and transforming power in the lives of the baptized.

Augustine's Pneumatology: "The Spirit Given to Us"

The Cappadocian defense of the Spirit's divinity proved normative in the Latin West as well as the Greek East. This is most evident in Ambrose's adaptation—with only a modest amount of editing—of Basil's *On the Holy Spirit*. However, the most important Western contribution to patristic pneumatology came, not surprisingly, from Augustine. In *On the Trinity*, Augustine places the Spirit as "gift" within his Trinitarian framework. "Father," "unbegotten," "Son," and "begotten" denote eternal relations that both distinguish the first two persons of the Trinity from each other and explain the interconnection between them.[4] Augustine identifies "gift" as the biblical term that sets the Holy Spirit apart as a distinct person

4. See chapter 6, pp. 264–72.

in the Godhead (*Trin.* 5.10). It might be argued that John 3:16, "For God so loved the world that he *gave* his only Son," makes "gift" an attribute of the Son as well as the Holy Spirit. The Son, however, is a "gift" only in the context of the divine economy; that is, he is given to the world for its salvation. Therefore, "gift" does not describe the Son's eternal relationship with the Father. In the case of the Holy Spirit, however, "gift" describes both the Spirit's place within the eternal relations between the persons of the Trinity as well as its role in the divine economy. Augustine makes this point by reading John 15:26, "the Spirit of truth, who proceeds from the Father," in conjunction not only with Romans 5:5 but also Romans 8:9, which identifies the "Spirit of God who dwells in you" as "the Spirit of Christ." The Spirit, therefore, is the love of God that the Father gives to the Son and that the Son in return gives to the Father. It is the gift that binds the Father to the Son and the Son to the Father in mutual affection; consequently, the Holy Spirit is "the inexpressible communion or fellowship of the Father and the Son" (*Trin.* 5.12). Gift is also an apt description of the Spirit economically. For the Spirit is not a mere "donation" that is conferred in time but is an everlasting gift that exists from eternity even before it is given to the Church (*Trin.* 5.16).

"Gift" is a relational term, Augustine explains, because "gift" implies both a giver and a recipient (*Trin.* 5.15). Although the Spirit "proceeds from the Father" as his gift to the Son, Spirit is not a second son begotten from the Father's nature. Because the Son returns the Father's gift of love, the Spirit is the product not of the Father alone but of the Father and the Son in their reciprocating love for each other. As Augustine puts it later, the Spirit is distinct from the Father and the Son because it is that which joins them together (*Trin.* 6.7). Yet even as he resisted arguments from 1 Corinthians 1:24 that risked reducing the Son to specific attributes, wisdom and power,[5] Augustine, like Basil, appeals to the doctrine of simplicity to argue that the Spirit, though principally understood as divine *caritas*, is equal in divinity with the Father and the Son, as they possess all the attributes of divinity. Indeed, the Spirit, Augustine writes, as the eternal communion between the Father and the Son, is the product of their reciprocal love of the properties they have in common, holiness and spirit (*Trin.* 5.12).

Point of Division: The *Filioque*

The year 1054 is the traditionally held date for the schism dividing the Roman Catholic Church and the Eastern Orthodox Churches. The exchange of excommunications between Pope Leo IX and Michael Cerularius, the patriarch of Constan-

5. See chapter 6, pp. 264–72.

tinople—excommunications finally lifted in 1965—may have been precipitated by a conflict over the control of churches in southern Italy, but it was the culmination of a growing divide between the East and the West over a host of differences ranging from clerical celibacy and the bread used in the Eucharist to the question of papal primacy. But among the most contentious issues was the wording of the third article of the Nicene-Constantinopolitan Creed. The wording set in 381 reads, "And I believe in the Holy Spirit, the Lord, the giver of life, who proceeds from the Father, who with the Father and Son is worshiped and glorified, and who spoke through the prophets." The issue was that the clause "who proceeds from the Father" was altered in the Latin West to include the words "and the Son," or in Latin *filioque*. The insertion of the *filioque* was first formally made at the Third Council of Toledo (589) when the Visigothic king Reccard converted from a form of Arian Christianity to Catholicism. In the eyes of the Eastern bishops, the introduction of the *filioque* was not only a novelty that was unfaithful to the judgment of the fathers at Constantinople, but it was a change made unilaterally by a Western council without any consultation of the Eastern bishops. The Western view was that it was merely a clarification of Constantinople rather than a substantive change and so did not need approval by an ecumenical council.[6]

As with most ecumenical councils, Toledo was not introducing an addition that was out of the blue; rather, it was simply confirming a common understanding in the West for over a century. The heart of the matter concerned how to articulate that the Spirit's relationship with the Father was different from the Son's. Since Christ is the "only begotten" (*monogenēs*) Son (John 1:18), the Spirit cannot be a second Son. If, then, the Spirit was not "begotten" by the Father, how was one to speak of the Spirit's origin? The scriptural answer lay in Jesus's Farewell Discourse in John's Gospel. There he speaks of the Spirit as being "given by the Father" (14:16), "sent by the Father" (14:26), and "proceeds [*ekporeuesthai*] from the Father" (15:26). Thus, the Spirit seems to be from the Father alone. Yet Jesus goes on to say that the Paraclete "will receive what is mine and make it known to you" (16:14), possibly implying that the Spirit comes from the Father *and* the Son. Basil, following Athanasius, viewed the Son as an intermediary between the Father and Spirit: "Through the one Son, the Holy Spirit is joined to the Father" (*Spir.* 18.45). And "the natural goodness, inherent holiness, and royal dignity reaches from the Father through the only begotten to the Spirit" (*Spir.* 18.47). The Son is mediating the divine nature of the Father to the Spirit. Here Basil is speaking economically. The Son is the middle rung of the Trinitarian ladder by which the divine is revealed to humanity and humanity ascends to the divine. Ultimately, in the East, Gregory of Nazianzus's voice,

6. For the best treatment, see A. Edward Siecienski, *The Filioque: A History of a Doctrinal Controversy* (Oxford: Oxford University Press, 2010).

especially on the Spirit, was authoritative: "The Holy Spirit is truly spirit coming forth [*proion*] from the Father, but not in the manner of a son or by generation but by procession [*ekporeusis*], if one must create a new term for clarity's sake" (*Or.* 39.12). Gregory, essentially at a loss for a term that is an alternative to "begotten," uses a neologism—*ekporeusis*—from the language of John 15:26 to convey the image of the Spirit as the breath of God breathed out on believers. While Gregory did not follow Basil in making the Son an intermediary, he nevertheless, like Basil, held the Father to be the sole source of the being of the Son and Spirit.

Two centuries later, Maximus the Confessor complicated the picture. Although the Father is the first cause from whom the Spirit proceeds, because the Son is always with and in the Father, the Spirit's procession from the Father implicitly includes the Son. For since the Father is always the Father in relationship to the Son, the Spirit comes from the eternally begetting Father. And since the Spirit is eternally with the Father and the Son, his going out is, in a sense, always from the two. This point Maximus makes explicit when speaking about the economic relationship of the Son and Spirit. Christ as the head of his mystical body, the Church, is the one through whom the Spirit is bestowed on the members of the Church. The Spirit is the Son's luminous divinity abiding in the Church that it might be a light unto the world. In this way, the Spirit may be said to proceed from the Father through the Son (*Quaest. Thal.* 63).

In the West, the tradition behind the *filioque* went back to Tertullian who described the relation of three persons using the metaphor of a fruit plant (*Prax.* 8). The Spirit is, he says, third in order, like the fruit that comes from the stem (i.e., the Son) that comes from the root (i.e., the Father). Thus, he says that the Spirit proceeds "from the Father through the Son" (*Prax.* 4). But the more developed view was provided by Augustine. Following Marius Victorinus and Ambrose, Augustine held that the Spirit proceeded from the Father and Son. The biblical warrant lay not in John but with Paul who spoke of the Holy Spirit as "the Spirit of Christ" (Rom 8:9–10; Gal 4:6; Phil 1:19). "Why," Augustine asks, "should we not believe that the Spirit also proceeds from the Son, since he is the Spirit of the Son? For if he did not proceed from Jesus, after the resurrection, showing himself anew to his disciples, he would not have breathed on them saying, 'Receive the Holy Spirit'" (*Tract. Ev. Jo.* 99.16.7). Augustine also reasons from Jesus's declaration that all that belongs to the Father has been given to the Son (cf. Matt 11:27; John 3:35; 6:37). If so, then the Son received the Spirit whom he then breathed on his disciples. Moreover, Augustine's view that the Spirit is the mutual love of the Father and Son requires that the Spirit be the product of the relationship of the two rather than being a unilateral gift.

Theological tension over the *filioque* built up over the centuries and came to a head in the Photian Schism of 867 when the Patriarch of Constantinople,

Photian, condemned and deposed Pope Nicholas. Photian's theological objection to the *filioque* was that it created two causes of the Spirit. Rather, he contended, the Father is the lone first principle and therefore the lone source or fountain of divinity. If the Spirit comes from the Son as well as the Father, that implies two causes. In effect, therefore, the Spirit becomes the grandson of the Father, which is completely unscriptural. Although Photian's condemnation was lifted and he was sent into exile by a synod in Constantinople in 869, the disagreement went unresolved. Indeed, in spite of efforts at rapprochement at the Council of Florence (1439), the enduring dispute over the *filioque* illustrated the theological, institutional, and cultural gulf between East and West that had developed over the course of the Church's first millennium.

Bibliography

Primary Sources

Aphrahat. *Demonstration 18: Against the Jews, Concerning Virginity and Holiness*. Translated by Adam Lehto. Piscataway, NJ: Gorgias, 2010.

Athanasius. *To Serapion*. Translated by Mark DelCogliano, Andrew Radde-Gallwitz, and Lewis Ayres. In *Works on the Spirit*. Yonkers, NY: St. Vladimir's Seminary Press, 2011.

Athenagoras. *Plea for the Christians*. *ANF* 2.

Basil the Great. *On the Holy Spirit*. Translated by David Anderson. Crestwood, NY: St. Vladimir's Seminary Press, 1980.

Brock, Sebastian. *Treasure-House of Mysteries: Explorations of the Sacred Text Through Poetry in the Syriac Tradition*. Yonkers, NY: St. Vladimir's Seminary Press, 2012.

Didymus the Blind. *On the Holy Spirit*. Translated by Mark DelCogliano, Andrew Radde-Gallwitz, and Lewis Ayres. In *Works on the Spirit*. Yonkers, NY: St. Vladimir's Seminary Press, 2011.

Ephrem the Syrian. *The Harp of the Spirit: The Poems of Saint Ephrem the Syrian*. Translated by Sebastian Brock. Cambridge: Institute for Orthodox Christian Studies, 2013.

Fenqitho. In Sebastian Brock, *The Holy Spirit and the Syrian Baptismal Tradition*. Piscataway, NJ: Gorgias, 2008.

Gregory of Nazianzus. Epistle 58 "To Basil." Translated by Brian E. Daley, SJ. In *Gregory of Nazianzus*. London: Routledge, 2006.

———. "On the Holy Spirit." Translated by Peter Gilbert. In *On God and Man: The Theological Poetry of St. Gregory of Nazianzus*. Crestwood, NY: St. Vladimir's Seminary Press, 2001.

Isaac of Nineveh. *Mystic Treatises by Isaac of Nineveh: Translated from Bedjan's Syriac Text with an Introduction and Registers*. Translated by A. J. Wensinck. Amsterdam: Uitgave der Koninklijke Akademie van Wetenschappen, 1923.

Jacob of Serugh. *The Epiphany Feast*. Translated by Mary F. A., Monica Mitri, and Michael Stefanos. Edited by Tadros Malaty. Alexandria: Saint George Church, 2021.

Narsai. *The Liturgical Homilies of Narsai*. Translated by R. H. Connolly. Cambridge: Cambridge University Press, 1909.

Origen. *Commentary on the Epistle to the Romans: Books 1–5*. Translated by Thomas P. Scheck. Fathers of the Church 103. Washington, DC: Catholic University of America Press, 2001.

———. *Commentary on the Epistle to the Romans: Books 6–10*. Translated by Thomas P. Scheck. Fathers of the Church 103. Washington, DC: Catholic University of America Press, 2001.

Philoxenus of Mabbug. *Memra on the Faith by Questions and Answers* (*Part 1. On the Indwelling of the Holy Spirit*). Published as *On the Indwelling of the Holy Spirit*. Pages 106–27 in *The Syriac Fathers on Prayer and the Spiritual Life*. Translated by Sebastian Brock. Cistcercian Studies 101. Kalamazoo: Cistercian, 1987.

The Syriac Versions of De Spiritu Sancto *by Basil of Caesarea*. Translated by David G. K. Taylor. CSCO 576. Leuven: Peeters, 1999.

Theophilus of Antioch. *To Autolycus*. *ANF* 2.

Secondary Sources

Beeley, Christopher A. "The Holy Spirit in the Cappadocians: Past and Present." *Modern Theology* 26 (2010): 90–119.

Briggman, Anthony. *Irenaeus of Lyons and the Theology of the Holy Spirit*. Oxford: Oxford University Press, 2012.

Brock, Sebastian. *Fire from Heaven: Studies in Syriac Theology and Liturgy*. Aldershot: Ashgate, 2006.

———. *The Holy Spirit and the Syrian Baptismal Tradition*. Piscataway, NJ: Gorgias, 2008.

Burgess, Stanley M. *The Holy Spirit: Ancient Christian Traditions*. Peabody, MA: Hendrickson, 1984.

Maspero, Giulio. *Rethinking the Filioque with the Greek Fathers*. Grand Rapids: Eerdmans, 2023.

Michelson, David A. *The Practical Christology of Philoxenus of Mabbug*. Oxford: Oxford University Press, 2014.

Miller, Micah M. *Origen of Alexandria and the Theology of the Holy Spirit*. Oxford: Oxford University Press, 2024.

Siecienski, A. Edward. *The Filioque: A History of a Doctrinal Controversy*. Oxford: Oxford University Press, 2010.

Wayman, Benjamin D. "The Transmission of Basil of Caesarea's *On the Holy Spirit*." In *The Use of Textual Criticism for the Interpretation of Patristic Texts: Seventeen Case Studies*. Edited by Kenneth Steinhauser and Scott Demer. Lewiston, NY: Mellen, 2012.

8

The Word Made Flesh

Theologies of the Incarnation, Fourth–Eighth Centuries

Counterintuitive though it may be, Arius possessed a high view of the incarnation. Largely through Athanasius's tarring his opponents with the label "Arian," Arius has assumed the role of "arch heretic" in the drama of early Christianity. It is easy, therefore, to forget the respects in which his doctrine of the incarnation was quite orthodox. After all, he was no Adoptionist; for Arius's Jesus was no mere man inspired to speak the word of God but the Father's Word united to a human body. Nor was he a Gnostic; for Arius, Jesus's body was no spectral illusion but real flesh and blood that really hung on the cross and really died and really rose on the third day. Ironically, Arius's error with respect to the nature of the Word was, in part at least, the result of his robust commitment to the reality of Christ's passion as well as his commitment to the uniqueness of the transcendent God (*Urk.* 14.37). In other words, it was precisely because the salvation of humanity was achieved by Christ's death on the cross that, for Arius, the Word that became incarnate could not be the unchanging and immortal God.[1] The Word had to be a creature—albeit a perfect creature who was the image of God—who was capable of change, able to enter into the suffering and death of a mortal man. By contrast, for those theologians who defined their position over against Arius by affirming the essential unity of the Father and his Word, the incarnation posed a greater theological challenge. Since the Son is consubstantial with the Father, sharing all the attributes proper to his divinity, that is, immutability, impassibility, immortality, and so on, how could the Son truly participate in the life of a human being whose creaturely nature was subject to change, suffering, and death? How then were Christians to think about the Nicene-Constantinopolitan confession that the "one Lord Jesus Christ" is "true God of true God" and that he "was made man . . . [and] suffered death"? How could these two claims be held together? How could Jesus be both the divine Word and a mortal man?

1. This motive for Arius's theology is presented in Robert C. Gregg and Dennis Groh, *Early Arianism: A View of Salvation* (Philadelphia: Fortress, 1981).

The challenges that a Nicene doctrine of the Word created for interpreting the incarnation were articulated as early as 357 when Phoebadius of Agen published his *Against the Arians* in response to the creed of the Council of Sirmium—or "the blasphemy of Sirmium," as Hilary of Poitiers dubbed it. Although the work was primarily a polemic against the Homoian theology, Phoebadius recognized that the logic of Nicaea required a different view of the union of the Word and humanity. The "Arian" Christ, he explained, was neither divine nor human but a *tertium quid*, that is, a hybrid of the perfect Word and passible humanity in which the natures were mixed together (Phoebadius, *C. Ar.* 5.1). This confused union negated the distinction of the Word and his humanity, making the Word the subject of suffering on the cross. Such a conception of the incarnation was untenable for defenders of the Word's divinity; for, Phoebadius reasoned, it would render God passible (*passus*) by "attributing to [the Word] the weakness of a human being . . . [such that] I do not see how he differs from any human being in whom such passions hold sway" (*C. Ar.* 22.4–5). Phoebadius's alternative was to distinguish "the twofold manner [*duplicem statum*] in which the Lord's power exists" (*C. Ar.* 4.8). Without employing technical language of "nature" to distinguish the divinity and humanity or "person" to speak about the union of the two, Phoebadius speaks of the incarnation as the conjunction (*coniunctus*) of the two substances (*substantiae*) of Spirit and flesh. This allows him to locate Jesus's suffering in the flesh while preserving the impassibility of his Spirit. But then, Phoebadius, in a move that anticipates Cyril of Alexandria, declared that Christ is the one man (*homo*) in whom the two substances are conjoined, who suffered and died in the manner of his humanity according to the weakness of his flesh. He defends this view by saying that when Paul says "*Christ* died," he did not mean simply the flesh alone but the whole man (*C. Ar.* 24.3–4). Thus, as Mark DelCogliano has observed, Phoebadius's early attempt at a Nicene Christology can sound conflicted at places appearing to divide the natures (i.e., dyophysite) and at other places uniting them in the single subject, the Christ.

As we have already seen, theological clarity—or at least the formation of normative boundaries for speaking about the mysteries of the Christian faith—often emerged out of controversy. In the late fourth century, the controversy that forced the Church to define the boundaries between orthodox and heterodox teachings on the incarnation centered, perhaps ironically, on the teachings of a student of Athanasius, Apollinaris of Laodicea.

Apollinaris and the Future of the Word-Flesh Christology

The son of a priest in the Syrian town of Laodicea, Apollinaris (b. 315) met Athanasius in 346 when, on return from his second exile, Athanasius stayed with Apollinaris's family. For their hospitality, Apollinaris and his father were rewarded with excommunication by the Homoian bishop, George of Laodicea. From that time on, Apollinaris remained a friend and ally of Athanasius. Not surprisingly, Apollinaris's Christology was strongly influenced by Athanasius's.

The governing principle of Athanasius's Christology was the Word's creative and redemptive role in the divine economy. Namely, the Logos, who created humanity in his image in the beginning, became incarnate in his own flesh that he might re-create humanity and restore to it the divine image (*Inc.* 7, 13) and deliver Adam's race from death by his own death and resurrection (*Inc.* 9, 27). Like Origen, Athanasius took John 1:14 as the starting point: the Word "was made flesh" so that he might offer humanity eternal life through the knowledge of the one true God whom no one had ever seen except the Son who made him known (*Inc.* 4). Because eternal life was possible through the knowledge of the Father revealed by his Word—"If you have seen me, you have seen the Father" (John 14:9)—Athanasius stressed the incarnation as God's self-disclosure through the work of the embodied Word (*Inc.* 15). Jesus's words and actions were salvific because they manifested the life-giving power and philanthropic character of God. Athanasius's emphasis, therefore, was not on Jesus's moral agency as a human being but on the agency of the divine Word. This emphasis led him to adopt a single-subject Christology. That is, the incarnation was a true union of divinity and humanity—human flesh, capable of dying, but governed entirely by the impassible Word.

The christological challenge was to articulate an account of the incarnation that preserved the Word's transcendent divinity while also affirming the Word's radical immanence in "becoming flesh." How might the Logos, who is consubstantial with the Father, be truly united to a mortal creature so that the creature might put on divinity but without the Word's immutability and impassibility being compromised? The first step lay in finding language that allowed him to make a clear distinction between Nicene orthodoxy and the errors of either Paul of Samosata or Arius and his allies. For the former, there was no real union of God and humanity, only the indwelling of the Word who spoke through Jesus, as in a prophet. For the latter, the union was real, but it was of creature with creature, not God with creature. Athanasius, therefore, used John 1:14, "and the Word became flesh," and spoke of the Word's "putting on flesh" to counter the Adoptionist language of "indwelling" that treated Jesus like an inspired prophet (Athanasius, *C. Ar.* 2.47; 3.30–32). For the Word did not simply inspire the man Jesus; he *became* the man Jesus. The flesh taken from Mary's womb was the body of the Logos. On the other hand, to preserve the immutability and impassibility of the Word, Athanasius on occasion deployed the image of a temple indwelt by the Word so that no one would misinterpret John 1:14 to imply that the Word was changed by its union with the flesh (*Ep. Adelph.* 7).

More than simply finding suitable language to speak of the traditional Alexandrian Word-flesh union, Athanasius's single-subject Christology confronted two significant challenges. The first concerned Jesus's passion and death. Since the Word was truly united to mutable flesh, how was such a union possible that did not compromise the Word's eternal and unchanging divinity? More to the point, since the Word was the single subject of all Jesus's activities, did not the Word experience the suffering of Christ's passion and death on the cross? This indeed was one of the Homoians' principal arguments against Nicene claims that the Son was equal in divinity with the Father. In the third book of his *Orations Against the Arians*, Athanasius gives a litany of key biblical passages that his subordinationist opponents of Nicaea cited as evidence that the Word was subject to creaturely change. Were the Word truly self-subsisting deity who lacks nothing but possesses all things in himself, they objected, Jesus would not have said, "All things have been delivered to me of my Father" (Matt 11:27), which implies some deficiency in the Word that the Father needed to fill. Similarly, speaking of Jesus's admission that his "soul is deeply troubled" (John 12:27) in the face of his imminent passion, the Homoians argued, "If he were power, he would not have feared, but rather would have supplied power to others" (*C. Ar.* 3.26). Athanasius's initial reply was to locate the fear of death in Jesus's body. Since some creaturely characteristics, such as change and the impulse for self-preservation, are inherent to the human nature, it was unavoidable that Jesus, who, unlike a gnostic Christ, was truly incarnate, would experience such bodily impulses (*C. Ar.* 3.55). This was, Athanasius argued, not different from his experiencing bodily growth from infancy to adulthood. Yet though the Word was the subject of his body, it was the body, not the Word, that underwent growth. So too, the body with its impulse for self-preservation was the locus of the emotion, not the Word. "If the speaker [i.e., Jesus] were a [mere] man," Athanasius writes, "let him weep and fear death; but since he is the Word in flesh . . . whom had he to fear since he was God? . . . [Indeed] when arrested he did not flee. . . . He could have avoided death, as he said, 'I have the power to lay down my life and I have the power to take it up again' (John 10:18)" (*C. Ar.* 3.54). Against a gnostic or Adoptionist two Christs—one earthly and one heavenly—Athanasius argued that there was only one Christ, the incarnate Logos. The Word, who created all things and was before Abraham and John the Baptist, was the very same Word who was the subject of Jesus's body that grew and suffered. Therefore, Jesus's words about fear, growth, and ignorance referred only to his life in the flesh and not to the Word himself (*C. Ar.* 3.55). That Jesus did not flee when the soldiers came to arrest him—something Jesus himself said he could have done—but submitted to his captors and then voluntarily gave up his spirit on the cross was evidence, for Athanasius, that the Word was not *subject* to passions of the body. Athanasius's logic seems to be that there is a difference between the involuntary impulses of the flesh and Jesus's ability to overcome those impulses.

Indeed, Jesus's triumph over the bodily emotions was evidence of the Word's divinizing power over the body. Although the Word, being impassible, did not suffer, Athanasius explains, these sufferings of the body were "done as from a man, that he might himself lighten these very sufferings of the flesh and free it [i.e., the body] from them" (*C. Ar.* 3.56). Commenting specifically on Jesus's prayer in the garden, Athanasius says that, although "the terror belonged to the flesh," Jesus's will was ultimately consistent with the Father's purpose in sending him. The power of the impassible Word enabled him to conquer the passions of his bodily nature: "For the sake of this flesh he combined his own will with human weakness, that destroying this affection he might in turn make man undaunted in the face of death" (*C. Ar.* 3.57). Jesus's triumph over this most basic of passions demonstrated the Word's divinizing power that was available to strengthen those who, by union with Christ, would themselves be empowered to resist the temptations of the flesh. Pointing to the example of the martyrs, Athanasius concluded, "Godhead was not in terror, but the Savior took away our terror. For as he abolished death by [his] death, and by human means [abolished] all human evils, so by this so-called terror did he remove our terror" (*C. Ar.* 3.57). Athanasius's Christology was less concerned about the Word's emotional experience than it was with the incarnate Word's display of a power capable of healing humanity's bodily weakness.

The second question for Athanasius's interpreters, especially when he is read through the retrospective lens of the Apollinarian controversy, is whether Athanasius's Christ had a human soul or mind. The question arises from the paucity of references in Athanasius to Jesus's human soul. Although, following the language of John's prologue, Athanasius primarily speaks of the Word's "flesh" (*sarx*) or "body" (*sōma*), he occasionally pairs "flesh" with "man" (*anthrōpos*), which suggests that "flesh" is synonymous with "humanity" or "human nature" (*C. Ar.* 3.55).

The closest thing to explicit evidence of his belief in Jesus's human soul appears in the *Tome to the Antiochenes* produced by a synod at Alexandria presided over by Athanasius in 362. Contrasting their view of the incarnation with an Adoptionist Christology, the *Tome*, likely authored by Athanasius, blended the language of John's prologue and the Christ hymn from Philippians: "the Word himself was made flesh, being in the form of God, took the form of a servant and from Mary after the flesh became man for us." Then the *Tome* goes on to qualify what sort of man the Word became. "The Savior did not have a body without a soul [*apsychon*] or without sensation [*anaisthēton*] or without reason [*anoēton*]. For it was not possible, when the Lord has become man for us, that his body should have been without reason, nor was the salvation effected in the Word himself a salvation of body only, but of the soul also" (*Tom.* 7). It is possible to read the *Tome* as simply affirming that the Logos, who is life and reason, is the source of both in Jesus's body. In the context, however, of describing the nature of Jesus's body, it would not have been necessary to explain that his body was not lifeless (a possible translation of *apsychon*)—as if the Word inhabited a lifeless corpse. Therefore, the clearest sense is that Jesus had a soul and with it the faculties of both the senses and the intellect. Moreover, the passage assumes there is a connection between the Word's body and the salvation of soul and body. The Word's divinizing effect on Jesus's humanity is paradigmatic for thinking of the Word's divinization of the soul and body of Jesus's followers.

Even so, the passage is open to conflicting interpretations. What is clear about Athanasius's Christology—a point that will become a point of critique by the Antiochenes—is that Jesus's soul, if he has one, contributes very little in Athanasius's salvation narrative. He was unconcerned with Jesus's human agency. Rather, his focus was on the Word's control and divinization of Jesus's human elements. It is the activity of the Logos, not a human soul, that is of theological consequence. For though essential for redemption, Jesus's humanity is almost entirely passive, existing in submission to the dominion of the Word. If Jesus had a soul, then, as Aloys Grillmeier puts it, "The brighter light of the Logos swallows up any created light [of the human soul]."[2] Sure evidence of this is that Athanasius clearly does not see fit to give a more developed account of the relationship between the Logos and a rational soul. Athanasius bequeathed this christological lacuna to his theological heirs, in particular Apollinaris.

Apollinaris's significance in the development of Christology is that he was the first to work out the logic of Athanasius's single-subject Christology. As with Athanasius's Christology, Jesus for Apollinaris is the impassible divine Logos united with a passible and mortal body (frag. 6). By this union, Jesus's body is purified through the *communicatio idiomatum* and so divinized that it is freed from the passions and mortality of fallen humanity. The Word takes on the human condition, conquering the passions and death, rendering his body as the temple in which the divine Logos dwells.

Noticeably absent from Apollinaris's account of the incarnation is a reference to a rational, human soul or mind. The Logos, for Apollinaris, served as the rational soul or *hēgemonikon* that is the source of all of Jesus's higher cognitive functions, for example, thought and speech, but also governed the nonrational soul animating Jesus's body. In this way, Apollinaris was able to explain Athanasius's account of the restorative revelation of the incarnation. Jesus's body governed by the Logos becomes the outward and visible form in which the invisible divinity of the Logos is revealed. And through it, believers were able to recover the image of God through the contemplation of the incarnate Word. As central as John 1:14 was for Apollinaris's Christology, so too was the Pauline motif of Christ as the second Adam (Rom 5:14; 1 Cor 15:45) that was so central to Irenaeus's Christol-

2. Aloys Grillmeier, *Christ in Christian Tradition*, vols. 1–2, parts 1–2, trans. Pauline Allen and John Cawte (Atlanta: John Knox, 1986), 1:325.

ogy. Jesus is the race of Adam refashioned perfectly, embodying the image and likeness of God. Therefore, Apollinaris drew on Paul's contrast between the first and second Adam in 1 Cor 15:45–47 to illustrate both the uniqueness of Jesus, in contrast with the prophets who went before, and the new humanity inaugurated by the incarnation. Here Paul contrasts the first Adam, who was "a living being" and "a man of dust" taken from the earth, with Jesus the "last Adam," who was "a life-giving spirit" come "from heaven." Apollinaris interpreted this to mean that the first Adam as a "living being" was a material creature ("from earth") animated by a rational soul, whereas Jesus the man from heaven possessed a "life-giving spirit," which he interpreted to refer to the higher or rational soul, in contrast with the nonrational or sentient soul (*Apod.* 26–29). Drawing together the prologue of John with 1 Cor 15, Apollinaris concludes that the Word is the "life-giving spirit" of the "man from heaven." "So Christ, having God as his spirit [*pneuma*]—that is his intellect [*ton noun*]—together with [a sentient] soul and body, is rightly called the 'man from heaven'" (*Apod.* 25). In other words, whereas the first Adam derived his rational soul from earth, the second Adam is the man from heaven because his rational soul was the divine Logos that governed the nonrational or sentient soul that animated the body. This distinction between the man from earth and the man from heaven allows him to draw a line between the old humanity that traces its origins to the first Adam and the new, divinized humanity inaugurated with the coming of the "man from heaven." Thus, although the first and last Adams share a common human form, their natures are different. "If Christ's nature is the same as ours, then he is the old man, a living being (soul) and not a life-giving spirit, and as such he will not give life. But Christ does give life and is a life-giving spirit. Thus, he is not of our nature" (*Anakeph.* 23). Thus, Christians, through their union with Christ, become partakers of the new nature of the "man from heaven" by receiving a share in his life-giving spirit. Unfortunately, Apollinaris's description of Christ's different nature as the "man from heaven" led critics, such as Gregory of Nazianzus, erroneously to attribute to him the view that Christ's flesh was not taken from Mary but belonged to him from eternity as Son of God (*Ep.* 102.2–4).

The chief reason guiding Apollinaris's Christology was his insistence on the absolute oneness of Christ. Jesus is a single person composed of Logos and flesh. Because the Logos is the sole governing principle or agent acting through Jesus's body, Jesus is neither divided nor conflicted; on the contrary, he possesses a single personality (*prosōpon*) that reflects the perfect harmony of the body with the Logos that exerted absolute power over it. By contrast, were Jesus to have a human soul, there would be two animating and governing principles, the Logos and a rational human soul. Jesus would have two, potentially conflicting personalities. Thus, interpreters of the Gospel narratives would have to discern which personality was active in any given episode. Moreover, since the soul was, as Aristotle had taught, the form of the body giving it the powers distinctive of a given nature, then a Jesus with a human soul as well as the Logos would have not one nature but two. On the contrary, Jesus, for Apollinaris, had a single nature or *mia physis* (*Ep. Dion.* 1.1–9). The Logos had knit the human body into single, perfect unity with itself through a special activity proper to the Logos's divinity. He goes so far as to say that Jesus is consubstantial with the Father through the Word and consubstantial with Adam's race through his human body (*Un. corp.* 8).

The presence of a human soul, for Apollinaris, would have contributed nothing helpful to the incarnation. For as is painfully obvious from the annals of human history, the rational, human soul had no power to control the body and rightly order it in obedience to God. On the contrary, the soul was itself overpowered by bodily passions; therefore, the soul could not function as a sanctifying governing principle. It could not purify the body of the passions. Only the Logos, which was not susceptible to the passions, could purify the body of the irrational and unholy desires and impulses that prevented perfect obedience to God's will. Christ's righteousness was not the product of human free choice—since man's free choice never made man righteous—but of the righteousness proper to the divine nature. This was the distinctive advantage Jesus enjoyed. He was able to prevail over the passions because his body is God's flesh. From the impassibility imparted to Jesus's body by the Word, this impassibility communicated to those who participate in Christ's body. Since through baptism the Christian is united to Christ as a member of his body and sanctified through feeding on Christ's flesh, his purified and divinized body is able to impart to the Christian the beginnings of that impassible divinity characteristic of the perfected body of the resurrection.

In addition to questions about the weakness of the rational soul, Apollinaris was also insistent on the uniqueness of Jesus. Were Jesus to have a human soul, then he would be a man, and the body would belong to that man. As such, it could not be worshiped; for the worship of a man's body would be idolatry. Since Jesus's body is God's body taken up into the Godhead, it is made divine and so is legitimately the object of worship. Making Jesus a man by attributing to him a human soul would have stripped Christ of the dignity that rightly belongs to the Logos. For a man, as a creature, is a slave to God. But Christ as the divine Logos, who is *homoousios* with the Father, is God; therefore, Jesus is rightly worshiped as Lord and God.

Furthermore, to attribute to Jesus a human soul skirted the threshold of Adoptionism. Were Jesus a human being having a human soul with his own will, he would be distinct from other people only in that God had united himself to Jesus and inspired him to speak his word. This was the Jesus preached by Paul of Samosata. Only the incarnate Word—without a human soul—was truly God in the flesh, truly unique, unlike Moses or any of the prophets whom the Word had only inspired and made his mouthpiece.

The Cappadocian Break with Apollinaris

Although Basil and Apollinaris had been allies of sorts in the pro-Nicene cause, a rupture in their relationship arose around 372 when an anonymous letter, likely circulated by Eustathius's camp, cast doubt on Basil's orthodoxy because of his connection with Apollinaris, which Eustathius and his allies saw as another form of Sabellianism. Only a few years earlier, Eunomius in his *Apology for the Apology* written in 370 attacked the partitive exegesis that Basil employed to refute Eunomius's subordinationist reading of Scripture. The result of Basil's distinguishing biblical descriptions of Jesus's divine attributes from his creaturely attributes led, Eunomius asserted, to Basil's division of Jesus into two Christs (Gregory, *Eun.* 5.2). Thus, Basil allegedly subscribed to a two-subjects Christology: a divine subject, the Word who was impassible, and a human subject, who did suffer and die. Such a view was anathema to Apollinaris. Consequently, Basil had to defend himself against charges of endorsing diametrically opposite Christologies: on the one hand, a single-subject Christology that did not protect the transcendence of the Word and, on the other hand, a two-subjects Christology that placed Jesus on the same plain as the prophets. Answering Eunomius's accusation fell to Gregory almost a decade later. Basil, however, rebutted the innuendo of the anonymous letter in a letter-writing campaign of his own in 377. Here Basil's goal was to separate himself from Apollinaris's several theological errors. Of these, two were christological. First, by denying that Jesus had a rational soul, Basil argued, the incarnation, according to the logic of Apollinaris's view, did not entail the true assumption of a human nature by the Word. Second, without a soul to experience Jesus's passions, the Logos would have been the seat of passion and thereby introduced change into the divine nature (*Ep.* 261.3; 262.1–2).

The initial condemnation of Apollinaris came in 377 at a synod in Rome convened at the behest of Basil to address the problem of heresies among the pro-Nicenes. The synod produced a letter authored by Pope Damasus condemning the views attributed to Apollinaris. Four years later, the Council of Constantinople included Apollinaris's Christology among the heresies condemned. However, as we have already seen with the lingering Homoian presence in the West after 381, formal conciliar condemnation did not automatically purge the church of the condemned views. The next year, Ambrose (*Ep.* 14) appealed to the emperor Theodosius to depose Apollinaris from his episcopal see. Apollinaris's support among key voices in the imperial court, however, was too strong. Therefore, his sustained influence was the lingering source of dispute that required more systematic refutation. This was to come from the Cappadocians.

After Gregory of Nazianzus left the Council of Constantinople, he withdrew from pastoral duties to allow his health to recover from recent illness. In his absence, the priest Cledonius assumed his pastoral and administrative duties. However, allies of Apollinaris used the bishop's absence to undermine Gregory's authority. Appraised of the situation by Cledonius, Gregory wrote a systematic refutation of Apollinaris's *Apodeixis*. Responding to the accusation that he preached "two sons," Gregory unequivocally affirmed that the Son of God was one entity worshiped "in undivided Godhead and honor" (*Ep.* 102.2). He illustrated the point by contrasting the Trinity with Jesus. Whereas the Trinity is not three in nature but three persons having one nature, the incarnate Christ is two natures but not two sons. The two natures are "one by coalescence, God being in-manned and man being deified" (*Ep.* 101.5). Apollinaris himself recognizes this distinction in his use of Gregory's own principle of partitive exegesis, which distinguishes between the two aspects of Jesus: on the one hand, his passion, death, and burial belonging to "his outer covering" and, on the other hand, the resurrection and ascension that were the result of "his inner treasure" (*Ep.* 102.8). Rather, Apollinaris's christological error of denying Jesus's rational soul was the result of an exegetical error. Namely, he construed John 1:14, "the Word became *flesh*," narrowly. Instead of equating "flesh" with the body, Apollinaris should, Gregory argues, have seen it as an instance of synecdoche in which a part is used to refer to the whole, as, for instance, when the psalmist similarly uses "all flesh"—"Let all flesh bless his holy name" (Ps 66:4)—to mean "all people" or "all creatures" (*Ep.* 101.11).

Gregory's primary objection, however, was what he took to be a serious flaw in Apollinaris's anthropology and his soteriology. He famously summed up his objection with what in time would be a christological maxim: "That which the Word did not assume he did not redeem, but what is united to God is also being saved" (*Ep.* 101.5). The fiery purity of the Word's divinity, like a glowing ember thrust into the hay, burns away the impurities of that to which it is joined. Since the first Adam fell, not in part but in his whole being, body and soul, then the second Adam must have both body and soul, if the whole of the new humanity was to be purified and divinized. Indeed, since human beings are distinguished from nonrational animals by the presence of a rational soul, if Jesus had only a nonrational, sentient soul and body, Gregory quips, then there would have been little difference between Jesus and a cow or horse (*Ep.* 101.5). One of the central points of disagreement concerned the source of sin. Apollinaris saw the body with its sentient passions, which the rational soul could not control, as the source of sin as well as that which experienced sin's corrupting consequence, death. By contrast, Gregory viewed the mind, not the body, as the source of sin; the body was dragged down by the disordered intellect. Precisely because the intellect was the higher nature intended to rule the lower, bodily nature and order it to the will of God, the act of disobedience lay in the will. So Gregory concludes, "The very thing [i.e., the mind] that transgressed stood in special need of salvation, [therefore] the very thing that needed salvation was assumed" (*Ep.* 101.9). The mind is redeemed because in Jesus the rational nature fulfills its end as God's instrument to rule and order the body. In Jesus, the Logos so dominates the mind that it is entirely conformed to and so absolutely submits to God's will. As the stars remain in their place in the day as in the night but cannot be seen in the day because their lesser light is swallowed up in the infinitely greater light of the sun, Christ's mind, though present, is overpowered by the infinitely greater light of the Word so that it is the Word that is seen in Jesus's words and actions (*Ep.* 101.7).

The mind of Jesus does serve one important function for the incarnation. It is the medium that bridges the divide between the Word's divine nature and Jesus's bodily nature (*Ep.* 101.8). Gregory's logic seems to be that, since the rational soul is simple and immaterial, even as the Logos is, then the Word, by virtue of their similar natures, is able to be united with mind and through the mind to the body. And through its divinization of his mind, the Logos was able to divinize Jesus's body.

Gregory of Nyssa, writing in the mid-380s, shared both Nazianzen's anthropological and soteriological critique of Apollinaris. His *Refutation of Apollinaris* and *Epistle to Theophilus* offered a defense of Diodore of Tarsus who assumed leadership of the pro-Nicene coalition after the death of Meletius (381). The result was a Christology that appears confused, if not outright contradictory, because of Gregory's insistence on both making a sharp distinction between Jesus's humanity and divinity and insisting on the divinizing unity of the two.

Like Nazianzen, Nyssen stresses the mediatorial role of the rational soul in the incarnation. Because the Word and the man are ontologically different, the Word cannot take the place of the human soul. Or if it had, it would have undergone an ontological change (*Antirrh.* 29; p. 250). Such change would have been unavoidable in Apollinaris's scheme. If the Word were the rational soul of Jesus's flesh, then by virtue of its union with the body, the Word would have experienced what the rational soul does as a result of its participation in the creaturely nature of the body: growth, ignorance, hunger, thirst, the pain of crucifixion, and death (*Antirrh.* 15; pp. 149–50). Rather, because Jesus's rational soul is the medium between the Word and the body, the rational soul acts as a kind of buffer between the two. Jesus's mind, not the Word, is the locus of Jesus's creaturely frailties and passions. Moreover, the presence of Jesus's mind alongside the Logos explains the presence of two wills in Jesus. Commenting on Jesus's prayer to the Father in Gethsemane, "Not my will but yours be done" (Matt 26:42), Gregory rhetorically asks, Who is praying: a man or God? Were it the divine Word, as Apollinaris's Christology necessitates, then the weakness belongs to the Word whose will diverges from that of his Father. Such would be absurd for a true defender of Nicaea, as Apollinaris claimed to be. To make his point, Gregory further asks, "How could God not have what is good within himself, but have to seek help from above? And how could God reproach his own will? Is what he wished for good or evil? If good, then why was what he wished for not fulfilled?" (*Antirrh.* 19; p. 171). The only solution is to recognize the prayer as an expression of Jesus's human will motivated by a natural fear of suffering and death. "Since in Christ the human intention is one thing and the divine another, he who speaks first does so as a human, saying what is appropriate to the weakness of human nature . . . then adds further words because, for the sake of the salvation of humankind, he wishes that sublime will . . . to be fulfilled rather than his human will" (*Antirrh.* 19; p. 172). This distinction between the human and the divine allows Gregory to preserve the transcendent immutability of the Word. Thus, although Gregory rejects the charge of holding that "it is the man who suffers, not the God," he says that Christ as the divine Word does not suffer on the cross but is "present in" the one who suffers (*Antirrh.* 28; p. 243). He explains this account of Christ's passion by making an analogy to other less controversial moments of the incarnation. Jesus as a human being was both born and resurrected; his eternal and immortal divinity needed neither. Nevertheless, by virtue of the union of the divinity and humanity in Mary's womb, the Word was present in the infant Jesus at his birth and in the crucified Jesus at his resurrection. It should not, therefore, seem strange then to say that the Word was present but was neither changed nor killed on the cross (*Antirrh.* 28; p. 245). Such a move sounded—and indeed today on this side of the christological controversy sounds—like the proto-Nestorianism or dyophysitism of Diodore of Tarsus.

To defend Christians against pagan accusations of worshiping a divine weakling who died on a cross, Diodore separated Christ's divinity from his humanity. Son of God and Son of Man both name the same person but are themselves not the same. The "only begotten" Son of God is divine and therefore not, properly speaking, born—in contrast with the Son of Man who was "firstborn" according to the flesh (*Comm. Ps.*; p. 354). Drawing on the soul-body analogy, Diodore argued that as the soul remains immortal while it endures the death of the mortal flesh, so too Jesus's flesh was mortal, but in his divinity, he retained his immortal nature. Therefore, technically only Jesus's flesh died (frag. 2 and 17; p. 356).

At the same time that Gregory, out of theological commitments, employed partitive exegesis to preserve Christ's impassible and immortal divinity, at other times, out of soteriological commitments, he championed a robustly—almost protomiaphysite—Christology that affirmed the oneness of Christ. Gregory offers a more developed account of the anthropology foundational to Nazianzen's claim that the locus of sin is the mind and not the body. Since the mind in its rational nature bears the image of the supremely rational and self-governing God, the mind is the locus of the "autocratic will" that makes human beings moral agents and therefore capable of sin (*Hom. opif.* 4). Unlike nonrational creatures driven only by instinctive responses to sensual goods, the intellect that alone apprehends the divine goods can choose to obey or disobey divine precepts. Therefore, the rational soul, and not just the body, requires healing through union with the Word. Since the intellect is able to direct the body in virtuous action because it is steered by God (*Antirrh.* 23; p. 200), the intellect, in order to participate in the glory proper to divine virtue, must be steered by the incarnate Word (*Antirrh.* 14; p. 144). Indeed, without a rational soul, the incarnation is not a full union of humanity and divinity. By Apollinaris's logic, what was produced in Mary's womb was not a human being but a hybrid creature, like the Minotaur, which was only part man and part something else (*Antirrh.* 25; pp. 229–30). By substituting the Logos for the rational soul of Jesus, Apollinaris rendered Jesus either subhuman because he lacked a human soul or suprahuman because his immortal nature was something greater than that of human beings. The alternative to this grotesque fusion of the Word with a human body was, for both Gregories, a true, organic mixture of divinity and the rational intellect. Only through a thorough integration of divine Word and intellect could the full purpose of the incarnation be realized in Jesus.

For Jesus does not merely possess the pure humanity of the first Adam before sin; he is the second Adam who by his death and resurrection is the "firstborn of the new creation." Thus, in Christ is divinized and perfected humanity revealed. Such perfection is not confined, as in Apollinaris's Christology, to the conferral of immortality and incorruptibility on the mortal and corruptible flesh. For Gregory, Christ's human nature—mind and body—is radically transformed by its union with the divine. Gregory writes, "[Christ] accepted being mixed [*epimixian*] with the lowliness of our nature; he took the man into himself and became himself within the man . . . [saying] 'I am in you and you in me,' that is, he made him [i.e., humanity] with whom he was mixed [*ton anakrathenta*] into what he was himself [i.e., divinity]" (*Antirrh.* 28; p. 241). Gregory's language of mixture has certain affinities with Stoic theories of mixture in which two substances are combined and formed into a new substance, yet with each retaining its distinctive properties. Yet, as Brian Daley has demonstrated, Gregory's view of mixture was decidedly different; for, in the mixture of the incarnation, the divinity and humanity do not coexist side by side. Rather, in the *communicatio idiomatum* that results from their union, the humanity so thoroughly participates in the Word's divinity that its creaturely attributes are replaced with divine properties. Juxtaposing Paul's declaration that Christ "became sin" (2 Cor 5:21) and a curse (Gal 3:13) with his earlier claim that in Christ what was mortal was "swallowed up by life" (2 Cor 5:4), Gregory concludes paradoxically that "[although] the human nature which was united to the Word was preserved . . . everything in our nature that is weak and mortal, having been mixed [*anakrathen*] with the Godhead, became that which the Godhead is" (*Theoph.*; Orton, 265–66). His most dramatic metaphor for the divinization of Christ's humanity is that of a bit of vinegar dropped into the vast ocean. Although the drop of vinegar becomes truly mixed with the sea water, the ocean completely subsumes the vinegar within its vastness even as the infinite divinity of the Word overpowers the bitterness of corruptible, mortal humanity (*Theoph.*; Orton, 266). As we shall see in later chapters, Gregory takes the full divinization of Christ's humanity revealed at his resurrection as paradigmatic for his theories regarding the salvation of our soul and body. For though ever remaining creatures, the saints' mortality, too, shall be swallowed up in divinity.

Gregory's christological concern for Jesus's rational soul and his soteriological concern for Christ's divinization of humanity through the Word's assumption of the whole person come together in his analysis of the biblical metaphor of Christ as the good shepherd (John 10:7–18) read alongside Jesus's parable of the lost sheep (Luke 15:3–7). Adam's race is the lost sheep that Christ, the pioneer of our salvation, rescues by raising up the whole sheep and carrying it upon his shoulders, that is, assuming the whole of our human nature. By contrast, Apollinaris's Christ did not rescue the whole sheep, Gregory scoffs, only its hide, leaving its entrails back in the wilderness. Then Gregory in an imaginative interpretation of the two parables says that Christ the good shepherd, in bearing the lost lamb upon his shoulders, became one with the sheep he carried. The shepherd himself becomes a sheep. Therefore, the sheep are able to recognize the voice of the shepherd: for the shepherd's voice has become that of a fellow sheep. "How," Gregory asks, "could our human weakness be adequate to comprehend an address by the divine voice? He speaks to us in a human way, that is, . . . in a sheep-like way" (*Antirrh.* 11; pp. 126–27). Thus, Christ is simultaneously the sheep and shepherd. As the sheep is carried on the shepherd's shoulders rather than walking under its own power, Jesus's humanity is moved back to the heavenly sheepfold not by its own strength but through the unseen footsteps (Ps 77:19) of the Word, not merely concealed in sheep's clothing but indwelling the whole sheep. Moreover, because the Word assumed a fully human nature, he is the good shepherd who "lays down his soul" for his sheep (John 10:17). Thus, Gregory concludes, "the author of our salvation becomes, in his human nature, both priest and lamb; he is able to share in suffering, and so also is able to incur death" (*Antirrh.* 11; p. 127). Gregory uses the good shepherd motif to express both his unitive Christology in which the Word is the single, unseen subject of Jesus's deeds as well as a proto–two natures Christology, like Diodore's, that allows him to articulate the paradox that the good shepherd is the priest who offers the sacrifice of himself as the lamb of God who takes away the sins of the world.

Gregory's response to Apollinaris generally and his specific reply to the charge of subscribing to two Christs reflects an early, clumsy attempt to affirm a unitive Christology that nonetheless preserves both the transcendence of the Word and creaturely attributes of Jesus's humanity. Gregory was clear what should not be said of Christ, in particular the problems intrinsic to Apollinaris's man-from-heaven Christology. Yet he fumbled when seeking an alternative description. Nevertheless, in his groping for the right language, one sees an emerging Christology that, though immature, possesses a coherence discernable in the light of Gregory's soteriology.

Antioch and Alexandria: Mary the God-Bearer and Clashing Christologies

The late fourth and first half of the fifth century witnessed an intensification of Christian veneration of Mary, the Mother of Jesus. Mary's place in salvation history had been highlighted, as we have already seen, by early theologians like Irenaeus who depicted her as the second Eve. Mary's belief in God's promise and her obedience that brought forth the Savior of the world were a recapitulation of the failure of the first Eve, whose lack of faith and disobedience brought death. Earlier in the mid-second century, the Gospel of James narrated the miraculous conception of Mary and her life of holy virginity. Though never canonized, this protogospel was widely translated and read. Mary's status became even more exalted two centuries later, when Ambrose articulated the doctrine of Mary's perpetual virginity and so lifted her up as the prototype for female monastics. Mary's developing status found its expression in new artistic representations. Before the fifth century, early Christian art depicted Mary in scenes from the biblical narrative. There she was not the central figure but only one actor in the biblical drama. In the fifth century, however, Mary became the centerpiece of images; she is the one on whom the viewer's eye focuses. Even as Christ the Pantokrator was depicted as enthroned in heaven ruling the cosmos, now Mary, too, was portrayed seated—enthroned (?)—holding the Christ Child on her lap. And the appellation *Theotokos*, or "God-bearer," became a common title for Mary. In the fourth century, the emperor Julian (331–363) complained that Christians "never stopped calling Mary *Theotokos*" (*Jul.* 8). Gregory of Nazianzus in his first letter to Cledonius virtually anathematizes anyone who does not recognize Mary to be *Theotokos* (*Ep.* 101.5). In Ephesus, which had once been the cultic center for the worship of the virgin goddess Artemis, Mary had replaced Artemis as the city's patroness. In Constantinople, the patriarch Atticus (406–425) promoted Marian devotion, especially among noble women in the imperial family, presenting her as an exemplar of faith after whom such noble women might model their lives. Among the Virgin's vociferous champions in Constantinople was the presbyter Proclus, who several times had been an unsuccessful candidate for the patriarchate, eventually being elected bishop of Cyzicus in 426, but who remained a prominent voice in the capital.

Against this backdrop of Marian devotion arose a controversy in Constantinople that challenged the Church, East and West, to address not only how it thought about Mary but how it should think of the union of the divinity and the humanity of Jesus. The Christian community in the Eastern capital was rife with division when in 428 the patriarch Sisinnius died and left the see open. Perhaps to avoid controversy by seeming to take sides among the ecclesial factions within the city, Emperor Theodosius II, who was then only fourteen, appointed a Syrian monk named Nestorius, who was renowned for his excellent oratory. Upon his consecration in April of 428, Nestorius immediately set about trying to promote unity. His first move was to order the monks, who had proven themselves a meddling nuisance in extraecclesial affairs, back into their monasteries. Consequently, instead of promoting unity under the patriarch's authority, Nestorius had earned the enmity of one of the powerful ecclesial factions within Constantinople. He also sought unity through a purge of factions that promoted what he deemed to be heretical doctrine that contributed to the division within the Christian community. He did this not only through antiheretical legislation but by promulgating a theology strongly informed by the teachings of the Antiochene luminaries, Diodore of Tarsus and Theodore of Mopsuestia.

Pushback against Nestorius's theological agenda came from leaders of the monastic faction who, perhaps wanting to bait Nestorius into a public controversy, asked for his position on the attribution of the title *Theotokos* to Mary. Nestorius foolishly took the bait. His chaplain, Anastasius, replied that, since the Logos was eternal and unbegotten by the Father, Jesus's divinity was derived from the Father, not Mary. Therefore, Mary could not be the mother of God; rather, she was the mother of Jesus's manhood. Consequently, she should be called *Anthrōpotokos*, or "Man-bearer." If the monks had hoped their question would stir up a hornets' nest in the capital, they succeeded beyond their least charitable imaginings. For the denial of the title *Theotokos* was instantly interpreted as a denial of the divinity of Christ. Nestorius tried to do damage control by arguing that both *Theotokos* and *Anthrōpotokos* were problematic because each was likely to provoke misinterpretation. *Theotokos* might be construed as either an attack upon God's transcendence—as Anastasius declared, "it is impossible for God to be born of a woman" (Socrates Scholasticus, *Hist. eccl.* 7.32)—or a denial of Jesus's humanity, while *Anthrōpotokos* might be taken to reduce Jesus to a mere man. The compromise alternative Nestorius offered was *Christotokos*. For Mary was neither the cause of God's existence nor the mother of a mere man. She was the mother of the Christ. As Brian Daley has observed, Nestorius's chief aim, like that of his Antiochene predecessors, was to speak with philosophical precision and avoid the imprecision they associated with the Alexandrian tradition, which was more concerned with being faithful to the language of the biblical narrative. The classic example of such problematic imprecision was Apollinaris's use of the appellation for Jesus, "Man from heaven" (1 Cor 15:47), which was open to the misinterpretation that Jesus's flesh descended with the Logos from heaven. However, *Christotokos,* rather than being seen as a more precise term for Mary, was seen to diminish the significance of Mary and of Jesus. Yes, she was the mother of the Christ, the Christ-bearer. But that title missed the greater significance of Mary as the one who bore the incarnate Word of God in her womb. The failure to recognize this significance was seen as demeaning to Mary. To call her merely Christ-bearer devalued her place in salvation history and as such was seen as an act of impiety. Nestorius, in his sincere desire for theological clarity, had failed to recognize the piety that was expressed by *Theotokos* and how pervasive this piety was in Constantinople. He had made the grave pastoral error of misunderstanding the sacred meaning that certain words had for his people. To step on them was to step upon the religious devotion on which his people, laity and clergy alike, staked their eternal salvation.

The controversy escalated when on the Sunday before Christmas 428, Proclus in the presence of the patriarch delivered a homily defending the practice of calling the Virgin Mary "Mother of God." Nestorius stood up to offer an immediate rebuttal, which was followed by a series of sermons defending Anastasius's rejection of *Theotokos*. In his first homily against *Theotokos,* he quoted Hebrews' description of Christ, "a high priest forever after the order of Melchizedek," as being "without father or mother or genealogy, and has neither beginning of his days nor of his life" (7:3). This, Nestorius declared, refers to Christ's divinity. One must conclude, therefore, that "a creature did not produce the Creator, rather [Mary] gave birth to the human being, the instrument of the Godhead" (*Hom.* 1; Norris, 124). She is the mother of the temple. Nestorius's homily then shifted from a discussion of Mary to a distinction between the divine Creator and the Creator's creaturely instrument. He affirmed the unity of Christ, stating that "Christ" applies to the two natures, both the form of God and the form of a servant. At times, however, his language separated Christ from his human instrument—as, for instance, when he said, "Christ assumed the person of the debt-ridden nature and by its mediation paid the debt back as a Son of Adam.... He assumed a person of the same nature [as ours] whose passions were removed by his passion" (*Hom.* 1; Norris, 126–27). The passion that liberated humanity from the passions, however, belonged to the instrument, not the Logos; for the incarnate God did not die but "raised up the one in whom he was incarnate" (*Hom.* 1; Norris, 125). Jesus's words, "Destroy this temple and in three days I will raise it up" (John 2:19), denote two natures: that fleshly nature of his temple, which was capable of destruction, and the indestructible divine nature that could raise the body from death (*Hom.* 1; Norris, 129). This distinction between the incarnate Logos and "the one in whom he was incarnate" sounds like Nestorius was speaking of two persons rather than one. In his effort to preserve the line between the Creator and the creature in the incarnation, Nestorius's language seems to distance the Logos from certain moments of the gospel narrative; since "that which was formed in the womb [was] not in itself God . . . [nor was] that which was buried in the tomb God" (*Hom.* 1; Norris, 130).

Nestorius's virtual anathematization of *Theotokos* was the flash point for a controversy that quickly reached beyond the question of which reverential title is most appropriate for the Virgin. This is not to diminish the significance of Mary or her place in fifth-century piety. Rather, it is to state the simple fact that the focus of debate shifts from Mary to the christological claims that were the foundation of Marian devotion. In other words, how one thinks about Mary is informed by how one thinks about the child conceived in her womb. Is Mary like Hannah, the mother of a holy prophet? Or is Mary sui generis among women because her child is unique among human beings? Fueling this debate was Nestorius's promulgation of Antiochene theology. While, as Aloys Grillmeier has made clear, there was sufficient difference of opinion among the so-called Antiochenes that it would be hard to think of them as a "school," if there was a common dimension in their identity—other than geography—it was their antipathy to two distinguishing features of Alexandrian theology: allegory and their divinization soteriology. The latter informed the eucharistic piety and Christology of Alexandrians such as Origen, Athanasius, and Apollinaris. Although Apollinaris's denial of Jesus's human soul had already been thoroughly repudiated, the suspicion lingered among critics that his Christology was merely the logical conclusion of the Alexandrian Word-flesh Christology, which, they believed, blurred the line between Creator and creatures. Therefore, in order to understand Nestorius's attack on *Theotokos* and the subsequent reaction of his archnemesis, Cyril of Alexandria, we need to examine the Antiochene roots of Nestorius's Christology.

Classic Antiochene Christology: Diodore of Tarsus and Theodore of Mopsuestia

The Christology of Diodore (d. 394) emerged as a reaction to the thought of two drastically different figures: Apollinaris and the emperor Julian. In the case of Apollinaris, Diodore was concerned that his description of Jesus as "the man from heaven" treated Jesus as a united organism that did not sufficiently distinguish between the divine Logos and the creaturely flesh. At the same time, Diodore wanted to counter those who denied the divinity of Christ, especially Homoians and pagan critics like Julian. The emperor sojourned in Antioch between 362 and 363, during which time he composed his anti-Christian polemic, *Against the Galileans*. The expressed purpose of the work was to expose Jesus, whom he called "that new-fangled Galilean god," as a small-time miracle worker and thus strip him of "the divinity falsely ascribed to him" (*Ep.* 55). While one would have expected a disciple of Neo-Platonism like Julian to have made the stock criticism that the crucified Jesus did not possess attributes proper to the divine nature (e.g., simplicity, immutability, impassibility), he does not offer a methodical, philosophical critique like that leveled in Porphyry's *Against the Christians*. Julian, however, is offended by Christian practice of "worshipping wretched men," who have imitated Jesus's death. Speaking of the cult of the martyrs, Julian complains, "You are adding more corpses to the corpse [i.e., Jesus] of the past." Since tombs are places of pollution (*akatharsia*), "How," he asked, "is it that you invoke God at them?" (*Gal.* 335b–d). The thought of associating immortal deity with death is clearly repugnant to Julian.

Diodore's agenda, therefore, was to defend the divinity of Christ against either those who said that an incarnation would be demeaning to God or those who said Jesus's birth and passion revealed that he was no God but simply a man. His strategy was to draw a clear line distinguishing Jesus's divinity from his humanity. Therefore, when he commented on Luke's description that the boy Jesus "grew in wisdom and in stature and in favor with God and men" (Luke 2:52), Diodore followed the basic principle of Gregory of Nazianzus's partitive exegesis; he attributed the growth to Jesus's humanity, not his divinity. Unlike the Word that is eternal, the humanity was a created thing that required time to grow and mature. Therefore, Diodore concludes, "the Godhead did not immediately impart to it all wisdom, but bestowed it upon the body in portions" (frag. 36). Similarly, suffering and death could not be ascribed to the immortal and impassible Word but to the mortal and passible flesh (frag. 17). What was for Nazianzen a mere conceptual distinction between divinity and humanity became in Diodore something bordering on a separation. He rejected speaking of Christ as a single hypostasis, because to hold that the Word and the man existed in an essential unity risked the passing of creaturely attributes to the Word. Therefore, he preferred describing the incarnation as the Word's indwelling the man Jesus, as a deity indwells a temple (frag. 1). This metaphor suited Diodore's concern. For the god is truly present in the temple but is not physically attached to the temple structure itself; therefore, the temple can be destroyed, but the indwelling deity remains unaffected. By this separation of God from temple, Word from man, Diodore was able to counter Julian's objections by attributing the suffering, which Julian found demeaning to God, to Jesus's mortal, corporeal nature rather than to the divine Logos who indwelt the human being. Thus, Diodore was willing to forgo a robust sense of unity for the sake of preserving the transcendent immutability of the Word.

If Diodore's exegetical method and his Christology were the seed of Antiochene theology, it fell to his student, Theodore of Mopsuestia, to nurture the seed's growth into a fully developed theological tradition. Becoming bishop of Mopsuestia a decade after the Council of Constantinople in 392, Theodore had almost three decades to refine and systematize Diodore's core ideas before his own death in 428.

Theodore's Christology was driven by a vision of salvation that focused heavily on what Rowan Greer has termed the "two ages": the present age of mutable creation ever in flux and the future age in which creation is renewed and rendered immutable. Jesus is the bridge between the two ages. He is the man of God's choosing who, through the indwelling of the Word, was perfected in his suffering (Heb 2:10–13; *Cat. hom.* 7) so as to pay humanity's debt of sin (*Cat. hom.* 6) and so abolish death itself (*Cat. hom.* 5). By his perfect submission to the Word, Jesus is "the pioneer and perfector of our faith" and the "captain of our salvation" who made a path for his followers through the wilderness of the present age to the immortal life of the age to come (*Dogm. fr.* 10). He is the second Adam. For while the first Adam was the principle (*archē*) of humanity's present existence, Jesus in his resurrection was the principle of the future life in which his followers united to him in baptism share in his resurrection to life eternal. Because his resurrection passes to his followers (*Cat. hom.* 8), baptism, in which believers are raised from the font, is a symbol of the new economy (*Cat. hom.* 6), that is, the reality of the second age where death no longer has dominion. As the firstfruits of the second age, the risen and ascended Christ is *the* model or type of the heavenly citizenship for which believers hope (*Cat. hom.*). Therefore, Theodore stresses that the Christian life in the present age involves a participation in the good things of the second age—that is, abiding in the "light of [God's] countenance" (Ps 4:6)—through the sacraments and by imitating him who is "the pioneer and perfector of our faith" (Heb 12:2).

This focus on Christ as the second Adam who inaugurates the economy of the second age led Theodore to give a more developed account of Jesus's humanity and the cooperative relationship between the divine Word and the man assumed by the Word in the incarnation than one often sees in the Alexandrian and Cappadocian accounts of the incarnation. Indeed, the agency of the man assumed is central even in the beginning, in God's election of Jesus to be the Christ. According to Theodore, God foreknew that the man Jesus would, when offered the special grace of communion with the Word and Holy Spirit, fully receive the grace assenting with all his will to the divine will of the Word. Based on this foreknowledge of Jesus's perfect conformity to God's will, God chose Jesus before the foundation of the world to be the one to whom the Word would be united (*Dogm. fr.* 7).

Theodore speaks of the incarnation as the union of the Word who assumed the man and the man who was assumed by the Word. This language of the "one who assumes" and the "one who is assumed" reflected Theodore's commitment to preserving the distinction between the two natures united in the incarnation. This serves his philosophical and pastoral commitments. Philosophically, Theodore is insistent on the absolute division between the Creator and the creature. The two natures, he insists, are so radically different that they cannot be concomitant in any way (*Cat. hom.* 4). Pastorally, Theodore interprets the New Testament passages where, he claims, the divine and human natures are distinguished in order that his catechumens might see Jesus as one of themselves and themselves as sharers in Jesus's humanity. For example, when he comments on John the Baptist's identification of Jesus as "the lamb of God who takes away the sins of the world" (John 1:29–30), Theodore says that the phrase "lamb of God" denotes Jesus's humanity that he offers up as a sacrifice for the forgiveness of sins. The clause "who takes away the sins of the world" refers to the Word who in his divinity alone has the authority to forgive sins (*Dogm. fr.* 10). Similarly, Theodore reads the Christ hymn of Philippians (2:5–11) in conjunction with the hymn of Colossians (1:15–18). The "only Son" who possesses "the form of God" is sui generis. But he who is "firstborn of all creation" and possesses "the form of a servant" has many brothers and sisters who, because they share his nature, will be reborn through resurrection just as he was (*Cat. hom.* 3). The Word who assumes confers benefits to the man who is assumed. And the man who is assumed is magnified by benefits conferred on him by the Word (*Dogm. fr.* 10). As the assumed man receives the benefits from the Word, so will the brothers and sisters of the assumed man receive similar benefits from the Spirit who unites them to him.

When Theodore describes the union of the Word who assumes and the man who is assumed, he draws on Diodore's metaphor of the temple to speak of it as an indwelling. The Word indwells the man whom he has assumed. His account of this indwelling is clear not to violate the ontological distinction between Creator and creature. Therefore, indwelling cannot be thought of as an indwelling of essence as if the infinite God could be contained or circumscribed within a finite, creaturely body. Nor is the indwelling simply another instance of God's indwelling of creation by his active operation that providentially orders and directs creatures for the fulfillment of his design. It is rather an indwelling "by his good pleasure" (*eudokia*). Rather than being the natural union of Creator and creatures, it is a special union granted to the saints who are zealously dedicated to God. Yet the Word's indwelling of the assumed man is unique. It is not like the Spirit's indwelling of the prophets and apostles. Rather, the Word's indwelling union with the assumed man is "as in a son." That is, the whole of the man is united to the Word such that the man shares *by grace* in all the honors that the Word has from the Father *by nature* (*Dogm. fr.* 7). Thus, there is an analogy between the relationship of the Father to the Son and the Son to the assumed man. As the Father indwells the Son so that he shares with the Son all the attributes proper to his nature, so too the Son who indwells the assumed man shares with him his own exalted status. And as the Father accomplishes all things through his union with the Son so the indwelling Son accomplishes all things through the man whom he assumed (*Dogm. fr.* 7).

This indwelling union is efficacious—indeed the thing that makes Jesus unique among men—because the union began in utero. There in Mary's womb the grace of the Word began forming the character of the yet unborn Jesus, imparting to him a preternatural inclination to the good (*Dogm. fr.* 7). When Theodore interprets Isaiah 7:15–16, "Before the child has come to know good and evil, he will reject the evil and choose the good," he applies this to Jesus, explaining that the grace of the Word created a virtuous intent in the assumed man so that he was predisposed to the good. This predisposition even in childhood enabled him to apprehend—as if by an intuitive judgment—the inherent goodness of the Word's will. Because of the conferral of grace by the Word, Jesus willingly submitted to the will and nudgings of the Word. While Theodore affirms the voluntary character of the assumed man's participation in Jesus's ministry, the Word's agency is dominant. "The Word governed everything [with respect to salvation]," Theodore concludes, "and urged him [i.e., the assumed man] on toward a larger perfection, while lightening for him the greater part of his toils . . . thus [the Word] prepared him for a greater and easier fulfillment of virtue" (*Dogm. fr.* 7). In Theodore, as in the Alexandrians and Cappadocians, the power of the Word accomplished the saving work of the incarnation. The critical difference is that, for Theodore, the relationship of the Word who assumed and the man who was assumed is a *cooperative* relationship. Whereas for the Alexandrians and Cappadocians the Word was the single subject who bore the mortal form of a human being and acted through it, for Theodore there were two subjects coexisting in an asymmetrical relationship. Theodore made this clear in describing the union of the assuming Word and the assumed man using the metaphor of marriage. The "unity of flesh" in husband and wife does not deny the "duality of subjects" (*Dogm. fr.* 8). That is, in marriage, the woman and man, though their natures remain discrete—one female, the other male—are united and become one at the level of their will and love for each other. So in the incarnation, the assuming Word and the assumed man, though remaining distinct in their natures—one divine, the other creature—are united at the level of will. Herein lies the perfection of Jesus that is paradigmatic for the eschatological life of the saints: a human will perfectly conformed in love to the will of God. There is an asymmetry to this cooperative relationship; the Word is completely dominant. Yet the assumed man retains his agency throughout the incarnation because his own will, informed by the gift of grace, *freely assents* to the will of the Word. To put it another way, grace enabled him to fulfill all righteousness by moving his will to embrace completely the righteousness of God. In sum, Theodore's theory of the union of the incarnation as a divine indwelling sought to make a place for the full humanity of Jesus that seemed missing in Alexandrian and Cappadocian narratives.

In his more theoretical description of the incarnation, Theodore speaks of this union as the conjunction of two natures in one *prosōpon* or "appearance" (*Dogm. fr.* 8). The term *prosōpon*, like *hypostasis* or *ousia*, is part of the technical vocabulary used to speak of the relationship between a species and its members. *Ousia* refers to the nature of a species that is composed of many individuals (*hypostaseis*). Among human beings, each person is a singular instance (*hypostasis*) of human nature (*ousia*). Each person (*hypostasis*), therefore, has attributes and faculties proper to the nature (*ousia*) shared by all people. Peter and Paul are distinct *hypostaseis* of human nature. Yet each person (*hypostasis*) also has a distinctive outward appearance (*prosōpon*) with unique features that separate them from others. Peter and Paul are two different individuals (*hypostaseis*) each with a different appearance or form (*prosōpon*). That appearance (*prosōpon*) will change over time as the individual grows from infancy to childhood to adolescence to adulthood. Behind the changes in appearance (*prosōpon*), however, the person (*hypostasis*) is the same. The person (*hypostasis*) is the subject who thinks and feels and acts. The *prosōpon*, therefore, is, as it were, the outward face an individual shows to the world and by which the world recognizes the individual distinguishing them from other individuals.

Within this scheme, Theodore understood the Logos who assumed the man and the man assumed by the Logos to be discrete *hypostaseis* of two different natures (*ousiai*), divinity and humanity. But in the incarnation, by their conjunction they appeared to the world as a single *prosōpon*, a single face. When his disciples beheld Jesus, they saw a single outward form. Jesus's *prosōpon*, therefore, consisted of his distinctive facial features, the qualities of his voice, his mannerisms, and his actions; these attributes constituted the *prosōpon* they called "Lord," "Rabbi," and "Master." This one *prosōpon* was the outward form in which the hypostasis of the Word manifested his power and authority by forgiving sins, walking on water, and raising the dead. Consequently, in this one *prosōpon* the disciples, regardless of whether they realized it at the time, encountered the Logos of God and a man perfected by the grace of the Logos.

Theodore wanted to avoid the Alexandrian language of "divinization" with all the metaphysical challenges of *communicatio idiomatum*; therefore, he had to seek an alternate way of speaking of participation. Here, too, the terminology of *prosōpon* served his purpose. Because the Word who assumed the man and the man who was assumed are *hypostaseis*, each also has its own distinctive form or appearance (*prosōpon*). Therefore, in the one *prosōpon* the Word and the assumed man share in the appearance (*prosōpon*) proper to the other. Thus, the Word reveals himself to the world in the *prosōpon* of the man assumed. So too, Theodore says, because of the unique character of their union, the man assumed is ultimately revealed in the *prosōpon* of the Word. Though the man assumed by the Word is distinct from the Word, the assumed man shares in the honor and glory and worship proper to the Word's divinity. An analogy Theodore uses to illustrate this is that of a king and his purple robe. The robe is not intrinsic to the person of the king; he remains king even when not wearing his robe. Yet the robe is part of the outward display of regal power and authority when presiding in public. The robe, therefore, is part of the king's public persona or *prosōpon*. Similarly, in the incarnation, the Word not only clothes himself with the form or appearance (*prosōpon*) of the man he assumes. At the same time, the Word clothes the man assumed with the honor, majesty, and worship proper to the divine form that belonged to the Word before the incarnation. On the Mount of Transfiguration and at his ascension, the man assumed receives the glory of the Word's nature in their shared *prosōpon* by virtue of his intimate union with the Word (*Eun. fr.*; Grillmeier, 433). In this revelation of Jesus's humanity adorned in the glorious *prosōpon* of the resurrection, the assumed man not only receives worship as God but also reveals the eschatological *prosōpon* of the citizens of heaven with which the saints shall be clothed at the resurrection.

Theodore's theory of the prosoponic union of the assuming Word and the assumed man made room for greater human agency than in Gregory of Nazianzus's description of the incarnation as a mixture of two natures under the hegemony of the Word. Yet it risked denying the uniqueness of Jesus. Although Theodore is explicit that the union of the incarnation is different from the Spirit's indwelling of the apostles, he is also explicit that the union is not a natural union but one according to grace, which is how God chooses to indwell exceptionally holy people, such as the prophets and apostles, as well as the saints eschatologically. Moreover, the union is effected by the conjoining of wills in perfect harmony just as in holy individuals. Theodore distinguishes the Word's indwelling of the saints through the Spirit from the Word's indwelling Jesus. In the case of saints, theirs is a particular participation in the Spirit through Christ. In other words, it is not a permanent indwelling but episodic—that is, whenever the Spirit chooses to speak through the prophet or inspire the apostle. By contrast, the Word's indwelling of Jesus is permanent, in which the whole grace of the Spirit is given to Jesus. There is, one might say, nothing in Jesus not under the influence of the Word's grace (*Dogm. fr.* 7). Nevertheless, since both the indwelling of Jesus and the indwelling of saints are an indwelling effected by the gift of grace, the union of the incarnation is different not *in type* but *in degree*. To his critics, it appeared that Theodore's Jesus was a superprophet distinguished from the others only by the amount and extent of the grace he received. Therefore, it sounded Adoptionistic; hence he was called a "man-worshipper" (*Dogm. fr.* 6).

Moreover, Theodore's language used to articulate the distinction between the divine and human natures also led to charges that he advocated a "two sons" Christology: the only begotten Son and the adopted Son. Indeed, when Theodore speaks of the Word as conferring grace on the assumed man, whom Theodore refers to simply as "him," the antecedent of "him" is Jesus (*Dogm. fr.* 7). That sounds as if Jesus is not merely distinct from but another individual separate from the Word. Further evidence for this interpretation lies in Theodore's account of Christ's passion.

Insistent that the assumed man was no phantasm, as Marcion and the Manichees taught, Theodore affirmed the reality of Jesus's suffering and death. He also affirmed that the prosoponic union was not severed or suspended during the passion: "He [i.e., the Word] was not separated from him [i.e., the assumed man] in his crucifixion, nor did he leave him at death, but remained with him until he helped him loose the pains of death . . . [and] made him immortal, incorruptible, and immutable" (*Cat. hom.* 5). Since the assuming Word is by nature incorporeal and immaterial, the Word in his divine nature did not experience death. Instead, it was the assumed man who was dissolved in death only to be raised and restored by the Word who assumed him (*Cat. hom.* 6). Here one sees Theodore's meticulous distinction between the mortal nature of the man and the immortal nature of the Word. Yet, although he insists upon the inseparability of the Word and the man, at times he fumbles for words to explain how the Word was present with the assumed man but did not himself experience death. Having affirmed that the Word strengthened the will and then gave life to the assumed man's body, Theodore comments that it was impossible for the assumed man to die "if (the Godhead) were not *cautiously remote* from him, but also near enough to do the needful and necessary things for the nature that was assumed by it" (*Cat. hom.* 8). Here Theodore affirms that even in the prosoponic union, the Word retains his transcendence such that his nature was not affected by the cross; while at the same time, he affirms that the Word was "near enough" to impart the grace necessary for the assumed man to remain ever faithful to God in fulfilling his role as sacrifice for the debt of sin. Theodore is able to make this claim precisely because the union was not a natural or ontological union—a mixing, as Nazianzen put it—but a union of wills through bonds fashioned by grace. Thus, the Word can strengthen the will of the assumed man without himself being affected by the thorns, nails, and lance that pierced only the flesh of the assumed man. A union of two wills, like that of husband and wife, necessarily implies two willing subjects. Such a view of the incarnation, however, raised the question posed among his critics, If there are two subjects, are there not two sons, two Christs? Indeed, Theodore's description of the "one who assumed" as "cautiously remote" from the "assumed man" came dangerously close to the account of Christ's passion narrated in the Apocalypse of Peter. There the man Jesus suffered on the cross while the spiritual Christ stood by laughing (Apoc. Pet. 83.1–3).

These were precisely the problems that Nestorius inherited from Theodore. Nestorius's attempt at a careful distinction between the humanity and divinity of Jesus did not satisfy Proclus and the defenders of *Theotokos*. Nor did the controversy remain local for very long. As copies of Nestorius's written statements spread, his arguments became the source of debate and controversy in other ecclesial provinces. Naturally, the bishops of those provinces, seeking to give doctrinal guidance to their flock, waded into the controversy. One such bishop was Cyril of Alexandria.

Cyril of Alexandria's Rejoinder

Well before the outbreak of the controversy around the title *Theotokos* and its christological implications, Cyril had articulated the classical Alexandrian soteriology and Christology in his biblical commentaries. The grand design of God's economy was the divinization of humanity by its participation in the divine nature through the union of the divine Word with mortal humanity. In Isaiah's vision in the temple (6:1–3), Cyril sees an image of the consubstantial relationship between the Father and the Son. The Lord seated upon his throne is the immutable and transcendent divinity of the Father who is above all creatures, and his glory that filled the temple is the Son (*In Isa.* 1.4, 173a). The minds of the seraphim, which can know neither the beginning nor end of God's ways, nevertheless burn with a fervent love for God that is nothing other than a participation in the fiery nature of divinity. The seraphim, therefore, serve as models of deified minds of those who cleave to God in love and so in their thoughts are raised in doxology above all that is base (*In Isa.* 1.4, 173c–d). The burning coal that seraphim held in the tongs of the alter and touched the prophet's unclean lips is a figure of Christ himself whom the Father gives as a sacrifice for the forgiveness of sins (*In Isa.* 1.4, 181b). The image of the burning coal—the means of Isaiah's purification—is, for Cyril, a figure of the incarnation. For coal is the union of two natures, fire and wood. As the fire penetrates the wood, filling it with heat, so the fiery divinity of the Son united to the material substance of a human being divinizes his humanity (*In Isa.* 1.4, 181d). And as when the coal purified Isaiah's lips with its touch, so too through the physical form of his body, the Word imparts his holiness to believers.

This is especially true in the case of the Eucharist. Commenting on Jesus's Bread of Life Discourse in John 6, Cyril draws a direct parallel between the union of the Word and flesh in the incarnation and the union of Christ and the believer in the Eucharist. Because in the incarnation the Word endows his human body with life, his incorruptible body gives life and incorruptibility to the believer's body as well (*In Jo.* 3.6, 324d–e). It is not Jesus's body in itself that gives life to the believer's body. Rather, through his body, the Word in his incorruptibility imparts incorruptibility to the soul and body of the one who feeds upon his flesh and blood in faith. Therefore, Cyril speaks of Christ's body as "a kind of coworker" with his divinity. As with the raising of Jairus's daughter (Luke 8:54), Jesus restored her to life not simply by the commanding power of his spoken word but by the touch of his hand (*In Jo.* 4.2, 361). Christ's flesh gives life because it creates a point of physical and spiritual contact between the divine Son and the believer. Cyril describes the divinizing of human nature with two important metaphors. First, even as water, though naturally cold, "forgets its nature" and becomes hot when, in a kettle over a fire, it receives the fire's heat, so too the believer's nature, which is naturally corruptible, forgets its nature and becomes incorruptible when it is united to the incorruptible incarnate Word (*In Jo.* 4.2, 362a–b). Second, as a glowing ember, like the burning coal that touched Isaiah's lips, is thrust into a pile of straw, ignites the straw, and burns it up, likewise in the Eucharist, Christ's body, when received by the believer, is mingled with the believer's body and burns up, as it were, the body's natural corruption and imparts to it a share in Christ's incorruptible divinity (*In Jo.* 4.2, 363e).

The divinizing power of the Eucharist, for Cyril, is possible only because of the nature of the union of the Word and flesh in the incarnation. Commenting on John 6:54, "He who eats *my* flesh and drinks *my* blood has eternal life, and I will raise him up at the last day," Cyril makes the point that the only way Jesus can speak of the flesh and blood as *my* flesh and blood is that they were genuinely his body and blood. That is, the incarnation is not the Word's *indwelling* a body, as when the Spirit indwells a prophet. For then the Word would merely *abide in* rather than being fully *united* to the body. When the body is united to the Word, the body becomes, as it were, part of the Word; it is the Word's body, no one else's. That is the significance of John 1:14 saying, "And the Word *became* flesh" (*In Jo.* 4.2, 363b). To be sure, Cyril recognized the addition of the words "and *dwelt* among us," viewing them as a necessary qualifier to prevent a misunderstanding. Here John joins the language of "becoming" with "dwelling" to hold two key christological points together. On the one hand, "becoming" rules out a "relative indwelling" as with prophets and saints, thereby affirming the uniqueness of Jesus as God *and* man. Were Christ's body not uniquely his, his body could not be worshiped; for that would be idolatry. On the other hand, the addition of "dwelling" excludes the possibility of someone's misinterpreting "becoming" to mean that the Word was *changed into* human flesh. Such is impossible since the divine Word is naturally immutable. Therefore, the Word retains the fullness of his divinity (Col 2:9) while dwelling in the temple that is his body taken from Mary (*In Jo.* 1.9, 96b–c). Here we see Cyril's classic deployment of paradox. It is for him one of the chief theological tools that holds together in a constructive tension two seemingly contradictory claims that, within the narrative of Scripture, necessarily coexist in the sacred mystery of the incarnation. Thus, in the incarnation, the Word dwells within his body as in a temple and yet does not merely indwell the body because the body is united to the Word more intimately than the way a deity inhabits a temple.

In this commentary written before the outbreak of the controversy with Nestorius, Cyril finds it easier to say what sort of union the incarnation is not—a "relative indwelling"—than to express in positive language the nature of the union. Amid passages of great clarity, he at times stumbles around to find the right words. For example, when explaining John 1:14, he writes, "the Word is God both in the flesh and with the flesh, since it is his own property, yet is conceived as something *separate* from it, and is worshipped in it and with it. . . . [Yet] God is in him, without *separating* the Word from the flesh" (*In Jo.* 1.9, 95d). Cyril's point, however awkwardly expressed, is that divinity of the Word is distinguishable from the flesh (i.e., each has different natural properties) and yet exists in a permanent union with the flesh (i.e., the Word's existence in flesh means that the incarnate Word's divine nature is always manifest in the flesh).

Cyril's interpretation of the Word's becoming flesh and dwelling in us followed the logic of Paul's Adam typology. That which was lost in the first Adam was restored in the Christ, the second Adam. "For we were all in Christ," Cyril writes, "The common element of humanity is summed up in his person, which is why he is called the last Adam: he enriched our common nature with everything conducive to joy and glory just as the first Adam impoverished it . . . so that through that one being who was 'designated Son of God in power according to his holiness' the whole of humanity might be raised up to his status" (*In Jo.* 1.9, 96d). By this "mystical union" of humanity and divinity in Jesus, the great exchange was accomplished. Those enslaved to sin and death could be set free and given a share in the richness of his divinity (2 Cor 8:9) by the one who became a servant. And when he who is the Son of God by nature became a son of Adam and dwelt in Adam's family, the children of Adam became children of God, crying, "Abba, Father" (Rom 8:15), because they have received his Spirit (*In Jo.* 1.9, 96e–97a).

This adoption of the members of Adam's family through the giving of the Spirit Cyril explains in terms of Christ's recapitulation of Adam's fall. He takes Isaiah's words, "There shall come forth a rod of Jesse, and a flower shall grow out of the root, and the Spirit of God shall rest upon him" (11:1–2), as a prophecy of Jesus's receiving and giving the Spirit. The theological issue here that Cyril sought to work through was why would Jesus who already was the incarnate Word of God need to be anointed by the Holy Spirit? Since the Son and Spirit are consubstantial, each fully possessing the same divine nature and authority, Jesus lacked nothing that he needed to receive from the Spirit (*In Jo.* 9.1, 810c). Cyril's answer is that the Spirit's anointing Jesus at his baptism revealed the restoration of the Spirit who abandoned Adam's race because of the fall. The breath, which God breathed into Adam at his creation (Gen 2:7), was, according to Cyril, the Holy Spirit. But because of the corruption of humanity through sin, the Spirit departed from Adam and his descendants. However, when the Word became a son of Adam, the Spirit found a sinless man worthy of making his resting place (*In Isa.* 2.4, 315c–d). The Spirit's anointing Jesus at his baptism did not contribute anything to Jesus that he did not already have. Rather, it marked Jesus as the second Adam, the progenitor of a new line of Adam's race and the one through whom the life-giving Spirit, who had been estranged from humanity by Adam's sin, was given afresh to believers in baptism (*In Isa.* 2.4, 315d–316a).

At first glance, it is obvious that Cyril shared with Theodore and Nestorius a number of essential orthodox views. They agreed that the Logos is the only begotten Son who is coeternal and consubstantial with the Father. Therefore, the Logos, like the Father, is immortal, immutable, and impassible. They agreed that the Logos's divine nature was not changed in the incarnation. Attempting to clarify his thought decades later, Nestorius used the analogy of water in its different forms to illustrate the immutability of the Logos. Even as the nature of free-flowing water in summer retains its nature when it becomes frozen in winter—free-flowing or frozen, it is still water—so too the Logos's divine nature was the same when he assumed the form of a servant as before the incarnation (*Heracl.* 1.1.11). Similarly, they were of the shared opinion that it was appropriate to distinguish the different properties of the divinity and humanity. The critical point of divergence concerned their differing theories of salvation and their understandings of the character of the union of the divinity and humanity. In short, for Cyril, an indwelling that is the mere conjunction or agreement of wills, however permanent, could not accomplish the divinization of Jesus's humanity necessary for his followers' sacramental participation in the divine nature that results in their divinization.

In the spring of 429, as the content of Nestorius's homilies against *Theotokos* made its way to Egypt, Cyril composed a letter to his priests and monks, refuting Nestorius's ideas, which he described as "dangerous murmurings . . . destroying simple faith by vomiting out a pile of stupid little words" (*Ep.* 1.3), before they could gain traction among less discerning minds. As an alternative to Nestorius's explanation of the incarnation as a conjunction of wills effected by grace, Cyril advocated that the incarnation involved a *natural or hypostatic union* of the Word and human nature to form a single subject. He begins his *Letter to the Monks of Egypt* by defending the term *Theotokos*; he asks very simply, "For if our Lord Jesus Christ is God, then how is the holy Virgin who bore him not the Mother of God?" (*Ep.* 1.4). He then proceeds to counter Nestorius's alternative *Christotokos* on the grounds that many figures in Israel's past—kings and prophets—had been called "Christ" or "Anointed

One." Therefore, the term *Christotokos* did not denote the unique status of Mary or of him who was in her womb (*Ep.* 1.10). Although the Word is the only begotten of the Father and therefore different from the flesh he assumed in the incarnation, the one whom Mary carried in her womb and to whom she gave birth was Emmanuel, "God with us." Emmanuel, though the union of the divine Word to a human soul and body, was not two things but one person. Cyril illustrates his point with an analogy that he will employ throughout his subsequent writings. Even though a human being is composed of two natures, an immaterial soul and a material body, one would not say that a mother gives birth to two things. Why? Because the two natures are naturally united to one another in a single person. In his typically acerbic tone, Cyril makes his point: "As I have said, a mother gives birth to one living creature skillfully composed from diverse factors and truly forming one man out of two things, each of which remains what it is while concurring, as it were, into a natural unity, and each one mingling its specific and proper characteristics with the other" (*Ep.* 1.12). As John McGuckin has clarified, Cyril is not here suggesting that there was mixing of the natures so as to form a third type of being, neither fully God nor fully human. Rather, Cyril, in using the soul-body union as an analogy for the natural union of the divine and human in Mary's womb, is able to affirm that the human and divine natures do not simply coexist, as in Nestorius's prosoponic union, but are *organically interwoven*, as it were, to form a single person. For in Cyril's thinking, a true *communicatio idiomatum*—sharing of characteristics proper to each nature—was possible only by such a union. As with the human person in whom two natures of soul and body are united though being conceptually distinguished from one another, so too in the incarnation, Emmanuel is one person, Jesus, even though the divine and human natures can be conceptually differentiated. Yet the divinity and humanity do not exist in a symmetrical relationship. The single person Jesus is the divine Word made flesh. Therefore, the Word is the single agent or cause responsible for all of Jesus's activities. It was the Word incarnate who with his own hands fashioned mud patties mixed with his spittle and applied them to the eyes of the blind man and with his divine power gave the man his sight. It was the Word *acting directly* through his body. Therefore, Jesus was not like Nestorius's Christ, a mere "God-bearing man" *inspired* by the indwelling Word to do thus and such; rather, he was "truly God made man" (*Ep.* 1.19). Jesus's body, therefore, could truly be said to reveal the invisible God because Jesus was Emmanuel; his body was the body of the Son of God (*Ep.* 1.20). Because it was the Word's body, the immortal Word, who in his divinity could not be touched by death, had the power both to hand his mortal body over to death on the cross and then, by his divine power, raise it up again (*Ep.* 1.24–25).

Nestorius countered that Cyril's unitary Christology that failed to distinguish between the natures of the one who assumed and the one who was assumed implied the passibility and mutability of the Logos (2 *Ep. Cyr.*; Hardy, 135–36). His logic was that if the incarnation were a natural union of the divine and human as the soul is united to the body, then, even as the soul suffers when the body is injured and the body bears outwardly the inner scars of a soul that suffers, the Logos would also share in its body's sufferings. Nestorius's two-subjects Christology allows him to quarantine the Word, protecting him from suffering by locating the suffering in the assumed man. But in Cyril's hypostatic union, there is only one subject of the suffering, the Word. It logically follows, for Nestorius, that Cyril's Word must be passible and mutable.

Since both Cyril and Nestorius affirmed the doctrine of divine impassibility (*apatheia*), it would be helpful to clarify the doctrine's origin and what it does and does not mean. First, as Paul Gavrilyuk has shown, early Christians ascribed to God *apatheia*, that is, freedom from suffering or from the passions, to distinguish the God of Jesus from the pagan gods of the Greco-Roman pantheon. In the stories of Greek and Roman mythology, particularly in the Homeric epics, Zeus and Hera and Apollo and Athena are not particularly virtuous. Rather, they are beset by all sorts of passions: sexual promiscuity, vanity, jealousy, unbridled wrath, and so on. By contrast, the God of Christianity is perfect holiness and goodness and therefore is not guilty of such pagan vices. Second, passion (*pathos*) was an emotional or psychic disturbance inflicted on the soul by external circumstances. *Apatheia*, as applied to God, affirmed God's transcendence and aseity or self-sufficiency. In other words, creatures are acted on and affected by things external to them such that their happiness—to a greater or lesser degree—is influenced or determined by external forces. God, by contrast, is entirely autonomous and therefore not subject to external forces. In order for God to be truly sovereign over creation, God must be autonomous and entirely self-sufficient, moved entirely by his own will, not by things in the world. Even in the Old Testament where various narratives depict God "repenting" and "changing his mind," God declares through the prophet Malachi, "For I am the Lord; I change not" (3:6). Hebrews explicitly ascribes such constancy to the Lord, speaking of "Jesus Christ, the same yesterday, today, and tomorrow" (Heb 13:8). Third, *pathos* was a corollary of change. To suffer harm was to suffer change. People are changed by catastrophic experiences. God, however, is immutable because he is eternal. That is, God did not come into being but always has been; therefore, change is not proper to God's nature. Immutability delimits the boundary between the Creator and the creature, between the one who eternally is and his many creatures that ever exist in a state of change and flux. Fourth, divine impassibility is an extension of divine perfection. That is, one feature of God's perfection, in addition to his perfect goodness, mercy, and so on, is God's blessedness. God is supremely and eternally blessed. Therefore, God's *apatheia* meant that God's perfect happiness is not compromised by the sufferings of the world. However, divine *apatheia* was never understood in Catholic circles as meaning that God is sublimely oblivious and indifferent to the sufferings of his creatures. Far from being impervious to injustice and sorrow, God's very transcendence of worldly sufferings was the source of the very hope that God in his strength and compassion was able to deliver humanity from miseries.

Against Nestorius's charge of theopassionism—the heretical view that God suffers—Cyril faced the challenge of affirming that Jesus was the single subject who was conceived in Mary's womb and hung upon the cross but also that neither the incarnation generally nor Jesus's death on the cross compromised the Son's impassibility and immutability.

Ever ready to go on the offensive, Cyril challenged Nestorius's prosoponic union, arguing that, although Nestorius claimed the union was permanent, in fact he was dividing Christ into two. Responding to Nestorius's claim, "There is no division in his being Christ, but there is division between the divinity and the humanity," Cyril counters that Nestorius's "indivisible conjunction [*synapheia*]" of the Word who assumes and the man assumed is merely a "casual joining" or "a conjunction of proximity or juxtaposition . . . [and] accidental" (*Nest.* 2.5–6). Rather, Cyril declares, "But when the mystery of Christ is set before us, our discussion of the union does not ignore the difference but nevertheless puts the division aside, not because we are confusing the natures or mixing them together, but because the Word of God, having partaken of flesh and blood, is still thought of as a single Son and is called such" (*Nest.* 2.6). Jesus does not speak of "our father"—the Father of the only begotten Son and of the adopted man who was assumed—but of "my Father" because he is the Father of the one Christ, the incarnate Word (*Pulch.*; Greer, 10). Therefore, the worship of Christ is not divided between the Word and the man who is honored because of his faithful adherence to the will of the Word (*Pulch.*; Greer, 24–25). Instead, "we worship him as one . . . believing that he is one and the same in his divinity and humanity, that is to say, simultaneously both God and man" (*Nest.* 2 proem).

Later, Cyril describes the hypostatic union as an "economic union" (*Pulch.*; Greer, 16), meaning the Word's "true" and "substantial" union in his salvific condescension in the incarnation. The language of "economic union" allows Cyril to distinguish the immortal nature of the Word from eternity and the Word's assumption of his mortal human nature in the Father's economic plan of salvation. This natural union of divinity and humanity, he insists, did not involve a change in the Word's divinity. For the incarnation did not entail a giving up of any property of his divine nature but the assumption of the weakness of fallen humanity. This, Cyril explains, is the meaning of the phrase in the Christ hymn, "he emptied [*ekenōsen*] himself, taking the form of a servant" (Phil 2:7). Paul's expression "self-emptying" (*kenōsis*) is synonymous with John's expression "became flesh"; therefore, the

Word's *kenōsis* occurs, not by subtraction from his divinity but by the addition of human limitations, "the poverty of human nature" (*Chr. un.*; McGuckin, 54–55). Among these limitations proper to human nature were changes that accompany the growth of the body from infancy to childhood to manhood. The Word could not clothe himself in human nature without also experiencing the changes that are part of being human. Yet the Word did not change in his divinity; it was only his body and soul that underwent the changes inherent to creaturely maturation (*Pulch.*; Greer, 11). Thus, the Word experienced the physiological changes in his body and psychic development in his soul, but without being changed in his divinity. As we shall see, this distinction between *experiencing change* in his body and soul and actually *being changed* in his divine nature will be critical for his discussion of Christ's passion.

The Word's kenotic assumption of human nature in a natural union, analogous to the union of soul and body, was necessary to liberate humanity from death and sin. Because the Word took to himself a human soul and body, such that they are truly his, he became a member of Adam's family. As a member of Adam's race, he took on himself *all* that belonged to Adam's family, including its collective sin that he condemned in himself—thus freeing his brothers and sisters from the law of sin and death. Moreover, by becoming one of Adam's family, he not only took all that belongs to Adam on himself, but he also confers on his sisters and brothers what rightly belongs to him, namely the riches of his divinity. Chief among these riches is immortality. How, Cyril asks, could humanity be healed of its mortal condition except that the Word assumed a mortal body to which he imparted incorruptibility? Moreover, the life-giving power of his divinity not only flowed from the Word to his body but flow from his body to the rest of Adam's race (*Chr. un.*; McGuckin, 60). By assuming a human body, the Word transmits to those, who through baptism are united to his body, the grace of sonship and the power to become children of God through his Spirit (*Chr. un.*; McGuckin, 63). Thus, because of this union of divinity and humanity, Jesus is the "new rootstock" or prototype of a new human race who, by abiding in him through the gift of his Spirit, share in his holiness and incorruptibility (*Chr. un.*; McGuckin, 64). In other words, unlike the mere conjunction of wills in Nestorius's prosoponic union, Cyril's hypostatic union with its organic integration of humanity and divinity in one person, the second Adam, creates an ontological connection between God and Adam's family. This ontological union creates the possibility for humanity as a whole to participate in Christ's Godhead. Thus, because of the hypostatic union, believers are able to see in Jesus a likeness of what they can become by their union with him through his Spirit.

Because both Cyril and Nestorius held that the divine and human natures had different characteristics and yet applied to Jesus, they both employed partitive exegesis, distinguishing when a given biblical description, such as thirst or foreknowledge, referred to Jesus's humanity or divinity. Nestorius's two-subjects Christology allowed him to attribute different characteristics to either the assuming Word or the man assumed. Cyril says that Nestorius "divides up the sayings in the Gospels, assigning them sometimes exclusively to the Word alone and sometimes exclusively to the man born from woman"; thus, the teachings from the Sermon on the Mount belong to the Word, while Jesus's cry of dereliction, "My God, my God, why have you forsaken me?" is that of the assumed man. Cyril's hypostatic union required that the different qualities or sayings apply to the same single subject, Jesus the Word incarnate (*Nest.* 2 proem). One example is Jesus's prayer in Gethsemane, "Let this cup pass from me; nevertheless, not my will but thine be done" (Matt 26:39). Here Cyril saw evidence of two wills, one human and one divine acting simultaneously in the one person. Because the Word assumed a human nature that is averse to pain and suffering, Jesus spoke the petition for the cup to pass from him out of the instinct or will for self-preservation inherent to human nature. Although the Word is immortal and cannot "cower before death," Cyril writes, "having come to be in the flesh, he [the Word incarnate] allows himself to experience the things proper to the flesh, and consequently, when death is at the door, to cower before it, that he might appear to be a real human being" (*In Jo.* 4.1, 331d–e). Yet as the Word incarnate, Jesus also shared the Father's will to redeem humanity, even by death on the cross. Therefore, the power of Jesus's divine will enabled him to restrain his natural human instincts and submit his human will to that of the Father's (*In Jo.* 4.1, 332a). This vignette was important for Cyril's soteriology. Jesus, as the second Adam, took on human weakness—such as the fear of death—but was able by his power as the Word incarnate to give strength to his human nature that he might act boldly and faithfully. Therefore, by the triumph of his divine will over his human weakness, Jesus revealed to his disciples the moral courage to overcome their creaturely fear and timidity that his Spirit would give them when they, too, faced death (*In Jo.* 8, 703e–704a).

This vision of Jesus, one man with two wills, as the revelation of a new humanity sanctified by the Holy Spirit was crucial for Cyril's response to Nestorius's charge of theopassionism. The basis for this charge lay with Cyril's own words condemning of Nestorius: "If anyone does not confess that the Word of God suffered in the flesh and was crucified in the flesh and tasted death in the flesh, and became the firstborn of the dead, although he is as God Life and life-giving, let him be anathema" (*3 Ep. Nest.* 12). Here Cyril was attacking Nestorius for attributing Jesus's passion to the assumed man rather than to the one Christ, the incarnate Word. Nestorius, on the other hand, saw the attribution of suffering to the Word as tantamount to a denial of the Word's impassibility and immutability. As one would expect, Cyril responded by going on the offensive. He objected that Nestorius's claim that "it is the temple that is capable of suffering, not the life-giving God of him who suffered," divides Jesus in two, "seeing that he who suffers is a separate subject, and he who is life-giving is another" (*Nest.* 3.1–2). On the contrary, Jesus is the one subject "who suffered death in a human fashion and rose from the dead in a divine fashion" (*Nest.* 4.6). Following in the tradition of Ignatius's battle against the docetic denial of Christ's passion, Cyril is committed to the arch of the biblical narrative: he who was truly made flesh was made capable of undergoing death and truly suffered for the redemption of mankind. Because of Cyril's understanding of the Word's "self-emptying" not as a loss of his divine capacities but an assumption of human limitations, he is able to think of the Word as experiencing the suffering of the body he assumed. At the same time, because he did not give up any element of his divine nature, his divine immutability enabled him to experience the passion of the flesh he assumed but without being changed by the experience. Even as Jesus experienced bodily growth as he matured from infancy to manhood without undergoing any change in his divinity, neither was his divine nature changed as his mortal human nature suffered bodily changes effected by the whip, nails, thorns, and lance of his persecutors.

Cyril captures the Word's experience of the passion in his humanity, but without change in his divinity, in the paradoxical expression "impassible suffering." Writing to Theodosius's highly influential sister, Pulcheria, and his wife, Eudoxia, Cyril opines, "since the Word of God is all powerful [he is also] stronger than death, beyond suffering, and completely without a share in the fear suitable to man. But though he exists this way by nature, still he suffered for us. Therefore, neither is Christ a mere man nor is the Word without flesh. Rather, united with a humanity like ours, he suffered human things impassibly [*pathoi apathōs*] in his own flesh" (*Pulch.*; Greer, 33). "Impassible suffering" makes both an ontological and a moral claim. Ontologically, the divine nature of the Word, who is the single subject of Christ, did not suffer change, although he experienced the suffering of the human nature he assumed. The Word indeed experienced death in that he descended to the dead to free those imprisoned in Hades; but his divine nature did not suffer death in the same sense that human beings lose their lives and pass away when they die.

The moral implication of "impassible suffering" is that Jesus's love of humanity, inherent to his divine will, was not diminished in the least—even for his persecutors—as a result of his passion. Rather, his divine desire for humanity's redemption remained, as was evident in his petition on the cross, "Father, forgive them" (Luke 23:34). And as the second Adam, Jesus's enduring compassion for humanity in the midst of his passion revealed how, by the gift of his Spirit, his followers might also persevere in their love of those who would persecute them as well. For immediately after invoking the expression "impassible suffering," Cyril tells the empresses, "Thus, these events [i.e., Jesus's passion] became an example for us in a human fashion" (*Pulch.*; Greer, 33), which echoes his earlier summation of the incarnation: "Surely it was the aim of the only begotten in having a likeness to us to suffer in a human fashion and to teach those familiar with him how they ought to approach the assaults of temptations . . . [and] to show how honorable the end of obedience is, so that we may be found excellent and wise imitators of what was done by him, and so that by following his footsteps we might be preserved in a life of glory" (*Pulch.*; Greer, 31). The hypostatic union in allowing Jesus's "impassible suffering" reveals God's transforming and divinizing power, which is the hope for believers seeking to persevere in loving their persecutors as Christ did.

Excursus: A Clarification of Terminology

The theological difference between Nestorius and Cyril is more profound than a difference of terminology. Yet the range of possible meanings for a single word clearly contributed to confusion between the fifth-century combatants and their modern interpreters. Therefore, at this point, it may be helpful to gain some clarity about how certain key terms are and are not being used. The term *hypostasis*, as used by Cyril, refers to a concrete, particular individual who is distinct from other individuals. In this sense, Peter and Paul are distinct *hypostaseis*. For although they share a common human nature, they are discrete persons separate from each other. Paul's body belongs to Paul, not to Peter. What happens to Peter happens to Peter, not to Paul. Even as Peter and Paul are separate persons who are the subjects of their own actions and experiences, so is Jesus a discrete individual or person who is the single subject of his actions and experiences. Because Cyril wanted to emphasize that Jesus is a single person or subject, he speaks of the union of the Logos's divinity derived from the Father and his humanity derived from Mary as a hypostatic union (*henōsis kath' hypostasin*). The confusion comes because Cyril uses the term "nature" or *physis* in two very different senses. Sometimes Cyril uses "nature" to refer to the essential features or characteristics that distinguish one sort of thing from another sort of thing. The body and soul are different sorts of things because they have different natures. The body is material and mortal; the soul is immaterial and immortal. Cyril, therefore, applies the term *physis* to refer to the difference between the immutable and impassible divine nature that the Logos received from the Father and the mutable and passible human nature he assumed in Mary's womb. This is the sense Cyril has in mind when he occasionally speaks of Jesus's "two natures" (*3 Ep. Nest.* 5).

Other times, however, Cyril uses *physis* as a synonym for *hypostasis*. In this case, "nature" denotes a single, concrete individual. Cyril uses "nature" in this sense when he wants to emphasize the *organic unity* of Christ as one person. Thus, he will speak of the incarnation as a "union in nature" (*henōsis kata physin*). Here "nature" or "natural union" stands in contrast with the *volitional unity*—on the analogy of the union of wife and husband—with which Nestorius described the prosoponic union of the human and the divine subjects. Thus, for Cyril, in the incarnation, the human and divine natures are naturally united even as the soul and body, which are of different natures and, nevertheless, form a natural unity (*3 Ep. Nest.* 4). This is the sense of *physis* Cyril has in mind when he uses the term *mia physis* or "one nature" to speak of Jesus. Although the term is traceable to Athanasius, it was problematically associated with Apollinaris. It did not, however, mean for Cyril what it did for Apollinaris. By *mia physis*, Cyril does not mean to suggest that Jesus was a single hybrid nature—like the mythical centaur—that is, a mixture, part divine and part human. Rather, he simply meant that Jesus was a single person or subject composed of two distinct natures, human and divine. Yet because Cyril alternated the meanings of "nature," sometimes referring to an individual and other times referring to essential properties, he created confusion among friend and foe alike.

As we shall see, when the Council of Chalcedon (451) would speak of Christ as having two natures, some of Cyril's heirs would misinterpret this to mean that Jesus was a union of two individual subjects. Conversely, Nestorius and his allies misinterpreted Cyril's use of *mia physis* to mean a blurring of the distinction between divinity and humanity through a mixing and confusing of the two natures in which each was changed and distorted.

Toward a Resolution? From Ephesus to Chalcedon

Tensions between Alexandria and Constantinople mounted early in 430 when, at Nestorius's invitation, Dorotheus of Marcianopolis preached a sermon anathematizing anyone who addressed Mary as *Theotokos*. Later that spring, Cyril composed the most extensive rebuttal to date in his *Five Tomes Against Nestorius*, which he promulgated widely in order to form a coalition against Nestorius. Persuaded by Cyril's *Five Tomes*, Pope Celestine in August 430 convened a synod in Rome of

Western bishops that condemned Nestorius. Cyril joined Rome's condemnation with a synod of his own in Alexandria that declared Nestorius's teachings anathema. As chair of the synod, Cyril composed the statement of condemnation that he sent to Nestorius in his famous third letter, which concluded with the *Twelve Chapters* that listed the twelve points of heresy for which Nestorius was excommunicated. Cyril's strong language left no room for Nestorius and Cyril to come to some reconciliation. Nestorius, however, was not without his allies. Andrew of Samosata and Theodoret of Cyrus, representing the Syrian churches, countered that Cyril, in failing to distinguish between the divine and human natures but affirming that Christ was one subject, was guilty of Apollinarianism. By December, the court in Constantinople was sensing the need for imperial intervention. The empress Pulcheria was pushing her brother to consider calling a synod in Ephesus because, as she knew well, Ephesus was a city renowned for its Marian devotion. In late spring of 431, Theodosius called a council to convene in Ephesus on Pentecost, 7 June. To oversee the council as his personal representative, he sent Count Candidianus with instructions not to become involved in the theological discussion but to ensure order so that the bishops might deliberate in peace. The council was to meet at the newly consecrated Church of Mary Theotokos.

One significant problem that would prevent the council from being, as Theodosius seems to have hoped, a forum for open deliberation among men of good will was that the June date did not give the Syrian delegation, led by John of Antioch, time to get to Ephesus. Cyril claimed that John had given written instructions that the council should proceed even if he and his delegation had not arrived by the appointed date. In the absence of Pope Celestine, Cyril, as bishop of the next most senior episcopal see, should preside. Count Candidianus, however, felt that meeting without John and the Syrians who were supporters of Nestorius was contrary to Theodosius's intent. As John's arrival was becoming later and later, Cyril decided to convene the council—even without John—on 21 June. Overruling Andrew and Theodoret, who declared that the council should try Cyril for Apollinarianism, Cyril summoned Nestorius to appear before the council to answer the condemnations from Rome and Alexandria. Nestorius refused the summons. In response, sixty-eight bishops who were supporters of Nestorius objected. Candidianus judged the council illegal and placed Cyril and his ally Memnon, bishop of Ephesus, under house arrest.

The council went ahead, establishing the Nicene Creed to be the standard of doctrine. Other documents were used as examples of the correct interpretation of Nicaea, namely Cyril's second letter to Nestorius and his letter to Pulcheria and Eudoxia, *On the Right Faith*, Gregory of Nazianzus's epistle 101 to Cledonius, and Athanasius's letter to Epictetus. Nestorius penned a seven-page statement of his Christology that was submitted in absentia. Of the 228 bishops assembled, 197 voted to condemn Nestorius.

Finally, on 26 June, John and his party arrived in Ephesus. Indignant that the council had proceeded without him, John convened his own council, known as the *Conciliabulum*, which rejected Cyril's *Twelve Chapters*, condemned Cyril and Memnon, and elected a new bishop of Ephesus. Theodosius accepted the judgment of both councils and excommunicated Nestorius, Cyril, and Memnon. Cyril induced allies at court, sometimes with material gifts, to apply pressure on Theodosius to reconsider. Finally, in September the condemnations of Cyril and Memnon were lifted, and Nestorius was sent into exile in his monastery in Antioch. The Syrian delegation refused to lift its condemnations of Cyril and Memnon. This meant that the churches of Syria remained estranged from Alexandria as well as Rome and Constantinople.

Under pressure from Constantinople, Cyril and John made steps toward reconciliation. John sent Paul of Emesa to Alexandria where he was welcomed by Cyril and invited to preach on Christmas Day 433. Paul presented a statement of the Antiochene position, which affirmed Mary to be "the God-bearing Virgin" of the "unique Son of God, perfect God and perfect man . . . consubstantial with the Father in Godhead and consubstantial with us in manhood." (This statement of dual consubstantiality is often called the "double homoousion.") As a bow to Cyril, the paper, likely composed by Theodoret of Cyrus, affirmed Jesus to be "one Christ, one Son, and one Lord," which was an "unconfused union" of two natures (*Ep.* 39; Hardy, 356). It also clarified the application of partitive exegesis: in scriptural descriptions of Christ, some refer to the one person, while others refer specifically to one nature or the other, the humility of Christ's manhood, the "God-befitting" ones of his Godhead. Cyril responded with a letter to John (*Ep.* 39) known as the *Formula of Reunion*, in which he accepted Paul's paper as "an unimpeachable confession of the faith." Cyril answered the charge of Apollinarianism by saying that only a fool would claim that "the holy body of Christ came down from heaven" and still call Mary, from whom Jesus derived his human nature, *Theotokos*. Cyril then affirms the immutability and impassibility of the Word while also making clear that the hypostatic or natural union did not entail a "mixture or confusion" of the Word and his flesh. Like all good diplomatic compromises, each side secured what was most important to them and was able to tell their supporters that the other side, not they, made the concessions. John and the Syrians secured Cyril's recognition of "two natures" language that preserved the distinction without confusion and that the Son's passion did not result in a change in his perfect divinity (*Ep.* 39; Hardy, 357). Cyril, on the other hand, secured what he most wanted, namely the affirmation that Christ is one person. Thus formally ended the mutual condemnations by Alexandria and Antioch.

As with most diplomatic compromises, however, not everyone was satisfied with the *Formula of Reunion*. Cyril himself was not content, fearing that the Antiochene de facto acceptance of Nestorius's condemnation was not enough without an explicit repudiation of the two-subjects Christology of Diodore and Theodore, who were viewed as the fathers of Syrian theology. This concern led to Cyril's composing *On the Unity of Christ*, which constituted his most developed rejection of the two-subjects Christology that was the foundation of Nestorius's thought. Unless Diodore and Theodore's views were condemned, then Nestorius's Christology had not truly been repudiated. Indeed, Nestorius's defense of his position in *The Bazaar of Heracleides* seemed to confirm that his Christology, though officially condemned, was far from dead. So incendiary were his subsequent writings that Nestorius was ultimately sentenced to live out the remainder of his unrepentant life in an Egyptian penal colony.

Among Cyril's more moderate supporters was Proclus who was patriarch of Constantinople in 434–446. In a sermon delivered in March 431, he employed language, likely taken from Cyril, that anticipated the language of Chalcedon twenty years later. Proclus unequivocally maintained Cyril's single-subject Christology. Having affirmed that Jesus was not merely a divinized man but the "incarnate God" in whom natures came together but remaining without confusion, Proclus introduced language of two natures. "There is only one Son," he declared, "for the natures are not divided into two hypostases, but the awesome economy of salvation has united the two natures in one hypostasis" (*Dogm. inc.*; Grillmeier, 520–21). Proclus, like Cyril, saw Theodore's two-subjects Christology in the background. Nevertheless, he recognized that an all-out attack on Diodore and Theodore would not build a spirit of reconciliation with the Syrians. So he encouraged Cyril to avoid direct references to either. Although Proclus was willing to critique Theodore in his *Tome to the Armenians* (435), his use of *hypostasis*, as Grillmeier has argued, matched the sense of "personal union" or *prosōpon* and so was acceptable to the Syrians.

After Cyril's death in June 444, his followers, who themselves were dissatisfied with the compromise negotiated between Cyril and John, were free to resume the battle. Dioscorus, who had served as Cyril's deacon and succeeded Cyril at his death as patriarch of Alexandria, thought that Cyril had conceded too much in the *Formula of Reunion* because he was advanced in years and was worn down by the protracted controversy. Specifically, by accepting the language of two natures, Dioscorus believed, Cyril had given up his theology of the "natural union," which produced a single nature (*mia physis*). Among the Antiochenes, Theodoret of Cyrus found no olive branch in the *Formula of Reunion*. In addition to his lingering view that Nestorius's condemnation was unjust and that Cyril should have been excommunicated as an Apollinarian, Theodoret recognized Cyril's position to be a rejection of Diodore and Theodore. In 447, he published his tome *Eranistēs*, which attacked any who affirmed that Christ had only one nature in which the divine Word suffered.

The tension between followers of Cyril, commonly referred to as "monophysites," who understood the Cyrillian language of one *hypostasis* to mean one nature, and the champions of Nestorius, who are called "Dyophysites" because of their insistence on the two natures or two-subjects Christology of Theodore, continued to simmer in the nearly two decades after the settlement between Cyril and John. The tension erupted into open conflict when, in November 448 at a gathering of bishops in Constantinople, Eusebius of Dorylaecum leveled charges of heresy against the aged monk Eutyches. Flavian, patriarch of Constantinople, convened the trial. Precisely what Eutyches held is uncertain. At the very least, he viewed the language of two natures as being open to a Nestorian interpretation against which he wanted to guard. A more extreme characterization of his theology, as presented by Theodoret, was that Jesus's human nature was "swallowed up" and transformed by the Word's divinity such that Jesus was not, properly speaking, consubstantial with the rest of Adam's family. Ironically, the monophysites took from this trial a useful formula used by Flavian: "We confess that Christ is *from two* natures [*ek dyo physeōn*] after the incarnation, confessing one Christ, one Son, one Lord, in one *hypostasis* and one *prosōpon*." The expression "from two natures" Eutyches either knew before the trial or quickly turned to his advantage (*Ep.* 28.6; Hardy, 368). He invoked the phrase to mean that the incarnation took two natures from the Word and Mary only to unite them into a single nature or *mia physis*. After ten days of the trial, Eutyches was found guilty of deviating from the *Formula of Reunion* and deposed as archimandrite or leader of his monastic community.

Eutyches promptly appealed to Pope Leo I. Flavian eventually sent Leo an account of the trial. Leo responded not as Eutyches had hoped, with an endorsement, but with a concurring censure. His reply, however, had far wider significance than this single case. The response, known as the *Tome of Leo*, was definitive of Western Christology and would be treated as having canonical authority on par with Cyril's letters as the controversy progressed. The *Tome* illustrates both an emerging linguistic and theological divide between the Greek East and the Latin West and at the same time certain shared christological sensibilities. For, on the one hand, Leo, understandably, seems to have no knowledge of the terminological confusion surrounding *hypostasis* and *prosōpon*. Nor does the *Tome* reveal any familiarity with the conflict between the two-subjects Christology of Theodore and the single-subject Christology of Cyril. On the other hand, Leo affirms the core claims that comprised the *Formula of Reunion*. His critique of Eutyches took as its starting points Scripture and the Apostles' and Nicene-Constantinopolitan Creeds. Moreover, the *Tome* affirms that Christ is one person, "the only begotten Son of God [who] was crucified and buried" (*Ep.* 28.5; Hardy, 366), while at the same time insisting upon the immutability and impassibility of Christ's divinity. Commenting on the line from the creed that Jesus was "born of the Holy Spirit and the Virgin Mary," Leo writes, "This birth in time in no way detracted from, in no way added to, that divine and everlasting birth [of the Word from the Father]; but extended itself wholly in the work of restoring man" (*Ep.* 28.2; Hardy, 361). Thus, Leo distinguished the Son's eternal nature from his economic assumption of human nature—an assumption though that in no way compromised his divinity. Christ's being two natures in one person was, for Leo, simply the logical extension of Scripture. Like Cyril, he was content to think of the two natures existing side by side in a salvific paradox: "the inviolable nature has been united to the passible . . . [so that] from one element [he is] capable of dying and from the other incapable" (*Ep.* 28.3; Hardy, 363). Leo denies any confusion of natures: "For each of the natures retains its proper character without defect . . . so the form of a servant does not impair the form of God" (*Ep.* 28.3; Hardy, 364). At the same time, he readily confesses that the incarnate Word did in flesh what the Word in his transcendence could not do: "the impassible God did not disdain to become passible and the immortal one [did not disdain] to be subject to the laws of death" (*Ep.* 28.4; Hardy, 364). Therefore, within the unity of the single person, the two natures remain conceptually distinguishable, which allows for, and at times requires, partitive exegesis. When commenting on the birth narrative in Matthew's Gospel, Leo distinguishes between two natures. The target of Herod's plot was the child Jesus in his humanity, whereas the worship of the magi was directed to Jesus in his divinity, to him who is "Lord of all" (*Ep.* 28.4; Hardy, 365). Thus, Leo held firmly to the undiminished immutability and impassibility of the Word without giving up Jesus's humanity as he accused Eutyches of doing. For at the heart of Leo's Christology was Jesus's salvific passion. If Eutyches affirmed, as Leo believed he surely must have, that Jesus's passion and crucifixion were real, then he had to acknowledge the reality of his passible flesh. The *Tome*, therefore, in its climax echoes Ignatius of Antioch's argument against docetic Christology.

In Alexandria, Dioscorus zealously embraced the role of Eutyches's champion and the defender of what he believed to be the miaphysite Christology of Cyril. He refused to recognize Flavian's and Leo's condemnations of Eutyches and, with the support of allies at court, persuaded Theodosius to call another council at Ephesus. Known as the "Robber Council" (*Latrocinium*), the Council of Ephesus was convened in August of 449 by Dioscorus, who presided autocratically. The discussion was entirely one-sided; Dioscorus refused to allow the delegates from Rome to read the *Tome of Leo*. Under coercion from Dioscorus, the council declared Eutyches innocent of heresy and rejected the *Formula of Reunion* with its two-natures language. Not surprisingly, Flavian, Theodoret, and Eusebius of Dorylaecum were condemned and deposed. The scene then turned violent when a mob of monks stationed outside of the church, at Dioscorus's instigation, stormed the building and brutally attacked Flavian while the archbishop clung to the altar for safety. The beating Flavian received was so severe that he died scant days later from his wounds.

The next year, Theodosius died in an equestrian accident. His sister Pulcheria married one of Theodosius's soldiers, Marcian, who was crowned the new emperor. Under pressure from Leo to overturn the travesty of the Robber Council and out of a desire to keep the peace within the empire generally and specifically between the sees of Rome, Alexandria, Antioch, and Constantinople, Marcian summoned a council that was convened at Chalcedon in October 451. With more than five hundred bishops, Chalcedon already had far more of an ecumenical character than did Second Ephesus, which had around 150 bishops. Even as the First Council of Ephesus began by designating certain texts as canonical for the purpose of deliberations, Chalcedon affirmed the sufficiency of the Nicene-Constantinopolitan Creed along with letters of Cyril and the *Tome of Leo*. The formal statement that emerged wove together the language of Cyril's letters, the *Tome of Leo*, the *Formula of Reunion*, and Flavian's formula read at Eutyches's trial. The Chalcedonian statement reads,

> Following therefore the holy fathers, we confess one and the same Son, our Lord Jesus Christ, and we all teach harmoniously [that he is] the same [being] perfect in Godhead, the same [being] perfect in humanity, truly God and truly man, the same [being] of a reasonable soul and body; consubstantial with the Father in Godhead, and the same [being] consubstantial with us in humanity, like us in all things except sin; begotten before ages of the Father in Godhead, the same [being] in the last days for us and for our salvation born of Mary the Virgin *Theotokos* in humanity, one and the same [being] Christ, Son, Lord, unique; acknowledged in two natures without confusion, without change, without division, without separation—the difference of the natures being by no means taken away because of the union, but rather the distinctive character of each nature being preserved, and each combining in one *prosōpon* and *hypostasis*—not divided or separated into two persons, but one and the same Son and only begotten God, Word, Lord Jesus Christ; as the prophets of old and the Lord Jesus Christ himself taught us about him, and the symbol [i.e., creed] of the fathers has handed down to us. (Hardy, 373, modified)

This statement, like the final creed of the Council of Constantinople (381) and the *Formula of Reunion*, was clearly a compromise formula that would satisfy the moderate heirs of Cyril and moderate heirs of John. Yet it was not a mere compromise. Rather, the Chalcedonian formula reflects a genuine evolution in Catholic Christology: a development in the understanding of what sort of language the Church uses about Christ and what that language may and may not mean. It affirms the absolute oneness of Christ advocated by Cyril while also being read so as to rule out the two-subjects Christology of Nestorius. The incarnation is no mere conjunction of wills. Jesus is not a superprophet distinguishable from other prophets and saints merely by the degree of grace given in the Word's indwelling. Rather, he is the unique union of divinity and humanity. By speaking of the union as in "one *prosōpon* and *hypostasis*"—to use the language of Flavian's formula—the council showed significant progress toward overcoming prior semantic misunderstandings. By treating the two disputed terms as virtual synonyms, *hypostasis* was understood to mean not a single nature, as it did for Eutyches and Dioscorus, but a single person or individual composed of soul and body, as was meant by *prosōpon*. At the same time, *prosōpon* was not understood in the Nestorian sense of the single likeness of a God-bearing man but as the one Lord Jesus Christ. Furthermore, the language of "two natures" from the *Formula of Reunion* was retained with the addition of four critical qualifiers that excluded the errors of Eutyches and Dioscorus ("without confusion, without change") and of Nestorius ("without division, without separation"). In this way, the formula affirmed Christ's unity—the *one* Lord who was truly crucified, dead, but raised—without compromising the immutability and impassibility of the Word. Finally, this affirmation of the oneness of Christ—one Son born of the Father from eternity and from Mary economically in time—meant Mary might continue to be called *Theotokos*.

Reaction to Chalcedon

Marcian's hope was that the judgment of the bishops at Chalcedon would set to rest the issue of Christ's identity and thus exclude the need for further discussion. The judgment of the fathers of Chalcedon was given the status of law in a constitution issued by Marcian in February of 452: "The struggle over the law of orthodox Christians is ended" (Grillmeier, 95). Moreover, Marcian declared that Chalcedon stood with Nicaea (325), Constantinople (381), Ephesus (431), and Rome (449) as authoritative. In the emperor's mind, Chalcedon's language of the two "natures" was simply an affirmation of the "truth" of Jesus's divinity and humanity. Therefore, rather than rejecting Cyril's understanding of *mia physis* as a synonym for *hypostasis*, Chalcedon merely rejected the Apollinarian or docetic character of Eutyches's Christology.

Yet what seemed intuitively obvious to Marcian—namely that Chalcedon, as a reaffirmation of Ephesus (431), was a vindication of Cyril and his single-subject Christology—was not at all obvious to others. In Jerusalem, a monk named Theodosius promulgated the view that Chalcedon had endorsed Nestorianism. This led to an uprising of the monks in Jerusalem who deposed the pro-Cyrillian archbishop of Jerusalem, Juvenal, and installed Theodosius in his place. Outrage among the Miaphysites spread, which led to the assassination of Severianus, bishop of Scythopolis. Violent protest broke out in Alexandria in response to the condemnation and replacement of Dioscorus with a pro-Chalcedonian bishop. This reaction was due in part to Marcian's own failure in his constitutions, which affirmed Chalcedon, to distinguish between Cyril's Christology and that of Apollinaris and Eutyches. As Grillmeier has noted, the attempt to promote Chalcedon by imperial mandate, rather than by an explanation of the formula through appealing to Cyril's own writings as interpretive documents, demonstrated Marcian's "untheological arrogance" that only fueled the anti-Chalcedonian reaction.[3] In declaring, "The citizens and inhabitants of Alexandria have been so infected by the poison of Apollinarius" (*Mar. imp. Pall.*; Grillmeier, 106), the emperor's apparent equation of Alexandrian theology with Apollinaris's Miaphysite Christology gave the understandable impression that Chalcedon was a condemnation of Cyril as well as his faithful interpreters, Eutyches and Dioscorus. Thus, Marcian found himself in the predicament of having to persuade the Alexandrians that Chalcedon was not what his own rhetoric had led them to believe.

Instead of creating ecclesial unity, the years following Ephesus (431) and Chalcedon (451) witnessed a hardening of ecclesial divisions. Between 484 and 486, Bishop Bar Sauma convened synods of bishops who were adherents of Diodore and Theodore's teachings, formally creating the Church of the East separate from the Syrian Orthodox Church. Meanwhile, the Imperial or Chalcedonian Church continued to be the Church of Byzantium and Palestine.

The Rise of Eastern Scholastic Theology

The term "scholasticism" is usually applied to the theology that developed in universities in Western Europe in the High Middle Ages. At its zenith in the thirteenth century, it is characterized, as Mark Clark has put it, by a shift from commentary on the biblical text to an analysis of the teachings of the masters such as Peter Lombard and Thomas Aquinas, and the use of categorical distinctions in order to arrive at ever more precise definitions. Theology in the East after Chalcedon can fairly be characterized in similar terms. Disputes centered on competing interpretations of early church fathers, especially Athanasius, the Cappadocians, and Cyril. And the arguments between the champions of Chalcedon and their miaphysite opponents hinged on the definitions of key terms (*physis*, *hypostasis*, *ousia*). Even as the scholastic disputes in the Latin West drew on distinctions using

3. Grillmeier, *Christ in Christian Tradition*, 2/1:108.

the traditional resources of Platonism or the categories of Aristotle whose works, once lost in the West, had made their way into Latin universities, the Eastern scholastics sought to clarify the distinctions between the terms of Chalcedon by appealing to the Neo-Platonic interpretations of Aristotle.

One such Eastern scholastic was the leader of the Miaphysites, Severus of Antioch (465–523). He defended the Cyrillian tradition with its emphasis on the Logos as the single subject of Christ and with it the language of "one nature" by arguing that the terms *physis* and *hypostasis* were synonyms. Severus—following Basil's examples of Peter and Paul, each of whom is a separate *hypostasis* (*Eun.* 2.4; *Ep.* 38.3)—uses *hypostasis* to refer to the particular individual in contrast with the genus or class (*Hom.* 125; Zachhuber, 123). Therefore, Christ can be spoken of as either one *hypostasis* or one *physis*. But Chalcedon's language of "two natures" (*physeis*) implies two hypostases or subjects; thus, the Chalcedonian formula is Nestorian. Severus's insistence on Jesus's particularity reflects, as Johannes Zachhuber has argued, the ontology of Gregory of Nyssa, which maintains that the universal can be known only through the individual because, as with Aristotle's ontology, the universal has no existence independent of its particular instantiations. The only way to know either the divine nature or divinized human nature was in the particular man, Jesus. Severus's emphasis on Christ as a particularity put him at odds with the pro-Chalcedonian theologian, John of Caesarea, also known as the Grammarian (490–570). John affirmed the "double homoousion" that Jesus as the incarnate Logos was consubstantial with both the Father and with human beings whose nature (*ousia*) he assumed (*Gramm.* 2.17; Zachhuber, 135). Because John equated *physis* with *ousia*, he interpreted *mia physis* to be a denial of the "double homoousion" in Cyril's *Formula of Reunion*. Here, however, was semantic confusion between Severus and John. Severus objected to John's use of *ousia* because, in Severus's thinking, it included the totality of individuals who were members of a particular class. In the case of Jesus, therefore, Severus understood John to be saying that all human beings were in Christ. Severus countered by applying the Trinitarian grammar to John's Christology. If *ousia* included all members of a class of things, and Jesus possessed the divine *ousia*, then not just the Logos but the whole Trinity was incarnate in Jesus. By extension, it was equally foolish to claim that all humanity was included in Jesus. Therefore, for Severus, it was better to dispense with the divisive language of the "double homoousion" in favor of the unitive language of *mia physis*.

Since, for Severus, the universal exists only in the particular, to say that Jesus was a single particular subject (*mia physis*) was tantamount to saying that he was also one nature. Yet his miaphysite Christology was distinct from the monophysite Christology of Eutyches and Dioscorus. For Eutyches's Jesus was neither fully God nor fully man but a third thing (*tertium quid*) altogether different from either.

He was a hybrid of the two natures, like a centaur, part man and part horse. For Severus, however, Jesus was "one composite, incarnate nature" taken "from two natures." In contrast with monophysites, Severus was able to affirm that Jesus was fully human—but understood entirely economically. That is, Jesus as the incarnate Logos acted in the world by exercising certain capacities proper to a human nature (growing, hungering, thirsting, suffering) so that he might reveal to the rest of Adam's family how their human nature might be sanctified by the Spirit. And in contrast with the Chalcedonian language of "in two natures," Severus was able to insist that Christ was one nature taken *from* the two natures united in the incarnation. Thus, he could affirm the full unity of divinity and humanity without any hint of a division in Christ between two natures or subjects that coexisted side by side *in* one person. Rather, the Logos was the single subject that exercised complete hegemony over Jesus's actions. Therefore, at times, Jesus acted as any human being composed of soul and body would; but the action did not arise from Jesus's rational soul or his body. Rather, these actions arose from the will of the Logos who decided such actions were necessary economically for humanity's salvation. Thus, the Logos allowed Jesus's flesh to experience and his soul to give verbal expression to the suffering of his passion and execution (cf. *Gramm.* 3.2; Grillmeier 2.2, 167). Severus could support this view by pointing to Isaiah 7:16: "Before he knows or chooses evil, he will choose the good." Although an infant is incapable of shunning evil because he cannot distinguish between good and evil, Jesus was able, even as a babe in the manger, to reject the evil in favor of the good because the all-wise Logos incarnate in the babe knew the good perfectly and so was able to choose the good. Thus, for Severus, miaphysite Christology best articulated Cyril's unitive, single-subject Christology.

In 531, a delegation of monks from Palestine arrived in Constantinople to participate in a synod summoned by the emperor Justinian I. It was composed of both defenders and critics of Chalcedon, and its purpose was to work out an understanding of Chalcedon that would be satisfactory to both sides. The leading voice in this Palestinian delegation, which was decidedly pro-Chalcedonian, was Leontius of Byzantium (485–543), who is often called the father of Neo-Chalcedonian Christology. Rather than a frontal assault against Severus, Leontius's approach was an indirect critique of Miaphysitism by attacking Nestorius and Eutyches, both of whom, Leontius says, were guilty of docetism. That is, each, though in opposite ways, denied the true unity of the incarnation: Nestorius by interpreting the two natures to imply two subjects, and Eutyches by imagining Christ to be something that is neither fully God nor fully human (*Nest. Eut.* 1; Daley, 128–30). With this oblique tack, Leontius sought to appeal to the Severans by clarifying how Chalcedon expressed a genuinely Cyrillian Christology that stood over against the Nestorians and monophysites.

Through his critique of Eutyches, Leontius argues that, in order to understand Chalcedon rightly, they needed to arrive at a clear understanding of the terms employed by the fathers, especially Cyril. This was particularly true of the meanings of *hypostasis* and *physis*. He grants Severus's claim that Cyril was not always consistent and that he at times treated *hypostasis* and *physis* as synonyms. That was fine; for in common, nontechnical Christian discourse, such as sermons, imprecision is acceptable as when one says, "God died on the cross." Yet when the grammar of dogma is being established, as Chalcedon sought to do, in the face of "struggles" and division, imprecision or ambiguity creates only erroneous theological ideas and further division within the Church (*Epil.* 3; Daley, 281–83). Even taking the route of silence about the union by speaking of it as an "ineffable and unnamable" union is, Leontius declares, hiding behind a dubious piety that only creates further impiety and confusion (*Nest. Eut.* 7; Daley, 165). Rather, a truly pious understanding of the incarnation required grounding the language in the doctrine of the Trinity. Therefore, Leontius sought to make the terms of Chalcedonian Christology consistent with the Trinitarian terminology developed in the fourth century. Father, Son, and Spirit are individual persons (*hypostaseis*) who share a common divine nature (*ousia*). Therefore, *physis* corresponded to *ousia*, meaning "nature," and *hypostasis* referred to the individual. *Physis*, like *ousia*, denotes the genus or general class, while *hypostasis* refers to a particular member of the class (*Nest. Eut.* 1; Daley, 133–35). Because a *hypostasis* possesses all the essential characteristics common to the beings of their class or nature, the persons of the Trinity possess all the qualities of the divine nature and so are said to be consubstantial (*Epil.* 2; Daley, 277). But because a hypostasis also possesses characteristics that distinguish it from other individuals, the Father, Son, and Spirit are not a single entity but three discrete entities. The hypostasis of the Father is distinct from the Son and Spirit because he alone is unbegotten, while the Son and Spirit are distinguished from the Father and each other because they are begotten and spirated, respectively. Thus, *hypostasis* is the term of individuation, and *physis* is the term of unity. Or as Leontius puts it succinctly, in the Trinity, "sameness of essence unites and difference of hypostasis divides" (*Epil.* 1; Daley, 273). He elaborates the point by using the example of a man, an ox, and a horse. Each is distinguished from the other by the defining characteristics of their different natures (*physeis*). Yet each is an individual (*hypostasis*) and so also possesses nonessential features that distinguish the individual man or horse or ox from other individual members of their respective genus (*Epil.* 2; Daley, 277).

When speaking of Jesus, the incarnate Logos, Chalcedon stated that he is one *hypostasis*, meaning he is a single individual who is the unconfused compound (*synthesis*) or product (*apotelesma*) of two natures (*physeis*) (*Epil.* 4; Daley, 285). Since *hypostasis* refers to a particular individual, Chalcedon's claim that Christ is one hypostasis is to say, contra Nestorius, that he is a single subject. This, Leontius says, is what the fathers meant when they spoke of the Lord as "one and the same" (*Epil.* 3; Daley, 281–83). Since a *hypostasis* is an instantiation of the genus or class, it possesses essential properties of its class or nature. Therefore, since Jesus possesses the essential properties of both God and man, he must be said to be "in two natures." Leontius proves the point by arguing that, since Jesus is the Logos, which according to its divine nature is immaterial and immortal, and yet also has mortal flesh proper to a human nature, Jesus must possess two different natures (*Nest. Eut.* 1; Daley, 131). Based on this application of the meanings of *hypostasis* and *physis* from the Trinitarian grammar, Leontius argues, it is incorrect for the Severans to speak of Christ as a single *physis*. In other words, when *physis* is rightly understood as corresponding to *ousia* or nature, the term *mia physis* cannot be applied to the unconfused union of the divine and human natures in Jesus.

One complication surrounding the term *hypostasis*, however, was that it had two different senses when transferred from the Trinity to speak of the incarnation. Within the Trinity, the Logos is a *hypostasis* inasmuch as he is the only begotten Son who is distinct from the unbegotten Father and the spirated Spirit. In the incarnation, however, the hypostasis of the Logos enters into hypostatic union. Therefore, the Logos simultaneously is a *hypostasis* with respect to the Godhead and, as Jesus of Nazareth, is a *hypostasis* in the sense that he is a discrete man distinct from other human beings. Leontius's point is that through the hypostatic union, the Logos, as a hypostasis distinct from though simultaneously united to the Father, is able to unite humanity to the Father (*Nest. Eut.* 4; Daley, 149). In this way, Leontius reaffirmed the "double homoousion" of the *Formula of Reunion*. Namely, the Logos, as the Father's coeternal Son, is *homoousios* with the Father and, as Jesus through the hypostatic union with human nature, is simultaneously consubstantial with humanity. Thus, the incarnation bridges the ontological divide between God and humanity.

The goal of Leontius's defense of Chalcedon was explicating the *unconfused* manner of this union, which, he says, is the mystery at the center of the Christian faith. Here, however, there is a key difference between Trinitarian grammar and Chalcedonian grammar. Whereas in the Trinity the nature (*physis* or *ousia*) is the principle of unity, and *hypostasis* is the principle of individuation that separates the persons, in the incarnation *hypostasis* is the principle of unity, and *physeis* refers to the "difference of essence that divides" (*Epil.* 1; Daley, 273). Leontius's challenge was describing how to think of these two natures existing in a true union that did not mix the natures in a way that compromised either Jesus's humanity or his impassible and immutable divinity. Central to this explication of the hypostatic union was elaborating on the meaning of Cyril's metaphor for describing the union, that is, the union of soul and body. Most basically, a person, as a particular individual, is a *hypostasis* that consists of both the essential characteristics of a human nature and the accidental characteristics particular to her as a unique individual. The person, as a hypostasis, is composed of body and soul but is not reducible to either. The person is not just her soul, nor is she just her body. She is the union of the two. So too, Leontius explains, the Logos, properly speaking, is not the Christ but becomes the Christ when he joins himself in a natural, organic union to a human nature in the incarnation (*Nest. Eut.* 2; Daley, 139). At the same time that a person is not reducible to either her soul or her body, the particular natures of soul and body are not confused in their union. That is, the union does not destroy either the distinctive nature of the soul or the distinctive nature of the body (*Nest. Eut.* 7; Daley, 175). On the contrary, the body maintains its material, sensible nature, and the soul retains its immaterial, rational nature (*Nest. Eut.* 2; Daley, 137). So too with Jesus. In the incarnation, the Logos does not give up its immortal and impassible nature, nor does his humanity give up its creaturely need for material sustenance or its ability to grow and change. Most of all, it retains its capacity to feel pain and to die. At this point, Leontius employs two other metaphors to reinforce the body-soul analogy of a union that does not confuse or destroy the natures in the compound: an oil lamp and a wooden torch. The lamp is composed of wick and flame, each having a distinctive nature. Yet, though the flame is joined to the wick on which it burns, the flame retains its ethereal, fiery quality, and the wick the properties of the fabric of which it is made. The same is true of a torch. Instead of negating the properties of the wood and the fire, the union of the two creates a complementary relationship, "each exchanging its characteristic with the other, both remaining in their unique, unconfused, individual existence" (*Nest. Eut.* 7; Daley, 171). The result of this union is a "woody fire" and "enkindled wood." Each imparts something to the other without fundamentally altering the nature of either the flame or the wood. Thus, the torch provides a model for thinking about the *communicatio idiomatum*. In the incarnation, the flame of the divine Logos abides in Jesus's humanity, so that when the woman with the issue of blood touched the hem of his garment, the indwelling healing power of the divinity passed through his body to her body.

The argument against these metaphors might be made that even as the wood of the torch is burned up because of its union with the fire, so the Logos loses its impassibility when united to passible flesh. Leontius anticipates this objection. He replies that every analogy has its limits because, as analogies, the lamp and the torch have more dissimilarities than similarities with the incarnate Logos. The wood can be burned up by the fire and the fire diminish with the burning up of the wood because both are creatures and therefore are inherently mutable. Similarly, in the case of the body-soul analogy, the soul suffers, Leontius observes, not because it is united to the passible body but because the soul "through its own nature" is passible. Here is where the union of divinity and humanity in the incarnation differs from the union of the fire and wood of the torch or of the soul and body in a human being. For in the case of the incarnation, the Logos by his very nature is immutable and impassible. Therefore, unlike the inherently passible soul or burnable wood, the divine nature of the Logos by its very nature is not and indeed cannot be changed or diminished by the union with the mutable human nature (*Nest. Eut.* 3; Daley, 143).

Leontius, echoing Gregory of Nyssa's argument that the greatness of God is that he is able to condescend and be joined to humanity's suffering without himself changing, turns the charge of theopassionism against his critics. To those who argue that a natural union would cause the Logos to suffer and be changed, Leontius says, "You are afraid to unite [the Logos] to flesh and to a complete man, lest he become necessarily circumscribed" (*Nest. Eut.* 3; Daley 141). On the contrary, the only change or diminution in the Logos would occur if he declined to condescend to human nature. If the Logos feared to be united to a body lest it suffer, then it would be inferior to the soul, which does not necessarily suffer with the body. Moreover, the only time the Logos would be said to suffer a passion would be if the Logos abandoned the *philanthrōpia* proper to his divine nature out of fear of personal suffering. That, however, would be a passion of which the Logos is incapable. For Leontius, as for Cyril, it is precisely through the hypostatic union with mortal human nature that the hypostasis of the Son is able to become Emmanuel, as Brian Daley expresses it, the God with us who makes humanity's vulnerability his own.

Leontius's definitions of *hypostasis* and *physis* based on the Trinitarian grammar allows him to counter Severus's replacement of "in two natures" with "from two natures." For "in two natures" means that in the incarnation, the human and divine natures are preserved as discrete but united in the compound; whereas "from two natures" implied that Christ is of a different nature entirely—a third thing resulting from the mixing of two natures, as when water is produced from hydrogen and oxygen. Christ, therefore, is truly one subject while also fully God and fully human.

In May and June of 553, the emperor Justinian I summoned the Fifth Ecumenical Council at Constantinople as an attempt to draw together the Miaphysites and the defenders of Chalcedon around their common opposition to Nestorianism. Second Constantinople issued fourteen canons, of which the last three were condemnations of Theodore of Mopsuestia, Theodoret of Cyrus, and Ibas of Edessa—the so-called Three Chapters—for their Nestorian tendencies. In the case of Theodore, the association with Nestorius is understandable since his two-subjects Christology was the foundation for Nestorius's theory of the prosoponic union. The charges against Theodoret and Ibas were less credible since Chalcedon had restored both men to their episcopal sees. For that reason, a significant contingent of bishops from northern Italy refused to subscribe to the condemnations because they saw them as an overturning of Chalcedon. In many ways, the canons of Second Constantinople had a largely negative character rather than contributing a positive explanation of the meaning of Chalcedon.

Its canons affirmed the double generation of Christ, first eternally from the Father and second in time from Mary. The third canon repudiated any separation of the Word from Christ's passion, thereby affirming that there was one subject of both the miraculous displays of the Word's divine power and his suffering on the cross. The fourth canon repudiated any description of the incarnation as a merely relational union by grace or activity (*energeia*) or through shared authority or equality of honor rather than Cyril's conception of a natural union. Rather than being two persons sharing one appellation "Christ," "Christ" denotes the one hypostasis who is a member of the Trinity and who in the incarnation assumed a human nature. Furthermore, it affirmed Justinian's so-called theopaschite formula that affirmed *unus ex Trinitate passus*, or "one from the Trinity suffered." Thus, it affirms that the Logos is the single subject who exists in a compound unity with his flesh that is neither confused nor separated (canon 4; Hardy, 379). The eighth canon affirmed that, because there is only one subject, no distinction should be made between the worship of the Word and of the man Jesus (canon 9). At the same time that the council repudiated Nestorius's two-subjects Christology, it also reaffirmed the condemnation of Apollinarianism through the council's affirmation of the "double homoousion"—Christ in his divinity is consubstantial with the Father, and in his humanity consubstantial with Adam's family (canon 8). One of the constructive moves of the council was its description of the union as synthesis (*synthesis*), which affirmed the presence of two natures while at the same time signifying that the two natures, though distinguishable in the believer's mind (*theōria*), were in reality inseparable (canon 7). Although Leontius was long dead by the time of Second Constantinople, his apologia for Chalcedon, though not ultimately proving persuasive for the miaphysite heirs of Severus, prepared the terminological clarity that paved the way for this fuller vision of Chalcedonian Christology.

The Church of the East: The Dyophysites

Syriac-speaking Christians had lived across the border of the eastern frontier of the Roman Empire that abutted the Parthian—later the Sasanian—Empire since the second century. By the early third century, there were an appreciable number of Christian communities—called East Syrian, as opposed to Western Syrian Christians living within the Roman world and centered at Antioch—that functioned semiautonomously. Because of their geographic location, they were less aware and therefore less under the direct influence of Constantinople. The Nicene Creed, for instance, was not officially accepted by the East Syrian churches until a synod at Selucia-Ctesiphon in 410, almost thirty years after Nicaea was reaffirmed at the First Council of Constantinople. By the fifth century, their bishops were chosen independent of consultation with Antioch. The real rift between the East Syrians and both the West Syrians and the church at Constantinople came in 431 after the condemnation of Nestorius at the Council of Ephesus. This marked a dogmatically determined division between the Church of the East and their Western counterparts. It is, however, inaccurate to refer to the Church of the East as the "Nestorian" church. The breaking of ties with the West reflected not a theological commitment to Nestorius per se but their devotion to the theology of Nestorius's teacher, Theodore of Mopsuestia. Theodore's works had been translated into Syriac by monks at the school of Edessa and gained almost canonical status among the East Syrians. While Nestorius was treated alongside Theodore and Diodore of Tarsus as one of the three doctors of the Church of the East, he was honored more because he was perceived as a martyr than because his writings were given an authoritative status.

In the years that followed the parting of the ways, the East Syrians began to expand upon Theodore's Christology. One of the leading voices in this process was Narsai, who after being expelled from the School of Edessa, reestablished the School of Nisibis. Strongly affirming the unity of Christ, Narsai was equally insistent that the divine and human natures needed to be distinguished: "in my confession I have not made any split, for it is in one Son that I confess, a single Lordship . . . one prosopon, of the Word and the temple he chose. . . . Perfect in his divinity, for he is equal with his begetter, and complete in his humanity, with soul and body of mortal beings" (*Hom.* 56; quoted in Brock, notes 34 and 36). Central to Narsai's position was, as Sebastian Brock has argued, the concern both to protect the Word's transcendent divinity from suffering and to preserve the full humanity of Christ. The latter was essentially a soteriological concern. Unless Jesus's humanity that was raised and glorified was truly human, that is, identical with that of all other members of Adam's family, then there was no true hope that mortals like us would also be raised and glorified. At a synod in 486, East Syrian bishops accepted Narsai's interpretation of Theodore's Christology as advocating two natures (Syr. *trēn kyānē*; analogous to Gk. *duo physeis*) unmixed, in union (Syr. *naqiputhā*, analogous to Gk. *synapheia*) in a single person. Thus, the East Syrians were called Dyophysites, in contradistinction from the West Syrian Miaphysites of the church in Antioch.

Though separated geographically and ecclesiastically from Constantinople and Antioch, the East Syrians were not unaware of the disputes between the Miaphysites and the Neo-Chalcedonians. Indeed, the arguments of Severus and

Leontius made their way east through the teachings of Ḥenana of Adiabene who introduced the doctrine of a single, composite hypostasis during his forty years as director of the School of Nisibis. The Dyophysite response was subsequently formulated in a tome entitled *On the Union* by the monk and theologian Babai the Great (c. 551–628) who studied at Nisibis before joining the monastic communities at Beth Zabdai and the Great Monastery of Tur 'Abdin, which he directed until his death. If one of the key features of Theodore of Mopsuestia's Dyophysite Christology was that he abandoned the Alexandrian divinization soteriology with its theory of *communicatio idiomatum*, Babai offers a thoroughly unitive Christology that does not avoid talk of natures and yet seeks to give expression to the transformation of Christ's humanity in the incarnation. In contrast with a Word-flesh Christology of Alexandria, Babai's is a *qnōmā-parṣōpā* Christology. Or to put it in a formula, Christ is two *qnōme* in one *parṣōpā*. The Syriac terms *qnōmā* and *parṣōpā* generally correspond to the Greek categories of *hypostasis* or *prosōpon*. However, *hypostasis* or *qnōmā* did not mean the same thing for Babai that it meant for Cyril or Leontius. Therefore, in order to grasp the subtleties of Babai's Dyophysite Christology, one must understand the distinct meanings that Babai applies to them when speaking of either the Trinity or the incarnate Word.

A *hypostasis* (*qnōmā*) is "an individuated *ousia*" that "subsists in itself" and "receives accidents" (*Lib. un.* 159.16–19). Babai, like Aristotle, maintained that universal natures existed but they did not exist as intelligible forms. Rather, the universal nature existed only in concrete instances. A hypostasis is this universal or common nature existing in a circumscribed individual located in place and time. Through the particular individual, the common nature is known. The *qnōmā* will manifest itself with the form distinctive of that nature. By contrast, the *prosōpon* (*parṣōpā*) consists of the set of accidents that an individual member within that class of beings possesses. As an illustration of the difference, Babai points to the sight of two figures walking toward you from a distance. They are close enough to be seen as two bipeds walking upright so you know that their *qnōmā* is that of a human being and not an elephant or a giraffe. But they are not close enough for you to see their distinguishing appearances (*parsōpe*) so as to tell whether they are Peter and Andrew or Mary and Martha. Thus, the *qnōmā* is both general and individual. For it is one instance of a common nature or essence (the human nature, for instance) in a discrete entity or individual (a particular person) that is different from others of the same class or essence. But the *parṣōpā* consists of the distinguishing features that make one individual different from all other individuals of that class.

The distinction between *qnōmā* and *parṣōpā* proved useful for Babai's explication of the Trinity. Each person is a *qnōmā* in the sense that each is a discrete instance of the divine nature or *ousia*. Yet what makes each person distinct from each other is their unique *parṣōpā* (*Lib. un.* 160.22). The Father's *parṣōpā* is his mode of being as the unbegotten. The Son's is his begottenness. And the Spirit's *parṣōpā* is his procession from the Father. Babai's notion of *qnōmā* fits nicely with the Nicene grammar of *homoousios* by allowing the common *ousia* to be individuated rather than being a fourth thing in which the three persons participate. Likewise, his concept of *parṣōpā* enabled him to express the unique feature or mode of being proper to each hypostasis.

The application of *qnōmā* and *parṣōpā* to the incarnate Word proved more difficult. On the one hand, *qnōmā* provided Babai with language to challenge the miaphysite account of two natures and their chief analogy of the soul's union with the body. Although soul and body are naturally different, he argued, human beings are not two natures but one nature or essence existing in a concrete individual. So too, Christ is not a compound in which the two natures or *qnōme* become dissolved into a new nature with its own *qnōmā*. Rather, he is the divine Word and a human nature conjoined in a single individual or *parṣōpā*. As such, the divinity and the humanity remain distinct at the level of *qnōmā*. Thus, Babai described Christ's humanity: "the human [...]—that is, Jesus of Nazareth—possessed a fixed *qnōmā* by which he is recognized and he possessed everything of the common nature in his *qnōmā*, which [Greeks] call an individual *ousia*" (*Tract. Vat.* 300.31–301.2).

To illustrate how the *qnōme* of divinity and humanity are joined but not confused, Babai adapted a common metaphor to fit his terminology of *qnōmā-parṣōpā*. A golden signet ring, as gold, is of a nature completely different from sealing wax and thus possesses a distinct *qnōmā*. The ring also contains the image of the king and inscribed words identifying the king. These are its *parṣōpā*, the distinguishing marks of this unique golden ring. When the ring is pressed into the wax, the wax receives the ring's *parṣōpā*, the imprint of the king's image and the accompanying words. The wax and the seal share, then, in a single *parṣōpā*. But it is not a union of the nature of the ring and the wax. For the gold proper to the *qnōmā* of the ring is not present in the seal. Nevertheless, the wax has taken on the marks of the ring with its image of the king and inscribed words (*Lib. un.* 165.5–9). The result of the joining of the ring and the wax is the creation of a wax form that carries all the authority of the king and demands respect of those receiving the documents to which the seal is attached as if the king himself were present to them. In other words, the wax gains a status and an authority that it would not have apart from the ring's impress (*Lib. un.* 165.11–13).

So too in the incarnation, the divine Word is conjoined to Jesus's humanity to form a single, kingly subject (*parṣōpā*) who bears all the marks of the Word's sonship. Yet even as the wax does not take on the gold proper to the ring's nature as a distinct *qnōmā*, the humanity of Christ does not become the divine *qnōmā*, nor is it subsumed within it. Babai sums up the point of the metaphor: "For God the Word, by participation through this conjunction gave to humanity his Lordship, his name, his adoration, all the exalted and unspeakable things which he possesses in his nature, except his nature and *qnōmā*, which cannot be given or received" (*Lib. un.* 165.25–166.1). Babai's distinction here between the things "in his nature" that are communicated to Jesus's humanity and the nature itself that is not communicated is confusing. He likely means that sonship of the Word and its authority are the consequence of the Word's being begotten from the nature of the Father. In the case of the incarnation, Babai's language preserves an absolute distinction between the creaturely nature and the divine nature. The former is not swallowed up in the latter, nor the latter changed into the former. Instead, Christ's humanity possesses this sonship and its authority not because it shares directly in the divine nature itself but because it is conjoined to the Word parsopically, in one person. Thus, there is only one *parṣōpā* of sonship in which the divine and human *qnōme* participate and by which the natures are manifested. Babai nevertheless distinguishes the manner in which each shares in the sonship: "The *parṣōpā* is one and the same but not in the same [respect]. One is natural and one [by] assumption" (*Tract. Vat.* 302.16–22). Thus, even if humanity is not assumed into the sonship of the Word through a natural union of the divine and human natures (as Cyril advocated in the hypostatic union), the conjoining of the Word and humanity in the incarnation fashioning a single *parṣōpā*, for Babai, nevertheless elevated human nature and conferred on it all the dignity of the Word's sonship.

The question lingers whether this elevation of humanity in the parsopic union is truly an instance of divinization or merely the nominal conferral of authority. One of the analogies Babai employs that strongly suggests a transformation of Jesus's humanity is the classic Alexandrian analogue of fire and iron. Jesus's humanity, Babai says, is not the mere humanity of Adam. Rather, it is a humanity full of divinity in the same way that the iron in the smithy's furnace is not mere iron but iron conjoined to fire (*Tract. Vat.* 300.16–17). As the iron does not lose its nature but takes on the qualities of the fire, the parsopic union of the Word and human nature allows the qualities of the Word's *parṣōpā* to pass on to Jesus's humanity (*Tract. Vat.* 304.11–29). While the natures are never conflated, there is a certain reciprocity in the union: "And thus divinity is not son without humanity from the union hence, and the humanity is not without the divinity separately mere [humanity] and ununited or called Christ, but in this one *parṣōpā*, they give and receive mutually. And this becomes that and that this parsopically, with this and that remaining in their individualized natures [*qnōme*] in this adored union of one *parṣōpā* of Christ, the son of God" (*Lib. un.* 172.10–28).

Babai's *qnōmā-parṣōpā* Christology had the advantage over Nestorius's prosoponic union that Babai was able to speak of a thoroughgoing unitive Christology complete with an exchange of characteristics of the two *qnōme* in the single *parṣōpā*. This was more than Nestorius's cooperative union of wills. Thus, he was able to come close to Cyril's almost organic characterization of the union using his own metaphors without falling into the difficulty of describing two natures. Though Babai shunned Cyril's paradoxical language—for example, suffering impassibly—his account of the exchange of parsopic properties included in Christ's sonship nonetheless gave his Christology a Cyrillian feel that came close to a divinization soteriology without the messy problem of explaining the unconfused union of two natures.

Maximus the Confessor and the Monothelite Controversy

In the first half of the seventh century, another attempt at rapprochement between the Chalcedonian and non-Chalcedonian churches was initiated by Sergius of Arsinoe, the patriarch of Constantinople. Desiring to reassure the Miaphysites of Egypt that Chalcedon's reference to Christ's two natures did not compromise the oneness of the person of Jesus, the Word incarnate, Sergius initiated a dialogue with the Egyptian bishop Theodore of Pharan. Out of their correspondence emerged a doctrine expressed in the document known as *Ekthesis*, which maintained that Jesus's activities were not divided between the Word and the man but were a single activity (*mia energeia*) accomplished by means of the human body governed entirely by the Word. Sergius referred to this single activity using the neologism, taken from Pseudo-Dionysius, of "theandric" or "divine-human" action (*theandrikē energeia*). This monoenergist Christology built on the logic of the theopaschite formula; if Christ is that one person of the Trinity who suffered and died, then there is one subject of all Christ's actions. Therefore, all Jesus's actions—eating and healing, suffering and preaching—were a single activity performed by a single subject. Emperor Heraclius (emperor 610–641) fully endorsed Monoenergism as a way to bind up the fissure between Alexandria and Constantinople. In June 633, Cyrus of Phasis, the patriarch of Alexandria, and Honorius of Rome affirmed Sergius's single action theory in the Formula of Union. Not everyone, however, was satisfied with Sergius's interpretation of *theandric activity*. John of Scythopolis interpreted Pseudo-Dionysius to mean by the expression "new theandric activity" that Jesus's actions were "new" because they represented a unique and unprecedented synthesis or compound of the divine and human actions. The ensuing divide between proponents of different interpretations of the idea of Jesus's theandric activity led to the question of the will of Christ. Did Jesus possess a single will that was the source of his single activity? Or did he possess two wills that corresponded to his two natures? The doctrine that Jesus had a single will, or Monothelitism, was seen by some as nothing other than a new iteration of Apollinarianism. Although the term "theandric" gestured to Jesus's human nature, in truth Jesus's humanity was reduced to the body that served merely as the physical instrument by which the Word accomplished his will. The debate that followed, the monothelite controversy, marked an effort among the Neo-Chalcedonians to understand implications of Chalcedon's "two natures" language within Cyril of Alexandria's theory of the hypostatic union.

One theologian who turned his considerable intellect to refute Monothelitism was Maximus the Confessor (580–662). Maximus's chief objection to *Ekthesis* was that its deficient depiction of Jesus's humanity could not provide a full and adequate account of salvation. That is, unless Jesus were fully human with a human will, then he could not be a model of redeemed and divinized humanity. Gregory of Nazianzus famously objected to Apollinaris's Christology, "That which the Word did not assume he did not heal," meaning if Jesus had no rational soul but only a human body, then only the body would be divinized by its union with the Logos. Maximus applied Gregory's logic in Chalcedonian terms. If Jesus possessed a fully human nature, then he possessed a rational human soul. Essential to that rational nature was a will capable of governing his human activities. Therefore, to claim that Jesus's single will was the will of the Logos was to deny that Jesus had a human soul. But without a human soul to be divinized by its union with the Word, Jesus could not truly be the second Adam who could reveal a purified and perfected humanity, which was the hope of salvation for his disciples.

Possessing a human will, for Maximus, fundamentally meant that Jesus's human will was able to carry out those functions proper to human nature. The *communicatio idiomatum* effected by the hypostatic union, Maximus insisted, did not "do violence" to Jesus's humanity by overriding his human will; rather, his will was restored to its natural, prelapsarian state (*Opusc.* 7; Daley, 220) so that it might then be raised into the highest communion with God, which was its ultimate telos. In other words, even as there was a divinizing communication of the divine power to Jesus's human nature, so too there was, as Cyril Hovorun has put it, a *communicatio voluntatum*. In the unmixed union with divinity and humanity, Jesus's natural human will was informed by and thus became conformed to his divine will. Maximus explained how this was possible by distinguishing between the "natural will" and the "gnomic" or postlapsarian will. The natural will referred to the innate inclination to pursue those goods necessary for the flourishing of one's nature. Because human beings were endowed with a share of the Logos, the natural will was, before the fall, governed by reason. In the light of reason, prelapsarian humanity willed creaturely goods appropriate for their well-being. However, with the coming of sin, the human mind was no longer guided by the pure light of reason, that is, a participation in the wisdom of the Logos. Therefore, Adam's race did not have sure knowledge of which goods were necessary and appropriate for their flourishing. The certainty and clarity of right understanding were replaced with the uncertainty of mere opinion (*gnōmē*). The result was an inner turmoil of conflicting opinions or impulses, as when Paul speaks of the law of sin in his members that war against the law of his mind (Rom 7:22–23). Without certain knowledge, human beings must deliberate within themselves about which goods they should pursue and which they should not. This deliberative process Maximus calls the "gnomic will." In the incarnation, however, Jesus experienced no inner uncertainty of opinion that produced a conflicted will. Rather, the grace of the luminous Logos imparted clarity to Jesus's rational faculties, which directed his natural will to those goods proper to his human nature and to the fulfillment of his earthly ministry.

The obvious counterexample was Jesus's prayer in Gethsemane: "Father, let this cup pass from me. Nevertheless, not my will but thine be done" (Matt 26:39). Maximus explained this seeming conflict by distinguishing between *different* wills and *opposed* wills (*Opusc.* 16). Jesus's two wills were not, he explained, opposed but simply different because of the different natures that were united in him (*Opusc.* 10). Different natures seek different goods and so will different things. In Jesus's human nature, therefore, he possessed a natural will that was directed to goods proper to a rational animal, for example, the desire to satisfy hunger, sleep, thirst, curiosity, and so on. These are different from what the Logos wills. For, in his divine nature, the Logos has no need of these goods. Therefore, the goods desired by Jesus's natural human will were not in opposition or contrary to the divine will—as a sinful desire would be—just different. Consequently, when explaining Jesus's prayer in Gethsemane, Maximus, following closely Cyril's interpretation, says that Jesus's natural will for self-preservation and his divine will for the redemption of humanity were not inherently in opposition. Jesus's dread at the prospect of his passion was perfectly understandable for a sentient creature. Nevertheless, the luminous grace of the Word allowed Jesus to see with clarity that the Father's will for deliverance of humanity through his death on the cross was a greater good than his natural will to avoid suffering and death. Therefore, Jesus's prayer did not reflect the confusion of a gnomic will. Rather, in the light of the sure knowledge provided by the Word, Jesus's divinized will conformed perfectly to God's will, and thus he chose to drink the cup of suffering (*Opusc.* 7).

The monothelite controversy illustrated how narrow the razor's edge was on which Chalcedon and Second Constantinople balanced the relationship of the one person and the two natures. It was easy for an emphasis on the single person of the incarnate Logos to minimize the role of the humanity the Logos assumed. Maximus's theory of Jesus's two wills affirmed a Cyrillian single-subject Christology while at the same time allowing Jesus's humanity to reveal both the fragility of human nature and at the same time its plasticity—that is, its ability to be transformed by the new communion between God and man inaugurated by the incarnation. As with Cyril's explanation of Jesus's Gethsemane prayer, Maximus's reading took seriously Jesus's agonized submission to the Father's will in a way that neither Apollinaris nor Sergius's Monothelitism did. He was able to describe the coexistence of the human and the divine in the single hypostasis that affirmed the balance between the single subject and the two natures that Chalcedon sought. He did so through a description of the great exchange between the two natures that resulted from their union in Jesus. Maximus maintained this balance by focusing his description on *how* the activities of each nature in Jesus was influenced by its union with the other. He famously said that Jesus acted "divine in a human way and human in a divine way." Though he was the incarnate Word, Jesus did not exercise his divine power by fiat as when God spoke the universe into being. Rather, his divinity exercised his immaterial power through the flesh of his humanity—that is, through the touch of his garment that healed the woman with the issue of blood or through his spittle mixed with earth to restore the sight to a blind man and through his voice that commanded demons to come out of the demoniac and that called Lazarus from the tomb. Most of all, Jesus, the Father's only begotten Son, displayed his divine compassion and mercy in the crucifixion of his body. *At the same time*, he lived out his sensual human life in a divine manner. Thus, at Gethsemane, Jesus, unlike the sleeping disciples whose spirit was willing but whose flesh was weak, faced fleshly human fears with a divine strength and resolute faithfulness—the faithfulness of the only begotten Son to his Father.

For Maximus, the monk and confessor seeking to lead other ascetics to perfection, this right reading of the hypostatic union was essential for their identity as Christians and the life they sought to embody through their ascetic regimen. Jesus's divine manner of living a human life was the example of the divine life to which the monks aspired. As the second Adam, Jesus was the prototype of a new, divinized humanity—a human life, like the angels, that reflected the glory of God. As Daley has put it, Maximus's Jesus was like an icon that revealed the divine glory, "an earthly reality charged with the energy and beauty of God."[4] Because he held the two natures so closely, Maximus's account of Jesus's two wills provided his disciples with the hope of how the divine energy of the Spirit might sustain them in their weakness that they might truly imitate his faithfulness even to the point of taking up their cross.

This theory of the two wills of Christ proved doctrinally definitive for the Imperial Church East and West but personally fatal for Maximus. In 626, he became caught up in the monothelite controversy when he fled to Carthage to escape

4. Brian E. Daley, *God Visible: Patristic Christology Reconsidered* (Oxford: Oxford University Press, 2018), 215.

the Sasanian incursions into Byzantine territory. There in 643 he engaged in a debate with the monothelite Pyrrhus, who was ultimately converted to Maximus's position. This debate proved influential leading to the adoption of the two wills Christology by a number of synods of African bishops. In 648, Emperor Constans II, wanting to put an end to theological disputes that divided the churches of the empire just at the time when he needed all Christians to unite against the threats from the Arab attacks from the East issued a decree, the *Typos*, that was a gag order prohibiting ecclesial debate about the wills of Christ. The next year, in direct defiance of *Typos*, Pope Martin I convened the Lateran Council that condemned the Monothelitism of the Imperial Church and established Maximus's two-will Christology as normative. This pitted Martin and Maximus against not only Sergius the patriarch of Constantinople but the emperor himself. Both men paid for their temerity. In 654, Martin and Maximus were seized by imperial troops and brought back to Constantinople. After a trial—likely accompanied by torture—Martin was sent into exile where he died. Maximus's trial came the next year. He was subjected to torture—his body grossly mutilated—and killed. For his suffering, Maximus earned the title, the Confessor. Within fifteen years, however, Maximus was vindicated in the eyes of the Church. On Easter 680, Pope Agatho convened a gathering of some 125 bishops to craft a confession of faith that condemned Monothelitism. Later that year, Emperor Constantine IV instructed George of Constantinople to convene at the capital what would be the Sixth Ecumenical Council. The statement of faith produced by Third Constantinople in 681 adapted the language of Chalcedon (451) to speak of "two natural wills and willings and two operations [*energeiai*] without separation, without change, without partition, without confusion . . . [shining forth] in his one hypostasis . . . each nature wills and works what is proper to it."[5] Furthermore, the council specified that the two wills are not contradictory but that the human will, though reflecting the impulses natural to human beings, followed the divine will without resistance or opposition.

John of Damascus and Christology in a Time of Transition

The labels historians apply to different periods are generally as artificial as the boundaries that mark the period. Indeed, to the people of a given period, the label would likely be unintelligible. The citizens of what is commonly today referred to as the Byzantine Empire did not speak of themselves that way; they were the Eastern Roman Empire and would be surprised to hear that the Roman Empire had ended in September 476. Nevertheless, there are occasionally events of such

5. Edward R. Hardy, *Christology of the Later Fathers* (Philadelphia: Fortress, 1954), 383–84.

sweeping import that the world after them is decidedly not the same as the world before. One such event was the rapid Arab conquest of the Levant in the seventh century. In 634, the armies of the Rashidun Caliphate commanded by Khalid ibn a-Walid that had swept up out of the Arabian peninsula defeated the Byzantine forces defending Damascus. Two years later at the Battle of Yarmouk, the Arabs routed the legions of Heraclius thus expelling the Romans from Syria. The next year, 637, Antioch, Jerusalem, and Gaza fell to the Muslim invaders. That same year other Arab armies commanded by Caliph Umar ibn al-Khattâb turned on the Byzantine's rivals, the Sasanians. In 642, at the Battle of Nihawând, the Sasanian forces were completely vanquished, which marked the end of the Persian Empire in the Levant. Although the Eastern Roman Empire had not yet suffered the fate of the Sasanians, Byzantium was on the defensive, feeling pressure from Muslim armies in Egypt, Cappadocia, and from the waters of the Mediterranean.

As the political map of the eastern Mediterranean world was rapidly being redrawn, the Christians of Syria and Palestine found themselves in a decidedly different social context. Ecclesiastically, the regions of the Church of the East, the Coptic Church, the Syrian Orthodox Church, and the Melkite Catholics were spread across lands no longer part of a Christian empire. Although some were martyred for the faith under Muslim rule, by and large, such persecutions were sporadic and isolated events. Nevertheless, for Chalcedonian Christians of the Melkite Church (i.e., the Imperial Church), their position of social and religious privilege was gone. Theologically, therefore, the agenda ceased to be devising formulae that would promote the unity of the churches in order to secure the unity of the Roman Empire. It was now apologetic in nature. Although rapprochement between Chalcedonian and non-Chalcedonian churches was not a realistic possibility, the Chalcedonians needed to equip their people with arguments against the critiques of their Miaphysite and Dyophysite neighbors. They also needed to defend Chalcedon against Jewish and Muslim theological attacks, such as the accusation that the use of icons in worship was idolatry.

Into the culturally and theologically pluralistic environment of Syria and Jerusalem in the seventh and eighth centuries appeared John of Damascus (675/680–749). The son of Melkite parents who served in the bureaucracy of the Umayyad Caliphate, John grew up in Damascus, which was the capital of the Caliphate. Although in Arab hands, Damascus remained a center of Greek culture that prepared him for life following in his father's footsteps and serving in the Caliphate's administration. Around 705, John left Damascus to become a monk in Jerusalem. It was then that he began his life as an apologist for Chalcedonian Christianity. Although the Melkites represented a religious majority in Jerusalem, Islam was attracting converts, some drawn to it theologically and others because it was the religion of the victors. In this context, John could neither simply argue by appealing to florilegia or handbooks containing passages from the heroes of Chalcedon, for example, Cyril and the Cappadocians, nor by following the Neo-Chalcedonian scholasticism that relied on Neo-Platonist interpretations of Aristotle to work out the relationship between universals and particulars, *ousia* and *hypostasis*. Rather, he needed to systematize the language of Chalcedon in a way that would give it greater clarity and coherence. Chief among his apologetic systematizations of Chalcedonian theology were three tomes collectively known as *The Spring of Knowledge*. Of the three, the third volume, *The Exact Exposition of the Orthodox Faith*, provides the Damascene's extended discussion of Chalcedonian Christology.

Foundational to John's defense of the unity of Christ was his ontological prioritization of the hypostasis or individual over the universal properties that comprised the individual. In his *Dialectic*, he defines *hypostasis* as an independent, concrete (*idiosystaton*), self-subsisting entity in which various properties of the general nature or class as well as particular properties unique to the individual inhere (*Dial.* 43; Zachhuber, 291). In other words, the properties of the *ousia* do not have an independent existence outside of the hypostasis of which they are an iteration. Since the parts or properties of an *ousia* do not subsist or exist independent of the hypostasis, they are called *enhypostata* (*enhypostaton* in sg.), that is, things existing in the hypostasis. The soul and body, therefore, are not separate from one another but exist enhypostatically in a person. Indeed, the whole person is greater than the combination of the properties of the soul and the properties of the body. Thus, the whole is not reducible to the sum of its parts. John goes on to say that, with the exception of the three hypostases of the Trinity that abide together in a perichoretic union, hypostases do not exist enhypostatically. That is, one hypostasis does not indwell another. Therefore, in the case of Christ, Nestorius's prosoponic union with its two subjects united in a permanent conjunction of wills (*synapheia*) is impossible. If a hypostasis or subject cannot be an *enhypostaton*, then there can be no mutual inherence of a divine subject (the Word who assumed the man) and a human subject (the man who was assumed). Rather, the humanity of Christ exists enhypostatically in the hypostasis of the Logos. Jesus's humanity, in other words, is an *enhypostaton* or cluster of creaturely properties that exists in the single hypostasis that is the incarnate Logos. At the same time, his enhypostatic ontology allowed him to rebut Miaphysites. By speaking of Jesus's divine and human natures as *enhypostata* (each existing in the single hypostasis), John was able to speak of a genuine reciprocity between divinity and humanity (akin to the reciprocity between the soul and body) without conflating them into a single nature. Thus, he was able to build on Maximus's view of Jesus performing human activities in a divine manner and performing divine activities in a human manner.

One of the critical distinctions in the use of the term *hypostasis* was how it was applied to the Trinity and to the incarnation. The Logos, as the eternally begotten Son of the Father, was a hypostasis distinct from the Father and Spirit. However, rather than identifying the Word as the Wisdom and Power of God, as Origen had done, John spoke of him as "the enhypostatic wisdom and power of God" (*Exp. fid.* 46; Russell, 164). By this, he interpreted 1 Corinthians 1:24 to mean that the properties of wisdom and power proper to the divine nature inhered in the hypostasis of the Son because he was consubstantial with the Father. In the incarnation, the Word incorporated the properties of Mary's human nature into his hypostasis (*Exp. fid.* 51; Russell, 179). Thus, the flesh came to subsist in and thereby be deified in the hypostasis of the Word. So, God was said to be "inhominated" (*enanthrōpēsanta*) (*Exp. fid.* 46; Russell, 165). Again and again, John stresses that this is not a union of natures. There are in nature, he admits, composite natures that are a mixing of properties. But in such cases, the composite nature is a thing different from the natures of the things that comprise the compound. It is a new nature altogether that is passed on to its progeny. The incarnation, however, was a "supernatural dispensation" and therefore a truly unique phenomenon (*Exp. fid.* 47; Russell, 168). When the Word was made flesh, his natures were united not in a composite nature but in a composite hypostasis that distinguishes him from the Father, the Holy Spirit, Mary, and the rest of Adam's family. In the hypostatic union, because the two natures remained distinct, each "preserved its own rule and law," which means that the divine nature preserved its properties and acted as divinity would and the human nature retained its properties and acted as a human being would. For such a union of natures into a single nature would entail a change in both. Moreover, since such a composite nature would be neither fully God nor fully human, Jesus would not have been consubstantial with either God or humanity. But in the hypostatic union, the coexistence of natures meant that neither nature was altered but remained fully what it was; "nor was he who is simple changed when he became composite. For change is a passion, but the impassible is necessarily immutable. . . . [Thus] when he was in the flesh, he performed [human] actions, but did not suffer" (*Exp. fid.* 51; Russell, 178).

At the same time that the natures are not confused but remain distinct, the hypostatic union results in the divinization of the human nature in the great exchange. "The Word," John writes, "appropriates [*oikeioutai*] what is human (for what belongs to the flesh is his) and communicates [*metadidoi*] his own to the flesh by the method of exchange [*kata ton tēs antidoseōs tropon*] on account of the parts cohering in [*perichōrēsin*] each other and in the hypostatic union" (*Exp. fid.* 47; Russell, 170). Here John employs the term *perichōrēsis* to draw an analogy between the union of the persons in the Trinity and that of the human and divine natures in the hypostatic union. Perichoresis refers to the mutual indwelling or coinherence of the persons of the Trinity to which Jesus gestures when he states, "I am in the Father and the Father is in me. I and the Father are one" (John 17:23). The language of perichoresis allows the Damascene to speak of a real union that explains how Jesus can also say, "He who has seen me has seen the Father" (John 14:8–9), without collapsing the persons into each other. One analogy he employs to illustrate the perichoretic union of the persons is that of three suns adhering so closely with each other that, though being truly distinct and unconfused, "there is one blending and union of the light" (*Exp. fid.* 8; Russell, 82). Thus, perichoresis allows the two natures in the hypostatic union to be mutually informing so that, under the rule of the Logos, Jesus's humanity is divinized. That is, able to participate in the properties of the divine nature and so perform actions beyond man's natural capacity. At the same time, perichoresis preserves the distinction between the natures; there can be a reciprocity that does not threaten the Logos's impassibility. Therefore, following Cyril and Maximus, John argues that because the divine nature, being uncreated, is immutable and therefore does not change in the hypostatic union, the *communicatio idiomatum* that results from the perichoretic character of the union is asymmetrical (*Exp. fid.* 48; Russell, 172). While the flesh becomes the vehicle through which the divine power of the Logos works, the human nature partakes in the divine nature and is divinized. But the divine nature, though acting through the flesh to which it is hypostatically united, does not participate in the human nature such that it is changed and becomes passible. John defines *theōsis* as the human nature's "participation in the glorious attributes of the divinity" such that the flesh of Christ is able to divinize those who partake of it. For the flesh of Christ "endows [us] with life, not by virtue of its own nature, but by its union with divinity" (*Exp. fid.* 51; Russell, 179). In this way, John's idea of perichoresis provides language with which Christians may speak about the power of Christ's body to convey the healing power of the Word's divinity to characters in the gospel drama by direct touch and to his eighth-century disciples through the sacraments.

Conclusion

Looking over the three and a half centuries from John Damascene back to Apollinaris of Laodicea, one sees retrospectively the dialectic of the cataphatic and the apophatic in speaking about the miracle declared in John's prologue: "And the Word became flesh." The challenge was the same for all these writers: how to describe this union of divinity and humanity in a way that explained the saving work of the divine Logos without compromising the very divinity that enabled Jesus's ministrations then and in the present to be redemptive of passible and mortal humanity. Chalcedon set the boundaries for such descriptions intended to rule out two errant interpretations of the gospel drama. Its affirmations that Jesus is "fully human and fully divine" and "perfect God and perfect man" also required the simultaneous negations, "without change, without mixture, without confusion." Regard for the wisdom of pre-Chalcedonian fathers by their heirs meant that the Chalcedonian formula did not stand on its own; its meaning was interpreted through the seminal writings of their forefathers, of Gregory of Nazianzus and Cyril of Alexandria. Yet words whose meaning in one context was innocent became vicious in another. Thus, Nazianzen's description of the incarnation as a "mixture" of the natures when employed by Eutyches and Dioscorus ironically came to describe a quasi-Apollinarianism that denied Jesus's full humanity but also his full divinity. Indeed, because Cyril himself was searching for the right terms with which to speak of the mystery of the incarnation, he too spoke—as indeed the authors of the New Testament and all preachers and theologians inevitably do—more poetically than precisely as he explored the permissible semantic range of Christian theological vocabulary. Yet such inconsistency and imprecision led to greater confusion and disagreement such that Cyril would be quoted by Leontius and Severus to justify mutually exclusive understandings. Yet Leontius recognized that in order for poetry to express the mystery and marvel of the incarnation without being misleading, there must be a recognition of the breaking point of all analogical discourse around Jesus's life from conception to ascension. Thus, certain key terms or expressions—Cyril's own words—had to be given more precise meanings, positively and negatively, so that the more poetic expressions in Scripture and the holy liturgy, in catechesis and homilies, might be more edifying than misleading. This was the Herculean labor left unfinished at Chalcedon that was taken up by subsequent generations—a labor that continues in modern ecumenical dialogue.

Bibliography

Primary Sources

Babai the Great. *On the Union*. Unpublished translation in Nathan Tilley, "Human Perfection in the Thought of Bābai the Great: Tradition and Development in East Syrian Theology." PhD diss., Duke University, 2023.

Cyril of Alexandria. *Five Tomes Against Nestorius*. In *Cyril of Alexandria*. Translated by Norman Russell. London: Routledge, 2000.

———. *Letter to the Monks of Egypt*. In *St. Cyril of Alexandria: The Christological Controversy; Its History, Theology, and Texts*. Translated by John A. McGuckin. Crestwood, NY: St. Vladimir's Seminary Press, 2004.

———. *Letter to Pulcheria and Eudoxia on Right Faith*. Unpublished translation by Rowan A. Greer.

———. *On Isaiah*. In *Cyril of Alexandria*. Translated by Norman Russell. London: Routledge, 2000.

———. *On John*. In *Cyril of Alexandria*. Translated by Norman Russell. London: Routledge, 2000.

———. *On the Unity of Christ*. Translated by John Anthony McGuckin. Crestwood, NY: St. Vladimir's Seminary Press, 2000.

———. *Second Letter to Nestorius*. In *On the Unity of Christ*. Translated by John Anthony McGuckin. Crestwood, NY: St. Vladimir's Seminary Press, 2000.

———. *Third Letter to Nestorius*. In *On the Unity of Christ*. Translated by John Anthony McGuckin. Crestwood, NY: St. Vladimir's Seminary Press, 2000.

Diodore of Tarsus. *Commentary on the Psalms*. In *Diodore of Tarsus: Commentary on Psalms 1–51*. Translated by Robert C. Hill. Atlanta: Society of Biblical Literature, 2005.

Gregory of Nazianzus. *Letter to Cledonius*. In *On God and Christ*. Translated by Lionel Wickham. Crestwood, NY: St. Vladimir's Seminary Press, 2002.

Gregory of Nyssa. *Epistle to Theophilus*. In *Anti-Apollinarian Writings*. Translated by Robin Orton. Washington DC: Catholic University of America Press, 2015.

———. *Refutation of Apollinaris*. In *Anti-Apollinarian Writings*. Translated by Robin Orton. Washington DC: Catholic University of America Press, 2015.

John of Damascus. *On the Orthodox Faith*. Translated by Norman Russell. Yonkers, NY: St. Vladimir's Seminary Press, 2022.

Leo the Great. *The Tome of Leo*. In *Christology of the Later Fathers*. Edited by Edward R. Hardy. Philadelphia: Westminster, 1954.

Leontius of Byzantium. *Against Nestorius and Eutyches*. In *Leontius of Byzantium: Complete Works*. Translated by Brian E. Daley. Oxford: Oxford University Press, 2017.

———. *Solutions to the Arguments Proposed by Severus*. In *Leontius of Byzantium: Complete Works*. Translated by Brian E. Daley. Oxford: Oxford University Press, 2017.

Maximus the Confessor. *Ambigua*. In *Maximus the Confessor*. Translated by Andrew Louth. London: Routledge, 1996.

———. *Opuscula*. Quoted in *Leontius of Byzantium: Complete Works*. Translated by Brian E. Daley. Oxford: Oxford University Press, 2017.

Nestorius. *The Bazaar of Heracleides*. Translated by G. R. Driver and Leonard Hodgson. Eugene, OR: Wipf & Stock, 2002.

———. *Second Letter to Cyril*. In *The Cambridge Edition of Early Christian Writings*. Vol. 3. *Christ*. Edited by Mark DelCogliano. Translated by Matthew Crawford. Cambridge: Cambridge University Press, 2022.

Severus of Antioch. *Against the Impious Grammarian*. Quoted in Aloys Grillmeier. *Christ in Christian Tradition*. Vols. 1–2. Parts 1–2. Translated by Pauline Allen and John Cawte. Atlanta: John Knox, 1986.

Secondary Sources

Beeley, Christopher A. *The Unity of Christ: Continuity and Conflict in Patristic Tradition.* New Haven: Yale University Press, 2012.

Blowers, Paul M. *Maximus the Confessor: Jesus Christ and the Transfiguration of the World.* Oxford: Oxford University Press, 2016.

Brock, Sabastian. "The Christology of the Church of the East." In *Traditions and Heritage of the Christian East.* Edited by D. Afinogenov and A. Muraviev. Moscow: Izdatelstvo "Indrik," 1996.

Daley, Brian E. *God Visible: Patristic Christology Reconsidered.* Oxford: Oxford University Press, 2018.

Gavrilyuk, Paul L. *The Suffering of the Impassible God: The Dialectics of Patristic Thought.* Oxford: Oxford University Press, 2004.

Grillmeier, Aloys. *Christ in Christian Tradition.* Vols. 1–2. Parts 1–2. Translated by Pauline Allen and John Cawte. Atlanta: John Knox, 1986.

Hainthaler, Theresia. "The Theological Doctrines and Debates Within Syriac Christianity." Pages 377–90 in *The Syriac World.* Edited by Daniel King. London: Routledge, 2019.

Menze, Volker. "The Establishment of the Syriac Churches." Pages 105–18 in *The Syriac World.* Edited by Daniel King. London: Routledge, 2019.

Twombly, Charles C. Perichoresis *and Personhood: God, Christ, and Salvation in John of Damascus.* Eugene, OR: Pickwick, 2015.

Wessel, Susan. *Cyril of Alexandria and the Nestorian Controversy: The Making of a Saint and of a Heretic.* Oxford: Oxford University Press, 2004.

Zachhuber, Johannes. *The Rise of Christian Theology and the End of Ancient Metaphysics: Patristic Philosophy from the Cappadocian Fathers to John of Damascus.* Oxford: Oxford University Press, 2020.

9

Ransom Captive Israel

The Cross and Atonement

In the year 71 BC, eight Roman legions commanded by the aristocrat Marcus Licinius Crassus confronted a ten-thousand-man army of slaves and their followers known as the *Spartacani*, after their leader, the former gladiator Spartacus. At the Battle of the Silarius River, Crassus's legionnaires routed the *Spartacani*, killing Spartacus himself and some four to five thousand of his troops and taking the remaining six thousand as prisoners. By his right as the commander on the field, Crassus could have sold the prisoners as slaves and pocketed the profit for himself or split it among his troops. As a man possessed of a vast fortune, Crassus did not need the money. Instead, he needed to make a statement. Crassus, therefore, chose not to sell the prisoners but to execute all the male rebels by hanging them from crosses that lined both sides of the Via Appia, stretching three thousand stadia—two crosses every two hundred yards—from Capua to Rome (cf. *Bell. civ.* 1.119–120). On those crosses, their bodies were left to hang. Crassus's goal was to deter any future slave uprising by stirring fear and instilling despair in the minds of the enslaved population of Italy that they might not be tempted to overthrow their masters and gain freedom by force of arms. Crucifixion was, in a word, state-sponsored terrorism. Mass crucifixions were not unknown in Palestine either. During a civil war in Judea (95–88 BC), the Hasmonean king, Alexander Jannaeus (Yanni), crucified some eight hundred insurgents. At the end of the first century BC, the Roman governor of Syria, Publius Quinctilius, put to death two thousand citizens of Jerusalem as punishment for a revolt against Roman rule. Perhaps most infamous was Titus's crucifixion of five hundred Jews a day for months after the fall of Jerusalem in AD 70 (*B.J.* 5.11.1). So shameful was the humiliation of crucifixion that it was an unthinkable fate for Roman citizens.

Jews, too, attached a similar stigma to such a death. In the prescriptions concerning execution of criminals, torah declares, "And if a man has committed a crime punishable by death and he is put to death, and you hang him on a tree, his body shall not remain all night upon the tree, but you shall bury him the same day, for a hanged man is accursed by God; you shall not defile your land which the LORD your God gives you for an inheritance" (Deut 21:22–23). The implication was that crimes worthy of such a curse have cut the criminal off from the community, and so even his corpse should be disposed of without delay.

Against this background, Jesus's crucifixion posed a theological and a missional problem best summarized in Paul's assessment to the Corinthian church: "For Jews demand signs and Greeks seek wisdom, but we preach Christ crucified, a stumbling block to Jews and folly to Gentiles" (1 Cor 1:22–23). For gentiles steeped in the erudition of the various philosophical schools, it was complete nonsense—metaphysically speaking—to claim that the immortal and eternal God *could* die, much more that he actually did. How could the gospel of Christ crucified even begin to be intelligible to the gentiles? For Jews as well as gentiles, the manner of Jesus's death called into question the essential claims of the primitive church about Jesus's identity. How could one who became accursed by God be the Messiah sent to liberate Israel? Yet this was precisely Paul's claim: "but to those who are called, both Jews and Greeks, Christ [is] the power of God and the wisdom of God. For the foolishness of God is wiser than men, and the weakness of God is stronger than men" (1 Cor 1:24–25). Paul's words to the Corinthians were an invitation to discover the logic of the cross that was deeper and more powerful than the logic of the conventional wisdom of Jews and Greeks. Paul went so far as to say that the cross was the indispensable lens without which one could not rightly see either Jesus's identity and with it the new covenant in his blood or the mission of the Church. For as he would tell the Corinthians in a later correspondence, "[Jesus] died for all, that those who live might live no longer for themselves but for him who for their sake died and was raised. . . . All this is from God, who through Christ reconciled us to himself and gave us the ministry of reconciliation" (2 Cor 5:15, 18). Early Christians took up this invitation, seeking to come to understand the wisdom behind the enigma of the cross. Consequently, as Robin Jensen has aptly put it, "this dreadful device paradoxically became the identifying badge of an emerging religious movement . . . reimagined and transformed from a totem of ignominious suffering into a trophy of triumphant victory."[1] One of the earliest moves at countering Jewish objections based on Deuteronomy 21 (cf. *Dial.* 32, 89) was reimagining Christ in terms of Jewish images of either the suffering servant and or the paschal lamb.

1. Robin M. Jensen, *The Cross: History, Art, and Controversy* (Cambridge: Harvard University Press, 2017), ix.

"Wounded for Our Transgressions": Christ the Suffering Servant

One of the earliest Christian explanations of Jesus's passion appeared in the figural interpretation of the hymn of the suffering servant in Isaiah 53. In Luke's Gospel, Jesus explicitly identifies Isaiah's description of the servant, "And he was reckoned with transgressors" (Isa 53:12), as a prophecy fulfilled in himself (Luke 22:35–37). In its sequel, the Acts of the Apostles (8:32–35), Philip in his conversation with the Ethiopian eunuch identifies Jesus as the one described by Isaiah, "As a sheep led to the slaughter or a lamb that before its shearer is dumb" (Isa 53:7). Later 1 Peter focuses on the substitutionary theme from Isaiah: "He himself bore our sins [cf. Isa 53:11] in his body on the tree. . . . [For] 'by his wounds you have been healed' [Isa 53:5]" (1 Pet 2:24). The Apostolic Constitutions, likely compiled and edited in the fourth century from early church orders, quotes the servant's hymn when explaining the duty of bishops to imitate Christ's suffering. As Christ "bore the sins of all and interceded for all," so bishops "take upon yourselves the sins of the laity" (Apos. Con. 2.25.11–12).

Cyril of Alexandria, in his *Commentary on Isaiah*, interpreted Christ's death on the cross by focusing on the words from Isaiah's Servant Song: "upon him was the discipline [*paideia*] of our peace" (Isa 53:5b LXX). The "discipline" refers to Jesus's being "wounded for our transgressions" (Isa 53:5a) and is the means for humanity's reconciliation or peace with God. Cyril explains that humanity's refusal to accept the "yoke of obedience"—a display of arrogance—created hostility between God and his creatures. Therefore, humanity could be reconciled with God only by being disabused of their arrogance by being humbled through discipline that they might once again submit to the yoke of obedience (*In Isa.* 53.5; CB, 419). Cyril likely has in mind the application of the tutor's rod to curb the high spirits of a disobedient student. If the student will not voluntarily submit to the teacher's authority, he will learn his place by being humbled with the rod. So too, proud humanity had to be humbled. By his voluntary submission to the discipline that all humanity earned, Christ endured suffering on behalf of sinful humanity. Indeed, all humanity in Christ was collectively disciplined and so taught humility. Christ, as the second Adam, performed the paradigmatic act of submission in which believers participate—that is, symbolically receive the discipline themselves—through baptism and the subsequent life of humble obedience. For Cyril, Christ's death was not, as in later substitutionary models, merely punitive or vindictive but pedagogical. Humanity had to be disciplined in order to be taught humility. But to save all humanity from the pain of that discipline, the Father, as an expression of his love for humanity (John 3:16), "'gave [Jesus] over to our sins' [Isa 53:6] in order that he might deliver us from judgment and save those who have faith" (*In Isa.* 53.5; CB, 419). For those who have faith in the crucified Messiah have learned the lesson of the humility from Christ's discipline. Indeed, the discipline of the cross contributed to the goal of *theōsis*. Of those same ones who are saved by faith, Cyril goes on to say, "Behold when they receive faith in Christ, they are transformed spiritually into his divinity and made exceptionally beautiful" (*In Isa.* 53.11; CB, 420–21). Thus, faith entails the humility necessary to seek and receive the gift of divinizing grace.

Augustine, too, interprets the Servant Song to express the idea of transformation. Reading Isaiah's metaphor of the servant as "a root in a thirsty land" (53:2) in conjunction with his later description, "He has neither fine appearance nor honor" (53:3), Augustine explains that Christ has no fine appearance because of the suffering and humiliation inflected on his human form by his persecutors. Yet how can the Son of God be said to be without comeliness? His answer is that in Christ's assumption of our corruptible nature, he was like a "root" that, in itself, is unattractive. But within the root is contained the potentiality for beauty, a beauty manifest in the tree that grows from the root. So too, from his divinized humanity springs forth the tree, the Church, which bears the beauty of the Word (*Serm.* 44.1–2).

Melito of Sardis: Christ the Paschal Lamb

One of the peculiarities of the Gospel according to John that distinguishes its narrative from that of the earlier Gospels of Matthew, Mark, and Luke is the time of Jesus's death. As we saw in chapter 1, whereas in the Synoptic Gospels Jesus is arrested after celebrating the Passover meal with his disciples and then crucified the next day, in the Fourth Gospel Jesus is put to death not on Passover but on the day of preparation, the time that the Passover lambs are being slaughtered for the Seder meal.[2] Thus, the time of Jesus's death fulfills John the Baptist's identification of Jesus as "the lamb of God who takes away the sins of the world" (John 1:29). This echoes Paul's similar identification of Jesus as "our paschal lamb" (1 Cor 5:7). Although the Letter to the Hebrews employs allusions to Jewish atonement sacrifice that presents Jesus as a high priest after the order of Melchizedek (Ps 110:4; Heb 7:1–3), one of the earliest and most extensive depictions of Jesus as the sacrificial lamb comes in the prose hymn, *On Pascha*, written by the second-century apologist, Melito of Sardis (d. 190).

Melito, a Jewish convert, was among those Christians in Asia Minor and Syria who celebrated Jesus's passion and resurrection on the fourteenth of Nisan, which corresponded with Passover on the Jewish festal calendar. They were, therefore,

2. See chapter 1, pp. 24–26.

called Quartodecimans. Pope Victor I of Rome, seeking to promote greater unity through regular practices throughout the churches, set the celebration of Easter—the Christian Pascha—for the Sunday after the first full moon after the spring equinox. Although Victor ultimately excommunicated the Quartodecimans, Melito's interpretation of Jesus's passion remained a classical example of early figural readings of the exodus narrative.

Since the Quartodecimans' celebration of the Christian Pascha coincided with the celebration of Passover by the Jews, *On Pascha* functioned as a reinterpretation of the Passover Feast against the backdrop of Jesus's passion and resurrection. Melito presents the Jewish Passover as a type or prefiguration of the reality of Christ's sacrificial offering. The Christian Pascha occurs at the same time as the Jewish Passover because the Christian Pascha has replaced the Jewish type (*Pasch.* 3). "Understand," he writes, "how the mystery of the Pascha / is both new and old / eternal and provisional / perishable and imperishable / mortal and immortal" (*Pasch.* 2). There is but one Pascha in two forms, Christian and Jewish. In its perfect Christian form, it is new because it is more recent but old because it is the ancient law. The Jewish Pascha, like the Law itself, was "provisional" (*proskairon*) because the imperfect type served only a period in history and passed away when the reality of Christ's salvific sacrifice came.

> For *then* the slaughter of the sheep was of value,
> *now* it is worthless because of the Lord's life. . . .
> The death of the sheep was of value,
> now it is worthless because of the Lord's salvation.
> The blood of the sheep was of value,
> now it is worthless because of the Holy Spirit.
> The temple below was of value,
> now it is worthless because of the heavenly Christ. (*Pasch.* 44)

The ritual of Passover, like the people of Israel and Torah, was of value because, as a type of true Pascha, it contained an element of truth that prepared humanity for faith in Christ (*Pasch.* 57). For it possessed a likeness to the reality that was to come as "a preliminary sketch" (*prokentēmatos*) of a building does to the edifice that will be constructed (*Pasch.* 40). Indeed, the truth of the type is not clear until one sees the reality of which it is an image as when "the analogy is brought to completion through the elucidation of interpretation" (*Pasch.* 43). In this way, Melito articulates the basis for Christian hermeneutics that both affirms the unity of the testaments and at the same time asserts the superiority of the gospel.

Melito's supersessionist assertion that the Jewish Passover is provisional rests upon his salvation history and Christology. Because of Adam's sin, he was "thrown out into this world, condemned as though to a prison" (*Pasch.* 48), bequeathing to his children "not freedom but bondage, / not sovereignty but tyranny, / not life but death, / not salvation but destruction" (*Pasch.* 49). Therefore, as children "dragged off a captive under the shadow of death," humanity's deliverance from the sufferings and death of the body required that "the paschal mystery [be] completed in the body of the Lord" (*Pasch.* 56). The Savior had to take upon himself humanity's mortality and its suffering.

> He accepted the suffering of the suffering one
> through suffering in a body which could suffer,
> and set free the flesh from suffering.
> Through the Spirit which cannot die
> he slew the manslayer. . . .
> He ransomed us from the worship of the world
> as from the land of Egypt
> and he set us free from the slavery of the devil
> as from the hand of Pharaoh. (*Pasch.* 66–67)

The pronoun "he" refers to the one from heaven, and the "suffering one" is his humanity; for the Word "wrapped himself in the suffering one by means of a virgin womb" (*Pasch.* 66). The suffering lamb, as an image of sinless sacrifice, was an apt symbol for Christ; but the reality far surpassed in greatness and wonder the analogy of the type: "He was born a son, and was led as a lamb, and slaughtered as a sheep, and buried as a man, and rose from the dead as God, being God by his nature and a man" (*Pasch.* 8). As man he was mortal and could be sacrificed like the lamb; but as God, Christ, unlike the lamb, could rise from the dead (*Pasch.* 9). Thus, while the lamb's blood smeared on the doorposts shielded the Israelites from the angel of death, Christ's death conquered death itself as demonstrated by his resurrection. As the blood of the lambs sacrificed at Yom Kippur brought forgiveness of sins, Jesus's passion together with his resurrection—celebrated by Christians on a single day as a single event—frees believers through the forgiveness of sin and deliverance from death through their union with his resurrected body. Thus, Melito concludes the hymn with Jesus's speaking to the congregation,

> Receive forgiveness of sins.
> For I am your freedom.
> I am your Passover salvation,
> I am the lamb slaughtered for you,
> I am your ransom,

I am your life,
I am your light,
I am your salvation,
I am your resurrection,
I am your King.
I shall raise you up by my right hand,
I will lead you to the heights of heaven
and there I shall show you to the everlasting Father. (*Pasch.* 103)

Origen: Christ the Peacemaker

Origen saw baptism as the sign of having been buried with Christ in his death to sin and united in his resurrection to new life in the Spirit. Through being dead to sin and reborn in the Spirit, the Christian is made righteous so as to enter God's peace. Since the true, inner baptism is a participation in Christ's death and resurrection, Christ's death, therefore, creates the condition by which the sinner might be reconciled to God. Origen explains this in terms of both what Christ has done on humanity's behalf and what Christ by his death and resurrection does in the life of the true disciple.

Although Origen has no single text devoted primarily to the subject of the atonement, his analysis of the salvific consequence of Jesus's death and resurrection is scattered throughout his *Commentary on Romans*. There Origen interweaves two images to describe Christ's atoning work: Christ as the second Adam (Rom 5:12–14) and Christ the destroyer of the dividing wall (Eph 2:11–18). Christ, the second Adam, offers humanity peace with God by tearing down the dividing wall of hostility between humanity and God (*Comm. Rom.* 4.8.1). For through "the blood of his cross" (Rom 5:10), those who were enemies of God were reconciled (2 Cor 5:20). The dividing wall of hostility Origen identified as the wisdom or lust of the flesh that refused to submit to the law of God. Although Origen does not take the word "flesh" to refer to the body per se, it does carry the sense of a lust for the goods of this world, an orientation of mind antithetical to the spiritual desire for peace and friendship with God in the heavenly commonwealth (*Comm. Rom.* 4.12.2–3). Since the sinful disobedience of the first Adam erected the dividing wall of sin that separated humanity from God and so brought death, Jesus broke down the wall through his perfect obedience, offering to God the obedience the first Adam owed but failed to pay. Therefore, by his obedience unto death, Christ the second Adam justified or reconciled humanity to God (*Comm. Rom.* 5.2.4). By his death and resurrection, Christ demonstrates that he who is life itself is more powerful than death, and he who is righteousness itself is greater than sin. Thus, Origen glosses Paul's words in Romans 5:12–14, "[Death] having received a beginning through disobedience of the one man, how much more powerful and deservedly will life reign through righteousness, receiving its beginning through the obedience of one man" (*Comm. Rom.* 5.2.5). Origen, therefore, understands Paul's paradoxical language, that by Christ's death was death put to death, to mean that the reconciling power of Jesus's death lay in his supreme act of obedience; "he died to sin itself, that is, like one who inflicted death upon sin by his own death. He is said to live to God, just as we too should live not for ourselves or for our own will but for God's" (*Comm. Rom.* 4.12.5). In shedding of this blood in obedience to the Father, Jesus lived his life entirely unto God, thereby fulfilling all righteousness on behalf of his fellow mortals.

Similarly, in his *Commentary on Matthew*, Origen identifies sin and death with the devil (*Comm. Matt.* 13.9). The Father, he explains, delivered Jesus into the hands of the devil who in turn used his minions, the "kings of the earth" who conspired against the Lord and his anointed (Ps 2:2), to make Jesus subject to himself even as he had the rest of Adam's race. Yet the Father delivered Jesus, knowing that his power was greater than the devil's and so would destroy the power of death (*Comm. Matt.* 13.8). Origen does not explicitly explain how Jesus's death destroys death. The implicit logic, however, is that the power of life proper to Jesus's divinity is greater than the devil's power of death through his promulgation of sin. What is important is that Origen holds together both motifs, Christ as the second Adam and Christ the victor over the devil. In the former, sin is conquered by Christ the righteous son of Adam. In the latter, death is conquered by Christ the life-giving Son of God. Thus, the Word made flesh prevailed because of the interconnectedness of life and righteousness.

Yet humanity's reconciliation to God, Origen insists, is accomplished not by Jesus alone but only by the double agency of Christ and of his disciples who imitate his faithfulness to God; "neither does our faith justify us apart from the blood of Christ nor does the blood of Christ justify us apart from our faith" (*Comm. Rom.* 4.11.5). Therefore, at the same time that he declares, "Not until then, when the hostility [wall of sin] had been destroyed in his flesh, did he reconcile men to God," Origen adds the stipulation, "provided that they keep the covenant of reconciliation inviolate by sinning no longer" (*Comm. Rom.* 4.12.4). Because human agency through the use of free will was central to Origen's accounts of both humanity's fall and restoration, Jesus's obedience on humanity's behalf was not a sufficient condition for humanity's deliverance from sin and death. Rather, what Christ did *on behalf of* Adam's children was efficacious because of what Christ's death accomplished *in them*. Namely, by his example, Jesus reveals how fallen rational beings might also become once again spiritual beings through living lives entirely oriented to God. Appealing to the Christ hymn of Philippians 2, Origen explains that Christ's taking "the form of a slave" and giving himself as a sacrifice through the offering of his blood exposed the difference between the wisdom of the world and the wisdom of God that is incomprehensible to the world. Christ gave himself up for humanity's salvation; the ruler of this world snatched greedily at what was not his (*Comm. Rom.* 4.11.4). Through his resurrection, Christ reveals to his followers that righteousness is more powerful than sin. Therefore, the strongman was bound and those held captive were freed. Thus, Christ's death and resurrection liberates humanity from the fear of death and teaches them to trust the strength of God's righteousness. In that knowledge, they discover that true life is found when, following Jesus's example, they no longer live but Christ in them (Gal 2:20) through his Spirit (*Comm. Rom.* 5.12.5).

Freed from the fear of death, they are emboldened to remain faithful to God even in the face of persecution by the same earthly princes who put Jesus to death (*Comm. Matt.* 13.9). Such courage, grounded in Christ's victory through the resurrection, allows his disciples to become spiritual beings whose hope is placed not in worldly security and comfort but in the peace of heavenly union with God. Origen makes this clear, as he explains how the lamb of God "takes away the sins of the world." From the very beginning of the incarnation, Christ was at work, taking away sin by removing sin from the lives of those who responded to his message. This, Origen said, is a process that continues until all sins have been taken away and the Son hands over to the Father a kingdom prepared for his rule. Purged of sin, one sinner at a time, the world will have no rival to God; then Paul's eschatological vision will be fulfilled when "God shall be all in all" (*Comm. Jo.* 1.233–234). The self-sacrifice of the martyrs is evidence of how Jesus's sacrificial example—a death to the wisdom of the world—ignites a holy contagion that gradually "destroys the evil powers . . . [and] blunts, as it were, the sharp point of the treachery of their enemies against their victims" (*Comm. Jo.* 6.273–281).

Gregory of Nyssa's Ransom Theory

Writing in the twelfth century in his monumental work on the atonement *Cur Deus Homo*, or *Why the God-man*, Anselm of Canterbury sought a single sufficient argument for the necessity of the incarnation. As he began laying out his satisfaction theory, that only the God-man could satisfy humanity's debt of honor to God, he begins by rejecting earlier, unsatisfactory theories, chief of which is a theory of ransom—that Jesus's death ransoms humanity from the devil (cf. *Cur Deus Homo* 7).[3] While Anselm does not attribute this view to any particular theologian by name, one likely author is Gregory of Nyssa.

3. Anselm's satisfaction theory is often mistakenly referred to as "penal substitution." It is a

The language of ransom is biblical. Jesus says of himself, "The Son of Man also came not to be served but to serve and to give his life as a ransom [*lytron*] for many" (Mark 10:45; cf. 1 Tim 2:6). Revelation even more closely identifies his death as a ransom: "You were slain and by your blood did ransom men for God" (Rev 5:9). While Gregory invokes the biblical metaphor of ransom, it appears so briefly in the course of three chapters in his *Catechetical Oration* that—if it is at all a *theory* of the atonement—it is not a highly developed theory. Nor does Gregory set out to explain the salvific value of Christ's death. Rather, his exploration of Christ's ransoming humanity from the devil grows out of a discussion of the unity of the virtues in God.

God, Gregory insists, possesses not only infinite power but all the other virtues, including justice, goodness, and wisdom. Unlike Augustine who reduces all virtues to one metavirtue, love, Gregory treats each of the virtues as distinct and yet necessarily united. In other words, in order to be truly virtuous, one must possess all the virtues together. For example, courage without moderation and wisdom, which temper one's zeal in the face of danger and determine the prudent course of action, is not true courage but rash or reckless behavior. So too with God. Goodness, for Gregory, is God's chief attribute: "We seek above all, in the case of God, signs of his goodness" (*Or. cat.* 20). However, goodness does not stand alone but is allied with God's wisdom, power, and justice. Gregory, therefore, seeks to understand how all the virtues work together in the economy of creation and redemption. God's goodness is unchanging. The very cause of his creation of the world in the beginning is not diminished by the rebellion of humanity. On the contrary, the greatest evidence of his immutable goodness is his refusal to abandon disobedient humanity that allied itself with the devil. Yet goodness must be grounded in wisdom, which, like the technical skills of a physician, is necessary to heal and restore humanity to the good that God willed for them in the beginning. Wisdom by itself is not a virtue without justice. In the concrete instance of Christ's redemptive work, Gregory asks, how do wisdom and justice ally?

If the redemption of humanity from the devil is to be just, it cannot be by the arbitrary use of power. One cannot, for instance, acquire possession of a slave by forcibly seizing him from his master. Rather, the master who has legal possession of the slave must transfer ownership voluntarily and at a price of his choosing. Compelling the master to give up his slave against his will or for an unfair sum

---

theory of vicarious atonement because Christ's redeeming action is performed on humanity's behalf. The God-man offers to the Father the supreme honor by his perfect and supererogatory obedience unto death so as to satisfy completely the debt of sin of all humanity. Unlike penal substitution, which holds that Christ endures the punishment of death on the cross to appease the righteous wrath of God, Anselm expressly says that the Father did not will Jesus's death per se, only the faithfulness by which the devil is conquered (*Cur Deus Homo* 9).

would be unjust. Gregory illustrates the conditions of justice by using the language of a slave economy because such language is consistent with Paul's descriptions of the condition of humanity as being a "slave of sin" (Rom 6:17, 21) and being "in bondage to beings that by nature are no gods" (Gal 4:8), and of Christ's work as setting creation "free from its bondage to decay" (Rom 8:21). Even if Scripture speaks of sinful humanity as being in a state of slavery, why does Gregory think that the devil has rightful claim over sinful humanity as its lord and master? Indeed, Anselm's argument against the ransom theory is that God does not need to compensate the devil for the release of humanity since God has rightful claim (*Cur Deus Homo* 7). God alone is the rightful master; sinful humanity should be thought of as runaway slaves. Captured runaways, like stolen property, must be returned to the one who holds original title and ownership. God the Creator has lawful title to his creation and so owes the devil nothing for humanity's release. Gregory, by contrast, assumes that the devil has a legal claim on sinful humanity. He writes, "when once we had *voluntarily* sold ourselves, he who undertook out of goodness to restore our freedom had to contrive a just and not a dictatorial method to do so . . . [i.e.,] to give the master the chance to take whatever he wants as the price for the slave" (*Or. cat.* 22). Why does the devil, not the Creator, have lawful title to Adam and his children?

The answer in many ways goes back to Gregory's high view of human nature. Free will and personal autonomy were natural extensions of humanity's being made in the image of God and endowed with godlike rationality. As rational beings, human beings are able to know the transcendent good and so are under no internal (e.g., instinct) or external (e.g., circumstances) compulsion in the choices they make. God, ever desiring a willing lover rather than an unwilling slave, asserts his authority over humanity not by force, which would compromise human freedom, but by persuasion. God's persuasive power lies in his goodness, which, when revealed in creation and in Christ, draws humanity to himself. To choose God, who is the proper end of human existence, is to gain life, blessedness, and to retain freedom. For by participating in God, the soul retains the knowledge of the good necessary to choose wisely. However, if the soul is excessively or inappropriately focused on the lesser, sensual goods of creation, rather than on the true good of God, it becomes attached to the world as with glue. Then the soul loses its freedom because it loses its knowledge of the true good. Instead, the mind serves the flesh and its rational powers and becomes bent on finding the means necessary for attaining those goods (*Hom. opif.* 18.3). But because these creaturely goods are not eternal but transient, the soul set upon these lesser goods has chosen the way of death rather than eternal life.

It is helpful here to remember that, though Gregory seems to have believed the devil to be a real being, he primarily uses the devil as the figure for speaking of death. For the devil is the one who deceived humanity into seeking transitory goods that lead to death rather than the eternal goods of God that lead to life. Therefore, since humanity has voluntarily given itself over to the devil and death, God respects that choice. In allowing itself to be deceived, humanity has chosen the life of slavery to a cruel master, the father of lies. He holds humanity captive not by the power of goodness but by the appearance of goodness. Like a fisherman who baits his hook with a delectable morsel of food, the devil cloaks vice—and by extension death—with sensual pleasure so as to make it appear beautiful and desirable (*Or. cat.* 21). Consequently, man has given himself over to the illusion that life and happiness can be found elsewhere other than God. By his free and foolish choice, man has given the devil rightful claim on his life. Moreover, living in the darkness of the devil's deception, human beings cannot of themselves know the liberating light that leads to life. Therefore, even as an addict is not free to liberate himself, neither can humanity free itself from its attachment to the things of death. Therefore, God must find a single means of redemption that satisfies two conditions. First, God must free Adam's race from the darkness of deception so that they may willingly seek the eternal goods of God. Second, at the same time, God must find a good so tempting to the devil that he voluntarily gives up his claim on enslaved humanity to get it.

In his clever wisdom, God turns the devil's own tactics against him. Just as the devil concealed his hook with the bait of sensual pleasure, God veiled his Son in human form. Jesus's human nature is the bait that concealed the hook of divine wisdom and power (*Or. cat.* 24). Since human beings were blinded by sin, they could not bear the glorious brilliance of God's naked power. Such glory and power was unapproachable because it filled sinful humanity with fear. The Israelites were terrified even of God's glory reflected in Moses's face. Therefore, divine power, like Moses's face, had to be veiled with a familiar, approachable form. The incarnation itself is, for Gregory, the supreme revelation of power conjoined with love: "God's transcendent power is not so much displayed in the vastness of the heavens, or the luster of the stars, or the orderly arrangement of the universe or his perpetual oversight of it, as in his condescension to our weak nature" (*Or. cat.* 24). That power, however, was not immediately obvious. Gradually, through his miracles of life-giving mercy, the healing power of divine light opened the eyes of sinful human beings, allowing them to see and so desire God's goodness. For human beings, divine power and wisdom take the form of the great physician: "Our nature was sick and needed a doctor. Man had fallen and needed someone to raise him up. He who had lost life needed someone to restore it. He who had ceased to participate in the good needed someone to bring him back to it. He who was shut up in darkness needed the presence of light" (*Or. cat.* 15). The death-dealing deception of demonic darkness was broken by the illumination of the one who is light and life (*Or. cat.* 17). The supreme revelation of God's life-giving power, of course, was Jesus's resurrection. Blinded no more by the apparent goodness of sensuality and vice, humanity's reason is freed to participate in God's wisdom. Now human free will, though not totally negated by the blindness of sin, is restored. Once again humanity is able to be the willing lover that God desired from the beginning. Thus, for Gregory, the eternal and incorruptible life is possible through participation in God's life to which humanity has access through Christ's revelation of the knowledge of the good (the divine hook) cloaked in human flesh (the bait).

The same baited hook that brought humanity deliverance through revelation of divine power stripped the devil of his power by its concealment of God's power. When the devil saw Jesus's miracles, he beheld a powerful human being unlike any other. So remarkable was his power, that the devil deemed him a prize greater than all the rest of humanity combined. Therefore, the devil greedily accepted Jesus as a ransom for release of all Adam's race. Yet like the greedy fish that unknowingly swallows the hook along with the bait, the devil devours what he cannot contain. For Jesus, the divine Word made flesh, is the complete antithesis of the devil. The power of God's luminous goodness and life inherent to Jesus's divinity dispels the darkness of deception and heals the decay and corruption of death. Since death cannot contain life and the darkness vanishes in the presence of light, the devil was stripped of his power over humanity. In this way, Gregory reasons, God redeemed humanity justly; the devil voluntarily accepted Jesus as payment for the release of captive humanity.

Gregory, however, imagines the objection that this salvific stratagem was not just because God overthrew the devil through deception. Even as the devil conquered humanity through deception by veiling vice with the appearance of goodness, God conquered the devil through deception by veiling divine power in mortal flesh. Such deception is incompatible with perfect divinity who is all truth and justice. This, however, is not the case. For one reason, the primary purpose of the incarnation was an accommodation of the weakness of sinful humanity. Since humanity could not behold God face-to-face, the divine Word needed to assume a human form. That the devil was deceived into thinking Jesus was a ransom he could possess was merely a secondary consequence. Second, and more importantly for Gregory's argument, the apparent deception of the incarnation was in fact a case of the devil's self-deception. The very cloak of human flesh that made God desirable, rather than terrifying, to humanity at the same time made him appear accessible to the devil. Although he had seen the mighty works of Jesus that revealed his divine power to people of faith, the devil was so desirous of power and so deluded by envy that he deceived himself into believing that he could control such power and use it for his own purposes. Indeed, the irony is that the devil, who controls man by blinding him to the knowledge of the good, is himself blind. The rebellion against

God was the result of his envy of the blessedness God willed for human beings. His rebellion was that he "closed his eyes to the good. He begot in himself the darkness of wickedness, and [was] sickened with the love of power" (*Or. cat.* 23). In a very real sense for Gregory, the devil's deception of humanity is a case of the blind leading the blind. The brilliance of God's wisdom was that he used the devil's own love of power, which was the source of his blindness and hubris, as the means of his undoing. His reach indeed exceeded his grasp. God, therefore, acted neither unjustly nor untruthfully. It was rather the devil's own blindness to the good that prevented him from seeing that Jesus's divine power, because it is always conjoined with life and truth, was inherently the undoing of death and deception.

Some three hundred fifty years later, John of Damascus (675–749) employed his own variation on Gregory's fishhook metaphor to explain the "harrowing of hell" and the liberation of those saints of the old covenant held captive until Christ's coming. John, too, invoked the language of "sacrifice" and "ransom," but the sacrifice of Christ's life that he offered up to death was a ransom offered not to the devil but to God so that humanity might be delivered from condemnation. Because Christ came in the form of mortal humanity, the devil, like the greedy fish, seized Jesus unwittingly, swallowing the Word as well. Because the Word is light and life, the devil—death and darkness personified—could not contain the Word. By gulping down "the bait of his body," John writes, "it [i.e., death] was snared by the hook of his divinity. After tasting his sinlessness and life-giving body, death is destroyed, and vomits up again everything that he swallowed long ago. For just as darkness disappears with the coming of light, so corruption is driven away by the assault of life. Life comes to all but death to the destroyer" (*Exp. fid.* 3.27). In vomiting up Christ—likely an image taken from Cyril of Alexandria (*In Jo.* 2.171; CB, 51)—death expels the patriarchs and saints of Israel who, in faith and hope, were joined to Christ and so freed from the bonds of death with Christ. With this image, John expresses the doctrine of the inevitable triumph of inexorable power of the one who is life itself and perfect goodness. Thus, for Gregory and John, the salvific work of the cross places less emphasis on the reconciliation effected by Jesus's faithfulness—given his divine holiness, that was a given. Instead, here their interpretation of Jesus's passion and resurrection emphasizes not only the self-destructive nature of sin but more important, the infinite power of Christ's divinity to liberate creation from the forces of death and restore the life God intended in the beginning.

Augustine: One Death Overcoming Two Deaths

Jesus's birth and death might appear to be contradictory moments—one the beginning of life, the other the end of life. For Augustine, however, Jesus's death on the cross was the moment of his perfect embodiment of his assumption of humanity in the incarnation. For his condescension in the form of a servant was his assumption of "the likeness of sinful flesh" (Rom 8:3) in order that "he who knew no sin might be made sin so that in him we might become the righteousness of God" (2 Cor 5:21). Augustine weaves together the Pauline themes of incarnation, sacrifice, and divinization in a way that unites Christ's work on humanity's behalf with his liberative work within the soul of individuals enslaved to sin.

In the fourth book of *On the Trinity*, Augustine describes the paradoxical condition of fallen humanity. On the one hand, Adam's children are afflicted by pride (*superbia*) in which, like their first parents, they are confident that they can exalt themselves and achieve happiness apart from the aid of God. On the other hand, in spite of the delusion of pride, they suffer from despair (*desperatio*) that is the source of what David Meconi calls "self-loathing." Under the conviction of sin by the law, individuals do not feel that they can presume to raise their gaze to the God against whom they have sinned and seek mercy (*Trin.* 4.1.2). Christ must overcome both pride and despair by revealing both the sufficiency of God's power and the truth of his love. He conquers pride by persuading human beings to trust in God's strength—manifest in his triumph over death at the resurrection—rather than their own. At the same time, he overcomes despair by revealing the extent of God's enduring love for humanity even in their sin. His display of divine power in the very assumption of human nature in all its fallen fragility reveals the liberating paradox that "in the weakness of humility, the power [*virtus*] of charity might be perfected" (*Trin.* 4.1.2). In other words, Jesus, the second Adam, revealed in his self-sacrifice God's love for humanity that overcomes the despair of estrangement from God while at the same time revealing the humility through which humanity may be partakers of God's blessings. Through this revelation, Christ clothes his fellow members of Adam's family in his righteousness. Thus, Augustine invokes the language of the "great exchange" (2 Cor 8:9) between God and humanity in the incarnation: "By joining us to the likeness of his humanity, he took away the unlikeness of our unrighteousness; and being made partaker of our mortality, he made us partakers of his divinity" (*Trin.* 4.2.4).

Augustine explains the great exchange as the elimination of humanity's "double death" by Christ's single death. Two deaths result from Adam's sin. The first is the soul's death by its estrangement from the God who is the source of life by the soul's ungodliness. The second is the corruption of the body by its separation from the soul that mediates life from God to the flesh. Thus, the body's death is the direct consequence of the soul's separation from God (*Trin.* 4.3.5). Christ's death on the cross is a single death—the separation of the soul from the body—because Jesus's soul was never separated from God by sin. His single resurrection creates the possibility for a double resurrection in the siblings of the second Adam. First, by the soul's repentance through faith in the one who died for the ungodly (Rom 4:5), it reunites the soul to God, which marks the renewal of the "inner man" (2 Cor 4:16). Second, the raising of the soul from spiritual death begins the renewal of the body—its liberation from corruption—which shall be perfected at the resurrection. Even as the corruption of the body was the result of the conflict between the sinful soul and God, so too the harmonic union of the godly soul and God restores a harmonic relationship between the soul and body. Thus, Jesus's cross and resurrection provided a type of the death and resurrection of the saints. For the saint's repentance is itself akin to Christ's death on the cross: "the crucifixion of the inner man [in baptism] is understood [to be] the pains of repentance, a certain wholesome agony of self-control, by which death the death of ungodliness is destroyed" (*Trin.* 4.3.6).

In sum, Christ's death and resurrection destroyed the object of human fear, namely death, so that people might shift their focus to the proper object of fear, ungodliness. In so doing, Jesus gives hope that by the humility of repentance, which trusts in the redeemer, they may be delivered from ungodliness and therefore also freed from death (*Trin.* 4.12.15). As the ungodliness of sin brought disunity, so Christ's death in righteous obedience is the sacrifice that restores unity: unity with the one *to whom* the sacrifice was offered, unity within the soul and body of the ones *for whom* the sacrifice was offered, and the unity *among those whom* he joins in his body. All this accomplished by the great high priest who is the lamb sacrificed in his humanity, by whom the holocaust is offered on the altar of his cross and is presented in the *sacra sanctorum* by his ascension to the right hand of the Father (*Trin.* 4.14.19).

Although Augustine speaks of Christ's death on the cross as sacrifice, the aim of the sacrifice was not appeasing God's wrath but reuniting the sinner with God by faith and godliness. For God had already loved sinful humanity and given his Son freely out of love for humanity's restoration. The crucifixion did not mark a change in God's disposition toward humanity. If his disposition needed to be changed from wrath to love, what, Augustine asks, made the Father offer up his Son in the first place (*Trin.* 13.11.15)? Rather, the cross is the expression of the very love out of which God willed to create humanity in the beginning. If God already loved humanity, how did the blood of Christ justify humanity and reconcile it to God?

Augustine's answer lies in his account of Christ's triumph over the devil. God did not give humanity over to the authority of the devil but permitted it to occur. That is, God allowed humanity to misuse its *liberum arbitrium* and then suffer the consequences. God's pronouncement of judgment on the serpent, "Dust you shall eat," signified the death of the body. But, as we have already seen, that death of the body was simply the logical extension of the death of the soul in sin. Yet God never completely abandoned his creatures; for they retained some knowledge of God and of the natural law. Nevertheless, God justly allowed Adam's race to be subject to the devil because Adam and the devil shared a common vice, pride (*Trin.* 13.12.16). Such pride is a perverse love of power, which is seen as the means to exalt oneself. It may take the form of the desire for autonomy rather than submission to God. Or it may find expression in the *libido dominandi*—the desire to exert power and control over others (*Civ.* 1, preface). It is not that Augustine believed power to be inherently evil and therefore something to be shunned altogether. The problem lay with power that was not subordinated to righteousness or justice (*iustitia*). Adam fell because he imitated the devil's love of power and rejection of justice, that is, the rightful submission to God (*Trin.* 13.13.17). Like Gregory of Nyssa, Augustine sees Jesus's liberation of humanity from the devil as the result of the devil's self-subverting power. The devil lost his power over humanity because he exceeded his power in putting to death one who was without sin (*Trin.* 13.15.19).

Augustine's account of the atoning work of the cross is more than the story of the devil's forfeiture of his claim on sinful humanity. Rather, Augustine separates Christ's work on the cross from the resurrection as a way of healing humanity of its prideful lust for power. God himself had the power to free humanity by conquering the devil by sheer force. That, however, would have only made power all the more alluring to humanity that was already unduly enamored with power. Therefore, in order to demonstrate the right relationship of power and justice, Christ conquered the devil first by his righteous life. That is, he resisted the devil's temptations by living in sinless obedience to the Father. His triumph over the devil was possible because of Christ's voluntary submission to the Father's will in assuming the weakness of humanity's mortal nature (*Trin.* 13.14.18). Only once he had conquered the devil by his righteous obedience unto death upon the cross did he then conquer the devil by his divine power at the resurrection. In doing so, Jesus disabuses sinful humanity of its perverse desire for power by revealing the right relationship between the Creator and the creature: through righteousness, one receives the gift of God's life-giving power. By Christ's death and then resurrection, humanity comes to a rightly ordered view of power. In the order of goods, power is subordinated to righteousness. Moreover, through Christ's double victory over the devil, humanity sees that it is only through righteousness that power can be rightly used and its benefits acquired. The cross and resurrection are a recapitulation of humanity's fall in Adam and therefore provide a new model for man's imitation. As Adam imitated the devil's unjust desire for power and fell into the suffering of slavery to sin and death, now the heirs of the second Adam may imitate Jesus by righteously submitting in humility to the Father who then raises them in power. Thus, through their imitation of Christ, the saints, too, conquer both the devil through righteousness and then death through the resurrection. In this way, the saints' souls are purified of their disordered love and come to begin the process of divinization that will be perfected only at the end of their pilgrimage when they finally rest in God as members of Christ's incorruptible body.

Augustine also plays with the paradoxical conjunction of humility and power in Christ, using the images of the lamb and the lion. Because the lamb of God who takes away the sins of the world is the lion of Judah, Jesus is unique, "the model of such humility in a king of such power and authority" (*Serm.* 375a.1). This is manifest in his passion: "He endured death as a lamb; he devoured it as a lion." Yet instead of dividing Jesus's lamb-like passion from his lordly resurrection, Augustine sees the contrasting qualities present in both his dying and his rising. In his passion, he was both the innocent lamb and the lion who slew death by death. In his resurrection, he reveals his everlasting innocence and everlasting might (*Serm.* 375a.2).

The whole discussion of the cross in *On the Trinity* 13 is a response to the philosophical question, How is the universal will for happiness fulfilled? Since immortality is necessary for happiness, Augustine responds, the Christian's will cannot be fulfilled in this life. Philosophical contemplation, in and of itself, cannot bring humanity to the *beata vita*. Only by faith in Jesus's victory over death (as lion) through his death on the cross (as lamb), not philosophy, does the Christian grasp the hope of immortality and happiness. Thus, Augustine, like Paul, pits the foolishness of the cross against the wisdom of the Greeks. The life of the Christian pilgrim, therefore, is living out the paradox of the cross: one gains one's life only by losing it, giving it up to the God whose power is revealed in apparent weakness and folly.

Conclusion

It is commonly observed that the early Church never convened an episcopal synod to establish a formula to define the salvific work of the cross. Although there was considerable conflict between docetic accounts of Jesus's crucifixion and Catholic accounts, the triumph of the Great Church over the ubiquitous sects of Gnostics resolved what was deemed "of first importance" (1 Cor 15:3), namely that Jesus's passion in the flesh and his bodily resurrection were real. *How* Christ's passion was salvific never became a divisive bone of contention. Perhaps this was because the cross was not treated as the singular locus of salvation but understood within the larger salvific context of incarnation—the re-creation and deification of humanity in the second Adam—with its climax in the resurrection and ascension. Nor does there appear, as with Anselm, to be the desire to discover a single, sufficient proof for the necessity of the incarnation. Rather, when early Catholic authors wrote of the cross, their approach was like that of a cinematographer splicing together, as it were, images from the Gospels, the Epistles, and the Old Testament Prophets to create a montage of Christ's passion. The conjoining of these images resulted in an unsystematic but nevertheless coherent picture that captured the power of the cross in its multiple layers of meaning. One such montage appears in Cyril of Alexandria's interpretation of the appellation "lamb of God." Having identified the sacrificial lamb prescribed in torah as a type of Christ, "the true lamb, the blameless sacrifice," Cyril proceeds with a long series of purpose clauses enumerating the many ways the lamb's death took away the sins of the world. He died

> so that he might conquer the destroyer of the world;
> so that he might abolish death, dying for all;
> so that he might break the curse over us;
> so that hereafter the words, "you are dust and to dust you shall return," might cease;
> so that there might be a second, Adam, not from dust, but from heaven;
> so that there might be the beginning of all good things for humanity's nature:
> deliverance from alien corruption,
> the gift of eternal life,
> the foundation of our renewal in God,
> the beginning of godliness and righteousness,
> and the way to the kingdom of heaven. (*In Jo.* 2.170)

Bibliography

Primary Sources

Augustine of Hippo, *On the Trinity*. Translated by Edmund Hill. Hyde Park, NY: New City, 1991.

Cyril of Alexandria, *Commentary on Isaiah*. CB.

———. *Commentary on John*. CB.

Gregory of Nyssa. *An Address on Religious Instruction*. In *Christology of the Later Fathers*. Edited by Edward R. Hardy. Philadelphia: Westminster, 1954.

Melito of Sardis. *On Pascha*. Translated by Alistair C. Stewart. Yonkers, NY: St. Vladimir's Seminary Press, 2016.

Origen. *Commentary on the Epistle to the Romans: Books 1–5*. Translated by Thomas P. Scheck. Fathers of the Church 103. Washington, DC: Catholic University of America Press, 2001.

Secondary Sources

Anatolios, Khaled. *Deification Through the Cross: An Eastern Christian Theology of Salvation*. Grand Rapids: Eerdmans, 2020.

Jensen, Robin M. *The Cross: History, Art, and Controversy*. Cambridge: Harvard University Press, 2017.

Meconi, David Vincent. *On Self-Harm, Narcissism, Atonement, and the Vulnerable Cross*. New York: Bloomsbury Academic, 2020.

Stewart, Bryan A., and Michael A. Thomas, eds. and trans. *John: Interpreted by Early Christian and Medieval Commentators*. CB. Grand Rapids: Eerdmans, 2018.

Wilken, Robert Louis, ed. and trans. *Isaiah: Interpreted by Early Christian and Medieval Commentators*. CB. Grand Rapids: Eerdmans, 2007.

Young, Frances M. *The Use of Sacrificial Ideas in Greek Christian Writers from the New Testament to John Chrysostom*. Patristic Monograph Series 5. Cambridge: Philadelphia Patristics Foundation, 1979.

10

"That They May Be One"

Ecclesiology in North Africa

Writing at the beginning of the second century, Ignatius of Antioch, who was a victim of the isolated and sporadic periods of persecution that characterized imperial-Christian relations, traveled to Rome to face sure death. In his letters to the churches of Asia Minor and Rome, he exhorted those congregations to preserve unity—a unity achieved through submission to the authority of the bishop who held the place of Christ in the community. Not only was the bishop, as the conduit for the teachings of Jesus and the apostles, the source of doctrinal unity, but he confirmed the hope preached by the Church through his faithfulness unto death. As martyr bishop, therefore, Ignatius preserved the unity of the Church at the levels of both correct teachings and faithful embodiment of those teachings. A century and a half later, a new round of persecution would challenge the unity of Christian communities throughout the empire by calling into question the place of the bishop as foundational to ecclesial cohesion. This was especially true for the churches of North Africa.

In December of 249, the North African aristocrat Cyprian—baptized only two years earlier—had been bishop of Carthage for little over a year when he was confronted with the challenge of leading congregations through the scourge of persecution. The new emperor, Decius, seeking to promote the unity of the empire amid the crisis of the third century, issued an edict requiring all people living within the boundaries of the empire to perform a ritual act of homage to the Roman gods (*vota solemnia*) for the emperor's well-being. Consistent with Rome's traditional policy of toleration and promotion of religious pluralism, devotees of other religions, including Christianity, were not required to renounce the gods they worshiped; they were simply expected to demonstrate civic *pietas*. For Christians, however, such worship of other gods was incompatible with the exclusive obeisance demanded by the one and only God. Cyprian, following the example of Polycarp's "martyrdom according to the gospel," fled into exile to avoid martyrdom. Other prominent bishops were not so fortunate. Dionysius of Alexandria also fled but was pursued and ultimately captured by authorities, while Fabian of Rome was executed. Five months after issuing the edict, Decius intensified penalties for those who refused to perform the obligatory sacrifices. These obdurate individuals were imprisoned where they suffered not only deprivation of food, light, fresh air, and water but were also tortured. These were called confessors, who even in prison shared the charismatic authority of being martyrs. But many Christians were not made of such sturdy mettle and submitted in order to avoid punishment. Thus arose the pastoral and theological question of how to treat the lapsed. In Italy, the policy set by the bishop of Rome was that the lapsed could be readmitted to communion after performing penance for their apostasy. Cyprian initially followed this policy. In this way, it was clear that the authority to bind or loose sins lay with the bishop. The challenge that Cyprian faced, however, was that some of the devout who were imprisoned and were likely to die a martyr's death issued letters of pardon (*libelli pacis*) to the lapsed. The logic behind the practice was that the supererogatory faithfulness of the martyrs earned intercessory status that allowed them to win the divine forgiveness of the lapsed. Cyprian recognized the pardon extended by martyrs to the lapsed who were near death themselves. But for the general population, he decided, absolution would be granted to the penitent at the end of the persecution. The theological question raised in the midst of this crisis was whether the martyrs, too, had the authority to forgive and offer sanctifying grace to sinners.

The double question of who had authority to forgive sins and what sins could be pardoned ignited division within the North African Church. Initially, a group of clergy, who were rigorist, defied a commission appointed by Cyprian to investigate various cases of the lapsed. Cyprian found himself in the middle between those who believed the letters of pardon from the confessors were sufficient and those who would deny the lapsed the hope of forgiveness. These positions amounted to either a usurpation of or an outright denial of episcopal authority to forgive. This disagreement resulted in a threefold schism: Cyprian and the Catholics against a group of North African rigorists who declared Maximus the bishop of Carthage but also by a group of the lenient clergy—called laxists—who supported Fortunatus. For the rigorists, forgiving a sin of the gravity of apostasy was a prerogative belonging to God alone. In that case, both the confessors and the bishops were overstepping their authority. For the laxists, on the other hand, Jesus had taught in his parable that the separation of the wheat and the weeds would come only at the final judgment. Therefore, objected the laxist bishop Pacian of Barcelona (*Ep.* 1.15), the rigorists' permanent excommunication of the lapsed in the present was contravening God's timetable.

The problem of how to deal with the lapsed was not confined to North Africa. The execution of Fabian created a vacuum of episcopal leadership in Rome.

One who stepped in to fill that vacuum was the presbyter and prominent theologian Novatian. In 251, a group of rigorist clergy, including three Italian bishops, consecrated Novatian bishop of Rome, thereby usurping the Roman see from Cornelius who claimed to be Fabian's successor. Although Cornelius was recognized by Cyprian and the majority of North African clergy, Novatian dispatched representatives who established congregations in Carthage that recognized him as the rightful bishop of Rome.

Whereas some rigorists, including Cyprian, would allow the lapsed to be restored to communion only on their deathbeds, Novatian absolutely refused readmission to communion even to the dying. Since no one could curse Christ while speaking in the Spirit (1 Cor 12:3), Novatian reasoned, then the lapsed who renounced Christ never had truly been born of the Spirit in the first place (*Ep.* 1.7). Furthermore, he contended that apostasy was the unforgivable sin of blasphemy against the Holy Spirit (Matt 12:32) because it was a refusal to listen to and be moved by the Spirit (*Ep.* 1.3; *Trin.* 14.10). Therefore, there could be no reconciliation with the lapsed since, as Hebrews declared, "it is impossible to renew them again to repentance, since they again crucify to themselves the Son of God and put him to open shame" (Heb 6:4–6).

The advent of rivals to the episcopal sees within Rome and Carthage raised an important theological question: Were schismatics merely heretics, or were they, as people who shared with Catholics a common confession of faith, an altogether different threat? Further related questions arose, specifically whether former members of these schismatic groups required rebaptism for admission to the Catholic Church. The issue of rebaptism provoked yet another split between Cyprian and the North Africans, on the one hand, and Stephen of Rome, on the other hand, who rejected Cyprian's innovative practice of rebaptizing schismatics. Ultimately, Stephen died and his successor, Pope Sixtus, was reconciled with Cyprian and the North African Catholics. These controversies surrounding episcopal authority forced Cyprian both to articulate the theoretical basis for Christian unity and to provide the theological foundation for his practical, pastoral policy concerning the treatment of the penitent lapsed and schismatics.

Cyprian and the Unity of the Church

In addition to his letters to fellow bishops, Cyprian articulated his ecclesiology in *On the Lapsed*, which was to be delivered to the congregations of Carthage in anticipation of his return from exile, and *On the Unity of the Catholic Church*, which was presented at the Council of Carthage in 251. There he described the contagion of schism as the devil's "new trick" to bring a "new darkness" into the world by deceiving people into believing that they were on the side of God because they saw themselves as upholders of faithfulness in the face of persecution and enemies of apostasy and laxity (*Unit. eccl.* 3). Far from being the champions of fidelity, however, both the rigorists and the laxists were adulterers who, leaving the Church that is Christ's bride, have forsaken the bridegroom and so have become outcasts, enemies of Christ, and therefore cut off from Christ's promise of salvation. Cyprian's logic rested on his conviction that the unity of the Church is derived from God's own immutable nature. Christians are united by their confession of the Trinity whose unity Jesus revealed when he declared, "I and the Father are one" (John 10:30). Because God is unchanging, the content of the Church's confession is also unchanging and so provides an unchanging principle of unity. Therefore, Christians, rather than being tossed about by ever-changing doctrinal claims, enjoy in Christ a share of his peace and stability. The peace and concord of the Church mirror the peace and unity of the Trinity. But the schismatics in breaking the peace and unity of the Church have, in effect, set some principle higher than the Church's confession of the Trinity. So, Cyprian concludes, "To break the peace and concord of Christ is to go against Christ. . . . He who does not keep this unity does not keep the law of God, nor the faith of the Father and Son—nor life and salvation" (*Unit. eccl.* 6). Interpreting Jesus's seamless garment "that was woven from the top throughout," which even his executioners decided not to tear apart (John 19:23–24), as a figure for the Church, Cyprian explains that in the incarnation, Christ mediates the unity of the Trinity to the Church, whose "wholeness and unity remained solid and unbreakable forever" (*Unit. eccl.* 7). Since Christ's garment, the Church, is indivisible, those who separate from the Church are necessarily separated from Christ as well. One cannot enjoy union with Christ without also being in communion with his Church. Thus, schismatics are cut off from salvation because the schismatic bishops lack the authority to consecrate sacraments by which participants receive life-giving grace. Cyprian finds a biblical warrant in Moses's instruction (Exod 12:46) not to eat the Passover lamb outside of the house, which he took to be a figure of the Church mentioned in the Psalms: "God . . . makes all men to dwell together of one mind in a house" (Ps 68:6). Therefore, the faithful have no home but the one Church (*Unit. eccl.* 8).

Even the shared agreement on points of dogma, according to Cyprian, was not evidence that the schismatics were the true Church and their sacraments valid. Although Tertullian accepted the baptism of heretics, the North African Church had years before Cyprian reversed Tertullian's policy. The heretics' baptism was invalid because it was not an initiation into truth but into error (*Ep.* 73.4–5). Cyprian went further, extending the exclusion to heretics and schismatics, including those like Novatian, who were orthodox in their dogmatic teachings such as the Trinity. To make his point, Cyprian drew an analogy between the Novatians and Korah (Num 16), who believed in the same God as Moses and Aaron and kept the religious laws like Aaron and yet whose sacrifices were invalid because he, like Novatian, presumed to make himself a priest rather than being chosen by God and set apart by Aaron. On this evidence, Cyprian argued that former members of the laxists and Novatian communities who sought admission to the Catholic Church had to be rebaptized since their baptisms were not efficacious (*Unit. eccl.* 18; *Ep.* 69.8). For the apostles received the authority to forgive and bind sins from Christ himself when he gave them the Holy Spirit (*Ep.* 69.8). Novatian, however, was not given that authority by bishops who already possessed the Spirit's authority but claimed it for himself.

The unity of the Church across time lay with the apostolic authority passed through a chain of episcopal succession. Although after the resurrection Jesus gave the redemptive power of forgiveness to all the apostles, he initially gave it to one man, Peter, when he said, "You are Peter and upon this rock I will build my Church . . . whatsoever you bind on earth shall be bound in heaven and whatsoever you loose on earth shall be loosed in heaven" (Matt 16:18–19). Although the power was held by all the apostles when the risen Christ breathed the Holy Spirit (John 20:22–23), the significance of giving it first to Peter, Cyprian claimed, was to show that it is a single power held in common by many (*Unit. eccl.* 4). This authority was then held by the college of bishops collectively and distributed to each bishop at his ordination. Therefore, it was incumbent upon bishops to act in concert and be in consultation with one another in order to preserve the unity of the episcopate and with it the Church. "The episcopate is a single whole, in which each bishop's share gives him the right to, and a responsibility for, the whole," Cyprian writes, "So is the Church a single whole, though she spreads far and wide into a multitude of churches as her fertility increases" (*Unit. eccl.* 5). The Church, though many, has one head, Christ, who, like the sun, is the sole source of light that is diffused throughout the world. The college of bishops, however, is the repository of that light, and the bishops individually are its many rays. Therefore, he declares, "Down the changes of years and successions, the appointment of bishops and the constitution of the church runs on, so that the Church rests on the bishops and every act of the Church is governed by these same prelates" (*Ep.* 33). Consequently, it is the bishops, not the confessors, who had the authority to pardon the lapsed. In a move that would have important implications for the North African churches in the centuries to come, Cyprian maintained, as Patout Burns has explained, that an individual bishop's personal fidelity—that is, they could not be guilty of apostasy—was necessary for the efficacy of the sacraments of baptism and Eucharist. The bishop's authority to forgive and sanctify lay in the college of bishops' gift of the Holy Spirit. Therefore, if a bishop were guilty of a serious sin, he ceased to have the basic level of religious integrity necessary for the Spirit's indwelling. Consequently, he could not be a vessel of grace for his people.

The Donatist Schism

Although Cyprian was martyred in 358 during another outbreak of persecution initiated by Valerianus, the rest of the third century was a period of relative peace between empire and the Church. On 29 May 303, however, Christian communities around the empire were caught completely off guard when the emperor Diocletian issued an edict directed against Manichees and Christians. The edict demanded the surrender of their sacred Scriptures, insisted upon the registration of church property, and called for the destruction of church buildings. This was followed up in 304 with a second edict requiring Christians to make sacrifices to the emperor on pain of death. Although the edicts were rescinded in March of 305, the different responses of clergy and laity created fissures in the North African Church. Some clergy handed over copies of the Scriptures for which they were branded *traditores*. Other more zealous clergy and laity not only refused but in an act of civil disobedience handed themselves over and confessed their refusal. These confessors were imprisoned, tortured, and in some cases executed. Although other more clever bishops surrendered texts by heretics that to the eyes of pagan authorities were indistinguishable from the real Scriptures, even the appearance of being unfaithful to Christ in contrast with the suffering of the confessors called into question the ecclesial authority of the *traditores*. Thus was renewed the conflict of the previous century between the rigorists and the lenient as to the condition for readmission to the Church.

The conflict simmered for years but did not erupt into outright schism until 312 with the election of Caecilian as bishop of Carthage. One of the chief agitators against Caecilian was Silvanus, bishop of the Numidian city of Cirta. He charged that Caecilian had been a *traditor* and guilty of impeding the flow of food relief to the confessors who were literally starving to death in prison. The Numidian bishop, Secundus of Tigisis, waded into the controversy, summoning a council of clergy that declared Caecilian's consecration invalid. On top of accusations, such as those put forward by Silvanus, Caecilian's consecration was invalidated on the grounds that he was consecrated by only three bishops, rather than the traditional twelve, and that one of the three, Felix of Apthungi, was a *traditor*. More than a matter of improper procedure, the belief was that a *traditor*, whose de facto apostasy rendered him unholy and therefore unworthy of the episcopal office, did not possess the apostolic grace to pass on to Caecilian but did transmit the guilt of his apostasy. Secundus's council, therefore, elected the presbyter Majorinus bishop of Carthage, creating rival bishops and therefore rival churches. The next year Majorinus died and was replaced by Donatus of Casae Nigrae who led the non-Catholic Christian community of North Africa for forty years. Consequently, the rival church took his name and was referred to as Donatist. Donatist ecclesiology followed Cyprian's view that the validity of the sacraments depended on the grace that had been conferred by Christ on the apostles and from the apostles to the faithful bishops who came after them. If, however, a bishop was guilty of apostasy, he was abandoned by the Spirit and, therefore, was not able to pass on the Spirit's grace in the sacraments. The same was true of bishops who, as supporters of Caecilian, shared in his sin. Thus, Donatists held Catholic baptisms and ordinations to be invalid because they lacked the grace to be efficacious. Consequently, the Donatists required Catholics to be rebaptized in order to be admitted into the Donatist church.

Although in the years to come, Felix of Apthungi was acquitted of the charge of being a *traditor*, Caecilian was vindicated by an imperial investigation, and Silvanus of Cirta was himself proven to have been a *traditor*, Donatist communities spread across North Africa. As W. H. C. Frend has shown, this was not only a conflict between rigorists and the lenient but also a clash between the Donatists who represented the lower classes of Numidia and the Catholics who were supported by the emperor. One of the strongest voices opposing the Donatist church—or schismatics in Catholic eyes—was Augustine of Hippo. Although Augustine's ecclesiology was not merely a reaction to the Donatists, his doctrine of the Church as Christ's body united by the Spirit in the bonds of charity was central to his rejection of the legitimacy of the Donatist church.

Augustine's *Totus Christus*

Augustine's ecclesiology was inseparably intertwined with his Christology. As the Word united himself to humanity in assuming the soul and body of Jesus, so in baptism believers become the earthly body of the risen Christ who is its head (*Enarrat. Ps.* 3.9). Augustine extrapolates from Paul's language of the head and body to articulate the unity of Christ and the Church in a doctrine known as the *totus Christus*. This doctrine holds that, because Christ is one person, wherever the head is located, there, too, is the body, and wherever the body is, there, too, is the head. Commenting on 1 Corinthians 12:12, "As your body is a unit and has many members, and yet all the members of the body, though many, are one body, so too is Christ," Augustine explains that Paul is not making a mere analogy; he is making a metaphysical claim about Christ, "All of [the body] simply is Christ . . . because the whole [*totus*] is Christ" (*Enarrat. Ps.* 142.3).

The doctrine emerged in Augustine's preaching on the Psalms, especially the psalms of ascent. The imagery of Israel ascending Mount Zion to gather together in the temple was an obvious figure of the Christian pilgrim's ascent to fellowship with God in the heavenly commonwealth. Such ascent is ultimately the work of love. Since love is the principle of motion, one's love either raises the soul to heaven or brings it down through fleshly longings. Augustine, however, recognized that this account of ascending through love was not as simple as it might at first appear. The problem lay in Jesus's words, "No one has gone up to heaven except the one who has descended from heaven, the Son of Man who is in heaven" (John 3:13). If the only one who has descended from heaven is also the only one who can ascend to heaven, then how can earthly creatures who have never dwelt in heaven ascend to the Father? Augustine finds his answer in the unitive nature of the incarnation. Drawing on Ephesians' interpretation of Genesis 2:24, "and the two shall become one flesh" (Eph 5:31), to speak of the relationship of Christ and the Church as that of husband and wife, Augustine applies this analogy both christologically and ecclesially. As Christ is the Word united to humanity, soul and body (*Enarrat. Ps.* 56.5), which are distinct yet united, so does Ephesians' marital metaphor illustrate not only the difference—"the distance between us [i.e., the Church] and the majesty of God . . . for we are not the Word, we were not with God in the beginning"—but also the unity: "But when we consider the flesh, there we find Christ, and in Christ we find both him and ourselves" (*Enarrat. Ps.* 142.3). The Word descended from heaven to assume a mortal body, thereby uniting himself with Adam's race. Thus, in a corporate sense, the incarnate Word, as the second Adam, became head of the body of the saints, the invisible Church. When, after his resurrection, he returned to the Father, Christ did not ascend as he descended, namely without a body. Rather, the invisible Word ascended with his glorified body. So too, in the collective sense, Christ "our head" ascended with his body, the Church. Because the head was not severed from his body, Christ remains united with his body the Church even in his ascension to heaven. Therefore, wherever Christ the head is, there too is his body the Church. There is, Augustine declared, "only the one Christ who both descended and ascended. The head came down, but he went up with his body; he went up clothed in the Church, whom he made ready for himself. . . . He is alone, yet he is with us, forming one person, and one forever. Unity binds us to the one Lord. The only people who do not ascend with him are those who refuse to be one with him" (*Enarrat. Ps.* 122.1). Therefore, the Church in a proleptic sense has already been raised to heaven with Christ at the same time that it abides on earth.

Augustine then presses the logic further. Since the head is not separated from his body, the ascended Word, at the same time that he is sitting at the right hand of the Father in heaven, simultaneously abides with his body below on earth. The scriptural warrant for this claim Augustine finds in the words of the risen Jesus addressed to Saul on the Damascus road, "Saul, Saul, why do you persecute me" (Acts 9:4). In persecuting the Church, Saul is persecuting Christ because Christ is one with the Church. To persecute the body is also to persecute the head. Thus, Augustine concludes, "[Christ] is still down here and we are already up there. He is down here by compassionate charity, and we are on high by hopeful charity, 'for in hope we have been saved' (Rom 8:24)." Then Augustine makes one of his strongest descriptions of the Christian life's proleptic orientation toward the heavenly commonwealth: "But because our hope, even though it bears upon the future, is absolutely certain, Paul's statement is made about us as though it were realized already" (*Enarrat. Ps.* 122.1).

The *totus Christus* became a hermeneutical principle for the Church's reading of the Psalms. The words of the psalmist are at once the words of Christ and of the Church. Because of the union of the Word and humanity in the incarnation, the voice of the head and the body are one: "There [in the psalms] Christ says many things in his own name as head and many other things in the name of his members, yet all of it is said as though one single individual were speaking. Wonder not that there are two with one voice, if there are two in one flesh" (*Enarrat. Ps.* 142.3). Christ speaks in the Church and the Church speaks in Christ (*Enarrat. Ps.* 56.1). With a single voice, the psalmist declares, "I rested and fell asleep, and I arose because the Lord will uphold me" (Ps 3:5). In the first clause, the voice is rightly both Jesus's and the Church's—Jesus speaking of his passion, and the Church of its experience of persecution and of death in this life. But then Augustine notes the conjoining of the past and future tenses in the second clause: "But in prophecy the future is quite rightly mixed with the past, because things which are prophesied are still to come in the future as far as time is concerned, but with regard to the knowledge of those prophesying, they are already to be considered over and done" (*Enarrat. Ps.* 3.5). Because the Church, as Christ's body, is united with the Word who is the head, Christ's passion and resurrection are the Church's. As all were in the first Adam, so are all the saints in Christ the second Adam. As all time is subsumed within God's eternity, so the Church as the body of the Father's coeternal Son sees itself linked in one moment to both the past and the future. Augustine imagines members of the Church triumphant singing with the Church militant the words of Psalm 124:1: "Let Israel now say, If the Lord had not been in us." The saints in glory sing as those who have escaped the sufferings and trials of this life. The Church militant, though mired in the sufferings of the present age, share vicariously in the saints' triumph in Christ. "Let us too," Augustine admonishes, "set up these triumphant heroes in our hearts and exult as though we were in their company. . . . Let us see ourselves included in the triumph to be celebrated in the world to come when we shall taunt death. . . . [For] the Lord, and no mere man, was among us and in us. . . . Because of him we, human though we were, became invincible" (*Enarrat. Ps.* 123.4). As such, the doctrine of the *totus Christus* provides members of the Church militant with the ability to live hopefully within the already–not yet tension that characterizes its present life on pilgrimage. Although the pilgrim recognizes that she is "on the way" rather than already "at home," she knows she can be confident of the way because Christ is *the* way. She is "on" the way because she, as a member of Christ's body, is "in" the one who is the way.[1] The Christian can have such confident hope both because "the king of our heavenly homeland has made himself our way" and because she abides in the Word through the word the Church proclaims. "The Word abiding in himself is the truth we are approaching," Augustine says, reassuring his congregation of pilgrims, "This is the truth that sets us free. But the word of faith preached to us, the word in which the Lord bids us abide in order to know the truth, is the Word made flesh who lives among us" (*Enarrat. Ps.* 123.2). The Word is the content of the words of truth. Even though she sees as in a glass darkly, the pilgrim, whose soul is formed by abiding in the Church's words by which it confesses the Word, can be confident that she is on the right way to her homeland.

Still, though, the Church suffers in the present. But because Christ is with his body suffering in the present, the psalmist's cries of lamentation are, for Augustine, those of the Church and of Christ suffering with his body (*Enarrat. Ps.* 56.10). The suggestion that the risen Christ continues to suffer with his earthly body the Church raises, as Augustine was fully conscious, questions about the Son's impassibility—questions that would dominate the debates in the Eastern church later in the fifth century. Augustine affirms the reality of both Christ's suffering in the union of the incarnation and the impassibility of his divinity. One example appears in his discussion of Psalm 131:2, where he quotes 1 Corinthians 3:2: "I gave you milk to drink, rather than solid food." There Augustine identifies the Christ with the bread—that is, the bread of heaven on which "intellectual spirits in heaven" are fed and nourished. Because of sin, however, humanity, "weak and engrossed in the flesh," like an infant who is incapable of eating bread, could not partake of the Word's divinity directly. Rather, like the child who feeds on the same bread her mother eats, which has been converted into the digestible form of breast milk, humanity partook of the same divinity of the Word as the angels but now in the Word's incarnate form. Because the Word assumed human flesh, Augustine proceeds to say, the Word himself was crucified. But neither the assumption of the flesh nor the crucifixion *changed* the Word's divine nature. There was rather an asymmetrical exchange in which "humanity was changed by its union with him . . . to become nobler than it had been before" (*Enarrat. Ps.* 130.10). This change did not constitute a conversion of human nature into "the substance of the Word." Thus, Augustine preserved the distinction between the natures; when speaking of Christ's crucifixion, he is clear that God experienced death but only inasmuch as his earthly body died. "God dies inasmuch as he was

1. This double entendre is implicit because in Latin *in* corresponds to the English prepositions *in* and *on*.

man, and man was raised up inasmuch as this man was God . . . we can say that God suffered, because God assumed that humanity, though he was not changed into humanity" (*Enarrat. Ps.* 130.10). He goes on to justify the language of God's suffering by comparing it to the language used to speak about being attacked by a mugger who tears one's clothes. Although properly speaking, only the clothes were damaged, we still speak of the person as having been attacked. By analogy, therefore, though the divine Word was attacked, only the outer form of his humanity suffered injury. He then shifts the metaphor to that of the soul and the body. As the latter may be killed but the former retain its immortal nature, so too the Word retained its immutable and impassible divinity even while his mortal humanity was killed. Because the immortal Word remains united to his mortal humanity, in his passions Jesus really experienced death and so was "dead"—because his soul and body were separated—even though his divinity retained its life. Precisely because the union of the Word and humanity remained even in his passion, the Word was in the tomb, in Hades, and with the Father simultaneously. Since a similar union exists with Christ and the Church, Augustine could speak of Christ even now as being in heaven and on earth. Christ's compassionate union with humanity endures even after his ascension.

The Eucharist, for Augustine, signifies and effects the unity of believers in the body of Christ. So Augustine exhorts his congregation, "eat what binds you together. . . . Just as [the body and blood of Christ] turn into you when you eat and drink it, so for your part turn into the body of Christ when you live devout and obedient lives" (*Serm.* 228b.3). As Ignatius of Antioch in the early first century saw the unity of the Church preserved in the communal participation in the Eucharist, Augustine, too, saw the gathering of the Church at Eucharist as the corporate enactment of its identity as the body of Christ. Commenting on Paul's words, "We, though many, are one loaf, one body" (1 Cor 10:17), Augustine reassures the newly baptized, "So you are beginning to receive what you have also begun to be, provided you do not receive unworthily" (*Serm.* 228b.4). He then explains the "worthy" manner of receiving: avoiding the yeast of bad doctrine and holding fast to the yeast of charity, which is the incarnate Wisdom of God (*Serm.* 228b.5). Charity as the criterion for embodying the reality of the Eucharist and the unity of the Church it represents was central in critique of schismatics, in particular the Donatists who refused to join in communion with those whom they considered unworthy of Christ.

Since ascending to the heavenly commonwealth is possible only by being united to Christ as a member of his body that he raises with him, those who are not members of his body, the heretics and schismatics, have no hope of ascending. In his homily on Psalm 131, Augustine shifts metaphors from that of the Church as Christ's body to that of the temple composed of living stones (1 Pet 2:5). Only the prayers spoken in the temple, Augustine says, are heard by God. Although he grants that even pagan prayers for temporal goods are heard and answered, the prayers for the supreme good of entry into the peace of the heavenly Jerusalem are efficacious only for those who worship God in spirit and truth—that is, those "within the unity of Christ's body" and "within the peace of the Church" (*Enarrat. Ps.* 130.1).

Donatists as Antichrists

Augustine's *Tractates on the First Epistle of John*, preached Easter week 407, articulated his essential ecclesiology by distinguishing the Donatist antichrists, as he called them, from the true faithful of the Catholic Church. The failure of the Donatists was not, strictly speaking, theological, for they shared with Catholics the common creedal confession. The first tractate begins by defining the Church in terms of the *totus Christus*. Because the Word joined himself to human flesh, "the Church is joined to that flesh, and Christ becomes the whole, head and flesh" (*Tract. ep. Jo.* 1.2). Though the Church of Augustine's day did not see that reality of the incarnation to which John bore witness (1 John 1:2–3), it is united in fellowship with the apostle because of its faith in his testimony (*Tract. ep. Jo.* 1.3). The problem was that the Donatists made the same claim. Since "no one can say that Jesus is Lord except by the Holy Spirit" (1 Cor 12:3), the Donatists appeared to have received the Spirit's witness and been born of the Spirit. Therefore, the mark of the antichrist was the denial of Christ. Even though the Donatists confessed Christ, they were, nevertheless, antichrists because they left the fellowship of believers (1 John 2:18–19). Their very act of schism was a sign that they were antichrists since those who are truly members of Christ's body remain in a sympathetic harmony—rejoicing with those who rejoice and suffering with those who suffer (1 Cor 12:26). The Donatists' withdrawal from the body indicated that they never were members of the body to begin with. Rather, they were like evil humors that the body is in the process of purging and from which it will be finally free at the resurrection "when they are vomited out [and] the body finds relief" (*Tract. ep. Jo.* 3.4).

Another indicator that the Donatists were not truly members of the body of Christ was their disconnection from the apostolic Church. Whereas the Spirit-anointed Church at Pentecost spoke in the tongues of many nations, the Donatists, Augustine observed, spoke not many languages but only Latin and Punic (*Tract. ep. Jo.* 2.3). This was significant for Augustine because it indicated that, though Donatists and Catholics both confessed Christ, the Donatists did not receive what he called "Christ's inheritance" (*Tract. ep. Jo.* 3.7). Based on his christological reading of Ps 2:8, "I will give you the nations as your inheritance," Augustine, following the logic of *totus Christus*, reasoned that, since the whole earth is Christ's possession, so too is it the Church's. Christ's body, therefore, is inclusive of all peoples and not confined to a single geographic region. Indeed, in their separation from the Catholic Church in Carthage, they broke unity with the Catholic Church in all the world. Because the Donatist church existed only in North Africa, it was neither apostolic nor Catholic but a provincial sect.

Because Christ, the head, is united to the body, only by being a member of the body is one also united to the head. To separate from the body, Augustine argued, was tantamount to a denial of Christ and therefore an act of apostasy. Moreover, it is a sin against the Holy Spirit. For schism, as a breaking of the bonds of charity with other believers, is a rejection of the Holy Spirit who, as Augustine repeatedly observed, is "the love of God poured into our hearts through the gift of the Holy Spirit" (Rom 5:5). The will is conformed to "love of God"—having both faith in God's love for humanity and a reciprocal love for God—through the indwelling of the person of the Spirit who binds the believer both to God and to neighbor. Consequently, the breaking of the love that binds fellow believers also breaks the love that binds the individual to God. In cutting oneself off from one's fellow Christians (the body), one cuts oneself off from Christ (the head). Thus, preserving the bonds of charity was paramount. Augustine the pastor knew that, given the enduring disorder of sin in the human will, there would be enduring disagreements between Christians—disagreements often arising from the scandalous conduct of members within the body. Nevertheless, even amid such scandals, unity must be preserved. Commenting on 1 John 2:10, "He who loves his brother abides in the light and there is no scandal in him," Augustine writes, "if you have maintained charity, you shall suffer scandal neither from Christ nor from the Church; you shall abandon neither Christ nor his Church. Those who cannot bear some things in the Church and draw back from the name of Christ or from the Church are the ones who suffer scandal" (*Tract. ep. Jo.* 1.12). They have been burned by the greater scandal of their division. To those who remain united, Augustine expresses comfort in the psalmist's words: "[God] is the shade on your right hand. The sun shall not burn you by day nor the moon by night" (Ps 121:6). "How then is there no scandal in him who loves his brother? Because he who loves his brother tolerates everything for the sake of unity, because brotherly love exists in the unity of charity. . . . How will they not suffer scandal unless they put up with each other?" (*Tract. ep. Jo.* 1.12).

In his discussion of charity, Augustine unites ecclesiology and moral theory. The exegetical challenge that prompted this discussion was how to reconcile 1 John's twin declarations that "no one born of God sins" (3:9) and "If we say we have no sin we deceive ourselves and the truth is not in us" (1:8). How can the "we" in 1:8 also be one who is innocent of the sin mentioned in 3:9? Since all have sinned and sin persists, what is the particular sin of which those who have truly been born of God are not guilty? Augustine's answer is that the "particular sin" that no one born of God commits is the violation of Jesus's new commandment (John 13:34) to "love one another" (*Tract. ep. Jo.* 5.2). Since God is love, love is the distinguishing marker of those born of God and partakers of the divine nature. Schism, however, which breaks the bonds of charity, is a sign that one has not been born of God; for schism, which is the shunning of one's neighbor, exhibits a lack of love if not also outright hatred. By contrast, the love of God and neighbor, which fulfills the law and all righteousness, offers forgiveness and absolves sins (cf. Matt 18:15–20; 1 Pet 4:8; *Tract. ep. Jo.* 5.3). Although perfect love is exhibited in the self-sacrifice of the martyr (*Tract. ep. Jo.* 5.4, 12), the Christian trains herself in such love by giving away her possessions in order to liberate her neighbor from material distress so that she might thrive (*Tract. ep. Jo.* 6.1–2). By defining schism in terms of a "breach of charity," Augustine named the profound contradiction inherent to the Donatist schism: they separated from the Catholic Church for the sake of preserving holiness yet in doing so broke the bonds of charity, which is the sine qua non of the imitation of the holy God who is love. Thus, when Augustine speaks of the Christian as the pilgrim who is traveling to her true homeland, the heavenly commonwealth, he is explicit that this pilgrimage entails not a movement in special location but a growth in charity. Progress in charity, however, cannot be achieved in isolation; it is possible only in the community of fellow sinners in whose company each is trained in love manifest in the virtues of patience, mercy, and forgiveness.

Conclusion

Augustine's doctrine of the *totus Christus* became the foundation for his sacramental theology with which he opposed the Donatists and therefore also the foundation of an ecclesiology that parted company with Cyprian. The dividing point between Augustine and Cyprian was over the contribution of the clergy in the sanctification of their congregations. For Cyprian, the college of bishops held the grace of Christ, which passed through the bishop to the people through the sacraments. However, the individual bishop had to be faithful in order to pass on the holiness to people. Therefore, an unfaithful priest was an impure vessel that could not convey holiness to the sacraments through which the people might be forgiven their sins and made holy. This was the foundational assumption of the Donatists' ecclesiology: the efficacy of the sacraments depended on the holiness of the clergy. On this point, the Donatist controversy led Augustine to diverge from Cyprian. It was not, however, a complete parting of the ways. Augustine's *totus Christus* followed the logic of Cyprian's claim that schismatics cut themselves off from Christ by separating themselves from the Church. Moreover, Augustine also agreed with Cyprian on the doctrine of apostolic succession. Unlike Cyprian, however, Augustine held that the bishops and other clergy do not possess a power in themselves—either collectively or individually—that is passed on from them to the laity through the sacraments. Rather, the grace that makes the sacraments, including ordination, efficacious is the direct work of Christ through the Holy Spirit. Therefore, the forgiving and sanctifying grace of the sacraments is not dependent on the fidelity or holiness of the priest. The priest, as Christ's instrument, simply announces what Christ through his Spirit is doing in the sacrament. This theology of the sacrament challenged the whole basis for the Donatist schism. Because the Donatists held that the efficacy of an ordination depended on the purity of the consecrating bishops, they denied that Caecilian's ordination was valid since one of the bishops was, they believed, a *traditor*. Since his ordination was invalid, they claimed, Caecilian was not the legitimate bishop of Carthage. For Augustine, however, this was a non sequitur. By focusing on Christ, not the priest, as the source of the sacrament's holiness, Augustine was able to argue that, even if Caecilian had been consecrated by a *traditor*, that bishop's lapse did not render Caecilian's ordination invalid. Therefore, Caecilian was the legitimate claimant to the see of Carthage and Donatus and his heirs were usurpers who divided the body of Christ.

More than a disagreement about the technical means for the efficacy of the sacraments, Augustine's departure from Cyprian offered a new vision of the Church. As "one, holy, catholic, and apostolic," the Church was holy because it was the body that derived its holiness from the holiness of its head, Christ. Its holiness did not reside in the members, including clergy, except that they were united to Christ through the Spirit. Holiness and ecclesial unity were inseparable. The holiness by which Christians might hope to ascend to the heavenly city was entirely dependent on unity with Christ the head through unity with the members of his body. That union was possible only through the bonds of charity forged by the Spirit. Therefore, the Church, far from being a fully sanctified community, was an assembly of pilgrims moving toward God in the holiness of Spirit-given love by learning the daily discipline of loving those whom God loves, both one's enemies and one's fellow pilgrims.

Bibliography

Primary Sources

Augustine of Hippo. *Exposition on the Psalms*. Translated by Maria Bolding. The Works of Saint Augustine: A Translation for the 21st Century 3/15–20. Hyde Park, NY: New City, 2017.

———. *Homilies on the First Epistle of John*. Translated by Boniface Ramsey. The Works of Saint Augustine: A Translation for the 21st Century 3/14. Hyde Park, NY: New City, 1990.

Cyprian of Carthage. *On the Unity of the Catholic Church*. Translated by S. L. Greenslade. Early Latin Theology. Philadelphia: Westminster, 1956.

Novatian. *The Trinity, the Spectacles, Jewish Foods, in Praise of Purity, Letters*. Translated by Russell J. Desimone. Fathers of the Church 67. Washington, DC: Catholic University of America Press, 1971.

Secondary Sources

Burns, J. Patout. *Cyprian the Bishop*. Routledge Early Christian Monographs. London: Routledge, 2002.

Burns, J. Patout, and Robin M. Jensen. *Christianity in Roman Africa: A Development of Its Practices and Beliefs*. Grand Rapids: Eerdmans, 2014.

Frend, W. H. C. *The Donatist Church: A Movement of Protest in Roman North Africa*. Oxford: Clarendon, 1952.

Papandrea, James A. *Novatian of Rome and the Cultivation of Pre-Nicene Orthodoxy*. Eugene, OR: Pickwick, 2012.

Ployd, Adam. *Augustine, the Trinity, and the Church: A Reading of the Anti-Donatist Sermons*. Oxford: Oxford University Press, 2015.

11

Debating Creation and Evil in North Africa

The Manichees and Augustine

Theodicy, as we saw earlier, was a dominant theological concern in the second and third centuries. How could one reconcile the confession of God's goodness, wisdom, and creative power with the presence of evil in the world he created? This question, arguably, lay at the very heart of the divergent cosmologies of Christians such as Irenaeus and Origen and their gnostic and Marcionite opponents. Even as cosmologies of the Gnostics posed a challenge for the Great Church in the eastern Mediterranean, forcing figures like Irenaeus to narrate the unity of creation and redemption in salvation history, the Latin West faced a similar challenge from Manichaeism.

Warring Kingdoms: North African Manichaeism

Around the year 290, Manichaean missionaries from the East arrived in Carthage within a generation of the death of the founder of their faith. Mani (216–277) was a Persian mystic and prophet whose family had been members of a Jewish-Christian sect, the Elchasaites. He saw his mission as completing the work of Buddha, Zoroaster, and Jesus—particularly the Jesus portrayed in the secret mystical knowledge taught by various gnostic sects—through synthesizing their teachings. Manichaeism, therefore, was self-consciously syncretistic and fluid. Its missionaries presented it in the language of the religion of the region where they taught. Among Christians, for instance, Mani was hailed "the Paraclete." Yet Manichaeism was larger and more encompassing than Christianity, Buddhism, or Zoroastrianism. "As a river is joined to another river," Mani taught, "to form a powerful current, just so are the ancient books [from other churches] joined in my writings; and they form one great wisdom, such as has not existed in preceding generations" (*Kephalaion* 154; trans. BeDuhn [2000], 6).

Despite, or because of, the many points of intersection between Manichaeism and Christianity, it remains fair to ask whether Manichaeism was a sect of Christianity or a different religion altogether. Based on Augustine's summary of *Capitula*, a book by the Manichaean teacher Faustus of Melevis (d. 390), Faustus identifies the Manichees as Christians because their lives reflect the teachings of Jesus: they are the poor, the meek, the peacemakers, and the persecuted; they left mother and father for the gospel; they have rejected silver and gold (*Faust.* 5.1). Yet Faustus, appealing to discrepancies in the genealogies in Matthew and Luke and the absence of birth narratives in Mark and John, denies that the divine Christ was born of woman (*Faust.* 3.1). Behind these arguments from Scripture lies a metaphysical objection born of the equation of the material world with evil: How could the Savior actually enter the pollution of the visible world and join himself to the dark matter to liberate humanity mired in its filth without himself being polluted? Moreover, Faustus rejected the Old Testament, which disinherited gentiles because they were excluded from the promises of Israel for not practicing the laws concerning the purity of things bodily: "This inheritance is so miserable, so bodily, so far off from what profits the soul" (*Faust.* 4.1). Although all of these deviations from Catholic Christianity are present in other Christian sects, Manichaeism's self-understanding as something larger than Christianity or Buddhism or Zoroastrianism—a perspective not shared by Marcion or the Valentinian Gnostics—makes it something other than a Christian sect.

One result of Mani's syncretism was the creation of a dualistic cosmology that depicted the visible world as a mixture of elements of light and dark, good and evil, that were constantly at war within the individual. The core of this cosmology was captured by Manichaeism's creation myth. In the beginning, before the visible world was made, there existed two realms of light and darkness—the latter being material, and the former consisting of a spiritual substance—that stood in radical opposition to each other. Certain entities dwelling on the fringe of the realm of darkness beheld the goodness of the light and were attracted to it. When they tried to cross over into the realm of light, God, seeking to prevent the corruption of the realm of light, sent an emanation from the light called primal man to repel the invasion. In the battle that ensued, primal man was captured and imprisoned within the material realm of darkness. Although he was eventually rescued, parts of primal man remained attached to the dark matter. This muddled mixture of spiritual light and dark matter—the remnants of primal man's bondage—resulted in the creation of the visible world. Human beings and all of creation are in differing degrees compounds of the dark substance and the luminous spirit, which are the source of an unceasing inner struggle. Like primal man, human beings live a captive existence in the material world and so have forgotten their divine identity, that imprisoned spark of light. Not too dissimilar from the *gnōsis* of the Gnostics,

Mani's teaching is intended to impart knowledge of an individual's true identity and awaken a God-self-consciousness, an awareness of their divine identity.

Salvation for the Manichees, therefore, was seen as reclaiming this divine identity through a slow, unending process of purification, purging—to a greater or lesser degree—the dark matter from one's soul and body. The dark element was responsible for the evil in an individual's thoughts and deeds. This did not mean, however, that the individual needed to be totally passive in her captivity. Rather, she could begin removing the material pollutants through ascetic disciplines, chief of which were abstaining from sexual intercourse and eating meat. The anthropology at the heart of this system held that an individual is an ever-changing organism in which the light and dark elements are ever flowing into and ever passing out of the person. Purification occurred by decreasing the intake of dark matter while at the same time increasing its expulsion. The goal was to lower the ratio of dark to light. Although all foods are a mixture of the light and the dark, certain foods, such as meat, contained more of the dark matter and others, like vegetables, contained less. By taking in less dark matter, over time the natural processes of ingestion and elimination of waste decrease the ratio of dark to light within the soul. Likewise, because intercourse involved an intense participation in the material, the more sexually active one was, the more dark substance penetrated the soul. Conversely, sexual abstinence decreased the flow of darkness and its imprisoning influence. Such asceticism was expected of the Manichaean Elect who were the teachers of Mani's doctrines. The other order of Manichees, the Hearers, who lived a less rigorous life, nevertheless derived salvific benefit through a partnership (*koinōnia*) with the Elect around the ritual meals and by their gifts of alms to care for the Elect.

Augustine's Response to the Manichees

Augustine, like the vast majority of the devotees of Manichaeism, never advanced beyond being a Hearer. Yet he was far from being a half-hearted, nominal practitioner. Consequently, even after his abandonment of Mani's teaching and eventual conversion to Christianity, Manichaeism remained a spectral presence in his theology. More than a decade after his departure from the religion of his early adulthood, he wrote *Against Faustus the Manichaean*, his most thoroughgoing refutation of Manichaeism. The impetus for writing this polemic—like the reason for writing *Confessions*—may have been a need to prove to his critics that he had completely renounced the errors of his youth. Nevertheless, the indictments against Catholic claims about creation and the Creator God leveled by the Manichees were so fundamental that they continued to gnaw at him. There could be no "think and let think" détente with the Manichees; for Augustine, the falsehood of their doctrines and flaws in their critiques of Catholic teachings had to be exposed and definitively refuted.

Scant months after his catechesis and baptism under Ambrose in the spring of 387, Augustine began composing his first critique of Manichaeism, *On the Morals of the Catholic Church and on the Morals of the Manichees*. The dual focus of his argument concerned the continuity of the ethics in the Old Testament and the New Testament, which the Manichaean dualistic reading rejected, and the superiority of Catholic asceticism to that practiced by the Manichees. Three years later, however, in *On True Religion*, Augustine took a different tack. The starting premise of *On True Religion* is that happiness is possible only if there is a principle of unity that is the common source of all things and gives coherence to reality. The one triune God who is the object of true worship by Catholics is that unifying principle. *On True Religion* retains his concern for the nature of the good and happy life that occupied his early writings composed during his sabbatical at Cassiciacum and shortly after his catechetical instruction and baptism by Ambrose. Yet the text marks an important development in his explanations of the *beata vita* and the cause of suffering in the world. Here his analysis expands from the problem of the transient nature of sensible goods to the paradoxical experience of the abundance of creation as a "plentiful poverty."

Rather than refuting the Manichees' dualistic cosmology head-on, he defends the Catholic faith against their critique that, by claiming God created *all* things, the Catholics make God the author of evil (*Ver. rel.* 9.17). He begins by repeating an argument he had previously introduced in *Morals of the Catholic Church* (*Mor. eccl.* 2.1.1–2.9.18), namely that evil is no thing but merely a privation of the good proper to God's creatures (*Ver. rel.* 20.38). Evil, therefore, is like darkness, which, though a reality of human experience, is not a thing in itself but merely the absence of light. That is, it does not have form or substance. Since all things that God created have form and substance (*Mor. eccl.* 11.21–22), evil, which has neither, is not one of the beings or substances in the world that God created. Augustine is not denying there is evil in the world, just that there is no such thing as substantial evil. Therefore, one need not explain evil by positing a realm of dark matter that pollutes and perverts the good, as the Manichees did. Augustine's account, however, leaves open the existential question, What is the source of evil? If evil is not a corrupting substance, what causes the loss of goodness proper to the things that God made? His answer is the wickedness (*nequitia*) of the will (*voluntas*) that turns from God, who is life, toward death (*Ver. rel.* 11.21) by seeking enjoyment in the creature rather than in the Creator. By "enjoying" (*frui*), Augustine means loving a thing as an *end* in itself rather than as a *means* to something else. Therefore, if one enjoys a creature, treating it as an end in itself, then one's love is wholly focused on the creature. One's affection does not rise above the creature to the Creator. Then the creature has become an idol, as it were, taking God's place in the cosmos as the highest good. But because the creature does not have existence in itself except by deriving it from God, "the fountain of life" (Ps 36:9), a creature cannot give life to another creature. Therefore, when human beings make intrinsically perishable creatures their supreme good, they have turned from the God, who is being itself and the source of life, to the nonbeing of death. Therefore, Augustine concludes that the sinful will, not God, is the cause of death: "And that is the sum total of what we call evil, namely sin and the punishment of sin" (*Ver. rel.* 12.23). This turn from God, far from being the cause of a dark force within a person's soul and body, is entirely the result of free choice: "So much is sin voluntary and deliberate an evil that in no way at all would it be sin were it not voluntary and deliberate" (*Ver. rel.* 14.27).

Even as God is not the cause of death, neither is God the cause of the suffering that results from sin's punishment. Such suffering is self-inflicted in two ways. First, sinful humanity suffers because it makes the mistake of seeking happiness in finite, transient creatures. Pointing to a doctrine common to Platonists and Christians, he writes, "it is given only to the rational and intellectual soul to enjoy and be influenced by the contemplation of [God's] eternity and to have the ability to earn eternal life. But it is wounded by love and by grief for things coming to birth and passing away" (*Ver. rel.* 3.3). Since human beings are made to enjoy the goodness of the God who is supremely good—the point with which he opens *Confessions*—they inevitably find no satisfaction for the soul's longings in finite creation, which does not possess the fullness of God's goodness. The imperfect beloved falls short of the lover's desire. When, therefore, in *Confessions* he describes the effect of pursuing his first love in Carthage, Augustine writes, "I rushed headlong into love, by which manner I was captured. 'My God, my mercy,' in your goodness you mixed bitter gall with that sweetness. My love was returned and in secret I attained the joy that enchains . . . with the result that I was flogged with the red-hot irons of jealousy, suspicion, fear, anger, and contention" (*Conf.* 3.1.1). Although God used the ultimate dissatisfaction with his newfound love to keep his restless soul seeking a worthy object of his complete devotion, his suffering came from seeking in another creature the fulfillment of desires that God alone can truly fulfill. Moreover, because the creatures are not eternal, like God, but transitory, they do not remain forever but eventually pass away. When the soul makes its happiness entirely dependent on a transitory being, it will inevitably experience the loss of the object of its love and with it the loss of whatever happiness it derived from it. The pain suffered at such a loss is, Augustine contends, the self-inflicted consequence of loving the transitory creature rather than the eternal God whose perfect goodness neither diminishes nor passes away.

The second way that disordered desire causes suffering is by loving *many* creatures rather than the one who is the source not only of life but of the cohesion and unity of creation. Augustine's argument takes as its starting point the declaration of Ecclesiastes 1:2–3, which is commonly rendered, "Vanity of vanities, all is vanity. What abundance is there for a man in all his toil, with which he toils under the sun." Augustine interprets "vanity of vanities [*vanitas vanitatum*]" as "vanity of vain people [*vanitas vanitantium*]." Augustine's translation implies that creation itself is not intrinsically vain and useless but that the problem lies with the disordered love of sinful people "who chase after the last and the least things [i.e., bodily goods] as if they were the first and foremost" (*Ver. rel.* 21.41). Vanity lies in the belief that happiness is found amid carnal pleasure rather than in the higher goods that sustain the soul. Were the goods of the body seen in their proper place in the hierarchy of creatures—those that serve the needs of the body subordinated to those that serve the needs of the soul—then the true beauty of bodily goods would be rightly appreciated. Then each thing would "manifest its beauty without deception." As it is, however, humanity is almost overwhelmed by the superabundance of beautiful forms in creation and so is pulled by greed in many different directions, often by mutually exclusive goods. Thus, human beings suffer from the distention of desire. In *Confessions,* Augustine describes his own life as "a distention in several directions," living "in a multiplicity of distractions by many things," such that he confesses, "I am scattered in times whose order I do not understand. The storms of incoherent events tear to pieces my thoughts" (*Conf.* 11.29.39). This is the vanity of the present age. The vain pursuit of happiness in the many, Augustine says, is "a toilsome abundance [*abundantia laboriosa*] and . . . a plentiful poverty [*copiosa egestas*], while one thing follows another and nothing remains with him" (*Ver. rel.* 21.41). Ecclesiastes, for Augustine, characterizes the condition of fallen humanity in terms of both time and abundance. The vanity of human labors is that one toils for goods that are not permanent. The fruit of one's efforts is quickly lost and must be replaced by yet further toil. Therefore, one does not see her life's work as a whole but only as a succession of gain and loss that ends in the final loss of death. Precisely because one labors for transitory goods that ever need replacing, there is always an abundance of goods that we desire. Such an abundance, however, becomes not the source of ease and happiness but a burden that produces misery. Without a governing principle that orders man's desires rightly, which unites and gives coherence to them, one seeks enjoyment in many goods that are more numerous than one is able to enjoy. At the same time, however, the laborer is miserable because she does not rightly value these transitory goods for what they are. Her abundance is toilsome (*abundantia laboriosa*) because all these transitory goods require continual labor to attain, preserve, protect, and replace. Yet because these many goods are not the eternal and perfect God, who alone is the ground of blessedness and security, the toilsome abundance turns out to be a plentiful poverty (*copiosa egestas*). The soul is impoverished because, for all its worldly possessions, it lacks the one thing needful for true happiness. Thus, humanity's disordered loves have left it in a fragmented existence lacking any real coherence.

Augustine's arguments in *On True Religion* counter the Manichees by providing an alternative explanation to the problem of evil. Evil need not be thought of substantially but as a failure of the will to love God above all and to love creation rightly. The evils of suffering and death are real, but they are self-inflicted because humanity fails to see that God and God alone is the source of happiness. The Catholic faith, therefore, proves superior to Manichaeism because of all religions, it offers access to the happy life, which is found in worshiping the one who is the origin and source of unity in the cosmos. Because, according to the Manichees, there is no single first principle from which all things come but two eternal first principles, light and darkness, God is locked in a ceaseless struggle with the kingdom of darkness. There is neither final triumph in which the enemies of light are vanquished nor an eschatological redemption in which humanity is definitively delivered from bondage to sin and death. By contrast, the triune God of Christianity is the first principle, the *principium*, who, as the origin of all things, holds all things together. Therefore, when the Christian loves God as the supreme good, she loves all that God has created and reflects, albeit imperfectly, God's goodness. She is, therefore, able to love the creature rightly as God's creature. Indeed, as Augustine will eventually come to say in *On Christian Doctrine*, she enjoys the creature *in God*. Because she loves the creature as a creature, she loves it not as an end in itself but as a part of the whole creation ordered by divine providence. On the whole, as narrated by Scripture's account of salvation history, she sees the artistry of the Creator who gives a role and value to each creature. Each creature is, as it were, a single tile that makes up a richly detailed and elaborate mosaic. Therefore, an individual's true beauty, what makes her really loveable, is seen only in her divinely ordained contribution to the harmonic beauty of the whole discovered in God. Yet amid the distention of the present, precisely because the many come from one source and not two conflicting first principles, Augustine can confess that "'[God's] right hand upheld me' in my Lord, the Son of man who is mediator between [God] the One and us the many," so that "leaving behind the old days I might be gathered to follow the One" (*Conf.* 11.29.39). Because the Savior is the *principium* (the beginning) in whom and through whom all things were made, Augustine can hope for the resurrection when the toilsome distention shall end, "when, purified and molten by the fire of your love, I flow together to merge into you. Then shall I find stability and solidity in you, in your truth which imparts form to me" (*Conf.* 11.29.39–40). This form imparted by the truth is, for Augustine, the very form that imparted existence to all creation in the beginning.

Light and Form: Augustine's Platonic Interpretation of Creation

Countering the Manichees was not as simple as refuting their idea of substantial evil through Augustine's theory of the will; he had to provide an alternate cosmology. Shortly after his conversion and around the time of his ordination to the priesthood, Augustine had tried to compose such a cosmology in two commentaries on Genesis (*On Genesis: Two Books Against the Manichees* and *On the Literal Interpretation of Genesis: An Unfinished Book*). Dissatisfied with these initial efforts, either because he failed to give an account of the literal meaning or because they raised more questions than they solved, he abandoned these projects. His mature accounts came almost a decade later, first in an abbreviated form in book twelve of *Confessions* (397–401), and then in *On Genesis Literally Interpreted* (401). Although Augustine was fully capable of offering a spiritual or figural reading of Genesis, what he wanted was to explain the literal meaning—that is, what actually happened. What are the heavens and the earth mentioned in Genesis 1:1? And what is the light that God created prior to the creation of the sun?

Behind Augustine's exegetical questions lay other questions rooted in his reading of Neo-Platonist accounts of creation based on *Timaeus*. There the demiurge creates by imposing order on the formless, chaotic preexisting matter by giving form based on the perfect archetypes or paradigms existing eternally in the intelligible realm. Unlike in the Manichaean myth, this matter, although it is a second first principle, is not evil; it is simply without form. The world created by Plato's demiurge, though fashioned from matter, is good because each creature reflects, albeit imperfectly, the perfect goodness of the eternal ideas that served as the model for the world. In other words, the world receives both being and goodness when it receives form from the Creator who beholds the forms. Plotinus expands upon Plato's hylomorphic theory of creation. The World Soul is the creative impulse that emanates from the Mind, the second principle, and is responsible for fashioning the material world. Mind, who in beholding the beauty of the One, gives expression to the beauty of the One in concepts or forms in Mind. These forms do not exist in the One who is simple and beyond being. Rather, they exist in Mind where each has a discrete form or character that distinguishes one from the other; thus, Mind is the intelligible realm of being. The forms are themselves not perfect as the One is perfect because the One's perfection lies in its absolute oneness and simplicity. Though inferior to the One, the forms in Mind are like the numerous, brilliant colors emanating from light that has passed through a spectrum. Because Mind loves the beauty of the One reflected in the forms, Mind generates Soul to create a world that resembles the beauty of the One reflected in the forms. The task of individual souls that are part of the World Soul, therefore, is to give existence to individual creatures by communicating form to matter. A soul exercises dominion over the body by simultaneously contemplating the beauty of the forms and continually keeping its body in conformity with its archetype. Should the soul become so absorbed in the material realm of the body that it does not exercise its rational nature in contemplation of the intelligible realm, then it "forgets" the exact image of the form. It cannot then communicate form to the body and the body's matter becomes deformed. Deprived of form from its soul, the body degenerates and becomes ugly. This privation of form means that the material body fails to reflect the goodness and beauty of the One reflected in Mind. Thus, Plotinus uses the categories of form and matter to explain both the goodness of creation and the origin of evil.

The Platonic hylomorphic theory was appealing for Augustine not only because—unlike either Aristotle's theory of the eternality of the world or the Stoic cosmology with its unending cycles of explosive generation (creation) and implosive conflagration (collapse of all things)—it was a theory of actual creation. But it also provided language to explain some obscure elements of the Genesis narratives that posed exegetical challenges, particularly the nature of the heavens and the earth mentioned in verse 1. First, how should one understand God's creation in the beginning of an earth "without form and void and darkness was upon the face of the deep"? The language from the book of Wisdom that speaks of "unformed matter" (11:18) combines with the narrative of *Timaeus* to provide a helpful explanation: the earth "without form and void" was the formless matter to which God gives form (*Gen. litt.* 1.1.2–3; 1.9.15). Though it is "a kind of formlessness without any definition," it is not "absolute nothingness" (*Conf.* 12.3.3). In *On Genesis Literally Interpreted*, the formless matter was not created first and then received form. Rather, the matter and the particular creatures composed of matter are created at the same time (*Gen. litt.* 1.15.29). The narrative order simply expresses the logical, rather than temporal, priority of form and matter to the things composed of them. *Confessions* is more ambiguous. There it appears that although matter had existence, it was no thing because it had not yet been shaped into the form of particular things. Ultimately, formless matter is Augustine's principle of mutability, which renders all things capable of being changed (*Conf.* 12.6.6). Indeed, the waters of chaos in their ever-changing fluidity are, Augustine says, an apt image for formless matter that is the source of all things, since all species emerge not from dry earth but from moisture (*Gen. litt.* 1.5.11). Yet, whereas in the Platonic tradition formless matter, which was the substrata of all corporeal creatures, was not created by the demiurge or soul but existed from eternity, for Augustine prime matter is not another first principle but is itself entirely God's creature; for God "made this next-to-nothing out of nothing" (*Conf.* 12.8.8). Thus, the very substance of all material creation is not some alien force on which God must impose his will but is an instrument of God's will because it is itself an artifact of divine wisdom and power.

A second exegetical knot in Genesis concerns the order of the creation of the heavens and heavenly bodies: if the firmament that was called "heaven" was not created until day two, and the moon, sun, and stars in the heavens not created until day four, what are "the heavens" spoken of in verse 1? To this, there is a related question: If the sun did not come into being until the fourth day, what is the light that shone in the darkness at God's command, "Let there be light" (Gen 1:3)? By reading Genesis through the lens of John 1:1–2, Augustine concludes that, since the Word (*Verbum*)—who is also called the "true light that enlightens every man" (John 1:9)—is the one who was in the beginning and through whom *all things* were made, the light created on the first day is not a reference to the Word. This is the case, Augustine reasons, both because John says of the Word, "without him was nothing made that was made," and because the Word itself was not made but begotten from the Father's being. If the light is not the Word, neither can it be the light apprehended with the eye since none of the heavenly luminaries were as yet created. Therefore, the light must be God's created wisdom spoken of in the Wisdom of Sirach: "Wisdom has been created before all things" (Sir 1:4). The Word is the Father's eternal Wisdom; the created wisdom is the first of God's creation because it is the source of the form that the Creator Word uses to fashion the unformed matter of earth into all the creatures made over the next five days of creation. Speaking of the formless earth, Augustine writes, "imperfect being . . . tends to nothingness because of its formless state," but, he continues, it comes to imitate "the exemplar in the Word . . . [and] receives its proper form and becomes a perfect creature" (*Gen. litt.* 1.4.9). Thus, the earth that was "without form and void" is "imperfect" until it receives form from the Word and becomes the "perfect" creature that God intended. This created wisdom is an *eternal* creation in the sense that it came into being before time, yet it is not coeternal with God, as is the Son, the Father's eternal Wisdom (*Conf.* 12.15.20).[1] Moreover, because the created light is the source of the form that gives structure to creation, created wisdom is also that with which the Son illuminates the intellect of "spiritual and rational creatures" and gives them understanding (*Gen. litt.* 1.17.32).

This interpretation of the light is critical to his adaptation of a Platonist illuminationist epistemology articulated in his early dialogue, *On the Teacher* (389). At the root of this theory of knowing are two questions. Can knowledge be taught?

1. Augustine can speak of a creation that is eternal—that is, outside of or prior to time—because he recognizes that time is merely the measurement of relative change or movement of things, such as the movement of the hands of a stopwatch and the body of a runner moving around a track.

Is it a thing that can be passed from one person to another? And how can one recognize a thing without prior knowledge of it? For instance, how can one judge an action to be unjust without first knowing what justice is? Yet people every day make this sort of judgment with only an intuitive sense of what justice is. So what is the source of that hazy sense of justice? For Plato, the answer lay in a theory of innate ideas, that inchoate sense of the ideal based on the soul's vision of the forms in the heavenly realm before its descent into the earthly realm and union with the body. Augustine agrees with Plato that knowledge is never simply transmitted from one person to another. Teachers use signs to communicate information to their students. Yet such signs are effective for communication only if the meaning of the sign is already known by the student. Therefore, signs do not convey knowledge but only remind the student of something already known. Like an orator's hand gesture, they direct the mind to look and see; in this case, to look within itself and discover in memory what the sign refers to. In the case of Scripture, the meaning of its words is given by an inner teacher, Christ, whose light reveals the meaning and truth of its signs (*Mag.* 11.38). Thus, Christ, the inner teacher, gives knowledge by imparting to the mind the created wisdom, which functions in Augustine's epistemology as the forms do in Plato's. For the intelligible created light is that wisdom, God's intention, that orders all the rest of creation according to his purposes. In that sense, created wisdom functions as the forms, both cosmologically as models for ordering the world and thus epistemologically as innate ideas that allow rational creatures to understand that order.

The light of created wisdom is critical for Augustine's understanding of human happiness. The perfect form of the divine Word derived from its eternal union with the Father is the source of existence and happiness. By contrast, rational creatures are given form, which imparts mere existence. Their existence, however, will be happy only when they turn to the Word who imparts to the soul that wisdom that gives godly form to the mind that it may live well in the world and share in the blessedness of God. Conversely, "when it is turned away from changeless Wisdom, its life is full of folly and wretchedness, and it is in an unformed state" (*Gen. litt.* 1.5.10). The existence of rational creatures begins with God's gracious act of creation but is truly complete only when the rational creature opens itself up to receive the form-imparting wisdom of the divine Word.

Augustine's interpretation of the light of Genesis 1:3 as "created wisdom" clearly reflects Platonic influence, but it is also significant because of its points of divergence from the Platonists. In *Timaeus*, the paradigms according to whose pattern the demiurge fashioned the world are eternal. For Augustine, the form that the Word imparts to formless earth is not eternal but created. Since the triune God exists in eternity, outside of time, the Father's creative command in the Word, "Let there be light," occurred in eternity, but the light's coming into existence occurred in time (*Gen. litt.* 1.2.6). Nevertheless, the light of wisdom is a creature. While the form by which the Word fashions formless earth is an expression of God's goodness, it is clearly something other than God. Therefore, it illustrates the gratuitous nature of creation. There was no coeternal principle from which God derived the model of the earth; the form came from a model of God's own making. Thus, God's plan of creation was conditioned by nothing other than his own will.

The light that is created wisdom is closely related to "the heavens" mentioned in Genesis 1:1. This heaven is spiritual, perfect in form, and existing timelessly "above" the material heaven that is the firmament containing the moon, sun, and stars (*Gen. litt.* 1.9.15). It is the "heaven of heaven" (*caelum caeli*), which, because it is spiritual, is not a place but a community of rational beings or angels who transcend time and abide in the light through their contemplation of the true and the real, that is, the light of created wisdom. The expression "Let there be light," Augustine explains, is the soundless communication of the timeless forms (*rationes*) impressed by God through his divine Word upon the minds of these spiritual creatures (*Gen. litt.* 1.9.17). Although "the heaven of heaven" is not coeternal with God, through cleaving to God in contemplation, it participates in God's eternity so that it is not subject to mutability or corruption (*Conf.* 12.9.9). This created heaven is in a certain sense eternal because it does not change. Since a rational nature conforms to what it thinks about, the *caelum caeli* never changes because its thoughts are eternally informed by its intellectual vision of the divine. God is the uninterrupted content of its thoughts. However, were these rational beings ever to turn their thoughts from God and so cease to be illumined by his light, they would cease to be eternal, becoming formless and chaotic (*Gen. litt.* 1.9.17). Although these angelic beings are rational creatures made from nothing, they do not grow in their knowledge of God; rather, they simply know God in a single moment, an eternal present without experiencing the passing or distention of time (*Conf.* 12.13.16). As such, "the heaven of heaven" is paradigmatic for the eschatological rest the saints will enjoy: "There [God's] delight is contemplated without any failure or wandering away to something else. The pure heart enjoys absolute concord and unity in unshakable peace of holy spirits, the citizens of your city in the heavens above the visible heaven" (*Conf.* 12.10.12). Thus, this heaven is the "house of God," in which the psalmist wishes to dwell all the days of his life (*Conf.* 12.15.20) and, as Augustine puts it, "Jerusalem, my homeland and mother" (*Conf.* 12.26.23).

Conclusion

The problem of theodicy was the vexing issue that drew the young Augustine to Manichaeism and that later occupied his theological project in his Catholic, post-

Manichaean period. But the theology that emerged was richer and more intricate than a simple definition of evil that exonerated God from the charge of being evil's author. In *On True Religion* and *On Christian Teaching*, he deepened his account of the enigma that is the soul of fallen humanity and the cause of its suffering. In the doctrine of creation developed later in *On Genesis Literally Interpreted* and in *Confessions*, he articulated not simply a Christian adaptation of Neo-Platonic cosmology but also a distinctly Christian eschatology. In so doing, he offered a vision of the blessedness for which God made man in the beginning and that will be the destiny of the saints who abide in the unity of God's oneness.

Bibliography

Primary Sources

Augustine of Hippo. *Answer to Faustus a Manichean*. Translated by Roland J. Teske. The Works of Saint Augustine: A Translation for the 21st Century 1/20. Hyde Park, NY: New City, 2007.

———. *Literal Meaning of Genesis*. Translated by John Hammond Taylor. Ancient Christian Writers. New York: Paulist, 1982.

———. *On Christian Belief*. Translated by Boniface Ramsey. The Works of St. Augustine: A Translation for the 21st Century 1/8. Hyde Park, NY: New City, 2005.

Secondary Sources

BeDuhn, Jason David. *Augustine's Manichaean Dilemma*. Vol. 1. *Conversion and Apostasy, 373–388 C.E.* Philadelphia: University of Pennsylvania Press, 2010.

———. *The Manichaean Body in Discipline and Ritual*. Baltimore: Johns Hopkins Press, 2000.

Kenney, John Peter. *The Mysticism of Saint Augustine: Rereading the* Confessions. New York: Routledge, 2005.

Smith, J. Warren. "Loving the Many in the One: Augustine and the Love of Finite Goods." *Religions* 7 (2016): DOI: 10.3390/rel7110137.

12

Divine and Human Agency

Questions of Free Will, Grace, and Election

Early in the fifth century, the British monk Pelagius heard a line from Augustine of Hippo's autobiographical prayer, *Confessions*, "Give what you command and command what you will" (*Conf.* 10.29.40), and was deeply troubled. Pelagius was a devout man widely admired for his personal holiness and piety. What concerned him was that not everyone in the Church shared his concern for rectitude and righteousness. Pelagius began with the premise that a person is morally obligated to do only that which is within her power. From that starting point, he interpreted Jesus's words in the Sermon on the Mount, "Be perfect even as your heavenly Father is perfect" (Matt 5:48), to imply that all people *could* and therefore *should* live lives of sinless perfection. Perfection, therefore, was not only an expectation; it was requisite for eternal life. Pelagius complained that bishops had not made this point clear to the neophytes entering the Church in large numbers. Because the clergy had failed to lay before these new converts the strenuous life of moral striving expected of them, they had given them a false hope of heaven.

Augustine's petition disturbed Pelagius because it presupposed that Augustine did not have it within himself to fulfill the Lord's commands but needed divine assistance in order to obey. This was problematic because it challenged Pelagius's understanding of the relationship between human and divine agency. By implicitly denying humanity's natural capacity to do what God commanded, Augustine had made God unjust for setting, and judging mortals according to, moral requirements that were unattainable. If people could not attain the prescribed righteousness apart from God's assistance, then the fault for their failure lay not with them but with God for not giving the needed aid. Therefore, Pelagius penned a response to Augustine entitled *On Nature*, arguing that the sin of the first parents had not altered human nature in such a way that inherent sinfulness was passed on over the centuries from generation to generation. Pelagius argued that the nature inherited by subsequent generations was essentially no different from that of Edenic humanity. True, the sons and daughters of Adam, unlike their parents in Eden, live under the shadow of mortality. That, however, was the result of living outside of paradise with its tree of life. Moreover, he contended, they were not being punished for the sins of their forebears. Every child was born in a state of innocence. Although "all have sinned and fall short of the glory of God" (Rom 3:23), this is because the innocent babe grows up in ignorance of true righteousness and so develops sinful habits by observing and imitating the sinful deeds of his parents. However, Pelagius stresses, there is no weakness inherent to human nature that makes an individual's fall into personal sin inevitable or necessary.

Augustine's plea "give what you command" was neither a thoughtless rhetorical flourish nor an expression of the pathos of his theologically immature self in his early thirties. Rather, it was the prayerful expression of his conviction that God's *grace* is a gift given to enable people to convert their will and fulfill the righteous demands of the law. It was the period after his ordination to the priesthood, in which he expounded the Christian Scriptures to his congregation in multiple sermons a week, that he began to attend closely to the account of grace in Paul's letters, especially Romans.

Arguments about the relationship between human and divine agency begun in the dispute between Pelagius and Augustine lasted for over a hundred years after Pelagius's and Augustine's deaths until they were formally settled at the Council of Orange in 529. The council's conclusion shows that while Latin Christendom had decided that Pelagius's anthropology was wrong, it was not entirely satisfied with all the implications Augustine drew from his doctrine of grace. Some of those conclusions would be points of contention for centuries to come in the Latin Church. The greatest dissatisfaction, however, came from critics in the Orthodox Churches of the East who saw Augustine's doctrine of original sin as lowering the standards of holiness to which Christ called his disciples.

Although the dispute over grace and free will would come to a climax in the Latin West during the Pelagian controversy of the fifth century, the relationship between divine agency and the extent of and condition for human moral responsibility was a point of contention that went back much farther in Christian history to the Great Church's disputes with both paganism and gnostic conceptions of election.

Divine Agency and Human Will for the Gnostics and Irenaeus

The second- and third-century debates around moral agency and free will stand against the backdrop of pagan conceptions of necessity (*anankē*). Although certain thinkers like Plato sought to link necessity with an individual's choices (*Resp.* 10 [617d–e]), necessity was commonly understood as referring to the influence of the celestial bodies on the lives of individual human beings. Perhaps the earliest sustained argument against fate and in favor of free will is preserved in a dialogue composed by a student of the Syrian teacher Bardaisan of Edessa (AD 154–222), entitled *The Book of the Laws of Countries*. Having been an astrologer before his conversion to Christianity, Bardaisan used his knowledge of arguments defending astral determinism to refute the Chaldean doctrine of fate. In his cosmology, the universe is ordered by natural laws established according to God's will. Nature is impersonal; all creatures live and operate within its structure. Nature sets a woman's child-bearing age, for example; mothers do not bear children either younger or older than a certain age (*BLC* 575). That is simply a fixed rule of nature. Fate is distinct from nature. It refers to the influence that heavenly beings, called rulers and guiding signs, exert on the lives of individuals. Sometimes their influence is benign, strengthening the natural constitution. Other times—more often than not—the rulers impede or disrupt nature (*BLC* 576). To some, fate gives robust health or wealth or power or numerous progeny, and to others, illness or poverty or destitution or infertility (*BLC* 570). For Bardaisan, nature refers to God's general providence, and fate to specific providence. At times, Bardaisan depicts fate as the result of how the rulers use the liberty given to them by God (*BLC* 579). Elsewhere, the rulers and guiding signs are instruments of God's will: "For that which is called Fate is really the fixed course determined by God for the Rulers and Guiding Signs. According to this course and order, the spirits undergo change while descending to the soul and the souls while descending to the bodies" (*BLC* 571). In other words, the rulers make changes in each soul as it is "descending" into its body, and these changes determine its future.

While the particular material quality of one's life is determined by fate, the individual still retains the freedom to determine the moral character of her life. In answering a student's question, "Why did God not make human beings incapable of sinning?" Bardaisan responds that eliminating the possibility of sin would reduce human beings to mere instruments of God, like a stringed instrument, which is worthy of neither blame nor merit. The musician, not the instrument, is praised for the beautiful music (*BLC* 544). Therefore, it is the gift of liberty that raises human beings above the stars and moon, which can do only as they are ordered. "Through this liberty," Bardaisan explains, "the individual justifies himself, leads his life divinely, and is associated with the angels, who possess a free will of their own" (*BLC* 548). The divine gift of liberty carries a responsibility but not an onerous one; in fact, "They are easy, and there is nothing that can prevent them . . . every human being with a soul can keep them with joy" (*BLC* 551–552). That is because doing good is connatural for rational creatures. By contrast, the works of evil result when a person has abdicated his self-mastery (*BLC* 555). While fate may disorder nature, free will enables the soul to resist fate and conform her life to the natural order of the cosmos. Evidence of humanity's freedom from the dominion of fate in matters of morality Bardaisan finds in a country's laws, which are an expression of God-given liberty. For although the stars determine different fates for different individuals, all those individuals conform to the moral standards determined by such laws, not the determination of the stars (*BLC* 583). Furthermore, even though men and women may share the same astral fate—that is, being born under the same constellation—their adherence to laws regarding the different conduct for men and women is proof that they are not compelled by fate to act the same (*BLC* 584).

As serious as was the Christian clash with pagan culture over astrology—a cause shared by adherents of the gnostic sects as well as members of the Great Church—the greater conflict about human freedom occurred between Christians. They clashed over how to interpret the Pauline language of election (Rom 8:29–30, 33; Eph 1:4; 2 Tim 2:10), especially when the distinction between the elect and the nonelect was mapped onto a division according to one's *natural* disposition between those who are spiritual and those who are fleshly (1 Cor 15:46, 50). According to Irenaeus, the "heretics" of the second century divided the human race hierarchically into three groups: at the bottom are the materially minded (children of Cain), next the psychic or soul people (children of Abel), and at the top the spirituals (children of Seth).[1] The descendants of Cain possess a carnal nature that has been irredeemably corrupted by their life in the material world. Because they never received a spark of Wisdom, they live in complete ignorance of the realm of true being that exists outside of material creation, and lacking the spark of light, they live under the illusion that the material world is all there is. Consequently, their minds cannot be turned to the light but face the destruction that comes to all material things. Abel's offspring possess the quality of soul but not spirit; therefore, they lack *gnōsis* necessary for full salvation. Instead of being guided by knowledge of true reality, they live by faith (*Haer.* 1.6.2). If they live well and perform good works, they will find rest in an intermediate place between the realm of light and the realm of destruction. If, however, they do not live justly but are absorbed in the material world as are the children of Cain, they will share the same fate, destruction (*Haer.* 1.7.5). The spirituals are the gnostic elect who have received a spark of light from Sophia (Wisdom) that allows them to attain perfect knowledge of God and be initiated into the gnostic mysteries (*Haer.* 1.6.1). Their salvation lies not in virtuous living but simply in their spiritual nature. Possessing in their nature the deposit of the spirit of Sophia, they are not deluded into thinking the material world is ultimate reality and so cannot be corrupted

1. Irenaeus's term "heretics" includes self-identified *gnōstikoi* as well as nongnostic sects, e.g., Marcionites and Ebionites, but the primary referent is the Valentinians.

by their contact with it any more than gold dipped in filth ceases to be a precious metal (*Haer.* 1.6.2).

Irenaeus's characterization of gnostic teachings is more or less consistent with the description of the human condition in the Apocryphon of John; there the descendants of Seth are "the immovable race upon whom the spirit of life will descend ... [which] strengthens that soul and nothing can mislead it into works of wickedness" (Ap. John 25.20–25; 26.5–20). Since salvation is not available to all because not all can understand the difficult parables and the enigmas that disclose the truth (Ap. John 25.18–20), the Gnostics did not reveal their special *gnōsis* openly (*Haer.* 1.3.1). The non-Gnostics, therefore, are enslaved to destiny and subject to the counterfeit spirit, which deceives the soul by fostering forgetfulness that prevents it from being awakened (Ap. John 26.35–27.2; 28.6–31).

This division between the gnostic elect and the nonelect reflected a fundamental disagreement in the interpretation of Paul's epistles. The Gnostics, especially the Valentinians, thought of themselves as standing in the line of apostolic succession from Paul (*Flor.* 7.9) since Valentinus was a hearer of Theudas, who was one of Paul's trusted disciples (*Exc.* 7.17). Being "all things to all people," Paul preached two versions of his gospel. One focused on the crucified Christ who was born and suffered; this was the message for the psychics. The other taught Christ according to the spirit; this was the secret oral tradition that Paul taught to Theudas, who passed it on to other pneumatics (*Exc.* 23.3–4). The interpretive key that Paul revealed to Theudas is that the terms "Jews" and "gentiles" do not refer to a racial division between the children of Israel and non-Israelites but are ciphers for speaking about two sorts of people, the psychics ("the Jews") and the pneumatics ("the gentiles"), Paul's foolish and wise in Romans 1:14. From this division of the human race, the Valentinians interpreted the "elect" of Romans 8:1–4 to be the pneumatics in whom the Spirit of God dwells and so do not fear condemnation under the law of the demiurge (*Haer.* 1.13.6). They are those foreknown by God and predestined to be conformed to the image of the Son, the pneumatic Christ (Rom 8:28–39). They are children of the promise (Gal 4:28) who are from the seed of Abraham and so, like the Savior, appear to be psychic but are in truth pneumatics. By contrast, the psychics, who are not among the elect, fear condemnation because they remain under the law of sin and death (*Comm. Jo.* 20.38). Valentinus speaks of the variety of people, whom the Word is coming to judge, as jars, some leaky or dry, others half filled, some full, and some simply broken (Gos. Truth 26.35–38). The pneumatics are the full and purified jars, while the psychics are cracked and half full. In the Gospel of Thomas, Jesus reveals that the Gnostics are "offsprings," "the elect of the living God," who are "from the light that we have come from—from the place where the light, of its own accord alone, came into existence" (Gos. Thom. 50, 41.30–42.4). The psychics, however, are not entirely without hope. Although not predestined, the psychics have received "a call" through the revelation of the psychic Christ, which the psychic Paul proclaimed "to my brothers, my kinsmen according to the flesh" (Rom 9:1–5). According to Heracleon, God has communicated with the psychic, but only a few have received the revelation (*Haer*. 1.7.3). Those few are the remnant of the psychics whom God has elected.

Alongside Romans, Ephesians was an important text for the Valentinian doctrine of election. According to Valentinus, Paul in this letter addresses both the pneumatics, who are the "holy ones," and the psychics, who are "the faithful in Christ" (Eph 1:3). The pneumatics have received the spiritual blessings from God the Father, who has elected them in Christ "before the foundation of the world" (Eph 1:4). In contrast with the "self-appointed wise people . . . who were not truly intelligent" and who rejected the Savior (Gos. Truth 19.21), the "living book of the living," which before the foundation of the entirety was among the Father's incomprehensibles, was revealed to "the little one to whom belongs acquaintance [*gnōsis*] with the Father" (Gos. Truth 19.27–20.1). Valentinus goes on, "Those whose names [the Father] foreknew were called at the end, as persons having acquaintance [*gnōsis*]. . . . For one whose name has not been spoken does not possess acquaintance. How else would a person hear, if that person's name had not been read out? For whoever lacks acquaintance until the end is a model form of forgetfulness, and will perish along with it" (Gos. Truth 21.25–37). The psychic Christ became an "adopted son" giving hope that they, too, might be adopted as psychic sons of the Father (*Exc.* 33.1–2).

Irenaeus begins his response to the Gnostics with an appeal to justice. All that is good is given by God as gift, but it would be unjust for a person to enjoy the benefits of the divine gifts unless he preserved that good within himself by voluntarily conforming to the good. In other words, the divine blessings must be merited, and such merit is accrued only if the individual could have chosen to do otherwise (*Haer.* 4.37.1). The ability to choose to conform to the good or not is the freedom of the will with which humanity was endowed when God made the first human beings in his image and endowed them with the same freedom God himself possesses (*Haer.* 4.37.4). Free will allows human beings to merit the blessedness of communion with God. If, however, one's obedience to God is not deliberate but simply the result of following one's natural inclination, there is no honor or merit in it. Only the willing obedience to the good God commanded—when one could have done otherwise—justly deserves the fruit of his fellowship.

The denial of free will not only denies the just moral order of the cosmos; it also questions the power and wisdom of God. If the children of Cain are by nature irredeemably sensual, then God is impotent to heal their nature and bring them to salvation. Furthermore, if God does try to turn them from the life of the flesh to the life of the Spirit by the exhortations of his prophets and apostles, then God is ignorant of their hopeless condition (*Haer.* 4.37.6). Such a quixotic venture would only reveal God to be a fool. On the contrary, that God has sent prophets and apostles to exhort sinners to repentance presupposes that they have a will capable of responding to exhortations and turning back to God (*Haer.* 4.37.2). Therefore, since all possess free will, no person's nature a priori excludes him or her from God's salvific work.

One text that Irenaeus says was "adduced by all the heretics in support of their folly" (*Haer.* 5.9.1) was 1 Corinthians 15:50: "flesh and blood cannot inherit the kingdom of God." This verse, read together with verses 44–48, in which Paul distinguishes between the psychic body (*sōma psychikon*) and the spiritual body (*sōma pneumatikon*) and the man of earth and the man from heaven, provided the warrant for the threefold division of humanity: the materialists, the psychics, and the spirituals. Irenaeus counters that body/flesh, soul, and spirit do not refer to three classes of people but to three dimensions of the complete person. Flesh is a person's material substance that is formed and animated. Soul is the animating principle that can be directed either to the things of the body or the things of the spirit. The spirit is from God's Spirit and preserves and fashions humanity for eternal life. Not all have spirit. This is not the result of a defect in their nature but a failure of their free will. People who are spiritual are those who *by faith* establish their lives in the Spirit of God, who raises the individual up into the life of God (*Haer.* 5.9.2). Yet faith—the faith by which one receives the gospel, repents, and participates in the life of God—is the product of one's free will. Quoting Jesus's words to the blind men who come seeking sight, "According to your faith, be it done to you" (Matt 9:29), and to the father of the boy with the dumb spirit, "All things are possible to him who believes" (Mark 9:23), Irenaeus concludes, "faith is a property peculiar [*propriam*] to human beings since human beings have the distinctive property of will [*sententiam*] . . . [thus] faith lies within one's own power [*potestas*]" (*Haer.* 4.37.5). Consequently, one is not spiritual by nature but by union with God's Spirit through an act of will, that is, by choosing to believe and receive. Irenaeus, therefore, interprets the "spiritual body" of 1 Corinthians 15:44 to refer neither to a class of humanity nor an immaterial existence after death but to the weak body of this life that has been given the strength of the Spirit through fellowship with the Spirit. "Spiritual body" refers to a "living person"—a "person" because she has the substance of flesh and "living" because she partakes of the Spirit (*Haer.* 5.9.2)—of which Christ Jesus, the man from heaven (1 Cor 15:49), is the prototype (*Haer.* 5.9.3). When Irenaeus turns then to interpret 1 Corinthians 15:50, "flesh and blood shall not inherit the kingdom of God," he says that strictly speaking, flesh, the body, does not inherit but "is inherited," even as a bride, properly speaking, does not wed but is wedded by the bridegroom. Human nature, particularly the body, rots unless it is inherited by the Spirit (*Haer.* 5.9.4).

This contrast between "inherit" (active voice) and "is inherited" (passive voice) gives greater importance to the agency of the Spirit than the active role of the will in attaining eternal life. Using Paul's analogy of the wild and domesticated fig trees (Rom 11:17–24), Irenaeus explains how the psychic body is transformed into the spiritual body: even as the substance of the wild fig tree is not changed when it is grafted onto the domesticated fruit tree, so too when the Christian by faith is grafted into the body of Christ through receiving the Spirit, she receives a new name and acquires new spiritual qualities evident in the spiritual fruit (Gal 5:22–24) she bears (*Haer.* 5.11.1). Thus, the mortal and corruptible nature puts on immortality and incorruptibility (1 Cor 15:53–54) proper to the second Adam and the Holy Spirit. In sum, although the will for Irenaeus is free to respond to God in faith, it is the Spirit alone that makes the believer spiritual.

Origen on Free Will

Free will has no higher place in Eastern Christian thought than in the theology of Origen. He includes it in his enumeration of the apostolic teachings that contain "the very words and teaching of Jesus Christ" and comprise the dogmatic core of Christian thought. Having explained that each soul shall be rewarded after death according to its deserts, he states, "every rational soul is possessed of free will and choice and is engaged in a struggle against the devil and his angels. . . . There follows from this the conviction that we are not subject to necessity, so as to be compelled by every means, even against our will, to do either good or evil" (*Princ.* 1. preface 5). Here is the core understanding of the will in Eastern Christian thought: unlike nonrational creatures whose experience of the world is confined to the material realm accessible through their senses, rational beings are capable of knowing intelligible, immaterial reality that is foundational for rightly understanding the cosmos. Nonrational creatures are subject to a certain necessity (*anankē*) because their actions are determined by instinctual reactions to their material circumstances. Rational creatures, by contrast, have the capacity to adjudicate between the material goods that serve the needs of the body and those goods of God in whom the soul finds its highest good (*Princ.* 3.1.3). Because the intellect can grasp the hierarchy of the cosmos, rational creatures can order their desires and actions according to this hierarchy rather than simply reacting to their perceptions of what is sensually pleasant or unpleasant. Able to judge what is true and truly good, the rational creature can see through the devil's deceptions and so overcome temptation.

More than simply serving the negative function of avoiding sin, God endowed rational creatures with free will primarily for the positive purpose "that the good that was in them might be their own" (*Princ.* 2.9.2). In other words, all rational beings were created in a state where they enjoyed immediate access to the goodness of God revealed by his Logos. This goodness might become *their own* when they chose it for themselves. Then the goodness of God ceased to be something external to them but became internalized, constituting the very content of their thoughts. Their minds were thus conformed to the goodness of the divine Logos because they chose this goodness for themselves. This union existed only as long as they *chose* to focus on God. At the resurrection, the rational creatures will return to the original harmony not because they are in any sense compelled against their will but because the motions of all their minds will lead to a common end in which "their wills should work subtly and usefully together to produce the harmony of a single world" (*Princ.* 2.1.1–2).

As we have seen from Origen's narrative of creation and fall,[2] free will stands together with equality as an essential corollary of divine justice. Since God is just, all the rational beings created in the beginning must have been created in a state of perfect equality. The unequal conditions of their present existence into which they have fallen correspond to the varying degrees of merit or demerit (*Princ.* 2.6.3). Whether the rational individuals came to indwell the bodies of the stars or angels or demons or human beings depends entirely on the degree to which their love of God cooled. Although it is hard to imagine how boredom born of satiation with the blessed life—his explanation for the fall of the rational beings—is a *choice*, Origen sees sloth, that failure to cleave to God in love, as a failure of the will to be attentive to the goods of God (*Princ.* 2.9.2). Such neglect is the voluntary failure to choose to contemplate the one who is the highest good and proper end of all rational beings.

Origen was cognizant of passages of Scripture that appeared to the intellectually simplistic and spiritually immature (*simpliciores*) to limit human moral agency. Texts like Ezekiel 11:19–20, "I will take away their stony hearts and will put in them hearts of flesh, that they may walk in statutes and keep my judgments," were, from Origen's perspective, misconstrued to imply that God's intervention, not an individual's choice, determines whether one is virtuous. Equally troubling was Paul's declaration (Rom 9:16) that God's compassion "is not of him that wills or of him that runs but of God that has mercy," which caused such people to doubt that "each person has freedom over his own will," thinking instead that it depends on the will of God "whether a person is lost or saved" (*Princ.* 3.1.7). Most troubling of all was God's hardening Pharaoh's heart in Exodus 4:21 and 7:3. However, the real problem that Origen had to address was not the simplistic interpretations by literally minded laypeople in the Great Church but the various sects of Gnostics

2. See chapter 3, pp. 89–91.

who employed such passages of Scripture to support their deterministic division of humanity—the fleshly, the psychics, and the spirituals—that, he believed, fundamentally denied moral freedom.

The thrust of Origen's critique targeted not primarily the distinction between the pneumatics and the psychics but the hopeless condition of the so-called children of Cain. The implication of the gnostic doctrine of election was that the possibility of salvation does not lie within the power of the individual; rather, being lost or saved was entirely a matter of the individual's nature or the nature of the individual's soul. There was no hope that the person whose soul was inclined to wickedness might turn to the good. They contended that God hardened the hearts of those who, like Pharaoh, possessed an earthly disposition but showed mercy to those whose soul possessed a spiritual nature. However, there was a basic flaw in the gnostic interpretation of the exodus narrative. If Pharaoh's nature was already earthy such that he was irredeemably wicked and unable to believe in God, then why did God need to harden his heart? Scripture's description of Pharaoh's heart's being hardened necessarily implies, Origen argues, that Pharaoh's nature, far from being permanently fixed, could undergo change. The biblical language of "hardening" presupposes that Pharaoh's soul was malleable, "capable of giving way when amazed by the signs and mighty works" of God (*Princ.* 3.1.8). The Gnostics may not have taken "hardening" to mean that God literally altered Pharaoh's fundamental disposition; rather, it may simply have been a figurative way of describing God's punishment of Pharaoh's wicked, earthly nature (*Princ.* 3.1.9). Such punishment would, according to the Gnostics, reveal that the God of Israel was *merely just* but not good. How can the Gnostics claim, Origen rhetorically counters, that the God who hardens Pharaoh's heart so as to cause him to do evil and then punishes him for evil he commits, not voluntarily but out of some divinely imposed necessity, be called just? In other words, Origen is willing to press the logic of the Gnostics' argument to an even harsher judgment of God in order to expose the inherently unjust character of the Gnostics' universe. This world of the gnostic myth and the Creator deity who stands behind it illustrates for Origen the radical difference between the Gnostics and Catholic Christianity. Yet if he was to defend the Catholic alternative—a God who is just *and* good—then Origen had to provide an alternative interpretation of the hardening of Pharaoh's heart.

Following the exegetical principle that Scripture should interpret Scripture, he reads Exodus 4 and 6 through the lens of Hebrews 6:7–8, "The land which has drunk the rain that comes upon it and brings forth herbs appropriate for those who till it shall receive blessings from God; but that land which bears thorns and thistles is rejected with a curse, whose end is to be burned." In his justice, God's blessing, represented by "the goodness and impartiality of the rain [that] visits all lands alike," falls equally on the field of all human hearts. Those souls—like the fields that have been carefully cultivated to capture the right amount of water, prevent erosion, and bear fruit—receive God's grace and bear spiritual fruit. Such a soul "becomes softer and brings itself into obedience with the whole mind, if it has been cleansed from its faults and carefully trained" (*Princ.* 3.1.10). By contrast, Pharaoh's soul—like the field that has not been tilled and, so suffering runoff and erosion, is baked hard by the sun—was "hardened by the mighty and wonderful works of God" because it was uncultivated in virtue and godliness with the result that he became "more savage and thorny than ever" (*Princ.* 3.1.10). Origen's interpretation renarrates the exodus story in a way that affirms the just impartiality of God's agency and places the responsibility for Pharaoh's disobedience squarely on Pharaoh himself. God reaches out to all souls through his self-revelation in what Origen, using the language of Acts 2:11, repeatedly refers to as the "mighty works of God" that give "proof of the spirit and of power" (*Cels.* 1.2). Such proof is necessary to draw fallen souls back to God. But the soul must be cultivated in order to recognize and submit oneself to the divine whom the mighty works reveal. The soul is cultivated through its formation in the virtuous life. Therefore, human wickedness, like that of Pharaoh's, is the consequence of culpable ignorance resulting from spiritual neglect.

Gregory of Nyssa: Free Will and the Image of God

Following the tradition of Origen, Gregory of Nyssa illustrates the relationship between human freedom and divine agency in his speculative analysis of the exodus narrative in his *Life of Moses*. As we have already seen,[3] Gregory, like Origen, envisioned the capacity for moral choice (*idios thelēmasin autokratorikōs*) and the resultant self-governance (*autexousion*) as divine endowments of human nature (*Hom. opif.* 4.1). They are corollaries of the rational nature that allow souls to participate in the divine nature and so reflect his image characterized by purity, freedom from passion and evil (*apatheia*), and blessedness (*Hom. opif.* 5.1). Gregory describes the soul's reflection of God's perfection as an eternal ascent into God.[4] Perhaps his most developed account of this ascent comes in *Life of Moses*. Here he offers a spiritual interpretation (*theōria*) of the orderly unfolding of Moses's narrative to serve as a model for the imitation of Christians seeking to attain the perfection of being a friend of God (*Mos.* 2.319–320). In this allegory, Gregory interprets Moses's birth in Egypt under the rule of tyrannical Pharaoh as symbolic of the life of subjection to one's material and passionate nature. Yet the

3. See chapter 3, pp. 91–98.
4. See chapter 13, pp. 483–91.

soul is capable of "birth" in virtue or vice by one's own choice (*ek proaireseōs*): "We are in some manner our own parents, giving birth to ourselves by our own free choice in accordance with whatever we wish to be" (*Mos.* 2.3). The rational faculties are the parents of virtue, and free choice of the will is the midwife "delivering amid great pain" (*Mos.* 2.4). The pain of childbirth is a figure of the hardship and austerity of life in which the virtues are cultivated. If the soul is to stay afloat in the turbulent waters of the Nile, that is, the tyranny of the passions and pleasures, then, like Moses in the ark, its choice for virtue must be buoyed up by education (*Mos.* 2.7–8).[5] Although Gregory himself was intellectually steeped in the Greek *paideia* or high culture, this is not the education he has in mind. For he treats Pharaoh's barren daughter, who raised Moses in the house of Pharaoh, as a figure for the barrenness of pagan philosophy, "which is in perpetual labor but never gives birth" (*Mos.* 2.10–11). This need not be taken as Gregory's wholesale rejection of philosophy but merely the recognition of its insufficiency to bring the soul into the realm of light. Reason alone may grasp partial truths that point to the light—that is, God—but not confer true knowledge of God. Thus, as Moses who nursed at his Hebrew mother's breast, the Christian, while studying philosophy, must drink the milk of her true mother, the Church, with its teachings and practices that are the means of ascending (*Mos.* 2.12). Ultimately, the Christian, like Moses after killing the Egyptian, who, for Gregory, is a figure of idolatry and heresy, must withdraw from the vices of pagan culture so that "the movements of [one's] soul are shepherded, like sheep, by the will of guiding reason" (*Mos.* 2.18). The teachings and disciplines of the Church purify the intellect that it may receive the light of truth necessary for spiritual ascent (*Mos.* 2.19). Moses receives just such illumination before the burning bush on Mount Horeb.

The light from the bush, "brighter than the sunlight that dazzled his eyes," drew him up the mountain where, Gregory says, "The light's grace was distributed to both senses, illuminating sight with flashing rays and lighting the way for hearing the undefiled teachings" (*Mos.* 1.20). Not surprisingly, Gregory sees the bush as a figure for Christ. Even as the fire's light radiated from the bush illuminating Moses's soul, the divinity of the one who is called light and truth entered the world through the womb of the Virgin who, like the bush that burned but was not de-

5. Gregory's account of the preparatory function of philosophy and classical learning reflects the earlier tradition of Clement of Alexandria, who described philosophy as the pure water that makes the spiritually arid soul disposed to receive the spiritual seeds of truth (*Strom.* 1.17.4). Philosophy, Clement contends, is analogous to the commandments of the Old Testament, which Paul in Galatians 3:24 had called the *paidagōgos*, or tutor and disciplinarian, that prepares the soul for the gospel (*Strom.* 1.28.2–3) by teaching it to grasp the hidden meanings of Scripture through the pursuit of intelligible truths (*Strom.* 1.20.3) and by teaching moderation, e.g., controlling the tongue as well as one's bodily appetites (*Strom.* 1.30.2). Cf. chapter 2, pp. 67–90.

stroyed, preserved "the flower of her virginity" even in giving birth (*Mos.* 2.21). The divine light instructs Moses to put off his sandals so his soul may "stand within the rays of the true light" (*Mos.* 2.22) and be taught the difference between the Creator, who is true self-subsisting being, and the creature, who has only the appearance of being but exists only by participation in God's being (*Mos.* 2.23–25).[6]

Here Gregory's figural reading of Moses's life narrates the relationship between divine and human agency. The story's order, always important for Gregory, follows a cyclical pattern of purification and illumination. The soul's purification from passion begins the reorientation of its desires from the sensual goods of this world to heavenly goods. Once the eye of the soul is directed heavenward, it is ready to receive spiritual illumination, which has the effect of further purification that in turn opens the way for an even higher degree of illumination. Gregory assumes that the initial cultivation of virtue—learning to be temperate in consumption of material goods—is within the natural capacity of Christian and pagan alike. One chooses whether she will or will not pursue virtue. That training in virtue, however, is not the natural unfolding of human nature but is guided by philosophy and, for the Christian, by the teachings and disciplines of the Church. Since all virtue is derived from God, even this elementary step is a participation in God's virtue. Thus, all virtue, for Gregory, is grounded in God. Once purified of vicious idolatrous habits of life and thought, the soul is prepared to receive the light of God that draws the soul to the Word made flesh who purifies the intellect that it may know the great I AM. Gregory is not preoccupied with the nature-grace question. His pastoral rhetoric balances the need for his reader to choose the way of virtue alongside the Christian's need to be liberated by God from the passions' tyrannical enslavement. Such liberation cannot be achieved on one's own. When the Christian, like Moses the liberator, has been illuminated by "the radiance which shines upon this thorny flesh and which is (as the Gospel says) the true light and the truth itself . . . [she] becomes able to help others to salvation, to destroy the tyranny which holds power wickedly, and to deliver to freedom everyone held in evil servitude" (*Mos.* 2.26). Because Gregory understands the cycle of purgation and illumination entirely within the context of the Christian's participation in the God who calls her back to himself, there is never for him a claim to moral self-sufficiency. God's revelation of the divine name "I AM THAT I AM" purified Moses's knowledge of God and of himself as God's creature. Only when the soul learns the difference between God

6. Because the sandals are made from animal hide, Gregory sees them as a figure for the "dead earthly covering of skin" with which God clothed Adam and Eve (Gen 3:21). In his lost *Commentary on Genesis*, Origen may have used this image to describe the mortal bodies with which fallen human souls were covered. Gregory, however, interprets the "skins" repeatedly as referring not to the body itself but to either mortality or the sensually minded habits, especially sexual desires, that accompany one's material existence (*Or. cat.* 8; *Hom. Cant.* 11).

as "true being that possesses existence in its own nature" and the creature who is "nonbeing . . . with no self-subsisting nature" can the Christian recognize her absolute dependence on God for existence and virtue. Any virtue the Christian has is solely through her voluntary participation in God's goodness.

Gregory died in 394; that very year on the other side of the empire in North Africa, Augustine began his first serious study of Paul's writings on grace and election. Augustine was in agreement with Gregory's model of participation; both men could quote Paul's rhetorical question, "What do you have that you did not receive [from God]?" (1 Cor 4:7). And both men spoke of the soul's movement to God in the language of an erotic desire for the divine. The question, however, that would trouble Augustine for the next thirty years—a question that seems not to have troubled Origen or Gregory—is whether, given the corrupting effects of sin, the will is naturally inclined to move toward God or whether even this most elementary desire for God must be given by God himself.

Manichaean Dualism and the Free Will Defense

As Augustine reflected on the flaws in Manichaean belief, the chief defect was the lack of a principle of cosmic unity and thus the absence of a coherent vision of salvation. In this respect, the teachings of Mani suffered from the same failing as pagan polytheism. Just as the world of pagan religions was governed by the many deities rather than the one true God (*Ver. rel.* 1.1), the Manichaean cosmos was divided between the light and the darkness, its two first principles, and thus lacked a unifying foundation that gave it coherence. The Manichees might have a more sophisticated, less anthropomorphic cosmology, but their world, because it had two irreconcilable first principles, was inherently and inescapably conflicted. Consequently, there could be no final peace, no ultimate resolution of the conflict, and thus no true salvation. At most, Augustine explains, the Manichaean salvation entails the dilution of the dark substance of the world by creating an admixture of the divine luminous substance and dark material substance (*Ver. rel.* 9.16). Yet the divine never fully overcomes the darkness; some residual evil penetrates the whole. Christianity, on the other hand, with its one God, from whom all things came into being, had a single first principle. Because God was the sole source of all beings, God was the source—the *principium* or *archē*—of that primal unity from which the many creatures came and by which it is held together even now. Therefore, only the one God could ultimately restore the world's fundamental harmony and unity that has temporarily been broken by sin.

The Manichaean cosmology had the advantage, in Augustine's adolescent thinking, of providing a ready explanation to the problem of evil. The dark material substance that coexisted with light was the source of ignorance, error, and passion. The challenge that the Manichees posed to Catholic Christians like Augustine was explaining the source of evil within their notion of cosmic unity. If all things come from one and the same source, then evil must as well; God must be the cause of evil as well as goodness. This was the theological issue that had troubled Augustine throughout his early adulthood. Before his baptism into the Catholic faith, Augustine had found in Platonism an easy counterargument: evil is merely the privation of the good. Even as darkness itself is *no thing* but only the word we use to describe the absence of light, evil, too, is nothing other than the absence of the good intrinsic to the natural world that God created. Evil is a perversion or distortion of a thing's goodness. That *diminished* goodness is evil. Evil, therefore, has no being in and of itself; it is always and only parasitic on some created good that itself actually exists. Existentially, the distortion of the goodness that God intended is very real, but ontologically speaking evil is nothing. Since evil is not a substance or a subsistent reality in the universe, it is neither one among God's many creatures, nor is it one of the twin first principles coextensive with God as in the Manichaean cosmology. While this answer went a great distance to address the metaphysical problem of evil, it did not entirely settle the problem of theodicy.

If evil is a privation of the good due to some perversion of the natural goodness of a thing, what is the source of the perversion? Augustine's answer was the human will (*voluntas*). Angelic and human beings, not God, were responsible for the coming of evil into the world. But God, who created angels and people with the capacity to choose (*liberum arbitrium*),[7] could be completely exonerated only if the will was free and not determined by some necessity derived from a defect in God's creation—in either the will itself or the world in which the angelic and human choices were made. Years after Augustine had seen the flaw in Manichaean cosmology and became confident that the will, not fate, was the cause of evil, he remained determined to prove definitively the error of the Manichees. The free-will defense, therefore, was the all-consuming theological concern of his early writings.

Writing in Rome the year after his baptism (387), Augustine launched the free-will defense in the first book of a treatise entitled *On Free Choice of the Will*, and the next year after his return to North Africa (388) in *On True Religion*. His anal-

7. For clarification of terms, *liberum arbitrium*, often translated "free will" or "free choice of the will," refers to the *capacity* to choose between goods, comparable to the idea expressed in Greek as *proairesis*. *Voluntas*, often translated "the will," refers to a *specific* choice of will, but it also may refer to a disposition or orientation of the soul toward certain goods. Ultimately, the will (*voluntas*) becomes for Augustine synonymous with love. The soul's loves determine the soul's choices.

ysis of evil and the will here grows out of his earlier inquiries in the Cassiciacum dialogues about the highest good (summum bonum) and humanity's capacity to achieve that end. That end, he had written in *Soliloquies*, is the knowledge of God and the human soul (*Solil.* 2.7) and to "see" the divine beauty so as to love it above all creatures (*Solil.* 7.14). Such knowledge is the highest good because true blessedness lies in possessing that which is perfectly and eternally good (*Beat.* 2.11). The antithesis of this happiness is suffering, which is commonly thought to be evil. Yet if God wills human beings' happiness and endows them with the capacity for happiness, why are they not happy? Augustine is not, he confesses, supremely happy, but his lack of happiness, his suffering in this life, is not due to some failure on God's part. Rather, his suffering stems from his love of imperfect, transitory goods that do not truly satisfy his soul's longings. By contrast, the blessed life is the life of the wise who love God's eternal Wisdom alone and for its own sake (*Solil.* 13.22). Such wisdom he describes as the true "measure" or just order of the soul, which avoids the love of worldly vanities that are the source of suffering; this wisdom is fullness given to the soul by God's indwelling presence (*Beat.* 4.35). In these early writings, Augustine speaks of the summum bonum both *anthropologically* as a condition of the soul—equilibrium or due measure resulting from wisely ordered loves—and *relationally* as fellowship with God himself who imparts wisdom to the soul. Already, Augustine has located human happiness and suffering as consequences of an individual's love, which itself has a volitional character.

Sin and its consequent suffering are entirely the result of the misuse of free will. Evidence for the existence of a will Augustine locates in a human capacity for self-transcendence or consciousness. The very desire to know whether there is a will indicates that rational creatures are not simply automatons. The will lies behind and moves the rational faculty in the pursuit of wisdom (*Lib.* 1.12.25). Moreover, the existence of the will is necessary if the world rests upon the eternal moral law according to which virtue is rewarded and vice punished (*Lib.* 2.1.3). Since God would be unjust for punishing someone for doing or not doing something over which they had no control, he declares emphatically, "Sin is so much a voluntary evil that it is not sin at all unless it is voluntary" (*Ver. rel.* 14.27). While he certainly recognized a division among people between the virtuous and the base, he insists, using John the Baptist's metaphor of the threshing floor, that people are either wheat or chaff not by some preordained station but entirely by their own will. When he offers his account of the volitional nature of happiness and sin, Augustine—like his Greek-speaking predecessors—grounds the autonomy of the will in humanity's rational nature. Since the human intellect is an image of God's virtue by which he orders and rules creation, humanity's rational nature, by its ability to distinguish what is truly good from what has only the appearance of goodness, is able to exert authority over the lower, carnal nature, even as it exerts dominion over nonrational beasts (*Lib.* 1.7.16–10.21). Therefore, the desire (*concupiscentia* or *libido*) to live, to be free from fear, to attain praise and glory, and so on does not have sufficient power in itself to exert control over the mind unless the intellect fails to assert dominion by its own free choice. Confident in this superiority of the mind, Augustine even went so far as to say that happiness, which consists in having a good will—that is, willing no one evil and giving to each his due (*Lib.* 1.13.27)—is entirely within the capacity of the will itself (*Lib.* 1.13.28–29). The basis for such a bold claim rests in his contention that happiness is loving that which cannot be lost or taken away (*Lib.* 1.4.10)—that is, loving only that which is entirely within one's control. One may not be able to fulfill the good that the good will wills, but one's happiness lies in the goodness of the will itself. In this respect, Augustine's eudaimonism resembles a Stoic view that the sage's happiness lies entirely in that which is within his power, namely his virtue, rather than in externals that are beyond his control. You may not have control over what the world does *to you*, but you do have complete control over *how you react* to the world. As we shall see, Augustine will eventually abandon and offer a harsh critique of this Stoic eudaimonism with respect to both the conditions for happiness and humanity's capacity to will the good. In these early writings, however, the possibility of such moral autarky was essential to his free-will defense.

Yet Augustine was haunted by an obvious question: If happiness is as easily attained as willing the good, why are so few actually happy (*Lib.* 1.14.30–15.31)? The explanation could be found in a failure to know the good and to cultivate the virtues necessary for willing the good. Although all creation retained a vestige of the truth of its origin in God so that even sinful humanity could not find an excuse in total ignorance of the good (*Ver. rel.* 29.72), the mind could be weakened by sin. Using the Stoic theory of moral choices as *assent* to perceptions scrutinized by the intellect, Augustine explains the mind's choice to seek the objects of base desire as its approving or assenting to falsehoods (*phantasiae*)—as if they were true—due to a sheer weariness of the mind (*Lib.* 1.11.22). Here sin is chosen as an act of free will, but the choice is dependent upon the judgment of the intellect. Thus, in these early writings, while Augustine employs the language of free will, he explains sin primarily as a failure of the intellect to judge rightly between the truly good and that which has only mere appearance of goodness. Therefore, the cardinal virtues (wisdom: knowing what is to be sought and avoided; fortitude: enduring loss and inconvenience; temperance: restraining desire; and justice: giving to each his due) were necessary for the mind to apprehend and will the good (*Lib.* 1.13.27). Yet Augustine understood the cultivation of these virtues, especially wisdom, as the result of the healing aid of God's grace. How? Although Plato's teaching about the one God who is ontologically distinct from the material creations was consonant with Christianity, it lacked the ability to heal the soul because it was "pleasant to read rather than potent to persuade" (*Ver. rel.* 2.2). The persuasive power that could heal the soul of its love of finite, transitory creatures and turn it back to God came through the special revelation, specifically the incarnation. Because we love material creatures and are distracted from the worship of the invisible God by their physical beauty, God uses sensible forms as "temporal medicine" to reorient and restore the soul to health. The belief in the incarnate Word is the authority that prepares the soul for reason's quest to understand the God in whom it believes (Isa 7:9; *Lib.* 1.2.4). Even as the love of temporal things makes those creatures in some sense part of the soul such that their loss causes pain in the soul (*Lib.* 1.15.33), the mind now set upon Christ, who is Wisdom itself, imparts wisdom to the soul, making the soul wise (*Ver. rel.* 16.30). Although the capacity of free choice remains even under sin, Augustine is also insistent, "Whenever a person falls, there she must lie until she is raised up" (*Ver. rel.* 24.46). The key point, however, is that at this point in his life, Augustine takes the model for thinking about the healing work of grace from his life as an orator who has no power to force his will on his audience. His only power lies in the force of his eloquence to persuade. So too, he concludes, "[God] did nothing by violence, but everything by persuasion and warning. The old servitude was past and the day of liberty had dawned and humanity was fitly and helpfully taught how he had been created with freewill" (*Ver. rel.* 16.31). The Word, in assuming human nature, persuades his disciples by opening their eyes to both the goodness of the transcendent God and the power of free will that God gave to rational creatures that they may be free from slavery to worldly pleasures and their manifold concomitant miseries.

Although Augustine dogmatically employs the free-will defense to defend Catholic Christianity against Manichaean fatalism, even in these early writings, he shows transparent candor in naming cracks in this account of the autonomy of the will. Scant weeks after reading the words of Paul to the Romans (Rom 13:14), "put on the Lord Jesus Christ and make no provision for the flesh in its lusts," and feeling that "all shadows of doubts [about his submission to the life of chastity] were dispelled," in the garden at Milan (*Conf.* 8.12.29), he felt licentious longings intruding—unbidden and contrary to his will—upon his mind as he lay in his bed at Cassiciacum (*Solil.* 14.25). If his will were autonomous and exerted control over the meditations of the mind and movements of the body, whence came these unwilled desires? By the time Augustine writes the second book of *On Free Choice of the Will*, six to seven years have passed, and one sees more doubts and misgivings about his earlier confidence in the autonomy of the will. If God created human beings with a will, the instability of which is the cause of evil, is not God at least indirectly responsible for the evil? Although he remained committed to the view that the will is necessary for the saints to merit reward (*Lib.* 2.1.3), Augustine had come to see the easily attained good will not as the locus of happiness itself but merely an intermediate good that allows the soul to cleave to the only unchangeable good, God (*Lib.* 2.19.52). Moreover, he repeats more firmly the infirmity of the soul under sin and its impotence apart from divine healing. Although he contends that the defective movements of the soul are voluntary, he also concedes, "Since a person cannot rise of his own free will as he fell by his own will spontaneously, let us hold with steadfast faith the right hand of God stretched out to us from above, even our Lord Jesus Christ" (*Lib.* 2.20.54).

Augustine's Early Reading of Romans

Augustine likely returned to the problem of the will in the second and third books of *On Free Choice of the Will* in 395, the year the bishop of Hippo Regius died and Augustine, much to his consternation, was elevated to the episcopal see. Around this time, he began his first systematic study of the Pauline corpus, especially Romans. Following his exposition on Galatians, he began a commentary on Romans but never got farther than 1:7 because he was distracted by the absence of any reference to the Holy Spirit in the salutation and discouraged by what he perceived to be the vastness of the undertaking (*Retract.* 1.25). Earlier, however, while a presbyter in Carthage, Augustine was asked by his fellow priests to address questions they had about Romans. The transcription of his answers, entitled *Exposition on Propositions from Romans*, laid out his first effort to make sense of the nature of the law, the relationship of faith and charity, and the turning of the will to God in faith.

Augustine had encountered the writings of Paul long before this in his time both as an *auditor* among the Manichees and as one of Ambrose's catechumens. With the Manichaean critique of the law and their appeal to Paul as justification for this view fresh in his mind, Augustine was particularly concerned with Paul's contrast between the letter of the law that kills and the Spirit that gives life in 2 Corinthians 3:6, a point that he seems to repeat in Romans 7:11: "Sin found opportunity to deceive me through the commandment and through it killed [me]." How can the law be good if it is the source of deception and death? The answer Augustine located in Paul's later comment: "We know that the law is spiritual, but I am carnal" (7:14), which placed the cause of death not with the law itself, which is good, but with the misuse of the law by the fleshly oriented soul. Commenting on Romans 3:20, "For no flesh will be justified before him by the law, for through the law comes the knowledge of sin," Augustine defends the goodness, if insufficiency, of the law and explains how Paul's view of justification through faith does not negate the freedom of the will (*Exp. prop. Rom.* 13–18.1). Although the law does not justify the sinner, its value for redemption can be understood within the fourfold *ordo salutis* by which the sinner comes to salvation: life before the law (*ante legem*), under the law (*sub lege*), under grace (*sub gratia*), and in peace (*in pace*).

The first stage is life before the law (*ante legem*) in which the individual is in a state of sin but is blithely ignorant. She does not know that her desires and actions are contrary to God's will and that she, therefore, stands condemned before God. Sin is motivated by fleshly longings (*concupiscentia carnis*) that love the "sweetness of temporal pleasures" (*Exp. prop. Rom.* 42), what Paul calls "walking according to the flesh" (Rom 8:3), and is led by "wisdom of the flesh" (*prudentia carnis*) that seeks to gain worldly goods and fears worldly pains and difficulties. At the same time that she is ignorant of her sin she nonetheless is aware of her mortality and the mortality of all that she loves. Therefore, out of anxiety for the fragile, transitory goods of this life, the sinner clings all the more tightly to them and desires to maximize her enjoyment of them (*Exp. prop. Rom.* 13–18.10 and 45–46.7). Thus, her will is evermore oriented, and her affections attached, to creatures rather than the Creator. In spite of the fear of death, the sinner *ante legem* does not experience any spiritual struggle. There is no inner conflict between her desires and some higher prohibition; rather, she readily consents to the impulse of carnal concupiscence. In other words, hers is a state of spiritual ignorance; she does not know her actions to be sin or herself to be a sinner. Curiously enough, Augustine makes no reference here to the natural law. Earlier, however, commenting on Rom 1:21, "Knowing God, they neither honored him as God nor gave him thanks," Augustine identified such impiety as pride (*superbia*), punishment for which is God's abandonment of the proud to the vain desires of their hearts (*Exp. prop. Rom.* 4–5). That is, if the proud desire to be their own masters and the source of their own happiness, God exposes their insufficiency precisely by letting them live as slaves of their own hubris.

In the second stage, *sub lege*, the sinner has received the law, which reveals her carnal desires as sin and therefore that she stands condemned before God her judge. While previously *before the law*, the sinner experienced no inner spiritual struggle; now since the law has given her the knowledge of sin and judgment, she feels the conflict between her habitual impulse to follow the carnal desires as she used to and her desire to resist those fleshly longings. She seeks to resist sin and follow the commandments of God, but she fails and is ultimately overcome by sin. Her resistance is futile. She fails for two reasons. First, because a person wills that in which they delight, the law, which forbids sin, paradoxically makes the sin appear all the more delightful. The carnal pleasures she had previously enjoyed before the law now have the added attraction of being forbidden fruit. Therefore, law intensifies carnal desires, and the sinner is evermore enslaved to them. But second, even her obedience to the law is ultimately an act of sin or carnal concupiscence because the motive for obedience is not love of God or of righteousness, but the love of self. The sinner's erstwhile obedience arises from the impulse of self-preservation and the desire to escape punishment. *Sub lege*, obedience is merely an outward, superficial compliance that fulfills only the letter of the law rather than a genuine inner desire for righteousness. Since all the law is fulfilled by the love of God and neighbor, the sinner who does not act out of this love cannot fulfill all righteousness. Therefore, her efforts—half-hearted at best—are in vain, and she remains condemned. What is more, because all sin arises from the delusional self-confidence of pride, the sinner *sub lege* trusts that she can fulfill the law by her own natural ability. Yet where there is no genuine desire, there is no heartfelt will or effort to obey the law, even in its outward demands. Consequently, all the sinner's efforts fail.

The knowledge of this failure, exposed by the law, creates an existential crisis for the sinner. Despite her best efforts to resist the carnal desires of her heart, she has failed, and that knowledge engenders both a frustration with her impotence and a fear of the punishment that awaits. Yet here, for Augustine, is the blessed paradox of the law. The law contributes to the sinner's salvation by exposing both her unrighteousness and her impotence to make herself righteous. She cannot save herself; this is the terrifying reality the law reveals. Thus, the crisis of the terrified conscience is the goal of the law. The knowledge of the impossibility of fulfilling the law—by sinners motivated by pride and carnal concupiscence—breaks the illusion of pride and engenders the self-despair of humility. Thoroughly humbled by the law, the sinner shorn of the self-conceit of pride now cries out to God for mercy and deliverance from condemnation. This is the turning point in the sinner's life. This is the point where the self-reliance of pride gives way to the trust of faith that relies entirely on God's gracious forgiveness.

Having cried out in faith for God's mercy, the believer enters the third stage of the *ordo salutis*, life under grace (*sub gratia*). This faith is an inner disposition that stands in contrast with self-assured pride in one's moral self-sufficiency (*Exp. prop. Rom.* 19.1–2 and 24). Faith at work in baptism unites the believer with God through Christ so that she is no longer merely one of God's precious creatures but becomes a child of God having received the Spirit of adoption (*Exp. prop. Rom.* 53.13–14). This faith merits the gift of the Spirit who pours out upon the soul the love of God, which merits the believer's justification. Grace brings forgiveness so that she experiences God's charity as well as justice and thus is freed from the fear of condemnation (*Exp. prop. Rom.* 13–18.7–8). The struggle against sin continues, but now *sub gratia* the struggle is profoundly different from the struggle under the law. Whereas under the law the resistance to sin was half-hearted and therefore was ultimately futile, under grace the believer, having experienced the goodness and mercy of God, possesses a love of God and neighbor—Augustine's definition of "spiritual grace" (*Exp. prop. Rom.* 2)—that allows her to obey not begrudgingly out of fear but willingly out of a genuine delight in God's righteousness. This willing obedience fulfills all righteousness.

Life under grace is not without struggle. The effort to resist sinful habits is still real; the believer may serve the law of God with her mind but experiences the law of sin in her flesh that wars against the law of her mind. Nevertheless, she prevails because she does not consent to the impulses of concupiscence (*Exp. prop. Rom.* 13–18.10). Grace enables her to resist sinful desires because by her union with Christ in baptism, Christ has put to death the "old humanity" with its carnal appetites (*Exp. prop. Rom.* 32–34.1.5). Since through grace the believer receives the Holy Spirit and thereby is made spiritual, like the law (Rom 7:14), she grasps the law's spiritual nature, and loving it, she "will easily fulfill what it prescribes" (*Exp. prop. Rom.* 41.2). Furthermore, with the gift of the Spirit, the Christian does not follow the wisdom of the flesh that seeks temporal goods. Instead, the carnal wisdom is replaced by a spiritual wisdom that, through the Spirit's intercession, makes the believer groan (Rom 8:23) for the unfading goods that await her at the consummation of all things (*Exp. prop. Rom.* 54.6–7). Moreover, because Christ has freed the believer from condemnation and broken the power of death, she is liberated from the anxiety about her mortality that caused her to hold onto and pursue temporal goods, which she feared losing, rather than the eternal God (*Exp. prop. Rom.* 48). The contest between the law of the mind and the law of the flesh continues until the final stage when the believer enters into perfect peace at the resurrection. Then she is healed of carnal concupiscence, and she is made whole. The harmonic, Edenic unity of mind and body is restored.

This text is important in the development of Augustine's understanding of the will both because of what he does say about the will and because of what he does not say. Here Augustine articulates the fundamental position on grace and free will that will extend throughout the rest of his writings. "Free will existed perfectly in the first man; we, however, prior to grace, do not have free will so as not to sin, but only so much that we do not want to sin. But with grace, not only do we want to act rightly, but we can; not by our own strength, but by the help of the Liberator. And at the resurrection, he will bring us that perfect peace which follows from good will" (*Exp. prop. Rom.* 13–18.12). This marks a decided shift from the view articulated in his confident free-will defense. Yes, happiness lies in a good will, but such a will is possible only because the will is healed of concupiscence by grace. And that healing will not be completed in this life. Humanity, therefore, is not able to will the good, which is the defining character of a genuinely free will, apart from grace.

What, in retrospect, is conspicuously absent from his account of the will and faith is a developed explanation of the source of faith that cries out to God for help. Is faith a natural capacity or a gift of grace? Does it arise spontaneously within the human will, or is it a response to some initiative on God's part? Is it a human work that merits God's grace or is it the work of grace upon the will? Augustine does declare, "By free will humanity has the means to believe in the Liberator and to receive grace" (*Exp. prop. Rom.* 44.3). That still leaves unclear whether the belief of free will is possible because of grace or whether the will is free to believe prior to and independent of grace. If faith and belief, which merit the gift of justifying grace, are capacities of free will, the implication is that faith is a human work and not a gift of grace. Moreover, if belief in the Liberator is a capacity of the free will prior to grace, how does one reconcile that claim with Augustine's previous claim that there is no free will apart from the healing of the will by grace? One explanation might be that the sinner, like a drowning person desperately waving to a sailor on the deck of a ship to throw out a lifeline, in her desperation hopes that God will be merciful, come to her in her cries, and deliver her from death. Such freedom of the will would, nevertheless, be quite different from willing the good in love, which comes only from the healing gift of grace. What is clear is that Augustine in this early examination of Romans is explaining his revised and qualified view of free will in *On Free Choice of the Will* book 2—namely, that a person cannot raise herself up out of her fallen condition by a simple act of will—within his construction of a Pauline *ordo salutis*. What is equally clear is that he has not yet developed an account of whether faith, by which the soul turns to the Liberator for help, is a spontaneous, natural act of will or the result of God's working upon the will.

Letter to Simplicianus, the Turning Point

In 397, Ambrose of Milan died, leaving his important episcopal see vacant. His successor was Simplicianus, a figure who makes only a cameo appearance in the drama of the early Church but whose role was not insignificant. To him had fallen the task twenty years earlier of catechizing Ambrose in the Catholic faith before his baptism and ordination. What Ambrose became as a theologian began with Simplicianus's teaching. Almost ten years later when Augustine came to Milan to teach rhetoric, the two met, and Simplicianus introduced Augustine to the story of the great orator and Neo-Platonist philosopher, Marius Victorinus, and of his conversion from paganism to Christianity—one of those conversion narratives that made a distinct impression on Augustine and, according to *Confessions*, moved him toward his own conversion experience (*Conf.* 8.2.3). The year before his elevation to the episcopacy, Simplicianus wrote Augustine, asking a series of questions about certain puzzling claims Paul makes in Romans. His reply to

Simplicianus (letter 37, known more commonly as *Ad Simplicianum*), coming a scant sixteen to eighteen months after completing *Exposition on Propositions from Romans*, reveals that Augustine had continued to reflect on his underdeveloped treatment of the will and faith.

The first question that troubled Simplicianus—and Augustine—was Paul's description of the conflicted nature of the will in Romans 7:7–25, especially his seeming confession, "I am carnal, sold under sin. I do not understand my own actions. For I do not do what I want, but I do the very thing I hate. So then it is no longer I who do it but sin which dwells in me" (7:14–15). Is Paul really talking about himself here? How can the apostle who was converted by a face-to-face encounter with the risen Christ (Gal 1:12 and Acts 9:1–5) and then elevated to the beatific vision in the third heaven (2 Cor 12:2) be so ruled by concupiscence that he continues to sin? Moreover, is this sin the product of his own will or due to a force within him—sin—that has power over his actions that his will cannot resist? If such were the case, then this passage would seriously undercut Augustine's earlier free-will defense.

Augustine initially repeats his explanation from *Exposition on Propositions from Romans* that, in his use of the first person, the apostle is not actually speaking about his present experience but has artfully adopted the persona of a person *sub lege* (*Simpl.* 1.1.1). Augustine goes on to defend the goodness of the law, insisting that it does not instill sin in the soul; it merely reveals sin's latent presence so that the sinner, now aware of her condemnation, may turn in search of grace (*Simpl.* 1.1.2). Sin "was dead" (Rom 7:8) before the law only in the sense that it was hidden and therefore did not inspire fear of punishment. The law, though by nature spiritual (Rom 7:14a), becomes the occasion for sin only because the awareness of sin and its prohibition makes sin desirable to the carnal will that both is habitually covetous and prizes its independence and autonomy above all else. The law, therefore, can be spiritually efficacious only once a person has been made spiritual; then the spiritually disposed will that has been enlightened by light of the Lord can take delight in the law. When Paul goes on in 7:15 to say, "I know not what I do. . . . It is not I but sin which dwells in me," he means that the person under the law does not consent to sin but is overcome by cupidity (*Simpl.* 1.1.9). Indeed, the sinner under the law finds it easy to will the good (*Simpl.* 1.1.12) but is overwhelmed by sinful concupiscence and so cries out, "Wretched man that I am! Who will save me from the body of this death?" (Rom 7:24). Stepping out of his persona, Paul declares the answer: "The grace of God through Jesus Christ our Lord" (7:25). Contrary to his supremely optimistic view of the will in the wake of his conversion, Augustine now affirms that willing the good, which is within humanity's natural capacity even *sub lege*, does not immediately confer happiness. Paul's words leave no room for self-righteousness or confidence in the power of the individual to fulfill righteousness. So Augustine concludes, "What in fact is left to free choice in this mortal life . . . but that by suppliant piety he may turn himself [*se supplici pietate convertat*] to him by whose gift he may be enabled to fulfill it" (*Simpl.* 1.1.14). Apart from grace, an individual cannot fulfill the good, but she can turn to God for help. To put it another way, *sub lege* the humbled sinner stands at the fork between the way of death and the way of life; which way she will go is entirely the free choice of her will.

When Augustine has to explain 7:14b, "but I am carnal," a shift begins to emerge. While "carnal" may describe the sinner *sub lege* who remains a slave to desire, it also may refer in Paul's corpus to the novice *sub gratia* who has been reborn by grace in baptism but whose soul still has carnal habits such that she is not yet ready for the "solid food" (1 Cor 3:2) of doctrine that has become palatable to the spiritually mature (*Simpl.* 1.1.7). While this interpretation is consistent with Augustine's earlier view that the believer *sub gratia* struggles but is not overcome, it marks his recognition that even the apostle after his conversion might have described himself as "carnal." The truly pivotal moment, however, comes when Augustine has to answer Simplicianus's concern about the thorny question of God's election of Jacob and rejection of Esau in Romans 9:10–29.

Having confessed his anguish over the rejection of Christ by some of his fellow Israelites, Paul explains his enigmatic comment, "Not all who are descended from Israel belong to Israel" (Rom 9:6b), by drawing a line between Israelites "according to the flesh" who have rejected Christ and Israelites who by their acceptance of Christ are "children of the promise" (Rom 9:7–8). What troubled Simplicianus and Augustine was Paul's justification of his division by appealing to God's declared election of Jacob over his older brother Esau: "Jacob I loved; Esau I hated" (Rom 9:12–13). What was particularly disturbing, however, was not God's love of one and hatred of the other but Paul's assertion that their election and rejection occurred "when they were not yet born and had not done anything good or bad" (Rom 9:11). How could they be either chosen or rejected before they had done anything either to merit God's favor or earn God's wrath? Admitting his puzzlement over this "exceedingly obscure" passage (*Simp* 1.2.1), Augustine says that Paul's main point is that "no one should boast of the merits of his work . . . [since] the grace of the gospel is not dependent on work; otherwise grace is no longer grace" (*Simpl.* 1.2.2). Grace, therefore, is not merited by works; rather, grace precedes the works that flow from faith. Augustine here is claiming the absolute priority of grace over merit. Yet he also sees grace as the reward for faith: "one cannot do good works unless she has attained grace through faith" (*Simpl.* 1.2.2). If, however, faith is a free choice of the will—as he just stated in his answer to Simplicianus's previous question—then faith would seem to be a work of the human will. Therefore, if grace is attained through faith, grace is the reward for the work of faith. That conclusion, however, would undermine his earlier claim—in the same passage—that grace that is dependent on works is not grace. To avoid this contradiction, Augustine immediately makes faith itself dependent on God's gracious initiative: "But a person begins to obtain grace when he begins to believe in God, having been moved to faith by either an *internal or an external urging*" (*Simpl.* 1.2.2). The grace obtained from the sinner's faith is God's pardoning and liberating response to the soul's penitential cry for mercy. This is the grace that forgives and then sanctifies through the gift of the Holy Spirit whose outpouring of love makes the believer actually righteous before God. But there is also another form of grace at work *before faith*. It is the prevenient or unilateral urgings of grace that move the will to faith. Augustine's point is that faith is indeed an act of the contrite will turning to God for mercy, and that movement of the will is itself a response to the call of God speaking to the soul through *outward* signs, such as the appearance of an angel or a word of Scripture, or through *inner* moments of illumination, or both. Augustine illustrates the point by appealing to the conversion of Cornelius (Acts 10:1–4). The good works of almsgiving and prayer, which Cornelius performed before he received the grace of baptism, were clearly expressions of his belief in God. Yet Cornelius's belief was the result of his having been called by God. Cornelius's faith before baptism is like the coming to being of a child at her conception; his life full of good works after baptism is analogous to the child's entry into the world at birth. "In order to arrive at eternal life," Augustine concludes, "one must not only be conceived but also born. But none of this is without the grace of God's mercy" (*Simpl.* 1.2.2). Here Augustine is expanding the meaning of grace to include the whole of God's merciful condescension including the call that turns and draws the sinner's will to himself (*Simpl.* 1.2.7).

Augustine works out the relationship of the believer's will and God's call as he further ponders Jacob's election: How could God make a just choice prior to and independent of any merit or demerit? Augustine's nonanswer is that God chose Jacob in order that he might be good (*Simpl.* 1.2.4). Since no one, he reasoned, can perform meritorious works prior to grace, God first chose to extend grace to Jacob so that he might become righteous. That answer, however only raised another question: Did God choose Jacob because God *foreknew* Jacob's faith? One thing is chosen over another thing because of some distinguishing feature or quality that sets one apart from the other. Therefore, it seemed to Augustine that the election had to be based on foreknowledge of Jacob's righteousness. Were that the case, however, the elect might be able to boast of their election as the result of their works, even works enabled by grace. Yet such a conclusion flies in the face of Paul's declaration that the elect were chosen "not because of their works but because of him who called them" (Rom 9:11b). The point of God's election is the revelation of "the generosity of God's gifts" completely independent of merit so that humanity might humbly trust God's mercy rather than trust their works (*Simpl.* 1.2.6). Consequently, if election is entirely gratuitous, then faith itself cannot be viewed as the meritorious work of the believer. Therefore, the gracious call of God that turns the will is not God's reaction to faith but is itself the cause of faith (*Simpl.* 1.2.9). "How will they believe him whom they have not heard? And how will they hear without a preacher?" (Rom 10:14). Thus, faith, though an act of the will, is entirely a response to the divine call (*Simpl.* 1.2.10). Indeed, the good will—the will that repents, the will that resists the law of sin, and the will that seeks righteousness—is the work of God. Glossing Philippians 2:13, "For it is God who, for the sake of a good will, works in you both the willing and the working," Augustine writes, "even a good will itself comes about in us through God's working . . . because the human will does not suffice for us to live in rectitude and righteousness unless we are aided by God's mercy" (*Simpl.* 1.2.12).

Yet over his analysis of Romans 9 hovered the theological specter that haunted his thoughts since his battles with the Manichees: how to affirm both the freedom of the will and God's sovereignty. Is the call of God irresistible, or is the will able to reject the call?[8] Following Jesus's words, "Many are called but few are chosen" (Matt 20:16), Augustine concludes that the call is not irresistible. It creates the possibility of faith, but it does not compel the will to turn. Rather, as in his earlier writings, the turning of the will is voluntary; it is persuaded, not coerced. Thus, "[God] has willed that our willing be both his and ours—his by calling and ours by following" (*Simpl.* 1.2.10). Human agency is preserved—the willing is genuinely "ours" because the consent is within the power of the believer. The call of grace, therefore, is a necessary, but not sufficient, condition for the conversion of the will. Yet in such a case, how is God's will sovereign? How is the election of the saints certain if they have the capacity to reject the call? If the call can truly be rejected, then the election is not sure, nor is God's will definitive. Augustine's answer to this conundrum is to say that, while all are called, the elect are called in a way that is appropriate to the character and condition of the would-be believer. This is often referred to as a "congruous vocation," which means that the manner of the call is effective because it is congruent with some element peculiar to the individual's will that attracts him or her to God. Such a call is not the general promise of mercy but addresses the particular desperate condition of the sinner's terrified conscience. Because of the particularity of the call with its offer of mercy

8. Although it is common in modern discussions of the will to ask, "Is the will *free* to reject God's call?" Augustine never uses that wording because, for him, freedom (*libertas*) does not refer to the ability to choose between opposing goods—especially life in God or death in sin—but the ability to cleave to God. Grace frees the will to choose the good; then and then only is the will truly free. By contrast, choosing sin and death reflects not the will's freedom but its bondage to concupiscence.

spoken directly to her, she finds the call so persuasive that she will not reject it (*Simpl.* 1.2.13). God's merciful call fills her with such delight in the promise of salvation that she desires in the depths of her being the righteousness to which her Liberator calls her.

God's rejection of Esau remained an unresolved question. If God hates none of his creatures and is able to move the sinful will with an irresistibly persuasive call, then why did God not call Esau in an efficacious manner (*Simpl.* 1.2.14)? Augustine prefaces any attempt to address such questions by reminding Simplicianus of God's absolute freedom, quoting Romans 9:14–15: "What then, shall we say, 'Is there injustice with God?' Of course not! For Moses says, 'I will have mercy on whom I will have mercy and I will show compassion to whom I will be compassionate.'" He then explains Esau's failure to respond to God's call by comparing it with the blindness of those who did not believe Jesus even though they had witnessed his miracles. As with Pharaoh's heart, the sinner's resolve not to believe is not the result of God's causing sin but God's giving the sinner over to the hardness of his sinful will as punishment (*Simpl.* 1.2.15). God does not compel; he merely withholds his mercy. This, however, does not answer why God showed mercy to Jacob and not Esau. Without articulating a developed doctrine of the fall, Augustine focuses on Paul's language of the "lump of humanity" (Rom 9:20–21). Jacob and Esau are members of the common lump of sinful humanity that as a whole owes a debt due to sin and so deserves punishment (*Simpl.* 1.2.16). Esau's hardness of heart is his just punishment for the sin that is the cause of injustice in the world (*Simpl.* 1.2.17). The punishment is not unjust; rather, the efficacious call of Jacob to righteousness is the inscrutable justice of God that replaces condemnation with mercy. Thus, the guilty cannot decry his punishment as unjust, nor can the believer saved through the gift of faith boast of her righteousness.

This explanation is not unproblematic. Augustine's justification for God's withholding grace is that it is the just punishment for the demerit of sin. However, if God withholds grace from Esau because Esau is a piece of the lump of sinful humanity, then Esau's nonelection is the result of God's foreknowledge of humanity's sin. In the case of Jacob, however, Augustine expressly denies that his election was based on God's foreknowledge of Jacob's righteousness. It seems then that God's election of Jacob was the unconditioned choice of God's free will with no regard for Jacob's merit, while God's rejection of Esau—before the foundation of the world—was conditioned by God's foreknowledge of sin. Augustine navigates this problem by anchoring his response on what he takes to be Paul's primary concern in Romans 9, namely disabusing Jews or gentiles of their self-righteousness. In the case of Jacob, who is also a sinner, God "loved in him not the guilt that he did away with but the grace that he bestowed . . . [that he] might be changed from wickedness and believe in him who makes the wicked righteous" (*Simpl.* 1.2.18). Jacob's election rests on the love of grace generally and not on Jacob's particular righteousness. Ultimately, the gratuitous nature of God's election of Jacob—and all the elect—lies in God's response to their sin with mercy rather than the condemnation that their sin justly merited. The nature and source of this sin shared by Jacob and Esau Augustine clarifies in the development of his theory of original sin in his dispute with the Pelagians about human nature and the need for infant baptism.

The Pelagian Controversy

The controversy around human moral agency and the role of divine assistance was ignited by one of Pelagius's disciples, Caelestius. The son of a noble Roman family, Caelestius was a zealous neophyte who championed Pelagius's rigorist perfectionism and the anthropological assumptions that were its foundation. In 411, when he arrived in Carthage, no sooner had he made landfall than Caelestius, not yet ordained, plunged headlong into theological disputations with North African clergy over the question of the soul's origin. Subscribing to Pelagius's view that human nature was not corrupted by the sins of one's parents in any way that would compromise one's natural capacity of free will, Caelestius argued that each soul was born newly fashioned by God. Having no life prior to birth, the soul was born in a state of innocence and therefore had no sin that needed to be washed away through the grace of baptism. This, it should be noted, was not a position explicitly advocated by Pelagius in any of his extant writings. But Caelestius's reputation for heterodoxy had followed him across the waters to North Africa. So when he applied for ordination in Carthage, he was denounced by Paulinus of Milan and tried by an ecclesiastical tribunal that found him guilty of heresy and excommunicated him. Although Augustine had not been present for the trial, it took little arm-twisting to persuade Augustine to weigh in on Caelestius's teachings. Marcellinus, the emperor Honorius's envoy sent to North Africa for managing the conflict between Catholics and Donatists, wanted Augustine to address the confusion among "our weak brothers" caused by the questions Caelestius raised. In his response, *Guilt and Remission of Sins*, Augustine grants that infants have certainly done nothing personally that is sinful. Nevertheless, since none can enter the kingdom of God unless he is reborn in Christ through baptism, infants are brought to the Church to be baptized that they may be healed by the great physician of the disease of original sin (*Pecc. merit.* 1.18.23–23.33). The key for Augustine is Jesus's words, "Those who are well have no need of a physician but those who are sick; I have not come to call the righteous, but sinners to repentance" (Luke 5:31–32). Therefore, to assert that infants do not need to be baptized is to claim that they have no need of Christ's mercy and that they are not among the ungodly for whom Christ died (Rom 5:6).[9] In this opening salvo against Pelagius's followers, Augustine, repeating a theme already articulated in *Letter to Simplicianus*, challenges their confidence in the power of free will apart from the influence of grace. People do not will the good either because they are ignorant of it or because they take no delight in it. Therefore, grace reorders the will by making that which we once viewed as unpleasant to be sweet and the source of our delight (*Pecc. merit.* 2.17.28–18.28).

Guilt and Remission of Sins, it should be noted, was not an attack on Pelagius himself. Although Augustine and Pelagius never met, they had a number of mutual friends among the Roman aristocrats who had been converted to Pelagius's demanding ascetic brand of Christianity. They also shared certain theological commitments, such as their mutual opposition to Manichaeism with its fatalistic denial of moral agency. In 414, however, Augustine turned his theological energies against Pelagius after reading his *On Nature*, given to him by two of Pelagius's former disciples. The dispute between Augustine and Pelagius gained visibility around the Mediterranean when, during an episcopal synod in Jerusalem in 415, one of Augustine's zealous protégés, Paul Orosius, announced to John of Jerusalem that Caelestius had been condemned in Carthage. He then proceeded to read portions of a letter from Augustine against the followers of Pelagius. When invited by John to lay out the case against Caelestius, Orosius, in a move guaranteed to strain relations between East and West, declined, saying that the Greek bishops should simply accept the judgment of the North African bishops, especially Augustine. In December of that year, two Gallic bishops leveled charges of heterodoxy against Pelagius. At a synod in Diospolis summoned to hear his case, Pelagius ably defended his position against the allegations against him and repudiated Caelestius. Largely due to Pelagius's insistence on the necessity of grace in order to attain sinless perfection, the fourteen bishops at Diospolis acquitted Pelagius of these charges. Upon receiving a detailed report of Pelagius's defense at Diospolis and the violence perpetrated by his followers in Palestine, Augustine countered with his *On the Deeds of Pelagius*. After two synods of North African bishops condemned Pelagius in 416, Pope Innocent confirmed the condemnations and excommunicated Pelagius and Caelestius in January 417. But shortly after Pope Innocent's death, his successor Zosimus reopened the case, ultimately exonerating Pelagius and Caelestius.

Leading up to the North African synods and Zosimus's judgment, Augustine had entered deeper into the fray. His conflict with Pelagius was fought on two theological fronts. The first front concerned the nature of nature and the effect of

9. For Augustine's doctrine of original sin, see chapter 3, pp. 104–14.

sin upon it.[10] The second front concerned the nature of grace. Although Pelagius maintained that human nature was endowed with the moral capacity to fulfill all righteousness without the aid of an added gift, he fully recognized the need for grace. But for Pelagius, since sin had not altered human nature and diminished the capacity for moral agency, there was no need for human nature to be *healed* by grace. Indeed, God was responsible for goods works because his construction of human beings with the capacity of free will was itself a gift of God's grace. Sin compromised the right use of free will only through the fog of ignorance. Because children imitate the conduct of their parents, sin spread by their imitation of their parents' sinful example. Therefore, though endowed with the capacity for moral perfection, all humanity has fallen into sin and so is in need of both forgiveness for its sins and an alternate moral example to imitate. This knowledge of true righteousness was given in the law of Moses and fulfilled in the life of Jesus. Thus, the law and Christ's example are the forms grace takes to reveal the moral good that frees humanity from ignorance. This is how Pelagius made sense of Paul's account of the saving work of grace.

Pelagius's essential failure, according to Augustine, was equating the law with grace. Knowing the good through instruction in the law is not sufficient for doing the good. Augustine laid out his argument in his treatise *On the Spirit and the Letter*. Second Corinthians 3:6 provides the immediate scriptural warrant as well as the rhetorical force for his argument: "[God] has made us ministers of the New Testament, not by the letter but by the Spirit; for the letter kills but the Spirit gives life." Augustine's explanation of how the letter kills and how the Spirit gives life rests upon his exegesis not primarily of 2 Corinthians but of Romans. When Paul speaks of the "letter" that kills, the apostle is not, Augustine insists, referring to the literal rather than the figural meaning of Scripture. "Letter" refers to the law of Moses read with a carnal disposition of mind. The law's prohibition against covetousness (*concupiscentia*) is to be taken literally by Christians as well as Jews (*Spir. et litt.* 14.24). Augustine determines then that the death-dealing "letter" in 2 Corinthians 3:6 is the law itself to which Paul refers in Romans 7:11: "Sin found opportunity to deceive me through the commandment and through it killed [me]" (*Spir. et litt.* 4.6). Since the law is intrinsically good, the letter kills because of a corruption in the will that prevents one from fulfilling the good that the law prescribes. Therefore, if the Christian is to escape the letter that kills, her will must be healed of its corruption, its disordered, self-centered love. This transformation of the will comes through the love of God poured out into the heart by the luminous presence of the Holy Spirit (Rom 5:5). For through the light of the Spirit, the soul

10. See chapter 10, pp. 104–14.

is enabled to behold and delight in the goodness of the law understood spiritually. Only when one delights in the law, can one fulfill the law willingly.

Augustine's logic rests upon Matthew 22:40, "In these two commandments [i.e., 'love the Lord your God with all your heart and all your soul and all your mind' and 'Love your neighbor as yourself] all the Law and the prophets hang," and Romans 13:9–10, "For the whole Law is fulfilled in one saying, 'You shall love your neighbor as yourself'" (Gal 5:14). "This love is not 'written on stone tablets' (2 Cor 3:3) but is 'poured out in our hearts through the Holy Spirit who is given to us' (Rom 5:5). The Law of God, therefore, is love.... [Then] it is the law of faith and the Spirit giving life to the one who loves" (*Spir. et litt.* 17.29; 36.64). Through the gift of the Holy Spirit, who is the love of God, one is actually made righteous. Loving God in whom the Christian delights and delighting in what God loves become a set piece; they are both one love. One primarily loves the righteousness that God loves and commands *because* God loves it. Ultimately, however, one comes to love the righteousness that God loves and commands because one sees that the righteousness commanded in the law is a reflection of God's righteousness.

The Christian's ability to fulfill the law depends on the Spirit's daily reforming her will with the love of God and his righteousness. This is the will-healing grace on which the Christian is absolutely dependent. For the Christian living under grace, there are two laws at play: the "law of works" and the "law of faith," the latter being the humble and plaintive spirit of Christians endowed with the wisdom of faith: "Accordingly, by the law of works God says: Do what I command! By the law of faith we say to God: Give us what you command! After all, the law commands in order to remind us of what faith should do" (*Spir. et litt.* 13.22). The law of works reveals the content of the righteous life, while the law of faith is the wisdom that seeks the aid necessary to live righteously. For Augustine, Pelagius's teaching that human beings have the moral sufficiency to fulfill what the law teaches—and this is the true death-dealing work of Pelagius's thought—promotes self-righteousness and pride in one's own moral autonomy rather than teaching the humility that causes one to cleave to God for the assistance necessary for living righteously.

This was a pastoral as well as theological concern Augustine had voiced early in the controversy. "God does not produce our salvation in us as if we were mindless rocks," Augustine had insisted; nonetheless, the Christian cannot deny the need of God's help. One cannot presume that "having received once and for all free choice of the will, we need not pray that God might help us not to sin" (*Pecc. merit.* 2.5.6). Augustine repeatedly used Jesus's parable of the Pharisee and the tax collector (Luke 18:9–14) to illustrate his point. Although the Pharisee is right in thanking God that he is not like the tax collector because of his works of the law, it is the tax collector, who prays, "Have mercy on me a sinner," who goes away justified before God because he does not presume on his own righteousness. For the Pharisee is guilty of pride for failing to ask for an increase in righteousness because he assumed incorrectly that by fulfilling the external works of the law he had fulfilled all righteousness (*Spir. et litt.* 13.22). Thus, for Augustine, the Pharisee becomes a cipher for Pelagians who give thanks for the gifts of free will and the law but do not ask for grace in order to accomplish the demands of the law. Indeed, the Pharisee is more righteous than the Pelagians because he at least recognized his fasting and tithing were not possible without God's help (*Pecc. merit.* 2.5.6).

In 416, Pelagius's rebuttal came in a treatise entitled *On the Defense of Free Will.* There he countered Augustine's charge of self-righteousness by arguing that God is to be praised for our righteousness because without his gracious endowment of human nature with free will, humanity could not fulfill righteousness; therefore, "we praise both human beings and God who gave them the ability for this will and action and who always assists this ability by the help of his grace—that human beings can will and accomplish what is good is *due to God alone*. . . . When we say that a human being can be without sin . . . there is no reason to praise people at this point, when God is the only cause under consideration" (*Lib. arb.* 3). Pelagius employed the very illuminationist language central to Augustine's account of the work of the Spirit: "We do not say as you suppose that [grace] consists in the Law alone, but we profess that it is also found in God's help. . . . For God helps us through his teaching and revelation, in *opening the eyes of our heart*, in disclosing to us what is to come so that we are not absorbed with what is present . . . in *enlightening* us by the manifold and ineffable gift of his heavenly grace" (*Lib. arb.* 1).[11] Pelagius here distinguishes law and divine teaching but does not say explicitly that such teachings are anything other than the teachings of the New Testament and of preachers. In his interpretation of Philippians 2:13, "God produces the willing and the act," Pelagius explains that God produces a holy will in the believer "by setting us on fire with the greatness of the glory to come . . . he does this by rousing the sluggish will to a desire for God through revealing his wisdom; he does this by urging us toward everything that is good" (*Lib. arb.* 3).

From Augustine's perspective, Pelagius was being deceptive by giving God alone praise for human good works by conferring both the *ability* not to sin and the *assistance* of grace that produced a good will. This assistance, however, was

11. *Lib. arb.* 1 quoted in *Grat. Chr.* 1.7.8; trans. Roland J. Teske, in Augustine, *Answer to the Pelagians I: The Punishment and Forgiveness of Sins and the Baptism of Little Ones, The Spirit and the Letter, Nature and Grace, The Perfection of Human Righteousness, The Deeds of Pelagius, The Grace of Christ and Original Sin, and The Nature and Origin of the Soul,* The Works of Saint Augustine: A Translation for the 21st Century 1/23 (Hyde Park, NY: New City, 1997), 394–95.

not the *inner* working of grace that healed the will as Augustine had described it in *On the Spirit and the Letter* but merely the *external* revelation of righteousness in the law. There was not a real distinction between the teaching of the law and the teachings of the Church; they are both *external* and therefore have only the power of persuasion. They are not the immediate inner healing of the will necessary for liberating the will from its captivity to sinful *concupiscentia*. Twenty years earlier in *Letter to Simplicianus*, Augustine had argued that grace worked in two forms: internal illumination and external revelations. Whereas earlier in *On True Religion*, the intellect acquires understanding that turns the will to the good, in *Letter to Simplicianus* there is no gap between seeing and willing the good. The illumination of grace conveys a knowledge of God's goodness and mercy that acts upon the will giving it the form of a holy desire for the Liberator. Seized by the conviction of faith, the soul is moved inexorably from a sinful will to a delight in and desire for the God whom grace has revealed. A case in point is Saul of Tarsus: "What did Saul want except to find, to seize, to overcome, and to kill Christians? How rabid a will, how ferocious, how blind. Nevertheless, by a single voice from above, he was laid prostrate, then such a vision [*visio*] prevailed upon him by which that mind and will broken by its savagery were turned violently and reformed for faith" (*Simpl.* 1.2.22). The violence of Saul's malicious will is overpowered not with intellectual persuasion as in *On True Religion* but by a violent vision of mercy that immediately transformed Saul's will and mind, which confers the gift of submissive faith. The Spirit's call—through a combination of inner and external *visa* (visions)—replaces the blindness of self-will with the sight of faith that apprehends the goodness of God and moves the will to cleave to the Liberator.

By 416, Pelagius's confusing language of "the help of grace" in the external form of the law and divine teachings forced Augustine to clarify the nature of grace. Specifically, he needed to stress the insufficiency of external modes of revelation independent of the immediate inner work of grace. This argument he presented in 418 with the publication of *On the Grace of Christ and Original Sin*. Law and Christian doctrine, he argues, show *what* the Christian should do without actually *assisting* her in doing it. In effect, the law includes all commands, all teaching that carries an obligation. Here Augustine falls back on his argument for the impotence of the law from twenty-four years earlier in *Exposition on Propositions from Romans*. The revelation of what *should* be done carries condemnation and so serves only to increase sin. Humanity's salvation, however, lies in the righteousness of God that is revealed separately from the law (Rom 3:19–21). This righteousness is the love of God, which is the gift of the Spirit (*Grat. Chr.* 1.8.9). Wisdom taught by human teachers likewise gives only knowledge of the moral imperative and so is no different from the law's commands. *Showing* believers the eternal goods of God's eschatological kingdom—prizes we should desire—is not the same as *giving* the believer love for God's eternal glory; Scripture's vision of eschatological glory is an *external* sign and, therefore, does not in itself convict the believer of the truth and goodness of the reality that it signifies. It does not give the conviction of faith. The divine teachings, even in the New Testament, are but the letter that kills. They become life-giving only when the Spirit allows the believer to delight in them. Pelagius, therefore, missed the mark by assuming that the teachings in their external form arouse delight *independent* of the inner illuminating witness of the Spirit. Apart from the light of grace, these teachings merely urge (*suadere*) the Christian to action; that is no different from exhortation, which is what the letter of Scripture already does ineffectually. Grace not only reveals the glory to come, but it convicts (*persuadere*) Christians of the hope of God's eschatological promises. This is the conviction of faith that is necessary for the revelation to be efficacious (*Grat. Chr.* 1.10.11). Only the Spirit's light mediates the truth of divine realities revealed in Scripture and a preacher's words. Only in the inner light of the Spirit does one delight in that truth. From the inner witness of the Spirit, the soul delights in God's righteousness so that its actions conform to his *iustitia*. Then the will experiences, as far as possible in this life, true freedom—*libertas* to cleave to God in love and conform to his will.

On the Grace of Christ and Original Sin thus marks the consummation of Augustine's developing narrative of free will and grace because it is the fullest integration of his illuminationist epistemology with the doctrines of justification and pneumatology that emerged from his ongoing interpretation of Romans. Augustine's doctrine of grace was not developed purely, or even largely, in reaction to Pelagius. Rather, the doctrine that emerged was an extrapolation of the interior working of grace through the irresistible, congruous vocation articulated in *Letter to Simplicianus*. Through this doctrine, Augustine believed he had developed a theory of grace that makes room for a truly free human will and yet excludes human pride and self-righteousness through an account of salvation that is entirely the work of God acting in the lives of the elect.

Moreover, his understanding of election as God's *predestination* of individuals to receive saving grace rather than the result of his *foreknowing* the sinner's response to grace made grace the first and sole cause of salvation. After all, were election the result of God's foreknowledge, then even the initial gift of grace would not be absolutely gracious but would have been merited by the individual's response. The works of charity that merit salvation are the work of grace in the believer. But in the order of salvation, the individual's good works, which God foreknew, would be logically prior to God's decision to give the grace necessary for those good works; therefore, God's will to give grace would be conditioned by the human will.

A Controversy Among the Anti-Pelagians: Augustine and John Cassian

By the end of the second decade of the fifth century, Pelagius's confident view of uncorrupted human nature and of the law and Christian doctrine as the forms of grace needed for perfection had fallen into theological disrepute in the West. For all his personal holiness, Pelagius's theological anthropology and doctrine of grace had been exposed by Augustine as contrary to the baptismal piety of the ancient church and the problematic source of a divisive spiritual elitism. The controversy that bears his name was over. Having largely accepted an Augustinian doctrine of grace, the Latin Church had still to work out certain implications of this doctrine. In particular, what was the place of human agency within this model of unmerited grace? It was precisely this question that exposed new theological fault lines in the Western church between followers of Augustine and those of John Cassian.

Raised on the Danubian frontier, Cassian as a young man had traveled among the monasteries of Syria, Palestine, and Egypt. Eventually making his way to Italy and Gaul, he established two monasteries in Massilia (modern Marseilles) modeled on Palestinian and Egyptian communities. During the mid-420s, some monks in the Massilian monasteries pressed the question, If the virtues that merit salvation are the work of God's unmerited grace in the believer, what is the salvific value of a monk's ascetic labors? The question arose precisely because of Cassian's firm doctrine of grace articulated in *Conferences* 11 (*On Perfection*) and 12 (*On Chastity*). Cassian, speaking in the voice of the Egyptian monk Abba Chaeremon, held that perfection in virtue was attainable but only through divine assistance. Perfection, the goal of the monastic life, was achieved through spiritual maturation, from the fearful piety of a servant, who obeys in order to escape punishment, to the hopeful piety of a hireling, who longs for heavenly reward, to the filial piety of a child, who loves God and virtue for God's own sake. Yet such progress, the aged monk says, is possible only "by God's help and not [by] relying on [one's] own laborious effort" (*Coll.* 11.9.1). The patience and mildness a monk must have to endure the annoying sins of his fellow monks come from a humility born of the knowledge that "he was saved by the Lord's pity." Then he will realize that "he was *not* freed from the assaults of the flesh *by his own efforts* but was saved by the protection of God," as the psalmist confesses, "Unless the Lord had helped me, my soul would soon have dwelt in hell (Ps 94:17)" (*Coll.* 11.9.1).

The question of the possibility of perfect virtue takes concrete form in *Conferences* 12 where Germanus, Cassian's longtime ascetic companion and Abba Chaeremon's interlocutor, asks about chastity. The possibility of being sexually chaste was the test case for the effectiveness of monastic disciplines because the impurity with which the monks wrestled was, generally speaking, not the physical act of fornication but the deep sexual desires manifest in dreams and nocturnal emissions. Was it possible to be free not only from unholy appetites that one did not consciously will but also from impure thoughts that involuntarily intruded upon the mind during hours of rest? Without diminishing the importance of ascetic disciplines, Chaeremon stresses the insufficiency of outward acts of mortification to produce inner chastity: "although we undergo all the rigors of abstinence . . . we are still unable to acquire perpetual chastity through these efforts unless . . . its incorruption [is] granted to us by the bounty of divine grace" (*Coll.* 12.4.1). It is the very unbidden nature of sexual dreams that, contra Pelagius, proves a monk's impotence to achieve the perfection Christ commanded simply by relying on his natural capacity of free will. The nocturnal ejaculation is evidence of the adulterous lust in the heart (Matt 5:27–28) that falls short of the perfect fulfillment of the law's prohibition of adultery (Matt 5:48). Through his endurance of the hardships of outward disciplines, the monk "will deserve to be freed from the assaults of the flesh"; nevertheless, Chaeremon cautions, "he must not believe that through these things he will attain by himself the unspoiled bodily chastity that he seeks" (*Coll.* 12.4.2). Far from being confident in the natural capacities of his will and proud of his self-control, the monk, who awakens refreshed from a night unspoiled by licentious thoughts, should give thanks to God rather than "trusting proudly in the knowledge of his own virtue . . . for he knows he will be [unclean] . . . if the divine protection departs from him *even for a little while*. Therefore, in all contrition and humility of heart, one must pray ceaselessly for perseverance in [chastity]" (*Coll.* 12.4.4). Purity of heart—the true mark of perfection in virtue—is possible only through the aid of God. Such knowledge—gained often from the experience of nocturnal emissions suffered during times of spiritual complacency—disabuses the monk of any delusions of self-righteousness or moral self-sufficiency. Creatures cannot achieve perfection on their own; that is ultimately the work of grace, a point no ascetic should forget. While Augustine, though granting, at least for a time, that grace theoretically could produce perfection (*Spir. et litt.* 1.1–2.2), doubted that anyone attained perfection in this life, Cassian's account of the absolute necessity of grace, the insufficiency of the natural moral faculties, and the importance of humility that continually prays for divine protection is in accord with Augustine's critique of Pelagian pride and moral self-confidence.

Given the insufficiency of ascetic disciplines and necessity of a divine gift that is beyond one's control—a gift for which one can only beg—the question remained, What is the value of human efforts? Do they serve only to teach the monk his moral impotence? How does this doctrine of grace not negate the value of all the monk's labors to be holy? These questions are the heart of Germanus's bold sally at the beginning of *Conferences* 13. With his claim that salvation is entirely the work of grace, Germanus charges, Chaeremon has "in a single assertion nullified the value of human effort" (*Coll.* 13.1). After all, Germanus says, a good harvest is attributable in no small degree to the toil of the farmer who tilled the soil and watered his crops (*Coll.* 13.2). Chaeremon counters that the farmer's toil would literally be fruitless if God did not send the right amount of rain and a moderate winter (*Coll.* 13.3.1). To be sure, a few pagan philosophers attained outward chastity, but they did not achieve the inner purity of heart that human frailty cannot attain without the purifying work of grace upon the soul. Therefore, he concludes emphatically, "without the help of God, human frailty can accomplish nothing which pertains to salvation" (*Coll.* 13.6.1); indeed, "The *whole* of our salvation must be ascribed not to our deserving works but to heavenly grace" (*Coll.* 13.18.3). However, Cassian, seeking to affirm the monk's moral agency, seemed to backpedal, affirming that salvation is the product of grace *and* human free will. Citing a long list of antinomies, for example, Romans 2:6, God "renders to each according to his works," and Philippians 2:13, "It is God who works in you both to will and to accomplish" (*Coll.* 13.9.2), Chaeremon argues that Scripture gives primacy to God's assistance but also makes it incumbent on the Christian to exert a discipline of will and effort to seek holiness.

The real seed of division among the anti-Pelagians was Cassian's further point that certain acts of human initiative could merit grace: "When his kindness sees shining in us the slightest glimmer of good will, which he himself has in fact sparked from the hard flint of our heart, he fosters it, stirs it up, and strengthens it with his inspiration" (*Coll.* 13.7.1).[12] In the monastic context where the monks had already been baptized and were striving for perfection, Chaeremon's word may be read as offering reassurance and encouragement to a monk who earnestly desires purity but whose will is weak. Yet Chaeremon goes on to argue that God's grace operates differently on different people. Some with an especially hardened will, like Saul of Tarsus, God chooses to save by overpowering his will; in such cases, grace is entirely operative, forcefully imparting belief and love "against their will" (*Coll.* 13.17.1). However, others, like Zacchaeus and Cornelius, he imagines were already inclined to virtue and were seeking salvation (*Coll.* 13.11.1–2). In such individuals, divine assistance *follows* upon human initiative: "When [God] notices good will making an appearance in us, at once he enlightens and encourages it and spurs it on to salvation, giving increase to what he himself planted and saw arise from our own efforts" (*Coll.* 13.8.4). For Cassian, the whole of salvation is the

12. I am intentionally avoiding the common labels "semi-Pelagian" or "semi-Augustinian" to describe this controversy for two reasons. First, not being coined until the sixteenth century during the controversy about grace between the Dominicans and the Jesuits, "semi-Pelagian" is an anachronism. Moreover, second, given Cassian's insistence on the necessity of grace for the healing of human nature in order to merit salvation, the label "semi-Pelagian" is an unfair characterization of his thought.

work of grace: the grace that endows human nature with free will, the grace that implants a seminal desire for virtue, and the grace that ultimately produces the fruit of virtue that merits salvation. Cassian has a strong sense of the prevenient character of grace. God "inspires the beginning of that holy desire and bestows both the commencement of a good work and perseverance in it" (*Coll.* 13.17.1). The titles "savior" and "protector" name God as the one who draws us to our salvation unwilling and unaware, while "supporter" and "refuge" names God who sustains our will in the midst of spiritual struggle (*Coll.* 13.17.2). He is clear that an individual is impotent to attain salvation without God's assistance. Even though an individual's efforts contribute to her salvation, "working [it] out with fear and trembling" (Phil 2:12), her role is minuscule in comparison to the infinitely greater role of God's grace (*Coll.* 13.13.1). Therefore, there is no warrant for human boasting or self-righteousness. Nevertheless, because the *Conferences* had primarily the pastoral aim of encouraging monks in the midst of ascetic struggle, he emphasizes the responsibility God places on people and the efficacy of labors of renunciation. A balance is struck: grace is not cheapened as the automatic gift of salvation for the lax and lazy (*Coll.* 13.13.1), while nevertheless being the source of hope to the struggling.

A critical difference from Augustine that allows Cassian to give greater weight to human agency is his more positive view of human nature after the fall. Unlike Pelagius, Cassian sees human nature weakened by sin so that it is dependent on grace. But, like the Augustine of *Exposition on Propositions from Romans*, Cassian allows that the soul is able of its own accord to cry out for deliverance: "For when God sees us turning in order to will what is good, he comes to us, directs us, and strengthens us, for 'as soon as he hears the voice of your cry he will respond to you' (Ps 50:15)" (*Coll.* 13.11.5). This is possible because humanity's rational nature allows it to retain, even in sin, some knowledge of the good. This is Paul's assumption behind his assertion in Romans 1 that the gentiles are able to do without the revelation of the law what the law requires (*Coll.* 13.12.2). This innate capacity to know the good is the seed of virtue implanted in human nature by God—a seed, however, that will never grow to perfection without the divine gardener's care and cultivation (*Coll.* 13.12.5–6). Though the non-Christian's pursuits of virtue—for example, desire for knowledge, love of courage, moderation of one's appetites, or contrition for injustice—do not merit salvation, they constitute a turn to the good that God's grace brings to perfection in the theological virtues. Therefore, contra Augustine, one cannot say that, apart from grace, human deeds are only bad or perverse (*Coll.* 13.12.5).

The issue where Cassian most clearly parts ways with Augustine is election and predestination. Cassian maintains that God desires the salvation of all. God did not create human beings in love only to will their destruction. Rather, God's original purpose in creating human beings to be partakers of his goodness has not been changed by sin (*Coll.* 13.7.1). "How," Chaeremon asks rhetorically, "can it be thought . . . of [God], who does not want a single little one to perish, that he does not wish all to be saved universally, but only a few instead of all?" (*Coll.* 13.7.2). This position is confirmed by Paul's declaration that God desires "all to be saved and come to the knowledge of truth" (1 Tim 2:4). Therefore, God extends grace to all people at all times—though in different ways according to the individual's disposition toward the good (*Coll.* 13.7.3). Cassian, however, does not advocate a universalist account of salvation. Grace is given that all *may* turn to God and go on to perfection. Generally speaking, grace calls, but it does not compel and override free will. The will may resist the call or, once having answered the call, may neglect grace and fall away from the love of God (*Coll.* 13.12.8). Thus, Chaeremon says that God calls and invites but also waits for the creature's free response (*Coll.* 13.12.11). Contra Augustine, there is no fraction of the human race to whom God does not extend grace; that grace, however, is not irresistible. Although Cassian maintains, generally speaking, humanity's capacity to reject God's offer of grace, he recognizes that there seem to be exceptions where God compels the conversion of some, such as Paul. Yet he does not explain why a God who desires the salvation of all would compel the acceptance of grace by some but not all. Such a case reflects the inscrutable diversity of means God chooses to use for the salvation of all that nonetheless respects human free will (*Coll.* 13.18.5).

About the same time as Cassian was composing Chaeremon's answer to Germanus, Augustine was encountering similar questions about grace and human agency from some North African monks in the town of Hadrumetum. One of their number, Florus read a letter (*Ep.* 194) Augustine had written in 418 to the priest Sixtus, who would in 432 become bishop of Rome. In it, Augustine had emphasized the gratuitous nature of grace and argued that the merit by which one is saved is attributed entirely to the work of grace in the believer. Valentinus, the abbot at Hadrumetum, wrote on behalf of his monks, asking Augustine for clarification of his position. Did the bishop of Hippo mean that the spiritual disciplines were of no ultimate value for salvation? If perfection in this life is impossible and salvation is entirely the gracious work of God, why should anyone perform the radical acts of renunciation these monks had? If the merit lay entirely with grace working in the monk, did that mean that the monk was, in effect, merely a puppet manipulated by the divine puppet master? Augustine responded in the treatise *On Grace and Free Will*. Grace, he argues, does not negate free will. On the contrary, the commands of Scripture assume the ability to obey (*Grat.* 2.2); thus, there is no excuse for sin, and God is without blame. But acting in accordance with God's will does not mean that a person can take credit for his good works (*Grat.* 2.4). Therefore, to whatever degree one affirms free will, one cannot eliminate the need for grace such that she glories in herself (Jer 17:5) rather than in grace. Merit, by which one is worthy of eternal life, is attained by the work of grace within the believer's will. In a sense, the reward of salvation is God's rewarding the merits of his grace active in the believer.

One of the Hadrumetum monks, who read *On Grace and Free Will*, refused to submit to the abbot's correction on the ground that, since perseverance in the good was entirely dependent upon grace, the correction was useless. Instead of punishing him, the monk argued, his abbot could only offer intercession that further grace be given. Augustine responded with *On Correction and Grace*. Appealing to 2 Timothy 2:25, he explained that the efficacy of gentle correction rested on the hope that God would, through the correction, bring the brother to repentance and the knowledge of truth. Indeed, those in Christ were given a more powerful grace than Adam enjoyed. This grace not only allowed them to remain in the good, but it placed the will to carry on to the end (*Corrept.* 11.31). Even though they lapse, this grace enables them to hold fast (*Corrept.* 11.32). Such confidence rested entirely on the permanence of God's election.

Two questions about election emerged. The first concerned limited election. Since God's grace gives to the believer's will the faith necessary to merit the gift of the Holy Spirit, why does not God move the will of all people in order that all may be redeemed? Such, for Augustine, is a mystery of God's inscrutable will. Moreover, he rejected universalist interpretations of 1 Timothy 2:4: "[God] desires all people to be saved." The "all" refers not to all members of the human race but to all nations and races of people (*Corrept.* 14.44). Equally problematic was Augustine's distinction between the visible and the invisible Church—the former being all the baptized, which included the elect and the nonelect, and the latter being only the elect known only to God. Though all who are baptized receive the gift of faith that works in love, God gives to the elect the grace of perseverance, enabling them to see their pilgrimage through to the end. Indeed, they cannot help but to persevere (*Corrept.* 12.34). But God withholds that grace from the nonelect who ultimately turn away from the life of faith and are not saved (*Corrept.* 6.10; 9.20). They could have persevered if they had willed, but they did not (*Corrept.* 7.11); yet they could not will to persevere without the grace of perseverance.

Augustine's writings to the monks at Hadrumetum had already begun to raise questions among Christians in Gaul before the arrival of *On Correction and Grace*. The layman Prosper Tiro of Aquitaine (390–455), who lived in Marseilles, found himself in the role of an apologist for Augustine, responding to questions of those troubled that Augustine's doctrine of grace compromised the place of human agency in salvation. But when Cassian's monks at the monastery of Saint Victor in Marseilles read *On Correction and Grace*, their suspicion that Augustine was advocating a fatalism akin to that preached by the Manichees prompted Prosper of Aquitaine to write Augustine and lay out objections of the monks of Saint Victor.

They agreed with Augustine that since all sinned in Adam, no one is saved by his own works but the grace of God that is the source of new birth. "Yet," they claimed, "all men without exception are offered the reconciliation that Christ merited by the mystery of his death, in such a manner that whosoever wish to come to faith and to receive baptism can be saved" (*Ep.* 225.3). This offer is entirely gratuitous, entirely prior to merit. They interpreted Paul's language of "the elect" to refer to those who God foreknew would choose the grace offered to them. Unlike Augustine's view that the call, though extended to many, was given in a manner effective only on the elect, for the monks of Marseilles, the call of God, who wills the salvation of all, is fairly extended to all. This call of grace is not irresistible but creates the possibility that all who receive the offer may repent and seek God's mercy. Moreover, all who have received the grace of regeneration in baptism have been given the ability to persevere in grace. Thus, all the baptized have the genuine hope of salvation. This position, the monks held, acknowledges the role of human agency and the necessity of grace for salvation; thereby they provided an alternative to Augustinian fatalism that "takes away from sinners an incentive for conversion and gives the pious occasion for lukewarmness. For both of them, exertion becomes superfluous if neither diligence can save a reprobate nor negligence ruin an elect" (*Ep.* 225.3). Decades later in 474, to counter an extreme doctrine of predestination being preached by a Gallic priest named Lucidus, Faustus of Riez (405–490) would argue a similar position. Influenced by both Cassian and Rufinus's Latin translation of Origen's *On First Principles*, Faustus sought to navigate his way between the Scylla of Pelagius's exaggerated optimism in the power of the human will and the Charybdis of Augustinian fatalism (*Grat.* 1.1). In his *On Grace*, he insisted that, while the human will was incapable of turning to God apart from grace, such grace was available to all.

Upon receipt of Prosper's account of the Gallic reaction to *On Correction and Grace*, Augustine responded with *On the Predestination of the Saints* (428–429). After acknowledging that the monks of Saint Victor's view of the necessity of grace places them far from the Pelagians (*Praed.* 1.2), he goes straight to the point at the heart of his doctrine of election: the complete and utter gratuity of faith (*Praed.* 2.3). Contrary to his early view that faith lay within the individual's natural capacity, his eyes were opened to the necessity of seeing faith as a gift of grace, espoused by Cyprian, who quoted 1 Corinthians 4:7: "we must boast in nothing, since nothing is our own" (*Praed.* 3.7). If, however, faith were from us and merited the pardon and sanctification of grace, then it would not be a gift at all but would be our own. Explaining Paul's words, "Not that we ourselves are sufficient as from ourselves but our sufficiency is from God" (2 Cor 3:15), Augustine says that, since belief is a response to some prior thought, our belief is necessarily dependent on God's call that conveys the hope of salvation (*Praed.* 2.5). Moreover, since the call is efficacious only in those who have received the grace that moves the will to respond to the call in faith, belief itself is a gift. Therefore, the merit of faith is a gift of God's mercy that enables the believer to live faithfully to the end (*Praed.* 3.7). The logic of grace requires that, contrary to his earlier view that the elect are chosen because God foreknows their belief and faithfulness, election is entirely a free choice of God's will. Because God predestines grace, it is truly a gift given with no regard to an individual's subsequent merit (*Praed.* 10.19). The reason why some are elected and others not lies veiled in God's inscrutable ways (Rom 11:23) that combine the mercy of liberation with the truth of just judgment (*Praed.* 6.11). For if election were based on God's foreknowledge, the cause of the election would be the individual's response. Therefore, the elect are foreknown not because God foresees the merit of their faith but because God knows what he has willed, that is, what he has predestined. Therefore, the believer has nothing in himself of which he can be proud. In fact, her recognition that faith is entirely a gift of God and that her election—if she is indeed among the elect—is independent of her merit is itself a remedy for the sin of pride (*Praed.* 4.8).

The critical divide between Cassian's monks and Augustine concerned scriptural passages that appeared to support a broader extension of grace to all people. Augustine's first response was to reaffirm the irresistibility of grace. Appealing to Jesus's words, "Everyone who has heard the Father and has learned, comes to me" (John 6:45), he argues that since no one who has truly heard the Father's call has failed to come to Christ, then the call given to the elect is irresistible (*Praed.* 8.13). Grace removes the hardness of the heart that keeps one from God so that all to whom grace is given ultimately, even if there has been a period of resistance, turn back to God. Thus, Augustine concludes that had God given grace to all so as to hear the Father's call, then all would necessarily have responded to the call. However, since obviously not all have returned to God in repentance and faith, not everyone has been given the grace to hear the Father. Yet if John 6:45 is read alongside Isaiah's declaration, "They all shall be taught by God" (54:13), then from Cassian's perspective, the conclusion is that, though the Father calls all, not all have heard and responded. Therefore, the call creates the possibility of repentance and faith but is not irresistible. Augustine responds that Isaiah 54:13 does not mean that the Father teaches all. Rather, all that are taught by the Father, namely the elect, hear and come to Christ (*Praed.* 8.14). Cassian's other key prooftext was 1 Timothy 2:4: "He wills all to be saved and to come to the knowledge of truth." Augustine takes advantage of a textual variant; his Latin text adds "these" (*hos*) to "all": "All these he wills to be saved" (*Praed.* 8.14). Thus, "all" does not mean "all people" but "all those whom God teaches."[13] He concludes therefore that God extends his irresistible teaching to all the elect whom alone he wills to be saved.

13. See William J. Collinge in *Four Anti-Pelagian Writings*, Fathers of the Church 86 (Washington, DC: Catholic University of America Press, 1992), 236 n. 94.

More important for the monks of Saint Victor's monastery than the question of human agency in the soul's conversion was the question of the believer's agency in her further journey to the city of God. What role did the believer's efforts play in her perseverance to the end? In a companion piece to *On the Predestination of the Saints* entitled *On the Gift of Perseverance*, Augustine returned to a theme from his earlier dispute with the Pelagians: God not only turns the will but gives the increase. Appealing to Cyprian's treatise on the Lord's Prayer, he argues that the petition, "Lead us not into temptation," presupposes that spiritual perseverance is the gift of grace. It also presupposes that perseverance is not something the believer can do on her own but only through the gift of grace. Why else would she pray to ask God to deliver her from evil and temptation if she could do it on her own? If the believer is delivered from temptation, Augustine explains, then she will not turn away from God but will persevere in her pilgrim's journey (*Persev.* 5.9). The grace of perseverance is necessary to complete the work of conversion. Such grace, however, cannot be gained or lost. It is intrinsic to election. God gives to all the elect the grace necessary to persevere. The paradigm case is Jesus. As Christ was predestined to persevere in the wilderness and during his passion, so too are the elect who are members of his body. Paraphrasing Psalm 79:18–19, Augustine concludes, "So when the hand of God is upon [Christ] that we not depart from God, then the work of God (for that indeed is what is meant by the hand) reaches indeed to us. . . . Therefore, it is by God's hand, not our own, that we do not desert God" (*Persev.* 7.14). Unlike Cassian, for whom grace creates only the possibility of repentance and perseverance in faith and love necessary for salvation, the grace of election for Augustine creates not the mere possibility but the absolute surety of perseverance unto salvation.

This account of election and perseverance raised two thorny problems. If both conversion and perseverance are entirely the work of the unmerited and irrevocable grace of election, how does one explain those who confess Christ and appear to turn to God in repentance and faith but do not persevere? Did God give the grace of justification but not the grace of perseverance? Second, if perseverance is an unconditional gift of election, then why do believers need to pray for it? Augustine does not give a clear answer to either question, yet in *On the Gift of Perseverance* and earlier works, he gestures toward fuller answers. With respect to the latter, Jesus's teaching of the Lord's Prayer is an exhortation reminding the believer not to be proud and trust in his own strength but to trust in grace as the means of her perseverance.

Augustine's arguments, however, provided only cold comfort to Christians, like the monks at Saint Victor's, who had made sacrifices in turning to Christ but who daily prayed for deliverance from temptation to the very sins for which they invariably would be asking forgiveness the next day. In spite of their baptism and ascetic rigors, they were painfully aware of how far from perfection they still were.

Such seemingly fruitless struggles might, within Augustine's scheme, be taken as a sign that they were not among the elect and that all their efforts were futile. Their sacrifices were for naught. They had no agency on this spiritual journey. It had already been preordained by the unfathomable will of God. Moreover, Augustine's view of grace and election raised serious questions about the efficacy of baptism. For the elect, baptism conveyed the grace that cleansed and healed the soul and was a sign of the grace of perseverance that would see them through to their arrival in the heavenly commonwealth. However, for the vast majority of the baptized, who were not of the elect, baptism was not a sign of hope but only an empty sacrament, mere water and words without the sustaining power of grace.

Disagreement over these issues in one iteration or other continued for another hundred years. The official resolution of dispute came at the Second Council of Orange (July 529). Called by Caesarius, the bishop of Arles, the most important episcopal see in Gaul, the purpose of the gathering was to counter the attack on Caesarius leveled against him by an assembly of Gallic bishops the previous year at Valence. The bishops at Valence, who rejected Augustine's mature doctrine of predestination, criticized Caesarius's view of grace, which was strongly influenced by Augustine but also reflected the practical pastoral need for moral exhortation by clergy and for moral agency by his parishioners. The canons of Orange were largely Caesarius's adaptation of a series of doctrinal statements or *capitula* from Felix IV of Rome. They were also informed by Prosper of Aquitaine's anthology of Augustine's doctrinal sayings, *Book of Sentences Extracted from the Works of Saint Augustine* (*Liber sententiarum ex operibus sancti Augustini delibatarum*).

The doctrine of grace and human agency that emerged from Orange was a softened Augustinianism: Before baptism, it is all the unilateral work of God, but with the reception of baptism, the Christian empowered by the healing illumination of grace regained that freedom of the will to cleave to God and persevere in grace. Orange repeated the rejection of Pelagius that prevailed for over a hundred years. Based on Romans 5:12, the second canon rejected Pelagius's view that Adam's sin affected him alone and instead affirms that the death of the body and soul are due to sin passed from Adam to the whole human race. Canon 5 repudiated the Pelagian claim that the beginning of faith as well as its increase lie within the individual's natural capacity. Quoting Philippians 1:6 and Ephesians 2:8, it affirmed that faith is the work of grace given as a gift through the inspiration of the Holy Spirit who turns the soul from unbelief to belief and ungodliness to holiness. For, as explained in canon 13, the freedom that was lost by man's sin can only be restored by the one who gave humanity *libertas* in the beginning. Moreover, canon 18 articulates the Augustinian conviction that God's conferral of grace is entirely prior to merit and that human beings are incapable of performing any meritorious works apart from the assistance of grace. Indeed, not only does God work good in the believer, but there is no good in the believer's actions for which God is not responsible (canon 20). Here the council sides with Augustine and rejects any possible intimation by Cassian that God's grace is a response to an incipient faith on the part of the would-be believer (cf. *Coll.* 13.11.5).

At the same time, however, the council qualified Augustine's view of election and grace that gave greater significance to the believer's agency after baptism. In its conclusion, the council expressly stated that, although perseverance (*fortitudo*) is the work of the love of God poured into the heart by the Spirit (canon 17), "having received grace through baptism, all baptized persons are capable and ought [*possint et debeant*], if they desire to labor faithfully, to perform with the aid and cooperation of Christ what is of essential importance in regard to the salvation of their soul." Here the council gives the pastoral reassurance, which Cassian's monks so wanted, that baptism confers on all initiates the grace necessary to persevere and attain eternal life. Thus, while the baptized remain dependent upon grace to merit salvation, they have received the ability to seek that grace. When God frees the will from captivity to sin, the believer's moral and spiritual agency are restored, and with it the responsibility to participate in the Church's instituted means of grace that enables them to endure to the end. This repudiates the later Augustinian view that not all the baptized have the hope of salvation. Indeed, if a believer turns away from the faith, the responsibility for that fatal transgression lies with the lapsed believer, not with God (*Persev.* 8.19). Any suggestion that God predestines anyone to commit evil—presumably including apostasy—the council roundly condemned.

Conclusion

The fifth- and sixth-century debates around grace and free will have, with the introduction of Augustine's doctrines of original sin and predestination, moved the Church's reflection on human responsibility for sin and agency in the process of salvation far from battles of second- and third-century Christians against pagan, gnostic, and Manichaean fatalism. No longer is it assumed that humanity's rational faculties in themselves confer freedom of choice and that the will is naturally able to respond to the call of God to repentance and holiness. Disagreement about the relationship of foreknowledge and predestination in the West would continue well into the High Middle Ages and the early modern period, as did arguments about the infallible results of divine aid and human freedom. Argument and counterargument were launched between Luther and Erasmus, Dominicans and Jesuits, Calvinists and Arminians, John Wesley and George Whitefield. Yet these disputes were implicitly or explicitly governed by the grammar of grace that came out of the Second Council of Orange. The question was not whether human nature needed to be healed by grace or whether grace was needed to fulfill the demands of righteousness. What remains is the persistent theological challenge of imagining the cooperative relationship between the will liberated by grace and the ongoing aid of grace by which the Christian lives into a life of holiness.

Bibliography

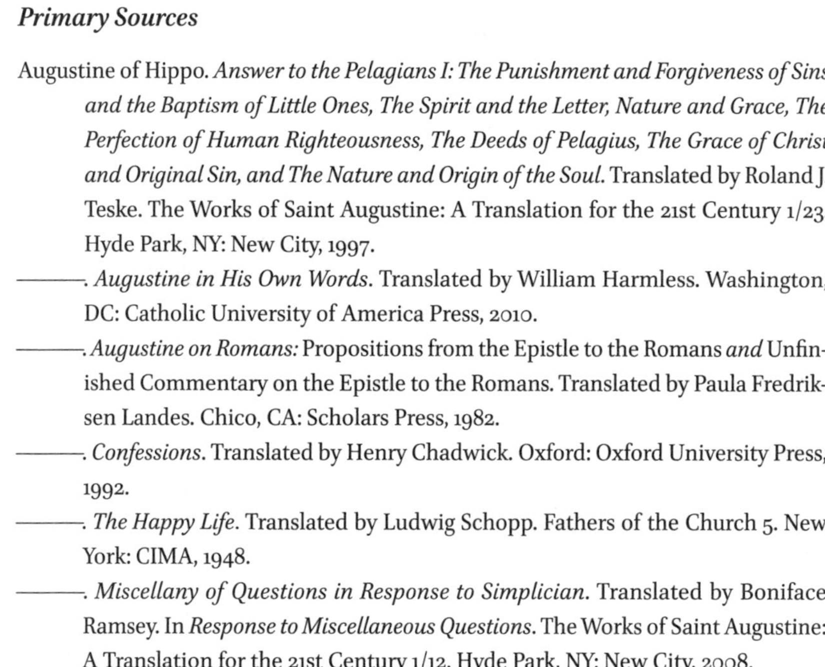

Primary Sources

Augustine of Hippo. *Answer to the Pelagians I: The Punishment and Forgiveness of Sins and the Baptism of Little Ones, The Spirit and the Letter, Nature and Grace, The Perfection of Human Righteousness, The Deeds of Pelagius, The Grace of Christ and Original Sin, and The Nature and Origin of the Soul.* Translated by Roland J. Teske. The Works of Saint Augustine: A Translation for the 21st Century 1/23. Hyde Park, NY: New City, 1997.

———. *Augustine in His Own Words*. Translated by William Harmless. Washington, DC: Catholic University of America Press, 2010.

———. *Augustine on Romans:* Propositions from the Epistle to the Romans *and* Unfinished Commentary on the Epistle to the Romans. Translated by Paula Fredriksen Landes. Chico, CA: Scholars Press, 1982.

———. *Confessions*. Translated by Henry Chadwick. Oxford: Oxford University Press, 1992.

———. *The Happy Life*. Translated by Ludwig Schopp. Fathers of the Church 5. New York: CIMA, 1948.

———. *Miscellany of Questions in Response to Simplician*. Translated by Boniface Ramsey. In *Response to Miscellaneous Questions*. The Works of Saint Augustine: A Translation for the 21st Century 1/12. Hyde Park, NY: New City, 2008.

———. *On True Religion*. Translated by Edmund Hill. In *On Christian Belief*. The Works of Saint Augustine: A Translation for the 21st Century 1/8. Hyde Park, NY: New City, 2005.

———. *The Teacher, The Free Choice of the Will, Grace and Free Will*. Translated by Robert P. Russell. Fathers of the Church 59. Washington, DC: Catholic University of America Press, 1968.

Bardaisan of Edessa. *The Book of the Laws of Countries: Dialogue on Fate of Bardaisan of Edessa*. Translated by H. J. W. Drijvers. Assen: Van Gorcum, 1965.

Canons of the Second Council of Orange. Translated by F. H. Woods. Oxford: Thornton, 1882.

The Gnostic Scriptures. Translated by Bentley Layton. Garden City, NY: Doubleday, 1987.

Gregory of Nyssa. *Life of Moses*. Translated by Abraham J. Malherbe and Everett Ferguson. New York: Paulist, 1978.

———. *On the Making of Man*. *NPNF* 2/5.

Irenaeus of Lyons. *Against Heresies*. *ANF* 1.

John Cassian. *The Conferences*. Translated by Boniface Ramsey. Ancient Christian Writers. New York: Paulist, 1997.

Origen. *On First Principles*. Translated by Henri DeLubac. Gloucester, MA: Peter Smith, 1973.

Prosper of Aquitaine. Epistle 225 in *Defense of St. Augustine*. Translated by P. De Letter. Ancient Christian Writers. Westminster, MD: Newman, 1963.

Secondary Sources

BeDuhn, Jason David. *Augustine's Manichaean Dilemma*. Vol. 1. *Conversion and Apostasy, 373–388 C.E.* Philadelphia: University of Pennsylvania Press, 2010.

———. *Augustine's Manichaean Dilemma*. Vol. 2. *Making a "Catholic" Self, 388–401 C.E.* Philadelphia: University of Pennsylvania Press, 2013.

Behr, John. *Irenaeus of Lyons: Identifying Christianity*. Oxford: Oxford University Press, 2013.

Brown, Peter. *Augustine of Hippo: A Biography*. Berkeley: University of California Press, 2000.

Burns, Patout. *The Development of Augustine's Doctrine of Operative Grace*. Paris: Études Augustiniennes, 1980.

Cary, Phillip. *Inner Grace: Augustine in the Traditions of Plato and Paul*. New York: Oxford University Press, 2008.

Harrison, Carol. *Rethinking Augustine's Early Theology: An Argument for Continuity*. New York: Oxford University Press, 2006.

Kantzer Komline, Han-Luen. *Augustine on the Will: A Theological Account*. New York: Oxford University Press, 2020.

Lewis, Nicola Denzey. *Cosmology and Fate in Gnosticism and Graeco-Roman Antiquity*. Leiden: Brill, 2013.

Pagels, Elaine. *The Gnostic Paul: Gnostic Exegesis of the Pauline Letters*. Philadelphia: Fortress, 1975.

Stewart, Columba. *Cassian the Monk*. New York: Oxford University Press, 1998.

Weaver, Rebecca Harden. *Divine Grace and Human Agency: A Study of the Semi-Pelagian Controversy*. Patristic Monograph Series 15. Macon, GA: Mercer University Press, 1996.

13

Partaking of the Divine Nature

Deification, Monasticism, and Mysticism

"If you would be perfect, go, sell what you possess and give to the poor, and you will have treasure in heaven" (Matt 19:21). These words of Jesus to the rich young ruler were being read when a young Egyptian from an affluent, land-owning family entered the cathedral in Alexandria. Curiously, he had just been meditating, as he walked to church, on how the apostles had left everything to follow Jesus and how the early Christian community described in Acts surrendered their possessions to be sold for the relief of the poor. This, he judged, could be no mere coincidence; rather, Christ was speaking these words specifically to him in that moment. They were an invitation to a different life (*Vit. Ant.* 2). The young man was Antony who, together with Paul the Hermit, came to be canonized in the Coptic Church as the fathers of the Egyptian monastic movement.

After entrusting his younger sister to a community of female virgins, Antony sold his family's estate and donated its proceeds to assist the poor. Then he sought some old hermits to teach him the way of the solitary life (*Vit. Ant.* 3). As Athanasius records in his *Life of Antony*, there were other Christians who, seeking perfection, entered into a life of voluntary poverty and the self-discipline of solitude. What made Antony different was that whereas these zealous souls lived on the outskirts of their village, none before had ventured into the utterly remote region of "the great desert." This radical pursuit of perfection through a life of rigorous self-denial made Antony a beloved, charismatic figure. But it was his retreat to the high desert that captured the imagination of many who sought to imitate his radical withdrawal from the world. As Antony's example attracted more and more men and women, the desert that was home to the demons was, as Athanasius narrates it, transformed into a city of monks. Antony and Paul were not the first monks, nor did the soil of the Egyptian desert become the seedbed whence all Christian monasticism sprung. About the same time, an independent ascetic tradition developed in Syria, which only later (sixth century) was influenced by the

Egyptian coenobitical monasticism of Pachomius. Nevertheless, the stories and sayings of Antony preserved in his vita and the *Apophthegmata* or *Sayings of the Deserts Fathers and Mothers* made him an exemplar of the monastic life in early Christian communities in Asia and Europe as well as North Africa.

Athanasius composed this vita not simply to provide an account of Antony's monastic practices but as a guide for those who would imitate his devotion. More than that, Athanasius used the life of Antony to illustrate the theological claim that was at the core of his christological argument against the subordinationists (e.g., the Eusebians and the Homoians) whom he called "Arians"—namely, that the Father sent his divine Son to reveal in human flesh the image of God that through him human beings might become partakers of his impassible and incorruptible divinity. Antony was the fulfillment of Athanasius's famous dictum describing the purpose of the incarnation: "God became human that human beings might become god" (*Inc.* 54; *Vit. Ant.* 74). He was proof of the Son's consubstantial relationship with the Father and the power of that reality to transform and perfect human nature—a transformation that in time Gregory of Nazianzus would refer to using the neologism *theōsis* or "deification."

The *Askēsis* of the Christian Gnostic

Nearly a hundred years before the Egyptian desert became populated by Christian monks, Clement of Alexandria appropriated notions of self-control or moderation (*sōphrosynē*) from various philosophical schools as a way of training Christians in the way of perfection. In Plato's account of Socrates's deathbed dialogue with his students before he drank the hemlock, Plato depicts the great teacher consoling his grieving students by saying that death, far from being an occasion for sorrow, was the culmination of the philosophical life (*Phaed.* 64d–65e). His argument for the immortality of the soul rested on a theory of the soul's preexistence before its fall into the body and with it into the realm of the senses. Since the material world experienced through the bodily senses was a place of suffering, deception, and irrational passions, Socrates explained that the goal of philosophy was the liberation of the soul from the body so that at death the soul would be pure and able to return to the heavenly, intelligible realm. The beginning of this separation was effected by the life of moderation (*Phaed.* 67c–68e). It prepared the soul by lessening its attachment to the sensible pleasures so that its higher, rational faculties might turn toward the contemplation of the true, perfect, and eternal realities. By exercising its contemplative faculty, the soul would attain a likeness to the divine so that it might break the cycles of embodiment and return to its proper abode in heaven.

Socrates's claim rests on the assumption that the soul takes on a likeness to the objects of its thought. Consequently, the more a soul has been preoccupied with things of the senses, the more like the material world it has become. Since at its death the soul returns to the place that is like itself (*Phaed.* 81a), the soul of the sensual person is reincarnated, dragged back down by the accretion of its "bodily element" into yet another life of imprisonment in the fleshly mire of the senses (*Phaed.* 81c–d). The philosopher does not experience this same fate. To begin with, the philosopher's simple life of moderation frees her soul from worldly demands and concerns so that she may devote herself to the life of contemplation—that is, the pursuit of what is true and real and eternal. Thus, the life of moderation minimizes the philosopher's attachment to sensual pleasures. At the same time, through the contemplative life of dialectic, the philosopher glimpses with the eye of her mind the intelligible, divine realities and so becomes conformed to the divine objects of its contemplation. Freed from the taint of bodily things, the soul's rational nature is both purged of sensual desires and reacquires a likeness to the intelligible things of heaven. Thus, the purified soul is freed to return to its heavenly point of origin (*Phaed.* 80b–82c).

Clement appropriated Plato's identification of human flourishing (*eudaimonia*) with attaining "the greatest possible likeness to God" (*Theaet.* 176b) to describe the philosophical character of a saint's life (*Strom.* 2.19.99). For the Christian, like the woman with the issue of blood, desires to touch "the fringes of God's power" (*Strom* 1.9.44) in order to be healed and become like God. Although his writings are peppered—somewhat pedantically at times—with allusions to Classical Greek literature and philosophy, Clement was of the view that pagan philosophy, though valuable for training the mind to distinguish the true and the false (*Strom.* 1.6.33–35) and to teach reverence for God (*Strom.* 1.4.27), was only a preparation for the higher truth contained in the special revelation of God's Logos in the incarnation (*Strom.* 1.1.17). Through the soul's consent in faith to the Logos (*Strom.* 2.2.8), the Christian became what Clement calls the "true gnostic" because she possesses the correct knowledge of God. Thus, he distinguished Christians of the "Great Church" from gnostic sects. Unlike certain of the *gnōstikoi* who held that the saving knowledge is accessible only to an elect few, Clement maintained that truth was available to all. Yet that wisdom could be attained only by those who labored to prepare themselves to receive the knowledge of God who lies beyond the grasp of human wisdom. Created beings may draw near to the uncreated God only by exercising the power of God himself given by the Holy Spirit through whom they "search out the deep places" (*Strom.* 2.2.7). Even then, God reveals himself to the Christian, as he did to Moses, in utter darkness "of unapproachable, imageless, intellectual concepts relating to ultimate reality" (*Strom.* 2.2.6). When Isaiah declares that "heaven is [God's] throne" (66:1), he is not naming a dwelling place; rather, he speaks of God's transcendence that is not contained in any space or located in time. Clement's "imageless concepts" are apophatic in nature because they mark a move away from an idolatrous piety dependent on physical images constructed by the human imagination that render God a fellow creature.

In his *Exhortation to the Greeks*, Clement declares that Christ is the true Orpheus whose song is the animating force of the new creation freeing gentiles from the petrifying effects of idolatry. Commenting on John the Baptist's declaration, "God from these stones is able to raise up children to Abraham" (Luke 3:8), Clement explains that the "stones" are a figure of the gentiles who worship stone idols. Not only has the idolatry turned them into beasts dominated by vicious passions, but they have also lost that capacity for wisdom and right understanding proper to creatures made in the image of the Logos. Clement explains that "the great dullness and hardness" of the gentiles "whose hearts are petrified against the truth" results from "trust in stone" (*Protr.* 1). By worshiping the lifeless and senseless idols of stone, the gentiles become ossified in their thinking because they think of God in material terms (*Protr.* 4). They find it hard to move from a materialistic conception of God to thinking of the deity as immaterial and incorporeal. The new song of the Logos reveals the order of creation and the transcendent otherness of the Creator, thereby freeing idolatrous gentiles from stone-like senselessness. In this true *gnōsis*, the believer's mind can be restored to its proper rational nature by being conformed to the divine Logos.

Although Clement affirms the importance of contemplation (*theōria*), conforming one's mind to the Logos, attaining the likeness of God entails an active imitation of Christ. Quoting Deuteronomy 13:4, "Walk behind the Lord your God and keep my commandments," Clement says that the believer possesses the "likeness" to God by "following" God. For, like Moses, likeness to God comes from seeing not God's face but his "backside," which is a figure for God's activities. Therefore, the "likeness" to God is manifest in the believer's imitation of her heavenly Father's mercy (*Strom.* 2.19.100). By imitating God's works, the Christian receives the "likeness" of God impressed upon her intellect (*Strom.* 2.19.102). The embodiment of the divine image, which could best serve as the example for the Christian gnostic to be imitated, was that of the holy martyrs. Indeed, martyrdom was, as Robin Darling Young has shown, an "imitative sacrifice," which, like the Eucharist, was a confession of Christian identity. But whereas the Eucharist was a confession symbolic and private within the community of the baptized, martyrdom was a public display or "spectacle"—what Origen called a "confession before men" (*Mart.* 35)—that bore witness to the martyr's identity by her literal embodiment of Christ's passion.

In addition to imitating God's works of beneficence, growing in likeness to God requires the soul's purification through the *askēsis* of moderation. Drawing on Socrates's description of the philosophical life as a preparation for death (cf. *Phaedr.* 81a), Clement understands moderation as "practicing dying" because it reorders the soul by replacing unworthy desires with "desires limited by nature, and not bursting natural boundaries into excess or running contrary to nature which is the seed of sin" (*Strom.* 2.20.109). Such moderation of desires, Clement explains, is what the apostle Paul meant when he spoke of putting on "the whole armor of God to be able to stand against the wiles of the devil" (Eph 6:11). For when one exhibits moderation, one is not governed by either pleasure or pain to which most people are enslaved. Rather, the moderate person's appetites are controlled by reason that directs them to natural goods. She is no longer a slave to the love of pleasure that nails the soul to the body (Plato, *Laws* 1.633; *Strom.* 2.20.108). Therefore, she is able to govern herself rather than being driven by impulses to seek what is easy and pleasing and avoid what is difficult and painful. This disposition, what Clement calls *apatheia*, is certainly necessary if one is to imitate the single-minded faithfulness of the martyrs in "following" Christ, the impassible God made flesh (*Strom.* 3.5.40; 3.7.57).

Athanasius's *Life of Antony*: Divinization in the Desert

In his *On the Incarnation*, Athanasius builds his Christology around the Word's condescension to human form to restore the image of God compromised by sin. As we have already seen,[1] Athanasius explains that the Logos, the Father's agent of creation, fashioned humanity after his image, imparting to the first people a share in his rational nature. Such rationality would allow them to transcend the realm of the senses and contemplate the invisible God (*Inc.* 4). For through such contemplation, they might participate in God's immutable nature and so be rendered incorruptible and immortal. Thus, they would be able to overcome their inherent creaturely instability and attain a godlike stasis (*Inc.* 3). Yet, in sin, their souls turned from contemplating God, and they fell into death and decay. Therefore, the Logos, who fashioned them after his image in the beginning, needed to refashion the divine image in them that humanity might once again know God and, through the contemplation of God the Father revealed in his Son, might once again participate in his divinity and so be delivered from death (*Inc.* 5). In the *Life of Antony*, Athanasius illustrates the character of such divinization. When a group of visitors knock down the door of Antony's fortress hermitage, they beheld the man himself not having changed physically since he was last seen twenty years before. His body showed no scars from battling the demons. Nor had he either

1. See chapter 5, p. 195.

grown fat from his sedentary existence or emaciated from fasting. The stasis of his bodily equilibrium was the result of a similar equilibrium within his soul. For he was unmoved by the intrusion of the visitors, becoming neither angry nor elated. Rather, his soul possessed the tranquility of one completely "guided by reason and steadfast in that which accords with nature" (*Vit. Ant.* 14). Thus, through his contemplative *askēsis*, Antony's mind had become conformed to the Logos and thus a partaker of the Logos's immutable divinity.

The *askēsis* of Antony's solitary life entailed a disciplining of the body through a simple diet, fasting, sleep deprivation, sexual abstinence, and so on. But, as William Harmless has observed, Antony's training, like that of all athletes, is primarily a disciplining of the mind and secondarily a training of the body. The desert was the training ground for both. The high desert was a place of withdrawal from the world—that is, the cities along the Nile, where one was distracted by the pursuit of mundane needs and worldly pleasures that surpassed the needs of nature. In the city, one could be self-forgetful and inattentive to the state of one's soul. Alone in the desert, one could not flee oneself. There were no escapist diversions of the city. In the desert, one could not evade confronting one's own unholy thoughts and desires. Thus, life in the desert both exposed the monk to himself and trained him to master himself.

While the desert was at one level a place of solitude ideal for self-examination, it was also a place of the demonic. Because the desert was the realm of the demons and wild beasts, it represented the world after the fall. The garden of paradise planted and ordered by the Logos was replaced by a barren wasteland populated by irrational beings. It was the antithesis of the city of God. Yet as these Logos-bearing monks made the desert their home and their voices chanting the psalms were carried on the wind filling its vast emptiness with the music of a divine choir (*Vit. Ant.* 44), the desert was being reclaimed by the Logos, and the forces hostile to the Logos were being expelled. Precisely because the desert was the domain of the demons, the desert was an ideal training ground for the mind in holiness. The demons, in effect, served as the monk's sparring partners.

The monk's struggle with the demons trained his mind in two ways. First, the demons exposed Antony's unholy desires by appearing to him as the incarnation of his passions in the form of a seductress or the likeness of something that aroused anger (*Vit. Ant.* 5–6). Thus, Antony was trained to recognize and resist the temptations to which he was most vulnerable. Second, battling the demons trained Antony's mind to see the world rightly. By taking the form of a terrifying wild beast, demons tested Antony's faith in Christ and the new creation inaugurated by his victory on the cross. In Athanasius's cosmology, demons were creatures of the air hovering between earth and heaven, thereby blocking the soul's ascent to God. Jesus, however, was on the cross lifted up into the air to do battle with the demons. By his victory over the demons, Jesus removed the demonic obstacle to the soul's ascent. Consequently, the demons have no objective power over human beings. The only power they had was to deceive people into thinking that they had power. By taking on the phantasmic image of a ferocious lion or bear, the demon tries to play upon Antony's fears—especially the fear of death. By striking terror in Antony's soul, the demon tries to deceive him into believing that the demon possesses a real power over him he in fact does not have. Antony, however, overcomes the demonic apparition by invoking the name of Jesus and making the sign of the cross. Immediately the demon withdraws. For Antony has spoken the name of the one whose true power vanquished the demons. Signing himself with the cross—the sign of the demons' defeat—is Antony's confession of faith in the triumph of Christ's death, by which the demons are rendered impotent. In his struggles with the demons, therefore, Antony trains his mind to see through the illusions created by the demons and recognize the new cosmos that Christ's victory over the demons established. Thus, Antony is liberated from fear and worldly desires. Through such training, Antony acquires confidence both in his own capacity to resist temptation through the cultivation of virtue and in the faithfulness of God who will empower him to triumph over the world. For he affirms that, since "the kingdom of God is within you" (Luke 17:21), the life of virtue requires only that the monk wills to be virtuous and his intellect is ordered according to nature, that is, toward God (*Vit. Ant.* 20).

At the same time, the monk should be confident that he will overcome sinful desires, grudges, and resentments that haunt the soul, because God is his "coworker" (*Vit. Ant.* 19). In one episode early in Antony's withdrawal, he was locked in struggle with a host of demons who tormented his body and caused him great pain. Antony resists their torments by mocking them, "'If there were some power among you [pl.], it would have been enough for only one of you to come. But since the Lord has broken your strength, you attempt to terrify me by means of a mob; it is a mark of your weakness that you mimic the shape of irrational beasts. . . . For faith in our Lord is for us a seal and a wall of protection'" (*Vit. Ant.* 9). Then a beam of light penetrated a hole in the roof, and the demons fled, leaving Antony whole and free of pain. When Antony inquires why God did not come sooner, God replies, "I was here, Antony, but I waited to watch your struggle. And now, since you have persevered and were not defeated, I will be your helper forever" (*Vit. Ant.* 10).

The ascetic struggle with the demons in grounding the monk's mind in the knowledge of Christ's redemptive triumph also purifies his emotions. One of the central disciplines by which the monks battle the demons—especially in times of weakness when one is most vulnerable—was the recitation of the Psalms (*Ep. Marcell.* 32). The book of Psalms is unique, Athanasius writes, because unlike narratives in which the reader is a passive observer, in the Psalms, especially in a liturgical context, the reader is an active participant. The worshiper, like an actor, takes on the words of the psalmist. They become her words, her emotions. Indeed, the Psalms are a mirror that reveals the worshiper's emotions to herself (*Ep. Marcell.* 12). Because the Psalms give voice to virtually every imaginable emotion, the one who recites the Psalms is confronted by those passions. The Psalms do not allow the repression of emotions, but being confronted by them enables the Christian to be brought both to repentance and hope. Moreover, the recitation of the Psalms contributes to the soul's deification through the healing of its passions (*Ep. Marcell.* 10). For the words of the psalmist are often Christ's words or prophecies about Christ (*Ep. Marcell.* 11). Therefore, when the monk recites the words of or about Christ, the monk's thoughts become conformed to Christ. Since Christ not only assumed human nature with its weakness and the accompanying emotions but purified them, so the monk is sanctified in the recitation of the Psalms as his emotions are healed and re-formed in the image of Jesus's own sanctified emotions (*Ep. Marcell.* 13).

Although Antony began his life in the desert as a hermit, his attraction of other seekers of perfection led to the creation of communities. Far from being a private blessing attained by individual monks, deification as the telos of the monastic life had a corporate dimension as well. To put it another way, salvation from sin and the passion was sought and achieved in community.

Redefining Perfection: Gregory of Nyssa on Mystical Ascent

By the second half of the fourth century, the monasticism of Egypt and Syria was having a profound influence on a number of major theological voices of the century. Macrina, the older sister of Basil the Great and Gregory of Nyssa, had converted their family estate in Annisa (Asia Minor) into an ascetic community for women. Basil and Gregory of Nazianzus had traveled widely throughout the Near East visiting ascetic communities and monasteries of Syria, Palestine, and Egypt. From these they derived models for their own communities of ascetics in Cappadocia. In the Latin West, Ambrose of Milan's earliest writings encouraged young women to pursue, as had his sister Marcellina, the life of virginity consecrated to Christ.

Although the practices and wisdom expressed in the sayings of the desert fathers and mothers that were collected, as well as the vitae that praised the lives of famous ascetics, rested upon certain implicit theological assumptions, there was a need for someone to offer a more systematized account of ascetic practices that linked them with theological anthropology. In other words, given one's understanding of human nature, the ascetic life enabled Christians to pursue that perfection to which Christ called his followers and that is the end God ordained for human beings. Gregory of Nyssa offered a systematic theological rationale for the ascetic life lived out in Basil's communities. As we have already seen, Gregory of Nyssa's anthropology,[2] developed in the late 370s and early 380s, gave a developed account of human nature that would provide the foundation for later ascetic theologians. In *On Virginity*, Gregory was writing to Basil's monks, exhorting them to stay the course of the monastic life but not be proud of their virginity. At the outset of his encomium, he says that virginity is a movement toward purity of soul and holiness achieved by participating in God's holiness (*Virginit.* 1–2). Therefore, when the monks are tempted by thoughts of the pleasant life they left to join the monastery, they should remind themselves of the hardships and misery that accompany the life out in the world. These range from passions stimulated by worldly activities, including sex, that repeatedly disturb the mind to the unpleasant family obligations, including the pursuit of worldly honors to please parents and in-laws. At the same time, they should see virginity as a "mean" (*Virginit.* 5) between, on the one hand, disparaging the goods of marriage and, on the other hand, becoming overly attached to the world through indulgence in sexual pleasures (*Virginit.* 4). Moreover, virginity is not an end in itself and is not sufficient for salvation unless it is partnered with the other virtues, most of all humility and charity to one's fellow monks (*Virginit.* 17).

At the heart of Gregory's praise of monasticism is his concern that the soul's desires act like an adhesive bonding a person to the objects of her love. Since all people have from birth been oriented to the temporal, sensual goods rather than the eternal, intelligible goods of God, an ascetic regimen of self-denial, prayer, and contemplative study of Scripture served to break the adhesive bond of sensual desire and reorient the monk's love toward God. In these ascetic writings, Gregory already had a notion of the life of holiness as a movement to the good, "a striving after the better" (*An. res.* 6.12; Silvas, 208). In his later years, the nature of the movement toward the better would become a central theme in the account of Christian perfection he would develop in his monumental works *Life of Moses* and *Homilies on the Song of Songs*.

Written as a guide either specifically for leaders of religious communities or more generally as a text to be read in monasteries, *Life of Moses* ostensibly is a response to a request for an outline of the perfect life (*teleios bios*). He begins with an ironic disavowal of the possibility of fulfilling the request. "It is beyond my power," Gregory explains, "to encompass perfection in my treatise. . . . Many great men . . . will admit that for them such an accomplishment is unattainable" (*Mos.* 1.3). Far from being a stock confession of his unworthiness to treat such a

2. See chapter 3, pp. 91–98.

lofty subject, these words make a bolder claim about the nature of Christian virtue. Gregory proceeds then to redefine perfection. In classical thought, especially that of Aristotle, the perfection of a thing is determined by some boundary or limit or telos. Physical movement is always toward a thing's end or telos; in the case of fire, for example, the flame moves upward toward the ethereal realm of the heavens whence it came. The telos sets a limit on movement; for fire ceases to move once it has reached the heavens because this is its proper place in the cosmos. There is no other place it could or should go. It has perfectly actualized all its potential for movement; so its perfection is absolute rest or stasis. Similarly, the perfection of a cubit is its exact measurement—nothing more, nothing less. Even in Aristotle's view of virtue, the golden mean is a bounded perfection because it is the appropriate action in the particular circumstances, bounded by the extremes of deficiency or excess.

For Gregory, however, perfection in virtue is fundamentally different because it is understood in terms of the rational creature's relationship with the Creator. Since God is absolute goodness, there is no defect in God that would limit his goodness. There being no limit to God's goodness, God's goodness is infinite (*Mos.* 1.7). Gregory had already begun working out his theory of divine infinity a decade earlier in *Against Eunomius*. Infinity is a corollary of divine simplicity; in Plotinian terms, God is the unconditioned condition of all else. Since God is not a creature, he is not conditioned by time (i.e., he did not come into being) or form or matter; therefore, he is eternal and unbounded or infinite. God, the great I AM, is eternal Being who abides in infinite and perfect stasis. By contrast, human beings, as creatures, came into being from nothing; therefore, change and movement—passing from one state to another—is inherent to their creaturely nature. Human beings are, Gregory says, "always coming to birth" (*Mos.* 2.3). For rational creatures, who were made for contemplative participation in the divine nature, it is a process of continually being formed and reformed through newer visions of the wonders of the divine nature. Consequently, continual re-creation through eternal participation in God means growing into greater and greater degrees of likeness to God. Yet since God is infinite and human beings are constantly in motion, there is no state of permanent rest for them.

This view of human nature, Gregory recognized, has two significant implications for the life of virtue. First, since human beings are constantly changing, they are necessarily changing either for the better or for the worse. That is, they are either moving toward the good or away from it. There is no standing still, no resting on one's laurels. "Just as the end of life is the beginning of death, so also stopping in the race of virtue marks the beginning of the race of evil" (*Mos.* 1.6). Therefore, the monk can never become complacent, thinking that holiness is something he *possesses*, but must persevere, making daily progress in the ascetic life. Second, since God's perfect goodness is infinite and unbounded, finite rational creatures will never attain a perfect likeness to God's perfection. However, as much as the soul advances in virtue (however much it embodies God's goodness), there will always be greater degrees of virtue (of likeness to God) into which the soul may grow. Human virtue will never be identical with God's virtue. Therefore, perfection is, as Gregory said in his opening disclaimer, unattainable (*Mos.* 1.9).

If perfection were absolutely unattainable, however, then Jesus's exhortation, "Be perfect even as your heavenly Father is perfect," would appear to be an impossible and unreasonable commandment. What then is the perfection Jesus expects of his followers? Gregory's solution was to distinguish between divine perfection and human perfection. Whereas God's perfection lies in his nature as *eternal Being*, man's perfection lies in his creaturely nature as *ceaseless becoming*. Therefore, perfection for human beings is not a stasis in virtue but an unceasing growth in virtue and godlikeness. *This* is an attainable perfection. Gregory finds supporting evidence in the life of Paul. Even though Paul had attained such purity of heart as to merit being drawn up into the third heaven and given the beatific vision, Paul denies that he is "already perfect [*teteleiōmai*]." Instead, he writes, "but one thing I do, forgetting what lies behind and straining forward [*epekteinomenos*] to what lies ahead, I press on toward the goal for the prize of the upward call of God in Christ Jesus" (Phil 3:12–15). On Gregory's reading, Paul recognizes that divine perfection is beyond his grasp. Yet his own life provides a model of the life of virtue as a "straining forward to what lies ahead." This verse from Philippians is one of the most frequently quoted passages of Scripture in Gregory's descriptions of the Christian life. Paul's perfection lies in ceaselessly seeking to be more conformed to Christ's perfection. Therefore, following Paul's example, Gregory exhorts his readers, "We should show great diligence not to fall away from the perfection which is attainable but to acquire as much as is possible: To that extent let us make progress within the realm of what we seek. For the perfection of human nature consists perhaps in its very growth in goodness" (*Mos.* 1.10). In other words, Gregory used the theological grammar that distinguished the Creator as *eternal Being* from the rational creature as *ceaseless becoming*, to redefine the character of perfection and with it his concept of the virtuous life. This definition of moral perfection as "straining forward"—a signature theme of Gregory's often referred to as *epektasis* or epectasy—is the soul's eternal movement into God's infinite being.

Gregory returns to the theme of Paul as an example of Christian perfection in his treatise from the same time, *On Perfection*. In baptism, one receives the name "Christian" and so is made to share Christ's name. Therefore, to understand what Christian perfection is, the baptized ought to embody all the virtues contained in the name "Christian." He then points to Paul's life as the guide that will teach its meaning. For the apostle "led the way by what he did to the sort of character one named by Christ ought to have . . . [and] so visibly imitated Christ that he displayed his own Master formed in himself" (*Perf.* 175; Greer, 25). Thus, Paul could say, "I have been crucified with Christ; it is no longer I who live, but Christ who lives in me" (Gal 2:20). As central to Gregory's theory of perfection as imitation or mimesis is, the life of perfection is not simply imitating Jesus's moral example. Rather, such imitation is possible in the Christian, as with Paul, because in praying to Christ and naming him "wisdom" and "power," the soul draws Christ into itself, making Christ the object and therefore the content of its thoughts. Then the mind is conformed to Christ because Christ is in the mind, and his divine power and wisdom within him. Thus, Christ's wisdom and power shape the mind so that the Christian receives the ability to live into her baptismal name by embodying the virtues of the one whose name she bears (*Perf.* 183; Greer, 29).

Gregory's *Homilies on the Song of Songs* expand his earlier insight into the implication of the metaphysical gap between the Creator and the creature for his understanding of the soul's participation in God. Whereas in *On the Soul and Resurrection* Gregory argued that eschatologically when God shall be "all and in all" the soul's desire for God will be changed into enjoyment,[3] by the time Gregory writes *Life of Moses* and *Homilies on the Song of Songs*, he recognized that the eschatological union with God does not negate the metaphysical difference between the Creator and the creature. God remains eternal and infinite Being, and human beings, for all their individual progress in the good, remain finite and eternally mutable creatures. Consequently, although the soul that abides in eternal fellowship with God the "all in all" is never separated from God, the essence of the infinite deity remains beyond human comprehension. An eternal gap exists between what the mind already knows of God and what there is yet to be revealed. Therefore, the soul will always lack a full knowledge of the divine. Since the soul's eschatological vision of God, though the source of supreme blessedness, is incomplete, the soul will desire to behold even more of God's yet unseen glory. In other words, the soul's enjoyment of God, rather than bringing an end of desire, serves only to arouse deeper desire for the divine. This insight he first articulated in the prologue to *Life of Moses*: "Since, then, those who know what is good by nature desire participation in it, and since this good has no limit, the participant's desire itself necessarily has no stopping place but stretches out with the limitless" (*Mos.* 1.7). The rational soul's love of God is essentially an erotic longing aroused by God's disclosure of his beauty in order to draw the soul eternally into the infinite wonders of God's goodness. Such is the love represented in Solomon's Song by the figures of the bride and the bridegroom.

Gregory describes the dynamics of the soul's erotic ascent into the divine as a dialectic of purgation and illumination that produces an ever-greater union with

3. See chapter 14, p. 519.

the God in whom the soul lives, and moves, and has its being. As narrated in Gregory's allegorical reading of Exodus, a precondition for the ascent is represented by Moses's fleeing Egypt—representing the errors of profane philosophy (killing the Egyptian) and the disquiet of conflicts with heretics (the dispute between the two Israelites)—to settle into the solitary life (i.e., single-minded devotion) in the wilderness (*Mos.* 2.18–19). Freed from such distractions, the mind quiet and peaceful is able to receive the rays of divine illumination, which, like the light from the burning bush on the slopes of Mount Horeb, draw the soul to God. This light of truth comes to the soul through Christ, who, like the burning bush, is the divine light manifest in a material form (*Mos.* 2.20–21). Illumination by the light of Christ is itself purgative. For as the voice from the bush instructed Moses to take off his sandals because he was standing on holy ground, Christ calls the soul to repent and put off the "dead and earthly coverings of skins," that is, the life of sin and corruption (*Mos.* 2.22). In the moral purification of repentance, the soul is also purified intellectually in its thinking about the Creator-creature distinction. As when God gives Moses his name, I AM, the soul learns the difference between true being and nonbeing. God the Creator is the source of all life because he is life itself. He alone is self-subsisting being (*to aprosdeēs tōn ontōn*); that is, he is dependent on no other for his being. By contrast, creatures have only the appearance of being self-subsisting when in fact they are entirely dependent upon God for their being. Therefore, in contrast with God's true being, Gregory classifies all creatures as nonbeing (*to mē on*). This does not mean that they do not really exist—like phantoms of the imagination—but that they do not in themselves possess life (*Mos.* 2.23–25). Creatures live by way of participation (*metousia*) in the divine life that is outside of themselves, whereas God's being is not derived by participation in anything outside himself; God simply is. When God illumines the mind with the distinction between true being and nonbeing, the Christian realizes that God alone is the proper object of her desire (*monon orekton*). Since creatures lack true being, they, unlike God, are not able to give life itself or the perfect goods the soul truly desires; these are to be found in God alone. Since desire (*epithymia*) is the soul's principle of movement, this illumination has begun to purify not just the intellect but the soul's desires so that it may advance on the upward way undistracted and undeceived by those things that have only the appearance of goodness.

Although the Christian's thinking about the good has been purified by her understanding of the creature-Creator distinction, her thinking about the Creator still needs further purification. For there still remains the tendency to imagine God in creaturely terms. The language used to speak about God—even the names given to God in Scripture—draws upon analogies: light, bread, water, breath, and so on. Such metaphors are at best a diaphanous veil that both reveals and conceals the deity. If one is to have a right knowledge of God and make right use of biblical language, there is a further stage of purification she must undergo. She must "wash from her understanding every opinion derived from some preconception and . . . [from] sense perceptions" (*Mos.* 2.157). That highest level of purification is represented by the theophany on Mount Sinai. Even as Gregory of Nazianzus in his second theological oration compared theology to the ascent of Sinai (*Or.* 28.2), Gregory of Nyssa similarly writes, "The knowledge of God (*theologia*) is a mountain steep indeed and difficult to climb—the majority of people scarcely reach its base" (*Mos.* 2.158). Unlike the theophany at the burning bush in which God revealed himself as light, at Sinai's summit he reveals himself to Moses in darkness, which is the inner sanctuary (*adyton*) or heavenly dwelling place of God (*Mos.* 2.164). The dark cloud represents the paradoxical experience of apophatic illumination. Such contemplation of God is apophatic because it negates or purges from one's mind not only sensual images but even abstract concepts or ideas that the intellect normally uses to reason about the divine. Then the soul experiences illumination because it discovers that the "invisible and incomprehensible" deity is not really light or bread or water or breath or anything else. Moreover, because the concepts used by the intellect are products of a finite creaturely imagination, God's being does not correspond to any of these either. In the recognition of God's absolute transcendence of human categories of thought and speech, the soul "sees God"; for this "true knowledge [of God] . . . is the seeing that consists in not seeing" (*Mos.* 2.163). In other words, the soul is simultaneously illuminated and purified in its thinking about God because it "sees" what God is not. It sees that it cannot see and so is purged of the temptation to the hubris of heretics, such as the Eunomians, who presume to know the divine essence. Gregory recognizes that theology that is not first purified by the apophatic stage falls into the dilution of idolatry of thinking that concepts (*noēmata*) fashioned by the finite intellect of man can capture in words the infinite and incomprehensible God (*Mos.* 2.165).

Yet apophatic illumination is not the end. The mind's entry into the darkness of Sinai is not the experience of God's absence. God is no thing; but he is not nothing. Rather, in the darkness of God's incomprehensibility, the mind must reach out in a different way, faith. For Gregory, faith is the mind straining forward beyond the analytical and conceptual resources of reason (*dianoia*) to the God whose incomparable reality surpasses the grasp of the uncomprehending intellect. Faith is the mind's holy curiosity, which in discerning the presence of the God whom the intellect cannot comprehend, it, therefore, bridges the epistemic gap between the intellect and God. When Gregory summarizes Exodus's figural account of the soul's ascent, he writes, "in the impenetrable darkness draw near to God by your faith [*dia pisteōs*], and there are taught the mysteries of the tabernacle and the dignity of the priesthood" (*Mos.* 2.315). Similarly, in faith the bride reaches for her bridegroom to draw him into the bridal chamber (Song 3:4): "[having] passed by everything in the creation that is intelligible and left behind every conceptual approach," the bride declares, "I found the Beloved by faith and holding on by faith's grasp to the one I have found, I will not let go until he is within my chamber" (*Hom. Cant.* 6; Norris, 195).

The Christian who in faith has passed into the darkness of the cloud is not left speechless. Nor is her mind blank when she hears the word "God." For, now that her mind has been purified of simplistic, material ways for thinking about God, she is ready to understand rightly the significance of the images by which Scripture offers a positive account of the God who truly is. In the darkness of the inner sanctuary, the soul sees the tabernacle (*skēnē*) not made with hands, which was the archetype of the earthly temple. Gregory then enumerates the decorations of the earthly tabernacle—golden pillars with silver bases and capitals, intricately woven tapestries of many colors, braziers, and candle sticks—of which he says in conclusion, "What words could accurately describe it all?" (*Mos.* 2.172). The tabernacle is Christ, who in his divinity was not made with hands but through whom all the universe was made, including his own body, his earthly tabernacle (*Mos.* 2.174). Although Christ is described in Scripture with many names, "all names have equally fallen short of accurate description" (*Mos.* 2.176–177). Yet Christ, as the wisdom and power of God, both is the tabernacle that encompasses all of creation and takes creation as his tabernacle. As Gregory of Nazianzus (*Or.* 28.3) allegorizes Moses's beholding God's glory by standing in the rock (the incarnate Christ) and contemplating God's train (his works in creation), Gregory of Nyssa uses the same image to convey a similar point. Once the intellect has been purified with the knowledge of its absolute impotence to define the divine essence with any word or concept, it is then free to know rightly the incomprehensible God by contemplating the ineffable Word made flesh.

Gregory's shift from the darkness to the tabernacle marks a shift from the apophatic to the cataphatic, from the invisible and ineffable to the visible and intelligible. The imagery of bright and vivid colors used in the decoration of the earthly temple—the very antithesis of the cloud's blackness—signifies the innumerable, visible works (*energeiai*) expressed in the biblical names or concepts (*epinoiai*). For Gregory, therefore, the cataphatic and apophatic, far from being mutually exclusive, are mutually informing within a dialectic of purification and illumination. The apophatic purifies the mind, readying it for cataphatic illumination. Perhaps Gregory's greatest insight on this point is his recognition that the Scriptures' numerous, positive or cataphatic revelations about God's nature taken together are themselves apophatic. It is *apophasis* of superabundance rather than the *apophasis* of simple negation. In other words, all the biblical names for God denote *propria* or real attributes of the divine nature. However, none is sufficient to encompass the totality of

God's infinite being. Therefore, when the Christian begins making positive claims about God, she does not stop with one or two *epinoiai* but builds upon the list of names or attributes that came before. Yet each additional attribute is implicitly a negation of the previous attributes in the list. For in seeking "another way to put it," she recognizes the inadequacy of each of the previous names, individually and collectively, to give a fuller account of God. Gregory writes, "For this reason, the bride contrives all sorts of word-meanings but every expressive power . . . falls short and is exposed as being less than the truth. The great David himself often does the same sort of thing: calling the divinity by a thousand names and then confessing that he has fallen short of the truth" (*Hom. Cant.* 12; Norris, 377–79). The endless names of praise are summed up for Gregory in David's apophatic doxology: "How wonderful is your name in all the earth!" (Ps 8:1).

Systematizing Ascetic Theology: Evagrius and Apophatic Prayer

While Gregory of Nyssa provided an anthropological foundation underlying the asceticism practiced in his sister's and brother's communities, the speculative character of his thought did little to connect his monastic theology with the practical experiences of monks. This task was taken up by Evagrius Ponticus (345–399). The son of a country bishop in Pontus, Evagrius early on came under the influence of the Cappadocians. He was ordained a lector by Basil and then deacon by Gregory of Nazianzus (then bishop of Constantinople) under whom he served as archdeacon. Following a scandalous connection with the wife of a prominent governmental official, Evagrius left Constantinople for Jerusalem. There he was invited into the monastic community supported by Melania the Elder (350–410) at the Mount of Olives. Later he journeyed south to the monastic communities of the Nile Delta at Kellia and Scetis where he encountered the monastic luminaries Macarius the Egyptian, Macarius the Alexandrian, and John Cassian, who would transmit Evagrius's interpretations of the monastic life to the Latin West. The most important writings that articulate Evagrius's ascetic and theological vision are his trilogy: *Praktikos*, which explained how the soul was purified by the monastic life, *Gnōstikos*, which discussed the life of prayer made possible by ascetic discipline, and *Kephalaia Gnōstika*, which, strongly influenced by Origen's thought and likely written while in Constantinople before he visited the desert communities, laid out his theory of salvation history. Ultimately, his adherence to Origen's thought embroiled him in the Origenist controversy that began in 394 and ended a hundred fifty years later at the Second Council of Constantinople with the condemnation of Origen, Didymus the Blind, and Evagrius himself.

Evagrius's account of asceticism and the life of prayer rests upon his concept of deification. Although he does not employ the technical term *theōsis*, the content of the idea is explicit in his writing. Based on Psalm 81:6 (LXX), "I have said you are gods," he qualifies "gods" by saying that human beings are divine "by grace" through participation in God (*Ep. fid.* 9) through the Eucharist (*Ep. fid.* 14). For he interprets Jesus's high priestly prayer, "that they all may be one" (John 17:21), to mean that God will restore the primal unity of rational beings (*Ep. fid.* 25). Here we see Origen's influence on Evagrius, who also maintained a theory of the preexistence of rational beings. Originally, they existed in contemplative stillness in God. But due to "carelessness," they became active with movements that turned them away. The result was a fall into the state of multiplicity characteristic of a bodily existence (*KG* 1.65). When, however, Christ, who abides in the perfect unity of the Trinity, comes to dwell in each rational being, the rational being becomes a Christ and so shares Christ's unity with the Father and Spirit. Even as Gregory of Nyssa famously described Christ's humanity as a drop of vinegar swallowed up in the vast sea of his divinity, Evagrius employs a similar metaphor to speak about the deifying unity of humanity and God,

> If this visible sea (which is one in nature, color and taste), when many rivers of different taste join it, not only is not changed to their qualities, but instead easily changes them completely to its own nature, color and taste—how much more so the intelligible, infinite and immutable sea, that is, God the Father? . . . [So when] the minds return to him, he completely changes them to his own nature, color and taste: in his endless and inseparable unity, they will be one and no longer many, since they will be united and join to him. (*Ep. Mel.* 27)

Thus, eschatologically human beings are restored to their original, purely rational nature, while bodies are "destroyed" through sublation, that is, the elevation into a higher level of being. Then the distention of the present life that results from the binary of soul and body is completely negated (*KG* 2.77). This process of being united with all other rational creatures in God begins through the union with God through the present life of prayer.

The goal of the ascetic life was, for Evagrius, to produce theologians. Not theologians in the modern academic sense but as those possessed of the mystical knowledge of God (*gnōstikē*) through a life of formless prayer. "If you are a theologian," Evagrius famously wrote, "you truly pray. If you truly pray, you are a theologian" (*Or.* 60). In contrast with *oikonomia*, which was knowledge of God's activities in history revealed in Scripture, *theologia* was discourse about God's nature itself. The knowledge possessed by the theologian, for Evagrius, was not discursive knowledge but the intuitive insight gleaned by prayer. For the essence of prayer was intimate intercourse with God (*Or.* 3) akin to the immediate communion with God enjoyed by the angels. Alluding to Jesus's promise that those found worthy in the resurrection shall be like angels (Luke 20:36), Evagrius says that the monk-theologian is "another angel [*isangelos*]" (*Or.* 113)—that is, one who attains the experience of God that the saints shall enjoy in the eschaton. Indeed, he speaks of prayer as "that country" where the purified soul ever abides in the presence of God (*Or.* 61).

Prayer, as practiced by the theologian, is not an episodic activity but a virtuous mental habit (*Or.* 150) or "state of mind [*katastasis*]" (*Skemm.* 27). By speaking of prayer as a state of mind, Evagrius meant that the mind was continuously conscious of standing before God. Like the angels who are made dazzling because they reflect the glory of the God in whose presence they eternally stand, the theologian's mind is similarly illuminated such that he or she can fulfill the role of *abba* or *amma* in the monastic community and lead other monks to God. For the theologian has attained true knowledge of God because his very manner of life is what Evagrius calls "true prayer" or "spiritual prayer." "True prayer" is the source of true knowledge because it is a formless or imageless mode of prayer (*Or.* 117). The difference between prayer that employs images and formless prayer is the difference between the analogy and the definition. The analogy does not say what a thing is but simply what it is *like*; the definition says what a thing *is*. Because God is incorporeal spirit, God is uncircumscribed and so has no form. Therefore, to pray using images is to think about God not as God actually is; it is to reduce the formless God to the status of a form-bound creature. Images, therefore, provide at best an imperfect analogy for thinking about God, and at worst, they are a barrier between the monk and the true, mystical knowledge of God. Therefore, the one who would know God truly and immediately must strip away all images in order to experience God in his formless otherness. Evagrius went so far as to say that prayer should be wordless. Words and even abstract concepts—what he calls "intelligible things"—do not belong to "the perfect place of God," because, while God is simple, words and concepts belong to the creaturely realm of multiplicity (*Or.* 57, 70). Even the holy names of God used in Scripture are incomplete, at most giving only a fragmentary glimpse of the divine. Informed by Cappadocian doctrines of divine simplicity and language, Evagrius maintains that in order to attain true knowledge of God, the monk must transcend the many, partial descriptions of God offered by words and instead encounter him in his perfect oneness. This is the theological basis of apophatic prayer.

Such knowledge of God is possible, Evagrius teaches, because the mind is made to experience the ubiquitous presence of God. In a state of pure nature, the mind would simply be continually reaching out for God and receiving from God the condescending disclosure of his presence (*Or.* 58). In other words, the human mind is hardwired for true prayer. The only reason most people do not enjoy this uninterrupted God-consciousness is that their minds are occupied with worldly matters and unholy passions. Indeed, for Evagrius, as Martin Laird has said, if only one could free her mind from the clutter of worldly distractions and desires, she would intuitively apprehend God's presence. How, therefore, can the mind be purified in order to attain the pure contemplation of God in imageless prayer? This is the task of ascetic discipline (*praktikē*).

The goal of this *praktikē* or *askēsis* was achieving *apatheia*. Drawn from Stoic moral philosophy, *apatheia* originally meant freedom from errant judgments that were the cause of *pathē* or psychic disturbances—for example, fear, lust, rage—contrary to virtue. Evagrius spoke of the passions as *logismoi* or "trains of thought" not rightly governed by the Logos. Vestiges of human fallenness, the *logismoi* were both impure thoughts that intruded upon a monk's prayer as well as the source of friction and conflict in the monastery as in the world outside its walls. For Evagrius, these passions were ultimately forms of ignorance of the Logos who reveals the patterns or ideals (*logoi*) on which all things were modeled. Through them one was able to know oneself and the world as God intended. Without the light of the Logos, human beings are ignorant of their own identity and the world in which they must live. In the place of knowledge from the Logos, human actions are guided by self-serving prejudices that are born of irrational *logismoi* and that create disordered relations between oneself and the world. The solution to the problem of *the* passions was the "ascetic struggle."

For Evagrius, the alternative to the psychic disturbances of the passions was *apatheia*, which he described as a calmness of soul (*Prak.* 52) given by God (*Prak.* 66) and cultivated through the "ascetic struggle" of the monastic life. The monk could achieve *apatheia* through obedience to God's commandments and the use of ascetic disciplines to cultivate a justly ordered and virtuous soul free of vice. Within Evagrius's anthropology, the soul was composed of three faculties (the rational, irascible, and concupiscible). The demons blocked the soul's ascent to God in prayer largely by suggesting unholy "trains of thought." An image of a former romantic interest might arouse lust in the concupiscible faculty as would the recollection of an injury or insult stir emotions of anger or resentment in the irascible faculty (*Prak.* 11). The more subtle insinuations by the demons would arouse in the rational part of the soul pride in having overcome the passions of the soul's lower faculties. Equally dangerous was the vice of vainglory that desired the praise of people more than divine approbation.

The *Praktikos*'s catalogue of vices provided monks with the self-awareness of both their vulnerabilities and the demonic stratagems that would play on those weaknesses. Such self-awareness enabled them to be sensitive to the subtle demonic intrusions upon their thoughts so that the monk would be equipped to parry the demon's blow. Three of the chief defenses against demons were singing the psalms, praying, and giving alms. Singing psalms provided encouraging words and sensually soothing music to counter the passion, especially anger burning in the "savage breast" (*Prak.* 15). The cooling effect of the psalms prepared the soul for prayer in which one in humility could call upon God's assistance (*Or.* 83, 85). Then in prayer the monk invokes the aid of the Holy Spirit who "takes compassion on our weakness, and though we are impure, he often comes to visit us. If he should find our spirit praying to him out of love for the truth he then descends upon it, and dispels the whole army of thoughts and reasonings that beset it" (*Or.* 62). Under the illumination of the Spirit, the demonically inspired phantasms are dispelled, and the monk discovers the tranquility of *apatheia* "seeing its own light"—that is, knowing its own luminous nature rightly as God intended even in the face of worldly temptations (*Prak.* 64). Through these disciplines, the monk who attains *apatheia* is prepared for formless contemplation of God because he has been trained to overcome the sensual phantasms that habituate the mind to thinking about all reality in material terms. Thus, the mind is prepared to think about the immaterial God without the use of material images.

Finally, giving alms to the poor counters demonic temptations, especially those of anger or resentment that are so contrary to the disposition of charity (*Prak.* 20). For, in giving to the poor, the monk sees himself and, more importantly, sees the poor person as he is, one like himself, bearing the image of God. Indeed, here the goal of *apatheia* is achieved. As theology is the goal of contemplation or true prayer, love (*agapē*) is the telos of the ascetic life (*Prak.* 81). Charity is the corollary of *apatheia*. If the monk has achieved the tranquility of not being moved to vices by demonic images, then his soul's faculties are governed by love. In other words, the purity of mind necessary for true prayer is nothing other than the proper love of God, neighbor, and all created goods. The monk who is ruled by *agapē* rises above even that most subtle of vices, vainglory, because, in the true knowledge of God, he realizes that the approval of God, not other human beings, is alone worthy of pursuit. In such freedom, the monk's mind has achieved that original purity by which it may live in a state of ceaseless prayer. This is the highest stage of the spiritual life, which Evagrius refers to as *gnōstikē*—that is, the apophatic contemplation of the formless God that deifies the mind and allows the monk to enter into the blessedness of God's own peace.

Pseudo-Dionysius and Divine *Erōs*

A century later, Origen's and Gregory's adaptation of Platonic *erōs* to describe a dynamic process of *theōsis* was transformed and made even more radical by a Byzantine known only by his pseudonym, Dionysius. This nom de plume was taken from the Acts of the Apostles (17:34), which speaks of a follower of Paul and first bishop of Athens as Dionysius the Areopagite. Pseudo-Dionysius—sometimes called Pseudo-Denys—drew directly on the Neo-Platonist Proclus's account of the erotically motivated overflow or emanation of being from the One to describe God's condescending, redemptive love (*erōs pronoētikos*). Although neither the Septuagint nor the New Testament uses the word *erōs*, likely to avoid confusing Christian love with the crude, sensual connotations of *erōs* in Greek mythology, Christians, as early as Origen in his homilies on the Song of Songs, recognized the erotic character of the soul's longing for God. Similarly, Dionysius uses *erōs* as the logic underlying the economy from creation to eschaton all while incorporating it into a strongly apophatic understanding of God.

His apophatic theology begins with the assumption that God is utterly simple. "In him there is no change, decline, deterioration, or variation. He is unalloyed, immaterial, totally simple [*haploustaton*], self-sufficient, subject to neither growth nor diminution.... He is defined by his singularity [*epitēdeios*] and his sameness" (*Div. nom.* 912b–c). Simplicity (*haplotēs*) had, since Plotinus, become the way to speak of God's transcendence, his radical otherness, and his self-sufficiency or aseity. As the first cause of all things, God is, as Plotinus put it, the unconditioned condition of all things. Therefore, God transcends all categories or predicates applied to creatures. God is "being" inasmuch as he alone truly exists because he is self-subsisting (*Div. nom.* 856b). Yet he is not one being among other beings; rather, as the cause of the being in which all existent things participate, God is "beyond being" (*Div. nom.* 588b, 824a). Confessing God's transcendence or otherness, however, raises an essential epistemological problem noted by Plato in his creation myth, *Timaeus*: "That which has come into existence must necessarily have come into existence by reason of some cause. Now *to discover* the maker and father of this universe is a difficult undertaking [but] having found him, *to speak* about him is impossible" (28c). If God is unlike any creature, then how is theology possible? How can names taken from human speech about creatures properly be applied to God? Dionysius's treatise *Divine Names* is essentially a Christian attempt to answer this question.

Precisely because God is "beyond being" and therefore beyond all earthly analogue, theology for Dionysius, as for Gregory of Nyssa, requires that the mind live within the tension between affirmation and negation, the back and forth between *kataphasis* and *apophasis*. Dionysius begins his *Mystical Theology* by invoking God's assistance in the soul's ascent: "O Trinity! Higher than any being, any divinity, any goodness! . . . Lead us up beyond unknowing and light, up to the farthest, highest peak of mystic scripture." Then, however, he concludes the invocation with the paradoxical description of the mind's experience of contemplation of

Scripture where "amid the wholly unsensed and unseen [the mysteries of God's Word] completely fill our sightless minds with treasures beyond all beauty" (*Myst. theol.* 997a–b). Moreover, even as the Cappadocians opposed Eunomius's reduction of God's essence to the negative term "ingenerate," Dionysius does not reduce theology merely to the act of negation. Therefore, his apophaticism seeks to rise above all human concepts—even negative descriptions. "There is no speaking of [the divine nature]," Dionysius writes, "Darkness and light, error, and truth—it is none of these. It is beyond assertion and denial. We make assertions and denial of what is next to it, but never of it, for it is both beyond every assertion, being perfect and unique cause of all things, and, by virtue of its preeminently, simple and absolute nature, free of every limitation, beyond every limitation; it is also beyond every denial" (*Myst. theol.* 1048b). And as Gregory of Nyssa described Moses's contemplating the tabernacle not made with hands that lies within the cloud of unknowing, Dionysius likewise compares the Christian's contemplation of God to that of Moses who did not behold God face-to-face but contemplated God "where he dwells" (*Myst. theol.* 1000d). The back-and-forth between seeing and unseeing, knowing and unknowing, in *Divine Names* takes as its starting point Paul's description of his own preaching, which depended "not on the plausible words of human wisdom but in the demonstration of the power granted by the Spirit" (1 Cor 2:4). That is, the Spirit conferred on the authors of Scripture a revelation of God "in a manner surpassing speech and knowledge" so that believers might attain "a union superior to anything available to us by way of our abilities and activities in the realm of discourse or of intellect" (*Div. nom.* 585b).

Taking this "scriptural rule" as the methodological assumption of *Divine Names*, Dionysius unfolds his theology by analyzing the meaning of the names given to God in Scripture (*Div. nom.* 588a). For, in the power of the Spirit, the divine names in Scripture act as a heavenly ray of light that descends from God upon the mind of the believer, filling her with reverent awe and raising her thoughts to God's heavenly splendor. This heavenly ray is the divinizing *erōs* of God by which God draws the soul upward into the perfection of union with himself (*Div. nom.* 700b–c).

All the biblical names he enumerates are bracketed by two primary names, "the Good" and "the One." For together they name God as both the *archē* or beginning and the telos or end of all things. God is "the Good" because he is the source of the being and goodness of all (Gen 1). God is "the One" because he is the single source whence come all things and thus is the source of unity by which the many creatures exist not in chaos but as ordered cosmos. God is also "the Good" and "the Beautiful" because his goodness is that end for which all things yearn and thus "bids all things to itself . . . and gathers everything into itself" (*Div. nom.* 701c). Therefore, God is also "the One" teleologically because he is the source of the harmonic unity into which God joins all things when they are eschatologically drawn together in him (*Div. nom.* 980c). Indeed, God as "the One" is the perfect "Good" because God as "the One" is he to whom all shall be united eschatologically and in whom all individual creatures within the order of the cosmos are already united to each other. In this way, Dionysius demonstrates the unity of God's creative and redemptive activities, both of which are expressions of and governed by *erōs*. The all self-sufficient God creates out of an ecstatic love. Following Plato's description in *Timaeus* (30a) of creation as the expression of God's self-diffusing goodness, Dionysius says that God creates out of a love for his own goodness:

> The divine longing [*ho theios erōs*] is Good seeking good for the sake of the good. That yearning which creates all the goodness of the world preexisted superabundantly [*kath' hyperbolēn*] within the good and did not allow it to remain without issue. It stirred him to use the abundance of his powers in the production of the world. (*Div. nom.* 708b)

Far from hoarding his goodness in a miserly way, God naturally desires to share the very goodness that is the object of his love. Out of his natural munificence, he fashions creatures to be the recipients of his goodness. Therefore, creation itself is an expression of both God's love of his own goodness and his generosity. It is the ecstatic outpouring of God's goodness in the form of beings who possess a likeness to their Creator in that they are capable of enjoying the Good as God himself does. That is, their likeness to God is their ability to imitate God's self-love. Sharing in God's goodness predisposes creatures to desire God as "the Good." Thus, the creature's eschatological return to God the Good is a mirror image of God's ecstatic fashioning of creation. Even as creation is the outward movement of God motivated by love for his goodness, the redemption of creation is the movement of the creature back to God motivated by the very love for God's goodness that was the impetus for God's creative movement in the beginning. He speaks of this process by using Origen's and Gregory's language of restoration or *apokatastasis*.[4] Thus, Dionysius explains the Platonic *exitus-reditus* model as governed by divine love for "the Good."

Although all of creation is naturally disposed to seek what is good, it is God who effects the return by his condescension to creation both through the heavenly rays' descending through the heavenly hierarchy of the angelic host and through the sending of the Son and Spirit. For Dionysius, Christ's *kenōsis* or self-emptying in the incarnation is the ultimate form of God's ecstatic love. In other words, the very ecstatic love that produced creation in the beginning is the same ecstatic love with which God perfects creation by drawing it back into unity with himself.

4. See chapter 14, pp. 528–33.

Herein lies the logic behind Dionysius's attributing *erōs* to God. Since, according to the Platonic understanding of *erōs*, erotic love was born of lack or deficiency, it seems an unfitting, indeed impossible, description for the love of God who is entirely self-sufficient and lacks nothing. Yet within Dionysius's *exitus-reditus* motif, what God loved was his own goodness that had gone out from him in creation. Nevertheless, this going out did not deprive God of his goodness; therefore, God's aseity was not compromised. Still, God's love was erotic in the sense that, within the economy of salvation, God's love, which reached out to creation, was a longing for his own goodness in creation and for what was his own to return and be reunited with him. Thus, the very love by which creation yearned to return to God was an image of the very love by which God descended to redeem and perfect creation. Therefore, Dionysius envisions the culmination of his plan of deification chiefly in terms of the union of creation with God or *henōsis*. God fulfills his goal of making his creatures participants in his divine nature and enjoying the blessedness of union with him through arousing in them the same ecstatic love in which God desired to create the world in the first place.

The soul's apophatic ascent into unity with God is central to *theōsis*. For the purging of false impressions of God that treat the divine as a being among beings purifies the mind and makes it conformed to the simplicity of God. From contemplating the brilliant beauty of God's dwelling place (cataphatic), the soul descends into darkness (apophatic) where words fall short and in humility the mind rests in silence (*Div. nom.* 1033b–c). This silence is not the experience of nothing; on the contrary, human voices become still because they "will finally be *at one* with him who is indescribable" (*Myst. theol.* 1033c). Whereas in the present the mind has used concepts to reach beyond the ontological gap between creatures and the transcendent God, eschatologically such categories and concepts will be unnecessary when the soul abides in the presence of the God that envelops the soul within its blazing light (*Div. nom.* 1.4). In union with God, the "All and in All," the mind will no longer need words or concepts to rise above the creaturely things that are not God (*Myst. theol.* 1033c–d; *Div. nom.* 648c). This eschatological union is the ultimate display of God's omnipotence by which God binds all things together in himself and sustains their union with himself and each other by creating a shared yearning for God (*Div. nom.* 937a). This union is not an absorption into God in which all particularity is negated. Rather, the many creatures exist in an unconfused union that preserves in each its distinctive reflection of the divine goodness—that is, each existing perfectly as God intended and eternally following the inherent motion that providence ordained for each nature and each individual (*Div. nom.* 952c–d). United in the One who is the principle of unity, all creatures, therefore, experience the peace of harmonious coexistence effected by the One's gift of his divine *erōs*.

Maximus the Confessor

Although Pseudo-Dionysius recognized the importance of the incarnation in his doctrine of *theōsis*, he gestured toward rather than offered a developed account of Christ's role in this salvation scheme. Writing a century later, Maximus the Confessor rectifies this deficiency by offering a grand, cosmic narrative that places Christ at its very beginning and end. As Paul Blowers has put it, for Maximus the divinizing work of God in the incarnation is "the christocentric plot of creation." The incarnation, especially at its climax in Christ's passion and resurrection, reveals the saving knowledge of God's plan for creation that is the source of hope and even joy amid the "ascetic struggle" of the present life. For the incarnation in its totality is "the divine sacrifice underlying the fabric of the cosmos" (*Theol. oec.* 1.66). Maximus's Neo-Chalcedonian understanding of the union of creature and uncreated deity in the single hypostasis of the incarnate Logos provided a model for understanding God's ordained telos for creation; this union is "at once the blessed end for which all things are ordained . . . [and] the divine purpose conceived before the beginning of created beings . . . the preconceived goal for which everything exists" (*Quaest. Thal.* 60). For in the hypostatic union, the Logos fulfills the goal of the cosmic drama in which all things are united in himself by bridging the cosmic divides—between uncreated and created, intelligible and sensible, heavenly and earthly, paradise and the present world, and male and female—that have separated humanity from God and human beings from one another (*Amb.* 41, 1305a). In other words, the *henōsis* that is the narrative's climax is but the actualization of the unity of all things implicit in the Logos in the beginning. Indeed, the creation finds its perfection in the recapitulation of creation's primal unity in the Logos in whom all things hold together. Such recapitulation in which the dividing walls of fallen creation are torn down in the incarnation is a form of re-creation in which Christ, the Creator-Logos, fashions "a fresh institution" of natures (*Amb.* 41, 1313a).

The process of rational creatures' deification results from their participation in the Logos through the life of ascetic struggle and contemplation. In *Difficulties* 10, Maximus refutes the misinterpretation of Gregory of Nazianzus that asserted that philosophical contemplation, that is, dialectic, was sufficient to achieve union with God without ascetic struggle. Maximus explains that the holy life by which one reflects the righteousness of the Logos and without which one cannot attain salvation requires that the *movements* of the body, as well as the mind, conform to the Logos (*Amb.* 10, 1108b). The contemplation (*theōria*) of the Logos rightly orders the movement of soul and body because the Logos contains within himself the *logoi* that are God's creative intentions for all beings. Ascetic struggle is, for Maximus, the mind's resistance to deception of pleasure and the movements of the flesh and its restoration of humanity's natural movements toward God. Through monastic disciplines, the monk's mental and bodily movements come in time to conform to the proper movements God intended for human beings from eternity. The virtues necessary for the ascetic struggle "raise the mind—mind now free and pure of any motion around any existing thing and at rest in its own natural activity—to God, so that in this way it is wholly gathered to God and made wholly worthy through the Spirit of being united with the whole Godhead" (*Amb.* 10, 1113a–b).

The *logoi* are not identical with Plato's forms (*eidē*) or models (*paradeigmata*) of universal natures after which the world was fashioned. Rather, for Maximus, because God eternally intended creation as the outward expression of his goodness, God willed not only the essence (*ousia, physis*) distinctive of each species of creature (*logos physeōs*) but also each individual creature (*hypostasis*) with its distinctive characteristics (*tropoi hyparxeōs*) or ways of embodying the universal. Since the *logoi* abide in the Creator-Logos, who is the wisdom and power of God, their actualization as concrete individuals means that creation is an incarnation—figuratively speaking—of the Logos. Indeed, the Logos's immanent or providential governance of creation's actualization of his will is through the divine *energeiai* associated with each of the *logoi*. One metaphor Maximus uses to illustrate the relationship of the Logos and the *logoi* is that of a book. The universe is the book whose author, the Logos, composed with words, that is, the *logoi*. The book of the cosmos is autobiographical in nature; for the Logos himself is the content of creation (*Amb.* 10, 1128d–29a). Creatures are distinguished from the perfect and absolute rest (*stasis*) of eternal deity by coming into being and therefore by movement (*kinēsis*). Therefore, Maximus speaks of the essential differences between the *logoi* in terms of their particular types of movements. In moral or ethical terms, this means that the life of virtue is engaging in those movements proper to human nature as rational, embodied beings, namely the particular movements that contribute to the soul's ultimate movement toward union with God. However, because of the sinful condition of humanity, which Maximus describes by using Paul's language of "flesh" (e.g., Rom 7–8; Gal 5:15), the mind is deceived by sensual pleasure such that the mind and body's movements are disordered, inclined to the transitory and sensual rather than the eternal and divine Good (*Amb.* 10, 1109b–c).

To break the unholy, habitual movements of "the flesh," the monk must know the divinely intended pattern of movements. These he apprehends through contemplating the *logoi* revealed in the incarnate Logos. As the union of creature and God, the incarnate Christ reveals the goal of all natural movements (*Quaest. Thal.* 60) and the character of deified creaturely movements. For since the Logos contains within himself all the *logoi* from the beginning (*Amb.* 7, 1081a), Jesus, who as the incarnate Logos did not suffer the confusion of fallen humanity's gnomic will, manifests the natural movements God intended for human existence (*Opusc.* 3, 48d, 53c)—what Maximus calls "well-being" (*Amb.* 10, 1116a–b). In this way, he is the recapitulation of the movements of the first Adam now perfectly conformed to the will of God. Therefore, the Christian comes to the knowledge of the *logoi* by contemplating Jesus's movements narrated in Scripture—movements in which the divine *energeia* is actualized (*Amb.* 7, 1097b–d). Through *askēsis*, the soul's practical reason reforms the movements of its body, ordering them to its knowledge of the *logoi* through contemplation of the Logos (*Amb.* 10, 1109b). The incarnation is the primary object of contemplation because the Creator-Logos descends to human flesh in order to reveal the *logoi* in himself as parents might condescend to "play" with their children (*Amb.* 71, 1413a–1416c). For in play, the parent enters into the limited world that lies within the child's scope of understanding and imagination. As such, the world of play is not the real world but the world of the child's imagination. Yet a child's play—whether caring for a baby doll or locked in combat against an imaginary foe—is an image of the real world in which the child will live as an adult. So too, in the incarnation, Christ participates in the world of the present age that falls short of the reality of the world in the age to come. At the same time, through the play-like enigmas of his parables, Christ trains his immature sisters and brothers to imagine the true cosmos that they shall inhabit in the age to come. While the incarnate Logos is the object of contemplation, the act of contemplation is not, for Maximus, simply exercising the faculties of one's contemplative intellect. Rather, it is possible only through the illumination of the Spirit. He compares the experience of contemplation to that of John the Baptist who, full of the Spirit, discerned—even in the darkness of his mother Elizabeth's womb—the presence of the incarnate Logos in Mary's womb (*Amb.* 6, 1068a–b).

Above all, it is the incarnate Logos's revelation of the divine beauty reflected in the unity of the *logoi* that divinizes the rational soul. In contemplating the narrative of the theophany on the Mount of Transfiguration (Matt 17:1–9), the monk becomes like the disciples who ascended the mountain with Jesus. For in contemplating the image of Jesus's brilliantly luminous face and clothes, the monk receives a vision of transformative unity of divinity and creature. His body is lit up, and the light of Jesus's divinity—a brilliance that transcends the intellect's comprehension (*Amb.* 10, 1128a)—radiates from his body, rendering it a luminous image of the Father's glory. At the same time, the monk discerns that Jesus's dazzlingly white garments are themselves a symbol both of Scripture itself through which the Logos reveals God's wisdom and of the clarity with which the saints shall behold Christ—the unity of all things in him—in the eschaton (*Amb.* 10, 1128b). Jesus's transcendent, divine beauty manifest in his transfiguration deifies the soul by arousing in its appetitive faculty a love for God's goodness that mirrors God's transcendent love for his goodness in the unity of the cosmos. This attraction to the beauty of Christ's divinity draws the monk closer into union with the Logos, whose beauty is manifest in the monk's virtuous life. For as the monk is enraptured with the divine beauty, the movements of his mind and body are governed by a rightly ordered love for God—virtuous movements that reflect a conformity with the *logoi* (*Amb.* 10, 1113b). Abiding in the Logos's unifying love is "well-being" (*Amb.* 10, 1116a–b; 1204a–b)—that is, not mere passive participation in being that all creatures have but existence that actively participates in God's goodness through conformity to the motions of the *logoi*. In this way, Maximus is able to rehabilitate Evagrius's adaptation of Origen in his account of the unity of the rational beings by placing Evagrius's thought within the logic of a Neo-Chalcedonian Christology.

Maximus explains the deifying power of love and its connection with the Logos in an early letter of pastoral guidance to John the Cubicularius and his fellow courtiers who sought his spiritual counsel. Love (*agapē*) is the highest degree of godlikeness (*Ep.* 2, 396a); for it is the source, the goal, and highest expression of God's goodness (*Ep.* 396a). Because God is one, his love unites lovers to each other in their common orientation toward God (*Ep.* 2, 397b). *Agapē* is the principle of unity; it is a single-minded inclination toward God that eliminates the divisive inclinations—the private, self-serving inclinations of self-love—and so "unites the torn fragments of nature" (*Ep.* 2, 404a). Maximus goes on to explain the relationship between deifying love and the ascetic struggle of all followers of the Logos. The disciplines of ascetic struggle allow the love of God to grow because *askēsis* curbs the pleasure-seeking inclinations by which the devil turns one's love from God, and by extension from the collective good of the whole creation, to the narrow love of oneself—that is, the seeking of private goods that serves only to promote fragmentation in which equal regard for one's neighbors (*Ep.* 2, 400a) is replaced by tyranny that uses the neighbor to satisfy nothing higher than one's personal desire for pleasure. When the disciplines of self-denial free the mind from the passionate habits born of self-serving love, the monk grows in a common love of God and neighbor. In this existence where one's movements conform to God's *logoi* out of love for his righteous intentions, one discovers the highest personal "well-being" in the fellowship and friendship of those who are united in Christ.

Conclusion

The ascetic movements of the late third and early fourth centuries were an expression of a twofold theological conviction: first, that Christians are called to imitate God's perfection—especially his mercy to the poor—and second, that in the incarnation, the Word's participation in human nature created the possibility that human beings might be partakers of his divinity and thus be perfected in his image. This doctrine of participation was the foundation for the doctrine of *theōsis*, and with it trust in the efficacy of ascetic disciplines proper to the monastic life. Since no doctrine stands alone but is implicit in all other doctrines, the Church's clarification of theological and christological matters naturally expanded the churches' conception of *theōsis*.

The second- and third-century vision of salvation as overcoming the passions and growing into the likeness of God expanded in the fourth through the seventh centuries as a result of theological developments during the Trinitarian and christological controversies. The incarnate Logos, being consubstantial in his divinity with the Father and Spirit and in his humanity with Adam's family, was able as the second Adam to inaugurate a new humanity, capable of participating in God's incorruptible and immortal nature. Such participation began with baptism, but through the monastic life of ascetic discipline the monk might attain that perfection to which Jesus invited the rich young ruler. If the idea of divinity was more elastic in the early fourth century and the boundary between the divine and human more porous, by the First Council of Constantinople in the waning decades of the century, the Cappadocians' debate with the Homoians and Eunomians had drawn a much sharper ontological distinction between the infinite and eternal being of the Creator and the finite and temporal nature of his creation. This clearer distinction led Gregory of Nyssa to reconceive not only the nature of Christian perfection but also how one's thinking of God must be purified in order to become conformed to the image of God in his simplicity. The ontological "gap" (*diastēma*) between God and humanity redefined perfection, not in terms of achieving stasis as conceived by Athanasius. Rather, it was to be thought of as an unceasing growth in God's likeness by eternally participating in God's infinite being. The implications of the ontological gap also challenged ascetics to reconsider the nature of prayer and contemplation by which the soul entered into divinizing communion with God. Thus, the mystical tradition with its roots in Neo-Platonism came to acquire its mature form as an apathetic theology firmly grounded in the Nicene-Constantinopolitan doctrine of the Trinity.

Building on the work of the Cappadocians, Evagrius reconceived Nyssen's view of *apatheia* not simply as a sublimation of the passions redirected to God but as a freedom from the passions that was necessary for true or formless prayer. Only by transcending images and words might the monk pray to God properly, knowing and coming to attain a godlike simplicity of heart. For Evagrius, this *apatheia* enabled the mind to once again attain knowledge of God in Godself and by this knowledge come to be mingled with God apart from the body in the age to come. Pseudo-Dionysius and Maximus, both informed by the ascetic and apophatic theologies of Origen, Gregory, and Evagrius, built upon Platonic cosmology and

Gregory's eschatological vision of God as "all in all" to present *theōsis* not simply as operating at the level of the individual soul but at the cosmic level with the union of God and the whole of creation. Drawing on the model of the hypostatic union central to Neo-Chalcedonian Christology, Maximus in particular was able to think of *theōsis* as the sacramental process by which rational beings through union with the incarnate Creator-Logos were able to actualize their inherent potential for union with the Father. Such a union, moreover, was no divine afterthought but the very heart of God's plan for creation from eternity. In the incarnation, the Father's plan was inaugurated; in the God-man Jesus was revealed God's plan of cosmic unity in microcosm. Moreover, through sacramental participation in Christ and the life of ascetic struggle, the Christian's mode of being was reformed through conforming to the godlike movements of the *logoi* revealed in Christ's life. Through this union with Christ, both individually and ecclesially, the Christian herself might become in microcosm an image of the eschatological union of all things in Christ.

The union envisioned by these theologians, except perhaps for Evagrius, was not simply the immaterial soul's return to union with the One, as in Plotinus, but the redemption of material creation as well. This Christian hope of the redemption of the cosmos was grounded in Christ's resurrection. The New Testament's witness to Jesus's resurrection and with it the promise of a general resurrection of the dead raised obvious exegetical and theological challenges for the early Church. How would mortal flesh that is subject to decay and decomposition as it becomes the food for worms be restored to life? How, in other words, could *theōsis* extend not just to the rational soul but to the material body as well? This is the central theological question we will examine in the final chapter.

Bibliography

Primary Sources

Athanasius of Alexandria. *The Life of Antony and the Letter to Marcellinus*. Translated by Robert C. Gregg. New York: Paulist, 1980.

Evagrius Ponticus. *The Gnostic Trilogy*. Translated by Robin Darling Young, Joel Kalvesmaki, Columba Stewart, Charles M. Stang, and Luke Dysinger. Oxford: Oxford University Press, 2024.

———. *The Praktikos and Chapters on Prayer*. Translated by John Eudes Bamberger. Collegeville, MN: Liturgical Press, 1972.

Gregory of Nyssa. *Concerning Perfection*. Translated by Rowan A. Greer. In *One Path for All: Gregory of Nyssa on the Christian Life*. Eugene, OR: Cascade, 2015.

———. *Homilies on the Song of Songs*. Translated by Richard A. Norris Jr. Atlanta: Society of Biblical Literature, 2012.

———. *Life of Moses*. Translated by Abraham J. Malherbe and Everett Ferguson. New York: Paulist, 1978.

———. *On Virginity*. Translated by Virginia Woods Callahan. In *Saint Gregory of Nyssa: Ascetical Works*. Washington, DC: Catholic University of America Press, 1967.

Maximus the Confessor. *Maximus the Confessor*. Translated by Andrew Louth. New York: Routledge, 1996.

———. *On Difficulties in the Church Fathers: The* Ambigua. Translated by Nicholas Constas. Cambridge: Harvard University Press, 2014.

———. *On the Cosmic Mystery of Jesus Christ: Selected Writings from St. Maximus the Confessor*. Translated by Paul Blowers and Robert Wilken. Crestwood, NY: St. Vladimir's Seminary Press, 2003.

Pseudo-Dionysius. *Pseudo-Dionysius: The Complete Works*. Translated by Colm Luibheid and Paul Rorem. New York: Paulist, 1987.

Secondary Sources

Bathrellos, Demetrios. "Passions, Ascesis, and the Virtues." Pages 387–406 in *The Oxford Handbook of Maximus the Confessor*. Edited by Pauline Allen and Bronwen Neil. Oxford: Oxford University Press, 2015.

Blowers, Paul M. *Maximus the Confessor: Jesus Christ and the Transfiguration of the World*. Oxford: Oxford University Press, 2016.

Brakke, David. *Athanasius and Asceticism*. Baltimore: Johns Hopkins University Press, 1995.

Corrigan, Kevin. *Evagrius and Gregory: Mind, Soul, and Body in the 4th Century*. Farnham: Ashgate, 2009.

Davis, Stephen J. "Deification in Evagrius Ponticus and the Transmission of the *Kephalaia Gnostica* in Syriac and Arabic." Pages 251–66 in *Faith, Reason, and Theosis*. Edited by Aristotle Papanikolaou, George E. Demacopoulos, and Ashley M. Purura. New York: Fordham University Press, 2023.

Harmless, William. *Desert Christians: An Introduction to the Literature of Early Monasticism*. Oxford: Oxford University Press, 2004.

Kalvesmaki, Joel, and Robin Darling Young. *Evagrius and His Legacy*. Notre Dame: University of Notre Dame Press, 2016.

Laird, Martin. *Gregory of Nyssa and the Grasp of Faith: Union, Knowledge, and Divine Presence*. Oxford: Oxford University Press, 2004.

Larchet, Jean Claude. "The Mode of Deification." Pages 341–59 in *The Oxford Handbook of Maximus the Confessor*. Edited by Pauline Allen and Bronwen Neil. Oxford: Oxford University Press, 2015.

McGinn, Bernard, and Patricia Ferris McGinn. *Early Christian Mystics: The Divine Vision of the Spiritual Masters*. New York: Crossroad, 2003.

Russell, Norman. *The Doctrine of Deification in the Greek Patristic Tradition*. Oxford: Oxford University Press, 2006.

Smith, J. Warren. "Becoming Men, Not Stones: *Epektasis* in Gregory of Nyssa's *Homilies on the Song of Songs*." Pages 340–59 in *Gregory of Nyssa:* In Canticum Canticorum*; Analytical and Supporting Studies; Proceedings of the 13th International Colloquium on Gregory of Nyssa (Rome, 17–20 September 2014)*. Edited by Giulio Maspero, Miguel Brugarolas, and Ilaria Vigorelli. Leiden: Brill, 2017.

Williams, Rowan. *Where God Happens: Discovering Christ in One Another*. Boston: New Seeds, 2005.

Young, Robin Darling. *Procession Before the World: Martyrdom as Public Liturgy in Early Christianity*. Milwaukee: Marquette University Press, 2001.

14

When God Shall Be "All and in All"

Eschatology

The nature of the eschaton—the last things—has from the earliest days of Christianity been a concern for those who professed a belief in Jesus's resurrection and eventual return. Its centrality for Christian belief is signified by the shift of the Sabbath worship for Christians from the seventh day to the first, the day of Jesus's resurrection. For Christians were concerned with Jesus's resurrection as the "firstfruits" (1 Cor 15:20) of his promises regarding the coming kingdom and with it the believer's deliverance from death and entrance into eternal life. In the earliest Christian writing—Paul's First Letter to the Thessalonians, composed around the year 50—the apostle speaks to worries in the community about those who had died before Christ's return (1 Thess 4:13–18). Later in his First Letter to the Corinthians, Paul addresses the apparent belief that Jesus's resurrection inaugurated a present spiritual resurrection, rather than a future bodily one. He counters this view by reminding the Corinthians of the gospel they first heard him preach and in which they placed their hope of salvation (1 Cor 15:1–2). Then he names Jesus's death and resurrection as among the things "of first importance" to this gospel (1 Cor 15:3–11). In the lengthy discussion that follows, Paul affirms that Christ's resurrection provides the Church with the hope that the dead shall be raised (1 Cor 15:12–19) and that this resurrection shall entail a transformation of the body that died from being perishable, corruptible, and weak into a spiritual body, rendered imperishable, incorruptible, and full of power (1 Cor 15:42–44, 53). Then Christ will have placed all things in subjection to the Father, and he shall be "all and in all" (1 Cor 15:28), and the prophecy of Isaiah (25:8) shall be fulfilled: "Death is swallowed up in victory" (1 Cor 15:54).

Paul's discourse on the resurrection, however, did not end questions about Jesus's parousia, or second coming, and the mode of the saints' existence at his return. Rather, it provided further grist for theological speculation. Indeed, the ensuing reflections about the eschaton by early Christian theologians were mostly commentary on Paul's suggestive words. One of the central questions was how to understand Paul's description of the resurrected body as "spiritual" (1 Cor 15:44). Did he mean that the body ceased to be a material body? Or did it mean that the body's matter would be transformed so as to be free from its present weaknesses? Yet these questions were only complicated by Paul's argument in Romans that the Christian life is *already* given a new character because of the resurrection (Rom 8:9–11). The hope of the Christian's resurrection is grounded in the moral transformation ("walking in the Spirit" [Rom 6:4; 8:4]) resulting from one's union with the risen Christ through the Spirit. In the Fourth Gospel, Jesus declares that those whom the Father had given him and who believe in him and eat his flesh and drink his blood shall be raised up to new life at the last day (John 6:39–44; 11:24). The logic in both Paul's letters and the Gospel of John is that resurrection is the result of participation in Christ, who gives to his followers a share in his life. And yet the wicked as well as the righteous shall be raised at a general resurrection (John 5:29; Acts 24:15). If the Christian is already "in the Spirit," what is the relationship between the spiritual life of the Christian in the present and the spiritual existence into which she shall enter at Christ's return?

Eschatological Hope of the Martyrs

For Ignatius of Antioch, writing in the first decades of the second century, the physical reality of the incarnation was inseparably linked to the hope of life beyond the gruesome death that awaited him in Rome. In his letter to the church at Smyrna, he reminds them that figuratively they have been nailed to the cross with Jesus who was "truly nailed in the flesh for us under Pontius Pilate . . . in order that he might raise a banner through his resurrection for his saints and faithful people" (Ign. *Smyrn.* 1.2). It is this banner of the resurrection, he says, that enabled the apostles, who touched Jesus's risen body, to "despise death . . . and prove its victors" (Ign. *Smyrn.* 3.2) when they faced execution for the faith. Then, imitating Paul's counterfactual flourish against the resurrection deniers in Corinth (1 Cor 15:12–19), Ignatius, thinking of those docetic Christians who denied the reality of the incarnation, death, and resurrection, rhetorically asks, "If what our Lord did is a sham, so is my being in chains. Why then have I given myself up, completely to death, fire, sword, and wild beasts?" (Ign. *Smyrn.* 4.2). Precisely because of the centrality of Jesus's resurrection for the hope of the Christian's resurrection, Ignatius was insistent that he must be allowed to see his martyrdom through to the end. For by his imitation of the apostles' courage and faithfulness in the hour of their death, Ignatius sought to confirm by his manner of death the eschatological hope he had preached.

Gnostic Resurrection

There are no extant texts left by Ignatius's docetic opponents laying out their eschatology. But among various second-century groups of Gnostics, one finds carefully developed alternative interpretations of Paul based on their dichotomous view of spirit and matter. Instead of a physical resurrection, their hope lay in the spirit's liberation from its imprisonment in matter and material concerns. One of their eschatological writings, the Treatise on the Resurrection, appears to be a response to a letter written from a Christian seeking clarification about Valentinian Christians' understanding about Jesus's resurrection. As becomes quickly apparent, Christ's triumph over death and that of believers are intimately connected. Jesus is not mentioned by name but referred to as "our Savior, our Lord, the King" (Treat. Res. 43.35). The Savior is incarnate, revealing himself as the Son of God and teaching about "the law of the natural order," which means death. In his divinity, he conquered death, and in his humanity, he returns to the Plērōma since "from the beginning he existed as a seed of the truth from above" (Treat. Res. 44.14–35). The Savior, therefore, is a prototype and forerunner of the gnostic who aspires to ascend through contemplation to eternal spiritual realities where, unlike the unstable material world that is constantly in a state of flux, the gnostic soul finds rest (Treat. Res. 43.35; 48.33). For through the Savior—in the form of a human child—came incorruptible light streaming into the corruptible world (Treat. Res. 49.1) that the elect might receive acquaintance or knowledge of "he who became death's undoing" (Treat. Res. 46.14–17). Appealing to the Pauline language of 1 Corinthians 15, the author says that the Savior has swallowed up death, incorruption has replaced corruption—the "visible [swallowed up] by the invisible" (Treat. Res. 45.13). That is, the illusory nature of the material world that is a mere apparition (Treat. Res. 48.16) is overcome by the revelation of the inner, transcendent spiritual reality manifest in the Savior.

The language of "resurrection" does not refer to the reunion of the soul and body. Rather, it is a taking off of the body (Treat. Res. 47.30–36). For the body is not proper to "the real you" but is a corruptible envelope of the soul into which it descended (Treat. Res. 47.15–18). Therefore, resurrection is the liberation of the Gnostic's spiritual nature from the body and the material world's death-dealing ignorance. It is when the intellect is "drawn upward" (Treat. Res. 45.39–46.1) through an "uncovering" of "the elements that have 'arisen'" (Treat. Res. 47.38–48.4). That is, the spiritual nature of the elect is no longer enveloped by the deceptive fog of the material realm. Therefore, the intellect no longer stumbles as it sleepwalks through life in ignorance but is awake to the knowledge of its true identity as belonging to the spiritual reality that is the Plērōma from which it came (Treat.

Res. 46.25; 47.27). Yet the author plays with the double meaning of "death" much as did Jesus (Matt 16:25) and Paul (Rom 6:8–10). The world is death, yet by dying, Christ overcame death. The gnostic, who in receiving the revelation of the risen Christ has a share in his resurrection, is no longer deceived into thinking that the realm of death is ultimate reality. Therefore, she "rushes to death" in the sense that she puts to death worldly hopes and ambitions and in doing so is liberated from her attachment to its transitory and ultimately unsatisfying pleasures that leave her unfulfilled (Treat. Res. 49.23). By dying with the Savior to the world, the gnostic attains true life. Thus, resurrection is not only an eschatological hope but a state of present enlightenment necessary for the return to the Plērōma after the death of the body. In this sense, the birth of the elect in the material world is a spiritual death that ends with the subsequent death of the material body, which is a resurrection or ascent back to the spiritual realm.

The Treatise on the Resurrection does follow the Pauline pattern in two respects. First, as already shown, it assumes a Pauline realized eschatology that results from participation in Christ. Second, neither is there a general resurrection unto judgment at which time the saints and the reprobates will be separated. Rather, resurrection is only a resurrection unto life. The nonelect, who are not raised to enlightenment, are simply left to endure the living death of their own ignorance. Yet the Treatise on the Resurrection does not ground its realized eschatology on the work of the Spirit; rather, it focuses exclusively on the revelation of the Savior.

Notable also is how Treatise on the Resurrection illustrates the diversity of thought among gnostic authors and how Christians engaged influential philosophical accounts of death and the life after. To begin with, Treatise on the Resurrection presupposes an account of the soul's origin that is markedly different from that in the Apocryphon of John. Whereas in the latter, human beings were entirely the creation of Ialdabaōth, in the former, the rational or spiritual element in human beings existed in the Plērōma before their incarnations. Nor in the Apocryphon of John does the saving descent of the Christ into the realm of darkness deliver the Gnostics from the material world in an eschatological resurrection. Salvation comes only in the form of true self-knowledge. In this way, the theology of the soul's origin and salvation articulated in Treatise on the Resurrection is closer to a descent-ascent or *exitus-reditus* model proper to Plato's theory of the transmigration of souls. For neither holds a place for the body's redemption. In whatever way bodily experiences of the world, which for Plato is an imperfect reflection of eternal paradigms, might be the grist for dialectic and the discovery of the Good, the body plays no such role for liberated souls of philosophers. Rather, the pure soul of Socrates and those like him—now free from the body and with it the distortions of the senses and the burdensome passions of the flesh—ascend to the intelligible heavenly realm to enjoy a *direct* vision of the beauty of the forms in all their perfection. The Treatise on the Resurrection, therefore, represents an interpretation of the Pauline language of dying and being raised in Christ entirely in a spiritual sense. Its primary concern is not the death and resurrection of the body but of the soul. Such an integration of the Pauline and the Platonic eschatologies in Treatise on the Resurrection is the reason the thought of Gnostics has by some scholars been pejoratively described as "hyper-hellenized Christianity."

Origen: Glorification of Spiritual Humanity

Growing up in a Christian community in the quintessentially Hellenistic city of Alexandria, Origen's anthropology, as we have already seen, was significantly informed by Classical as well as Pauline writings. The same was true for this eschatology. Yet although the Valentinians and Origen followed Paul's connection between moral transformation in the present age and spiritual transformation in the eschaton, Origen distinguished himself from both the gnostic and Platonic traditions with his understanding of the spiritual body of the resurrection. For Origen, resurrection was not the restoration of the soul's godlike wings after its liberation from the fetters of the fleshly body; resurrection entailed the transformation and glorification of the body as well as the soul.

Origen's account of the resurrection is notoriously difficult to reconstruct. For the modern reader is almost entirely dependent on Rufinus's bowdlerized Latin translations of *On First Principles* and *Commentary on Romans* in which Rufinus may have omitted various of Origen's speculations, the orthodoxy of which Rufinus questioned. Nevertheless, in both these works, one finds the repetition of certain key themes that influence Origen's soteriology across his corpus. Therefore, instead of trying to reconstruct his vision of the eschaton—as if Origen had a single, final interpretation of any passage of Scripture—it is more helpful, as Thomas McGlothlin has argued, to notice the recurring themes that connect these texts.

Origen thought of the resurrection of the dead as the glorification of the bodies of the saints as a result of the moral transformation effected in them by Christ's own death, resurrection, and ascension to glory. Origen's cosmology and soteriology were both governed by his absolute commitment to God's justice and humanity's free will. Therefore, Jesus's death proved salvific not because he did something *on behalf of* humanity but because of what it does *in* and *to* the believer. At one level, Jesus redeemed humanity because he is "the lamb of God." His blood, shed in his sacrifice upon the altar of the cross, conquered the prince of this world, rendering him and his minions powerless over humanity. Thereby, the cross created the condition for the possibility of humanity's liberation from the devil's temptation to sin. At the same time, Jesus's fortitude and faithfulness to the Father in resisting the devil's temptations even to the point of death both provided an example of moral courage and with it aroused in believers confidence that they, too, might overcome the power of temptation even to the point of imitating Christ's death. Those souls, therefore, who use their natural freedom and the example of Jesus to reject sin have turned their hearts from the world in all its carnality. With the aid of the indwelling Holy Spirit, the soul is freed from its fleshly orientation and passions and becomes *spiritual* with minds that are reoriented to Christ's heavenly kingdom. This transformation of the soul's character from being carnal to being spiritual allows it to participate in Jesus's resurrection and ascension. As the crucified Jesus was raised and experienced a progressive transformation in glory from his resurrection to his ascension on high, the liberated soul also undergoes a progressive transformation that Paul described as "walking in newness of life" (Rom 6:4) and being "changed from glory into glory" (2 Cor 3:18) through the daily renewal of the "inner man" (2 Cor 4:16; Col 3:10). For this reason, Jesus's ascension is every bit as important as the resurrection for the mind's reorientation from the sensible world to the invisible things of heaven. If the resurrection gives hope for believers' deliverance from death, the ascension gives hope of the glorious existence that awaits them. Based on Ephesians 2:6, "[God] raised us up with him and made us sit with him in the heavenly places in Christ Jesus," Jesus's ascension points his followers to their telos and with it effects a reconception of their lives. By seeing their lives through the lens of their eschatological telos, they become detached from worldly matters and set their minds upon the things above (Col 3:1). Yet if the Christian's life is not transformed and the "old self" not put off in the hope of resurrection and ascension, Jesus's resurrection is of no effect. "Christ justifies," Origen writes, "only those who have taken up a new life by the example of his own resurrection and are casting off their old garments of injustice and iniquity" (*Comm. Rom.* 4.7.8). This moral transformation is important because of Origen's conception of the relationship between the moral or spiritual condition of the soul and that of the body.

As we have already seen,[1] all creatures for Origen exist in bodies. Only God is truly incorporeal. Bodies' different constitutions enable different souls to inhabit different environments for which they were made. In the case of rational beings, all were created in the beginning with the same ethereal body suitable for inhabiting the heavenly realm where they might enjoy the blessedness of contemplat-

1. See chapter 3, pp. 89–91.

ing God. The lightness of the ethereal body reflected the lightness of the mind's likeness to God's incorporeal being (*Princ.* 2.2.1; 2.3.3). The coarse material bodies that human beings and demons occupy now was the result of a degenerative moral transformation of the mind. As the rational mind *cooled* in its love for God, it was transformed into soul—*psychē* from *psychesthai*, which means "to cool"—and with it the body was also changed. No longer light and ethereal, the body of the fallen soul, which itself was growing heavier in its waning interest in God, was now a heavy, material body fit for the life not in heaven but in a material world. Each soul's body differed from those of other souls based on one's relative diminished love for God. Thus, the diverse conditions of the bodies reflected the fallen moral character of their soul (*Princ.* 2.9.6). The transformation of the light, ethereal body into a dark, murky, material body burdened with pains and passions was the self-inflicted suffering that resulted from the mind's failure to cleave to God in love. Yet this transformation also reflected God's merciful use of the material body born of sin for humanity's redemption and restoration. Therefore, unlike for Plato and the Gnostics, the material body, though the product of the fall, was for Origen not so much a prison as a hospital or rehabilitation center for the soul. For the conjunction of bodily suffering and the revelation of the Logos in Jesus sanctified the soul, making it spiritual, by arousing a fiery longing for God whereby the mind might once again be made fit to return to fellowship with God. Since the condition of the body was contingent upon the condition of the soul, the restoration of the mind's spiritual character through the indwelling of the Spirit meant that the body, too, would once again become spiritual and ethereal.

The transformation of bodies at the resurrection reverses the degenerative transformation of the fall. Origen explains Paul's description of the mortal putting on immortality and the corruptible putting on incorruptibility (1 Cor 15:52–53) as precisely that transformation of the body's constitution. In other words, the change in the body is the result of the soul's transformative restoration to a spiritual mind filled with warm desire to be reunited with God in heaven. Thus, there is a direct connection between the constitution of the perfected soul and its body. Because in the present life the soul is perfected and transformed by putting on Christ, clothing itself with Christ's incorruptibility, then at the resurrection the body of a perfected and incorruptible soul itself becomes incorruptible (*Princ.* 2.3.2). This is the logic of Origen's interpretation of Paul's description of the resurrected body as spiritual (1 Cor 15:44). When the carnal soul is transformed into a spiritual mind, then its body will be spiritual as well (*Princ.* 2.10.3). And since the spiritual mind shall also ascend to heaven, as did Christ, to sit with Christ, contemplating the Father through his Word and Wisdom, so too its body will also be returned to its ethereal constitution fit for its heavenly abode. Thus, for Origen, the body is integral to the creaturely nature of the mind and so is not abandoned but redeemed along with the mind. Conversely, for those souls who in this age do not use the life in the body to become spiritual but continue to "love the shadows of error and the night of ignorance"—so becoming more morally degenerate—their body in the subsequent age will take on a more degenerate physical form (*Princ.* 2.3.2).

One of the enduring eschatological questions was how to preserve an individual's continuity between the present age and the eschaton if the body undergoes a radical transformation in the resurrection. If a person's body is no longer heavy and coarse but ethereal and resplendent, reflecting the Father's glory, how is the person the same person? What is the principle of continuity? Origen's answer had been that, even as a plant contains a *ratio* that, at God's command, governs its development from the seed to the mature plant, so too each person had such a *ratio* that was constant from creation in the beginning to resurrection. Moreover, though the body's substance was changed at the resurrection from earthy matter to heavenly ether, it retained the same form or *eidos*, the pattern of which was preserved in the soul. It was this enduring form that makes the person recognizable in the resurrection (*Princ.* 2.10.3). Although Origen maintains that all rational creatures will be transformed and raised, his commitment to free will, as we shall see, complicates his hypothesis as to how and when this resurrection occurs.

Methodius and the Purification of the Temple

Although Origen's theory of resurrection affirmed the goodness of the body and gave it an enduring role in the life of redeemed rational beings in a way absent from gnostic accounts, his critics objected that he had not gone far enough. One such critic was Methodius of Olympus. Against the Gnostics, Origen and Methodius were in full agreement that the misuse of man's capacity of free choice (*eleutheros*), not matter or the physical creation, was the source of sin (*Arbitr.* 16.2). Methodius, however, contended that the material body of the present age, though in need of purification and healing, was itself part of the creation that God pronounced good in the beginning. He objected that Origen did not recognize the material body's goodness except as it was a place for the soul's convalescence. The physical body for Origen was a mere epiphenomenon that could be replaced with a radically different body once the soul was healed and ready to return to its spiritual existence in the heavens. Therefore, Methodius's eschatology sought to preserve a continuity between the good, material creation in Genesis 1 and the redeemed and glorified creation in Paul.

In his treatise *On the Resurrection of the Dead*, Methodius explained the necessity of death in humanity's deliverance from sin. Drawing on Paul's description of sin in Romans 7 in which the apostle spoke of the law of sin in his members that was at war with the law of God in his mind, Methodius contended that sin, though originating in the will, was an invasive presence that inhered in the body. Although his free-will defense affirmed that evil was not itself a substance but merely a privation of the good, he never articulated an ontology of sin but tended to speak of it in reified terms. The metaphor he employed to describe the body's sin-infested condition was that of a temple in which had grown a fig tree. As the fig tree grew, its branches filled the temple (*Res.* 1.41). More pernicious, however, were the roots that spread throughout the foundation of the temple, reaching in and filling every nook and cranny. Although the branches of the fig tree, which represented the outer works of sin, could be pruned, the tree would remain as long as the roots remained. The only way to save the temple, paradoxically, was to tear the temple down, stone by stone. Then, once the stones were separated from the fig tree's roots, the builder could reassemble the stones according to his original design. So too, Methodius explained, in death God frees the body from the sin that has infested its members in order to rebuild the body according to his purpose. Without the corrosive presence of sin in the body's members, the body is freed from the cause of death and regains its original, inherent stability and immortality (*Symp.* 9.2).

The metaphor of the fig tree and temple carried several important implications. First, the body of the resurrection will be the same body that one possesses in the present—except that it will be free from sin—because its substance will be the same. Thus, one's identity—that which is the same in the present age and in the age to come—includes the material elements of the body as well as the soul. Second, since the goodness of the material body as God designed it in the beginning will be restored, Methodius, unlike either the Gnostics or Origen, affirmed an essential continuity between God's creative intention in the beginning and his salvific work through Christ's death and resurrection.

There was, however, one implication of the metaphor of the temple and the fig tree that seemed to deviate not only from Origen's integration of the soul's moral transformation and the transformation of the body but also from Paul's view of resurrection as the result of participation in Christ. That implication was that all people, the unrepentant as well as the righteous, will die and be raised—raised free from sin. Whereas in the Gnostics' reading of Paul, only the spiritual who have put on Christ shall be raised, Methodius made resurrection an act of divine fiat, independent of the spiritual condition of the soul. At first glance, it appears that Methodius leaves little room for human agency in determining one's eschatological fate. Yet although both Origen and Methodius engage Daniel 12:2–3, Methodius construes it to mean that, while all will be resurrected, not all will enter into blessedness (*Comm. Rom.* 5.9.12).

Appealing to Paul's distinction in Romans 9:21 between earthen vessels of honor and of dishonor, Methodius contends that, although all will be raised, some will be raised in honor and others in dishonor (*Res.* 1.44.2). In his dialogue *Banquet of the Ten Virgins*, a dialogue between virgins extolling the virtue of chastity, Methodius compares the resurrection to the Jewish Feast of Tabernacles (Lev 23:39–43) in which the temple is adorned with firstfruits of the harvest, branches from palm trees, and the shoots of willows. Methodius interprets the feast to be a figure of the wedding banquet in the resurrection (*Symp.* 9.2). The righteous, whose lives of virtue—especially the virtue of chastity—freed them from the dominion of the passions, have good works with which to decorate the temple of their resurrected body (*Symp.* 9.4). By such good works, the temple of the Lord is honored, and they are prepared to partake of God's blessedness. By contrast, those who never cultivated the virtues have no good works with which to beautify their temple. They cannot participate in the feast, for their souls had not acquired that holiness and strength of spiritual sight necessary to behold the brilliant glory of God (*Symp.* 9.5). These individuals, though their bodies are free of sin and once again immortal, are consigned to perdition. Although the cultivation of virtue is not, for Methodius, the cause or precondition of the resurrection into spiritual bodies—as it was for Paul, the Gnostics, and Origen—the degree of virtue attained in the present age determines the character of one's life in the resurrection. Thus, human agency is not lost. For while resurrection is entirely the product of the re-creative power of God, the level of blessedness the resurrected experience is determined by the individual's moral and spiritual preparation through setting her mind upon the things of God and living in hope of the blessedness of the angels (*Symp.* 9.4–5).

Gregory of Nyssa and Glorifying the Material Body

As with many features of his thought, Gregory of Nyssa's eschatology was heavily influenced by Origen both positively, having features he retained, and negatively, features he sought to correct. One of the latter was his account of the resurrection. One critical point where Gregory's eschatology diverges from Origen's concerns the nature of the body that is raised at Christ's second coming. Whereas Origen interpreted Paul's metaphor of the grain (1 Cor 15) that is changed into an ear to mean that the material body of the present life will be transformed into a spiritual or ethereal body in the resurrection, Gregory insisted that the body of the resurrection must be the same material body of the present, only healed and glorified. This, however, was not always the case. In an early work, *On Those Who Have Fallen Asleep*, Gregory affirmed that in the resurrection, human beings will be "changed from this life to one spiritual and incorporeal" (*Mort.*; Greer, 94). By the time he writes his main works on anthropology and eschatology, *On the Making of Humanity* and *On the Soul and Resurrection*, he distinguishes his view from Origen by denying the preexistence of the mind (*Hom. opif.* 28) and by affirming the bodily nature of the resurrection. Although he speaks of the eschaton as the restoration of paradise, complete with the tree of life, he concedes that, at some level, the nature of that life is "another kingdom, of a description that belongs to unspeakable mysteries" that is beyond the life as he knows it now (*Hom. opif.* 21.4). Nevertheless, the resurrection entails not only the reunion of the soul with the body as in Jesus's resurrection but also the reassembling of the body's elements into the form of the person to whom they belong (*Hom. opif.* 27.1; *An. res.* 2.53–9; Silvas, 187). One metaphor Gregory employs to describe the body of the resurrection is that of the broken clay pot whose many fragments are perfectly reassembled by the skilled potter (*An. res.* 5.8–11; *Or. cat.* 7). This reflects Gregory's insistence that, in contrast with Origen, the body that God created and pronounced good was a material body. Therefore, if the resurrection is a restoration and a perfection of God's original creation, then the body that is restored must be a material body. Only if the material body has a place in the new creation can the first creation be thought truly good.

Although themes of eschatology recur throughout his corpus, Gregory's most extended speculation about the nature of resurrection occurs in *On the Soul and Resurrection*. Written around the same time as *On the Making of Humanity* and *Life of Macrina*, *On the Soul and Resurrection* is a dialogue between Gregory and his sister, modeled on Plato's *Phaedo*. Like the *Phaedo*, its dramatic setting is Macrina's deathbed—the time shortly after the death of Basil. Upon seeing Macrina's wasted frame, Gregory is reminded of his brother's death. The sorrow still fresh from Basil's passing wells up in Gregory's soul. Macrina, ever acting as grief counselor, reins in her brother's *pathos*, reminding him of Paul's words: "One ought not grieve for those who have fallen asleep like those who have no hope" (1 Thess 4:13). She then assuages her brother's grief by renewing his hope in the immortality of the soul and the resurrection of the dead.

In the case of the soul, Gregory, speaking in the *dramatis persona* of Macrina, refuted Epicurean and Aristotelian views of the soul's mortality, arguing that the soul, like God, is simple in substance and therefore cannot die by being broken down into many pieces as the body can (*An. res.* 1.11–12; Silvas, 174). Therefore, even when the body dies and disintegrates, the soul endures. Although the argument from simplicity was a condensed form of Plato's argument in *Phaedo* (78c), Macrina's more developed argument rested on a comparison of the immaterial soul and incorporeal divinity. Christians believe in a God who cannot be seen because of signs of divine power that can be seen in creation. Similarly, the Christian can still believe in an invisible soul because its active powers are visible in the body (*An. res.* 1.29–32; Silvas, 177–78).

As the dialogue unfolds, a more serious issue emerges regarding the soul's eschatological participation in God. Macrina had earlier drawn a sharp distinction between the rational faculties of the soul that are the locus of the image of God and the nonrational faculties, which human beings share with the beasts. The latter consist of the powers of perception as well as the appetitive faculty, which is the source of desire (*epithymia*), and the spirited faculty, which is the emotion of fight or flight (*thymos*). Together they are the soul's principle of motion. When desire is aroused, the soul is oriented and begins to seek the good it desires. Spirit, also called irascibility or gumption, is the drive to overcome all obstacles in order to attain the good. They are also the source of all emotions, both virtuous emotions, love and courage, and the vicious passions, lust and wrath. Because the nonrational faculties are alien to the divine nature, Macrina says that they are not essential to the human soul made in the divine image but are mere ancillary faculties residing on the "borderland" of the soul.[2] Following the underlying assumption that "like is known by like," Macrina reasons that in order for the soul to possess that likeness to God—a purity of heart and soul—necessary to receive the eschatological vision of God, it must be purified of all that is alien to the image of God. Her brother, never a passive interlocutor, objects that, if the soul is purged of the nonrational faculties that contain the principle of motion, the soul will not be able to participate in the divine, ever changing into greater degrees of likeness to God (*An. res.* 6.12; Silvas, 208). Already one sees here the seeds of Gregory's theory of the soul's perfection, epectasy—that is, the soul's growth in likeness to God through an eternal movement into God's infinite being.[3]

Not all movements of the soul, Macrina replies, are forms of desire and gumption. Contemplation, for instance, is a movement proper to the rational soul (*An. res.* 6.13; Silvas, 208) that does not require the aid of desire or spirit; it is a pure, cognitive activity. Eschatologically, when God is, as Paul says, "all and in all" (1 Cor 15:28), there will be no evil obstacles that frustrate the soul's participation in God. Therefore, there will be no need for courage to resist the temptations of the devil. More importantly, because the purified soul will "be joined" to God and eternally abide in the presence of the divine beauty, God will be immediately present to the soul. There will be no sin that keeps the soul at a distance from God. Therefore, since the soul will not lack for God's fellowship, the soul will not desire God. For one desires only that which one does not have; but when one possesses the object of desire, desire is replaced with enjoyment (*apolausis*) (*An. res.* 6.14–15;

2. For a more developed account of Gregory's anthropology, see chapter 3, pp. 91–98.

3. See chapter 13, pp. 483–91.

Silvas, 208–9). In this life, the Christian's love of God has the erotic character of desire for the beloved to whom she is not yet united. This desiring love is born of hope for that which she has been promised. But the promise is not yet fulfilled. Therefore, she longs for its fulfillment. Eschatologically, the promise is fulfilled with the soul's union with her beloved. Even as faith and hope will be changed to sight, so the character of the Christian's love for God is transformed from erotic longing into contemplative delight. Gregory's insight, spoken through Macrina, is that the purification of soul comes not from a change in human nature itself but in the soul's experience of God. When evil is no more and God is unceasingly present to the soul, then the character of the soul is changed. In the present age, the soul has lived as a creature of time whose passions have been shaped by its recollections of the past and its anticipation of the future. But in the eschaton, when God is all in all, the soul will abide in the eternal now. For in the presence of God's perfect beauty, there will be neither nostalgic longings for the past nor the distraction of desire for some better day to come. Instead, the soul will be perfectly content in fellowship with God.

Even Gregory's vision of the soul's eternal enjoyment of God is haunted by the ghost of Origen. For in Origen's theory of creation, all the rational beings enjoyed just such contemplative fellowship with God. But eventually, all of them—all except the mind of Jesus—became satiated with God and, in greater and lesser degrees, turned from God. Gregory, therefore, needed to explain why the soul in this eschatological blessedness would not suffer the same satiation as Origen's rational beings. To put it another way, why won't there be a second fall? This question is even more complicated given Gregory's anthropology. As creatures who came into being from nothing, humans are beings in constant motion—changing all the time. How, therefore, can a creature of constant movement ever rest content in God? Why won't the soul become bored in paradise? Gregory finds his answer by grasping the dynamic relationship between God's infinite being and humanity's creaturely becoming. Love is aroused by what is beautiful. Because God's beauty is infinite, having nothing to limit it, there will also be no end of the soul's love of God's infinite beauty (*An. res.* 6.32–34; Silvas, 211). Since the soul is, as Gregory says, a mirror bearing the image of that which it contemplates, the more the soul contemplates the beauty of God and the beauty of God's love for humanity, the more the soul grows in its likeness to God. Following the principle that like not only knows like but is attracted to like, Gregory envisions the soul's movement in an eternal cycle of greater and greater attachment to God. For the more the soul grows in the knowledge of God's glory, the more it loves God's beauty. As its love for God grows, the soul comes to bear greater and greater likeness to God; for it possesses the very love that God has for God's own goodness. The more the soul mirrors the perfect goodness of God, the greater its capacity to receive the vision of God's glorious goodness. The more of God's wondrous being the soul is able to see, the purer is its love of God. Since God's beauty and love are infinite, eternally arousing greater degrees of love for God, the cycle never ends. And where love is ever growing, the relationship between the lover and the beloved will never be stagnant. God's infinite beauty will eternally bind the soul to God, eliminating the possibility of satiation and boredom that characterizes life in this age.

Gregory's ontological division of God's infinite and eternal being and humanity's infinite becoming creates, as we have seen,[4] the foundation for his theory of *epektasis*, the eschatological perfection of human nature. In his later *Commentary on the Song of Songs*, Gregory modifies this account of the soul's eschatological participation in God. Since writing *On the Soul and Resurrection*, the subject of divine infinity assumed a greater significance in his thought. Although sin created a gap of unlikeness that separated sinful humanity from holy God—this gap would be entirely bridged in the resurrection—there remains an ontological gap. In the eschaton, as in the present, God is infinite; therefore, God's infinite being will always remain beyond human complete comprehension (*katalēpsis*). That is, the human intellect will never know God in the totality of his being (*Hom. Cant.* 8; Norris, 259). Because this is an essential difference between God and humanity, the gap between who God is and what the human mind may know of God will endure even in the resurrection. The beatific vision will transform the soul, eternally changing it from one degree of glory into another without end (*peras*); this is Gregory's idea of eternal creation (*Hom. Cant.* 6; Norris 185–87). Here lies a key difference between Gregory and Origen. For Origen, the rational being's contemplation of God leads to union of the divine and human in which the human mind appears to be absorbed into the divine mind. For Gregory, however, because the metaphysical gap remains, the boundary between Creator and creatures is never obscured. That is, eschatologically God is what he always is, eternal and unchanging being, while the eternal life of human beings in the resurrection is an eternal becoming (*Hom. Cant.* 8; Norris, 259). Although human beings forever remain creatures of change, their eternal participation in God creates a kind of rest or stasis in God—what Rowan Greer calls a "stable motion"—because they will abide unswervingly and unchangeably in the good (*Hom. Cant.* 8; Norris, 265–67). Eschatological perfection, therefore, is paradoxically the unceasing contemplative communion with God that produces an eternal change in the soul from greater to even greater degrees of likeness to God.

Gregory's mature theory of *epektasis* led to the transformation of his understanding of the eschatological relationship of desire and enjoyment. Whereas in *On the Soul and Resurrection* he had argued that when God is all and in all, desire

4. See chapter 13, pp. 483–91.

will be replaced by enjoyment, in his *Homilies on the Song of Songs* Gregory realized that because the metaphysical gap between Creator and creature remains even in the resurrection, then the soul's enjoyment of God's goodness will never be complete. On the contrary, each vision of God's perfect beauty is a foretaste of even greater visions to come. Therefore, the soul's eschatological enjoyment of God is not the end but only the beginning. He writes, "the Good alone is truly pleasant and desirable and loveable and [its] enjoyment is the ever available opportunity of a yet nobler desiring because by participation in good things it stretches and expands our longing" (*Hom. Cant.* 1; Norris, 33). Unlike the present life, however, where the soul's desire is motivated by lack or by separation from the God it loves, eschatologically its ascent is motivated by its perfect enjoyment of divine abundance—the abundance of God whose beauty is without end.

The doctrine of the resurrection was the touchstone for Gregory's reflection on the nature of the Christian life in the present. His brother Basil and Gregory the future bishop of Nazianzus had understood their life together in Athens as practicing the virtues proper to their eschatological life (*Or.* 43.20). Macrina and fellow female ascetics, through their life of chastity, prayer, and worship, embraced the angelic existence of the resurrection (*Macr.* 13.6; Silvas, 122). Gregory used the model of the resurrection to rethink the nature of human social relations, especially that of master and slave. Famously, in his fourth homily on Ecclesiastes, he argues from his doctrine of the *imago Dei* that God endowed humanity with the irrevocable gift of liberty. If humanity is made in the image of God in order to govern creation, who would presume to make such a rational creature a slave, like dumb beasts? (*Hom. Eccl.* 4.335, 337). Although Nazianzen, Chrysostom, and Augustine deny that slavery is a natural state and even, in the case of Nazianzen, implicitly condemn slavery, Gregory is the only figure within the patristic tradition explicitly to repudiate chattel slavery. In his Easter homily *On the Holy Pascha*, he shifts the basis of his critique to the liberty of the resurrection and the ecclesial practices at Easter. Quoting Psalm 117:24 (LXX), "This is the day that the Lord has made, let us rejoice and be glad in it," he observes that on the feast of the resurrection all Christians gather as one household to sing a single song in harmonic praise. It is a day of rest for all, "oppressive duties have dispersed like a winter storm at the coming of spring . . . the poor is as fine as a rich man [and] the rich man appears more splendid than ever" (*Sanct. Pasch.*; Hall, 8). This prefigures the universal gathering of humanity at the resurrection. So, for Easter, slaves are set free from work but also from the threat of public beatings and humiliations and insult even as they will be at the resurrection. Yet the resurrection brings both liberation and judgment. So reminding the master that "at the resurrection, in likeness of which we honour this day, he needs also the indulgence and generosity of his master [i.e., Christ]," Gregory exhorts him to "take away the pain from oppressed souls as the Lord does the deadness from bodies" (*Sanct. Pasch.*; Hall, 9). Since the peacefulness of Easter is an image of the life of the resurrection that all Christians desire, masters should, he says, live every day as Easter and grant to all the liberty and honor they hope will be granted to them in Christ's kingdom. Gregory, the master orator, is never so flat-footed as to explicitly command masters to manumit their slaves. He is more subtle. Yet the inescapable implication is that masters should give to their slaves the freedom proper to their nature if they, too, desire to be free from their heavenly Master's judgment.

Augustine: Full and Certain Peace

The fall of the first human beings, for Augustine, marked a fundamental disruption of the cosmic order and a corresponding corruption of human nature. The internal conflict between the law of sin that abided in the members of the body and the law of the mind mirrored the rebellion of the human creature against the Creator whose law should govern all his creatures. Moreover, the stasis of incorruptibility that Adam and Eve would have been given if they had remained faithful and obedient to God was postponed until a distant future. For the time being, the life in paradise was replaced by that of "wretched pilgrimage" (*Civ.* 17.13). It is precisely because of the disordered relationship between the soul and the body, which is an image of the disordered relationship between the sinner and God, that the resurrection is essential for humanity's entrance into the "full and certain peace" (*pax plenissima atque certissima*) that God originally intended (*Civ.* 19.10). Such peace is full and certain because it is no longer the unrealized object of hope in the midst of the saints' vigilant watch and daily struggle in the present life. Gone are the temptations born of disordered and conflicting desires. Gone are the physical and emotional sufferings inherent to mortality. For there is no outward peace where there is an inner rebellion of the body against reason (*Retract.* 1.19.1). But eschatologically, there will be no inner conflict; the body of the saints will be made subordinate to the mind as their mind will be subordinate to God. When, in *City of God*, he lists the ten types of peace, Augustine begins with the peace of the body, that is, "a tempering of the component parts in duly ordered proportion," and ends with the peace of the whole universe, that is, "the tranquility of order . . . the arrangement of things equal and unequal in a pattern which assigns to each its proper position" (*Civ.* 19.13). The eschatological peace of the body is the peace of the universe in microcosm. This peace achieved through right ordering of the individual body and the whole cosmos is the hope of the resurrection.

Augustine distinguishes two resurrections that correspond to two deaths. The first resurrection occurs in baptism where God in his mercy counters the first death, that is, the soul's separation from God. This resurrection belongs to those who "hear the voice of the Son of God" and obey and believe and who persevere to the end; these have "passed from death into [eternal] life" (John 5:24). This first resurrection Augustine calls the resurrection of the soul. The second resurrection occurs at the end of history when the souls of all will be reunited with their body. Then those who did not hear the voice of the Son and undergo the first resurrection will face a second death—that is, "the last and great judgment" (*Civ.* 20.6). Here Augustine, like Methodius, breaks with the Pauline model in which the resurrection of the body is the consequence of participation in Christ as members of his mystical body. For the wicked as well as the righteous will be raised in the second resurrection to face judgment. Commenting on the scene of the last judgment in Revelation when "the books were opened" (Rev 20:12), Augustine says that "the books" refer to the record of each person's life that will in a single moment be clear to them as they stand in the presence of the divine judge: "Each one's knowledge will accuse or excuse his conscience and thus each and all will be judged simultaneously" (*Civ.* 20.14). To the saints in whom the Spirit planted the love of God's righteousness, their consciences will bear witness to their righteousness. Therefore, to them, this vision of God will be blessedness itself and peace because it will be the fulfillment of their most deeply desired hope. To the damned, however, whose conscience will bear witness to their unrighteousness, the vision will be terrible.

Following the judgment in which the damned will be cast into the lake of fire (Rev 20:15), there will be a great conflagration that will usher in the new heaven and the new earth (Rev 21:1). The "fire" from heaven, signifying God's sweeping purification of the world, will transform the present qualities of the material creation purging the corruption that results from sin (*Civ.* 20.16). Although the bodies of the wicked are freed from the infection of sin and so made immortal—ironically becoming like God, as the serpent promised—the incorruptible nature into which they are transformed allows them to endure the pains of their punishment without the hope of liberation in a final disintegration. The purified bodies of the righteous, by contrast, find their habitation in the new Jerusalem, which will radiate with the divine light reflected in the body of the saints. The descent of the heavenly city, however, will not have begun with the re-creation of heaven and earth. Rather, the new Jerusalem, Augustine explains, has already been descending even in the present age as it has been populated by those who have received the "'washing of rebirth' in the Holy Spirit" (*Civ.* 20.17).

Although Augustine speculates about how a material body might exist in heaven (*Civ.* 22.4), he, like Methodius and Gregory of Nyssa, rejects Origen's view of the resurrection as the conversion of the material body into an ethereal one. The material substance of the body in the resurrection is purified and transformed—radically so—like the rest of earthly creation, so as to be capable of immortality, but it remains essentially a terrestrial body, only perfect. Although the mature Augustine of *City of God* repudiated the disparaging of the body in his early writings (cf. *Solil.* 1.14.24), he retained a Platonic critique of the body in its postlapsarian condition. Consequently, the resurrection was necessary to bring about the healing and perfecting of human nature "when 'the corruptible body no longer weighs down the soul' (Wisd. 9:10) . . . [and] when the body, freed from corruption, offers no hindrance to the soul" (*Civ.* 22.29).

The resurrection and perfection of the body are essential as a sign of God's sovereignty. Humanity's rebellion did not thwart God's plans. In bringing humanity to incorruptibility, God ultimately fulfilled his original purpose for creating humanity for the peace of paradise. The resurrection of the body, however, is not an end in itself. The summum bonum that awaits the vigilant pilgrim is the beatific vision of God. The resurrection is merely the necessary condition for the enjoyment of that paradisaic peace that is God himself (*Civ.* 19.26).

The nature of the beatific vision is a point where Augustine's thought diverges from Gregory of Nyssa's. Neither holds that God's infinite being will be comprehended by finite minds. Yet, as Hans Boersma has explained, Augustine is comfortable saying that the saints shall see God's essence. Because God is simple, their perfect encounter with the merciful love of God will be a vision of God's essential being. Augustine proceeds to offer an analogy. As the angels now see God, so too will the saints when they are raised and become fellow citizens with the angelic hosts.

This, however, raises the question, In what sense shall the saints "see" the invisible God? In the perfected condition, Augustine says, the saints will have no need of bodily eyes, for the power of God, who shall be "all in all," will so pervade all, uniting the saints in himself such that they, as the prophet Elisha (2 Kgs 5:26), will see and know each other immediately in their hearts (*Civ.* 22.29). Yet the restoration of the eyes of the spiritual body cannot be to no end. For while God will always be seen in the spirit, the saints' bodily vision will be given "an extraordinary potency" not like the sharper vision of raptors but like that given to Job (42:5) and promised by Paul (1 Cor 13:12), namely the ability to see the immaterial God "face-to-face." This perception of immaterial, spiritual realities by the spiritual body is analogous to one's present perception of the life that animates the body. One is able to tell the difference between a lifeless corpse and living body; we apprehend with bodily eyes the presence of something—invisible though it be—in the latter that is palpably absent in the former. Thus, Augustine concludes, "it is indeed most probable that we shall see the physical bodies of the new heaven and the new earth in such a fashion as to observe God in utter clarity and distinctness, seeing him present everywhere and governing the whole material scheme of things by means of the bodies we shall inhabit and the bodies we shall see wherever we turn our eyes" (*Civ.* 22.29). This implies that the physical eyes of the spiritual body—and not just the inner eye of the mind—will have an intellectual quality capable of perceiving the immaterial. Since, however, such a conjecture cannot be supported by Scripture, Augustine offers a simpler alternative: "[God] will be spiritually perceived by each one of us in each of us . . . wherever the eyes of the spiritual body are directed with their penetrating gaze" (*Civ.* 22.29).

Augustine's eschatology has implications that touch upon a number of key, and recurring, theological concerns. First, his account of the spiritual perception in the resurrection not only addresses the interpretive problem of understanding the Pauline language of seeing God "face-to-face," but more importantly it explains how eschatologically saints shall rightly love the beauty and goodness of creatures without falling into the idolatrous love of worshiping the creature instead of the Creator (Rom 1:25). In other words, it solves the dichotomy between the love of God and the love of neighbor. The neighbor is loved and enjoyed not as an end in herself but is rightly enjoyed *in God* (*Doctr. chr.* 1.7–8). Thus, the hierarchy of loves corresponds to the hierarchy of being so that the Creator's love of his creatures conditions the creatures' love for one another. For, second, it promises that in the beatific vision, the saints shall see rightly the unity of all things. God, as the one source of all things, is the source of the light of heavenly wisdom by which we might rightly know the natures of all creatures generally. But in seeing God actively indwelling each creature governing the whole creation, the saints grasp the individual value of the many parts of creation in the interconnected cosmic unity (*Civ.* 14.1). In this way, *City of God* expands his earlier account of the "eternal life of the saints" revealed to him and Monica in their joint vision at Ostia. There, Augustine spoke of the experience of God as eternal life and wisdom "in the region of inexhaustible abundance where you feed Israel eternally with truth for food" and transcend the company of all creatures—even the self—and are unmediated by created signs or symbolic utterance (*Conf.* 9.10.25). Here in *City of God*, however, the "wisdom by which all creatures come into being" (*Conf.* 9.10.24) is experienced in the creatures, especially in the community of the saints. Thus, third, Augustine preserves the corporate experience of God anticipated in the unity of the Church. The pilgrim partners joined to each other in the present life through virtue—the virtues of a shared love for God and hope in his promises—shall eschatologically enjoy God together. Then the miserable pilgrimage, though not the fellowship, will be at an end. Finally, the journey, the striving, the toil of pressing on will be over; the eternal Sabbath will have come when "now restored by him and perfected by his greater grace we shall be *still* and *at leisure* for eternity, seeing that he is God, and being filled by him when he will be all in all" (*Civ.* 20.30).

Babai the Great and Syriac Eschatology

The Syriac-speaking churches largely followed the view of resurrection expressed by Greek fathers, like Gregory of Nyssa, in affirming the redemption and transformation of the material body. Babai the Great's eschatology, however, was something of an outlier, and in it one sees the breadth and diversity of early Christian eschatologies. The chief differences were twofold: first, his account of Christ's resurrection, and second, his use of quasi-divinization to describe the saints' raised bodies.

Whereas a commonplace, East and West, was to view the marks of Jesus's crucifixion as permanent features of his raised and glorified body, Babai held that the appearance of the scars seen by the apostles was not permanent but a miracle to persuade the disciples of Jesus's identity (*Lib. un.* 190.24–29). Babai maintained that Jesus's resurrected body was of such a subtle composition that it could pass through doors and his luminous divinity was able to shine forth as at the transfiguration, which foreshadowed his glorification (*Lib. un.* 191.26–27). The light of his divine nature, however, was not immediately manifest at the resurrection but remained cloaked until his ascension. Although his resurrected body retained the general features proper to his human form (*qnōmā*) and the specific facial features identified him as Jesus (*parṣōpā*), it was fully healed of mortality and corruptibility. The healing of the wounds inflicted by the nails and the legionnaire's spear was necessary as a sign of the complete healing of the body brought by the resurrection. The miraculous appearance of the scars, therefore, revealed the marks of his mortality that had been fully healed. Thus, it served both to confirm Jesus's identity to the disciples and to give them the hope of transformative healing that awaited them at the general resurrection.

As Jesus's glorified body shone with the light of his divinity—the very light encountered by Moses on Sinai and Saul of Tarsus on the road to Damascus—so, Babai maintained, would the raised bodies of the saints, like Moses's face, become luminous (*Lib. un.* 5.19). But unlike those who, following Origen, hypothesized that the body of the resurrection would be perfectly spherical (*Princ.* 4.6), Babai held that the resurrected body would retain its *qnōmā* and the particularities of its *parṣōpā*, just as with Jesus's resurrected body. Also like Jesus's glorified body, the bodies of the saints would shine forth with a divine radiance. This aura was the product of a bodily change produced by the Spirit's indwelling of the saint. The light was from the Spirit's divinity, but it was manifest in the resurrected body because of the change wrought in the body by the Spirit. The luminous divinity of the Spirit so thoroughly filled the saint that her nature was swallowed up and transformed even as the nature of iron is transformed when thoroughly suffused by the heat of the blacksmith's furnace (*Comm. KG* 6.58). Babai's logic is that the light proper to the divinity of the Spirit enlightens the soul through its indwelling presence in which the soul encounters the Trinity. The resurrected body in turn bears the radiance of the Spirit's presence as did Jesus's glorified body. This eschatological transformation is, Babai claims, manifest proleptically in the lives of the martyrs. In Babai's hagiographical narrative of the martyrdom of Saint George (d. 615), he recounts that George's crucified form "put on bodily glory" like the glory of the "new man" put on at the resurrection (*Vit. Georg.* 69).

Apokatastasis: The Final Restoration of All Things

Central to the eschatologies of Western and Eastern fathers was the idea that creation and redemption were plots within a single narrative composed by a single divine author. Unlike the salvation stories of Gnostics and Manichees, the Catholic and Orthodox salvation story maintained that the Savior was the very Creator himself. For them, the eschaton was the consummation of God's creative purpose in the beginning. At last, creation would be free from sin, and, in its complete subjection to God, his sovereignty would be manifest. One expression of this idea was the theory of *apokatastasis* or restoration of all things.

Although its origins in Stoicism predate Christianity, *apokatastasis*'s most notable early Christian advocate was Origen. The foundation of Origen's doctrine is his interpretations of Paul's declaration, "When all things are subjected to him, the Son himself will also be subjected to him who put all things under him, that God may be all in all" (1 Cor 15:28). Since God is perfect goodness, he reasons, Paul's words imply the elimination of evil in every form:

> God will be "all" in individual beings in the sense that when the rational mind is freed from the dregs of vice and has the clouds of wickedness swept away . . . evil will be nowhere to be found; for God is "all" to the creatures, and there is no evil in him. . . . When all sense of evil is removed and swept away to produce holiness and purity, only the God who is one and good will be all to the creatures. It is not in a number of creatures, whether many or few, that God will be "all," but "in all," since there will be no death, no sting of death and no evil at all. Thus, truly God will be "all in all." (*Princ.* 3.6.2–3)

Whereas in the beginning the rational beings that fell were distracted from the goodness of God, in the eschatological restoration God will be the sum of all consciousness. The *logikoi*'s attention will be fixed entirely upon God. Then the rational beings shall be returned to their original state in which, without distinction, they shall reflect the splendor and glory of the goodness of the God in whom they participate (*Princ.* 4.4.8). Yet if the resurrection is merely the *restoration* of the way things were in the beginning, does not such a restoration simply set the stage for a repeat of the fall? What prevents the rational beings from misusing their free choice to turn from God a second time and creating a condition in which the cosmos is locked in an eternal cycle of fall, redemption, and repeated fall?

Origen's solution was to explain that *apokatastasis* will not simply be a return to the beginning but rather that the end shall be *like* the beginning. "Like" implies a notable difference between the life of rational beings in the eschaton from that of the original creation. That difference will be that, whereas the *logikoi* had fallen through complacency with the blessed life of beholding God's glory in the heavenly classroom, in the resurrection the souls, having passed through the trials and sufferings of their life in exile in the material world, will have acquired a newfound appreciation for the blessings of heaven. Having been made homesick for their heavenly home, rational beings will now be filled with an even hotter ardor for God—an ardor that will cause them freely to cleave to God whom they now recognize as the lone source of happiness. Origen's theory rests in part upon the logic that the beginning of all things establishes in their nature the telos toward which each is ultimately predisposed. The incarnation of the Logos both reveals this telos and enables humanity to move toward it. This explanation enables Origen to reconcile the tension between two of his chief commitments: human free choice and divine sovereignty. Through his creation of rational beings in the image of the Logos and Christ's redemptive condescension in the incarnation, God demonstrates his sovereignty while at the same time respecting the capacity of free choice with which he endowed the *logikoi* from the beginning. Building on the work of his Alexandrian predecessor Clement (*Protr.* 12.120.3–4), Origen understood Christ's work to bring immature humanity made in God's image into the perfect likeness of Christ's spiritual nature. Thus, as Ilaria Ramelli has demonstrated, *apokatastasis* and *theōsis* were synonymous in Origen's thought.

Two related implications inherent in Origen's theory of *apokatastasis* proved troubling for many who came after him. The first implication, which Origen acknowledged, is that all rational beings shall be saved. In *Against Celsus* 4.99, Origen responds to Celsus's claim that God is concerned for creation as a whole and not individuals. Although he agrees with Celsus that "all things have been made . . . so that this world, as God's work, may be made complete and perfect in all its parts," Origen argues that, while God rightly punishes all according to their deserts, "even if some part of [the world] becomes very bad because the rational being sins, God arranges to purify it, and after a time to bring the whole world back to himself." Biblical references to hell refer not to an eternal damnation but to the suffering concomitant with the purgation of evil. The second, infinitely more controversial implication was the salvation of the devil and his minions. Because evil has no independent subsistence but is simply a privation of the good that God created, the essential goodness of all creatures remains. The evil that is destroyed in the eschaton is not the creature that God made but the perverse will that is itself evil (*Princ.* 3.6.5). Therefore, the devil, in his essence, remains an archangel. Since free choice is inherent to the goodness of the rational nature of an archangel (*Princ.* 1.8.4), the devil retains the ability to turn back to God. Furthermore, since all evil will be eliminated when God is "all in all," it is not the devil who will be destroyed but his evil will. Although Origen scholars today debate whether he actually held to this view, the logic of his argument certainly led his critics to attribute such a view to him. For it, among other things, he was eventually condemned at the Second Council of Constantinople (553).

Although Gregory of Nyssa repudiated Origen's version of *apokatastasis*, which, on Gregory's interpretation, entailed the transmigration of souls (*Hom. opif.* 28), he shared with Origen a doctrine of *apokatastasis*, according to which all human beings shall be redeemed. In *On the Soul and Resurrection*, he interprets the reference to those "under the earth" whose knees bow and tongues confess Christ as Lord (Phil 2:10) to mean that "nothing shall be left out of the good," and "every reasoning creature in the restitution of all things is to look towards him who presides over the whole" (*An. res.* 4.17; Silvas, 199). Gregory's universalism is based on two principles. First, God's infinite being encompasses all things. Although sin is a movement away from God, because God is infinite, he circumscribes the whole of creation. Therefore, however far the soul seemingly moves *away from* God, eventually its movement turns out to be a movement *toward* God (*Hom. opif.* 21.2). Second, the restoration of all things entails the postmortem purification of those who, in the present life, have not purified themselves of sinful passions. His universalism raised an exegetical challenge: If all humanity ultimately returns to God, how should one interpret Jesus's teachings about hell (*An. res.* 5.47; Silvas, 206)? Gregory's answer is that "hell" describes the suffering inherent to the process of the purification endured by the soul that was not purified in the present life. Since the soul is incorporeal and so cannot be confined to a place, the souls of the wicked are separated from the souls of the righteous—as are the rich man and Lazarus in Jesus's parable—not physically but by the orientation of their respective desires. Since desire binds the soul to the object of its love, the desires of the wicked, who in this life loved the things of the world more than God, remain bound to the world even though in death they are unable to enjoy the worldly objects they love. By contrast, the souls of the righteous, who through disciplines of self-denial in this life reoriented their desires from the transitory things of the world to the eternal things of God, are able to enter into the blessedness of fellowship with God at death. Therefore, death is, so to speak, a psychological hell for the wicked because their souls are torn from the bodily pleasures and social goods that they love. Death is like tearing flesh as it is ripped from a piece of wood to which it has been glued (*An. res.* 6.4; Silvas, 207). Postmortem torture of the unrighteous is not God's punitive action; rather, it is a self-inflicted consequence of mistakenly loving the world as if it were eternal. In order for the souls of the wicked to come to the blessings of fellowship with God, therefore, their loves must be purified—reoriented from a longing for the world they have lost to the God who is the source of true happiness. To speak anachronistically, the soul of the aesthete is like the drug addict who must endure a period of detoxification—and with it the painful withdrawal symptoms—as he is cleansed of the hold the drug has on him. The soul *will* be purified, if not voluntarily in this life, then through a more painful, involuntary separation after death. Such purification, Gregory says, applies even to the devil (*Or. cat.* 26).

Although Gregory employs the language of "restoration" (*apokatastasis*), the beginning that shall be restored will not be the heavenly classroom where rational beings in ethereal bodies would be absorbed in contemplation of the divine. Rather, the beginning that shall be restored, for Gregory, is the creation that God intended in the beginning—a creation of embodied rational animals perfectly bearing the image of God through an unending participation in the infinite being of God.

In the preface of his treatise *On the Making of Humanity*, written in that period of almost frenetic productivity following the death of his brother, Basil, and his sister, Macrina, Gregory establishes the resurrection—that consummation of God's creative and redemptive work—as the hermeneutical lens through which one can interpret God's creative intentions in the beginning. As we have already seen, Gregory, based on his interpretation of Genesis 1:26–27, distinguished between God's original intention for human beings to be made in his image and God's subsequent decision, in anticipation of the fall, to divide humanity into male and female for sexual reproduction (*Hom. opif.* 16.8–9).[5] Yet gender and this bestial mode of procreation were, for Gregory, alien to the divine image, in which there is neither gender nor sensual passion. Moreover, sexual reproduction motivated by a desire for sensual pleasure is, Gregory says, the source of humanity's sensual passion (*Hom. opif.* 17.4–18.1). Therefore, the gendered humanity that God actually placed in Eden was not the sexless, rational humanity God originally intended.

Nevertheless, in Adam, God created, at the level of his foreknowledge, the fullness (Plērōma) of the human race—that is, all people that ever shall live. In the fullness of time, all those whom God foreknew according to his creative purpose shall be born, actualizing God's purposes for humanity. Even as Gregory speaks of the Plērōma as having been in Adam at the beginning, he speaks similarly of the whole human race in the resurrection as being one man. "So I think," Gregory

5. See chapter 3, pp. 91–98.

writes, "that the entire plentitude of humanity was included by the God of all . . . in one body . . . the man that was manifested at the first creation of the world, and he that shall be after the consummation of all [*synteleian*] are alike: they equally bear in themselves the divine image" (*Hom. opif.* 16.17). In other words, all humanity existed in potentiality in the first Adam and is being actualized over the course of history. The consummation will be when eschatologically all humanity abides in and is united in the second Adam, Christ. When all those whom God foreknew in Adam shall be born, the human race will have attained its ordained limit or size; then the resurrection will come (*An. res.* 9.20–21). When Gregory says that eschatological humanity shall be like humanity of the "first creation," he is not referring primarily to the particular man, Adam, but the human nature God intended when he said, "Let us make man in our image." Based on Jesus's description of the resurrection in his debate with the Sadducees—those worthy of the resurrection "shall not marry nor be given in marriage . . . because they shall be equal to the angels" (Luke 20:35–36)—Gregory concludes that in the resurrection, human beings will possess the likeness to genderless angels that humanity would have had in the beginning had God not foreseen the fall. Since the resurrected body, though transformed, will have its original physical features, in the resurrection people will not be genderless. Nevertheless, though the marks of gender will remain, human beings, no longer needing to procreate, will be devoted entirely to the contemplation of God rather than partaking in sexual relations. This is why Gregory depicts the life of sexual chastity and contemplation practiced by Macrina and the women in her monastic community as being like the angels (*Macr.* 13.6–7; Silvas, 122). The resurrection, therefore, is not strictly speaking a *restoration* of Eden but the *perfection* of Eden—that is, the fulfillment of God's original purpose. Finally, humanity, free from nonrational passions, will enjoy the blessedness proper to beings that have been formed in the image of the supremely blessed God.

The end of history for Maximus the Confessor is the consummation of God's plan described by Paul in Ephesians 1:10: "to unite all things in him [i.e., the Logos], things in heaven and things on earth." In the incarnation, the union of the *logoi*, which were in the Logos in the beginning, was a revelation in microcosm of God's plan to draw back to himself all things that were "in him [i.e., the Logos] before the foundation of the world" (Eph 1:4). The eschaton will be the perfection of creation because it is the actualization of the unity of all things in the one in whom they were united at the level of God's intention in the beginning. Maximus's vision of the eschaton is grand. While he preserves the ontological distinction between Creator and creature, creation is divinized through and through:

> And finally, beyond all these, the human person unites the created nature with the uncreated through love (Oh the wonder of God's love for us human beings),

> showing them to be one and the same through the possession of grace, the whole wholly interpenetrated by God and becoming completely whatever God is, save at the level of being, and receiving to itself the whole of God himself, acquiring as a kind of prize for its ascent to God, the most unique God himself, as the end of the movement of everything that moves toward it, and the firm and moving rest of everything that is carried toward it. (*Amb.* 41, 1308b)

Maximus can speak of creation's perfect reflection of the divine nature because its movements conform to the *logoi*, which are the image of the Logos and contain the proper pattern of movement that God intended in the Logos for all creatures. All things in the end will abide in the perfect harmonious unity prefigured in the unity of the *logoi* in the Logos. Drawing on Gregory of Nyssa's idea of *epektasis*, Maximus describes this perfected movement of the rational creatures as "ever-moving rest" (*akinētos stasis*)—"rest" because it is eternal union with God but an "ever-moving" rest because it is an eternal participation in and growth in the knowledge of the infinite deity (*Quaest. Thal.* 59, 65).

Although the eschatological unity of all things in God will be the completion of the unity first actualized in Christ, Maximus also speaks of it as "restoration." Commenting on Gregory's theory of *apokatastasis*, he makes a threefold distinction between types of restoration. The first is the life of virtue attained through the participation in the Logos. The second is the restoration of humanity through the resurrection. Like Origen, Methodius, and Gregory, it is the bodily resurrection of all. Finally, *apokatastasis* is the restoration of "the [original] powers of the soul that fell into sin" (*Quaest. dub.* 19). Even as human nature must be restored to a state of incorruption through bodily resurrection, so too the soul can be restored through being purged of the memories of evil and the attainment of "full understanding" so that it may participate fully in God. The evil memories, according to Andreas Andreopoulos, likely refer to the gnomic will, whose choices are based upon deliberation around one's *uncertain* opinion. The "full understanding" is likely the natural will whose choices are based in a *certain* knowledge of the good derived from its life in the Logos. As with Origen and Gregory, the logic of Maximus's interpretation of the universalist language of Ephesians is that all shall be redeemed (*Quaest. Thal.* 21, 43). Yet elsewhere he does speak of an eternal punishment (*Quaest. Thal.* 59; *Amb.* 42, 65).

Conclusion

If the writings of Maximus have left modern readers with uncertainty about his view of universal salvation, no such ambiguity exists in Augustine's thought. Pastorally, Augustine counsels that, since God alone knows those whom he has graciously chosen to redeem for blessedness and those whom he has consigned to perdition, it is best in practice to assume that, like Saul of Tarsus, each sinner is among the elect who will be saved. Yet his reading of Scripture compelled him to reject any notion of universal salvation. Against universalist interpretations of 1 Timothy 2:4, "[God] desires all men to be saved and to come to the knowledge of the truth," Augustine says that "all" does not mean "all people" but all those whom he wills to be saved (*Praed.* 8.14). He also rejects any suggestion, as Gregory's speculation, that the torments of hell are but a short-term punishment intended for the soul's purification. Unless the will of the damned is fixed and their punishment in hell eternal, Augustine counters, how can we cling to the hope that the will of the saints is fixed and their blessedness is eternal? If not, such a pedagogical view of damnation creates the possibility of a second fall (*Civ.* 21.17). Toward the end of his life, writing his *Retractions*, he qualifies his earlier view of the resurrection, drawing a clear line between Origen's universalism and his doctrine of election (*Retract.* 1.7.6). Ultimately, for Augustine, the mystery of salvation was not why God in his inscrutable wisdom would save some and damn others. Rather, it is that God in his mercy would choose to redeem any portion of thankless, rebellious humanity. And it is a sign of his infinite power and sovereignty that he would not allow sin to contravene his purposes but clothe the pilgrim saints with Christ and make them partakers of his holy and incorruptible nature as he willed before the foundation of the world.

Bibliography

Primary Sources

Augustine of Hippo. *City of God*. Translated by Henry Bettenson. London: Penguin Books, 1972.

———. *Revisions*. Translated by Boniface Ramsey. The Works of Saint Augustine: A Translation for the 21st Century 1/2. Hyde Park, NY: New City, 2010.

Babai the Great. *Liber de Unione* [*On the Union*]. Edited by Arthur Adolphe Vaschalde. CSCO 2/61. Leuven: Secrétariat du Corpus Scriptorum Christianorum Orientalium, 1915.

———. *Life of George*. In *Portraits of Spiritual Authority: Religious Power in Early Christianity, Byzantium, and the Christian Orient*. Edited by Jan Willem Drijvers and John W. Watt. Leiden: Brill, 1999.

Gregory of Nyssa. *Catechetical Oration* [*GNO* 3/4]. Pages 268–325 in *Christology of the Later Fathers*. Edited by Edward R. Hardy. Philadelphia: Westminster, 1954.

———. *Homilies on Ecclesiastes* [*GNO* 5:277–442]. In *Gregory of Nyssa: Homilies on Ecclesiastes*. Translated by S. G. Hall. New York: de Gruyter, 1993.

———. *Homilies on the Song of Songs* [*GNO* 6]. In *Homilies on the Song of Songs*. Translated by Richard A. Norris. Atlanta: Society of Biblical Literature, 2012.

———. *On the Holy Pascha* [*GNO* 9:245–70]. Pages 5–23 in *The Easter Sermons of Gregory of Nyssa*. Edited by Andreas Spira and Christopher Klock. Translated by S. G. Hall. Cambridge: Philadelphia Patristics Society, 1981.

———. *On the Making of Humanity* [*GNO* 4/2; PG 44:125–256]. *NPNF* 2/5.

———. *On the Soul and Resurrection* [*GNO* 3/3]. Pages 171–248 in *Macrina the Younger, Philosopher of God*. Translated by Anna M. Silvas. Turnhout: Brepols, 2008.

———. *On Those Who Have Fallen Asleep* [*GNO* 9:28–68]. Pages 94–117 in *One Path for All: Gregory of Nyssa on the Christian Life and Human Destiny*. Translated by Rowan A. Greer. Eugene, OR: Cascade, 2015.

———. *Oration on the Savior's Nativity* [*GNO* 10/2:233–69]. In *The Cambridge Edition of Early Christian Writings*. Vol. 3. *Christ*. Edited by Mark DelCogliano. Translated by Andrew Radde-Gallwitz. Cambridge: Cambridge University Press, 2022.

Maximus the Confessor. *Maximus the Confessor*. Translated by Andrew Louth. London: Routledge, 1996.

———. *On Difficulties in the Church Fathers: The* Ambigua. Translated by Nicholas Constas. Cambridge: Harvard University Press, 2014.

———. *On the Cosmic Mystery of Jesus Christ*. Translated by Paul M. Blowers and Robert Louis Wilken. Crestwood, NY: St. Vladimir's Seminary Press, 2003.

Origen. *On First Principles: A Reader's Edition*. Translated by John Behr. Oxford: Oxford University Press, 2019.

Secondary Works

Andreopoulos, Andreas. "Eschatology in Maximus." In *The Oxford Handbook of Maximus the Confessor*. Edited by Pauline Allen and Bronwen Neil. Oxford: Oxford University Press, 2015.

Daley, Brian E. *The Hope of the Early Church: A Handbook of Patristic Eschatology*. Cambridge: Cambridge University Press, 1991.

Greer, Rowan A. *Christian Hope and Christian Life: Raids on the Inarticulate*. New York: Herder & Herder, 2001.

Hunter, David G. "Books 21 and 22: The End of the Body; Heaven and Hell." In *The Cambridge Companion to Augustine's* City of God. Edited by David Vincent Meconi. Cambridge: Cambridge University Press, 2021.

Ludlow, Morwenna. *Universal Salvation: Eschatology in the Thought of Gregory of Nyssa and Karl Rahner*. Oxford: Oxford University Press, 2000.

McGlothlin, Thomas D. "Augustine's Resurrection Framework: Clarifying and Connecting Senses of 'Resurrection.'" *Augustinian Studies* 55 (2024): 25–42.

———. *Resurrection as Salvation: Development and Conflict in Pre-Nicene Paulinism.* Cambridge: Cambridge University Press, 2018.

Moreira, Isabel. "Book 20: The Last Day; Judgement, Purification, and Transformation." In *The Cambridge Companion to Augustine's* City of God. Edited by David Vincent Meconi. Cambridge: Cambridge University Press, 2021.

Moss, Candida R. *Divine Bodies: Resurrecting Perfection in the New Testament and Early Christianity*. New Haven: Yale University Press, 2019.

Ramelli, Ilaria L. E. *The Christian Doctrine of Apokatastasis: A Critical Assessment from the New Testament to Eriugena*. Leiden: Brill, 2013.

———. *Social Justice and the Legitimacy of Slavery: The Role of Philosophical Asceticism from Ancient Judaism to Late Antiquity*. Oxford: Oxford University Press, 2016.

Walker, Caroline Bynum. *The Resurrection of the Body in Western Christianity, 200–1336.* New York: Columbia University Press, 2017.

Acknowledgments

Now a word of thanks. This section, of necessity, must be short; as such, however, it fails to do justice to my sense of gratitude to the people who have made this book possible. The model for this project I took from the patristic history assigned my first year in seminary, J. N. D. Kelly's *Early Christian Doctrine*, a volume to which I referred repeatedly especially in preparation for my preliminary exams in historical theology. There were also Jaroslav Pelikan's *The Emergence of the Catholic Tradition (100–600)*, and R. P. C. Hanson's *Search for the Christian Doctrine of God*. More recently, my students have benefited from Robert Wilken's *The Spirit of Christian Thought* and *The First Thousand Years*, as well as Frances Young's *From Nicaea to Chalcedon*, John Behr's *The Nicene Faith*, Lewis Ayres's *Nicaea and Its Legacy*, and Khaled Anatolios's *Retrieving Nicaea*. These works have been invaluable resources over my three decades of teaching. I have not tried to duplicate them here but have found them repeatedly helpful in thinking and rethinking how to narrate the complicated world of early Christianity.

Although I settled down to begin writing this book five years ago, there are sections of this book that I salvaged from deleted sections of previous writings. I am, therefore, indebted to colleagues with whom I engaged in lengthy email exchanges about various topics even before this volume was a twinkle in my imagination. Others offered themselves as conversation partners along the way. And still others have read chapters or sections of chapters and offered helpful suggestions, editorial and substantial, to correct my omissions and commissions: Khaled Anatolios, Lewis Ayres, Michel Barnes, Christopher Beeley, Paul Blowers, Brad Boswell, Anthony Briggman, Thomas Breedlove, Patout Burns, Aaron Butts, Mark DelCogliano, Philip Cary, John C. Cavadini, Thomas Clemmons, Stephen Cooper, Maria Doerfler, Milanna Fritz, Erin Galgay Walsh, Reinhard Hütter, Judith Heyhoe, Robin Jensen, Han-luen Kantzer Komline, Jackson Lashier, Greg Lee, Morwenna Ludlow, Bruce McCuskey, Cullen McKenney, Tom McGlothlin, Jillian Marcantonio,

Heather Moffitt, Peter Morris, George Parsenios, Zlotko Pleše, Andrew Radde-Gallwitz, Taylor Ross, Kavin Rowe, Nathan Tilley, Charles Twombly, and Daniel Williams. To you I am extremely grateful for your counsel, your willingness to let me add many emails to your inbox, and most of all for your friendly support and encouragement through the process. This would have been a long and less enjoyable undertaking without you. My thanks also go out to students who have served as my research assistants most recently: Christopher Albert, Bobby Douglas, Nathan Porter, Jackson Shepard, and Abigail Smith. I should also thank my students across the years at Wabash, Yale, and Duke whose provocative questions forced me to hone my teaching of early Christian theology on which this book was constructed. To James Ernest, thank you for believing me capable of undertaking such a vast project and being patient with the speed or lack thereof with which I brought it to completion. Thanks as well to Jennifer Hoffman and Justin Howell for their editorial labors and Heather Brewer for her creativity in designing a cover that captures the spirit and content of the book. And as always, I am grateful to Kim, Katherine, and Thomas for your patience—especially your understanding when, in the midst of writing, I have responded to a family summons saying, "Let me finish this one thought. I'll be there in just a minute," and for patiently understanding that in a moment of concentration "a minute" is no more precise a measure of time than "forty days and forty nights" and at times may feel as long. You are better to me than I deserve and dearer to me than you know.

Super omnia, Deo omnia gloria et honor et laus.

Index of Modern Authors

Index of Subjects

Index of Scripture